The Holiday Which? Guide to
GREECE
and the Greek Islands

The Holiday Which? Guide to
GREECE
and the Greek Islands

Edited by Ingrid Morgan

Published by Consumers' Association
and Hodder & Stoughton

ACKNOWLEDGEMENTS TO *Rosalyn Belford,
Val Campbell, Stephanie Ferguson, Adam Hopkins,
Adam Ruck, Andrew Ruck*

Which? Books are commissioned and researched by
The Association for Consumer Research
and published by Consumers' Association,
2 Marylebone Road, London NW1 4DX, and
Hodder & Stoughton, 47 Bedford Square,
London WC1B 3DP

Typographic design by Tim Higgins
Cover artwork by Neil Pinkett
Maps by David Perrott Cartographics

First edition 1989

Copyright © 1989 Consumers' Association Ltd

British Library Cataloguing in Publication Data

The Holiday Which? guide to Greece and the Greek
   Islands – (Which? Books)
   1. Greece. Visitors' guides
   I. Morgan, Ingrid II. Consumers' Association
   III. Series
   914.95'0476

ISBN 0 340 50433 1

Typeset in Linotron Aldus and Optima
by Wyvern Typesetting Ltd, Bristol
Printed and bound in Great Britain
by BPCC Hazell Books Ltd
Aylesbury, Bucks

Contents

About this guide 7
Introduction 9
Choosing a holiday 20
History, art and architecture 31
Mythology 42
Wild flowers 58
Eating and drinking 64
Map of Greece 74

The Mainland
Athens and Attica 79
The Peloponnese 127
Central Greece 178
Macedonia and Thrace 231

The Islands
Corfu and the Ionian Islands 257
The Peloponnese Islands 321
Evia and the Sporades 353
The Cyclades 384
Crete 482
Rhodes and the Dodecanese 525
The North-East Aegean Islands 594

Information 647
Glossary 1 *Art and architecture* 693
Glossary 2 *Food* 695
Index 701

About this guide

Holiday Which? first visited Greece and its islands in 1973. Corfu, Crete and Rhodes were some of the first places to become popular mass tourism destinations, and were the first islands to which we gave our attention; in later years we visited the smaller islands, some already popular, others still remote and unfrequented. As our visits to Greece continued, we observed changes on a far greater scale than in countries more developed for tourism. New roads and airports where previously there was nothing have altered not only the pattern of tourism but the pace and style of local life. In other places, while the aspect of the village or resort may not appear to have altered substantially, its tourism has.

For this book we have revisited the Greek mainland and all the islands described.

The guide is divided into three main parts: some short chapters giving background information on history, architecture, Greek mythology, wild flowers and eating and drinking; a section with practical information at the back of the book; and eleven chapters of area descriptions, divided into 'mainland' and 'island groups'.

Each chapter includes hotel recommendations, the result of first-hand inspections. Unlike in the other *Holiday Which?* guides (to France, Italy, Weekend Breaks), our descriptions of hotels are brief. The nature of Greek hotels means that very few can be singled out as being exceptional in any way; most of those listed in this book should be considered only as suggestions of simple, clean establishments in places where you are likely to want to spend a night or two. They will generally have been selected not for any high degree of stylishness or abundance of facilities but because they are in convenient and attractive locations. The hotel's official category (Luxury, A, B, C, D or E) which appears in parentheses after its name serves as an indicator of price, if not necessarily of style or facilities. In our section on Hotels on page 664 we have attempted to describe the characteristics of Greek hotels in the various categories, and our generalisations hold true for much of the hotel accommodation throughout the country.

The dearth of highly recommendable hotels, particularly of the old and charming type such as can be found in many other European countries, should not be seen as totally negative, and need not put you off a touring holiday. Greek resorts and towns almost always have some simple modern hotels which are perfectly adequate for a night or two; and for a stay-put package holiday, modern hotels in the higher classification categories provide accommodation which is on a par with other Mediterranean holiday areas, provided your requirements are reasonably modest. On the islands, private rooms in family homes constitute a sizeable amount of the available holiday accommodation,

7

and can be an enjoyable way of getting to know the host nation more intimately than is usually the case on holiday.

In the text, we use the device of SMALL CAPITALS when referring to places which are described more fully later in the chapter, and which merit a gazetteer entry of their own – either because they are major resorts or sights, or because they can be singled out in some way from the surrounding resorts or area.

The spelling of Greek place-names is a subject which has exercised many minds, not least of other guidebook writers. The statements of an early-19th-century traveller that 'It is impossible in any manner to avoid inconsistency' holds true today, and the recent official attempts at standardisation have served mainly to add to the confusion for a traveller. The complexities of spelling start with the problem of two alphabets – Greek and Roman – which do not directly correspond. To this one must add a whole list of factors: modern Greek is not the same as Ancient Greek; modern Greek developed into two distinct forms – the *katharevousa* of the educated, and the *dimotiki* of the rural population (the latter form has since 1976 been imposed as the official language); place-names, as other nouns, decline (a traveller asking the way to Delphi should expect directions to 'Delphous', and a street named after Hermes will be called Ermou); and many place-names are derived from Frankish, Venetian, Albanian or Turkish roots and their Latin form follows appropriately different rules to those with Greek roots. Changing fashions in transliteration have meant that for a while the Greek Y (the capital of *upsilon*) was rendered as 'I' (Mikonos, Zakinthos), but the more traditional 'Y' is now gaining ground (Mykonos, Zakynthos). Finally, many places have a known anglicised form used by classicists and archaeologists (Athens, Corinth, Thebes, Salonika, Boeotia). To the complexities of transliteration can be added those of usage or preference. For instance, the island of Santorini (or Santorin, or Santorine) is variously known as Santorini (by most Greeks), Sandorini (on a Greek National Tourist Organisation map), Thera, its official (ancient) name, or the alternative Thira (which appears on maps and airline timetables). Its capital town appears as Thira, Thera, Fira, or Phira; and, in common with other island capitals, may be referred to as *Chora* on signposts. Its ancient capital may take any of the former spellings, plus Thyra.

In this guide, our preference has been to adopt the known English or Latin form where this exists for ancient sites or towns (Bassae and Mycenae, instead of the phonetic Vassae and Mikinai, and Corinth instead of Korinth, despite the fact that a hard 'c' does not exist in Greek), and in all other cases to use the most commonly found version, be it on local signposts or maps, in books or tour operator brochures; we give alternative spellings where these are substantially different. The appropriate local spelling is given for a modern town or village which has become established near an ancient site (for instance, Delfi and Dhafni near the ancient sites of Delphi and Daphni). Finally, we have preferred to transliterate the Greek *gamma* as 'g' instead of 'y' in the words *Agios* or *Agia*, although the pronunciation is closer to *Ayios* as the 'g' is silent.

Introduction

The equation of Greek with alien – as in 'It's all Greek to me' –
flies in the face of reality. We may have a different alphabet,
but our vocabulary is full of Greek words and our culture and
outlook on life are full of Greek ideas and ideals. Philosophy,
democracy, geometry, drama and marathons are only a few
Greek corner-stones of the edifice of western civilisation.
Modern Greece may be a pale shadow of its glorious ancient
self, but there is nothing tarnished about the beauty of the
landscape – the wild grey peaks of western Crete and the Pindos
Mountains, the rolling woodlands of Arcadia, the Mediterranean
symphony of shimmering silver olives and solemn dark
cypresses, the unique clarity of the Aegean sky and dazzling
brilliance of the blue and white island landscape. The settings of
many of the great classical sites – Cape Sounion, Delphi,
Phaistos – bring home the force of the argument that Ancient
Greek civilisation and the Greek landscape are inseparable, or
would be in an ideal world.

But separation has been the hard rule of history. In the
Middle Ages Turks raided Greece to carry off women and
children to the harems and slave markets of the east, and
continued to demand a human tax when Greece was part of the
Ottoman Empire. In the 18th and 19th centuries acquisitive
European connoisseurs descended on Greece in a race to export
movable works of art. Edward Clarke went to Patmos in 1799
and described his visit to the monastery library: 'a domed room
full of books and manuscripts, many of them lying on the floor
prey to moths and mould.' Clarke, like Lord Elgin in Athens,
saw where his duty lay and arranged for some of the most
precious manuscripts, including the 24th Dialogue of Plato and
the Lexicon of Cyril of Alexandria, to be smuggled out of the
monastery in a bread basket. Not all collectors were so
scrupulous. Landing at Delos in the late 17th century, an
Englishman called Simon, captain of the *Santa Barbara*, tried to
carry off a 7th-century statue whose inscribed base can still be
seen *in situ*. Finding it impossible, he broke off the head, arms
and feet and took those.

The British Museum, the Louvre and many other of the
world's great museums bear witness to the Greek achievement
and to the removal of works of art from Greece. The

9

displacement still goes on: important artefacts are taken from local sites to museums in Athens or other cities, and, with some notable exceptions, tourists on the spot have to be satisfied with lesser items.

Not that sightseeing in Greece is a disappointment. On the contrary: from the ruins you can resurrect ancient civilisations in your imagination, marvel at their sophistication, ponder all the unanswered questions. You will also find, perhaps with some surprise, that there is much more to sightseeing in Greece than antiquity. Go to Crete and you may be delighted to discover that the frescoed medieval churches hidden away in the olive groves give as much pleasure as Knossos and the other world-famous Minoan sites. The same goes for the other great sightseeing treasure store of Greece, the Peloponnese, where the churches of Mistra, the fortress of Nafplion and the warlike tower-houses of Vathia are not eclipsed by the glories of Mycenae and Olympia. Kos and Rhodes have a similar rich mixture of ancient and medieval remains, with mighty forts built by the crusading Order of the Knights of St John, Christendom's front line of defence against the Infidel in the 14th and 15th centuries.

In Greece one is never more than 60 miles from the sea, a key ingredient of the most celebrated Greek landscapes. It was also a key element of ancient Greek civilisation whose basis was maritime trade and colonising and the cultural exchange that went with them. The sailors in turn depended on the weather, the northern *meltemi* which blows southwards across the Aegean reliably from spring to autumn. 'Without this prevailing wind,' wrote the great sailing writer Ernle Bradford, 'Greek civilisation and Greek culture might never have arisen.' The sea and the wind have star parts in the rich fabric of Greek myths, where history and invention are so teasingly interwoven. They also feature high on the list of Greece's attractions to tourists. At a conservative estimate the country has 10,000 miles of coast, excluding 1500-odd islands. The sea, the islands and the wind make Greece a holiday paradise for the recreational sailor and the beach lover. A must for historically aware tourists, Greece is also a wonderful country for those who seek nothing more demanding than a place in the sun, with a bottle of wine, a breeze and a strip of beach.

There is a special quality of life that sets Greece apart. If you have ever been there, you will have your own trigger mechanism that will transport you instantly back. It may be sinking your teeth into the salty flesh of an olive or a gluey cube of almond *loukoumia*, tasting the harsh tang of resin in the wine, hearing the spiky melodies plucked on the *bouzouki*, the foul smell of the mosquito coil or the blast of hot air that hits you on the gangway at Athens airport, a rich mixture of the sea, sweat, pine, eucalyptus, oil on hot tar, exhaust fumes, builders' dust. You can probably also summon up some thoroughly unpleasant sensory memories of the country, but even these will elicit a smile of happy recall. For in Greece, where the first words of English on every local's tongue are 'No problem, my friend', you have been relaxed and content. The weather has a lot to do with this, of course. But it is the Greeks themselves who are chiefly responsible. In many contexts 'My friend' has a distinctly menacing ring to it, but in Greece they mean it. *Xenos*, the foreigner, is a friend until proved enemy. Because we find tourism an ugly phenomenon, it is easy to assume that the Greeks must resent tourists. They do not.

If holidays are a dream commodity, Greece is a dream come true. The sea and the sky are as blue as they are in the brochures, the sugar-cube villages as white. On the taverna terrace octopus is pegged out to dry on the line. The old women are broad and beaming, the old men toothless and unshaven, the beach bodies gleaming and beautiful. The waiter downs his tray to put on an impromptu dancing display. The peasant goads his lazy mule up a stony hillside, breaks some bread, anchors the beast by tying a rear to a front leg and snores the afternoon away in the shade of an olive tree. Fishermen sell the night's catch, still flapping, on the quay and spend their afternoons in the timeless fiddly ritual of netmending. The warlike Cretan's high brown boots and baggy breeches; the pink slash of oleander in a river gully like an open wound in the parched hillside; the monks and mules, caiques and cats, worry beads and windmills; and, of course, the wine-dark sea and rosy-fingered dawn: all are as they should be. As you drift in and out of sleep to the rhythmic sound of a fisherman beating an octopus against a rock, it may occur to you that 3000 years ago an Ancient Greek was probably beating an octopus against the same rock.

With all its islands, the country is uniquely rich in small, simple, intimate, slow-moving ports topped by ruined fortresses and little domed chapels outlined against a sky broken only by a few wheeling gulls. Small islands, where life revolves around the water-front and the comings and goings of fishing fleets and ferries, have a special concentrated charm. For many visitors this is the special essence of Greece. High up on the hill is the old village, a half-deserted labyrinth of staircase streets full of sly cats and nervous chickens, where the islanders lived in the days when the waters of the Aegean were thick with unbridled pirates. It is a stiff walk up from the port, not something you undertake in the heat of the day. From high up, rough tracks take hikers down to empty coves where the sea washes the stones and broken columns of some ancient city, and to silent monasteries which come to life for one day a year, when the entire island population treks across the hills for the local festival. Impatient visitors can buzz and rattle their way to the wildest corners of the island on a rented motor-bike, freedom for a few pounds a day. An enterprising local has set up a ramshackle cafe on a far-off beach and runs boat-trips from the port. Such are the simple pleasures of a small-island holiday.

But Greece is more than a collection of calendar photographs and the clichés of promotional tourist literature, the new mythology. It has an agitated modern history and contemporary political, economic and social problems which, if they are not the main concerns of a holiday guidebook, are highly relevant to the experience of the country. 'No problem' is not the whole truth for the country, nor for the tourist. Greeks remember not only the deprivations and heroics of the Second World War but also civil war in the years immediately afterwards and junta rule in the 1970s. Even now, the dispute with Turkey about rights in the Aegean rumbles on unresolved and threatens to erupt at any moment. Many of the prettiest islands bristle with soldiers.

In the space of a generation, Greece has joined the EEC and, with its eyes on Europe, undergone a rapid process of modernisation: industrialising, urbanising and speeding communication with new roads, airports and TV. Out of ten million Greeks, three million now live in Greater Athens, many of them first- or second-generation migrants from rural Greece. Yet 30 per cent of Greek employment is still in agriculture and 30 per cent of the population still lives in communities of fewer than 2000 souls. These figures alone point to a remarkable polarisation of the country and explain how a profound social transformation can have done surprisingly little to change the physical appearance of Greece beyond the spreading Athenian megalopolis.

Modernisation is unpicturesque, and it is easy for us to see ways in which the new wealth is poorer than the old poverty. Enter a cafe in a remote village and you are quite likely to find the villagers not locked in heated argument about some political issue as Greek cafe patrons are supposed to be, but tamely engrossed in an episode of *The Good Life*. Get chatting to a taxi driver and you may find it hard to distract him from a proud recitation of British football teams. Share a remote beach or the deck of a ferry with a group of Greek teenagers and you may be driven off by blaring rock on the ghetto blaster. Young people ape western European and American fashions. The news-stands on Constitution Square are full of pornography. A recent survey of church attendance among Athenians found that only 9 per cent go to church every Sunday, although 60 per cent go to weddings and festivals. Monasteries are falling empty.

Much of this has its roots in city life, a shift in the balance of the conflict between the liberal ideas of a westernised Athenian elite and the ultra-conservative attitudes of country people dominated by the anti-European tradition of the Orthodox church. The conflict goes back at least as far as national independence in the mid-19th century. Urban values now reach the remotest corners via television and those who return home from Athens, New York, Melbourne or Munich. The ugly proliferation of pubs and fast-food restaurants might seem to be a product of foreign tourism, but usually it is not. Expatriates return to start small businesses and, to their way of thinking, this is the smart modern style. Jimmy's Hot Dog Heaven is as likely to be in a tourist-free country village as in a busy international resort, and it is as authentically Greek as a rustic open-air taverna with retsina from the barrel. In many resorts you will find an evening contraflow, with locals migrating from the run-down area where they live to the cocktail bars in the modern hotel zone, while discerning tourists stroll down to the much more authentic local restaurants by the smelly old fishing harbour.

In a developing economy with a chronic imbalance of payments problem and few natural resources other than scenery, seasides, sunshine and sightseeing, tourism has inevitably played a big part in the modernisation process. From 450,000 in 1961, the number of annual visitors has risen to over 8 million, not far short of parity with the population. The visitors bring nearly $4 billion a year to Greece and employ 8 per cent of the labour force in summer. The development boom has been very rapid, inadequately controlled and not at all pretty. As well as the sheer ugliness of big hotel blocks and permanently unfinished tourist rooming buildings with bare wires, bare bulbs and roofs sprouting construction rods, there have been infrastructure problems (not enough water) and understandable concern about the corrosive influence of the behaviour of arrogant and disrespectful tourists who sunbathe naked, sleep around, get drunk, go into churches in a state of undress, and take photographs without asking. Greece is cheap and cheap tourism is a blunt instrument with which to solve economic problems.

The moral dimension can be exaggerated. Greeks themselves have few rivals as litter louts, noise polluters and ignorers of notices about dress requirements at monasteries. Fishermen ruin their own livelihood by using dynamite to destroy all marine life, while tourist islands risk ruining theirs by pumping untreated sewage into the harbour. Most of the complaints about foreign tourists come from other tourists, not local people, who have much more sympathy with the young and the outlook summed up as the hippie mentality than is commonly supposed, which is why Greece became so popular with free-spirited travellers 20 years ago and why students still flock there to hang out in summer. Most Greeks, with the notable exception of the military, queue up for the camera. They love loud music and riotous celebration. And if they take exception to your clothes in church, or to the noise you're making at siesta time, they will leave you in no doubt about their objections.

There is a beach overlooked by a monastery on the distant island of Karpathos, a favourite destination for Crusoe-esque escapists. Nudism Strictly Forbidden and Nudism For Ever graffiti are splashed across the rocks in a ferocious propaganda war. On the monastery terrace above the beach stands a monk with a pair of binoculars ever alert to the possibility of being scandalised. Tourism in Greece is big business. It is also great fun.

In the Romantic age poets went to Greece in a nostalgic mood, musing along the lines of Byron's 'Fair Greece! Sad relic of departed worth!'. It is once again a fashionable tune, with newspaper travel pages filled with similar nostalgia for a Greece of yesteryear, before tourism ruined everything. The writers were young and carefree once, mostly in Greece. Now they are older and cynical, and imagine Greece has lost its innocence. It is easy to forget that, without tourism, many once-idyllic corners of rural Greece would be deserted, not blissfully unchanged, for tourism is the one thing that has reversed the trend of migration to Athens.

When we complain about how tourism ruins a country it is not out of concern but selfishness. Donkeys are more picturesque than tractors. We prefer not to share beaches or archaeological sites with other people. We go on holiday to escape familiar surroundings and the faces we see on the 8.05 to Waterloo, and we do not like the sight of hotels along the back of the beach, especially if we knew the beach before the hotels were erected. This may not be an easy attitude to justify, but it is easy to share, and it is a fact. In this guide we have tried to refine our judgements further than the assumption that touristy is bad and untouristy is good, but it is not part of our purpose to promote mass-market package tourism to those who want a different style of holiday.

Over 8 million tourists a year is also a fact, which means that the satisfaction of having places to yourself is increasingly hard to achieve in Greece, at least in the most beautiful coastal areas in high summer. It also makes the whole question of 'what sort of people go there?' – a minefield of class and racial prejudice – unavoidable. In Greece today, tourists are as much part of the landscape as the mountains, olive groves, beaches and ancient theatres, and greatly outnumber the local people in most resorts – by ten to one on the island of Rhodes, which has a relatively large local population. If it is reasonable to dwell on the friendliness or otherwise of the local people, it is at least as relevant to attempt to convey what the other 90 per cent of the company is likely to be. Ask people about their holidays and, as likely as not, it will not be the sightseeing or the scenery they talk about, but the people. The place was full of fat Germans or lager louts or yuppies or Henrys and Carolines. In this guide we have not attempted to skirt this minefield, but have done our best to tiptoe carefully through it. Not to do so is to risk total irrelevance, along the lines of Lawrence Durrell's remarks on Ios, the disco capital of modern Greece: 'One should make every attempt to step ashore here and taste the felicity of its silences, fractured only by some distant church bells or the braying of a mule. Even the wind seems lulled and in Ios one sleeps the full sleep of early childhood.' Step ashore on Ios between May and October and it is not the silence that will be fractured, but your ear-drums.

Inexpensive and easily accessible, Greece now has few places with an exclusive, or even a smart, atmosphere: not Mykonos, not Hydra, not Lindos, not Elounda, nor any of the other places where the jet set was to be found a few decades ago. Hotels on Crete that were once filled with merchant bankers on honeymoon are now filled with groups packaged by the world's biggest tour operators. It is hard to see that this constitutes ruination.

But there are certainly big differences of style between resorts and their clientele, as there are everywhere in the Mediterranean. Some resorts are all-new colonies of big hotel blocks or sprawls of nose-to-tail self-catering studio blocks, punctuated by discos. Others have grown out of old villages and have managed to retain their village looks, with tavernas, old men's *kafeneions*, fishing harbours and a colourful variety of packaged and independent tourists. Others are dominated by colonies of windsurfers and sporty sailing people.

Villages also look very different from region to region. The classic whitewashed cube and chapel villages on all the calendars are few outside the Cyclades. In northern Greece and other island groups you find pitched roofs of old rough-stone or new red tiles, and handsome timbered mansions in Turkish style. There are 19th-century British colonial buildings on Corfu, pre-War Italian colonial buildings in the Dodecanese. Large areas of the country have been flattened by recent earthquake and have no old buildings at all.

There are big variations in the national make-up of the tourist population, which influences the style of tourism. For Greece as a whole, Britain is the number one source of tourists (1.8 million in 1988, 23 per cent of the total): wherever you choose a resort, you are unlikely to lack the company of compatriots. The Britishness is particularly dense on Corfu and the Ionian Islands, whose inhabitants are well used to us, having suffered (as they will remind you at every opportunity) British rule for half of the 19th century, when the rest of Greece was newly free. Over 90 per cent of the charter flight arrivals on the island of Cephalonia are British, and the figures for Corfu and Zante, the most developed of the Ionians, paint a similar picture – about 80 per cent British business. On these islands there is not much room for independent travellers in high season, with accommodation in big hotels and cheap, shoddy little purpose-built holiday rooming blocks or so-called villas, an alluring word that covers a multitude of architectural sins. In developed areas of the mainland coast of northern Greece (Halkidiki), on Rhodes, Kos and Crete the style of resorts is not very different but the tourist population is much less dominantly British. On Kos, Rhodes and Crete we account for about a third of the tourist population, on the increasingly busy island of Samos less than 10 per cent.

The Cyclades islands of the central Aegean are the realm of the footloose backpacking young ferry travellers, who make their way to Greece on a shoestring, set sail for the islands and hop from one to the next, sleeping on deck, on the beach, in campsites or in simple village rooms, moving on after a night or a month, depending entirely on how the mood takes them. The popular islands get impossibly crowded and are certainly very touristy, but there are few big hotel blocks and, visually, these islands have lost none of their beauty. When the summer season is finished, tourism recedes without a trace.

In the curious world we inhabit, there is now no longer a small minority taste but a mass taste for holidays away from the masses. Desperately fleeing our own shadows, we demand the illusion of doing things differently from other people, not being tourists at all. A place only has to establish itself as popular for us to want to go somewhere else. And yet we also want to be flown to within half an hour of our destination, we want others to make all the arrangements and we certainly do not want the worry of not having pre-booked accommodation. Our schedules are too tight, our need for freedom from stress and any decision-making agonies absolute. We look to the mass media for advice about where to discover the undiscovered, and we look to tour operators for package holidays in places unspoilt by package tourism.

Tour operators are happy to oblige, and brochures now provide a mixture of resorts styled either as lively, for those who are not put off by the idea of rubbing shoulders with tourists, or as unspoilt, for those who are. There is a growing number of small operators who specialise in holidays for those who like to think of themselves as travellers. It is easy to pour scorn on the pandering to travel snobbery and the meaningless promises of discovering the real Greece, but the product is often good: relaxing beach and taverna holidays in pretty, small, quiet places. Many of these places are in the busiest tourist areas, such as Corfu and Crete.

However, the search for new destinations is beginning to reach a barrel-scraping stage, with uninteresting and often unattractive destinations presented to the discerning public as the last word in unspoilt Greece. So off-putting is the idea of tourist development that potential visitors may be tempted by dead-end places that have very little to offer (and are now not even free from tourism), and diverted from the most deservedly famous, beautiful and historically fascinating places in Greece, simply because these places are reported to be overrun. This is madness.

Sanity lies in not being obsessed by the need to escape tourists and not selecting resorts simply on the basis of their being undeveloped. It is no coincidence that the most beautiful and interesting places in the country are those that have been developed for tourism: Crete, Rhodes, Kos, Corfu, Mykonos, Santorini, Paros. It would be odd if they had not. This is not a reason to stay away, but a reason to choose your holiday, and especially its timing, with care. Nowhere in Greece is overrun by tourists outside July and August. Unless you positively enjoy boring your friends with droning stories about how things have changed, do not revisit old favourite haunts, but seek out new places; that way, you won't be disappointed by how your own Greece has changed and will be able to enjoy the underlying beauty of the place.

Whether they admit it or not, most people are likely to have more fun in a resort than in a village or town with no tourism at all. Tourism brings more comfortable accommodation, much better restaurants, yoghurt and honey for breakfast, excursions to even the most inaccessible sites, dinghies and windsurfers for hire, better plumbing. But if you do want to get off the beaten track and discover the other Greece, pick up your sunbed and go out and look for it. However important for the country tourism may be, it affects only small areas of the mainland coast and almost none of the interior except the immediate neighbourhood of a few of the best-known archaeological sites. No one could complain that independent travel in Greece is arduous. Cheap flights are widely available, despite the moderately strenuous attempts of the Greek authorities to block them on the probably spurious grounds that seat-only travellers are hooligans. Scheduled flights bought well enough in advance are not much more expensive. Public transport is comprehensive and very cheap. Accommodation is easily found. Every village has its English speakers, and in most places people are wonderfully friendly. The climate is ideal for summer holidays taken outside the hectic peak season months of July and August. Walkers, botanists, fly-drive tourers and sightseers can rejoice in the fact that the best months for them are when tourism is at a low ebb.

The other Greece still exists. But do not imagine you will find it by buying a package holiday from a tour operator, not even the one with the scruffiest brochure and the most plausible patter about holidays for independent travellers who like to get off the beaten track. Part of the fun of travelling in Greece is the freedom to do as you please, head off on unexpected tangents, change plans at a moment's notice. There are headaches and hassles, but the rewards always outweigh the inconvenience. Making your own arrangements will bring you into contact with other people than the tour operator's rep, and your holiday will be the richer for it. Package holidays have much to commend them, especially if you have children to cope with, are stuck with July/August or want a cruise or a specific activity holiday. But if you want to enjoy Greece in the round, there is no better way than a DIY holiday.

Tourism in Greece is entering a new phase. The Greeks say they no longer want to play the numbers game but instead want to play the upgrading game, which means improving quality, earning more from each tourist, pricing itself out of the hooligan market. This makes good sense, now that Greece is no longer the cheapest place in the Mediterranean for a basic sun-and-sand package. More money is to be made available for improving accommodation than for putting up new buildings. Greek hotels will have tennis courts and swimming-pools and jacuzzis. New marinas are being built. The result will be a more varied and less ugly leisure product.

Despite the talk of saturation having been reached and the

application of brakes, the development process that many lovers of the country regard as little short of sacrilege is sure to continue. The policy emphasis has shifted towards spreading the tourists around the country more evenly, so remote areas will go on getting the treatment: new island airports, new roads and big hotels on hitherto empty bays. Ikaria, Syros and Naxos are next on the airport hit list. No tears need be shed for Ikaria or Syros, but Naxos . . . now there is a place where nostalgia has a great future.

Another result of the new tourism may be a greener Greece. Having done serious surveys of what their visitors care about, the Greeks are now talking loudly about learning from mistakes and correcting them (although it is not clear how they propose to correct places like the Athenian Riviera), and of recognising that the country's most valuable natural resource is a clean sea. Athens is at last to have a sewage plant, as is Corfu. Throughout the country, hotels old and new are to be equipped to treat sewage. Everywhere, they say, new hotels and tourist rooms must be in a style that fits in with traditional local architecture, not just four storeys of bare concrete. Things are beginning to happen: ruined tower-houses of the Mani and timbered mansions of the Pelion have been restored and converted into holiday accommodation, and dying villages resuscitated.

There is a big gap between posturing and implementation but, if the Greeks mean what they say, it could just be that tourism will be a force for conservation and environmental awareness, not destruction and desecration. If so, Greece will have more to thank us for than our foreign exchange.

Choosing a holiday

Like most other popular holiday countries, only perhaps more so, Greece caters for many different tastes in holiday-making, from mountain hiking to sailing, from beach lazing and disco bashing to temple spotting and museum gazing. About the only generalisations to be made are that holidays are cheap (unless you hire a car), the sun shines from mid-May to mid-October, and accommodation and cuisine are simple. If you want a holiday in the lap of luxury, look elsewhere, and if a Greek hotel is presented to you as luxurious, be sceptical. The essence of enjoying Greece is enjoying the simple life.

A few areas, such as Crete, combine most of the different styles of activity and inertia. But the diversity of the country means that holiday-makers with different priorities will find their ideal Greece (and their ideal Crete, for that matter) in different places: one Greek resort is certainly not like another.

Scenery, architecture and historical background vary enormously from west to east, mainland to island, and even from one island to its close neighbour. There are areas rich in history and sightseeing interest, others more or less devoid of either monuments or even any old buildings, earthquakes having comprehensively and repeatedly flattened them. Some parts of Greece have vast sandy beaches, others only rocks; some stretches of coast where busy tourist resorts have been built have no good bathing at all. Holiday resorts may be big towns, small fishing villages, purpose-built hotel and apartment colonies or self-contained all-in-one hotel resort complexes. Some resorts have watersports facilities, organised excursions by boat and bus, and discos galore. In others you should expect to do a lot of reading.

The following lists of places recommended for certain kinds of holiday are intended as a short cut to relevant descriptive sections of the guide, which may in many cases contain important qualifications to the inevitably rather vague general recommendations.

Sightseeing

The three richest areas are Athens, the Peloponnese and Crete. The national capital is no place for a summer holiday, although all travellers interested in Greek antiquity will want to visit the

Athens Acropolis and National Archaeological Museum, where most of the important finds from sites throughout Greece (except Crete and Macedonia) are housed.

A touring holiday is much the best way to make the most of the Peloponnese and Crete, although on Crete most of the important sites can be visited on excursions from the main resorts. Crete and to a lesser extent the Peloponnese have good beach holiday resorts and are thus excellent places for holidays combining sightseeing with lazing around. Enervating mid-summer temperatures and crowds, however, can make the driving and sightseeing elements of the holiday a bit of a slog. All in all, spring and autumn are ideal times for a visit to either place; autumn is better for bathing, spring better for landscape beauty. Crete is one of the few parts of Greece much visited in winter, and is well worth considering: there is plenty of life in its towns, snow (and even skiing) in the mountains and, often, summer weather on the south coast.

The main sightseeing attractions on the mainland outside Athens and the Peloponnese include Salonika, Meteora, Delphi and the monastic peninsula of Mount Athos. The Peloponnese islands are all (except Kithira) well placed for mainland excursions – to Athens as well as the Peloponnese. Day-trips to Turkey are organised from some of the eastern Aegean islands (Samos to Ephesus, for example), but the rules are volatile.

Apart from Crete, the most rewarding islands from a sightseeing point of view are:

Cyclades Naxos, Delos, Santorini
Dodecanese Rhodes, Kos, Patmos, Symi
Ionian Islands Corfu
North-east Aegean Chios, Samos, Samothrace
Peloponnese Islands Aegina, Hydra

The list needs to be extended to include the most picturesque old island villages (not including any on the islands already mentioned), among the most famous and photographed of Greek beauty-spots:

Cyclades Mykonos, Sifnos (Kastro), Paros (Parikia and Naoussa), Folegandros
Dodecanese Karpathos (Olymbos), Chalki
North-east Aegean Lesbos (Molyvos)
Sporades Skyros

Picturesque Greek island charm

Many people's ideally indolent Greek holiday formula features a
small white village on a small rural island, with donkeys, fishing-
boats, beaches, waterside tavernas and a not overwhelming
amount of tourism. The following islands fit the bill nicely:

Cyclades Andros, Kea, Naxos, Serifos, Sifnos, Folegandros, Amorgos,
Astypalaia
Dodecanese Nisyros, Patmos, Karpathos, Symi, Tilos
Ionian Islands Paxos, Ithaca
North-east Aegean Limnos
Peloponnese Islands Kithira
Sporades Skyros, Skopelos, Alonnisos

Similar, with lots of tourism and lively nightlife:

Cyclades Paros, Ios, Mykonos, Santorini
Peloponnese Islands Hydra, Poros, Spetses
Sporades Skiathos

Scenery

All the mainland regions have some areas of beautiful high
mountain scenery, as do the largest islands – Crete and Evia. Fine
mountain scenery can also be enjoyed on Karpathos, Naxos,
Santorini and Nisyros; the last two are spectacularly volcanic.

Otherwise, the fundamental distinction is between islands that
are abundantly green – the Ionian Islands and the Sporades – and
those that are sparsely vegetated and, from late June to October,
parched and brown – the Cyclades. To the green party should be
added the thickly wooded islands of Thassos (despite recent fire
damage), Spetses and Poros. In addition, there are large areas of
fertility and forest on most of the big islands: Crete, Rhodes, Kos,
Karpathos, Lesbos, Samos, Chios, Naxos and Evia. Other islands
with beautiful pastoral landscapes (not only in spring, when much
of Greece goes through brief periods of brilliant colour) include
Tinos, Andros, Kea and Sifnos.

Beaches

A small stony cove to yourself with a few overhanging pine trees
and crystal-clear water may seem preferable to vast wide sands at
a busy resort, packed with tavernas and ranks of loungers and
umbrellas, its waters thick with skiers and pedalos; also, a
wonderful beach in June may be insufferable in August.

Beach connoisseurs may totally disagree about the different
factors that make a good beach: texture, colour, steepness under

water, shelter from wind, size, popularity, facilities (food and drink, lavatories, loungers and umbrellas, showers, watersports), shade and ease of access are all matters of personal taste, and beauty is a concept that seems even more nebulous than usual when applied to beaches. About the only matters unlikely to be questioned are the desirability of clear water and an unlittered beach, and the undesirability of sea-urchins and jellyfish.

All too often remote and little-visited beaches reached with some difficulty turn out to be covered in garbage instead of virgin clean. If you have observed the amount of rubbish chucked into the Mediterranean from ships and pumped into its harbours, this will come more as a disappointment than a surprise. All the rubbish has to land somewhere, and much of it is washed up on beaches exposed to the prevailing winds, which means north-facing beaches in the Aegean. Those who run tavernas or watersports operations are often obliged to clean their beaches.

The dream of finding a beautiful, completely deserted beach in summer now rarely comes true in Greece, unless you have your own boat. But many islands have the sort of remote or secluded sandy beaches appreciated by those who like to shed all clothes. There is nothing very defined or permanent about where nudity is and is not tolerated, and references to 'official' nude beaches mean little. Hardly anywhere in Greece is naturism institutionalised. Nude bathers simply go to remote beaches or the remote end of long beaches, where other nude bathers go, and these places become well known locally and in a few cases on the international beach bums' grapevine. Toplessness is now a matter of routine in almost all resorts, and is no longer confined to foreign tourists or the well proportioned.

The following inevitably subjective list of best beaches distinguishes between resorts with good beaches and islands with good beaches away from the main resorts. For the purposes of this selection, big and sandy is good. We have not counted beaches with a few rooms or hotels as resorts, although holidays in such places may be sold by tour operators.

Best resort beaches:

Mainland Tolon, Methoni, Stoupa, Loutra Kaiafas, Vouliagmeni
Crete Mallia, Rethymnon, Plakias, Matala, Paleohora
Cyclades Naxos, Ios, Serifos, Andros (Batsi), Sifnos (Kamares), Santorini (Kamari, Perissa)
Dodecanese Kos (town, Kardamena), Karpathos, Rhodes (all east-coast resorts)
Ionian Islands Corfu (Kavos, Sidari, Agios Stefanos west, Glifada, Agios Gordis), Cephalonia (Skala), Zante (Laganas, Alikes)
North-east Aegean Lesbos (Sigri, Eressos), Limnos
Peloponnese Islands Aegina (Agia Marina), Kithira (Kapsoli)
Sporades Skyros

Best out-of-town beaches:

Mainland Parga, Sivota, Arillias, Halkidiki (hotel complexes), Pylos
Crete
Cyclades Mykonos, Naxos, Paros, Antiparos, Serifos
Dodecanese Kos, Karpathos, Rhodes, Tilos
Ionian Islands Corfu, Zante, Lefkas, Cephalonia
North-east Aegean Samos, Ikaria, Limnos, Thassos
Sporades Skiathos, Skopelos

Watersports

Nearly all popular beaches have watersports operators, renting
pedalos and windsurfboards by the hour from June to September.
Waterskiing, parascending, jetskis and other refinements are less
widespread but still common. Unsurprisingly, the busier the
resort, the wider the range of facilities you are likely to
encounter.

If you want to go to Greece specifically to learn to windsurf, it
is probably best to go on a windsurfing package holiday, provided
you are prepared to devote most of your holiday to the sport. The
relevant operators usually have a choice of centres chosen with
beginners in mind. If you aren't tempted by the idea of an
intensive watersports holiday, almost any resort in the Sporades,
Peloponnese Islands or Ionian Islands (where winds are generally
modest) will have boards to rent and instruction. Beginners
should avoid the Cyclades and Dodecanese in July and August.

For the experienced watersporter, the great attraction of a
specialist package is being able to use a variety of good equipment
rather than the basic boards rented out by most beach operators,
with some exceptions. Some tour operators offer dinghy or
catamaran sailing as well as windsurfing.

If you are already accomplished and want to combine an island
holiday with some sport, we offer the following tentative shortlist
of islands with a good combination of wind, beaches and hire
facilities.

Crete
Cyclades Paros, Naxos, Santorini (Kamari), Mykonos
Dodecanese Kos, Rhodes
Ionian Islands Lefkas
North-east Aegean Samos (Kokkari)

The Greek National Tourist Organisation can provide details of
specialist tour operators offering watersports holidays.

Sailing holidays

If you want to sail around a group of islands by yacht, as opposed to sailing dinghies from an island or mainland coastal base, you can buy a flotilla package or charter your own yacht. The most popular areas for flotilla holidays are the Ionian Islands, the Sporades and the Peloponnese Islands (and the mainland around Porto Heli in the Peloponnese), all offering safe and relatively straightforward sailing. If you want to tackle the greater challenge of the open seas and stronger winds of the Aegean you need to be an experienced yachtsman and charter bareboat or charter a skippered yacht.

The flotilla holiday is designed for modestly experienced and even inexperienced sailors, and is as much a social as a sports holiday, although the quality of the sailing depends entirely on the wind, which is less predictable than many tour operators imply in their brochures. Flotillas of a dozen or so four- to six-berth yachts follow set itineraries, meeting up in the evening. Flotilla operators may offer bareboat charter, combined shore-based and flotilla holidays and training sessions in Britain before departure.

The Greek National Tourist Organisation can provide details of tour operators offering flotilla holidays and of yacht charter operators. See also page 348.

Nightlife

Greeks are animated and often unstoppable conversationalists. After the twilight *volta*, or parade along the water-front, the typical summer evening consists of a protracted meal outside a taverna followed by a protracted nightcap outside a cafe. Most tavernas have some music and occasionally dancing breaks out, but wild bacchanalian nights of music, dancing and plate smashing usually take place in rural tavernas rather than in resorts, except at festival time. Tour operators may organise evening excursions from busy resorts to these country tavernas with locals on hand to demonstrate and lead the dancing.

Many resorts have open-air cinemas and even the most peaceful Greek seaside village resort has an open-air disco, usually on the outskirts of the village; many of these establishments amount to little more than a concrete dance pad and a ramshackle shed, and come to life only for a few weeks in mid-summer. In resorts that see a lot of international tourism, nightlife is much noisier, if not always particularly diverse, and the lively season much longer. As well as discos there may be cocktail bars and pubs playing rock, jazz and even classical music.

Best resorts/islands for lively nightlife (bars and discos):

Mainland Tolon, Glyfada, Vouliagmeni
Crete (Hersonisos, Mallia, Agios Nikolaos, Agia Galini, Matala)
Cyclades Santorini (Fira, Kamari), Ios, Paros (Parikia), Mykonos, Naxos (town)
Dodecanese Rhodes (all resorts), Kos (Kos and Kardamena)
Ionian Islands Corfu (Ipsos, Benitses, Moraitika, Kavos, Kassiopi, Paleokastritsa), Zante (Laganas)
North-east Aegean Lesbos (Plomari), Thassos (town, Limenaria), Samos (Pithagorio, Kokkari)
Peloponnese Islands Hydra, Spetses, Aegina (Agia Marina)
Sporades Skiathos, Skopelos, Skyros

Island-hopping

An island-hopping holiday means nothing more complicated than a holiday spent visiting a series of islands, ideally in your own or a chartered yacht, but more likely on the ferries; it is the insular equivalent of a touring holiday on the mainland or Crete, with the considerable advantage that you don't have to hire a car or make long stuffy bus journeys, but do your touring cheaply and (generally) enjoyably, on deck.

The essence of such holidays is freedom to move on or stay put at your whim, and it would be perverse (and needlessly expensive) to limit your options by buying an island-hopping package holiday, although some operators do offer such things. The only exception to this is for travel in August, when finding accommodation is extremely difficult.

Most of the small islands can be fully explored in a few days, and it is quite possible to visit half a dozen in a fortnight without undue rush, although you may well find that the charms of an island detain you for longer than expected.

The ideal island-hopping group is the Cyclades, where lots of small islands and very good summer ferry- and excursion-boat connections make it possible to construct a variety of different itineraries, combining the most famous beauty-spots (Paros, Mykonos and Santorini) with remote and little-visited islands, whose charm is less obvious but no less certain.

Island-hopping holidays traditionally start and end at Piraeus. Save time and a very tedious first leg to the journey (even the closest of the Cyclades are a half-day's sail from Piraeus) by flying to an island, either direct from Britain or by internal flight from Athens. Always allow a generous margin for delay at the end of a trip. An increasing number of Cyclades ferries use the mainland port of Rafina, which has a number of advantages over Piraeus, despite being marginally less convenient for central Athens and the airport.

If you develop a taste for island-hopping, you will probably want to explore the other groups. It is not as easy to ring the changes of itinerary as in the Cyclades, but travelling between the islands is neither difficult nor expensive, even in the north-east Aegean, where distances between islands are long and the main islands are large and interesting enough to merit a longer visit than a day or two.

The Ionian Islands see little island-hopping tourism: ferry services are not totally straightforward, and the islands are short of the cheap rooms beloved of island-hoppers; hotels block-booked by tour operators tend to be expensive for independent travellers passing through for a night or two. Crete or the Dodecanese can be combined with a Cyclades tour or reached direct from Britain or Athens (by plane or ferry). To do justice to Crete requires far more than a few days, but the Dodecanese lend themselves well to the island-hopping treatment, with a great variety of scenery and beaches, and exceptional historical interest. Kos and Rhodes, however, are ever-increasingly dominated by package tourism. The Sporades are an attractive leafy quartet with good ferry and hydrofoil connections between them, but have no easy connections with other groups. The same is true of the Peloponnese Islands.

August

Advising people not to take holidays in August is like advising city dwellers not to choose weekends for day-trips to the coast: splendid, if fairly obvious, advice for those able to make use of it, as many are not.

Overcrowding in resorts is much more severe in August than in July, because many Greeks take the whole month off, and large numbers of expatriates return to spend the month with their families on holiday or on their native islands. Not only are there more people in the resorts and on the beaches, but the supply of rooms for rent in private houses is actually reduced.

For independent travellers, there is no escaping the accommodation problem. High season may be a good time to visit remote and undeveloped islands which come to life only at this time of year and which still seem peaceful and relaxing, but the supply of rooms, restaurants and water is as likely to be overstretched as in big resorts.

Travel in August is a constant battle in temperatures unconducive to battling: people push to be first on the ferries in the hope of finding a seat, and push to be first off so as not to miss any rooms on offer. You tramp the streets for hours looking for a bed, fight for a place on the bus, and queue for a restaurant table hours earlier than you would like to eat, for food runs out early. By the end of the week you will need a holiday.

The solution is not to plan a touring or an island-hopping holiday, but to book a package well in advance and stay put. Car hire should also be booked in advance. A villa holiday is a good way to escape the worst of the high-season stress.

If you are travelling around in August, take a sleeping-bag. If at all possible, avoid making ferry journeys that involve arriving late in the day. Unless you want to witness the most famous pilgrimage in Greece, when pilgrims camp out in the streets, avoid the Cycladic island of Tinos on and around 15 August. In general, the first and last weekends in August are particularly hectic on the ferries.

Family holidays

The best formulae for families with children are either a self-contained beach hotel with good facilities of its own or a villa to rent somewhere easily accessible, with a good safe beach near by. The best places for the second option are northern Corfu, Zante and Skiathos.

The best places for self-contained beach hotel complexes, with a pool and other sports facilities, restaurants and nightlife on-site are:

Mainland Halkidiki, Tolon, Sivota
Crete
Dodecanese Rhodes, Kos
Ionian Islands Corfu, Zante
North-east Aegean Limnos, Samos (Pythagorio)
Sporades Skiathos

Accessibility

Whoever said travelling is better than arriving cannot have taken a package holiday. In these days of air traffic jams and charter flights leaving at two in the morning (when on time), travelling is the worst thing about holidays. Not surprisingly, for many holiday-makers the question of accessibility comes right at the top of the list of factors influencing decision-making; an uncomplicated journey is not so much a high priority as a non-negotiable requirement.

In Greece, where so much of the tourism is on islands, there is a sharp distinction between places with and without direct flights from Britain. Although there is a big variation in the degree of remoteness of islands without these direct flights, the distinction is still important: even the most straightforward ferry, hydrofoil or internal flight connection can involve long hours of hanging around or an overnight in transit. In the context of a short holiday this is a serious annoyance, whether or not aggravated by a heatwave, heavy luggage and overtired children. If the onward connection seems to dovetail neatly and avoids the need for a long wait, the chance of the connection being missed because of delayed departure looms large and menacing; if there is more than one leg to your journey, the knock-on effect of delayed departure can assume nightmare proportions.

On the other hand, if you book a holiday on a small island such as Skiathos, Mykonos or Santorini, you will have the consolation of knowing that, however protracted the business of getting away from Britain may be, when you do arrive it will be to within a quarter of an hour of your holiday accommodation. With so many island airports, Greece has an exceptional number of holiday destinations with admirably short airport-to-resort transfer times.

There is a price to be paid for convenience, of course. Having an airport capable of receiving direct charter flights is symptom and cause of a boom in local tourism: if you want to escape masses of other tourists, you should not expect to be able to do so on a small island with direct flights from Britain. The list of direct charter airports suggests a few areas which have the advantage of convenience without, so far, large numbers of people taking advantage of it. These are the places where tourism is most likely to expand rapidly over the next few years, except Paros, which has already developed a large volume of ferry-borne tourism. Naturally, the number of tour operators offering flights to these minor destinations is few.

There are various degrees of easy accessibility:

Scheduled flights from Britain Athens, Salonika (Thessaloniki), Corfu
Direct charter flights Mainland and island airports in descending order of passenger numbers (949,000 people arrived at Heraklion in 1988, and 1000 in Limnos): Heraklion (Crete), Athens, Rhodes, Corfu, Kos, Salonika (Thessaloniki), Zante, Chania (Crete), Samos, Skiathos, Cephalonia, Lesbos, Mykonos, Santorini, Preveza, Araxos (Patras), Kavala, Kalamata, Karpathos, Paros, Chios, Limnos
Internal flights All the airports with direct charters also have internal flight connections with Athens, except Karpathos (connections with Rhodes and Crete). In addition, the following islands have airports with internal flights (to and from Athens unless stated otherwise) but no direct charters: Kassos (connections with Rhodes and Crete), Kastellorizo (connections with Rhodes), Kithira, Leros, Milos, Skyros
Hydrofoils With frequent and swift hydrofoil connections with Piraeus, the Peloponnese Islands of Aegina, Poros, Hydra and Spetses are at least as accessible as the islands served by internal flights.
Other A few islands have very short and frequent connections with

airports served by direct charter and internal flights. Skopelos and Alonnisos are very easily reached from Skiathos, Thassos from Kavala, Kalymnos from Kos.

Evia and Lefkas are linked to the mainland by road. The transfer time from Athens to Evia is at least two hours. Lefkas is very close to its nearest airport (Preveza).

History, art and architecture

Prehellenic

From 3000BC Bronze Age civilisations in Cyclades and Crete.

Decorated fired-clay **pottery***. Small semi-abstract figurines, mostly female in form, made of local Naxos/Paros marble.* [Museum of Cycladic and Ancient Art, Athens; Naxos Museum]

2000–1500BC Golden age of **Minoan** civilisation on Crete. Palaces built c 1900BC, and destroyed – probably by earthquake – c 1700BC; rebuilt with wall-paintings, again destroyed c 1450BC by fire, probably connected with massive volcanic eruption on Santorini and consequent tidal wave c 1500BC.

Building of elaborate unfortified **palaces** *on Crete. Complex, labyrinthine plan: varied rooms on several levels, stairs and linking passages, light-wells and courtyards. An efficiently piped water supply. Colourful* **wall-paintings** *in lively, sensuous style, and sculpted low relief. Elegant* **pottery** *with vigorous, inventive decoration, especially the later vases with octopus and marine themes. Bulls a* leitmotif *in Minoan art and possibly religion (Minotaur legend).* [Archaeological Museum, Heraklion]

c 1500–1100BC **Mycenaean** (or Achaian) civilisation based in Peloponnese conquers Minoan Crete, and extends trading empire throughout eastern Mediterranean. Possible siege and conquest of Troy, related in Homer's *Iliad*. Mycenaeans adapt Minoan script into Linear B, first written Greek. Decline and destruction of Mycenaean settlements between 1200 and 1100BC; invasion and settlement by mountain tribe of **Dorians** from the north.

On the mainland, fortress-walls and citadel-palaces of massive **masonry***, sited for defence, with villages below. Royal dwellings a simple rectangular layout of hall (***megaron***) with central hearth; entry through spacious outer vestibule; private apartments behind. Palace art and pottery generally derivative of Minoan style, with additional* **battle and hunting themes***. Artefacts and ornaments of* **gold***, seemingly much in use and beautifully crafted, buried with the royal dead in three types of graves: pits, sepulchres or beehive-domed 'tholos' chambers – first known as 'treasuries'.* [National Archaeological Museum, Athens]

1150–750BC **'Dark age'** of economic and trading decline; return to pastoralism. Gradual emergence of **city-states** after c 1000BC. Refugee Mycenaeans (known as Ionians) settle on Aegean islands, in Asia Minor and in Attica; **Athens** becomes leading Ionian city. In the Dorian city of **Sparta**, Lycurgus instigates a totalitarian military regime. Swift and successful expansion from Greece to coastal settlements around the Mediterranean and along the Black Sea. First official celebration of the pan-Hellenic Olympic Games in 776BC.

Decoration on pottery limited to lines and circles, called **geometric**. *Gradually, funerary, battle and dance themes incorporated into the designs on red terracotta vases.* [National Archaeological Museum, Athens]

Archaic

c 750–500 BC The epic poems of **Homer** – the *Iliad* and the *Odyssey* – tell the story of the Trojan War and the subsequent adventures of Odysseus, King of Ithaca. Power-struggles between mainland city-states. Oligarchies replaced by single **tyrants**, some enlightened, including Peisistratos of Athens. Increasing creativity in the literary arts. Unity of Greek speakers, in Greece or settlements; others termed 'barbarians'.

Influence of Egypt in architecture, sculpture, pottery and script. Replacement of wooden structures with stone. Monumental **temples**, *derived from the rectangular 'megaron' throne-room; rows of columns, supporting sloping roof. The* **Doric Order** *(c 650BC, Peloponnese) was the earliest and plainest style of column, the* **Ionic** *(c 600BC, eastern Greece) added decorative scrolling (volutes) at the top of the shaft. Sculpture ornamented the* **frieze** *between columns and roof and the triangular* **pediment** *below the gable end.*

The first life-size or larger **statues**, *in standard pose (one foot forward, hands held close to body), with stylised hair and smile; distinctive types were the* **Kore** *and* **Kouros**, *clothed maiden and naked youth.*

Oriental decorative motifs on pottery, followed by **black-figure** *style on red clay, then more flexible* **red-figure** *on a black ground (c 500BC): formal patterns, running friezes of animals, dramatic narratives of gods and mortals. Innumerable examples survive, a major source of our illustrated knowledge of Greek religion and history.* [Corinth Museum; National Archaeological Museum, Athens; Acropolis Museum, Athens]

Classical

500–400BC Emergence of democracy in Athens. Period of outstanding intellectual and artistic creativity: philosophy (Socrates, Plato), drama (Aeschylus, Sophocles, Euripides, Aristophanes), history (Herodotus, Thucydides), sculpture (Pheidias).

Expanding **Persian** empire overruns Greek colonies in Asia Minor. At **Marathon**, Athens defeats a Persian invasion (490BC). In 480, at **Thermopylae**, King Leonidas and his 300 Spartans die delaying the infantry of Persian Xerxes; Athens evacuated and destroyed before combined Greek fleet defeats Persians at sea battle of **Salamis**.

Athens' walls rebuilt (478–476BC) at start of 50-year period of **Golden Age**, culminating under leadership of **Pericles** (died 429BC). Lavish reconstruction of the city and building of temple complex on the Acropolis. Peace ends with outbreak of **Peloponnesian Wars** between Athens and Sparta in 431, which finally end in 404. **395–338BC** Various wars among Athens, Sparta, Corinth, Thebes. **Sparta** finally destroyed by Thebes at Battle of Leuktra (371BC). Athens' battles with encroaching **Philip II of Macedon**, who finally defeats a belated combination of Greek forces and becomes their overall commander.

The age of architectural and sculptural masterpieces. **Temples** *incorporate theoretically ideal proportions and subtle design mathematics to give a harmonious appearance.* **Theatres** *for drama exploit natural contours, with tiers of seats and retaining walls. In sculpture, after a transitional period,* **Pheidias** *(490– 430BC) and* **Polykleitos** *introduce a new canon of ideal beauty, liberated from conventions of Archaic style. Pheidias sculptor-in-chief of the Parthenon and other temples on Athenian acropolis; personally responsible for huge gold and ivory (chryselephantine) statues of Athena and 42-foot Zeus at Olympia, all lost.* **Parthenon marbles** *best surviving evidence of his style.* **Corinthian Order** *(acanthus leaf decoration of capitals) first used c 450BC (temple of Apollo at Bassae).*

Further evolution of sculptural style towards greater naturalism culminates in supremely graceful work of **Praxiteles** *(370–330BC). Statue of Hermes at Olympia his only certain surviving work; otherwise known through Roman copies. Statues usually painted. First female nudes. In bronze,* **Lysippus** *was a master of portrait sculpture.*

Hellenistic

336BC Philip II murdered.
334–323BC His successor, **Alexander the Great**, extends empire as far as India. Dies young, in Babylon.
323–225BC The Greeks fail to exploit fragmentation of Alexander's empire under his successors. Under Macedonian kings, Greek the written language of the civilised world, Athens its leading university city, influential in Egypt, Asia and young Rome. **Rhodes** emerges as important maritime power and cultural centre. Greek colonies in Italy threatened by Rome. King Pyrrhus of Epirus sent to their aid, winning only 'pyrrhic' victories.
215–146BC Increasingly dominant involvement of Rome in Greek affairs, at first by participating in **Macedonian Wars** between Philip V of Macedon and rival Greek Aetolian and Achaian federations. Philip forced into alliance with Rome c 200BC. Macedonian kingdom destroyed 168BC. Sack of Corinth 146BC. Formation of **Roman provinces** of Macedonia and Achaia.

c 300–100BC *Hellenistic city and sanctuary building makes much use of the* **stoa** *(a long, colonnaded portico backed by rooms) as meeting and working place. Temples refurbished; theatres given raised stages. Sculpture enters post-Classical phase: less balanced and generalised representations of ideal beauty, more elaborate physical and emotionally expressive detail. Laocoön [Pio-Clementino Museum, Vatican], Winged Victory of Samothrace and Venus de Milo [Louvre, Paris] among many masterpieces surviving outside Greece. Colossus of Rhodes lost (c 280BC).*

Roman

180–86BC Greece suffers as battleground of wars between Rome and Asia Minor kingdoms. Heavy taxation, sanctuaries plundered and treasures sent to Rome.
48–31BC Rome's civil wars, also partly acted out in Greece; successive defeats of Pompey, Brutus and Cassius, Antony and Cleopatra (at Actium, 31BC).
From 31BC Prosperity and settled conditions of Augustus's **Pax Romana**. Greece insignificant in the Empire, but Athens still the fashionable seat of learning.
AD49–54 Visits of **Saint Paul** to Salonika, Athens and Corinth.
120–150 Prestigious Roman rebuilding, especially in Athens by Emperor **Hadrian** and philanthropic banker **Herodes Atticus**.
c 170 Pausanias's *Description of Greece*: travel writing for the Romans, a comprehensive guide to the sites.

200–300 Spread of Christianity and growing menace of Goths on northern frontier.

313 Constantine's Edict of Milan, which declares freedom of worship.

330–395 Under Constantine, Byzantium (renamed **Constantinople**) becomes the new capital of the Roman Empire. Under Theodosius I, **Christianity** is adopted as the official state religion (380), and pagan rites are forbidden. Formal division of Roman Empire into Latin west and Byzantine east.

395 Alaric's **Goths** devastate Athens and the Peloponnese.

Enlargement and redecoration of Athens and important sanctuaries. Wooden-roofed theatres (odeions) supplement open theatres. Corinthian style widely used. Neo-classical sculpture, and much copying of Greek masterpieces. Lifelike portrait-statues and busts.

Byzantine and Medieval

From 395 Unlike Rome and western Empire, Constantinople secure against outside attack but consumed by doctrinal disputes between different national churches. Raids of Goths and Vandals in mainland Greece.

527–567 Emperor **Justinian** temporarily effective against the barbarians. Salonika becomes second city of Byzantine Empire.

529 Athens' schools of philosophy closed – Plato's Academy and Aristotle's Lyceum.

565–1025 **Slavs** invade and settle Greece, eventually becoming Christians. Saracens and Bulgars new threat to Macedonian emperors (Basil the Bulgar-slayer).

681–1054 Increasing controversies between east and west churches, notably over role of religious imagery (with opposing factions of iconoclasts and iconodules), culminating in formal separation of Latin and Greek churches.

1050–1200 Sicilian Normans invade mainland Greece. Venetians begin to annex islands. The eastern Empire is overrun by **Turks**, against whom the Papacy summons Crusades in 1095, 1147 and 1187.

1204 Constantinople taken and sacked by the discreditable **Fourth Crusade**; Franks and Venetians found the **Latin Empire**.

1210–1262 Feudal territories in Greece: Attica and Boeotia under Duke of Athens (the de la Roche family), the Peloponnese under Prince of the Morea (the Villehardouins); islands mostly Venetian.

From 1261 Constantinople taken by Anatolian Michael Paleologos, who re-establishes Greek control. Byzantine reconquests in the Peloponnese, where **Mistra** becomes an artistic and intellectual centre.

1262–1355 Greek, Frankish, Venetian and Genoese factions constantly in conflict, employing Catalan and Turkish mercenaries. Expelled from Holy Land, **Knights of St John** take over and fortify Dodecanese islands (after 1309).

1355–1400 Increasingly expansionist Turks take over much of mainland Greece.

1402 Temporary lull in Turkish momentum when Sultan Bayazet defeated and captured by the Mongols under Tamerlane. The Byzantine Empire is reduced to Constantinople, Salonika and the Peloponnese.

1453 Sultan Mehmet II takes Constantinople; Turkish occupancy of Greece.

Temples converted into Christian **churches**. *The first brick-built basilicas developed from the civic* stoa, *with wooden-roofed nave and two aisles. Oriental influence in the dome, symbol of heaven. Interior decoration of* **mosaic** *on arches and upper walls, sculptural decoration on capitals, cornices and the screen dividing church and sanctuary (iconostasis). Under Justinian, magnificent mosaic art: cubes of vividly tinted glass, leaves of silver and gold, stone tiles used only for pale flesh tints.*

Much destruction from 7th to mid-9th centuries. A new period of church building in the more settled conditions under the strong Macedonian emperors in the mid-9th to 12th centuries: small churches built of brick and ancient stone in Greek-cross shape (four arms of equal length) with a central dome. Internal decoration followed standard liturgical scheme: Christ Pantokrator (Almighty) central in dome, Virgin in apse; angels, apostles, saints and dignitaries placed hierarchically.

After 1300 elegant, complex churches built, combining basilica and Greek-cross structures, with external brick and tile ornament and several small domes. Mosaic too costly for impoverished Empire; replaced by **frescoes** *characterised by movement and expression within the liturgical composition.*

Fortresses *in key strategic locations are repeatedly strengthened and adapted by their various occupiers. Byzantine/Frankish/ Venetian fortifications on Ionian and Aegean islands, and in Peloponnese; especially impressive fortress town at Rhodes, occupied by Knights of St John in 14th and 15th centuries.*
[Byzantine Museum, Athens; churches in Salonika, Mistra and on Crete; monasteries at Ossios Loukas, Daphne, Mount Athos and on Chios; fortresses at Chlemoutsi, Koroni, Methoni and Nafplion in Peloponnese; houses in Nafplion and on Corfu]

Turkish occupation

1453–1832 Greece part of Ottoman Empire. Most Aegean islands taken in 1460s and 1470s, except Rhodes (1522), Chios and Naxos (1566), Cyprus and Samos (1571), Crete (1669) and Tinos (1715). Ionian islands except Lefkas (Ottoman rule from 1479 to 1684) revert to Venice after brief period of Ottoman control. Well-fortified island of Corfu remains under Venetians until 1797, but often raided and sacked.

Turkish rule generally fairly remote and confined to tax collection, especially on the islands and the Peloponnese, where local representatives effectively autonomous, often ruling in semi-feudal style. Climate of greater religious tolerance than under Venice, with a patriarch of the Orthodox church in Constantinople. But general discrimination against Greeks, whose only prospect of advancement in the Empire is via the 'tribute of children' (one male child in five taken to serve in the elite corps of Janissaries); numerous instances of sporadic unprovoked violence, and savage reprisals following any resistance. Turks offer no control of **piracy** in the Aegean, a constant scourge; many islanders abandon coastal villages for less vulnerable inland sites. A number of islands (Skopelos, Aegina, *et al*) completely abandoned after intensely destructive raids of Khaireddin Barbarossa, a Muslim convert from Lesbos with a navy of North African pirates. Notably violent tenor of life on Crete (where Turkish rule persists until the 19th century), with fiercely unsubmissive elements of local population.

1687 During a campaign which temporarily regained the Peloponnese, Venetian artillery touches off a Turkish powder store and largely demolishes the **Parthenon**.

18th century On the retreat in Europe, Ottoman Empire suffers increasing land shortage for imperial officials. Greeks expropriated and reduced to serfdom; many take to the mountains as brigands (**klephts**). Orthodox church in Constantinople increasingly corrupt and discredited. Growth of Greek trading activity in Mediterranean; big armed **merchant fleets** of islands of Hydra, Spetses, Psara. Russia foments unrest in Greece; unsuccessful uprising in Peloponnese under Count Orlov (1770). Refugees from reprisals flee to islands.

1789–1815 The French Revolution inspires expatriate Greeks with ideas of liberation. Napoleonic Wars greatly increase British involvement in the Mediterranean.

1814 Foundation in Odessa of the **Philiki Etairi** (Friendly Society) with specific aim of liberation of motherland.

1815 Ionian islands given independent constitution under British protection.

1821 War of Independence begins with roughly co-ordinated uprisings all over Greece (National Independence Day, 25 March). Only success in Peloponnese: Nafplion blockaded and taken with help of Spetsiots under leadership of Lascarina Bouboulina, first islanders to join independence movement.

European public opinion increasingly engaged following widely publicised massacres of over 25,000 Greeks on Chios and Psara (1822). Philhellene Lord Byron resides in officially neutral Ionian islands and attempts to mediate between the argumentative Greek factions; crosses to Greece to join besieged Greeks at Missolonghi and dies there, April 1824.

1825 Peloponnese re-taken by Ibrahim Pasha, followed by sustained period of ferocious reprisals. Ailing Greek cause rescued by decisive intervention of allied British, French and Russian force; Ibrahim's fleet annihilated at sea battle of **Navarino Bay** (at Pylos, in the Peloponnese).

1827 Greek leaders appoint Corfiot Ioannis Capodistrias as first president of independent Greece; Aegina becomes his capital. Autocratic style of government widely resented; Capodistrias assassinated 1831. Young Bavarian prince, Otto, deemed acceptable by all the Great Powers, becomes first king of Greece in 1833.

*Little creativity in new building or general cultural activity under Turkish rule. Flourishing of the arts on Crete when artists and scholars flee Constantinople after 1453. New elegance in fresco and icon painting ('***Cretan school***'), well represented in churches on the island, and later in those of the Meteora and Mount Athos, to which it migrated.* **El Greco** *a product of the school before going to Venice and Spain. After fall of Crete (late 17th century) artists evacuate this style of painting to Ionian islands.*

Elegant Venetian baroque churches and urban architecture in Ionian islands largely destroyed by war and earthquake, except at Corfu.

Domestic architecture varies considerably from region to region. Timbered Turkish-style **houses** *with projecting wooden upper storeys survive in some parts of northern Greece (Kastoria and Pelion) and Crete (Rethymnon). A number of island towns that grew rich from maritime trade in Turkish period have kept their imposing town* **mansions***: Hydra, Patmos, Simi, Lindos (Rhodes) best examples. Unique geometric style of external decoration on village houses of southern Chios still employed. Typically Cycladic whitewashed* **cube architecture** *often harmonious and very picturesque, although lacking much architectural refinement: finest examples on Mykonos, Paros, Sifnos, Folegandros, Skyros.*

Few monuments of Turkish rule survive, except in areas more recently joined to Greece: **mosques** *and* **minarets** *in Ioanina, on Kos, Rhodes, Lesbos, Chios; Turkish* **graveyards** *on Chios and Rhodes. In many places de-minaretted mosques have been secularised* [Chania tourist office, Nafplion cinema] *or left abandoned* [Chalkis, Evia]. *Elsewhere, buildings converted by the Turks have reverted to original role of Christian churches.*

Frontiers of independence

1830 Frontiers of new Greek nation established to include part of central Greece, the Peloponnese, the Cyclades, Evia and the Sporades. Ionian Islands and Kithira (1864); Epirus, Macedonia, north-east Aegean islands and Crete (1913); Thrace (1923); Dodecanese (1947). Large body of Greek opinion retains visionary 'Great Idea' of restoring old Orthodox eastern Empire based in Constantinople ('the city').

1843 Otto, compelled by an army-backed demonstration in Athens to abandon his Bavarian advisers, convenes a **National Assembly** and forms a constitution.

1853–7 Otto's abortive attempt during **Crimean War** to invade Thessaly and Epirus annoys France and Britain (allied with Turkey against Russia) who occupy Piraeus as a guarantee against 'brigandage'.

1859 Otto becomes even more unpopular by supporting Austria rather than the Risorgimento in Italy.

1862–4 Army-backed rising deposes Otto; young Danish prince accepted and proclaimed **George I of the Hellenes**; new democratic constitution. Britain cedes **Ionian Islands**.

1864–1913 Gradual economic development and expansion of frontiers whenever Balkan politics provide opportunity. Thessaly and Crete change hands or status more than once. Under Cretan prime minister **Venizelos**, Greece doubles in area by end of two Balkan Wars.

1913 George I, murdered by a madman, succeeded by son Constantine I.

1914–18 In **First World War** Constantine (married to Kaiser's sister) wants Greek neutrality, but Venizelos determined to support Allies. Constantine and crown-prince George leave the country; younger son Alexander regent. Greece fights; spectacular gains at subsequent peace treaties, including Smyrna in Anatolia.

1920–23 After the early death of Alexander, King Constantine recalled by plebiscite. Venizelos loses an election, but not before initiating a war with Turkey: Mustapha Kemal (Ataturk) victorious, Smyrna sacked. The **territorial settlement** then enforced by treaty applies today (apart from Dodecanese and Cyprus). The struggle to extend Greek frontiers ended by a compulsory **exchange of populations**: 1½ million Christian refugees arrive in Greece, and about 380,000 Muslims leave for Turkey.

King Otto brings German architects to Athens, and their neo-classical style is used for public building on the mainland, while economics allow. [Royal Palace, University, Academy, National Library, Athens]

Modern politics

1924–35 After the Smyrna defeat five political leaders are executed; the king is deposed again and a military coup declares a republic. Brief dictatorship of General Pangalos, then unstable gamut of political parties from monarchist to communist. New king, George II, restored by 97 per cent plebiscite.

1936–41 Deaths of several leading politicians. Monarchist **General Metaxas** inherits and exploits parliamentary impasse; **dictatorship**.

1940 Greece enters **Second World War** on Allied side when Metaxas rejects ultimatum from Mussolini to allow right of way for Italy's army. Metaxas's 'No!' ('Ochi') gives Greece its second national day, 28 October.

1941 Germans advance through Yugoslavia and take Salonika. Combined British, Australian and New Zealand expeditionary force joins Greeks in a series of heroic but unsuccessful rearguard actions, but is unable to hold the country. Crete last major part of Greek territory to fall.

1941–44 King and government in exile during **German occupation**. Varied **resistance** groups (including a strong Communist faction) in klepht (brigand) tradition remain active in many areas, particularly vigorous in Crete and Dodecanese after ill-fated Allied campaign there in 1943.

1945–49 After liberation, **civil war** between Communists and the government backed by Britain and USA. Paul I succeeds his brother to the throne. The **Truman Doctrine** commits the USA to preventing Soviet control of Greece or Turkey.

1949–55 Cold War; American aid, military and civil, to Conservative government. Greece joins NATO. Dodecanese islands have been ceded to Greece, but in Cyprus – under British protection since 1878 – the campaign for **enosis** (union with Greece) is just beginning.

1955–63 Economic reconstruction under Conservative leader **Karamanlis**. Problems include Russian threats to US bases – Kruschev mentions bombing the Acropolis – and terrorism in

Cyprus, which becomes an independent republic in 1960 under Archbishop Makarios.

1963–7 End of American civil aid increases hardship. Strikes, demonstrations, political trials, unstable governments. New king, young Constantine II.

1967–74 Smooth military coup installs totalitarian junta of **the colonels**. Constantine deposed after failed counter-coup. Dissent and intellectual activity suppressed, heavy press censorship, stagnant government under **Papadopoulos**. In 1973 brutal suppression of student demonstrations at Athens Polytechnic; second coup, harsher regime, under chief of military police **Ioannides**. After his attempt to have Archbishop Makarios assassinated, Turkish forces land on Cyprus, and finally occupy 40 per cent of the island. On the point of war with Turkey, Ioannides loses all support. Junta collapses; army and politicians dismantle dictatorship.

1974–75 All political prisoners are released and the Communist party legalised. New Democracy party led by Karamanlis wins the first election for ten years; Greece votes against the return of King Constantine and becomes a **republic** with an elected president.

1975–81 Continuing problems with Turkey over Cyprus and the Aegean – control over air-space, territorial waters and (following discovery of oil deposits) the sea bed. New Socialist party PASOK led by **Papandreou** gains ground in opposition: anti-Turkish, anti-American, anti-European.

From 1981 PASOK wins election. Leading Greece's first Socialist government, Papandreou becomes more moderate: Greece goes ahead with progress towards full EEC membership, does not leave NATO and remains narrowly at peace with Turkey. Campaign for return of Elgin Marbles led by Minister of Culture, former film and pop star Melina Mercouri, one of many distractions from tough deflationary regime. Socialist government wins diminishing support for carrying out non-socialist policies and is further undermined by financial and personal scandals. June 1989 election returns New Democracy as biggest single party but without overall majority. Interim coalition government set up under Tzannis Tzannetakis.

Mythology

The religion of Ancient Greece began with the worship of a Great Goddess and gradually changed to incorporate male-dominant cults. Greek gods were immortal projections of human virtues – and vices – and their powers were the violent forces of nature. The myths and legends which evolved around them illustrated recurrent moral themes, such as the punishment of pride or jealousy, and the tragic inevitability of the struggle against destiny.

The Romans took over the whole pantheon, giving each god and goddess a Latin name and suitable worship. But to the Greeks they were less abstract – almost very distant ancestors, whose legends had real and actual locations. Myth and history had a meeting-point.

There is no definitive version of any Greek myth. Variations in the stories are commonly covered by interesting but cumbersome addenda beginning 'but some say . . . but others believe . . . but according to X . . . but the account in Y . . .'. This chapter attempts only a simple introduction to (or reminder of) some of the characters and plots.

Creation

In the beginning, Earth and Uranus (the Sky) emerged from chaos. Ocean's stream swirled around the horizon where they met, and beyond it lay the Underworld whose lowest depth was Tartarus. Mother Earth had many children, from plants and beasts to a race of Giants, and her last 12 were the Titans. Uranus, fearing his children's power, imprisoned the Giants in Tartarus and swallowed each Titan at birth until Kronos, the youngest, castrated and overthrew him. Kronos took as consort his sister Rhea, and their offspring were the first six gods and goddesses. Fearing his own overthrow, Kronos five times took his child at birth and swallowed it. The sixth time Rhea deceived him into swallowing a stone, and the youngest child, Zeus, grew up at a safe distance. Then, with his mother's help, Zeus brought Kronos a drink of nectar and herbs which caused him to vomit up first the stone then five full-grown immortal children. The gods and goddesses claimed their inheritance. Rhea and Zeus released the Giants to fight on Zeus's side; the war between gods, Giants and

Titans rocked the universe, but the Titans were defeated. Down to Tartarus they were banished, all but a few, and the reign of the gods began.

The Olympians

Zeus and his brothers Poseidon and Hades drew lots: Zeus won control of the sky, Poseidon the sea and Hades the Underworld. Each was all-powerful in his kingdom; on earth they held power in common. Zeus set his court on Mount Olympos. He took his sister Hera as consort, but had many more children than hers. Hera resented his love affairs and his power, but attempts at rebellion failed, and all the gods accepted his overriding authority.

The gods and goddesses of Olympos (and their Roman names) are:

Zeus (Jupiter) All-powerful, arrogant, prolific; his thunderbolt is the ultimate weapon.

Hera (Juno) Powerful herself but subdued by Zeus; jealous and frequently shrewish. Patroness of marriage.

Poseidon (Neptune) Rules over all water, salt or fresh; produces springs or catastrophic tidal waves with his trident; enjoys earth and Olympos more than his palace under the sea, and is associated with horses.

Athena (Minerva) Chaste goddess of victory and wisdom, patroness of sciences, arts and crafts. She goes armed and helmeted and her symbol is an owl.

Aphrodite (Venus) Beautiful goddess of love; her magic girdle instantly inspires it, and her infant son **Eros** shoots arrows of desire.

Ares (Mars) God of war, who loves battle for its own sake, taking sides indiscriminately, and delighting in slaughter. His sister **Eris** (goddess of argument) is a troublemaker.

Apollo (Phoebus) Archer-god of music, medicine and prophecy, with a care for flocks and herds; quickly angered and cruel in youth, but later moderate in all things. The most famous oracle, at Delphi, is his.

Artemis (Diana) Apollo's sister, a huntress with a silver bow and arrows; she and her nymphs remain virgin, but children and childbirth are under her protection.

Demeter (Ceres) Sister of Zeus, powerful goddess of agriculture, corn and harvest. Her daughter **Persephone** (Proserpina) is the wife of Hades (see below).

Hestia (Vesta) Sister of Zeus, peace-loving goddess of hearth and home, welcome everywhere on earth.

Hephaistos (Vulcan) The smith-god, strong but lame and misshapen. He is craftsman to Olympos, and married to Aphrodite.

Hermes (Mercury) An entertaining latecomer to Olympos, full of trickery and an accomplished thief from babyhood. Zeus made him herald of the gods and gave him winged golden sandals and helmet. Goat-footed **Pan** is his son.

Dionysos (Bacchus) Another latecomer: Hestia, preferring earth, gave him her place on Olympos. The inventor of wine, he is god of intoxication and ecstasy and became patron of drama and the theatre.

Hades (Pluto) Remained in his Underworld, visiting neither earth nor Olympos since the occasion he abducted Persephone to be his queen. The grief of Demeter, her mother, so blighted the earth that Zeus persuaded Hades to let her go; but because she had eaten the food of the dead – albeit only seven pomegranate seeds – she was obliged to return to him for a part of each year. Ever since, nothing grows in the winter months when Demeter mourns again.

The making of mankind

Prometheus, a Titan friendly to the gods, made for their amusement clay figures of men, and a delighted Athena breathed life into them. Prometheus proceeded to endow his protégés with the skills and pleasures the gods enjoyed; but Zeus, displeased, contributed all the miseries of the human race. He made a woman, **Pandora**, and set her down on earth with a box he warned her not to open. But, woman-like, she did, and out flew old age, disease, despair and all the rest. From Prometheus, mankind's last gift was fire. This he had to steal from the gods: the light and warmth of the divine spark Zeus had expressly withheld from mortals. Enraged, Zeus blasted Prometheus with a thunderbolt, and though he could not kill him punished him cruelly. Prometheus was chained to an icy mountaintop, where each day an eagle came to tear his flesh and devour his liver, renewing great wounds that healed each night.

   Then Zeus turned his anger on the human race, whose impious quarrels offended his ears, and caused a great flood. All on earth perished, except one man and one woman. **Deucalion**, forewarned by Prometheus, built an ark and survived with his wife **Pyrrha**. When the waters subsided they prayed humbly to Zeus. He relented and allowed them to renew the human race, by casting behind them 'the bones of your mother' – the stones of Earth – which sprang up as men from Deucalion's hand and as women from Pyrrha's. Ever since, mankind has offered the gods their due prayers and sacrifices.

Gods and mortals

The Olympians had their own rivalries and jealousies, and
meddled enjoyably in mortal affairs. Poseidon hankered after
earthly kingdoms and claimed Attica; he gave Athens a well. But
it was of seawater, and Athena's gift of the olive was judged more
useful. Athena, supreme mistress of spinning and weaving, once
lost her temper with a princess called **Arachne** who wove a
faultless cloth depicting the gods, and turned the poor girl into a
spider. Apollo heard one **Marsyas** boasting that his music was as
fine as the gods', and challenged him to a contest; Apollo won,
and flayed Marsyas alive for his presumption. Artemis, bathing
with her nymphs, found a hunter called **Actaeon** watching
enthralled from a thicket. She turned him into a stag and let his
own hounds kill him. And there was a foolish king called **Midas**
who earned a favour from Dionysos; granted one wish, he asked
that whatever he touched might turn to gold. His joy at untold
wealth was brief, as even his food and drink became metallic.
Dionysos released him from his wish, but Midas was later
afflicted by Apollo with the ears of an ass, for supporting Marsyas
in the music contest. The ears could be concealed from all but his
barber, who let out the secret, and Midas expired from shame.

Love affairs between gods and mortals seldom caused jealousy,
but once there was scandal up on Olympos. Aphrodite took as her
lover the swaggering Ares and was seen at her sport by **Helios** the
sun, who told her husband. Hephaistos made a net of bronze,
gossamer-fine but unbreakable, and trapped the lovers in his
marriage-bed. Then he called in all the gods to witness his
dishonour, demanding the return of the marriage gifts he had
paid to Zeus before he would release Aphrodite from her public
embarrassment. But the gods looked, and roared with laughter.
Apollo and Hermes agreed aloud that they would relish being in
Ares' position, net and all; Poseidon offered to pay up and marry
her himself, if Ares defaulted; and Zeus refused to intervene. In
the end the net was lifted and nobody paid, for Hephaistos was
too much in love with Aphrodite to divorce her.

Hephaistos made weapons, toys and marvellous inventions for
the gods; mortals commissioned such things from **Daedalus**, a
smith almost as ingenious. While he was working for King **Minos**
of Crete, the king's wife **Pasiphaë** angered Aphrodite and was
punished by falling into a monstrous passion for a huge white
bull. Daedalus made her a hollow imitation cow, which the bull
obligingly serviced while Pasiphaë lay inside. In due course she
gave birth to the **Minotaur**, with bull's head and man's body. King
Minos imprisoned it in the most secret chamber of a labyrinth,
also devised by Daedalus, and refused to let the craftsman leave

Crete. So Daedalus constructed wings, for himself and his son **Icaros**, out of willow and feathers and wax; and they flew off from the island like gods. But Icaros soared so high that the sun's heat softened the wax, his wings loosened, and he fell into the sea and drowned. Daedalus reached Sicily, where his workmanship was much appreciated.

Years later, Minos caught up with him. Visiting Sicily, he offered a reward to anyone who passed a thread through the labyrinthine spirals of a triton shell, knowing Daedalus alone could do it. When the king of Sicily brought the problem to him, Daedalus fastened the thread to finest gossamer and the gossamer to an ant, then lured the ant through the shell by smearing honey round the exit hole. Seeing the threaded shell, Minos knew he had found his man. But Daedalus was never recaptured: he killed Minos in his bath by pouring boiling water on him through a hidden ceiling pipe.

Death and punishment

Minos, who had been a mighty law-giver, became one of the judges of souls in the Underworld. Dead souls from earth crossed the river Styx, paying a copper coin to **Charon** the ferryman. Guarded by **Cerberus**, the fierce three-headed dog, the dead awaited judgment in the Fields of Asphodel, sometimes forever, drinking forgetfulness from the river Lethe. Good souls passed on – unless their bodies lay unburied – to Elysium, a land of pleasures and perpetual sunshine. Evildoers went down to Tartarus, the place of punishment.

Tantalus had invited the gods to a banquet and served them his son Pelops cut up and stewed. For this and other crimes he was forever tormented with hunger and thirst, grasping for dangling fruits and lapping water seemingly in reach but always eluding him. **Sisyphus** had prospered by treachery, robbery and murder – he crushed his victims under stones – until he betrayed some secrets of Zeus. In Tartarus he struggled forever to push uphill a huge rock, which would crush him if he stopped, knowing his punishment would end if he got it to the summit, knowing too that each time he almost succeeded it would topple back to the bottom.

Only a handful of living men visited the Underworld and survived. The unhappiest was **Orpheus**, a music-maker taught by Apollo himself, who charmed birds, beasts and forests with his songs and won the woodnymph **Eurydice** for his wife. She died of a snake bite, and caring nothing for life without her he won over Charon, the dog Cerebus and Hades himself. Hades agreed to release Eurydice, but there was one condition: Orpheus must not look upon his wife until he had led her back into the upper world, or he would forfeit her. So Orpheus, rejoicing, retraced his steps as if alone. But when daylight shone from the entrance he had to know if she had followed. He turned; he caught one glimpse of her; and then she vanished, this time lost forever.

Sometimes the punishments of Tartarus began on earth: the **Furies**, three dog-headed crones, could haunt the dreams of an evil-doer or hound him day and night. Above all, they pursued those who murdered blood-relatives, such as the luckless **Oedipus**. As soon as his mother **Jocasta** had given birth to him, Oedipus was exposed on a mountainside to perish, because his father **Laius**, king of Thebes, had been warned by the oracle at Delphi that he would die by the hand of his son. The baby was found, and taken to the childless king of Corinth, who named him and brought him up as his own. When Oedipus reached manhood he paid a visit to the oracle, and was told that he was fated to kill his father and marry his mother. Stricken with horror and determined never to return to his parents in Corinth, he went on foot toward Thebes.

In a narrow defile he met his real father Laius, a stubborn old man who ordered him off the road so arrogantly that Oedipus tangled him in his own chariot reins and whipped up the horses to drag him to his death. Uncaring, Oedipus approached Thebes. The city was beset by the **Sphinx**, a monster with woman's head and lion's body, who each day devoured a citizen for failing to solve its riddle: 'What has four legs in the morning, two at noon and three in the evening?' Oedipus answered it: 'Man; he crawls on all fours as a baby, walks erect in youth, and uses a stick in old age.' The Sphinx, defeated, dashed itself to pieces down a cliff. The grateful Thebans acclaimed Oedipus their king, and he married their recently widowed queen, Jocasta, his real mother, and had children by her.

Terrible plague descended on Thebes. Oedipus sent to consult the oracle, who instructed him to punish the murderer of Laius; Oedipus duly laid a curse and sentence of exile on whoever it was. Soon there came dreadful revelations. A renowned seer proclaimed the blood-guilt of Oedipus; and from Corinth his foster-mother sent him the story of his discovery as a baby. Jocasta realised the full truth from many details, and hanged herself for shame and grief. Oedipus in frenzy blinded himself with a pin from her garments. He left Thebes and wandered the earth in torment, hounded for years by the Furies, until he died in exile.

The absolute power of the Furies lasted until the case of **Orestes**. He had deliberately killed his mother, and there was no more appalling blood-guilt than matricide; but there were mitigating circumstances and the gods fought for him. His mother **Clytemnestra**, with her lover **Aegisthus**, had murdered his father **Agamemnon** on his return from the Trojan War. For seven years the two ruled Agamemnon's kingdom, Mycenae. Then Orestes, who had been brought up by his grandparents, learned from Apollo's oracle that he was destined to end the long chain of treachery and murder in his accursed family by avenging his father's death. He must kill his mother, and face the Furies.

Urged on by his sister **Electra** from her unhappy life at Mycenae, Orestes came to the palace in disguise, took Aegisthus off guard and despatched him first. Then his mother recognised him and begged for mercy, but he stabbed her to death. The madness and agony of the Furies began from that moment: they tracked Orestes wherever he went, visible in their ghastliness so that all men turned away from him in fear and loathing. They fell asleep once, while he was in sanctuary at Delphi; but Clytemnestra's ghost came to rouse them and they pursued him to Athens.

In Athena's temple he was given a trial before a jury of citizens. The Furies demanded their rightful prey, and Apollo appeared for the defence. Voting was equal; then Athena's casting vote released Orestes to go in peace to claim his kingdom. As for the Furies, Athena placated them with new and benign powers to invoke fair winds, fine harvests and fruitful marriages. She gave them a shrine under the Acropolis, and their suppliants prudently called them 'the Kindly Ones'.

Heroes and monsters

Bellerophon, a particularly handsome prince, was sent monster-hunting as an unjust punishment for trying to seduce his hostess (whose advances he had in fact rejected). His quarry was the **Chimaera**, a fire-breathing medley of lion, serpent and she-goat. A seer told him where to find a wonderful winged horse, called **Pegasus**; with Athena's help Bellerophon caught and mastered the horse, and was then able to overcome the Chimaera from his airborne mount. After this and other exploits his reputation was cleared and he prospered. But he kept Pegasus, and one day tried to ride up to Olympos; for this presumption in a mortal Zeus made him fall off. Bellerophon ended his life a crippled beggar.

Perseus had better prospects from the start. His father was Zeus, who visited his mother **Danae** as a shower of gold. Because of a prophecy that Danae's son would kill his grandfather, she and the infant Perseus were cast out to sea in a wooden chest, but they were rescued and given a home by a king called **Polydectes**. In due course, Polydectes wanted to be rid of Perseus, the better to pay court to his mother, and he tricked Perseus into a boast that he would bring home the head of **Medusa**, the Gorgon. Medusa had deadly snakes for hair and a face so terrible that to look upon it was to turn instantly to stone: Perseus needed help from the gods.

Hermes provided winged sandals, a helmet of invisibility, an adamantine sickle to cut off the head and a magic wallet to carry it in; Athena a brightly polished shield, and the essential advice that Perseus should use it as a mirror, and look only at the reflection of the Gorgon. Thus abundantly equipped, and after interim adventures, Perseus collected Medusa's fearsome head. On the way back with it he saw a beautiful naked girl chained to a rock in the sea: she was **Andromeda**, set there as a sacrifice to placate a sea monster who devastated her father's kingdom. Perseus fell in love at first sight, killed the monster and married Andromeda. Arriving home in triumph, he found his mother Danae hiding in a temple from the unwelcome attentions of Polydectes and his friends. So Perseus, averting his eyes, held high the Gorgon's head in the king's banqueting hall, and all present turned to stone. Perseus went on to become a great king, and found a dynasty. As prophesied, he did kill his grandfather by accident, with an unlucky discus-throw at the games; and when he died he went to Olympos, as befitted a son of Zeus.

Herakles (Hercules) too was a son of Zeus, conceived from no light amour but with the deliberate intention of putting on earth a champion of the gods against all enemies. Herakles was born heroic – he strangled in baby fists two lethal serpents sent to his cradle by the jealous Hera – and grew up talented, immensely strong and invincible with his bow. Youthful exploits included impregnating in a single night the 50 daughters of a neighbouring king. He lived a life of honourable battles until Hera made him temporarily mad and he killed some of his own children. In penance, he had to perform 12 tasks – the **Labours of Herakles** – for the feeble king **Eurystheus**. These were long and wearisome safaris and Herakles used to take time off in between to join other heroes' quests. Eurystheus, who dreaded his triumphant returns, hid in a huge half-buried bronze jar from each terrible beast he brought back.

The first was the Nemean lion, weapon-proof; Herakles wrestled it to death and wore its pelt. The second, the nine-headed venomous Hydra, provided him with poison for his arrows. Then he chased for a year the swiftest hind in the world, brought her back gently and let her go; and the man-eating boar which came next gave him no trouble. The fifth labour was to clear in one day the massively filthy Augean stables, accomplished by diverting two rivers through them; the sixth, to deal with the man-eating flock of brazen Stymphalian Birds, which Herakles failed to kill but drove far away with sheer noise.

For his seventh task he captured the Cretan bull that sired the Minotaur, and for his eighth he mastered four savage mares. Then Eurystheus demanded as a present for his daughter the golden girdle of Hippolyta, queen of the Amazons who made war more fiercely than men. Herakles made a leisurely quest of this with a crew of friends and many adventures on the way, and in the event Hippolyta offered him her girdle as a love-gift.

The tenth labour, much less fun, was to steal the giant Geryon's cattle from the western brink of the world. Herakles cut a short sea-route from the Mediterranean, setting up the Pillars of Herakles to hold back Europe and Africa; but he had immense trouble driving the herd back overland. Next he had to fetch the Golden Apples of the Hesperides from their dragon-guarded tree in the mountains. Nearby, Atlas the Titan stood where Zeus had set him after the early wars, bearing the weight of the sky forever on his shoulders. Herakles offered to take the weight for a while if Atlas would do him the favour of picking the apples, and Atlas obliged. But delighting in his freedom he then declared he would take the apples himself to Eurystheus, and Herakles had to trick him back into holding up the sky. On another mountain, Herakles found Prometheus still bound in agony and persuaded Zeus to set him free. The twelfth and final labour was to bring out of the Underworld the dog Cerberus, a task achieved by brute force rather than guile.

Freed at last, Herakles settled various old scores (one entailed an early sack of Troy), and assisted the gods against restive Giants. He married **Deianeira**, who unwittingly caused his death. **Nessus**, a centaur (friendly but uncivilised creatures, half-man and half-horse) tried to rape her and was shot by Herakles. Dying, Nessus told Deianeira to keep some of his blood, which rubbed into a shirt Herakles wore would keep him faithful to her. In due course Deianeira took offence at the latest of Herakles' mistresses, and anointed his shirt with what she assumed was a love-charm. But the blood of Nessus was poisoned, and the shirt burned Herakles and stuck fast to his flesh. In agony he lay on his death pyre and ordered its kindling; when eventually someone was persuaded to obey him, he died and was warmly welcomed to Olympos.

Theseus was of mortal birth, but the rumour that Poseidon had fathered him was spread, to cloud the circumstances – **Aegeus**, king of Athens, had enjoyed a drunken night with the daughter of a neighbouring king. Theseus was sent by his mother to Athens as Aegeus had instructed in the event of a promising son. He performed on the way several 'labours', in emulation of his admired cousin Herakles, clearing the coast road of a string of well-established bandits. After proving his identity in Athens he dealt heroically with an invading army, and recaptured the Cretan bull which Herakles had let loose. Then, to his aged father's distress, Theseus joined the seven youths and seven maidens who were sent periodically to Crete, a tribute exacted by King Minos, who used them for ritual sports in the bullring and then fed them to the Minotaur. The Athenian tribute ship bore black sails of mourning; Theseus swore he would bring all back safely under white sails.

In Crete, luck and Aphrodite were on his side: the king's daughter **Ariadne** fell in love with him, and gave him a magic ball of thread made by Daedalus. Tied at the entrance of the labyrinth it unrolled before Theseus to lead him down to the lair of the Minotaur; and when he had killed the monster it guided his return. The Athenians escaped the same night, taking Ariadne with them. On the island of Naxos, where their ship halted, Theseus abandoned her, sailing away while she slept. The god Dionysos consoled her as she wept for vengeance, and Theseus did not go unpunished: he forgot the promised white sails, and as the black ones were seen approaching Athens his despairing father leapt to his death from the rock of the Acropolis.

Theseus, now king, was an excellent ruler of Athens, though he frequently absented himself in search of adventure. Joining Herakles, he won himself an Amazon wife and had a son, **Hippolytus**; later he married **Phaedra**, younger daughter of Minos of Crete. His great friend was **Pirithöus**, king of the Lapiths, who had a stimulating feud with the Centaurs since they got fighting drunk at his wedding. When Pirithöus required a second bride he proposed a raid on the Underworld to capture Persephone, and as a last fling Theseus went. The two reached the kingdom of Hades with suspicious ease and were offered hospitality. But the seats they took were thrones of rock to which they instantly stuck fast; and there they remained for four years, lashed by the Furies, until Herakles found them on his visit to steal Cerberus. Herakles tore Theseus free from the rock by brute strength, leaving behind painful amounts of flesh. But Pirithöus, originator of the blasphemous plan, he could not free.

Theseus returned home aged, crippled and out of luck. He had been supplanted on the throne of Athens. And Phaedra, his wife, had fallen desperately in love with Hippolytus, his son, who would have nothing to do with her; she killed herself, accusing Hippolytus of rape. He fled in his chariot, and the outraged Theseus called on Poseidon to kill him. Poseidon obliged: from the sea reared a monster which terrified Hippolytus's horses. Beyond control, they bolted until the chariot was shattered and their master dragged in the reins to his death. And Theseus, ex-king of Athens, met an ignominious death in exile: the king of Skyros pushed him over a cliff.

Joint enterprises

The first invited gathering of heroes was the hunting of the
Calydonian Boar. The king of Calydon had neglected Artemis in
his sacrifices, so she sent a gigantic boar to ravage his lands; no
man could tackle it alone, and word went out to summon the
bravest in Greece (Herakles was detained on a Labour, but
Theseus came). The hunt was led by the king's son, **Meleager**. At
his birth, the Fates had visited his mother, and told her the baby
would survive only as long as the brand of wood burning on her
hearth; she snatched it from the fire, and hid it away.

One maiden came to the hunt: **Atalanta**, devotee of Artemis,
who could run more swiftly than any man. Mixed feelings
greeted her arrival. Meleager was entranced, but two brothers of
his mother were among those who thought she would cause
trouble. The chase claimed several victims before Atalanta
wounded the boar, and Meleager finished it off. He awarded its
pelt and tusks to Atalanta, but his outraged uncles took them
away from her. In love and furious, Meleager killed his uncles.
His mother, when she heard what he had done, took out the old
brand and laid it on the fire; as it burned to ash, Meleager was
stricken and died.

Atalanta was the cause of many deaths. Urged by her father to
marry one of her suitors, she made each run a foot-race with her,
to win her or die if he lost. All comers lost and died, until one
brought with him three golden apples Aphrodite gave him. As he
ran he dropped them, one by one, at Atalanta's feet; unable to
resist pausing to pick them up, she finally lost the race.

Fifty heroes assembled – this time including Herakles – for the
quest of **Jason and the Argonauts** to fetch the **Golden Fleece**. The
fleece hung in distant Colchis on the Black Sea, where an ancestor
of Jason's had flown on the back of a miraculous ram; the quest
would appease the ancestor's ghost and save the family fortunes –
or at least get rid of Jason, which suited his wicked uncle, **Pelias**.

On the outward voyage the ship *Argo*, with its 50 oars, came
through all hazards. At Lemnos, Jason had some difficulty getting
his men back on board: they were joyfully repopulating the island
at the request of its women, who years before had killed off their
menfolk for complaining they stank. In Mysia they lost Herakles,
who went off to resume his Labours. They encountered the
Stymphalian Birds he had dislodged, and they only just survived
the Clashing Rocks at the entrance to the Bosporus.

Confronting the king of Colchis, they gained an unexpected
ally, his daughter **Medea**, who fell in love with Jason. She was a
witch-priestess, and in return for a promise of marriage she
helped him complete the impossible task the king set him: in a

single day to plough a vast field with fire-breathing bronze bulls, sow it with dragons' teeth, and destroy the army which sprang from them. Finding her father still had no intention of giving up the golden fleece, Medea took Jason to steal it, putting a spell on its guardian dragon. They fled with the Argonauts, and the king pursued them. Medea slowed down the swift Colchian galleys by a grisly variant of Atalanta's apples. She had brought along her little brother, and she chopped him into pieces and threw them overboard; his father had to stop to gather them for burial.

The gods, disgusted at this deed, drove the *Argo* with storms from sea to sea until Jason and Medea sought purification; then on their homeward course the Colchian fleet caught up, and only Jason's immediate marriage to Medea deflected their claim to both her and the fleece. So he brought her home, and she dealt with his uncle Pelias. In her witch-priestess garments, she demonstrated her power to restore youth, by cutting up and boiling a ram which seemingly leapt from the pot a young lamb. When Pelias eagerly submitted himself for the treatment Medea handed the knives to his daughters who obediently cut him up.

In spite of her repellent practices Medea kept Jason's love for ten years. Then he divorced her to re-marry; she caused the hideous death of wife and wedding guests before departing. Jason's own death had an odd pathos; he revisited his old beached ship the *Argo*, and was sitting in its shade when its crumbling timbers finally disintegrated and fell on his head.

The Trojan enterprise

The gods took a hand from the start: the ten-year war between Greeks and Trojans which killed so many princes was willed by Zeus, who found the princes over-mighty. The object of the war was **Helen**, the most beautiful woman in the world, daughter of Zeus and **Leda**, whom he overwhelmed in the form of a great white swan. When Helen grew up every prince in Greece came as her suitor; and they all swore an oath to defend her chosen husband against any who envied and wronged him. She married **Menelaus**, king of Sparta.

Arguably the most handsome man in the world was **Paris**, a prince of Troy. He was neither cowardly nor stupid, but Zeus put him in an impossible situation: Paris was required to compare the charms of Hera, Athena and Aphrodite, awarding one of them a golden apple which had lately appeared among the gods inscribed 'For the Fairest'. The three goddesses were not above bribing Paris. Hera offered him riches, Athena victories; but Aphrodite offered him the most beautiful woman in the world. Paris promptly awarded her the apple – and Hera and Athena from then on were enemies of Troy. Under Aphrodite's guidance Paris visited Sparta, Helen fell in love with him, and they eloped. He took her back to Troy, where everyone immediately adored her, and King **Priam** swore never to let her go.

Then Menelaus summoned all the princes who had sworn the oath, forming an army under his brother **Agamemnon**, high king of Mycenae, to fetch Helen back. Some were reluctant. The warrior **Achilles** had to be retrieved from his hiding-place, dressed as a woman among palace maidservants – a stratagem of his mother. (Though she had bathed him in the river Styx as a baby and rendered him invulnerable except for the heel by which she held him, she knew he was fated never to return from Troy.) And the wise **Odysseus** (Ulysses), forewarned of dismal years ahead, unsuccessfully feigned madness in an attempt to stay at home. Others came willingly, including **Ajax**, second only to Achilles in valour. Agamemnon himself, told by a priest that his fleet would not get the favourable wind until he sacrificed his fairest daughter, did just that.

So the Greeks sailed and a vast army occupied the plain before Troy where Priam awaited battle. His eldest son **Hector** was Troy's greatest warrior; only his daughter **Cassandra** had no hope of defeating the Greeks. Apollo, to win her love, had given her prophetic powers; but when she refused him he added the curse that nobody would ever believe what she prophesied. It was a war of siege and skirmishes, so equally balanced as the gods took sides that it went on for nine years; Hera and Athena did their utmost for the Greeks, while Aphrodite, Apollo and Zeus aided Troy. There were single combats – Hector and Ajax had one and ended up sworn friends; in the Greek camp there were complex rivalries, quarrels and betrayals. By the tenth year the Greeks were near despair. Hector was dead, but so was Achilles – from an arrow guided by Apollo to his vulnerable heel. Paris was dead, but so was Ajax. And Helen was still defended inside the walls of Troy.

The **Wooden Horse** was Odysseus's solution to the stalemate. Twenty-four Greeks climbed up through a trap-door and hid in its huge hollow body; the rest set fire to the camp, and overnight took their ships out to sea, waiting out of sight behind an island. The Trojans woke to an empty plain and the awesome horse, inscribed with a dedication to Athena 'in anticipation of a safe voyage home'. There was an uproar of debate, the majority opinion being that Athena's property should be treated with respect, and the horse taken to the citadel. Dissenting voices urged that in honour of Poseidon it should be burned where it stood. Cassandra announced that the horse contained armed men, but nobody listened. A priest called **Laocoön** declared that Greeks were not to be trusted, least of all when they brought gifts. He was preparing to consult Poseidon when from the sea came two enormous serpents, who swiftly coiled around him and his two sons, crushing them to death. This appalling retribution persuaded the Trojans to accept the horse: they dragged it, with great difficulty, inside the city walls. Odysseus and his men lay still inside the horse while the Trojans, celebrating the end of the war, passed from feast and revelry to drunken sleep. Then the trap-door was opened, and the fleet summoned with beacons. The Greeks poured in through the breached wall: after ten years of siege, a single night of burning and butchery completed the sack of Troy.

Homecomings

When all was over **Menelaus** took Helen back to Sparta. He had indeed intended to kill her for all the trouble she had caused, but her beauty remained irresistible.

He and his brother never met again, for Agamemnon, after a swift and prosperous voyage home, was murdered by his wife **Clytemnestra** and her lover **Aegisthus**. Aegisthus, a cousin of the high king, played his part for power, continuing a grisly family saga; but Clytemnestra had added reasons. She hated Agamemnon, who had killed her former husband and married her by force. He had also killed their youngest daughter, in sacrifice to summon a wind for his Trojan enterprise. He had neglected his kingdom for ten years, and now she heard he was bringing back the princess Cassandra as his war-prize. So Clytemnestra set him up: she greeted him as a triumphant hero, with banquet prepared, and luxurious bath. Cassandra would not enter the palace, crying that she smelt blood – but nobody listened. Agamemnon wallowed in his bath, then eager for the banquet made to emerge, and his wife entangled him in a net instead of a towel. Aegisthus' sword struck him back into the bath, and Clytemnestra beheaded him with an axe. Then, covered in blood, she ran outside and killed Cassandra.

Odysseus had small interest in prizes, compared with the prophecy that ten more years would pass before he got home to his kingdom of **Ithaca**. The winds first drove his ships south to Africa, where looking for water he nearly lost men to the lotus-eating habit – it induced euphoria and amnesia. Seeking food, they found an island full of sheep and cooked themselves a meal in a well-stocked cave. Its owner proved to be **Polyphemus the Cyclops**, a giant one-eyed son of Poseidon, who closed his cave with a vast rock and proceeded to eat the intruders. Odysseus got them out by tricking and blinding Polyphemus, and from then on was given a hard time by Poseidon.

At one point in the voyage his ships were within sight of Ithaca, with all winds but the favourable westerly safely on board in a bag; but his feckless crew opened the bag, and the winds slammed them far away again. In the next calm anchorage, cannibals stove in his ships and massacred his men – only Odysseus had moored far enough out in the harbour to escape. His remaining crew were then turned into swine by the enchantress **Circe**, but Odysseus was given a plant (called moly) by Hermes to keep him immune from her spells. Under duress, Circe released all her victims and enabled Odysseus to seek advice – in Tartarus, no less – concerning the rest of his ordeals.

Thus he survived the sweet, shipwrecking song of the **Sirens**; lashed to the mast, he listened himself, but the ears of his crew were plugged with wax. In the dreadful passage between the monster **Scylla** and the whirlpool **Charybdis**, he lost only six men. But he came to grief in Sicily, where his hungry crew against his orders slaughtered some of the cattle of Helios the sun. A thunderstorm promptly destroyed his ship and all but Odysseus drowned.

He was washed up on an island where **Calypso**, a beautiful nymph with youthful immortality in her gift, detained him for seven years before Zeus ordered her to let him go. He proceeded on a makeshift raft, but Poseidon spotted him and sank it. Odysseus swam for two days and nights before being cast naked and senseless on an island near his own, called Phaeacia. Here he was discovered by the princess **Nausicaa**, given a royal welcome, and finally with many gifts ferried home.

In Ithaca, his wife **Penelope** was besieged by over 100 insolent young suitors urging that Odysseus, so long absent, must be dead; and that she must decide on a second husband. For some years she had promised to do so on completion of the cloth which she was weaving, and every night delayed it by unpicking her work; but now her stratagem was discovered and she was desperate. Her only champion was **Telemachus**, the grown son whom Odysseus had left a baby. Son now met and recognised father through the intervention of Athena, and they made a plan.

Disguised as a beggar, Odysseus was sitting in his own banqueting hall when (at Athena's prompting) Penelope from her chamber sent word she would accept the man who could string and use the bow left behind by her husband. None could even bend it; Odysseus, amid jeers, took possession of it. Telemachus had removed other weapons from the hall and armed the few faithful servants. Odysseus shot his first arrow through the chief suitor's throat and proceeded to pick off the rest, while those who tried to escape were hacked to pieces. Then, his house cleansed and his kingly appearance restored, Odysseus at last rejoined his wife.

Though the slaughtered suitors' kin rebelled against him, Odysseus prevailed. Even the gods had grown tired of war: Zeus and Athena together imposed peace, on earth and on Olympos.

Wild flowers

Most people enjoy the sight of wild flowers: meadows coloured with buttercups or poppies or ox-eye daisies, woods carpeted with bluebells or anemones, king-cups or cowslips. These are familiar friends. But the wild flowers of Greece are something else. Their variety is astonishing – around 6000 species compared with the British total of something like 2000 (and the area of Britain is nearly twice that of Greece). This great variety relates to the character of the country, and in particular to its climate and its structure. The north of Greece has a Balkan climate, with very cold winters and rainfall more or less the year round; the south of Greece has a Mediterranean climate, with a mild, moist winter and spring, and a very hot, dry summer.

In its structure Greece is very rocky, mostly of limestone, and the majority of the countryside is unsuitable for cultivation, leaving large wild areas where flowers can flourish. As well as these features, the land mass of the country is very convoluted, so that there are many mountains and islands, and several thousand miles of coastline with beaches, sheltered bays and inlets, all of which are likely to have a specialised wild flower population of their own.

In Greece there are not many months when there are no flowers, because the late-flowering crocuses and autumn cyclamen flower on until November, and tulips, snowdrops and early crocuses and anemones are in flower in January. But it is in spring that one should look for flowers – from March to May much of the countryside is luminous with a riot of colour.

For a start, you should go to the wild, uncultivated lowlands, which can be found anywhere about 150 feet above sea level. They have their own varieties of habitat – stony and not-so-stony hillsides, scrubby woods with sunny glades, and open grassland often with coppices on the boundaries. All these have their particular communities of wild flowers.

Among these different habitats there will be an abundance of flowers, including cyclamen, crocuses, paeonies, tulips, irises, crimson poppies, grape hyacinths and orchids. Many of them will be familiar, but among the strangers will be the snake's head iris *Hermodactylus tuberosus*, with pale yellow-green and purple-black flowers, and the beautifully marked woodcock orchis *O. scolopax* as well as several yellow-marked orchids *O. lutea*. Out in the rocky ground the euphorbias will make their display; one of them, *E. acanthothamnos*, makes low and extremely prickly cushions showing small yellow flowers, and others, different sub-species of *E. characias*, send up tall stems with conspicuous green or yellow flowers. These are much cultivated in gardens around the Continent.

Some of the less stony hillsides will be covered with a yellow sheet of Jerusalem sage *Phlomis fruticosa*, which is cultivated in many European countries and here reminds one of the show that ragwort can make in England. One of the first spring sights on the hills is the deep pink flowering of the Judas tree *Cercis siliquastrum*, whose flowers precede the leaves. The legend is that the flowers used to be pale, but when Judas hanged himself from its branches the tree blushed for shame (but there is also a white-flowered, presumably shameless, form).

Towards the end of the spring the bright pink flowers of the rock rose *Cistus incanus* make a fine show on waste land. While many plants stop flowering during the hot, dry season, there is still a good deal of colour left from several varieties of (mostly pink) bindweed, larkspur and love-in-a-mist, and on a taller scale assorted mulleins *Verbascum spp* with yellow or purple flowers. There are also some very fine thistles, such as the milk thistle which rejoices in the name *Silybum marianum* and stands over six feet high; it has huge leaves beautifully variegated with deep green and white, and fearsome spikes behind its flowers. Another thistle *Onopordum acanthium* is as tall as the milk thistle but is more slender and without spikes; instead it has very conspicuous purple and white scales behind the flowers. After this late summer flowering the new season starts with the autumn crocuses and cyclamen. This sequence of flowers is general for lowland Greece. It will vary with local differences such as latitude, flat or hilly land, east or west (east being drier and west being warmer and wetter), but the variations will not be fundamental and will be within the pattern described.

As the lowlands rise towards the mountain heights, the wild flowers change, first to woodland species and then – above the tree line – to alpines. As plants grow higher, their flowering time becomes later, so that summer rather than spring becomes the time to go looking for most of the alpines. Many of these highland plants grow in relatively inaccessible places, but the mountains around Athens, although not especially high, do have a good variety of flowers and can be easily reached from the city.

Woodland flowers include the blue trio of scilla, anemone and willow gentian *G. asclepiadea*, and two lilies (turk's cap and martagon) as well as wintergreen *Pyrola rotundifolia*. They also include two plants which are great rarities in Britain – red helleborine and *Daphne mezereon*. On the mountain peaks there is a great variety of alpines, whose distribution varies between the north of the country and the Peloponnese. A representative selection is: assorted crocuses, tulips and cyclamen; the bright blue spring gentian *G. verna*, which is found over most of Europe; a pink corydalis *C. solida*; a blue and white columbine *Aquilegia ottonis*; and occasionally one of the most attractive alpines in Europe, the lavender-blue soldanella *S. alpina*.

Priorities for most visitors are to see some of the historic sites and some of the islands. Each of these have rich wild flower populations, but for very different reasons. The historic sites (mostly on the mainland) are usually protected from grazing, and many of their plants have therefore had an exceptional opportunity to flourish undisturbed. The islands, because of the sea around them, have milder winters than the mainland, and in addition their individual isolation has led to the evolution of some different species on different islands (a mini-Galapagos situation).

Of the many places which can be visited, only a few can be described here. At Delphi, anyone who wants to have a rest in the theatre must be careful not to sit on the cheerful ebullient campanula *C. rupestris*, which rampages all over the rocky seats, and which has as its neighbour the elegant golden drop *Onosma frutescens*. Outside the theatre and the stadium the tall golden spikes of asphodel *Asphodeline lutea* make a bold display.

Cape Sounion, with the beautiful temple of Poseidon on its headland, has a very fine show of wild flowers. One of the more distinctive plants is giant fennel *Ferula communis*, which grows on the cliffs and has very large yellow umbels carried on an eight-foot hollow stem. The story is that the god Bacchus used to order his minions to collect the long dry stems in the autumn and use them as staves to bring to order any unruly Bacchanalians who had stepped out of line at one of his parties – the staves being so light that nobody could be hurt.

Delos is an island full of history. It was a small barren island when Leto gave birth to Apollo under the shade of one of its date palms. On the instant, the island was transformed, flowers and fruit bursting from the rocks; and the palm tree became sacred to Apollo. Today one thinks of Delos as the island of a thousand lizards; it is also bright with stock *Matthiola incana*, which makes large and brilliant pinky-mauve clumps on top of the old walls, with the lions looking on.

Most of the islands have plenty of flowers, but the larger the island the greater the variety. Consequently, Crete, Rhodes, Samos and Lesbos are especially worth a visit. On Lesbos, snowdrops, tulips and cyclamen grow well on the slopes of Mount Olympos, and by the sea is the only European site of the yellow azalea *Rhododendron luteum*. The tall white and yellow iris *I. ochreoleuca*, much cultivated in other countries, also grows near the sea.

Samos is a green and pleasant island famous for the beauty of its scenery and for its flowers. In spring the pine woods of the mountain slopes are carpeted with the blue anemone *A. blanda*, often interspersed with several different species of crocus. Many orchids join in the spring flowering, including the conspicuous mirror orchis *O. speculum*, which has a bright blue patch on its lip. In summer the cliffs by the sea are ablaze with broom, and on the hillsides on the coast the very tall trio of hollyhock, mullein and thistle are eye-catching. Autumn by the sea brings a fine show of the blue autumn squill *S. autumnalis* and the much more surprising sight of the sea squill *Urginea maritima*, which sends up three-foot spikes of densely packed white flowers out of a very large bulb. Over the years these bulbs have been put to many and varied uses, including cough mixture, sheep wash, rat poison and the marking of boundaries.

Rhodes is the most eastern of the islands, and many of its flowers have an Asian association: one of the most conspicuous is the turban buttercup *Ranunculus asiaticus*, usually scarlet-flowered on Rhodes as distinct from its Cretan cousins. The spring flowering on the hillsides is very fine, and is distinguished on Rhodes by a white paeony exclusive to the island, *P. rhodia*.

Crete, because of its size, its southerly position and mountains, has a large and varied wild flower population, with more than 100 species which grow nowhere else. Of these, the early flowers include two tulips, the pink *T. saxatilis* and the white *T. cretica*, as well as a white cyclamen *C. creticum*. The turban buttercups flower pink, white and yellow. In May Crete is a good place to see the widely distributed and strange-looking tongue orchids *Serapias ssp.* Their rusty red flowers, sometimes marked with green or ochre and pointing spikily to the sky, make them hard to see. When one plant has been found you are likely to find another half-dozen in the same area (many plants have this elusiveness; in Britain the fly orchis is a perfect example). Another of Crete's specialities is the Cretan ebony *Ebenus cretica*, which in June in the south of the island shows conspicuous flowers with dense spikes of pink, resembling a concentrated version of the British sainfoin. Crete's mountains have a selection of alpines which is partly distinct from that of the more northerly mountains; it includes more Asian- and African-related species. The small blue *Chionodoxa nana* (often in British rock-gardens) is one such Asian-related plant. Among the variety – which includes a beautiful white crocus, a yellow flax and a maroon-tinted corydalis – one of the most distinctive is mountain bugloss

Anchusa caespitosa, which shows its intense deep blue flowers high among the rocks.

The coastline and shores of Greece and its islands have distinctive communities of wild flowers, not only on the shore itself but also on the backland just behind it. In the spring the beach will often be carpeted with the pink and yellow flowers of *Silene colorata* and *Medicago marina*, often with chamomile *Anthemis tormentosa* growing with or near them. On the rocks just above high-tide level Virginian stock *Malcolmia maritima* shows its large pink or white flowers and appears to be immune from any wave spray problems. On the cliffs and rough ground behind the beach there is usually a great deal to see. Crown daisy *Chrysanthemum coronarium* is all over the place, and there are many familiar plants – mallow, mignonette, storksbill, bugloss and lupin. Less familiar are honeywort *Cerinthe major*, with yellowish bell-shaped flowers, and salsify *Tragopogon porrifolius*, with purplish dandelion-like flowers and, later, very large 'dandelion clocks'. Its roots make a delicately flavoured vegetable said to be much less used than its flavour deserves. Behind the beach there may also be unusual-looking large areas where a mat of green is studded with small deep blue flowers: this will be blue pimpernel *Anagallis foemina*, which otherwise looks just like scarlet pimpernel. Hottentot fig *Carpobrotus acinaciformis* is a plant which no one will ignore. An immigrant from southern Africa, it has now established itself along the coastal areas of the Mediterranean and Aegean. Though not elegant, it creeps over stony ground with very thick leaves, sending up eye-catching three- to four-inch flowers of a garish puce-magenta. It often grows in large and spectacular colonies, sometimes with or near a related yellow-flowering species.

Later in the year there are familiar plants too: snapdragon, samphire, sea lavender and sea holly. But two deserve special mention. Squirting cucumber *Ecballium elaterium* looks like a courgette at its flowering stage, then produces a small oval hairy fruit (not at all like a cucumber). As this ripens, high pressures are built up in the liquids inside the fruit. When ripe, the fruit breaks off the stem and the seeds are blown out two to three yards away. Mandrake *Mandragora officinarum* is a plant of the nightshade family living on rough ground generally near the sea, with a rosette of rough green leaves from which come short-stemmed blue flowers. It is mandrake's history which is remarkable: the ancients valued it as an anaesthetic, but in the 4th and 5th centuries AD it was surprisingly recommended as an aphrodisiac (its fruits were known as devil's apples – presumably relating to the latter use). Finally, at the very end of the season, one of Greece's loveliest flowers can be seen. The sea daffodil

Pancratium maritimum, which grows along many of the southern coasts, produces clusters of very sweetly scented daffodil-shaped flowers. It is not rare, but is always a joy to find.

Wild flowers do not grow evenly over the countryside; there will be places where they are in special abundance, perhaps due to favourable soil variations or to a particular micro-climate. There will often be some local inhabitants who know of such places, particularly anyone who has acted as a guide to tourist parties; enquiries can be very rewarding. But enquiries must be responsible, and if there is any suspicion that plants are likely to be collected, no information will be forthcoming, and quite rightly. The trowel and spongebag practices which once were common, regrettably, are now becoming illegal in an increasing number of countries – after some of their finest flowers had been collected to extinction. To uproot plants and take them to another country almost always leads to their death in an alien environment. It must be a rule to leave them where they belong – so that they can flourish and flower for next year's visitors.

A very useful guidebook, illustrated in colour, is *Flowers of Greece and the Aegean*, by Anthony Huxley and William Taylor, published by Chatto and Windus.

Eating and drinking

Like the tantalising image of intense heat on a dull British summer day, the memory of a Greek meal taken in a happy throng on a balmy waterside terrace under the stars may assume a greater degree of enjoyment than the actual experience of the meal. Greek food isn't about scaling gastronomic heights, and the increasing availability of ready-made Greek dishes in British supermarkets serves only to emphasise the relatively poor quality of many of those dishes in an average Greek taverna. It's unfortunately only too easy to find synthetic pink taramosalata, shrivelling moussaka and lukewarm kebabs; and the ubiquitous Greek salad may be delightfully novel for a day or so, but can soon become oh-so-boring. In package-holiday hotels, the fare is often even worse: limp wiener schnitzel and soggy chips, tinned Russian salad, ungarnished pork chops, and a few stuffed vine leaves thrown in for good measure.

It's a vicious circle: hoteliers and restaurateurs serve up 'international' food because they think it's what British tourists want, and the tourists eat it because they think there's nothing better. Graecophiles argue that you have only to be more selective or adventurous in your choice of restaurant to find good, traditional cooking; and that for every ten tavernas with dry chicken and steak and chips there's one where you can find the real thing – if you're prepared to look and to abandon some assumptions about how and what to eat.

One of the main criticisms levelled at Greek food is that it's always cold. This is largely correct: Hellenic eating habits differ from ours. Greeks think tepid food is better for the digestion, and the climate calls for cool food as well. They don't feel the need to stoke up on piping-hot meals as we do, except in winter. And the pace of life is different: there's no rush, and Greeks like to linger over meals. In theory this is all very understandable. But in hygiene terms it's hard to find justification for the commonly found practice of cooking food in the morning and leaving it to cool (unrefrigerated) or to swelter for several hours before dishing it up lukewarm in the evening. After a recent survey into holiday health hazards, *Holiday Which?* advised against eating food which had been lingering on the hotplate all day.

Another criticism is that Greek food is always swimming in oil – also true. It would be unthinkable for Greeks to cook without olive oil. They consider it healthy and cannot understand our preference for boiling vegetables in water. A rich, oily, tomato sauce is a staple for almost all stews and ragouts of meat and vegetables; if you don't like olive oil, you'll need to stick to simple grills or roasts.

Traditional cookery is important to Greeks. Like the people themselves, it has been influenced by the Turks, the Middle East and Italy. But, as Greek cookery writer Rena Salaman explains in her excellent book *Greek Food* (Fontana), the main influence has been rural peasant roots. 'Greek cooking is not aristocratic; it reflects not the European tastes of the elite, or their metropolitan preferences, but the traditions and resources of a rural people. Greek cooking is the people's: simple and straightforward.' Recipes are handed down from grandmother to granddaughter, usually over a hot stove; they aim at making the best of what is fresh and in season – fish from the sea, lamb from the mountains, olives and herbs from the groves. Traditional food preparation may not be for the squeamish. Particularly in the more remote parts of Greece, food comes on the hoof, on the wing or in the net. Those little rabbits hopping around the village are there to hop into the pot, and at Easter the same goes for the paschal lambs. It's not uncommon to see creatures despatched in front of tavernas during the day to turn up on the menu at night; and the washing line of octopus becomes a familiar sight.

When eating out in Greece, it's well worth your while to be adventurous. Beware the places with pristine tablecloths and posh cutlery; when in doubt, follow the Greeks. A backstreet taverna with a loud local clientele may turn out to be just the place for an authentic evening. Greek meals are informal, often boisterous, and nearly always communal. It's quite usual to see whole families – including small children – at vast tables; if a few friends arrive too, chairs are dragged in to enlarge the circle. Sociability and sharing are the key words; you pour wine for each other and drink constant toasts. Table manners differ from our own more reserved ways, and it's quite acceptable to pitch into someone else's plate or offer choice morsels to a neighbour. Greeks eat with forks or fingers, and side-plates for bread are rare. Dinners are often punctuated by fiery discussions or bursts of song or dance. It's all to do with the spirit of bonhomie, *kefi* to a Greek, and the more company around the table the merrier.

For many visitors to Greece, this eating *en masse* is part of the appeal. The Greeks cannot imagine eating alone; to them a table for one is a piteous sight. So don't be surprised if you get invited to join a party at a local taverna, especially when the retsina is in full flow. Greeks are naturally hospitable, and it is also a question of honour, *filotimo*, to make visitors feel at home in their

country; the word for a guest and a stranger (*xenos*) is the same.
Zeus himself decreed the code of *philoxenia* (hospitality), turning
up incognito from time to time to test mere mortals. It's both a
virtue and an obligation to offer refreshment to travellers, and
Greeks will often not hear of foreign guests parting with a
drachma. If you are offered hospitality – a glass of water and a
few olives, coffee and a dish of fruit conserve, or perhaps an ouzo
and a sliver of octopus – it's an insult to refuse.

The Greek climate calls for late eating hours. Lunch, generally
eaten at home, is rarely before 2 p.m. and is followed by a siesta;
dinner is usually at around 10 p.m. (though restaurants catering
mainly for tourists will keep earlier hours). Meals are lingered
over until the small hours. When in Greece, it makes sense to
follow suit. The evening ritual of aperitifs and sundowners begins
with an ouzo, usually taken with a little water and a range of
nibbles, *mezedes*; Greeks never drink without eating. At an
ouzerie – like the *kafeneion*, usually a male preserve – you will be
offered olives, feta cheese, a bit of fish or aubergine, perhaps some
octopus or squid or chunks of cucumber. (In a number of places
they have cottoned on to the fact that tourists come and drink
ouzo, which is very cheap, simply for the *meze*, and either charge
extra for the side-plate of snacks or charge a special price for ouzo
and *meze*, giving you a small bottle of ouzo instead of a single
measure and managing to justify a high price for the package.)

There are two main types of eating place: the *estiatorio*, or
restaurant, which could also be a *psistaria*, specialising in grills;
and the *taverna* (or *psarotaverna*, specialising in fish). In many
places, particularly on the smaller islands, the distinction between
them is blurred. The *estiatorio* is generally open all day, and is
particularly busy at lunchtime between 2 p.m. and 3 p.m., when
there is a wide range of dishes simmering away in the kitchen,
and often a grill on the go as well.

After the evening stroll or *volta*, everyone heads for the
taverna. The taverna lies at the heart of the Greek holiday
experience: it's the basic supplier of meals and evening
entertainment. Most can provide menus, but rarely do so. Menus
show two prices for everything, a serious waste of some scribe's
time since the tax-free lower price is of no relevance. Nor does
the difference between the two levels of prices ever seem to
coincide with the quoted rate of tax. Never mind: Greek food is
very cheap by the standards of other European countries. A
service charge is added by law, and prices are controlled according
to the five categories of eating place – from D at the bottom to A
and Luxury. Fixed-price meals are rare, as are frozen foods, which
must be indicated on the menu with the letters KAT.

On arrival, preferably before installing yourself, go and look at the food in the kitchen. This standard procedure will not cause offence and solves problems of menu translation. Often only the trays of cooked food will be on display, with fish and fresh meat out of sight in the fridge unless you ask to see them. Only in very crowded touristy restaurants are you likely to be told that the kitchen inspection system does not apply. The reason for this may not be sinister – the cooking areas may be cramped and the staff overworked without having to answer queries from diners. Sometimes you will be invited to order at the same time as inspecting the food, but not always.

Go early if you want some choice and hot food: ideally, eat your main meal at lunchtime when most of the day's cooking is done. Steaks, chops, kebabs (*souvlakia*) or fish are the best things to ask for if you want something cooked to order. Fish is usually priced by weight rather than by the portion, and is always much more expensive than meat.

Everything you order will be served together. If you don't want your *tsatsiki* (a starter of yoghurt, garlic and cucumber) at the same time as your moussaka, the only solution is not to order the moussaka until later. Unless it actually has to be cooked, it will come straight away anyway. Service in tavernas is always said to be incredibly slow. In fact, it is merely unpredictable and may be lightning fast in an uncrowded restaurant. It can come as a bit of a shock, if you are ready to settle in to a leisurely water-front supper, to find the whole meal plonked in front of you within two minutes of placing your order. Getting the bill (*logariasmo*) is often more of a problem than getting food.

It's quite usual for a taverna to provide entertainment. There might be organised music – for a name day or festival – or an impromptu session with a local plucking a *bouzouki* or *lyra*. If you are lucky there will be dancing, the style of which differs according to the region. Most people recognise the Zorba-style *hasapiko*, or butcher's dance, from Crete; it's also the dance most suitable for tourist participation. Others are the elegant circle dances, the *kalamatianos*; the fast and furious *souta* or Cretan *pendezali*; the Greek belly dance, the sexy *tsifteteli*; or the acrobatic *tsamikos*, with the leader turning somersaults. An old man might suddenly take to the floor in the slow, elegant rhythm of the *zembekiko*, expressing his joy or sorrow. His supporters will kneel, forming a circle around him, clapping the rhythm. Almost certainly, drinks will be ordered in his honour and plates smashed to the floor (breakages, *spasimo*, are added to the bill). Spontaneous outbursts like this beat organised Greek Nights hands down.

Breakfast

Greeks rarely eat breakfast; in high summer they often rise with the sun, and make do with coffee and perhaps a hoop-shaped biscuit (*koulouria*). In a hotel you will probably be offered 'continental-style' breakfast, often of mediocre quality – instant coffee, tinned fruit juice, dull rolls or bread with jam, perhaps a hard-boiled egg. In major resorts you can usually find places which serve 'English breakfast' – toast and bacon and eggs fried in olive oil. British-style cereals are rare, and pricey in shops.

Plenty of tourists like to think of orange juice, yoghurt and honey as an authentic Greek breakfast, and these are now served by breakfast cafes in sophisticated tourist spots. Another place for a do-it-yourself breakfast is a dairy – *galaktopoleion*. Creamy Greek yoghurt – cows', goats' or ewes' milk – is very good, particularly when it's fresh local produce. Bread (*psomi*) hot from the village bakery can be delicious, preferably just as it comes, without butter (which usually isn't very tasty).

Coffee time

Greek days are punctuated by drinking coffee, *ena kafedaki*, sometimes at the *kafeneion* – traditionally an all-male domain, where old men smoke cigarettes and play with worry beads, and young men read newspapers or play backgammon. Greek coffee (the same as Turkish, although never referred to as such) comes in tiny cups with thick grounds. Ask for *glyko* if you want it sweet, *metrio* for medium (which is pretty sweet) and *sketo* for without sugar (which the Greeks find utterly incomprehensible). French-style filter coffee is difficult to come by. If you want ordinary coffee, you'll generally have to have instant: ask for 'Nes', the nationally acknowledged abbreviation. The Greek version is 'classico', stronger than ours, and comes in sachets; the waiter will bring hot water so you can make your own. 'With milk' is *may gala*; 'without milk', *horis gala*. Tea, *tsaï*, comes in bags, and is drunk with milk or lemon. Infusions of wild thyme (*faskomilo*), considered good for the digestion and for colds, are sometimes available. In summer, iced coffee frappé, instant given the frothy treatment (with sugar unless you specify otherwise and with or without milk), is a popular drink.

Lunch and dinner

A typical Greek meal consists of bread, a selection of communal starters, salads and a main course. Only tourist-orientated restaurants serve puddings, although you will sometimes be able to have fresh yoghurt or fruit.

A Greek menu starts with the **Orektika**, appetisers. Some things such as *taramosalata* (pink fish roe with oil) and *tsatsiki* (yoghurt, cucumber and garlic dip) may be familiar from British supermarkets. Others include *dolmades* (rice-stuffed vine leaves), *patzaria me skorthalia* (beetroot with fierce garlic sauce), *melitzanosalata* (creamy aubergine dip), *saganaki* (fried cheese), *kolokithakia* (fried courgettes), *marides* (a kind of whitebait) and *htapodi* (roast octopus). There are, of course, regional specialities, and you may find *kohlioudes* (snails), *petalides* (limpets) or even lightly battered and fried courgette flowers.

Soupes (soups) are often substantial meals in themselves, and with bread and a salad make for cheap eating. They include *avgolemono* (egg and lemon), *faki* (thick lentil), *kakabia* (spicy fish stew), *fasolada* (bean and tomato), *magiritsa* (Easter soup made from lambs' intestines and offal), *patsa* (tripe soup) and *psarosoupa* (made from different kinds of fish). When eating the last-named it's customary to take out the fish, put it to one side and drink the broth first, then tuck into the fish.

Next on the menu you'll come to **Psaria** (fish), which also includes seafood such as *garides* (prawns and shrimps), *kalamari* (squid), *astakos* (lobster), *htapodi* (octopus) and *karavida* (crayfish). Astonishingly, local fish is expensive in Greece, and often there is little available on menus. The main types of fish you'll see are *barbounia* (red mullet), *xifias* (swordfish), *sinagrida* (sea-bream), *glossa* (sole), *sardelles* (sardines) and *gopes* (like large sardines).

Ladera refers to dishes cooked in olive oil, such as *fasolakia* (fresh green beans), *gigantes* (butter beans) or *bamies* (okra), all cooked in a rich tomato sauce. Portions tend to be large, and these all make good main courses as well as starters.

Kymades means minced meat dishes and tend to include the *yemistes*: stuffed tomatoes, peppers, perhaps aubergines, usually filled with a combination of mince, rice and herbs. *Moussaka*, Greek shepherd's pie, probably needs little introduction; ideally it should feature layers of minced lamb, aubergine and potato, topped by a thick béchamel sauce, made in a tray and cut into squares. The Greek version of spaghetti bolognese comes in this section, and you may find *pastitsio*, a pie of macaroni and mince with a rich sauce. 'Eggplant shoes' are sliced stuffed aubergines that look like slippers.

Entrades are entrées or main courses. What's on offer depends on where you go and at what time of year. On some barren islands which rely on supplies being shipped in, menus may be limited. Beef, *vodino*, is rare; you are more likely to be offered veal (*moskhari*), lamb (*arnaki*) or pork (*hirino*).

Popular main dishes include *stifado* (a stew of veal with baby onions – and sometimes octopus, rabbit or hare is done this way), *yiouvetsi* (lamb or veal baked in a clay bowl or oven tray on a bed of tear-drop pasta), *arnaki exokino* (spiced lamb baked in a paper bag), *soutzoukakia* (minced meat balls with cumin in tomato sauce), *keftedes* (lamb rissoles with herbs), *kokoretsi* (spit-roasted liver and offal) and *garides pilafi* (prawns in a pilaff).

Regional and seasonal specialities might include lamb in lemon sauce, pork casserole with olives or giant butter beans, beef and quince casserole, lamb with okra, Kos lettuce or artichokes, and game, such as partridge in lemon sauce, pigeon in wine or hare with green olives.

Chicken is widely available and nearly always free-range, so it is generally far tastier than a British battery bird. You might find it with a walnut sauce, courgette and lemon sauce or spiced pilaff rice; generally, though, it comes barbecued or roasted dry.

The menu will generally also feature **Psita**, grills or roasts of veal, lamb or chicken. You pay by weight, and a price slip is usually attached to the serving dish. Takeaway barbecues or grills (**Tis Oras**) are popular. In addition to the ubiquitous *souvlakia* (kebabs of veal, lamb and sometimes pork on a skewer) you can find *brizola* (chops – often pork), *païdakia* (lamb cutlets), *biftekia* (hamburgers), *sykotaki* (liver) and various grilled fish.

Salates, salads, range from plain tomato and olive, *domata me elies*, to the varying *horiatiki*, or Greek village salad. A good one should consist of ripe tomatoes, cucumbers, olives, onions, olive oil and feta cheese topped with oregano. Variations include peppers and in some places bits of lettuce, *marouli*, greens, *horta*, and perhaps *caperi*, a thorned plant which looks like a rose bush. A large salad and bread can provide an adequate holiday lunch, although a Greek would never dream of ordering a salad alone.

Puddings (**Glyka**) are almost non-existent in Greek restaurants, although resort restaurants will have a small selection of *baklava* (honey and nut cakes), *pagoto* (ice-cream) and even cream caramel.

You will generally find cheese, **Tyria**, on the menu; *feta* (white creamy goats' cheese) is the most common, but you might be offered *kasseri* (light yellow and creamy), *graviera* (Swiss-style like Gruyère, from Corfu and Crete), and *mizithra* (soft cheese made from ewes' milk). Yoghurt, *yaourti*, may be included in this section.

Some restaurants offer **Frouta** (fruit) such as *mila* (apples), *peponi* (melons), *karpouzi* (water-melon) and *stafilia* (grapes).

Only tourist-orientated tavernas serve coffee. Eating out is a movable feast in Greece, and after dinner you go to a bar for coffee and a brandy, or to the *zakharoplasteion* for puddings, cakes, ice-cream, coffee and liqueurs. You might like to round off your meal with *loukoumades* (honey fritters with cinnamon), *galaktobouriko* (custard pie), *kataifi* (like giant shredded wheat with honey) or *rizogalo* (rice pudding, which can be true ambrosia).

The bill, *to logariasmo*, will probably be totted up at your table. Tipping over the service charge already included isn't widespread, but you may like to give a few drachma to the *mikre*, the youngster who helps in family-run tavernas, cutting the bread, clearing the dishes and acting as a subsidiary waiter. Never snap your fingers for service: a nod or excuse me – *signomi* – will suffice. You'll probably get *oriste?* (what is it?) or *amessos* (immediately) in reply. Don't take that literally – Greek service can be slow.

Snacks

Although western-style fast-food joints and hamburger chains are springing up in the cities, the Greeks have had their own versions for years. A *souvlakia* or kebab with pitta bread makes a cheap snack: you can either buy little skewers of meat or have a *gyro*, a donner-kebab version carved from a spit-roast of layered meat, wrapped in soft pitta bread with salad, onions and *tsatsiki*, yoghurt dressing.

A 'toast' or 'tost' means a toasted sandwich (usually cheese), not very substantial or appetising but often all you can get, on a ferry for example. Otherwise pies containing cheese, spinach, chicken or meat – *tyropitta, spanakopitta*, *kotopitta* and *kreatopitta* – are popular nibbles. A good cheese pie with herbs and feta in light filo pastry takes some beating.

Drink

Although a poor relation of France and Italy in wine terms, Greece has a fairly wide range of wines from which to choose – some renowned, like the Muscat of Samos, some very drinkable, and some like turps. Greek vineyards produce more than a million gallons of wine a year, and Attica, Corfu, Crete, Epirus, the Peloponnese and Aegean Islands can produce reasonable vintages.

Wine (*krasi*) may be *mavro* (dark red to almost black), *kokkino* (lighter red), *aspro* (white) and *roze* (rosé). It may be *ksero* (dry) or *glyko* (sweet). Just to add to the confusion, wine labels are printed in formal *katharavousa* Greek, in which *oinos* is wine, *lefkos* is white. Nowadays you're just as likely to see Vin Rouge or Blanc too.

Greek wine bottles – *boukali* – hold slightly less than French ones, about 67 cl. The most common and often cheapest wine is *retsina*, resinated white – sometimes red – which originated 3000 years ago when wine jars were sealed with pine resin plugs. The pine flavoured the wines, the Greeks developed a taste for it, and now resin from pine needles is added at the fermentation stage as a preservative. It's an acquired taste – you either love it or loathe it. Like most local products it tastes better on a balmy night beneath a Greek firmament than it does at home, partly because its astringency is the ideal foil for the oiliness of Greek cooking. It's best to start off with a young *retsina* from Attica; Kourtaki and Cambas are light and fresh. In some tavernas retsina and house wines come from the barrel, draught (*khyma*), and are served in metal jugs. For bottled retsina the everyday half-litre ('half-kilo') metal-capped variety is ideologically sounder, cheaper gulp for gulp, and usually better than retsina in corked bottles. It is increasingly common for restaurants in tourist resorts not to serve retsina at all. Whatever you think of the wine, this is a fair indication of a tourist trap.

Demestica – dubbed Domestos by most British holiday-makers – is a straightforward dull red or white table wine with national distribution. Achaia is better, particularly the white. Boutari and Rotonda wines from Naoussa in Macedonia are a good bet. Look out for Lac des Roches, a good dry white, Boutari Rosé, and dry red Naoussa. Boutari Special Reserve is also a good buy.

Many islands produce their own wines, and you can try out the local product in Zante, Kos, Andros, Naxos, Samos, Ios and Milos. Islands noted for their red wines are Corfu, Paros and Evia; and Lefkas produces Santa Mavra, a very dark red. Wines from Santorini are often powerful – about 17 per cent proof. The red Robola from Cephalonia can be very good. Crete produces big, strong reds, such as Mavro Romeika.

On Rhodes CAIR produces some excellent wine. The prize-winning white Ilios and red Chevalier are both VQPRD – similar to the French VDQS classification, which specifies the area of origin. CAIR also do cheap and palatable sparkling wines – ideal for Buck's Fizz. Dry whites Lindos and Rodos are also acceptable. The dessert wine Mavrodaphne, a sweet red from the Peloponnese, and the sweet white Muscat from Samos and Muscat Rion from Patras are well known.

Ouzo is to Greece what malt whisky is to Scotland. Superior brands of this aniseed-based spirit are distilled at Plomari on Lesbos. It should be 50 per cent proof, but you'll find it in varying strengths. Ouzo is transparent until mixed with water, when it goes milky, like French pastis. It is also served neat, with a separate glass or jug of water and, often, a saucer of seafood snacks. Some islands go for flavoured or liqueur ouzos. In Crete they drink *raki* and *tsikoudia*, both strong spirits; Rhodes has *suma*, equally lethal. Many areas have their own liqueurs: Chios has Mastika, a sweet mastic-scented aperitif; Naxos, Kitro, a sweet citrus liqueur; Corfu, a brandy made from kumquats; Rhodes, Koriandolino, made from local fruits.

Greek brandies – such as Botrys and Metaxa (three, five and seven star) are sweet and not very refined, but can be acceptable with post-prandial coffee. Metaxa mixed with coke is a popular drink. Samos and Parga produce good local brandy with a strong coffee taste.

Water is *nero* and ice *pago*. Beer (*bira*) is now usually imported lager, but Greek brands such as Hellas are worth a try.

THE LEGEND OF DIONYSOS

The Greeks tell the story of how the god of intoxification discovered the vine on his journey to Naxos. Taking a rest, he saw a strange plant and uprooted it. To protect it, he packed it into the bone of a small bird. It grew so quickly, however, that he was forced to put the lot into the bone of a lion. The plant started to sprout from each end of the bone, so again he re-planted it, this time in the bone of an ass.

When Dionysos got to Naxos the plant wouldn't budge from the bones, so he planted it as it was. It grew grapes, from whence flowed the first wine. And that's why when people drink they sing like birds, get as bold as lions and then make asses of themselves.

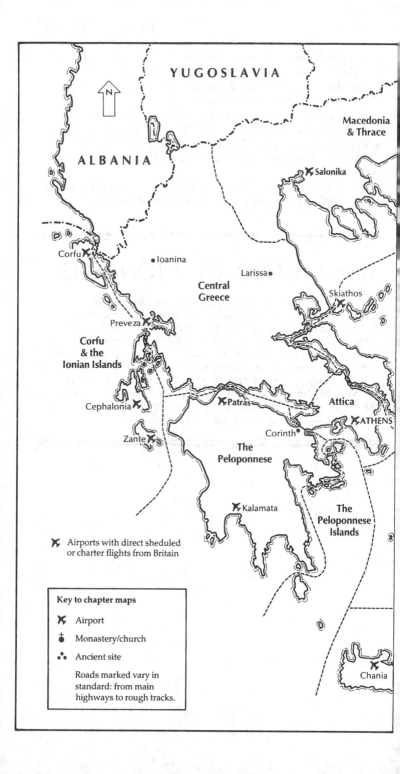

YUGOSLAVIA

Macedonia
& Thrace

✈ Salonika

ALBANIA

Corfu ✈

● Ioanina

Larissa ●

Central
Greece

Skiathos

Corfu
& the
Ionian Islands

Preveza ✈

Cephalonia ✈

✈ Patras

Attica

✈ ATHENS

Corinth ●

Zante ✈

The
Peloponnese

Kalamata ✈

The
Peloponnese
Islands

✈ Airports with direct sheduled
or charter flights from Britain

Chania ✈

Key to chapter maps

✈   Airport

‡   Monastery/church

∴   Ancient site

    Roads marked vary in
    standard: from main
    highways to rough tracks.

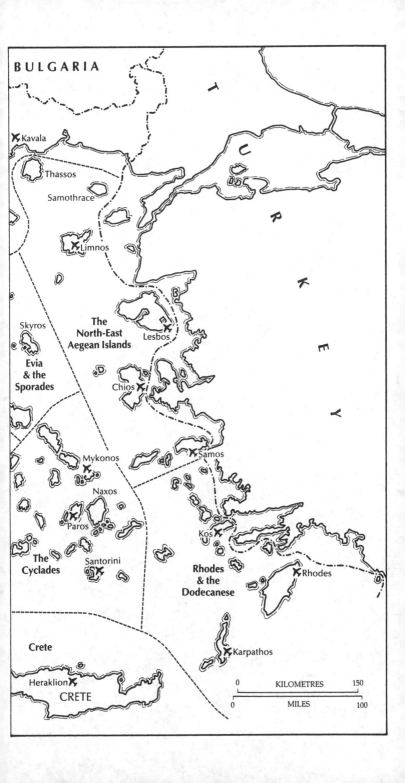

THE MAINLAND

ATHENS
AND ATTICA

Athens, the cradle of Western civilisation, is currently the most polluted city in Europe. An acidic smog created by the fumes of over 60 per cent of Greece's cars and 70 per cent of the country's industry frequently hangs over the city, trapped by the hills that encircle it. This cloud, *to nefos*, eats away at the marble of the city's temples, rasps the throats of its three million inhabitants, and has caused more damage to the Acropolis in the past 40 years than had occurred in the previous 24 centuries.

Recently measures have been taken to reduce pollution. In Greater Athens a system of alternate days for cars with odd and even numberplates has been introduced, the use of crude oil in domestic heating banned, and the most intensely polluting factories closed. However, with such density of population and industry, only a drastic measure such as mass de-urbanisation could even begin to solve the problem.

Unlike other European capitals, Athens retains little of its former dignity and character. Marble temples are cruelly juxtaposed with six-storey apartment blocks; the excavated foundations of the ancient city are fringed by congested roads; and the views from the Acropolis and the hills that punctuate and encircle the city are of an endless and brutally ugly conurbation.

The development of the city is recent. In the last century, when Athens became the capital of modern Greece, the population was a mere 10,000, and the famous city little more than a shabby village. Greece's first king, Otto of Bavaria, attempted to create a new town of neo-classical buildings of which the newly liberated country could be proud. The royal palace, university and elegant embassies remain, but the broad avenues have now become multi-lane thoroughfares constantly choked with traffic.

Despite Otto's efforts, and the city's prestigious architectural past, Athens never became an elegant European capital. After the population exchange with Turkey in the 1920s thousands of refugees flooded into the city, to live in squalid shanty towns that eventually grew into the dismal suburbs that sprawl around today's Athens and Piraeus. In the post-war years the refugees were joined by Greeks from rural areas, who, finding it increasingly difficult to make a living from the land, came to Athens to seek work in its new factories. The smaller houses of Otto's reign were replaced by blocks of flats, the plain around the city engulfed by industry, and hotels constructed to house the ever-increasing number of tourists.

Although it is possible to get away from the city chaos by taking a funicular up Lykavittos Hill or wandering around the National Gardens, Athens as a whole is a frenetic and singularly unrelaxing place. The two central squares, Syntagma and Omonia, are nightmarishly congested with traffic; the old working-class quarter, the Plaka, is traffic free but too frequented by tourists to have any authentic atmosphere; and the pavement cafes of elegant Kolonaki Square are more suitable for car-spotting than people-watching. The one place worth escaping to is the garden suburb of Kefalari, near Kifissia, where luxury hotels and decorative neo-classical villas lie along peaceful avenues shaded with eucalyptus, citrus and palm trees.

The city is never quiet, but is at its most palatable in the winter. In mid-summer it is at its worst – heat, traffic, carbon monoxide fumes and droves of tourists combine to make it an urban hell. Unless your budget is really tight, count air-conditioning and a private shower in a hotel as a necessity rather than a luxury. A rooftop swimming-pool (mainly in Luxury-category hotels) will also do much to make your stay more pleasant. If your hotel is on one of the main streets or squares, it's worth forgoing a view for the peace of an inward-facing room.

As few tourists stay in Athens for long, and as the number of travellers passing through *en route* decreases as the number of internal Greek airports increases, most of the larger hotels have geared themselves up for business people and the conference trade. The hotels are comfortable, and often rather luxurious, but if you have children or have left your smart clothes at home you could feel a bit out of place.

The reason that tourists from all over the world tolerate Athens is, of course, the city's history – going back to its mythological kings, and the goddess Athena's contest for it with Poseidon, won by her gift of the olive tree. Theseus the Minotaur-slayer, Athens' tenth king, is credited with uniting all Attica into a city-state. Athens drew riches from fertile plains, a long coastline of useful trading harbours, and above all from the silver-mines in the Laurion district; but all the wealth belonged to the ruling aristocracy which replaced the ancient kings. By the 7th century BC, when money replaced barter, the gulf between rich and poor was huge, and farmers were reduced by debt to slavery. Athens' rigid laws were recorded in 621BC by Draco, whose name lingers adjectivally – 'draconian' still means 'harsh'. Yet less than a century later, Athens was history's model of democracy.

Change began with the merchant-philosopher-statesman Solon, who was given by agreement of opposing factions ten years' dictatorial powers to solve Athens' unrest. He promptly abolished enslavement for debt. Then he put agriculture on the sounder footing of imported grain and exported olive oil, and boosted industry and craft, particularly pottery. The constitution he gave Athens in 594BC allowed for a gradual shift of electoral power from a few noble families to a wider, property-qualified group. Having set up his reforms, Solon left; he spent the rest of his life travelling.

In 560 Peisistratos seized power, as Athens' 'tyrant'. Many Greek states had these; the word originally conveyed single and absolute power without the modern implication of odious cruelty. Under Peisistratos Athens became a city of international importance through her arts and culture, from supremacy in vase-painting to the development of public drama and the great festivals of poetry and tragedy.

Peisistratos's son was a tyrant in the oppressive modern sense, and was driven out in 510. A third great Athenian statesman, Kleisthenes, took much further the moderate progression of the constitution of Solon. He minimised the powers of Athens' upper house, the Council of the Areopagus, and made the citizens' Assembly the sole legislative body. And in place of ages-old family groupings he created new electoral 'tribes', each consisting of parishes (*demes*) which were not contiguous but a social mix, drawn systematically from the coast, the plains and the city. A citizen now voted, fought and applauded at festivals by tribe; his loyalties no longer tied to his village or his occupation, he was an Athenian democrat.

Without petty rivalries, the Athenians with new-found confidence took on the invading armies of the Persians, who began attempts to add Greece to their empire. At the Battle of Marathon in 490BC Athens' army stood alone; at Salamis in 480BC her navy and that of Sparta together defeated the Persian fleet.

It was during and after long years of war that the city reached its zenith. It was then that you could have wandered down to the market place and chatted to Socrates while doing your shopping or having your shoes repaired; then that you could have visited the theatre to see the latest tragedy by Sophocles or Euripides; and then that you could have looked up to the Acropolis and seen what were to become the most famous buildings in Europe under construction.

From 442BC the catalyst behind these city improvements was

the statesman Pericles. Anxious to provide employment for the unskilled masses who could not serve on military campaigns, he set the Athenians to work on improving their city. The most vivid account of what he and they achieved is by Plutarch. 'He boldly laid before the people proposals for immense public works and plans for buildings, which would involve many different arts and industries and require long periods to complete . . . The materials to be used were stone, bronze, ivory, gold, ebony and cypress wood . . . So the buildings arose, as imposing in their sheer size as they were inimitable in the grace of their outlines, since the artists strove to excel themselves in the beauty of their workmanship.'

The buildings on the Acropolis were still incomplete when the Peloponnesian War with Sparta broke out in 431BC. Athens

Visiting Athens and Attica

Athens has a magnificent sunshine record, but is extremely hot during late June and in July and August, with average daily maximum temperatures of 30 to 33°C (91°F). April, May, September and October are much more comfortable and are the best time for sightseeing, although the city is no less crowded than in high summer. Mosquitoes are a nuisance at times.

Athens features on the itinerary of many organised European tours, and plenty of tour operators offer stay-put packages of three or more nights. Most have a selection of A-, B-, or C-category hotels and a few pensions. You can also combine a few nights in the city with a week on an island or a classical tour. It's well worth going independently to Athens if you plan to stay in simple hotels or pensions, as the choice of this type of accommodation is much wider than that offered by tour operators and there are plenty of cheap flights. Conversely, for Luxury, A- or B-category hotels, a package can be cheaper than going independently.

The Apollo Coast, also known as the Athenian Riviera, is offered by several tour operators as a stay-put seaside destination. Brochures tell you about fashionable and lively resorts within easy reach of Athens; what they don't always spell out clearly are the drawbacks – the noise from aircraft flying in and out of Athens airport, the busy coastal road, the lack of good sandy beaches. So, although the idea of combining a beach holiday with sightseeing in Athens may sound tempting, we don't think the Apollo Coast is where you should head for. A two-centre package offering Athens in conjunction with a resort on the island of Evia is a more pleasant option, and enables you to visit the sights of Attica just as easily.

There are direct scheduled flights to Athens daily from London (Heathrow), and one or two a week from Manchester. Charter flights leave from London (Gatwick), and in summer from regional airports

surrendered in 404BC and never really recovered, although philosophy and the arts continued to flourish under Plato and the great sculptor Praxiteles.

In 338BC Philip of Macedonia beat the Athenians at the Battle of Chaironeia, and seized the city. The Macedonians ruled until 168BC, when Athens fell to Rome. Its fortunes then depended on the character of the current Roman power – Sulla looted it, the Graecophiles Hadrian and Herodes Atticus redeveloped it, and the Christian Justinian closed the 'pagan' schools of philosophy and converted the temples into churches.

In the Middle Ages, after a brief period of Frankish rule, Athens fell to the Turks; the temples were converted into mosques, gunpowder stores and harems, a garrison was installed on the

including Birmingham, Luton, Manchester and Glasgow. Elleniko Airport, the East Terminal, is about 10km east of the city centre; it serves international flights operated by non-Greek airlines. The West Terminal is exclusively for Olympic Airways, and is the one you use for internal flights. A regular bus service (day and night) connects the two terminals with each other and with the city centre. The journey to Amalias Avenue (near Syntagma Square) takes about half an hour.

The Greek National Tourist Organisation (EOT) is at 2 Amerikis (telephone 3223111/9). Information offices are at: the National Bank of Greece on Syntagma Square (telephone 3222545), both airport terminals, and in Piraeus (Zea harbour). They should all be able to provide a free map, a general information booklet and useful factsheets about museum opening times, ferries and so on; and they will find you a room free of charge. Tourist Police usually speak English and can help with general queries and accommodation. They are based at 7 Singrou Street and in Akti Miaouli Street (Piraeus). You can contact them by phoning 171 (24 hours). *Athens News* is a small English-language newspaper; *This Week in Athens* is a useful free booklet.

Getting around

The sightseeing area of Athens is quite compact and is easily covered on foot, but there's an efficient and inexpensive public transport system. Buses (and trolley buses) are frequent and the standard fare (which you put in a box by the driver) is extremely cheap; the system is easy to master provided you have the free tourist office map which shows the routes. The metro system is also simple – just a single line which runs from the northern suburb of Kifissia through the city centre to the port of Piraeus. Fares and operating hours are the same as for buses. The two most useful central stations are on Omonia and Monastiraki Squares.

In the heat of summer, taxis prove useful; they are also cheap, and it's usually easy to find one. It can, however, be difficult to telephone for taxis at shift-change time (about 2 to 4p.m.); and they are notoriously

Acropolis, and the once-great city declined to little more than an obscure village largely forgotten by the outside world.

In the 17th century some of the more intrepid Grand Tourists began to visit Athens, but it was in the 18th century that a craze for all things Greek hit Britain, following the publication of Fénelon's *Les Aventures de Télémaque*, a continuation of the *Odyssey*. The architects Stuart and Revett spent two years in the city producing four volumes of architectural drawings, and copies of Athenian buildings sprang up all over Britain, culminating in the (unfinished) monuments on Calton Hill in Edinburgh.

The Napoleonic Wars of the late 18th and early 19th centuries

---

Getting around continued

unpunctual. Taxi-sharing is a common practice, so it's worth hailing them even if they are occupied; but you'll probably still have to pay the full fare. Ensuring that the meter is switched on is particularly important if you are travelling to or from the airports – it has been known for foreigners to be taken for a ride in more ways than one.

There are many excursions available from Athens, including classical tours of the Peloponnese and Attica, which last anything from one to nine days. If you're taking a guided tour, find out whether admission charges are included in the price and how well qualified your guide is.

Our experience of guided tours has not always been satisfactory: some allow little time at sights and over-generous halts at roadside shops or cafes. Our advice is to consider a do-it-yourself excursion using taxis or public transport.

The public bus service for destinations in Attica is fairly comprehensive. The National Tourist Organisation has a list of bus numbers, prices and destinations. The following places can be reached quite easily: Daphni (bus 373 from Deligiorgi, south-west of Omonia); Eleusis (bus 862 or 853 from Eleftherias Plateia); Glyfada (bus 121, 128, or 129 from Vas. Olgas, south of the National Gardens); Loutsa (bus 304, 305, 306, 316 from Eptahalkou below the Hephaisteion); Varkiza (bus 115, 116, or 117 from Vas. Olgas, south of the National Gardens); Vouliagmeni (bus 110 or 153 from Vas. Olgas); Lavrio, Rhamnous, Sounion, Vravrona (bus 14, from Mavromateion, behind the National Archaeological Museum); Marathon, Nea Makri, Oropos, Rafina (bus 29, from Mavromateion).

If you're travelling further afield, long-distance buses leave from one of two terminals: *A* at 100 Kifissou (for the Peloponnese, Epirus and Salonika); *B* at 260 Liossion (Delphi, Volos, Trikkala, Evia). You can reach both terminals by an express bus from Syntagma or Omonia (bus *A* for terminal *A*, *B* for terminal *B*).

The two railway stations are very close to each other. Larissa Station serves northern Greece and the rest of Europe. The Peloponnisou station serves the Peloponnese.

closed off much of Europe to the Grand Tourists, and they turned their attention to Greece. Artists churned out landscapes with ruins as the focal point, and controversy raged about the respective values of art and nature. Byron, the most famous of the 19th-century Graecophiles, was characteristically scathing about those who came out on the side of nature. 'Am I to be told that the "Nature" of Attica would be more poetical without the "Art" of the Acropolis? of the Temple of Theseus? and of the still all Greek and glorious monuments of her exquisitely artificial genius? Ask the traveller what strikes him as most poetical, the Parthenon or the rock on which it stands?'

Not all the Grand Tourists, Byron included, were content to paint or wonder at Athens' ancient ruins, but carted off choice objects to grace their cities or homes. The most notorious of these was Lord Elgin, who removed most of the Parthenon's sculpted frieze, but bankrupted himself in the process and was forced to sell the pieces to the British Museum, where they still remain.

One of the Grand Tourists' favourite and most painted sites was not, in fact, in Athens. The temple of Poseidon at Sounion, perched on a rocky bluff above the sea, is probably the most spectacularly positioned in Greece, and is understandably the most popular day-excursion from Athens. Other places to which you can take an excursion include the sanctuary of Demeter, overshadowed by the factories of industrial Elefsis, and the Byzantine monastery of Daphni sandwiched between a hectic motorway and a pine-clad hill. Attica also has more hidden treasures. The ancient fortress at Phyli stands above a sheer gorge on Mount Parnes, and the remote sanctuary of Nemesis at Rhamnous lies above a wild ravine which runs down to the sea.

With three million Athenians anxious to escape the heat of the city in mid-summer, the demand for a space on the beach is great. Most of the beaches on the so-called Apollo Coast (south-east of Athens) are rather dirty stretches of sand and shingle, and the heavily developed urban strip suffers greatly from aircraft and traffic noise, none of which seems to deter it from being offered as a holiday resort area. Vougliameni is the most pleasant resort; further south the coast becomes quieter. To the north-east of Athens the tiny beach at Rhamnous is one of the few in the area to remain undeveloped.

The city of Athens is bounded to the east by Mounts Hymettos and Pentilikon, and to the north by Mount Parnes (1413m) – wild and attractive, with a winter sports centre and a large casino hotel. But much of inland Attica is rather bland and bleak, and even when you leave behind the vast conurbation of

Greater Athens the villages and towns are not attractive –
particularly on the huge and vacant Marathon Plain with its
soulless shack villages.

Though most people head to the port of Piraeus for their
island ferry connections, there are more pleasant embarkation
ports which offer the opportunity to see some of Attica on the
way: Rafina serves the Cyclades and Evia, which is also
accessible from Agia Marina or Oropos.

ATHENS

Modern Athens is not a city to wander around. A grey sprawl
of closely packed square blocks, it's crowded and chaotic at most
times of the year; in summer it becomes almost unbearable.
Six-lane highways lead into the centre from the outskirts, and
in the centre there is a fairly complicated one-way traffic system
with big main roads and a maze of smaller backstreets; making
use of taxis between sites and museums is a sensible way of
conserving energy.

Two abrupt green hills rise above the dense concrete and
provide the city's major landmarks and (smog permitting)
spectacular views: the pine-clad Lykavittos (Lykabettos) and the
Acropolis, best known of all ancient sites. Athens' other sites
are scattered, often hemmed in by all the new buildings; and
there's no river to provide a focal point. In these ways, Athens
contrasts sharply with other major European cities, such as
Rome, where the sites form part of the modern city. The central
part of the city, where most of the sights are situated, is fairly
small, so it is reasonably easy to get around. From this point of
view it does not really matter where you stay.

Athens' old quarter, the **Plaka**, nestles below the eastern
slopes of the Acropolis. It's a labyrinth of cobbled streets
winding through a haphazard cluster of neo-classical villas,
shack-like shops and tacky 1960s hotels. Entering the Plaka is to
step back in time – not, as you might expect, into the working-
class Athens of the last century, but into the backpackers'
Athens of the hippie era. The poet sandal-maker visited by John
Lennon still plies his trade on Pandrossou; façades are concealed
behind racks of floppy, fringed and faded clothes; and gathering
dust in the cavernous shops are hookah pipes and strings of love
and worry beads. Some gentrification has taken place, with a
shrewd eye on the more affluent tourists of the 1980s, and there
are expensive antique and jewellery shops and up-market
restaurants alongside the basement tavernas, cheap leather
stores and shops selling mass-produced 'traditional rugs'.

Redevelopment of the Plaka began about 25 years ago when many of the elegant neo-classical villas were pulled down to be replaced by hotels. As the hoteliers and 'craftsmen' moved in, the original inhabitants moved out, and the Plaka's life now stems from the tourists. Recently local government bowed to pressure and put a stop to the ruthless development. In a new spirit of conservation, many of the old houses are undergoing restoration, traffic has been banned from most of the streets, and the number of loudspeakers and neon signs strictly controlled. The Plaka remains the city's most appealing quarter: wandering its streets, lazing in cafes, rummaging in antique shops and haggling over the price of rugs and leather goods is without doubt the best way of recovering from an overdose of culture and exhaust fumes. This is also the most pleasant place in which to spend your evenings, for the shops stay open late and there are plenty of tavernas – ranging from tourist traps where you'll end up paying a steep charge for watching displays of Greek dancing and listening to *bouzouki* crooners to colourful and steamy cellars which are cheap, cramped and frequented by as many Greeks as foreigners.

The main shopping street of the Plaka, with the greatest concentration of souvenirs, hippie clothes and 'I love Greece' T-shirts, as well as some excellent and surprisingly reasonable leather goods, is Adrianou. Voulis, which runs into the Plaka from Ermou, has some tempting rug shops, as well as jewellery, furs and leather. Ifestou, named after Hephaistos, patron of metal-workers, is now given over to shops selling fake antique copper goods, jewellery, army surplus and, at the Ermou end, motor spares and strange bits of machinery. Haggling over prices is standard practice; in fact, you'll often find that merely showing an interest in an item hanging outside a shop is enough to bring the owner scuttling out with the offer of a discount. Many of the leather shops and most of the jewellery shops take credit cards.

There are a couple of pretty Byzantine churches in the Plaka. The most interesting is the Old Metropolitan, which stands on Plateia Mitropoleos in the shadow of the ugly 19th-century neo-Byzantine cathedral; various archaic fragments were incorporated into its walls, including a zodiac calendar. The tiny Kapnikarea (Our Lady of the Robe) is a gem of a Byzantine church surrounded by modern shops on Ermou. There are also a couple of small museums: the Centre for Folk Art and Tradition, and the Museum of Greek Popular Art.

The Plaka is one of the most attractive parts of Athens in which to stay, and all the city's main archaeological sites are within easy reach on foot. The hotels in the area are generally

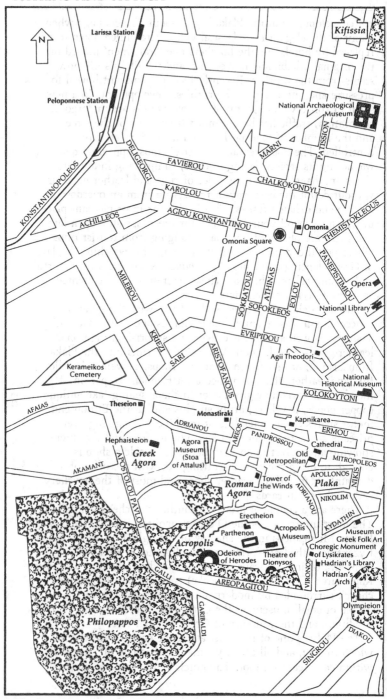

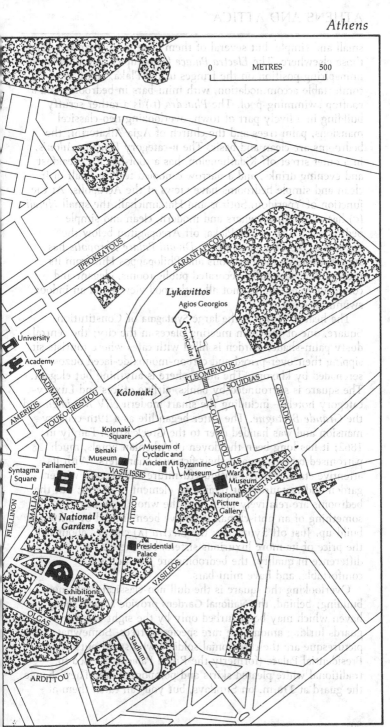

small and simple, but several of them have more character than those elsewhere. The *Electra Palace* (A) occupies a convenient if uninspiring position on the fringes of the Plaka, and has comfortable accommodation, with mini-bars in bedrooms and a rooftop swimming-pool. The *Phaedra* (D) is a rather scruffy building in a lively part of town, overlooking neo-classical mansions, palm trees and the church of Agia Aikaterini; the bedrooms are clean and basic. The B-category *Pension Adonis*, in a quiet street off Kidatheneion, has a roof-bar for breakfast and evening drinks, and a narrow canopied terrace. Half of its clean and simple bedrooms have views of the Acropolis. At the junction of Yperidou, Sotiros and Hatzimichali, the small *Nefeli* (C) has welcoming owners and modern, clean and simple bedrooms. South of the Plaka, off Areopagitou below the Acropolis, the Luxury-category *Divani Palace Acropolis* has superb views of the Acropolis and Philopappos Hill from its roof-garden, tastefully decorated public rooms, elegant and comfortable bedrooms (not all with good views) and an indoor swimming-pool.

The heart of town is the large **Syntagma** or Constitution Square, one of the main meeting places in the city; the central dusty palm-shaded garden is filled with cafes where tourists sit sipping their over-priced and carbon-monoxide-laced ouzos serenaded by klaxons. The atmosphere is anything but elegant. The square is surrounded by banks, airline offices and Luxury-category hotels – including the smart modern *NJV Meridien* and the *Grande Bretagne*. The latter began life as a 19th-century mansion and was handed over to the Greek Royal Family in 1862; it has long been the doyen of Athenian hotels, much patronised by writers and their fictional characters. With its attentive staff, restored antique furniture and elegant winter garden and restaurant, it retains an element of charm; but the bedrooms are relatively plain, and the whole may come as something of an anti-climax if you've been enticed by a literary build-up. Just off Syntagma, the *Electra* (A) charges about half the price of its more luxurious sisters, but there's little difference in quality; the bedrooms are spacious and comfortable, and have mini-bars.

Overlooking the square is the dull neo-classical Parliament building; behind, the **National Gardens** provide a cool, shady haven which may be disturbed only by the sight of armed guards lurking among the rare species of trees. Somewhat more picturesque are the ceremonial soldiers who stand outside the Presidential Palace (formerly the Royal Palace), dressed in traditional white pleated skirts and pompom shoes. They change the guard at 11a.m. on Sundays, but you can catch them at other times goose-stepping outside the gates, resolutely ignoring the giggles of tourists. Overlooking the palace is the ultra-modern and sophisticated *Astir Palace Hotel* (Luxury-category), favoured by diplomats and politicians. Along the western side of the gardens, Amalias Avenue leads down to the Olympeion and the arch of Hadrian, as well as to Piraeus and the West airport; it's one of the city's busiest roads.

Several of the museums, including the Benaki and the Byzantine Museums, are along or near **Vasilissis Sofias**, which is · lined with elegant neo-classical villas housing embassies. Just north is one of the least claustrophobic areas of central Athens, with hilly, tree-lined streets and a spacious, well-heeled air. In the pedestrianised sidestreets around **Kolonaki Square** are Athens' smartest shops. The square itself, inevitably choked with traffic, is flanked with expensive pavement cafes.

A few blocks from Kolonaki is the steep pine-clad hill of **Lykavittos**, crowned by a modern white chapel. It is the highest hill in Athens and is an understandably popular summer weekend retreat from the heat and fumes of the city. Views from the top are magnificent, and there is a cafe-restaurant and the Lykavittos Theatre on the summit. A road leads up to a viewpoint near the theatre, and paths wind around the hill. If you're feeling lazy, you can take a funicular railway from the end of Ploutarchou. At the foot of the hill, in a pleasant setting only a short walk from the Kolonaki shopping area, the Luxury-category *St George Lykabettos Hotel* has a stylish interior, plenty of facilities including a roof-garden and swimming-pool with views of Lykavittos and across to the Acropolis, and comfortable if rather plain bedrooms.

The main reason for heading west from Syntagma along the busy avenues of Stadiou and Venizelou is to visit the National Archaeological Museum. The avenues converge at Omonia, Athens' second square.

Omonia is gaudier, seedier and sleazier than Syntagma. A major focal point of the city, it's lively and bustling by day when the fountains play; the area is also very busy at night, but the atmosphere is distinctly unsavoury. To the west a grid of fairly uninteresting and densely built-up streets stretches towards the railway stations. South, towards Ermou and the Plaka, the area becomes more colourful (though not prettier): dozens of shopkeepers and tradesmen sell their wares and make furniture, clothes or ironmongery in little workshops. There are several lively street markets here and lots of food shops, and the air is thick with the pungent smells of herbs and spices. The east side of Omonia Square is much smarter: a busy shopping area around Stadiou; bookshops and a scholarly atmosphere

around the university; and, northwards, a quiet, leafy
residential sector near the Archaeological Museum. There's
quite a range of hotels in the area around Omonia, from the
seedy and dubious ones on and near the square itself to modest,
good-value places just a few streets away, and some rather
smart establishments on the east side of Eolou.

About half an hour on the Underground from the centre of
Athens is the suburb of **Kifissia**; just outside (about 15 minutes'
walk) is the leafy and elegant area of **Kefalari**, a fine place in
which to stay in style and comfort. The avenues are lined with
eucalyptus, palm, pine, orange and olive trees; Italianate villas
stand in luxuriant gardens; and, best of all, the air is fresh and
the pace unhurried. There's a park, cafes and restaurants, and a
small complex of designer shops and patisseries. The Luxury-
category *Pentelikon Hotel* is set in a secluded street just a few
minutes' walk from the park. It's one of the few hotels in
Greece as attractive outside as it is inside. Buttermilk-washed,
with wrought-iron and frescoed balconies, it stands in a pine-
shaded garden with a swimming-pool and elegant pavilion. The
interior has been refurbished by an Italian designer in subtle
pastel tones; there's a restaurant, cocktail bar and cafe, and the
bedrooms are tasteful and unfussy. Overlooking the park, the
Semiramis (A) is a family hotel with a homely atmosphere and
many long-term guests. It is currently undergoing some much-
needed refurbishment. The bedrooms that have been redecorated
are tasteful, while others are rather worn at the seams; all have
mini-bars. There's a terrace, garden and swimming-pool, and
aerobics, gym and Greek lessons are laid on.

Athens: sights

The Acropolis

The most famous ancient site in Europe, whose rocky platform is
polished by the feet of four and a half million visitors a year, rises
above the grimy chaos of modern Athens: classic, refined and
awesomely beautiful. No matter how many times you've seen the
Acropolis, how busy it is, whether you're sweltering in the mid-
summer heat or shivering in the icy winds of winter, it never ceases to
impress. British soldiers risked their lives to see it in the strife-torn
Athens of the Second World War; backpackers spend their last
drachmas on its entrance fee; and it is this, above all, which makes
hordes of tourists feel that spending part of their holiday in the most
polluted city in Europe is worthwhile.

The Acropolis hill has been inhabited since a Neolithic tribe was
attracted to its easily defended slopes in 5000BC. From then its history
becomes a confusing blend of fact and fiction. During the reign of King

Cecrops, who lived around 1700BC, the Acropolis was supposed to have been the scene of a competition between Poseidon and Athena for the honour of protecting the city. God and goddess each struck the rock, Poseidon producing a great gush of saltwater, and Athena the world's first olive tree. Not surprisingly, as the uses of saltwater are limited, Athena won, and the Acropolis was decreed to be her territory.

Sanctity to Athena, however, came a poor second to the need to defend the city, and it was not until the 6th century BC, when the Delphic Oracle decreed that the Acropolis should be occupied only by gods, that the kings and tyrants moved out and the building of temples began.

Nothing remains of the first temples, for they were razed to the ground by the Persians when they entered Athens in 480BC. Those that have survived date from the mid-5th century, when Pericles decided that the beautification of the city would be an excellent way of showing the defeated Persians that the Greeks were undaunted by the devastation wreaked by the Persian Wars.

Ironically the buildings of the Acropolis were still incomplete in 431BC at the outbreak of the Peloponnesian Wars with Sparta which necessitated a cut in expenditure. The bulges on the outer blocks of the Propylaia, for example, are the lifting bosses which would normally have been chipped off. These imperfections, however, are as nothing compared with the damage caused to the monuments by Franks, Turks, Venetians and Lord Elgin.

Under the Franks the monumental entrance, or Propylaia, was used as a palace, and the Parthenon and Erechtheion temples as churches; the Turks converted the Erechtheion into a harem, used the Propylaia as a powder magazine, and transformed the Parthenon into a mosque. Consequently, when the diplomat Hugo Favoli visited in the 16th century, he found the Acropolis 'looming beneath a swarm of glittering golden crescents'. The golden crescents were still glittering a century later when the gunpowder in the Propylaia exploded after being struck by lightning. The Parthenon then had to double as mosque and magazine, and it too exploded when hit by a Venetian cannonball some 30 years later. Once the Venetians had taken the Acropolis, they wreaked further havoc on the Parthenon by smashing a statue group of Athena and her chariot in the process of attempting to remove it. The most thorough pillager of the Acropolis, however, was Lord Elgin, British ambassador to the Turkish Empire (the Porte) in the early 19th century. After gaining permission to take as many antiquities as he liked, he removed most of the frieze, 15 metopes and pedimental figures from the Parthenon, as well as one of the caryatids from the Erechtheion.

The restorers of the last century attempted to strengthen the temples by inserting iron rods inside the columns. These have rusted and swollen and are cracking the marble. The ancient builders were somewhat more sophisticated, for they too used iron rods to strengthen the joints, but encased them in lead so that they would not rust. The current restoration work has involved X-raying the buildings in order to discover which joints are wrapped in lead and which not. The rusty 19th-century rods will be removed and replaced by non-corrosive titanium, which experts reckon will last 3000 years. The work is due to be completed in 1993.

The Acropolis is approached up a steep and slippery marble path on the north-west slope of the hill beyond the Odeion of Herodes Atticus. The site is entered through the Roman Beulé Gate, once flanked by two towers. This, however, is dwarfed by the massy, monumental gateway of the Propylaia, which you'll have plenty of time to admire while queuing to buy your ticket. The tiny temple of Athena Nike is perched alongside the Propylaia, although you may not have much time to look at it in between watching where you put your feet and dodging the irritatingly persistent vendors and unofficial guides.

Acropolis: highlights

● **Propylaia** Work began on the Propylaia, the entrance to the Acropolis, in 437BC, after the completion of the Parthenon. Its axis is aligned to that of the Parthenon – the first time that two buildings were erected in direct relationship to one another.

The Propylaia consists of five entrances divided by Doric columns, with the widest, in the centre, reserved for the Panathenaic procession. Its steps, now encased in wood to protect them from tourists' feet, are shallow so that the sacrificial beasts could cope with them.

It was originally sheltered by a coffered marble ceiling, with gilded stars on a blue background, supported by slender Ionic columns – another piece of architectural trail-blazing on the part of the designer, Meneskles, for it was the first time that two different orders of columns were combined in one building. Only one corner of the ceiling survived the explosion of the 17th century, and this is currently masked by scaffolding.

Building the Propylaia was not without its problems, for Meneskles's original design, which included two symmetrical flanking wings, enraged the priest of the adjacent temple to Athena Nike, as the southern wing would have encroached on his, or rather the goddess's, territory. Consequently, the southern wing is narrower than the northern, and doubtless as a way of placating the priest was used as a waiting-room for pilgrims wanting to visit the temple. A thousand years later Acciaolo, the Florentine Duke of Athens, established himself in the southern wing, adding a second storey, battlements and a tower (all removed during the 19th century).

● **Temple to Athena Nike** This small, beautifully reconstructed temple perched above the Propylaia was taken to pieces by the Turks to make room for a gun emplacement. In the 19th century the fragments were pieced together by archaeologists.

The temple once housed the famous relief of Athena, bringer of victory, fastening her sandals, wingless to prevent her flying off to another city. This is now in the Acropolis Museum (see page 98).

According to the travel writer Pausanias, it was from this rock that Theseus's father leapt to his death – Theseus had gone off to kill the Minotaur in Crete, and had told his father that if he succeeded he would change the black sails on his ship to white. In the thrill of beating the Minotaur he forgot, and his father, looking out to sea and seeing the black sails, assumed that he had been killed, and committed suicide.

● **The Parthenon** The most famous and photographed building in Greece, Pericles' temple to Athena has also been one of the most misused – as it was long before the temple exploded while being used as a gunpowder store.

In the 4th century BC King Demetrios kept his courtesans in it and held wild parties there; in the 5th century AD it was converted into a church, and the east pediment destroyed to make room for an apse; in the 10th century the re-dedication to the Virgin Mary involved daubing the interior with frescoes; in the 15th century it was transformed into a mosque, and a minaret appended to the south-west corner; and in the 17th century the Venetian Morosini, not content with the fact that his army had fired the mortar which caused the explosion, shattered the west pediment in the process of attempting to remove it to embellish Venice.

The early 19th century saw Elgin's visit, and an attempt at restoration by strengthening the columns with iron clamps, which rusted and made the marble crack. Now, in the 20th century, tourists and acid rain are eroding it. The interior is closed to the public.

The miracle of the Parthenon, however, is that its beauty has overridden adversity, and that even in its damaged state it remains sensational. What makes it special is that the designers, Pheidias, Iktinos and Kallikrates, realising that straight columns appear thinner in the middle when seen against a bright background, decided to correct the optical illusion. They achieved this by making the columns, and the platform on which they stood, slightly convex. The effect is difficult to pin down, and is most easily appreciated if you've seen the Hephaisteion (see page 102), which has none of the Parthenon's lightness and delicacy.

There are forty-six fluted Doric columns, eight at each end, and seventeen along the sides. The entrance was at the east, with a space inside, known as the *pronaos*, where offerings to Athena would be placed. From here a door led into the *naos* or *cella*, an inner chamber which contained a giant statue of Athena by Pheidias, made of ivory and over a tonne of gold. Behind the *naos* was another chamber, inhabited by the priestesses of Athena. This was the Parthenon proper, for the name originally meant virgins' apartment, and it was only later that it came to be used for the whole temple.

In its heyday the Parthenon looked quite different from the way it does now, being brightly painted and gilded. The pediment statues and battle scenes on the metopes which surrounded the temple were painted blue on a red background; inside was a marble coffered ceiling decorated with roses and foliage; and it is likely that even the columns were painted.

Although few of the metopes and only fragments of the pedimental sculpture have survived, descriptions by Pausanias and sketches by later travellers have made it possible to work out the decorative scheme. The east pediment showed the birth of Athena from the head of Zeus, and

THE ELGIN MARBLES

'The Elgin Marbles' is what Britain calls them; to the Greeks they are the Parthenon Marbles. They are 76m of sculpted marble figures – chiefly from the frieze – which once adorned the Parthenon, and they may well be the masterwork of its master-architect and sculptor, Pheidias.

When the seventh Earl of Elgin became ambassador to Turkish-occupied Greece in 1799, the Parthenon was in a distressing state. An explosion in a Turkish powder magazine there in 1687 had blown it apart, and a Venetian commander had tried to remove sculpture from the west pediment only to see it dropped and smashed. By the mid-18th century a mosque had replaced a church, built among the ruins. In 1801 Lord Elgin – who both studied and collected classical sculpture – obtained from the sultan a permit to remove from the Parthenon 'some blocks of stone with inscriptions and figures'. The Marbles were in due course shipped to England and in 1816 sold to the British Museum, where by Act of Parliament they remain 'inalienably': the museum cannot dispose of them.

But Greece wants them back. A long but low-key controversy over the question of returning the Marbles to Athens has been reopened with vigour in the 1980s by a socialist Greek government, and particularly by its Minister of Culture, Melina Mercouri, former actress and film star, MP for Piraeus since 1977.

The retrospective arguments, covering the actions of Lord Elgin, are bitter. His permit from the sultan was unspecific about removing fallen sculpture from the ground or taking it from buildings still erect; there

the west the contest between Athena and Poseidon for the possession of Athens. The metopes all showed battle scenes – on the west that of the Atticans against the marauding (and, in classical Greek terms, terribly unfeminine) Amazons; on the north the Siege of Troy; on the east the Battle of the Giants; and on the south the Battle between the Lapiths and Centaurs.

The inner frieze was badly damaged in the 17th-century explosion, but as there are 76 metres of it in the British Museum and 53 metres in the Acropolis Museum, as well as some fairly comprehensive sketches by Carrey, a 17th-century traveller, archaeologists have a fairly clear idea of its content. It showed the annual Panathenaic procession, and includes horsemen, musicians, men carrying trays of cakes and honeycombs to be offered to Athena, and sheep and heifers being led to sacrifice.

● **Erechtheion** This temple to Athena and Poseidon was built at the end of the 5th century BC on the most sacred part of the Acropolis. It was here that Athena and Poseidon were supposed to have held their rock-striking contest, and here that Athena's venerated olive tree grew. The tree was still standing in the courtyard of the Erechtheion when

seems little doubt that all his operations had official approval – at their height he was employing 500 local men – but the Greeks say he bribed local officials to let him take whatever he pleased, even if in so doing he further damaged the temple. Britain's Lord Byron was among those who thought – and publicly said, in his case in verse – that Lord Elgin was merely a plunderer. Yet Elgin can also be considered a preserver (which is how he regarded himself): as early as 1872 there was photographic evidence showing the dramatic deterioration of sculptures left in the Parthenon compared with those in the British Museum, and that was before modern air pollution really got going.

Today, it is not envisaged that the Marbles should be replaced in their original setting, exposed to Athens' smog, but that they should be displayed in a new Acropolis Museum equipped with anti-pollution filters. But possession is nine points of the law, and in this case British law confirms the tenth point. It is argued that in the British Museum this part of 'the glory that was Greece' is both better preserved and visible to many more people; that cultural sharing is more civilised than national possessiveness; and that to undo the 'inalienable' aspect of the British Museum's charge would be a disastrous precedent. What would happen to the great museums of the world if every country demanded its treasures back?

The arguments for the return of the Marbles to Athens are ethical, political, passionately felt. A foreign museum is no place for objects of such unique significance. Integral parts of the great temple should be gathered in the city that built it, where both scholars and the public can better appreciate the total impact – not 3000 miles away. The bottom line is the enormous importance to Greece of the Parthenon as a symbol: of former greatness, and now of national pride and identity.

Pausanias visited in the 2nd century AD, and within the temple was a well that echoed the sound of the sea when the wind blew south.

There are confused legends about its name. One states that Erectheus, a king of Athens, introduced the joint worship of Poseidon and Athena; another that the saltwater stream that Poseidon produced was known as the Erectheïs.

The sanctity of the site called for ingenuity on the part of the Erechtheion's architect, for the pre-existing shrines could not be demolished. The structure of the temple incorporates different floor levels and two asymmetrical wings.

Like the Parthenon, the Erechtheion was elaborately decorated – the capitals were adorned with bronze ornaments inlaid with fake gems, and the panelled ceilings of the porticoes were painted blue and studded with gilded bronze stars.

This glitzy décor, if it had survived, would have made quite an appropriate setting for the harem which the Turks established in the temple. However, by this time the decoration had long disappeared, and the Turks felt it necessary to deface the south entablature with inscriptions. This has now been replaced by a copy (minus graffiti), as have the six caryatids supporting the southern portico. One of these was removed by Elgin, and as acid rain was eating into the features of her five sisters they were transferred to the safety of the Acropolis Museum.

- **Acropolis Museum** Set in a dip behind the Parthenon, the museum contains statues, pottery and carvings from the site. Rooms 1 and 2 contain fragments of **pedimental structure**, still bearing traces of paint, from the 6th-century BC temple to Athena destroyed by the Persians. The best preserved is of Herakles fighting the Typhon, a monster with three smiling, blue-bearded male heads and a snake's tail. Serpentine monsters were much favoured by Archaic sculptors as they fitted neatly into the corners of pediments.

In the centre of room 2 is another smiling statue, the so-called **Moscophoros**, a man carrying a calf on his shoulders to be sacrificed to Athena.

In Room 4 there is a collection of *kouroi* and *korai*, Archaic (6th-century BC) male and female statues dedicated to Athena. You can follow the development from the early stiff, static and smiling figures to the more sophisticated statues in which elaborately gathered soft gowns or *chitons* are used to break up the vertical line. However, most retain a stylised pose, with their hands clenched by their sides and with one leg in front of the other – if you look carefully, you can see that the extended leg is actually longer than the perpendicular one.

In Room 6 is one of the first surviving statues to break out of the static mode of the Archaic *kouroi* – the **Kritian Boy**. The lines of this naked youth's body are fluid and relaxed, his head is inclined to one side, and he leans forward with his weight shifted on to his slightly bent front leg.

The miserable and much-battered fragments which have survived from the Parthenon pediment are in Room 7. It is these, rather than the temple itself, which bring home the temple's trouble-ridden history. Slabs from the inner frieze of the Parthenon showing the Panathenaic procession are displayed in Room 8. They were blown clear of the building in the 17th-century explosion and buried. There are animated horses and riders whose voluminous cloaks fly behind them, giving a real impression of speed; old men bearing olive branches; and sensitive and pensive-looking youths carrying pots and leading heifers to sacrifice.

Perhaps the most beautiful relief in the museum is that of the so-called **Wingless Victory** (in Room 9) which was in the temple of Athena Nike. Her smooth body is at times revealed, at times concealed by the soft folds of her diaphanous *chiton*. Almost as lovely, although severely damaged, are the five **caryatids** from the Erechtheion, which have been placed behind glass for protection. They too are draped in flimsy *chitons*, whose folds manage to echo the fluting of columns without appearing unrealistic.

- **Theatre of Dionysos** On a lovely site, carved into the southern slope of the Acropolis hill and screened from the road by trees, is the 4th-century BC theatre of Dionysos.

The first theatre on this site consisted of nothing more than a circle of pressed earth: until wooden seats were erected at the beginning of the 5th century BC, the spectators would sit on the grassy slopes. The theatre may have been unsophisticated, but the dramas certainly were not. For it was here that the great tragedies of Aeschylus, Sophocles and Euripides were first performed against backdrops of wood and canvas in the annual theatre festival.

As drama increased in popularity a stone stage was erected, complete with flying devices, cranes and a platform which could be let down from the ceiling so that gods could make sudden appearances. Eventually, in the 4th century BC, tiers of stone benches were set into the slopes, with room for 17,000 spectators. Twenty-five of the original 64 tiers of seats survive, including the elaborate thrones on the front row, reserved for the priests, whose names were carved on them. The most ornate, in the centre, was reserved for the priest of Dionysos; it is carved with lions, griffins, satyrs and grapes (the details are difficult to see at present, as the seat is roped off).

The theatre was rebuilt by the Romans. The orchestra was paved and the 4th-century BC drainage channel covered with perforated slabs which could be plugged so that the arena could be flooded for aquatic games. The Romans were also responsible for the sculpted frieze along the stage front, and a barrier to protect spectators during blood-sports.

From the theatre you can walk alongside the crumbling arches of the **Stoa of Eumenes**, a once-covered promenade, towards the Roman **Odeion of Herodes Atticus**. This is now used for the Athens Festival and has been rather brutally reconstructed, with tiers of pristine marble behind its massive arched façade. It is closed except for performances, but you can see it clearly as you climb up to the Acropolis.

Greek and Roman agoras

The ancient market place of Athens has been likened to a bomb site. After centuries of sackings, scavengings and rebuildings, only foundations remain, and the site is, to say the least, confusing. But it can also be one of the most rewarding, and as long as you arm yourself with a plan and visit the excellent museum first (which has exhibits ranging from a child's potty to a sausage griddle) you should have little difficulty in bringing it to life in your mind.

The most vivid evocation of life in the *agora* is by the comic poet Euboulos:

> *In one and the same place you will find all kinds of things for sale together at Athens: figs – Policemen! Grapes, turnips, pears, apples – Witnesses!*
> *Roses, medlars, porridge, honeycombs, peas – Lawsuits! Milk, curds, myrtle-berries – Allotment machines!*
> *Bulbs, lamps – Water-clocks, laws, indictments!*

Replace porridge with rice pudding, lawsuits with newspapers, allotment machines with lotteries, and water-clocks with digital watches, and the scene is not so different from a modern Athenian market.

But the *agora* was far more than a place at which to shop and gossip. It was the political as well as the social and commercial centre of town, and here the Athenians would come to stand for jury duty, to find out whether they'd been called up for military service, and to check out the agenda for the regular meetings of the citizens' assembly.

Nor was the conversation all idle gossip. Here the philosopher Socrates, less interested in trading goods than in trading ideas, spent his days in dialectical arguments around the tables of the money-lenders and in the workshops of craftsmen. It was here too that he was imprisoned, condemned to death and executed on a charge of insulting the gods and corrupting the young.

Athens' first market place lay just outside the entrance to the Acropolis, but in the 6th century BC its booths and tents were moved down to the flat land below the northern slope of the Areopagus. By the Classical period the stallholders had grouped themselves into circles – specialising in anything from fish, meat, wine or oil to horses and slaves. The few buildings to be erected in this period were destroyed or badly damaged in the Persian sack of 480BC. As part of the ambitious city-improvement plans of the mid-5th century BC they were restored and new public buildings erected and the temple of Hephaistos begun. Three hundred years later vast colonnades or stoas were erected, including the Stoa of Attalos which once sheltered 42 shops. (This has now been rebuilt, using ancient methods, to house the museum.)

The Greek *agora* was sacked by the Romans in 86BC, and in AD267 by northern 'barbarians', who scavenged the ruins and used column discs and fragments of friezes and architraves to build a defensive wall. The cycle of rebuilding and destruction continued right up until the 19th century, when the area was covered with modern houses. When excavation began, 400 buildings had to be demolished, and silt to a depth of 12 metres removed.

There are a number of entrances to the ancient site of the Greek *agora*. This itinerary begins at the entrance at the end of Polignotou to the west of the Roman *agora*.

Greek agora: highlights

● **The south** Right by the entrance is a chunkily paved section of the Panathenaic Way which led from the Dipylon Gate to the Acropolis. This was the route followed by the four-yearly Panathenaic procession. It is thought that the grooves along the north-east side of the Way were designed to take stands for spectators. The most dramatic feature was a race that involved the competitors leaping off and jumping back on to speeding chariots.

The south side was enclosed by three parallel stoas in the 2nd century BC, with fountain houses at either end of the outermost one. Walking along the foundations, you reach the **horos**, a small stone block near the corner of the middle stoa, above the junction of two long drainage channels. Inscribed on the *horos* are the words 'I am the boundary of the *agora*'. The *agora* was considered to be a sacred pre-cinct: criminals were banned, and anyone entering had to purify them-selves at a water stoup, whose stumpy pedestal stands above the *horos*.

From the *horos* a path leads outside the *agora* to the foundations of the **prison** where Socrates spent his last days. His death from hemlock, which involved gradual paralysis, is poignantly described by Plato in the *Phaedo*.

The *horos* stands next to the foundations of a row of shops and houses. In one of them hob-nails and eyelets for shoes were found, along with the base of a clay cup with the name Simon scratched on it – making it virtually certain that this was Simon the Cobbler's. Socrates often visited the cobbler to discuss philosophy, and Simon was the first person to take notes of the dialogues.

• **The west** To the left of the *horos* the foundations of the circular **Tholos** are clearly visible. This was the headquarters of the Council (Boule) of 500, elected annually from all male citizens. Each of the city's ten tribes was represented by a unit of fifty councillors, each unit taking on the presidency (*prytaneis*) for a tenth of a year with a third of its members on duty and in residence at the Tholos at all times. The foundations of a kitchen, shopping lists inscribed on shards of pottery, and an order for new beds were unearthed on the site, suggesting that the councillors on duty slept and ate there.

The Boule's duties included preparing legislation for, and convening the citizens' assembly. All male citizens were supposed to attend, and were paid half a drachma, about half the daily wage for a skilled craftsman. Public slaves would be sent to the *agora* armed with ropes whose ends had been dipped in red dye. They would swing these around to round up the citizens, and anyone found playing truant from the assembly with red stains on his clothes would be fined.

Other duties of the Boule included supervising the confiscation of property from wrongdoers, checking up on market stallholders with the set of standard weights and measures found in the Tholos, and running the treasury.

Their meetings were held next door to the Tholos in the **New Bouleuterion**, and their detailed records housed in the **Metroön** below it, under the protection of the mother of the gods. The most interesting of these records concerns the confiscation and selling of the property of Alkibiades and his friends as a punishment for supposed vandalism. They were said to have mutilated the Hermai, square pillars carrying busts of Hermes, the traders' god, which stood throughout the city.

Opposite the Metroön is the long pediment of the **Ten Eponymous Heroes**, so called because the ten divisions of Athens were named after them. Their bronze statues have been replaced by chunks of concrete. The monument served as a noticeboard, and here drafts of new laws, lists of men called up for military service and lists of lawsuits would be written on whitened boards and hung on the pediments.

Beyond the ten heroes is a statue of the self-styled hero Emperor Hadrian, somewhat robbed of his dignity by being headless and legless. He has been identified by the relief of Athena standing above the wolf suckling Romulus and Remus, symbolising the 'union' of Athens and Rome.

North of the Metroön are the foundations of the **Stoa of Zeus**, whose northern end has been cut off by the Athens–Piraeus railway. Socrates spent much time in philosophical discussion in the shade of its colonnade, and two of his dialogues are recorded as having happened there. His experiences were less pleasant in the **Stoa Basileios** (Royal Stoa), for it was here that he was summoned to appear before Athens' chief magistrate on the charge of impiety and corrupting the young, which led to his imprisonment and execution. This stoa, excavated in 1970, is not yet open to the public but is visible from the railway bridge.

- **The Hephaisteion (Theseion)** Echoing with birdsong, the best-preserved temple in Greece stands on a small hillock above the *agora* surrounded by a formal garden. The garden dates from the 3rd century BC, when plants were grown in sunken pots aligned with the Doric columns of the temple; as far as possible it has been replanted with the same kinds of plants that were there over 2000 years ago.

From the Middle Ages the temple has been known as the Theseion. It was here that the bones of Theseus were supposed to have been buried, and in the 19th century the French consul buried an Englishman here, as an excuse to dig – unsuccessfully – for the bones of Theseus. Not until the 1970s was it established that this temple was dedicated to Hephaistos; the resting-place of Theseus – and thus the site of the true Theseion – remains a mystery.

The temple was finally identified after the Royal Stoa had been excavated – for Pausanias described the temple of Hephaistos as standing above it. In addition, Hephaistos was the patron of metal-workers, and many foundries and metal workshops have been unearthed on the slopes of the hill around his temple. Their successors still ply their trade, or rather sell mass-produced beaten copperware, in Odos Ifestou, below the Hephaisteion.

The temple lacks the harmony and delicacy of the Parthenon, but it does retain much of its coffered ceiling, and many of its metopes carved with the Labours of Herakles and Theseus. It suffered far less than the Parthenon, although it still retains the barrel vault above the *cella* from its period as a church. A service was held in the temple-church in 1934 to mark the centenary of the last one – a Te Deum celebrating King Otto's arrival in the capital of the newly formed Greek state.

- **Odeion of Agrippa** Dominating the centre of the *agora* are the monumental statues of giants and tritons erected in AD150 to adorn the façade of the Odeion of Agrippa. This was a concert-hall built in 15BC by Agrippa, son-in-law of Emperor Augustus, with seating for 1000 spectators. In its day it was considered remarkable for not using supporting columns. Unfortunately, this piece of architectural bravado didn't work, and it soon collapsed. It was rebuilt in AD150, burned to the ground in AD267 and a gymnasium built on the site. The result is that the ruins are virtually impossible to make sense of.

- **Agora Museum** This is housed in the Stoa of Attalus, built in the 2nd century BC by Attalos, King of Pergamon, who had studied in Athens. It has been completely rebuilt, using ancient methods whenever possible, and now houses the wonderful Agora Museum. Items are labelled in English.

Of the numerous **funerary offerings** on display, the most interesting

are the plain vases from Middle Helladic (2000–1550BC) tombs on the
north-west slope of the Acropolis. A nice example of prehistoric
economy, they were covered with foil so that they looked like silver.
More poignant are the offerings from children's graves dating from the
Mycenaean period, including a spouted feeding bottle, and miniature
terracotta dolls.

The north-west slopes of the Acropolis were still being used as a
cemetery in 900BC, although by this time cremation had been
introduced. The body was burned on a pyre and offerings of food and
drink in vases thrown into it. When the fire went out, the ashes were
gathered into an urn and buried in a small pit along with other
offerings. One such cremation was of a warrior craftsman, identified by
the fact that the offerings included iron tools and weapons. The most
amazing relics, however, are the charred remains of figs and grapes.

A tiny **medicine bottle** was discovered in the cistern of the prison
where Socrates was executed by drinking hemlock. It is likely that he
would have drunk the hemlock out of just such a bottle.

Next to the Stoa of Attalos are the foundations of a **library** built in
the 2nd century AD. A tablet has been found inscribed with the library
rules and opening times: 'No book shall be taken out, since we have
sworn it. It will be open from the first hour to the sixth.'

The **standard weights and measures** were kept in the Tholos. The
weights are made of lead, and their denomination was indicated by a
small symbol in relief. A knucklebone weighed one *stater* (841.5
grammes), a dolphin roughly half a *stater*, a tortoise a quarter of a
stater and, logically enough, a half-tortoise an eighth of a *stater*.

One of the exhibits is a **water-clock**, used for timing speeches made
by plaintiff and defendant in court cases. Both would speak for
themselves, though usually reading pieces prepared for them by an
orator. The water-clock consists of two terracotta bowls with small
holes near the bottom. The upper bowl was filled with water, and when
the speaker began the hole was unplugged. He could speak for the six
minutes it took for the water to trickle out.

In the 5th century BC, as a measure against tyranny, all citizens were
allowed to vote to ostracise any man whom they feared. The name of
the relevant person was written on a pottery shard (**ostrakon**), and as
long as at least 6000 citizens had voted, the man who received most
votes would be ostracised for ten years. Many of the shards found were
written on by just six people; they would have been prepared by
political agents to be used by the illiterate. An enclosure was set up in
the *agora*, and the citizens would go inside, giving their vote to an
agent at the entrance. They had to remain inside until all the votes had
been counted. Themistokles is the name found most frequently on the
ostraka. He was a radical politician who campaigned to have the
Athenian navy strengthened. This made him unpopular with the rich,
who would have had to finance it, and his name came up for ostracism
year after year. They never succeeded in ostracising him, however – in
fact, on one occasion the anti-Themistokles faction was left after the
election with 190 unused *ostraka* on their hands, and dumped them in
a well where they were discovered by archaeologists.

Plenty of examples of everyday **domestic equipment** can be seen, helping to bring to life the picture of life in a Classical Athenian house. There's a sausage griddle, a portable clay oven, and best of all a terracotta potty with the photograph above it of a long-suffering toddler demonstrating its use.

Roman agora: highlights

Just east of the Greek *agora*, the Roman *agora* is smaller than the older market, but what remains is appealing. By the entrance are the foundations of a **public lavatory** with four stone seats intact. It was originally roofed except for the centre which was open to give ventilation and let in light.

Beyond is one of the city's most ingenious buildings – the **Tower of the Winds**, an octagonal white marble tower which housed a water-clock. It was built in the 1st century BC and is named after the winged figures on its eight faces, each of which personifies a wind direction. Water was channelled from a spring on the north slope of the Acropolis into the semi-cylindrical tank attached to the back of the tower. From there the water trickled in a steady stream into a cylinder inside the tower. The level of the water indicated the time, and the door of the tower was left open so that people could come and consult it. In the 6th century the building was a chapel; under the Turks it became a Muslim *tekke* (house of religion), occupied in the 18th century by whirling dervishes.

The rest of the *agora* is less impressive. Around the paved forum which retains a few columns from its colonnade you can make out the foundations of shops, and at the far end is a rather rickety triumphal arch.

Other classical sites

● **Hadrian's Library** At the end of Adrianou in the Plaka is Hadrian's Library, founded by the emperor in 132BC. It is closed to the public, but is visible from the street above. When Pausanias visited, a 'hundred splendid columns' surrounded the courtyard; although only a fraction remain, many retain their Corinthian capitals, making its former glory clear. Through the undergrowth you can just about make out the shape of the oval pool which was sunk in the centre of the courtyard and surrounded by gardens, and to the east are the foundations of the library proper.

● **Choregic Monument of Lysikrates** On the fringes of the Plaka, overlooked by neo-classical houses, is a strange and rather ugly cylindrical monument. It was erected in 334BC by Lysikrates, a wealthy Athenian who had financed the production of a drama which won first prize in the annual festival. It is decorated with a frieze showing Dionysos changing pirates into dolphins.

In the 17th century it was incorporated into the library of the Capuchin convent, which later gave hospitality to Byron, and it is said that the poet used it as a study while writing *Childe Harold*. Byron's lifestyle in the convent was hardly monastic – he surrounded himself with youths and schoolboys, amused himself by watching Albanian washerwomen teasing his servant by 'running pins into his backside' and gave a dinner party for a couple of influential Turks who 'made themselves beastly drunk with raw Rum'. Fortunately for Byron, the head of the convent was not averse to a bit of alcoholic dissipation, and got as drunk as the poet and his guests.

● **Kerameikos** In downtown Athens, approached via the second-hand furniture and engine-part shops of Ermou, is the ancient Kerameikos cemetery. It was in use from the 12th century BC until the Roman period, and graves and funeral monuments from most periods have been unearthed. Despite its unprepossessing surroundings, the Kerameikos is a peaceful site, and has the same feel as a modern cemetery.

The main attraction is the 4th-century BC **street of the tombs**, a funereal avenue on which the richest Athenians were buried. There are all sorts of funerary monuments, ranging from imposing marble bulls and lions to simple urns – but the most moving are the *stelae* carved with scenes showing the dead with their families.

The cemetery stood just outside the Sacred Gate, which spanned the road to Eleusis, and the Dipylon Gate, which guarded the road from Piraeus. The foundations of both remain on either side of the massive site of the Pompeion, where equipment was stored and preparations made for the annual Panathenaic procession, which began at the Dipylon.

Though the most valuable of the finds from the cemetery are housed in the National Archaeological Museum, there's a collection of minor finds in the site museum.

● **Hadrian's Arch** Rising from the traffic-laden Leoforos Amalias, this will be the first ancient monument you see if you approach Athens from the airports. It was built by Emperor Hadrian in AD132 to mark the boundary between the ancient city and the new city, which he somewhat immodestly named Hadrianopolis. So that no one could be in any doubt about the fact, one side is inscribed with 'This is Athens, the ancient city of Theseus' and the other with 'This is the city of Hadrian and not of Theseus'.

Hadrianopolis extended from here to the banks of the Ilissos, and by all accounts was rather a pleasant place, with temples, villas and bath-houses surrounded by gardens.

● **Olympieion** All that remains of the Olympieion, the largest temple in Greece, are 15 fluted columns soaring up behind Hadrian's Arch on a stretch of dry wasteland flanked by some of the busiest roads in Athens. It appears all the more lovely for the fact that it rises out of so much ugliness and grime, and is especially beautiful in the late afternoon, when the sun mottles and intensifies the fluting with shadows.

Work started on the temple in the 6th century BC but was interrupted when the Peisistratid tyrants were overthrown. It remained untouched until 174BC when Antiochus Epiphanes, King of Syria, commissioned a Roman architect to rebuild it; over 100 columns were added. But the Olympieion remained unfinished when Antiochus died, and some of the columns were carted off to Rome. It was finally completed in the reign of Hadrian, who erected a gold and ivory statue of himself alongside that of Zeus. Later, it was wrecked by barbarians and used as a stone quarry in the Middle Ages.

Museums

● **National Archaeological Museum** The biggest, best and busiest museum in Greece can also be the most overwhelming. It is advisable to go early – not only to avoid the worst of the crowds, but also so that you feel fresh enough to tackle it. Even so, it would be unwise to attempt to see everything, and you'll appreciate what you see far more if you select just a few rooms on which to concentrate.

You could choose to trace the development of Greek sculpture or ceramics; wind down in front of the refreshing frescoes from prehistoric Thera; and, until the collection is moved to the new museum at Mycenae, lose yourself in the opulence and intricacy of Mycenaean art. However alert you're feeling at the beginning of your tour, be prepared to be drained by the end. A good plan is to take a break in the basement cafe half-way through.

Below we give details of some of the many highlights.

In Room 6 is the **Cycladic Collection**: white marble figurines from the prehistoric civilisations of the Cycladic islands. The most famous are the almost translucent sculptures of a harp player and flute player, and the life-size figure of a woman standing on tiptoe as if about to dance. All are virtually abstract, and will remind you of works by Picasso and Modigliani, both of whom were deeply influenced by Cycladic sculpture.

The **Mycenaean Collection** is in Room 4. 'I found an immense treasure of archaeological objects of pure gold . . . sufficient to fill a large museum which will be the most splendid in the world.' So wrote the archaeologist Heinrich Schliemann to the king of Greece in 1876, after discovering five royal graves containing a wealth of golden objects along with twenty bodies which he assumed were those of Agamemnon, Cassandra and their court, murdered by Clytemnestra and her lover (see page 141).

Although subsequent tests revealed that the skeletons uncovered by Schliemann predated the era of Agamemnon and Clytemnestra by two centuries, his discoveries remain spectacular, and have indeed done much to make the National Museum one of the world's most splendid.

You could easily spend hours in the Mycenaean room, for it is crammed with beautiful objects ranging from tiny signet rings engraved with religious and battle scenes to golden cups and fragments of frescoes, including the famous and refined Mycenaean Lady. As space is limited, Schliemann's finds are not displayed to their advantage, but they are to be moved to a purpose-built museum at Mycenae itself (planned for 1990).

The highlights are a tiny and rather arrogant-looking seated gold bull (Case 1: 2947) with gold discs dangling from its ears. Bulls, along with lions, were a popular theme in Mycenaean art, for in the war-torn centuries of the 2nd millennium BC, physical strength was much admired. Another example is the silver bull's head rhyton (Case 27: 384), a flask used for libations, embellished with gold sun, horns and muzzle.

Of great excitement to historians was the discovery of a miniature ivory warrior in a boar's tusk helmet (Case 20: 2468). It is exactly like a helmet described in Homer's *Iliad*: 'On the outside the tusks of a white-toothed boar, thick set, ran in contrary directions.' Fully dressed warriors are shown departing for war on the sides of a ceramic crater (1426); and inlaid on the blade of a dagger (Case 27: 394) is a scene of men fighting a lion, protected by body-length shields, like the one given by Hector to Ajax in the *Iliad*.

The single most famous find from Mycenae is the so-called mask of Agamemnon (Case 3: 624). Schliemann removed the mask, and found himself staring into the perfectly preserved eyes of a 3500-year-old king, whom he took to be Agamemnon. He kissed the mask, and that evening is supposed to have sent his famous but possibly apocryphal telegram (of which no trace has been found) to the king of Greece: 'I have gazed on the face of Agamemnon.'

The bodies of two babies (Case 28: 146) wrapped in gold were discovered alongside those of three women. The fragments of these gold sheets are perhaps the most poignant of all the Mycenaean finds, for they still bear the forms of tiny toes, fingers and ears.

In another woman's grave an exquisite rock crystal vase (Case 5: 8638) was found. It is in the shape of a duck, with the body forming the case, and the head and tail turned inwards to form the handle.

Rooms 7 to 21 are devoted to **Ancient Sculpture**. In these rooms you can follow the development of ancient sculpture from the stiff, stylised and two-dimensional statues of the 7th century BC through the fluently sculpted statues of the Classical era to the pseudo-Classical Roman statues. The following is a representative selection.

Room 7 has a 7th-century BC metope of a goddess from a temple of Athena at Mycenae. At first sight she appears Egyptian, for she is wearing a head-dress similar to Tutankhamun's. In the 7th century BC the Greeks were trading with and working as mercenaries in Egypt and were no doubt influenced by Egyptian funerary art. Another Egyptian-style goddess is the full-length and rather rigid statue of Artemis from the island of Delos.

While you're here, don't miss the Dipylon Vase, a geometric funerary vase with a panel showing a funeral procession among the dizzying strips of meanders and zigzags.

In Room 8 the late 7th-century BC Kouros of Sounion stands over 3m high; it was discovered at the temple of Poseidon at Sounion. His crimped hair resembles a Cleopatra-style wig, and his body, with its incised anatomical detail, is stiff and angular.

The mid-6th-century BC Kouros of Volomandra is a far more realistic and sophisticated sculpture (in Room 10). The musculature and bone structure are an integral part of the body instead of being carved on afterwards. The contours of the face are especially delicate, and you begin to get a sense that there are bones beneath the marble skin.

In Room 13 the Kouros of Aristodikos dates from about 500BC; it was found in an Attican cemetery. The crimped Egyptian locks have been replaced by short curly hair, and although he still stands in the traditional *kouros* pose (with his hands by his side and one foot in front of the other) his slender body is fluid, realistic and works from three dimensions.

The powerful mid-5th-century BC bronze statue of Poseidon (Room 15) was hauled out of the sea near Evia by fishermen in 1926. The bearded god stands with his legs flexed and arms outstretched, captured in the moment before he hurls his (missing) trident. The body is perfectly tuned and balanced, compelling you to walk around it to enjoy the ever-shifting, but always perfectly harmonious, perspectives.

A galloping bronze horse with its tiny jockey (in Room 21) was found in the same shipwreck as Poseidon. Dating from the mid-2nd century BC, it's an exquisite and moving work, in which the fragility of the delicate jockey is juxtaposed with the power of the muscle-straining horse. In the same room is a 1st-century BC copy of a 4th-century BC bronze statue of Chthonian (Underworld) Hermes. With its relaxed body, fine curly hair, sensitive face and cloak casually tossed over its shoulder, it is the epitome of Classical beauty.

Room 22 is known as the **Epidavros Room**. The sections of the lion frieze from the Tholos, and the reliefs and statues from the temples of the sanctuary of Asklepios at Epidavros, will mean most if you've already visited the site (see page 146). Nevertheless, the statue of a woman sitting on a horse is lovely, though damaged – her flimsy *chiton* clings and gathers to reveal and conceal her body.

In 1900 the cargo of a shipwreck was discovered off the island of Antikithira, to the south of Kithira (see page 338). The booty included the shattered fragments of a bronze statue of a youth, which has now been completely reconstructed. The identity of this youth with the wavy hair and mesmeric green eyes (in Room 29) remains a mystery, as does what it was he was holding in his raised right hand.

Room 32 is devoted to the **Eleni Stathatou Collection**: gold jewellery from the Bronze Age to the Byzantine era. The most interesting finds are from 3rd-century BC Thessaly. These include gem-encrusted snake bracelets, a gold necklace of acorns and bulls' heads suspended from rosettes, and a unique miniature golden temple with a relief of Dionysos and a satyr.

The **Dodona Room** has mainly minor items from the oracle of Zeus at Dodona. The most interesting finds – jewels, fragments of votive tripods, and statuettes – are housed in the museum at Ioanina (see page 221).

Similarly, the best of the objects excavated at **Olympia** are in its own museum (see page 168). In the **Olympia Room** there are some bronze offerings to Zeus, including animals, weapons, cauldrons and tripods, along with others from the Acropolis.

On the upper floor, Rooms 49 to 56 house an extensive collection of **ceramics**, starting with the primitive proto-Geometric pottery of the 11th century BC and finishing with refined white *lekythoi* from the 5th century BC. You can follow the development of pottery in the

Geometric period from the early vessels decorated with a few wavy lines, stripes and concentric arcs painted with a comb-like brush to the final complex designs. On Geometric vases there is scarcely a centimetre which is not covered with bands of meanders, zigzags, diamonds, stripes and triangles.

In the early 8th century BC tiny geometric people and animals with triangular torsos, blob heads and stick limbs begin to make an appearance. The most famous of these is the Dipylon Vase now kept in Room 7, but there's a far more engaging one (990, in Room 50), also from the Dipylon cemetery. Below the funeral procession, where triangular-bodied women with bulging marrow-like thighs and calves raise their hands in anguish, is a chariot-race. Pairs of horses with spindly legs, fish-like heads and spiky manes pull chariots on which warriors perch precariously.

In the late 8th century and 7th century BC Attic potters abandoned the Geometric style in favour of vases with large polychromatic figures painted on a pale background. There is still some geometric decoration, but the main point of interest in the so-called Proto-Attic pottery are the pictures. The most beautiful examples here are the Amphora from Melos (911; 640BC), on which a winged horse draws Apollo on his chariot, and the Amphora of Nessos, which shows Herakles killing Nessos the centaur, and below him three gorgons flying, with their legs bent, over an ocean represented by leaping dolphins.

By the end of the 7th century BC Athenian potters had completely abandoned the Geometric style in favour of vases decorated with black figures with the details etched on; this is the so-called black-figure Attic pottery. Two of the most appealing are in Room 53 (Case 51). Both come from the cemetery of Anagyron near Vari (inland from Varkiza); one shows a bull and a lion, the other Hermes flanked by sphinxes.

Developments in art rarely happen overnight, but it does seem that the invention of red-figure pottery around 530BC was an exception. Pots suddenly appeared with their backgrounds painted black and the figures left in the bare red of the clay. Details could be painted in far more quickly than was possible when they had to be engraved, and by using thinned-down paint it was possible to represent flowing drapery, hair, the strings of lyres and minute archaeological detail.

The final rooms of this section are devoted to white *lekythoi*. These tall cylindrical urns, which enclosed a small perfume container, would be brought to graves by relatives of the dead. Their decoration was unlike that of other pottery, for the whole vessel was painted white. On this background, figures were painted in fine, delicate outline, and filled in with various colours.

White *lekythoi* were exclusively used by Athenians, and those that have been found elsewhere (for example in southern Italy and Cyprus) are thought to have been taken there by colonists.

Room 48 houses finds from **Thera**. In 1967 a prehistoric city which had been destroyed by an earthquake and volcanic eruption in 1500BC was discovered at Akrotiri on the island of Thera (Santorini; see page 447). As no corpses were found buried in the lava, it is thought that the inhabitants may have abandoned their city after an earthquake 50 years earlier.

The most important items from Akrotiri are the frescoes found on the walls of the houses. There are scenes of delicate antelopes, slinky blue monkeys and, in the fresco named Spring, swallows flying above flowers. But the frescoes are more than merely beautiful – the scene known as The Lady's Room and the narrative Sea Battle offer valuable information about the kind of clothes and ships used in prehistoric Akrotiri. The most engaging fresco, however, is the scene of two young boys boxing. Though only fragments were found, enough of them remained to reconstruct the contours, features and elaborate snaking locks of the sparring youths. One of the boys is wearing anklets and armlets of beads, together with heavy-duty boxing gloves.

• **Benaki Museum** A real treasure trove of a museum, the Benaki is the Greek equivalent of London's Victoria and Albert. The collection ranges from delicate Mycenaean jewellery to Arabic surgical instruments, and the best plan is to browse until you find something that catches your eye. The choice is vast, and you can spend your time examining the miniature details of oriental ceramics, Persian textiles and enamelled goldwork, Coptic embroidery, Byzantine silverwork, or regional costumes and jewellery.

The collection was left to Athens by Anthony Benaki, a Greek born in Alexandria, and is still kept in his elegant neo-classical villa. Other antique-collecting Greeks added to the collection, and consequently the Benaki is short of space. It is currently undergoing major restoration and extension, which will last for at least five years, and during this period there will be no entrance charge, but only a representative selection of the best items will be on show.

The shop is well worth a visit, for there is a good selection of books in English; tasteful but expensive reproduction jewellery; some lovely postcards; and a wide range of regional folk records.

• **Byzantine Museum** This museum is housed in a 19th-century villa which was once owned by Sophie de Barbe-Marbois, an eccentric French aristocrat who dressed as a Greek, kept the embalmed body of her daughter in a crystal coffin, and had a passion for fasting, which she inflicted on her guests. Her entourage included a dozen Pyrenean mountain dogs, who lived in the wings of the villa and terrorised anyone who met them.

The museum, the only one in Europe to concentrate exclusively on Byzantine art, was set up in the 1930s, bringing together collections which had been dispersed around the city. It is currently undergoing major restoration, so a number of rooms are closed, and the courtyard, which has been laid out like a cloister, has become a noisy building site.

The collections of icons and frescoes is very extensive, and a number of rooms have been laid out like Byzantine churches in order to create an appropriate environment for the lavish exhibits. The greatest attraction of the museum, however, is the opportunity to examine the minute details of sculpture, embroidery and metalwork at close quarters.

• **Museum of Cycladic and Ancient Art** A small, ultra-modern museum in which a collection of exquisite Cycladic sculpture and ceramics is imaginatively displayed in dark, spotlit rooms. The displays are labelled in English. The modern setting is appropriate, for the most beautiful items in the collection are the white marble sculptures of female figures, whose abstract forms had a profound influence on Picasso, Modigliani and Henry Moore.

The figurines date from between 3200 and 2000BC, and were found in graves on the Cycladic islands. Their significance is unclear: they may have represented fertility goddesses, or have been placed in graves to satisfy the sexual needs of the dead.

If their ancient significance remains a mystery, their modern influence is clear, and many are so well preserved that they could have been sculpted by a contemporary artist. The figurines are extremely simple, with long, smooth bodies, budding breasts and folded arms. The most distinctive feature, however, and the one most familiar from 20th-century art, is the form of the head: almond- or lyre-shaped, with backward-sloping forehead, bisected by an elongated nose in high relief.

It is only in this century that the beauty of the 5000-year-old figurines has been appreciated – in the pre-abstract world of the 19th century, an archaeologist described a life-sized head found on the island of Amorgos as 'repulsively ugly'.

As well as the figurines, there is a small collection of ceramics, including some so-called 'frying pans'. The only thing certain about these shallow pots is that they were not used for frying. As only the exteriors are decorated, it is thought that they may have been filled with water and used as mirrors, or that animal-skin was stretched over them to make drums.

On the second floor there is a miscellaneous collection of ceramics, gold, bronze, glass and marble work, covering the period from 2000BC to the 4th century AD. There are miniature pots which were found in children's graves, cooking utensils, southern Italian fish plates painted with fish and with a dent in the centre to take the sauce, and iridescent glass perfume containers.

On the top floor reproductions of Cycladic-influenced works by Picasso, Modigliani, Moore and Giacometti are juxtaposed with photographs of the sculptures that inspired them.

The shop sells tasteful and expensive reproductions of the sculptures, and has a good selection of art books in English.

• **Museum of Greek Folk Art** This has a small but well-presented collection ranging from elaborately embroidered household linen and regional costumes to ceramic wine jugs bearing rhyming couplets on the delights and hazards of alcohol. Don't miss the masquerade costumes, with grotesque masks and extraordinary head-dresses which are still worn at carnival time; they were originally designed to ward off evil spirits, in the hope of securing a trouble-free sowing and harvest.

• **War Museum** War planes and cannon stand on guard outside this austere museum, founded during the dictatorship of the Colonels to chart the development of Greek armies from the age of bows and arrows to the era of the machine gun. It doesn't glorify war as much as you might expect, for among the Mycenaean suits of armour, shelves of rusting shells, cases of gleaming bullets, and models of Ancient Greek ballistic engines, there are photographs from the Second World War of malnourished children, devastated villages and executed members of the Resistance.

The displays are not labelled in English, which is a pity, as there are detailed battle plans ranging from those of Alexander the Great to those of the Balkan Wars. Fortunately, a command of Greek is not necessary to appreciate the juxtaposition of ancient weapons with reproductions of sculpted battle scenes which show them in action.

Attica

Daphni

The monastery of Daphni, containing some of the most significant and sumptuous mosaics of the mid-Byzantine era, stands between the Athens–Corinth motorway and a pine-wooded hill, about six miles from Athens.

Controversy surrounds the origin of the monastery's name, which means laurel but was also the name of a queen as well as the nymph whom Apollo attempted to rape. It is most likely that the monastery was named after a temple to Apollo Daphniphorous ('Apollo wearing a laurel crown') which once stood nearby. A more melodramatic though less likely possibility is that it was founded by a queen Daphni in gratitude for being rescued, along with her 12 coffers of money, after being shipwrecked in the Bay of Phaleron. She allegedly used the contents of seven coffers to finance the church, and buried the rest in the grounds.

What is known is that the current church was built in the 11th century on the site of a 5th-century church which had been destroyed by barbarians. Its history, even before the building of the motorway, was anything but peaceful. It was sacked by Crusaders, captured and set alight by Turkish troops trying to melt the gold out of the mosaics, and was used as a barracks and lunatic asylum before finally being declared a historic monument at the beginning of this century. Not surprisingly, the mosaics suffered somewhat, although the Turks' attempt to milk its gold signally failed. The Christ Pantokrator in the dome, lit by the light from 16 windows, is particularly memorable – with a furrowed brow, eyes deepened by heavy eyebrows and dark rings, and craggy bony hand gripping the Book of Judgement. This is one of the most austere and intimidating creations of Byzantine art. In contrast, many of the other scenes are lyrical, tender and set in pastoral

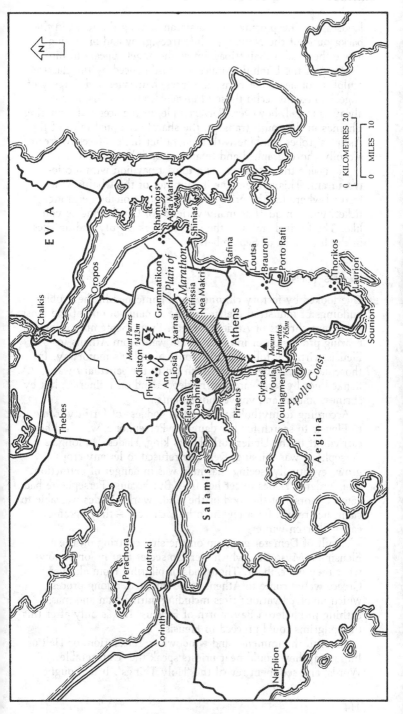

landscapes. Sheep drink from a stream among the rocks in the background of the Nativity, while trees grow and birds sing above the head of Saint Joachim as the angel appears to him.

Many of the Daphni mosaics were influenced by the classical sculpture of nearby Athens: the faces, hairstyles and drapery of angels and saints echo those of ancient statues. This doesn't always succeed, however. For example, in the scene of Doubting Thomas in the south transept, the sharply sculpted folds of the disciples' robes combine with their rather lifeless faces to create a coolly choreographed and totally emotionless tableau.

Alongside the monastery is a tourist pavilion with a cafe-restaurant. This is the scene in summer of the Dhafni wine festival where for the price of the (very reasonable) entrance ticket, you can quaff as many varieties of Greek wine as you like. The festival starts in the second week of July and finishes in the first week of September.

Eleusis (Elefsis)

Overlooked by factory chimneys and enmeshed in the grubby buildings of industrial Elefsis are the remains of one of the most important shrines of Ancient Greece. Every September a torch-bearing procession of initiates would walk from Athens to Eleusis, virtually following the route of today's motorway. In those days the Sacred Way which led to the sanctuary was flanked not by scrapyards, lorry depots and oil refineries, but by shrines, statues and votive monuments.

According to mythology Demeter, goddess of fertility, came to Eleusis to search for her daughter Persephone, who had been carried off to the Underworld by its king, Hades. As long as Persephone was missing, Demeter refused to let any crops grow; eventually, seeing that man was in danger of extinction, Zeus ordered Hades to set her free. But because Persephone had eaten a morsel of the food of the Underworld, Hades was able to claim her return for a few months each year – they became earth's barren winters.

A cult of Demeter grew up on the site, centring on the Eleusinian Mysteries, which were so secret that no one knows what they were about. Thousands of pilgrims from all over Greece would come to Athens to be initiated, a long process which involved various rites including purification and mass-bathing in Phaleron Bay, north of Piraeus. It was only after this that pilgrims could proceed to Eleusis.

Here, in the immense and windowless Telesterion, or Hall of Initiation, they would hear priests speak the 'Unutterable Words' and see them reveal the 'Holy Things'. It is thought that there was also some kind of play re-enacting the story of Persephone, and that the pilgrims would leave convinced and comforted that in the afterlife they would be able to commune with the gods. The cult was still thriving in Roman times, and after taking part in the ceremony Cicero wrote that he had learnt 'not only to live in joy, but also to die in greater hope'.

As the site was founded in the 15th century BC and was still central to Greek life in the Roman era, it was rebuilt on numerous occasions. The result is that the ruins can be somewhat confusing, so it's advisable first to visit the museum, which has reconstructions of the site in various stages. The architectural fragments and statues also help make the site come alive, despite that fact that many are copies, as the most important originals are in the National Archaeological Museum in Athens.

Eleusis: highlights

Inside the entrance is the **Great Forecourt**, paved with marble, where the pilgrims would gather for the final purification rites before being allowed to enter the sanctuary. It was laid out in the Roman era in the reign of Antoninus Pius. On the far left-hand corner is the **Kallichoron Well** beside which Demeter is supposed to have sat and grieved for her daughter before being cheered up by the Eleusinian girls performing a dance.

Once purified, the pilgrims would walk up the steps into the **Great Propylaia**, also laid out by the Romans. It was based on the Propylaia of the Acropolis in Athens: if you've seen this, it will help you make sense of the thresholds and column stumps which are all that remain of this once-magnificent outer entrance to the sanctuary. Propped up on one side is a stone medallion out of which glares the swarthy face of Antoninus Pius's successor, Marcus Aurelius; and scored on the floor are crosses made by Christians still scared of the power of the pagan spirits. Right until the end of the 19th century, peasants continued to visit Eleusis to place lighted lamps before a statue to Demeter, until the statue was removed to the British Museum.

The pilgrims, no doubt tense with anticipation, would then proceed to the Hall of Initiation, or Telesterion, passing through the **Lesser Propylaia**, or inner entrance. There are fragments of a frieze with carvings of corn, Demeter's symbol, on the ground by the entrance.

Before going to the Telesterion, it's worth walking along the short stretch of the Sacred Way, paved by the Romans, to see the caves hollowed out in the hillside to represent the entrance to Hades.

The **Telesterion** was an immense and once-splendid building in which the mysteries were revealed. It was divided by six rows of columns, and had room for 3000 initiates on its raked seating. Most of what remains today dates from the time of Pericles and was designed by Iktinos, one of the architects of the Athens Parthenon; but there are traces of earlier buildings, which can be somewhat confusing.

Piraeus (Piraievs)

The one reason for visiting Piraeus, Greece's main port, is to catch a ferry. The sleazy water-front is crammed with travel agents, shipping offices and sleep-crumpled travellers queuing or hanging around for early-morning ferries.

All ferries and the hydrofoil to Aegina leave from the main port; other hydrofoils leave from the smaller Zea harbour on the eastern side of the peninsula, ten minutes' walk away. A third harbour, the relatively tiny Mikrolimano, which once could accommodate 82 triremes, is now used by yachts; its many fish restaurants, though expensive, are the most pleasant places in which to while away time, and are popular with Athenians.

Around the other side of the peninsula, cargo vessels await loading and unloading. Piraeus is still an important hub of the shipping world; on Akti Miaouli Street the offices of Greek shipping magnates keep a watchful eye on the port activities.

Away from the harbour, Piraeus has a quiet residential area of hilly grid-like streets lined with apartment blocks. But there's very little hotel accommodation, a situation which is hard to comprehend in a port and staging-post of this importance. Independent travellers with ideas of overnighting in Piraeus before catching an early-morning ferry should bear this in mind and stay in Athens instead.

Piraeus is reached by green bus service (040) from Athens: from Filellinon, off Syntagma Square, day and night; and from Omonia and Monastiraki from early morning until midnight.

Perachora

As an escape from Athens, the sanctuary of Hera outside the village of Perachora, on the northern coast of the Corinthian Gulf, is hard to beat. Beyond the ugly high-rise resort of Loutraki, famous for its bottled water and for being the epicentre of the earthquake that destroyed Corinth in 1981, is **Lake Vouliagmeni**. It is highly popular with weekending Athenians, who come to laze on the small shingle beaches, idle at the fish tavernas, and take their motor-boats out or swim in the blue waters. There is one seasonal hotel, the *Philoxenia Motel*, with 14 simple and tastefully decorated bedrooms, and two campsites.

The **Heraion** is a short drive beyond the lake, on the tip of the Perachora peninsula. The road ends directly above the site, and a steep path runs down to it. Little but foundations remain of the temple and the settlement that grew up around it, but the setting, among craggy hills, is lovely, and you can swim in the cove from the tiny shingle beach below the platform of the temple (you should not, however, venture out beyond the cove as the currents are strong).

The cove was the only place on the rocky coastline where it was safe to dock ships in ancient times, and it is thought that the many votive offerings around the temple were to the goddess Hera by sailors relieved to have survived the currents and sharks of the gulf.

It takes very few people to make the site and beach seem crowded, and in summer there are usually a few escapist Greeks camping among the ruins or sleeping in the tiny Byzantine church above the cove. Solitude is at hand, however, on the other side of the peninsula, reached by a narrow path from the right of the road. The sea is often dramatically rough, with waves thrashing the rocks. There are good views down the Corinthian Gulf, fringed by the mountains of the Peloponnese and mainland, but the place is particularly evocative in the late afternoon. The soft dusky light transforms the ugly resorts below Corinth into gleaming white villages overlooked by the grim shadowy bulk of Acrocorinth; as the sun sets, the sea is tinged with coral. If you stay until after sunset, take care as you climb back to the car-park, for it is easy to lose the path and there are some sudden drops into rocky clefts. There's a harrowing account of getting lost here in *An Affair of the Heart*, the description of the discovery and excavation of the Heraion by Dilys Powell, who was married to the archaeologist Humfry Payne, Director of the British School at Athens.

The Apollo Coast

East of Piraeus stretch the resorts of the Apollo Coast, in a more or less continuous strip of urban sprawl. It has little appeal as a holiday destination, at least along the part nearest to Athens. **Glyfada** in particular is a resort to avoid unless you have a perverse desire to lie supine on a beach and gaze up at the under-carriages of aircraft. Hotel bedrooms throb, echo and vibrate with every boom, shriek and roar from the East Airport, ten minutes' drive away. The only solution is to spend as much of the night as possible in a club, flooding your ears with booms, shrieks and roars of the disco variety.

If it weren't for the noise, Glyfada would be quite a pleasant resort, for its boutiques and jewellery shops are good for window shopping and its sand and shingle beaches are reasonable (the best is the Astir, to the south of the resort, a pay-beach of fine sand and a sprinkling of gravelly pebbles, with a good selection of watersports).

Voula is a dreary and rather run-down resort which is virtually a continuation of Glyfada. The beaches are of soft sand scattered with pebbles, but are scruffy and littered. A small and pleasant but very popular resort which gets packed at weekends is **Varkiza**, whose main attraction is a long soft sand and pebble beach which is well maintained by the Greek National Tourist Organisation. There are tennis courts, a few swings for children and a modest selection of watersports. Although you're unlikely to want to base yourself in the resort, it's a good choice for a day on the beach, and its pizzerias, hamburger bars and ice-cream parlours are an added attraction if you can't face another Greek salad.

Vouliagmeni is a smart resort with a lovely beach at the head of a long, deep inlet sheltered by two promontories. Aircraft noise is no worse here than anywhere else with an airport nearby; but, as the most attractive resort of the Apollo Coast, Vouliagmeni gets extremely crowded, especially at weekends.

The small free beach – a scruffy triangle of hard-packed sand – is not worth bothering with, for the large main beach run by the Tourist Organisation is well worth the small entrance fee. The soft sand and shingle is backed by shady trees, among which there are tennis courts, water-chutes and a volleyball court. If you want more excitement, there's a waterskiing school between the two beaches which also has catamarans and windsurfers. Two minutes' walk from the beach is the *Hotel Armonia* (A), a sparkling lego-land trapezoid set back from the main road. The large airy reception area with a cafe-bar opens on to a terrace and swimming-pool. The bedrooms are tastefully furnished and the restaurant has a no-smoking area.

Just outside the resort is **Vouliagmeni Lake**, a natural and non-smelly sulphurous pool surrounded by sheer cave-pocked cliffs which is reckoned to be beneficial for skin diseases, rheumatism and arthritis. The temperature of the lake rises from 20°C in winter to 26°C in summer, and the overflow runs into the sea, making it just about warm enough for a winter swim.

There's little to detain you along the southern stretch of the Apollo Coast, for most of the beaches are rough, grey and littered, and the resorts ugly. The most depressing is at Anavissos, a once-beautiful bay backed by humped mountains but ruined by tenement-like flats and hotels. Nor is the large beach attractive – for it's composed of hard and rather muddy sand, fringed by strips of shingle and hard-packed sand.

Things improve beyond Legrena (whose polythene-strewn beach is the worst on the Apollo Coast) when you get your first view of the white columns of the temple of Sounion, spectacularly positioned on a rocky promontory above the sea.

Sounion

Place me on Sunium's marbled steep,
Where nothing, save the waves and I,
May hear our mutual murmurs sweep;
There, swan-like, let me sing and die.

So wrote Byron after one of his many visits to the temple of Poseidon at Sounion, superbly sited 60m above the sea on the craggy tip of the Attica peninsula. Today the sounds of murmuring waves are lost in the polyglottal babel of day-tripping tourists, and unless you manage to get there at opening time and are lucky enough to have it to yourself, you may find it more evocative from a distance.

The temple, with 16 of its creamy-white marble columns re-erected, would be beautiful anywhere. It was designed by the architect of the Hephaisteion in Athens, but has none of the latter's earth-bound solidity. Sounion's slender, elongated Doric columns soar up into the sky, lending it a rare, almost fragile delicacy, especially when seen from afar.

Sadly, however, any romantic 'spirit of place' evaporates when you have to share the site with coachloads of others, and find yourself having to squeeze through hordes of camera-clickers in order to stand pressed up against the protective ropes to see it properly. Nor is there any chance of getting close enough to see Byron's name, which he scratched on a column base. But even Byron wasn't always able to retreat into poetic reveries when he visited. On one occasion he and his party escaped attack from pirates only by showering them with bullets.

Sounion is no stranger to violence. The first temple, begun shortly before 490BC, was destroyed by the Persians while it was still being built; in the 2nd century BC it was captured by a thousand slaves who had escaped from the nearby silver-mines at Laurion; and in Roman times it was already well known as a haunt of pirates.

Nor was the reason for building the temple a peaceful one. As Athens' naval power increased in the 5th century BC, it was considered vital to have the sea god Poseidon on their side. Consequently, the temple was built in the hope that he would create conditions favourable to the Athenians in their sea battles. Sounion's clifftop position also made it a valuable vantage point in war, and in 412BC, during the Peloponnesian War, the temple was fortified so that the Athenians could control the entrance to the Evian and Saronic Gulfs and, equally importantly, protect the Laurion mines, a vital source of Athenian wealth.

Below the temple is a soft sand and pebble-strewn beach. It's nothing special, but is invested with a romantic magic at dawn, when you have a chance of having it to yourself, before climbing up the path to the temple. By the beach is the *Hotel Aegeon* (A), an ageing low-rise ochre-washed 1960s hotel. The rooms are small, plain and simple, and the public areas and restaurant clean but rather dingy and dowdy. There's a small children's playground, changing cubicles, and a bar on the beach. Though the bay is not particularly attractive, the views of the temple are superb.

The East Coast

The landscape of the eastern side of Cape Sounion is greener and more pleasant than that on the west. Not far north of Sounion is the small scruffy town of Lavrion, which owes its existence, like its ancient predecessor, to the nearby mines of **Laurion**. The mines are no longer exploited for the silver which financed the construction of the Athenian naval fleet in 483BC, but for cadmium and manganese, and the town is surrounded by tall candy-striped smelting chimneys belching pink smoke.

Nothing remains of ancient Laurion, but many of the ancient mines remain in the Berzeko valley, south of Kamariza, 5km to the west. The shafts are up to 100m deep, and from them radiate galleries only 1m high. The mines reached their peak in the time of Pericles, when over 20,000 slaves were forced to work there.

To the north of Laurion a conical hill crowned by an overgrown acropolis rises from the Evian Gulf above an immense power complex. This is **Thorikos**, where a military garrison was stationed to protect the mines and guard the ports into which wood for the smelting works was shipped from Evia. It's a melancholy, brooding place, and clambering up to the bleak acropolis and wandering around the foundations of workshops in which the ore was crushed and washed it's only too easy to speculate on the miserable lives of the ancient inhabitants. They did, however, have some relief from their dreary tasks, for the best-preserved feature of the site is a theatre. This is no elegant arena, but a clumsy elliptical structure built of rough-hewn stone, with no stage but just an altar on which sacrifices to Dionysos would be made before performances.

On the Evian Gulf due east of Athens airport lies **Porto Rafti**, a popular resort spread around the head of a long, sheltered inlet, where many Greeks have holiday apartments. At the mouth of the inlet is the island of Rafti, on which a 3m-high

Roman statue sits cross-legged. It is known as the 'tailor' (*rafti*) but probably held lamps and was used as a beacon.

The beaches are rather poor, mainly of shingle and pebble, except the northernmost one which is fringed by a sandy strip. The sea bed, however, is pebbly, and as the bay is used by the occasional cargo ferry and as a small boat anchorage, the swimming is not ideal. There are a couple of nightclubs and lots of shops, snack bars and tavernas; the simple fish taverna along the road to the southern end of the bay is a pleasant lunch stop. Although the resort gets busy in high season, it makes a convenient base for exploring this part of Attica.

On a plain fringed by low hills 9km north of Porto Rafti are the fairly substantial remains of a sanctuary to Artemis, goddess of virginity, at **Brauron** (Vravrona). According to legend, the cult was introduced to Attica by Iphigenia, the daughter of Agamemnon and Clytemnestra, and sister of Orestes.

Female animals, like the she-bear and hind, were sacred to Artemis, and when Agamemnon killed one of her sacred hinds he was doomed to atone for his sin by sacrificing his daughter. But according to one version of the myth, Artemis took pity on Iphigenia, who, swearing to remain a virgin, was sent to work as a priestess at Artemis's shrine at Tauris on the Crimean peninsula. There Iphigenia remained until the shrine was visited by Orestes, seeking forgiveness for having killed his mother. He recognised Iphigenia and brought her back to Attica, where she founded the sanctuary.

The cult of Artemis reached its height of popularity during the 5th and 4th centuries BC. Every five years a festival was held which involved girls aged between ten and fifteen dressing up as bear-cubs in yellow robes and performing a ritual bear dance. Young girls also worked year-round in the sanctuary in the service of the goddess. Behind the foundations of the temple to Artemis are the dining-rooms (complete with stone tables) and dormitories in which they lived, set around a large courtyard, some of whose columns have been re-erected.

A cleft in the rock which rises behind the temple is known as the Tomb of Iphigenia. Worship began here in the 8th century BC, long before the temple was built, and many votive offerings, including red and black figure vases, were found inside.

Many of the finds from the site are housed in the small museum. The most beautiful are the delicately carved statuettes and heads of the little girl 'bears'.

Loutsa, a mixture of working town and holiday resort, has the best beach near Brauron. This is not the beach to the south of town, which is littered and pebbly, but the beach of soft, very fine sand backed by pines and dunes to the north. Although this too has some litter and a sprinkling of tiny pebbles, the sea bed is smooth, and the strip of sand nearest the sea moist enough for sandcastle building. There are plenty of cafes and bars across the road from the beach, but further along they are replaced by shack-like chalets, and the beach and sea bed become more pebbly.

To the north is the ugly port town of **Rafina**, from which ferries go daily to Andros, Tinos, Mykonos, Paros, Naxos and Siros, as well as to Evia.

At the edge of the Bay of Marathon, **Mati** is an unwelcoming resort which lacks focus. There are a few hotels and a lot of exclusive summer villas set in secluded grounds. The beach is long, narrow and backed by red cliffs, and for most of its length is rocky; there is a short sand and shingle stretch, but the sea bed is pebbly and there are rocks offshore. The views across to Evia from the beach and from the small harbour are pleasant; but there are no cafes or tavernas here, and the beach is backed by unattractive hotels.

Even better views up the sweep of Marathon Bay can be had from the small resort of **Zouberi**, which has a rough sand and shingle beach. It makes for a pleasant lunch stop, but the sea bed is too rocky and weedy for swimming.

The most substantial resort on this stretch of coast is **Nea Makri**, which is much used by British tour operators. There are plenty of hotels, snack bars, pubs and restaurants. The rough sand and shingle beach is long and narrow, but there is a reasonable selection of watersports.

The vast **Plain of Marathon** is the site of one of the most famous battles in ancient history. In 490BC over 20,000 Persians landed at the Bay of Marathon to march on Athens, but were met by 8000 Athenian hoplites (foot-soldiers). Their general, Miltiades, knowing that the Persians would put their strongest archers in the centre, arranged most of his troops on the flanks, leaving just a thin screen of soldiers in the centre. The Athenians marched on the Persians, destroyed the weak Persian flanks, and converged behind the Persian centre. The Persians stampeded back to their ships, trampling on each other and being cut down by the Athenians in the process, with the result that 6400 of them were killed, compared with only 192 Athenians.

A runner, Pheidippides, was dispatched to Athens with the news; having run the 42km non-stop, he collapsed and died as soon as he had given his victory message. Pheidippides did, however, inspire the present marathon race, which was established as an Olympic event at the first modern games at Athens in 1896 (appropriately, a Greek won).

Cabbages, lettuces and olives now grow on the battlefield, and even the **Marathon Tomb**, a grassy hump erected over the bodies of the 192 Athenians who died, is unspectacular. It is signposted off the main road, and is clearly visible from outside its fence, so paying the entrance fee is unnecessary.

On the other side of the main road is another tumulus. You can actually go inside it to see eight graves with skeletons, thought to belong to soldiers of Plateia, the only other Greeks who came to Athens' aid in time. Beyond it is a small museum, whose collection of burial objects is really of interest only to enthusiasts.

Of more contemporary interest is Marathon itself, a modern agricultural village. At the entrance is a concrete platform surrounded by flagpoles, the starting-point for an annual marathon.

The best beach of Marathon Bay is at **Shinias**, near the northern end: a long stretch of soft sand with a sprinkling of pebbles and a pebbly sea bed. But the surroundings are rather desolate: the hinterland of the Marathon Plain is flat and dull, and there's only a small and ageing snack bar.

The road continues past a military airport to the northern end of the beach, sheltered by a low hilly tongue of land. Backed by pines, and with plenty of tavernas and grills, this is a more pleasant if busier spot, but the sand is harder.

Off the Marathon to Rhamnous road, a turning leads to the small port of **Agia Marina**, which has frequent ferry connections with Evia. It's a lovely place, with just a few houses and a cafe set on a small rocky bay with a minuscule sand and shingle beach, and enticing views of Evia. Make sure, however, that you take the first and not the second turnoff to the bay – the latter leads to a small naval base.

In a remote and silent site, the scant ruins of **Rhamnous** are scattered over a hill of prickly bushes above a wild gorge on the rocky coast 17km north of Marathon village. The savagery of Rhamnous's setting is appropriate. It was the site of a shrine to Nemesis, goddess of vengeance. Anyone guilty of a crime, of pride, or even of enjoying too much wealth and happiness lived in fear of retribution from the goddess. The defeat of the Persians at Marathon has been put down to Nemesis, for they were so confident that they would be able to march unhindered on Athens that they stopped off at Rhamnous to steal a marble block out of which they intended to make a victory monument. Whether as a punishment for the theft or for their pride, they were heavily defeated, and in gratitude the Athenian sculptor Pheidias carved the block into a statue of Nemesis, fragments of which are now in the British Museum.

Although only knee-high foundations remain of the temple to Nemesis, and of another to Themis, goddess of world order, the site is evocative and there is no better contrast with the commercialised ruins of Athens.

From the temples an ancient path leads past the remains of a Roman cemetery to the fortified town, built by the Athenians in the 5th and 4th centuries BC to guard the shipping lanes between Attica and Evia. Within what remains of its walls are the ruins of Hellenistic and Roman houses, a gymnasium and a theatre. Above are the overgrown remnants of an acropolis.

If you're more interested in spectacular routes than in ancient sites, you can drive to the coast below Rhamnous along a rough track which cuts along the opposite side of the gorge. The track begins in the small town of **Grammatikon**, 9km north of Marathon village. On entering the town, take the first right, turn right again and then left up a very steep concrete track. This soon becomes a pitted and rutted red rubble road, and you have a bumpy ride above gorges silvery grey with olives and spiked with cypresses. At the first fork take the lower track, which runs above a steep white rocky gorge at the end of which you have a fine view of Evia. After passing some stumpy bollards protecting a particularly narrow stretch of road, take the lower fork which descends steeply to a tiny beach of large white pebbles backed by an abandoned chapel. Sitting in solitude on the beach, or swimming in the deep-turquoise sea above gleaming white rocks, it's hard to believe that this secluded spot is less than 40 miles from Athens.

Due north of Athens, and reached by motorway and a fast new road, is the small resort of **Oropos**. This is a convenient place for a stop-over if you're intending to visit Rhamnous or Mount Parnes, but it is not appealing enough for a long stay.

The sea-front is lined with shops and eating-places, including fish tavernas and a couple of burger bars and pizzerias. There's no beach in the centre of the resort, just a concrete platform where you can sit and eat or drink. Next to the coast road to the south is a long, narrow and pebbly beach which is quite adequate for a couple of hours' swimming; this is where there are several large hotels. The small, basic *Avra* on Odos Kontinou, just off the coast road in the centre of the resort, is one of the few to remain open all year.

Mount Parnes (Parnitha)

Mount Parnes is the highest mountain in Attica (1413m). It's reached from the south, and is signposted from the outskirts of Athens. The nearest town is Axarnai, a scruffy industrial centre

with slate and marble works. Escape is rapid into the dense
conifer forest (scattered with the occasional beech), with picnic
areas in the clearings. A cable-car travels up to the ski slopes
and hotel near the summit, which has a radar station and is
inaccessible. Beyond the bottom station, the road climbs in
broad hairpin bends, and then makes a circuit of the mountain.
Hotel Mount Parnes (A) is a comfortable halt for an overnight
stay away from the heat and bustle of the city, in a peaceful
setting outside the village of Agia Triada. The exterior is ageing,
but inside the hotel is relaxed, with friendly and efficient staff.
Bedrooms are small and simple, and the restaurant and cafes
open-plan. There is a fairly large swimming-pool and terrace,
and a casino (open every night except Wednesday from
7.30p.m. to 2a.m.; to enter you need your passport, and men
must wear collar, tie and jacket).

There are lots of hiking possibilities on the pine-forested
mountain, the most interesting of which starts at the two
chapels of Metohi below the casino. The route follows a gorge
across to the spectacularly positioned **monastery of Kliston** and
the fortress of **Phyli**, reached in around two hours. The hike is
described in detail in Marc Dubin's *Greece on Foot*.

If you don't want to walk, both the monastery and fortress
are accessible by car. The road starts outside the industrial town
of Ano Liosia, linked by road with Axarnai, but the signposting
is misleading. Ignore the signs to Phyli, and turn left at the
roundabout and then right when you reach the main road.
There is then a short, depressing ride through the shanty
outskirts of the town, which are soon left behind for the rocky
and shrub-covered foothills of the western side of Mount
Parnes, and the dispersed village of Phyli which abounds with
yoghurt stalls. Beyond Phyli the Kliston monastery is clearly
signposted, and the road winds up to the sheer rocky and cave-
pocked gorge at the head of which the monastery stands.

The gorge and the shallow caves, in which hermits used to
live, are more impressive than the modern whitewashed
monastery, which retains little of its original 14th-century
structure. Fortunately, the ancient fortress of Phyli, a short
drive away, more than compensates.

To get there, return to the main road and continue along it to
the fork marked Klimenti Bari. Unless you want to stop at its
seasonal taverna, carry on along the main road and turn off at
the rough track to the left (not the track directly opposite the
turnoff) taking the lower branch when it forks. There, above the
grassy parking area, the fortress rises, wild, remote and
forbidding. It's an evocative spot for a picnic, although you're
unlikely to be alone on summer weekends as it's an
understandably popular excursion from the heat of Athens.

The fortress is pentagonal, and built of immense blocks of stone whose edges are still sharp. Though the walls have collapsed in places, some sections stand to 12 courses; as many of the drops are sheer and unprotected, you should take care. The fortress was built by the Athenians in the 4th century BC to guard the narrow pass into Boeotia, a direct route from Athens to Thebes. Its position was well chosen, for there are extensive views on all sides, most sensationally into a deep, spiky-rocked gorge from the one gate which retains its massive lintel.

Nearby are the remains of another summit fortress, presumed to be the one occupied in 404 BC by Thrasyboulos. The Athenian general, having witnessed a breakdown of democracy, went into exile and established himself and 70 followers in the fortress, just ten miles from Athens. Aided by a heavy snowfall, Thrasyboulos and his men easily repulsed an attack by the army of Athens' 30 tyrants. Back in Athens, other democrats heard the news and hurried to join him, swelling his forces to 1000. They then marched on Piraeus and, aided by gangs of rooftop stone-throwers, beat the 3000-strong army of the dictators; eventually, with the help of Sparta, they were able to enter Athens and restore democracy.

THE PELOPONNESE

Attached to the mainland only by the narrow isthmus of Corinth, the four-clawed peninsula of the Peloponnese is mountainous, beautiful and peppered with ancient sites. Some of the sites are famous from history and legend; others are hidden away and undisturbed by coachloads of whistle-stop tourists. There are medieval villages to be explored in the almost Alpine landscape of the Aroania mountains, and clusters of gaunt tower-houses to wonder at in the wild southern peninsula of the Mani. Rough roads, in places barely more than tracks, wind up mountains and down steep gorges, passing villages where strangers are rare. Outside the Greek holiday season of mid-July to mid-August you can find empty beaches; if you prefer your Greece more populous and civilised, you can base yourself in elegant coastal towns such as Nafplion and Pilos.

Of course not all of the Peloponnese is so idyllic. Earthquakes, and the Turks retreating after the War of Independence, have destroyed many of the old towns – Kalamata, one of Greece's main producers of olives, is still in the throes of reconstruction after the 1986 earthquake, and such famous centres of civilisation as Sparta, Corinth and Argos are now unappetising sprawls of featureless modern blocks. Nor does the story stop here. In the 1960s and 1970s the north coast and much of the Argolid peninsula were insensitively built up with ugly holiday resorts; tiny, once secluded coves have been ruined by dilapidating quick-rise concrete monsters.

While the tourist industry is responsible for ruining some of the coastline and promoting the building of unsightly villages around the major archaeological sites, it has also brought some much-needed prosperity to the region as well as comforts to the traveller. It wasn't long ago that uncomfortable beds and primitive plumbing were the norm, but now most hotels and rented rooms are clean and adequate. The concrete monstrosities of thirty years ago have given way to a new style of relatively inoffensive small hotels, rooms and apartments, generally good value and of a

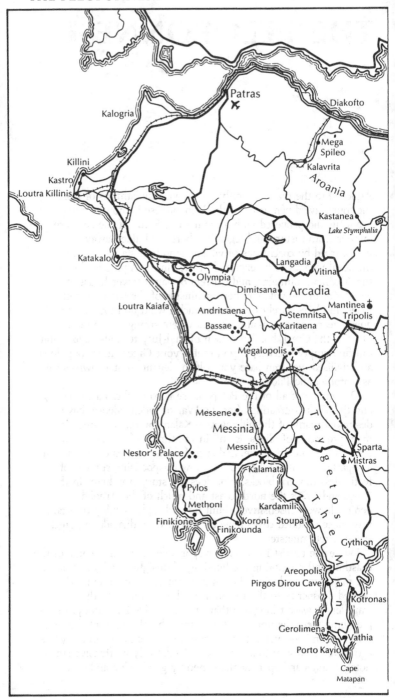

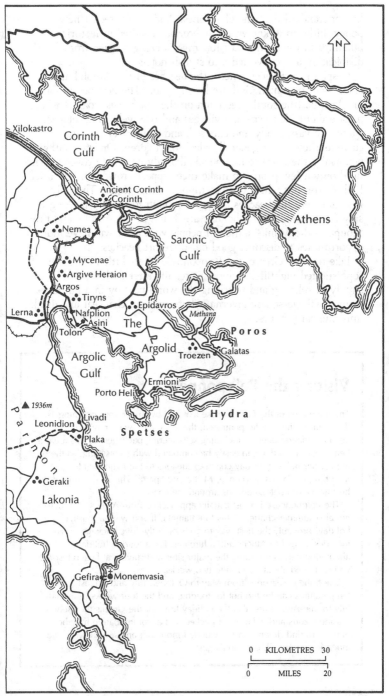

higher standard than the older ones. And a very recent new policy, hitherto unknown in Greece, has resulted in historic buildings in the Mani and Monemvasia being rescued from dilapidation and converted into stylish hotels.

Despite resort development, the beaches of the Argolid and along the Corinthian Gulf are largely poor. The best beaches are in Messinia (the south-west) and on the north-west coast – where most are outside towns and villages and relatively undeveloped. Many are vast, sandy and exposed, and as there are strong currents they're not generally ideal for children. On the southern peninsulas there are some fine small sandy or pebbly coves which need only a few people to make them appear crowded in the brief high season but which can be empty at other times. The only resorts where the beaches are good enough to merit a prolonged stay for a sun-and-sand holiday are Tolon in the Argolid and tiny Stoupa in the Mani – although people with a car will have more opportunities to discover good out-of-resort beaches.

Like most of Greece, the Peloponnese offers little in the way of sophisticated nightlife. In most places life after dark consists simply of relaxing and watching the world pass by in a harbour-front or village-square taverna, where you can chat, eat and drink until the early hours.

Visiting the Peloponnese

The main area of the Peloponnese featured by British tour operators is the south of the Argolid peninsula; there's a fairly wide range of accommodation offered, including self-catering packages. In this area, a beach-based holiday can easily be combined with sightseeing, as there are regular half-day or day coach-excursions to the major sights, including Epidavros, Mycenae, Mistra and Sparta. This is also one of the best areas for boat-excursions around the coast.

The Peloponnese is most usually approached from Athens, but there are also summer charter flights to Kalamata. If you want a touring holiday, probably the best way to go is on a fly-drive package. This includes a flight to Athens and a hire car. For a touring holiday alternating between visiting the major sites and staying at beach resorts, you will need about 10 days to two weeks.

The holiday season is from May to October. July and August temperatures can be too hot for touring, and the four weeks from mid-July to mid-August are also the holiday time for the Greeks themselves – seaside resorts and villages get packed and accommodation may be difficult to find. Inland, in the wooded mountain areas, it's cooler and much less crowded, even in August.

Most visitors to the Peloponnese intend to include some sightseeing in their itinerary. The region was ruled by a succession of ancient city-states followed by waves of colonisers: Mycenaeans, Ancient Greeks, Romans, Byzantines, Franks, Venetians and Turks have all left their architectural mark, either building their own strongholds or taking over and adding to existing ones. Hilltop Acrocorinth, for example, was used for over 2000 years by all the region's invaders. Fortresses ranging from those of the Bronze Age at Mycenae and Tiryns, through Byzantine Monemvasia and the Venetian castles at Nafplion, Methoni and Koroni, are all relics of the Peloponnese's strife-torn past. The fighting went on into the last century, with the Turks commandeering medieval strongholds in their battle to retain control of the region in the War of Independence; and the isolated southern peninsula of the Mani continued for considerably longer to be wracked by inter-familial vendettas, fought from their heavily fortified tower-houses. Thankfully, there are more than power-struggles to the history of the Peloponnese. The most moving monuments are those that testify to the highly civilised way in which the Ancient Greeks lived when they weren't involved in inter-state conflicts. From this period date the beautifully preserved mountaintop temple of Apollo at Bassae, the magnificent and perfectly proportioned

Getting around

Getting around by car is relatively easy. Most of the main roads are tarmac, with some rough stretches only on the less-frequented routes. There's a motorway from the Corinth Canal to Patras; it has only one lane and a hard shoulder (which is used for overtaking) each way, but it runs through attractive landscape and bypasses the built-up northern coast. A new motorway is being built across the Peloponnese to Kalamata in the south. Signposting is generally good: suggested speeds and bend warnings are accurate and should be respected. On the main roads, signs in Roman lettering follow the signs in Greek – often too late, just by the relevant turning. On minor roads, being able to read Greek placenames comes in very handy. There's no shortage of petrol stations and garages, even in the smallest villages.

Travelling by public transport requires careful planning and ample time. If you have only two or three weeks, it is wise to concentrate on one area such as the Argolid Peninsula. Each administrative region of the Peloponnese has a comprehensive local bus service, radiating from the main town – from Kalamata throughout Messinia and the Mani, for example. Timetables are devised to suit locals rather than tourists and often are not easy to come by – enquire at the bus station in the main towns or ask the locals. Some buses are air-conditioned and are worth the small extra charge.

continued

theatre at Epidavros, and the ruins of Olympia, where the four-yearly Games were held through war and peace for over 1000 years.

It is the well-explored and well-presented sites that are rewarding, in spite of the crowds they attract; however famous, unexcavated sites (like that of Menelaus's palace in the hills south of Sparta) are mainly of interest to archaeologists and passing walkers.

The Peloponnese has a variety of types of holiday resort, only a few of which are characterised by large-scale tourism or featured by package-tour operators. One such is Tolon, which has managed to retain some fishing-village charm as well as cater successfully for a good mix of holiday-makers seeking a varying blend of sightseeing and sun-lazing. Tolon and the fine coastal town of Nafplion make excellent bases for visiting the big-name archaeological sites of the Argolid.

In the south, two good, large seaside resorts are Methoni and Pylos – the latter close to the archaeological site of the palace of Nestor and an attractive town in its own right. In the scenic Mani peninsula there are some attractive coastal villages which function as small resorts in high season, as well as some newly created hotels in the atmospheric and almost depopulated remote inland hamlets.

Getting around continued

There's a railway along the north coast, south to Kiparissia, and east across to Kalamata and Argos. It's cheaper and slower than the buses, but a real experience, taking you through some of the most beautiful countryside.

Taxis are widely used for travel between villages, to beaches not on a bus route, and for excursions to the archaeological sites near towns. The Flying Dolphin hydrofoils link various places in the Peloponnese – Nafplion, Tolon, Porto Heli, Ermioni, Monemvasia, Leonidion and Neapolis – and go to Piraeus and the Peloponnese Islands.

There's a regular ferry service across the Corinthian Gulf to the mainland, handy if you want to take in Delphi on your way back to Athens. Ferries from Rio (just east of Patras) to Andirrio run every 20 minutes in the high season; there are also four ferries a day from Egio to Agios Nikolaos – nearer to Delphi than Andirrio.

It's sensible to avoid the Nafplion to Corinth Canal road on Friday and Sunday evenings; crowds of weekenders from Athens can make it a very slow journey. In hot weather always travel with water bottles – a raging thirst can prove unquenchable at siesta time or on a feast day when everything is closed, or after clambering around a cafe-less site. When sightseeing, go early in the morning, and take a sun hat and good walking shoes (most sites involve hill-climbing).

Many of the major sites in the Peloponnese have new purpose-built tourist developments nearby; but it's almost always possible to find places that are rather more atmospheric or comfortable for a holiday base.

Other options for touring accommodation include the large and generally dull but conveniently situated towns of Sparta and Kalamata; the fairly remote coastal resort villages of Githion and Leonidion; and the splendidly situated medieval villages of inland Arcadia.

The Peloponnese is most easily and rewardingly explored by car: while there are excursions from the resorts to all the main sights, public transport is geared to local rather than tourist use, and services to the mountain villages are very infrequent. If you need to rely on public transport, it's advisable to select just one area to explore, say Messenia or Lakonia, and to be prepared to plan carefully. Indeed, with or without a car, the Peloponnese is a region to be savoured slowly; tourists who confine their excursions to the well-beaten trail around the big-name sites will miss much of the most beautiful mountain scenery.

Corinth and the Argolid Peninsula

The road to the Peloponnese from Athens and northern Greece crosses the 23m-wide Corinth Canal and leads to **Corinth**. The port and ugly modern city, about 7km from its ancient counterpart, has been built to resist the earthquakes to which the area is prone (the latest was in 1981), some of which largely destroyed the previous cities. Despite several important sights – particularly ANCIENT CORINTH and the fortress of ACROCORINTH – it's not a place in which to linger.

The greatest concentration of archaeological sites of the Peloponnese is among the restful, but not overly interesting, low scrub-clad hills and fertile plains of the Argolid; the most famous are MYCENAE, TIRYNS and EPIDAVROS. This and the ease of access from Athens combine to make it the most visited area of the Peloponnese, and much of the coast is affected by rather unattractive small resort development – with the exception of the fine old town of NAFPLION and nearby lively TOLON, which successfully combines village charm with an array of tourist facilities, including a wide programme of coach-excursions for those without transport. Another large beach resort much used by tour operators is bustling **Porto Heli**, near the southern tip of the peninsula, on a pretty and almost enclosed bay. It's better for sailing than a sunbathing holiday – local beaches, mere strips of sand, are widely scattered. To the east, the little village of **Ermioni**, on another very enclosed bay opposite the island of Hydra, is fast becoming swamped by new development. There are no beaches in the village itself, but nearby are several large beach holiday complexes. The port of **Galatas** is chiefly a transit point for ferries, a rather unkempt contrast with the prosperous sprawl of Poros visible across the narrow strait.

Between Galatas and Ano Fanari, the winding coast road has splendid views over the islands. **Troezen** makes a pleasant inland detour: beyond the rudimentary site of Theseus's palace a rough track climbs up to the narrow Devil's Bridge (*Diavolo Gefiro*), which spans a deep, impressive gorge. To the north, the peninsula of **Methana** is an extinct volcano joined to the mainland by a causeway. On it are several small settlements and a spa with a yacht and fishing port whose most noticeable feature is a rotten-egg smell from the warm sulphurous waters of an open-air pool. Methana's main attraction is its novelty value.

Despite its high sightseeing interest, the Argolid is not a particularly rewarding area to tour. The landscape is rather bland, the villages neither old nor very attractive, and most of the beaches are poor and choked with ageing campsites. If your priorities include fine scenery and picturesque villages, you would do better to head to inland Arcadia in the north or to Lakonia and Messenia in the south.

Nafplion (Nauplia)

Nafplion is the most attractive town on mainland Greece, largely thanks to the Venetians who had two periods of occupation. Its ancient history as an Argolid port is thoroughly obscured by medieval and modern building, beginning with the Franks who began the dominating Palamidi fortress in the 13th century. Venetians and Turks extended this citadel and its sister eminence Its Kale (Three Castles), which is now occupied by hotels.

Nafplion escaped the destruction inflicted on other towns in the Peloponnese: in the War of Independence the Greeks took it from its Turkish garrison after a year's siege and made it the temporary capital of their liberated country. In the streets and alleys of the steep old town there are elegant houses dating from this brief period. Some have terracotta figurines balancing on their cornices, some stencilled eaves, and others elaborate balconies. Narrow streets are lined with stuccoed houses dripping with plants, and sheltering tavernas and cafes; and steep stepped streets climb the hill towards Its Kale. Best of all is Syntagma, the intimate and beautiful central square of the old part of town, paved with gleaming stone, illuminated at night by cascades of wrought-iron lamps and the soft lights from canopied tavernas. It's dominated by the arcaded façade of the sturdy Venetian arsenal which now houses the archaeological museum (see below). In the south-west corner is a domed mosque with scalloped oriental niches; when Nafplion was the capital of the newly independent Greece (1827–1834) this was where the parliament met.

Below, on the pedestrians-only part of the busy sea-front, stylish pavement cafes add splashes of colour to the buttermilk-washed Venetian houses with wrought-iron balconies, looking across to the crenellated island fortress of Bourdzi in the bay. It's always a flurry of activity, with fruit and nut vendors, Flying Dolphin hydrofoils and the turnout for the evening *volta*. Further round is the commercial harbour, whose practical concrete is backed by good simple fish tavernas. Modern Nafplion extends on flat land from here, its broad main arteries relieved by an opulent belt of palms.

The *Hotel Athena* (C) on Syntagma square can be recommended only for its position; it's dingy, and at present there are no rooms with wcs – although the owners are planning to install them. Hotels at the back of Nafplion town are quieter than those on the harbour-front, but quite a climb. The best of the hotels in the modern part of town is the *Elena* (C) just off Merarchias, one of the central avenues; it's clean, quiet and comfortable. Behind it is the *Nafplio* (C), more expensive and not as comfortable but more than adequate.

Built within the walls of the Turkish fortress of Its Kale is the *Xenia Palace* hotel and bungalow complex (Luxury-category). Bedrooms are large and comfortable, suites immense, and all rooms have balconies (though these are dangerous for small children). The style of décor leaves much to be desired and the atmosphere is in parts reminiscent of a villain's fortress in a 1960s sci-fi film, enhanced by a coffin-shaped swimming-pool and fake medieval torches protruding from the walls of the reception area. Lower down the same hill, the more modest *Xenia* (A) has large rooms overlooking the sea, or over the roofs of the old town to the sea, but is showing signs of wear. The hotel has a charmless sand and shingle beach, so tiny that it's been extended by a concrete platform.

The town beach is poor and rocky, but there are sandy ones nearby. At **Karathona**, just 4km out of town, there's an enclosed cove with a coarse sand beach reached along a road winding down from the Palamidi fortress.

There are small seasonal cafes, a taverna and a modest selection of watersports. The tree-shaded picnicking and parking area gets crowded with camper vans in high season. Tolon (see below) is a short car or bus drive away.

135

The fort of Tiryns is just up the road, and Mycenae and Epidavros make easy day-trips. If you don't have your own transport there are excursion coaches to the big sites – but it's cheaper to take a normal service bus to Tiryns and Epidavros. In high season there are boat-trips around the harbour and the islet of Bourdzi.

Nafplion: sights

● **Palamidi** A complex of forts encircled by crenellated walls crowning a steep hill and dominating the peninsula. You can climb up to it by a long flight of stone steps (estimates range from 850 to 1000) or, if you don't feel up to it, there's a road. At the top you can turn your back on the fort for extensive views over Nafplion and the Peloponnese coastline, or relax on the terrace of the bar.

Palamidi was the key to the control of the Peloponnese during the War of Independence and was subsequently used as a political prison, and until the 1920s for convicts – you can still see the remains of bars in the windows of the cells. The smallest and dankest of these held Palamidi's most famous prisoner, the formidable Klepht leader Kolokotronis, who did much to liberate Nafplion from the Turks. He objected to the fact that the new Greek government was about to limit his powers, and registered his disapproval by kidnapping four of its members. Imprisoned and sentenced to death, he was eventually reprieved and reinstated as a hero. His statue now stands under trees in the town.

● **Archaeological Museum** A small and easily palatable collection of finds from Mycenae, Tiryns and other Argolid sites. Look out for the spooky ceremonial masks discovered at Tiryns – fanged, with bulging eyes and bulbous noses. A more practical aspect of life at Tiryns is represented by an ingenious terracotta cooler. It consists of a large bowl with the top half of a jug fused to its sides. Wine, or anything else that had to be kept cool, was poured into the jug, which was then surrounded by water.

To give an idea of what the Mycenaeans looked like in battle, there's a distinctly uncomfortable and restrictive suit of Mycenaean armour made of body-wrapping bands of bronze, and a helmet, re-lined with leather.

There are fragments of frescoes from Mycenae itself, the best preserved being the almost Picasso-like 'lady of Mycenae' painted in profile with an exaggerated eye, large nose, receding chin and elaborate head-dress. And offering some insight into the religion of the Mycenaeans are a number of idols – grotesque faces, and coiled terracotta snakes, a symbol of the mother-goddess whom they worshipped.

Finally, don't miss the museum's most prosaic but pleasing exhibit – a terracotta bath with a raised seat inside for maximum comfort.

● **Museum of the Peloponnesian Folklore Foundation** Voted Europe's best museum in 1981, this is imaginatively laid out, with detailed explanations (in English) of the processes of cotton, wool and silk production, brought to life with the equipment used, examples of fabrics, and photographs of peasants at work. Inevitably, certain things stand out – the description of how poverty-stricken peasants made fabric out of broom leaves, for example, or of how aprons were embroidered with symbols designed to protect a woman's virginity or to aid her in childbirth (the apron was laid over her stomach during labour).

Upstairs, there's a collection of regional costumes, some intricately woven, others sumptuously embroidered, ranging from the oriental veiled dresses of eastern Thrace (now in Turkey) to the embroidered bodices worn by the women of western Thrace, complete with slits to facilitate breast-feeding.

There's a small shop in which you can buy rather more modestly embroidered purses, Greek coffeepots, and bags of herbs and mountain tea; and a cafe which serves traditional preserves of bitter oranges and quinces.

● **Agios Spiridon** A whitewashed Venetian church, outside which Capodistrias, first president of the Greek republic, was assassinated in 1831. The graze made by the bullet is protected by a plate of glass.

● **Shrine of Agios Anastasios** A huge and ancient olive tree from which Anastasios, patron saint of Nafplion, was martyred.

Tolon

Tolon is the largest resort on the Peloponnese, and already popular with the British. It's a well-organised place, with a wide selection of watersports, including para-gliding, and is well placed for exploring the sites of the Argolid. Though Tolon gets packed in July and August, it feels relatively sleepy in other months, and it's nowhere near as frenetic and rowdy as the big resorts on the islands.

The beach is long and sheltered and curving between two promontories. It's soft, sandy and backed by dunes in the south, but skimpy and hard-packed in the north near the small harbour. Beyond the southern headland of Asini lies a long rough sand or shingle beach, backed by campsites but not crowded.

There are plenty of good-quality hotels, rooms to rent, a string of campsites, almost a hundred tavernas, fifteen bars, three discos, and even the rare luxury of a launderette.

It's worth exploring the wild and jagged **Asini** headland, which was the site of an important Mycenaean city. There's not much left because Argos destroyed it after Asini sided with Sparta; but it's a peaceful and evocative site, with a couple of hundred yards of cyclopean wall and a scattering of later medieval ruins.

Excursions (by coach or taxi) are laid on to most of the sites of the Peloponnese, and there are boat-trips to the islands of

Hydra and Spetses. Avoid the day boat-trips across the Argolic Gulf to Paralia Tirou and other settlements – they do not add up to the 'small fishing villages' described in the brochures. There are also regular buses to Nafplion.

Recommendable hotels include the *Minoa* (c) on the skimpy stretch of beach near the harbour, smartly decorated in gleaming white and aquamarine; the price includes the luxury of breakfast in bed. The English-speaking owner can organise rooms too: the new *Festos Rooms*, with pine furniture and private bathrooms, are tucked away by a hill at the southern end of town, 500m from the best stretch of beach. The grounds are immature, and the view of the olive- and scrub-covered hill is uninspiring, but there's a swimming-pool and bar, and it's a good bet if you want some peace.

Further up the beach from the Minoa and much smaller is the *Knossos* (c), with cosy décor, including traditional flotaki rugs.

On the main road close to the good, southern stretch of beach is the *Maria Lena* (D). The rooms are good value, and all have balconies and bathrooms; there's a communal fridge on the landing.

On a hill at the edge of town, a short walk from the best stretch of beach, the *Barbouna* (D) is simple, friendly and awash with flowers.

Ancient Corinth

With interruptions, this strategic spot controlling access to the Peloponnese has been occupied since the mythological times preceding the Mycenaean era and earliest Greek history. Doric settlers re-founded the site, and by the 8th century BC Corinth was a sea power with her own colonies; by the 6th she dominated trade, hosted the Isthmian Games and was renowned as a luxurious playground for all who passed through. Her patron goddess was Aphrodite, whose sacred courtesans were the aristocracy among 1000 city prostitutes. Eclipsed by Athens in trade, Corinth kept her reputation for pleasure until razed to the ground by the Romans in 146BC. The fine site remained derelict until Julius Caesar rebuilt it in 44BC as one of his veterans' colonies; within a few years, Roman Corinth was as famously frivolous as its Greek predecessor, much to the distress of Saint Paul, who spent 18 months in the city attempting to mend the Corinthians' ways. The letters he wrote afterwards, railing against them for adultery, homosexuality and sleeping with their mothers-in-law, suggest he made little impact.

The passage across the Isthmus between the Ionian and Aegean Seas was a valuable source of toll-revenue to the

Corinthians. By the 6th century BC there was a portage road, along which ships were dragged on rollers, thus saving ship-owners the time and trouble of sailing right around the Peloponnese. Even at this date a canal was envisaged, but the first actual, short-lived attempt at one was Roman – the emperor Nero swung a golden pickaxe at a ceremonial opening. Nineteen hundred years and several abortive plans later, the modern canal was opened in 1893.

Post-Roman Corinth was ravaged by Goths, earthquakes and plague. Under Franks, Venetians and Turks, malaria was the chief natural drawback. In 1858 a major earthquake wrecked the ancient site and the very battered adjacent town. A new Corinth was built on the coast, only to be itself destroyed by an earthquake in 1928. Rebuilt again, on anti-seismic principles, unappealing modern Corinth escaped relatively lightly from the latest earthquake in 1981.

Ancient Corinth is about 5km inland from the modern port. Apart from the picturesque and much-photographed temple of Apollo in its midst, only foundations remain, overlooked by the grim mountaintop fortress of Acrocorinth. It's an atmospheric place, especially in the late afternoon with the sun setting behind the temple's seven columns. Next to the site is a small village, with tavernas, souvenir shops and a few rooms to rent.

Ancient Corinth: highlights

• **The Roman town** The layout is clearly visible from the modern road above it. A paved road which originally ran across the plain to the harbour of Lechaion on the Corinthian Gulf leads up to the market place with its row of shops. Outside the main site is the *odeion*, a theatre partly scooped out of the rock, with room for 3000 spectators, and below it you can see the shape of a larger theatre carved on to the side of a hill. Originally Greek, it was redesigned by the Romans – the stage was enlarged to make room for gladiators, and could even be flooded for mock sea battles.

Inside the main site is a **museum**, with a collection of Corinthian pottery, the city's main export in pre-Roman times. The slapdash quality of some of it indicates the pressures the potters were under to keep up with the demand. Animals were sometimes elongated to take up more space around the vases, and if you look carefully you can distinguish some distinctly wobbly lines in the geometric designs.

Neither are the Roman mosaics, found in a villa on the outskirts of the town, particularly accomplished, although they are well preserved. One is of a naked flautist rounding up cattle, the other a head of Bacchus surrounded by a complicated geometrical design.

The **agora** was the large market place and the centre of town. The so-called shops, only one of which retains its vaulted roof, included taverns. Cups were discovered in them, and most have their own well, probably used to chill drinks. There was a second storey above the southern row, which probably had rooms for the pleasure-seeking businessmen.

On the corner of the *agora*, next to the paved road, is the **Peirene fountain**. The water, from a natural spring, was stored behind a six-arched arcade and channelled into the rectangular pool in front. The pool is now dry, the water running along modern pipes to serve the village.

• **Acrocorinth** A steep and narrow road winds up to Acrocorinth, following the route Ancient Greek men took on their way to the prostitutes in the temple of Aphrodite. A less luxurious spot cannot be imagined. Fused on to steeply pitched rock almost 600m above the town, Acrocorinth stands desolate, brooding and defended by broken-toothed crenellations. Behind the three gates are 60 acres of crumbling ruins, choked by wild grasses and prickly undergrowth. The views are wonderful – across fertile plains to the Gulf of Corinth in the north, to the Saronic Gulf in the east, and on a clear day as far as Athens and the Parthenon – and made the citadel a crucial key in the defence of the Peloponnese.

Originally a Greek acropolis, Acrocorinth has since been occupied by a string of colonisers – Romans, Byzantines, Franks, Venetians and most recently the Turks. Rooting around the ruins of the Turkish quarter, just inside the third gate, you'll find the remains of a mosque, bath-house and even a truncated minaret. Overlooking it is the keep of a Frankish fort and, to the east, the summit which held Aphrodite's temple where the sacred prostitutes worked.

Nemea

Herakles slew the Nemean lion – one of his 12 Labours – in a cave nearby, dressed himself in its skin and, according to legend, founded the biennial Nemean Games. Nemea, like Olympia (see page 168), was a sanctuary with sports facilities, but was built on a far smaller scale and is less well preserved. As at Olympia, the prizes were symbolic – here, the simple wreath for the victor was of wild celery.

The site is dominated by three slender columns of the temple to the Nemean Zeus, re-erected and surrounded by a heap of tumbled column discs. Apart from the stadium (to the left of the approach road) which still has the starting-line *in situ*, the rest of the site is confusing. However, with the help of a plan, and a visit to the site museum, which has a model of what the sanctuary looked like in the 5th century BC, you can make out the foundations of a *palaestra* (exercise ground), *xenon* (hotel) and bath-house.

Nemea's sweet, potent red wine, known as the 'blood of Herakles', is famous throughout Greece, and worth sampling.

Mycenae (Mikene, Mikinae)

Spread over a bare rocky hill at the foot of dark barren mountains, an air of tragedy hangs over the stony remains of Mycenae.

The tales of crimes of passion that occurred among the Mycenaean royals read like an X-rated Ancient Greek soap opera. In this 3000-year-old citadel King Atreus murdered his nephews and served them to their father, Thyestes, at a banquet; Atreus was then killed by Thyestes's revenge-seeking son Aegisthus. Here the beautiful Helen married Atreus's son, Menelaus, before running off with Paris and provoking the ten-year-long siege of Troy; and here Agamemnon, Menelaus's brother and leader of the Greek forces at Troy, returned victorious, only to be killed in his bath by his wife, Clytemnestra, who had since taken Aegisthus as her lover. Not that it did Clytemnestra much good – she and Aegisthus ended up being killed by her son, Orestes.

Some knowledge of its history, together with an ample imagination, will help to make the site come alive. For though the treasures discovered here in the last century by Heinrich Schliemann are both opulent and archaeologically important, they are at present in the National Archaeological Museum at Athens. A site museum is currently under construction, but until it's open – possibly during 1990 –you'll have to make do with photographs and plans in the guidebooks on sale.

There is no shade on the site, and the stones are slippery. There are some refreshment wagons in the car-park, but these are closed out of season. In the nearby village, the little hotel Bellehelene has photographs and signatures of many visiting notables.

Mycenae: highlights

• **Lion Gate** The mighty walls that encircle Mycenae, in some places 9m wide, are pierced by the Lion Gate. An immense lintel (a single block of stone weighing an estimated 20 tonnes) supports a triangular pediment carved with two sleek and powerful but now headless lions. You normally have to queue to get through – for the gate is approached through a narrow path between high walls. This is a defensive measure. Invading armies would be slowed down – no doubt squashed into a huddle like impatient tourists – giving the soldiers time to attack.

• **Grave Circle A** A double circle of upright slabs enclosing six royal graves. In one of them Schliemann found three male bodies, their faces covered with golden masks and their chests with golden breastplates. When he unmasked the first two their skulls crumbled to dust, but the face of the third, complete with eyes, mouth and '32 beautiful white teeth' remained intact, so well had it been embalmed. This Schliemann took to be Agamemnon. He kissed the mask, and that night dispatched a now-famous telegram to the king of Greece: 'I have gazed on the face of Agamemnon.' Sadly, Schliemann was mistaken, and the burials have since been proved to date from 300 years before the Trojan War. Agamemnon is more likely to have been buried in one of the immense *tholos* (beehive) tombs outside the walls.

● **Royal Palace** Most of it has slipped down the hillside, but the foundation of the courtyard, porch and *megaron* (great hall) are still visible. To the right, steps lead down to a series of small rooms, in one of which a drain was discovered, leading to the romantic speculation that it was the bathroom in which Agamemnon was murdered.

● **Secret Cistern** Vital for holding out against an enemy during long sieges, the secret cistern is the best-preserved and most memorable part of the site. A hundred steps lead along a dank narrow passage carved in the rock to an underground spring. Don't go far without a torch, for there are long drops straight into the water.

● **Treasury of Atreus** Not a treasury, but an immense *tholos*, or

DISCOVERING THE MYCENAEANS

The Mycenaean civilisation of mainland Greece developed, flourished and declined at the end of the Bronze Age, and was at its height between 1400 and 1200BC. It overlapped and outlasted the Minoan civilisation on Crete, which was its great formative influence. There were three major differences. The mainland Mycenaeans were more warlike – probably by nature and certainly by circumstance – than the island Minoans, and they built great fortifications unknown on Crete. The Mycenaean religion involved masculine gods of the sky and the elements, inherited from their invading nomadic forebears, while Crete's settled agricultural communities worshipped the great goddess, a version of mother-earth. And the Mycenaean language, unlike the Minoan, was an early form of Greek.

This ancestry of Ancient Greece is known chiefly through the Iliad, *written some time in the 8th century* BC *by Homer. This epic poem about the Trojan War, and its companion-sequel the* Odyssey, *are the earliest surviving written product of an oral tradition: myth, legend and history were remembered through the generations of Greece's Dark Ages only by formulaic repetition, embellished with narrative twists or regional emphasis by each storytelling bard. Homer lists many Greek kingdoms who sent men to fight at Troy, and describes many palaces, some of which undoubtedly existed. But how much of Homer can be taken as factual history?*

beehive tomb, which could just possibly be the site of Agamemnon's burial. It's some way down the road from the citadel, and has a separate entrance, so you need to keep your ticket. Almost 14m high and 15m in diameter, the tomb is beautifully constructed of curved stone blocks. Its most notable feature, however, is the echo – stamp your foot in the dead centre and the entire tomb shudders with the sound of a muted machine gun.

Argos

The capital of Ancient Argolis, Argos is now a modern and undistinguished town with few visible traces of its history. What remains is of interest mainly to enthusiasts – the ruins of an immense theatre, which had room for 20,000 spectators (6000 more than at Epidavros) and a complex of Roman baths. The museum also has a limited appeal, but its contents are well displayed. There are Roman mosaics, a vase depicting Theseus

---

In 1873 Heinrich Schliemann, an untrained pioneer archaeologist with total faith in Homer, discovered and investigated Troy in western Turkey. He dug through several cities stacked in layers at the site, in search of Priam's palace; and he found a treasury of gold, with diadems and bracelets worthy of Helen herself. Though later archaeology demonstrated that this treasure-level was that of an earlier Troy than Homer's, it seemed at the time that Schliemann's faith was vindicated. He turned his attention to the ruins of Mycenae, always 'rich in gold' to Homer: the palace of Agamemnon, 'king of men'.

Unlike Troy, this site was well known. The walls and the Lion Gate of the citadel had never been hidden; and the enormous beehive-shaped tombs outside the walls were long rifled and empty. But Schliemann excavated inside the citadel, putting his trust in Pausanias, a Greek historian who visited Mycenae in the 2nd century AD. There he found graves where the bodies of men, women and children were clad and adorned and surrounded with gold. Schliemann lifted a golden death-mask and reported, 'I have gazed on the face of Agamemnon' – but again he was wrong. These 'shaft' graves proved to contain an earlier royal Mycenaean dynasty than Agamemnon's.

Subsequent finds at Mycenae – not only in the citadel and palace but in lesser houses – revealed through their materials, style and workmanship much about the wealth, the preoccupations and the far-reaching trade of this people. Other important centres, particularly Tiryns and Pylos, confirmed the links and the time-scale of a coherent civilisation.

and the Minotaur, and some terracotta figures playing blind-man's buff. The highlight, however, is an 8th-century suit of armour, similar to those described by Homer.

Nine kilometres north-east of Argos lie the scant ruins of the sanctuary of Hera (**Argive Heraion**), which was the centre of a cult designed to initiate participants into the mysteries of death. There is nothing necromantic whatsoever about the site, just long views over the Argive plain, and some welcome peace and quiet.

Ten kilometres south of Argos, the main site of **Lerna** is strictly for enthusiasts: the remains of Neolithic houses and pre-Mycenaean fortifications, protected by concrete canopies and close to a bog. In fact, the marshes are more evocative than the site – the Ancient Greeks thought they were bottomless and led to the Underworld, and within them Herakles attacked Hydra, the multi-headed water-snake. Every time he hacked a head off,

---

DISCOVERING THE MYCENAEANS continued

From the Minoans the Mycenaeans learned the art of writing. On Crete it had developed from hieroglyphs carved on small stones and seals to a cursive script, which the archaeologists called Linear A, found on vases, on bronze and stone objects and on clay tablets. Other clay tablets bore a more advanced script, christened Linear B. These were found not only at the Cretan palace Knossos but on the mainland too. The Minoan language of Linear A remains undeciphered but in 1952 – an astonishing year for archaeology with major finds at Mycenae – Linear B was deciphered, from the hypothesis that it might be Mycenaean Greek.

What survived in writing was chiefly to do with trade: inventories, owners' names, lists and quantities of the commodities that passed between Crete and the Peloponnese. At Pylos, however, a whole archive of fragmented tablets was found, from which it was possible to learn about the social structure and military arrangements of a Mycenaean kingdom – and to speculate on what might have caused its end.

The inscribed tablets were marked with a stylus while the clay was fresh and soft – once it dried out no mark could be corrected. The clay was not deliberately fired; but those tablets that survived to be read in the 20th century rather than crumbling to dust had come through catastrophic fires. The palace of Knossos was thus destroyed, in about 1400BC, possibly by Mycenaean action. Around 1150BC, about 50 years after the fall of the relevant Troy, the centres of Mycenaean civilisation were all deserted within something like a decade. Pylos,

---

another grew in its place, but he eventually succeeded in burning off all but her immortal head, which he buried under a rock.

Tiryns

The fortress palace of Tiryns is a contemporary of Mycenae, more modest, but less visited. This strangely atmospheric if somewhat oppressive place stands on a low hill surrounded by a plain, and though not particularly impressive from a distance is one of the finest examples of Mycenaean military architecture. Homer refers to 'wall-girt Tiryns'; it is here that you can best understand why the early Greeks thought only giants, the Cyclops, could have manoeuvred such enormous blocks of stone. Tiryns' Cyclopean walls are in places 11m thick – though now only about half their original height of 20m. The rest of

---

Mycenae, Tiryns and several others were burned, the rest simply abandoned and left derelict.

Theories vary about this abrupt and violent dispersal. It may have been the outcome of earthquake devastation, or even a drastic change in climate. There may have been internal uprisings or civil war, after the Greek leaders had over-extended their resources in a Pyrrhic victory at Troy. Instead – or as well – there may have been a swift and concerted invasion from the Dorian people of the north-west, who were the next to inhabit Mycenaean territory. And a third possibility involves the mysterious 'Peoples of the Sea'. These were migratory tribes, perhaps driven from their homelands by famine, who had become expert mariners. They first served greater powers as merchants and mercenaries, and later attacked them: they destroyed the Hittite kingdom and major centres of Syria and Palestine, and they were eventually defeated in a great sea battle with the Egyptians. It is completely unprovable that the Peoples of the Sea attacked the Mycenaeans, but the tablets at Pylos do indicate from which direction trouble was expected. From the palace, administrative headquarters for the southern Peloponnese, high-ranking men of the court were liaison officers with strategic coastal stations. All around the coast, watchers were on duty. The written numbers and depositions indicate a man every 200 metres.

After whatever catastrophe it was, Dorian incomers overran the Peloponnese – with the possible exception of Athens, which claimed never to have fallen to them. Archaeology offers no evidence of any Dorian culture, be it pottery or jewellery, weapons or burial customs. The next few centuries were to be Greece's Dark Ages.

---

the buildings are marked only by stumpy foundations, and trying to make sense of them without a plan is not easy. Little is known about Tiryns' early history, but according to legend Herakles was born here, the result of Zeus taking advantage of the beautiful Alkmene in her husband's absence. Herakles proved his demi-god status when only 18 months old, strangling a snake sent by Zeus's furious wife, Hera, to kill him.

The entrance to the fortress, up a sloping ramp, is the same that Tiryns's enemies would have had to use. As an invader approached, his right (unshielded) side would always face the walls, exposed to the projectiles hurled and shot by the defenders. If he made it so far, he would then have to turn a sharp corner, only to find himself facing a heavily defended gate, with walls rising on either side, no doubt bristling with more armed soldiers.

Inside the gate is a vaulted corridor set into the thickness of the wall. More recently, the corridors provided shelter for sheep, and the walls, polished by generations of fleecy coats, gleam in the dimness.

Only the foundations of the courtyard and great hall remain, but the clay hearth can be seen in the latter, and just off it is a bathroom, paved with a single stone flag, with the drain channels still visible.

A 'secret' staircase leads down to a postern gate, from which you can walk around the immense fortress walls. As you reach the corner, opposite a modern ochre-washed house, there are two tunnels leading to secret cisterns, each retaining a perfectly preserved stretch of its massy vaulting.

Epidavros (Epidauros)

The theatre at Epidavros is the most famous, most perfectly proportioned and best-preserved theatre in Greece. But though the star attraction now, it was only part of what originally went on at this site. For 1000 years from the 6th century BC, Epidavros functioned as a sanctuary dedicated to Asklepios, the god of healing. Initially, the cures were effected by Asklepios appearing to the ill in their dreams, after their imaginations had been inflamed by initiation rites and the experience of sharing their dormitory with holy snakes (the symbol of Asklepios). Not surprisingly, there were a few failures, and with the development of medicine scepticism over miracle cures increased. So the priests became proto-Freudian analysts, interpreting their patients' dreams, and prescribing various forms of therapy.

This is where the theatre comes in. The experience of

watching a tragedy or comedy was reckoned to be therapeutic, elevating the spirit and purging it of destructive passions (what Aristotle called catharsis). In fact, one of the greatest Greek tragedians, Sophocles, worked in Epidavros as a priest.

In addition to the theatrical cures, sport, dance, music, baths and even diet cures were prescribed, all designed to bring about the harmony of mind and body.

Under the Romans, faith in holistic medicine declined and more scientific methods were introduced. Baths were installed for spa therapies, purgatives administered, surgical operations performed, and sport and theatre became mere entertainments.

If you want to explore more of Epidavros than the theatre, a plan is useful, for only the foundations of the sanctuary have survived. The museum is between the theatre and the sanctuary, and its reconstructions of some of the buildings help to make sense of the site.

Epidavros: highlights

• **Theatre** Carved into the side of a pine-wooded hill, the theatre's contours echo those of the smooth sweeping mountains across the valley. The 55 limestone rows are arranged in two tiers, divided into wedge shapes by staircases, and have room for 14,000 spectators. The acoustics are astounding – drop a coin in the dead centre of the orchestra and it can be heard on the top row. More interestingly, you can eavesdrop on your compatriots' conversations.

Behind the orchestra are the foundations of the *skene*, or stage. In front of it was the forestage, and half way back you can see where four columns stood. Inserted between these were triangular-shaped scenery stands. Each side had a different background painted on, so there could be three scene changes.

An annual festival of ancient drama was re-introduced in 1954. There are performances every Saturday and Sunday evening from the end of June to mid-September. Tickets are sold out quickly, so if you want to be sure of a seat, buy one in advance from the Athens Festival Box Office, 4 Stadiou Street, Athens (telephone 3221459). Otherwise the box office at the site is open from around 5p.m. on the day of performance.

• **Museum** In the first hall are stone plaques covered with inscriptions. These list the more miraculous cures effected by Asklepios, some of them reading like stories from one of the more lurid Sunday newspapers. One woman, pregnant for five years, spent just one night in the sanctuary before giving birth to a boy, who immediately sprang up, washed himself and went for a walk. Another came because she was unable to get pregnant, but produced twins after sleeping with a snake.

Cures under the Romans were more prosaic. One Marcus Julius Apellas was healed of dyspepsia by eating bread, cheese, lettuce and celery, taking hot baths, sprinkling himself with sand, showering in wine, and going for long walks. Other Roman patients had less laughable treatments, which included scalpel, tweezers and a particularly nasty-looking saw.

In the next rooms are statues draped with curative snakes, and sections of the Tholos (see below) frieze supporting a segment of the majestic stone-coffered ceiling, studded with flowers. Part of the floor has been reconstructed, its black and white checks curving towards one centre, only to be interrupted and replaced by a movement towards another. Dizzying even now, the effect on patients dazed by mysticism can be imagined.

• **Gymnasium** Huge, with many rooms opening off a central courtyard, but the foundations are only knee-high. Unceremoniously plonked in the middle is a small Roman theatre (*odeion*).

• **Stadium** Built in a natural dip, with some stone seats remaining on the left slope, and the starting- and finishing-lines still visible. An underground passage (held up by modern wooden scaffolding) leads straight to the *palaestra*, where the wrestlers and athletes trained.

• **Tholos** A circular temple, once surrounded by two rings of columns and paved with the deliberately disorientating pattern of black and white tiles mentioned above. The central panel could be lifted up, giving access to a labyrinth, whose walls still stand. This is thought to have been a snake-pit, and according to one theory was used for a spine-shuddering form of shock therapy. Patients would grope their way in the dark through the labyrinth, and emerge in the centre to find themselves surrounded by a squirming (but harmless) tangle of snakes.

• **Abaton** A long dormitory where patients would sleep after their initiation rites, hoping for healing dreams. The mystical effect would be heightened by glimmering oil-lamps and the releasing of snakes later in the night.

The South

The southern Peloponnese is rich in scenery as well as architecture. The intimidating mountain ranges of Parnon and the Taygetos loom up from a gently undulating landscape of orchards and golden grasses, splitting into the peninsulas of Lakonia and the Mani. To the west of the Taygetos is the blunt Messenian peninsula.

The landscape of the central peninsula, the Mani, is unforgettable. Narrow and bony, it's formed by the last, threadbare peaks of the Taygetos. The region is divided into two parts. In the wealthier Outer Mani, to the north-west, where the foothills are gentle and fertile and the coastline is beautifully indented, the villages turn into small resorts in high season, popular with independent travellers and Greeks alike. The INNER MANI, the peninsula to the south, is remote, barren and subject to hot, dry African winds. Numerous barrel-vaulted chapels and domed Byzantine churches testify to the Inner Mani's prosperity in the 10th and 12th centuries. But now the isolated and deserted villages that spike the landscape of dry-stone walls and prickly pears are as severe and wild as the mountains glowering down above them.

Here the Maniots lived in a feudal time-warp, isolated from the rest of the country and grouped together in tribal villages, waging vendettas well into the last century. Houses were fortified and increased in height in relation to their owners' position in village society. It's a fascinating if sobering area to explore: many villages have been virtually abandoned to a few ageing Maniots scraping together a poor living from the infertile land.

Only KARDAMILI in the more open Outer Mani and GITHION on the east coast get really busy, and though the days of STOUPA as an undiscovered resort are about to end (it's being used by British tour operators), you can still find tranquillity.

At the head of the Mani peninsula, overlooked by the sheer rocky heights of the Taygetos, the large market town of **Kalamata**, famous for its olives, is in the throes of reconstruction after a severe earthquake in 1986. Shanty villages line the road south through the olive groves, skeletal shattered houses stand among the new blocks, and the town is still studded with dusty building-sites. Though you're unlikely to want to stay, there are lots of hotels and campsites along the sea-front and by the gritty beach to the east of town.

The landscapes of Lakonia and the Messenian peninsula are gentler than that of the Mani. Messenia is the more attractive, with the stylish town of PILOS lying on the vast sweep of Navarino Bay, and the pretty resort of METHONI dominated by a rambling Venetian fortress. There are good beaches, and both towns are convenient for visits to the site of NESTOR'S PALACE, described in Homer's *Odyssey*.

The road from Methoni to Koroni, Methoni's twin fortress on the eastern side of the peninsula, runs through low grassy hills and olive groves with tracks running down to two sand and shingle bays just before the village of **Finikione**: one isolated and without facilities, the second slightly busier, with a campsite and a small hotel. There are three more beaches at the small resort of **Finikounda**, which is popular with Greeks but gets few foreign visitors.

Koroni itself, with red-roofed whitewashed houses tumbling down beneath its fortress (more ruined and less imposing than that at Methoni) to the harbour, is neglected, and many of the old houses are in need of restoration. Once a wealthy port, there's now an air of poverty hanging over the streets, although it's appealing in a rough, earthy sort of way. There's a fairly good, long, sand and shingle beach 2km out of town to the south of the fortress, but it's not worth going out of your way for.

Lakonia is flanked to the north by the Parnon and Taygetos ranges; in the south it spills into a low, fertile peninsula, with a spine of gently undulating mountains. Tumbling down a great red rock off the shore of the Lakonian peninsula is the popular village and sight of MONEMVASIA, a ruined Byzantine port.

East of the mountains, in the fertile valley of the Eurotas, lies the dull modern city of SPARTA, which holds no clues to the austere and powerful civilisation that dominated and for a short period ruled the whole of Greece, but which survives only in name and reputation. The only reason for staying in Sparta is so that you can make an early start for Byzantine MISTRA 5km away.

Pylos or Navarino

With its plant-shaded *plateia* surrounded by whitewashed porticoes, gardens shadowed by palm trees and flopping banana trees, and lovely views across the vast sweep of Navarino Bay, Pylos is a stylish and attractive town, ideal as a base for exploring the southern Peloponnese or just for lazy lingering.

The natural harbour of Navarino Bay, almost enclosed by the island of Sphakteria, is 5km long and in places 60m deep. It was the scene of the famous battle between an allied fleet (British, French and Russian) and a Turko-Egyptian fleet, which helped to secure Greek independence from the Turks in 1827. The bay has also provided the setting for several movies. Today, even the occasional tanker plying across its glassy waters does not disturb the peace. The 'sights' of Pylos include a rambling and overgrown Turkish fort, a modern mosque-like church with a flashy silver dome, and a pretty white Turkish aqueduct.

There are several pleasant hotels. The *Karalis Beach Hotel* (B) overhangs the sea ('beach' is a misnomer), and the small rooms have good views of the bay, as does the roof-garden. The *Karalis* (C) also has small rooms, half of which have sea views; however, as it's on the main approach road, and heavy lorries pass even on Sundays, the back rooms are quieter. *House Philip*, a good simple 'pension', is also on a main road, and quite a haul from the harbour, but it too has excellent views across the bay. Pylos has no beach, although you can swim from a concrete platform to the left of the *plateia*. However, there are some good beaches to the north, easily accessible by car or boat: near the small resort of **Gialova**, where the *Hotel Helonaki*, close to the beach, has clean and modern rooms; and at the sleepy village of **Petrochori**, where the soft sandy beach (unfortunately with some rubbish and traces of tar when we visited) sweeps around a small lagoon, backed by waves of sand-dunes, and overlooked by a cliff topped with the remains of Paleokastro, a Venetian castle (see below). A couple of kilometres on, Agia Sofera and Paralia Mati share a fine long sandy beach with a good access road.

Pylos: sight nearby

• **Paleokastro** (reached via Petrochori, 15km from Pylos, then on foot; or by boat to Porte de Junch, and then on foot) Exploration of the castle is difficult – you can just about clamber up and make a cautious circuit of the walls, but the interior is virtually inaccessible because of undergrowth, no doubt concealing unprotected wells. Beneath the castle is a cave, reached by a narrow track. Inside, stalactites resembling animal hides hang from the walls (bring a torch), giving rise to the legend that King Nestor used it as a cowshed.

It's tempting to conclude that the beach below the castle, to the north, was the one mentioned in Homer's *Odyssey*, on which Telemachus, accompanied by the goddess Athena, moored his ship when he came to visit Nestor, seeking news of his father, Odysseus. They discovered Nestor and his men sacrificing 45 jet-black bulls to Poseidon on a sandy beach, and were immediately invited to join in the subsequent banquet of roasted bull and sweet wine before being taken to Nestor's inland palace. Indeed, there are few more evocative spots for an early-evening picnic, even if you can't follow Nestor's example.

Nestor's Palace

In the *Odyssey*, after the seaside barbecue (see above), Telemachus was led by Nestor to his hilltop palace, some 10km inland. Here Telemachus was treated to ten-year-old wine before being put to bed alongside the king's son in the 'echoing porticoes'. The next day he was bathed and massaged with olive oil by Nestor's beautiful daughter before attending a feast. Appropriately enough, a decorated terracotta bath-tub is among the objects excavated here. Unfortunately, the ruins of the palace itself are less likely to convey an image of life in Telemachus's time.

It's advisable to visit the museum first, 4km away in the village of Hora. Here there are reproductions of the colourful frescoes that adorned the walls, and perspective scenes of the *megaron* (great hall) and courtyard. Having seen these, and armed with a plan (books are on sale at the entrance), it's not difficult to understand the layout. The walls now stand at about three feet. They were originally half-timbered like Tudor houses and had two storeys, but all except the stone foundations were destroyed by fire in the 12th century BC. The main palace is in the centre, consisting of 45 rooms, halls and courtyards. To the left of it is a smaller and earlier palace, and to the right a series of small rooms thought to have been either workshops or guardhouses.

There are no powerful fortifications here: the palace is entered through a series of internal courts. To the left of the main court is a pantry, with wine jars and cups, thought to have been used to offer refreshment to visitors waiting in the room next door to see Nestor. Across the hall is the famous bath, in what were probably the queen's apartments. Fragments of frescoes were discovered in her hall – mostly of animals, including life-sized lions and griffins.

Audiences with Nestor were held in the *megaron*, its central circular hearth still existing, with traces of a flame-like pattern painted around its rim. The wooden columns that stood around it were destroyed in the fire, but you can see the imprints where their stone bases stood. They probably stood at the corners of an open shaft, to let light in and the smoke out.

The floor was decorated with painted stucco tiles, all geometrical designs, except for a life-like octopus which stood in front of the throne on the right-hand wall. A channel to the side of the throne was probably used to pour offerings of wine to the gods. However, as the messy business of sacrificing and roasting animals also occurred indoors, it could well have had a more functional use – the ceremony performed by Nestor in the palace when Telemachus was there involved scattering grain, sprinkling water and wine, bleeding a heifer, and chopping up the flesh and wrapping it in fat, after which the floor was no doubt in need of thorough mopping.

The site is covered by a canopy shelter which gives some welcome shade.

Methoni

The small market town of Methoni, guarded by the immense walls of a Venetian fortress, is an attractive resort which has become popular with windsurfers (and ageing hippies). There's little sea-front focus – just two converging streets. The main street is lined with whitewashed houses, many built in a Venetian style with wrought-iron balconies, shutters, and scalloped cornices echoing the contours of the wavy red roof-tiles. Rambling banana trees, palms and exotic flowering shrubs add a touch of tropicana, and the pavement cafes on the central *plateia* are perfect for leisurely breakfasts or wine-sipping evenings. Although there are modern houses, most of them are inoffensive and many have rooms to rent. The gently shelving beach of wet, hard-packed sand is backed by a scruffy campsite and small children's playground; it's not particularly attractive, and is used by traffic going to the small fishing harbour.

There are several pleasant hotels. On the beach and overlooked by the fortress is the *Methoni Beach* (B), rather overpriced but with light and airy if somewhat small bedrooms. The communal areas are dingy. About ten minutes' walk from the beach but close to the centre of town, the compact but comfortable *Albatross* (D) has the relaxed and welcoming atmosphere typical of the resort. There are mini-bars in all rooms, and mosquito-killers and fans are provided. There's some street noise in all the front rooms, and ground-floor ones open straight off the bar.

Methoni: sight

● **The fortress** Built of creamy, crumbling stone and licked on three sides by the sea, the fortress is reached across a multi-arched bridge spanning a dry, grassy moat. It's ringed by a wobbly oval of jagged walls enclosing an overgrown precinct, dotted with the occasional bath-house and tracings of knee-high ruins, and the main attraction is balancing along the narrow ramparts for the views.

Walking between the tall circuit walls, you pass the entrances to dank, smelly underground passages, used for positioning underwater mines, designed to destroy enemy mines by explosion. As the passages open straight into the sea, exploration is not advisable.

Ostensibly a stop-over for Italian pilgrims *en route* to the Holy Land, Methoni was really used by the Venetians to keep an eye on the southern Ionian, and it and its twin fortress at Koroni on the eastern side of the Messenian peninsula were known as 'the eyes of Venice'. A number of battles were fought over it, evident from the sections of walls that have been blasted away, some tumbled down on to the rocks, others lying some 2m inside.

Dizzying flights of steps lead up to the unprotected path along the walls, punctuated by small rooms once used by soldiers for shooting enemies, and now by camera-clickers for shooting atmospheric seascapes.

A causeway runs out to a domed Turkish fort. In 1500 Methoni fell to the Turks, who ruled it until 1828; among its prisoners was Cervantes, who later wrote about his experiences in *Don Quixote*. Today the only other signs of the Turkish regime are the baths, entered through tiny doors, and with their domes perforated to let the steam escape.

Kardamili

An almost cloying perfume lingers in Kardamili; backed by a cliff spiked with cypresses, it has streets shaded by willows, black pines and rubber plants, and gardens spilling with bougainvillea and citrus trees. The fine houses, built of rubble and mortar with subtle grey cornerstones and window-frames, were once colour-washed and still glow with a pleasing peachy-pink hue. Though relatively commercialised, with the obligatory tacky 'Greek art' shop, pizzeria and snack bars, and very crowded in mid-summer, it remains idyllic out of season and makes a good base for exploring the Mani.

There's a pretty little harbour looking out to an offshore islet; it's backed by old houses, many of which have been restored and have rooms to rent. One such is the *Castle*, where small apartments have slate floors, whitewashed walls and polished wood fittings. All have a fridge, sink and gas rings.

You can swim off the rocks below the *Taverna Leila*, the nicest place at which to stay on the picturesque harbour-front. The beach is pebbly but good for swimming, and there's another small pebbly bay further north.

Stoupa

Stoupa has three golden sandy beaches, the texture of cornmeal, two of which are the best on the Mani peninsula. The village itself is just beginning to be developed, but the new apartments are in pleasant whitewashed villas with wrought-iron balconies and wooden shutters, and merge quite acceptably with the older houses. There are plenty of rooms to rent. The central bay is picturesque, with a sweep of sand and small rocks jutting out of the water, and it's backed by simple tavernas and an ice-cream parlour. There is one disco. The northern bay is also lovely – a sandy semi-circle in a sheltered cove – and there's a tiny beach to the south, an idyllic hideaway if you can get it to yourself. The friendly pension-hotel *Lefktro*, up a shady lane from the beach, is attractive and excellent value. Nearby **Agios Nikolaos** is an earthy fishing village with a scruffy sea-front and an enclosed harbour on a rocky coast. As yet there's little development, just a few rooms to rent, the best being above the *Faros* restaurant, adequate for an overnight stop. There is no beach, but just some rocks to swim off.

Beyond the village the old coast road (a mere track in places) runs along the base of sheer cliffs, passing caves and precariously overhanging rocks to a fairly large pebbly and rocky beach.

The coast road south loops and twists through hills terraced with olives and barbed with the occasional abandoned tower-house to **Nomitsi**, a small sleepy village, unremarkable except for its two churches. At the entrance, there's a tiny rubble and mortar Byzantine church inlaid with criss-cross red tiles, capped by a pepperpot dome, and with frescoes in its cave-like interior. The Metamorfossi church beyond is less appealing from the outside, but inside are some animated pillar capitals, including a pair of griffins biting their tails and, in the true spirit of Maniot aggression, a cockfight. There are also some damaged frescoes – a wizard-like Abraham with a long pointed beard, and an Annunciation, faded to a ghostly transparency.

As you approach the Inner Mani, threadbare peaks soar above the road, a sombre background to the fine views down to the coast, while the terraced tower-houses of **Langada** and the evocative roofless ruins of **Agios Nikon** add perspective to the landscape, their weathered stones harmonising with the natural rock.

The Inner Mani

The peninsula of the Inner or Deep Mani, stark, remote and bathed in the blood of a violent history, is one of the most intriguing areas of the Peloponnese to explore. The final fling of the Taygetos mountains rises bleakly from the sea, their foothills terraced with olives or snail-trailed with dry-stone walls. Until very recently the most backward part of Greece, the Mani was a stormy feudal oligarchy of powerful families who waged vendettas on one another in their fight for land. They built tall tower-houses in which they would remain holed up, firing on their neighbours during the day, and emerging only at night to bring in supplies of food and ammunition or to rebuild damaged towers.

A truce would be called at harvest time, or whenever the whole community was threatened by invaders. Fierce enough when they were fighting one another, their ruthlessness knew no bounds when they were faced with an outside enemy – one Maniot nailed the heads of all Turks killed in a battle to the walls of his tower-house until it was studded with skulls.

The vendettas ended some time after Greece won its independence from Turkey, and the area is now severely depopulated, many Maniots having left the infertile Taygetos for an easier life in the cities. Tourism has brought some much-needed income to the area, as well as a very recent asphalt road around the peninsula. Now the Greek National Tourist Organisation is beginning to convert tower-houses into traditionally furnished hotels (at present there are two, at Areopolis and Vathia; see below). The area gets very busy in August, and you may have difficulty in finding a room.

The Mani can be approached from the town of Kalamata, in

the nook between the Mani and Messenian peninsulas, or from Githion at the head of the east coast. Both the coast road and that running across the high moorland between Githion and Areopolis are good, but there are occasional rough tracks running off towards the coast.

Areopolis, the city of Ares, god of war, could hardly be a more appropriate name for the capital of the vendetta-obsessed Maniots. It's a convenient place at which to stop over, although the modern town which has grown up around the old Maniot capital is unattractive, and the main square is surrounded by modern concrete buildings. Many of its old tower-houses, at the end of the tawdry main street, have been spoiled by over-enthusiastic restoration, and their rubble pointed by garish salmon-pink mortar. One which has been subtly restored (by the Greek National Tourist Organisation) is now the *Tower Hotel*. The interior is whitewashed, the floors and furniture are made of dark polished wood, and the upholstery woven to traditional designs. There's also a lower second block with a flat roof for sun-soaking. The cathedral, with its rough apricot-tinged creamy stone and tapering arcaded tower, is the most interesting building – though it was undoubtedly more so when Patrick Leigh Fermor (*Mani, Travels in the Southern Peloponnese*) visited, when it was a riotous triumph of bad taste, with mauve pilasters supporting apricot panels, and the apse moulding painted bright yellow. However, the carvings remain entertaining – there are pudgy-eyed and broadly grinning suns, stiff-armed warriors holding their weapons out at either side and riders superimposed on top of their horses rather than sitting astride them – all looking as if they'd been created by primary school children.

Just to the north of Areopolis is the sheltered **Limenion Gulf**, where Napoleon stopped off on the way to invade Egypt. On the north side, the pebbly beach is backed by a bare knuckle-duster of a mountain, Pentadaktilos (it means five-fingered), and there's a fish taverna and a few rooms to rent. On the other side of the bay is **Limeni**, the tiny port of Areopolis. The village of **Vitylo**, once important as the gateway between the Inner and Outer Mani, is now a sleepy place; it's divided by a ravine, on one side of which are splendid walls – the remains of a huge 17th-century Turkish frontier post.

On the coast just south of Areopolis in the red rocks of the horseshoe cove at **Pirgos Dirou** is a network of sea caves, the single most popular sight of the Mani. Understandably so, as you are rowed by boat into an enchanting underworld kingdom in which the dark glassy waters perfectly mirror the twists and folds of stalactites. A little of the magic is lost when it's busy –

so if you're there in high season try to go early (they open at 8a.m.). Outside the caves there's just a beach of pebbles and small rocks, a self-service restaurant and a small concrete hotel, so you're unlikely to want to linger.

Half-way between Areopolis and the southern headland, an easily missed side road leads down to the small fishing village of **Mezapos**, flanked by tiny coves and dramatic sandstone cliffs, sea-gouged into jagged, tooth-like strata. Across the bay is **Tigani**, literally 'the frying-pan', a white spit of rock leading to a cliff capped with the barely visible ruins of the medieval castle of Maina. A fisherman may be prepared to convey you by boat. Alternatively, drive back to the main road and take the small turnoff to Stavri. The path starts below the church at Agia Kyriaki; though it's only about 2km to the castle, don't attempt it without strong boots, as the 'handle' of Tigani is spiked with sharp jags of rock. Among the medieval fortifications are the ruins of a large Byzantine church, possibly one of the earliest Christian basilicas, dating from the 5th or 6th century; and in the south-west corner is a stretch of Bronze Age cyclopean wall. As if the place weren't dramatic enough, with the sheer cliffs below what's left of the castle walls plunging into the sea, there's a legend to add extra spice. When inhabited by a solitary princess, the castle was invaded by a king, and the princess, rather than fall into his clutches, mounted her white horse and leapt into the sea. Fortunately for her, the horse was a strong swimmer and bore her safely to land.

A short distance away, on a hill overlooking Tigani, lies the 12th-century church of **Episkopi**, which contains some fine frescoes. East of the road to Gerolimena lie almost deserted villages of tower-houses; **Kita** in its heyday had a population of almost 100 families; **Kato Boulari** retains one of the oldest towers (17th century) and **Ano Boulari** has a domed 11th-century cruciform church with a 12th-century cycle of frescoes.

The small southern port of **Gerolimena** is a desolate huddle of dilapidated houses below an eerie grey flat-topped cliff, strangely veined, cracked and scored. There are two very basic tavernas, a *kafeneion* and a couple of very simple pensions. Nine kilometres away, **Vathia** is the most dramatically sited of the Maniot villages, standing atop a bare hill, its tight cluster of towers lancing the sky. The smashed towertops are due not to natural decay but to the fact that the most prestigious way of scoring a point off an enemy was to smash his marble slab roof. For this reason it was a distinct advantage to have a tower taller than one's neighbours – and during sieges the nights were used to add extra storeys. Vathia today has been largely abandoned, but there's no more atmospheric place at which to stay while touring the Mani since the conversion of seven tower-houses into a hotel (*Vathia*), where traditional furnishings are combined with modern comforts. The entrance hall, stone flagged and beamed, is dominated by a massive olive grinder and oil-press. The rooms are all different, some still with ancient beehive fireplaces and a third bed in an open-sided loft reached up a ladder (although there's a barrier, it's not suitable for small children).

A short drive from Vathia are the two dark sandy grass-tufted beaches of **Marmari**, separated by a gloomy promontory. At this point it's only about 2km across the peninsula to the depressing village on the beautiful natural harbour of **Porto Kayio** on the east coast.

Rather than go to Porto Kayio, take the rough track which branches off the road as it reaches its highest point. The track is just about drivable until you reach a cemetery on a hill. From here it's a (tough) hour's walk to **Cape Tenaro** (or **Matapan**), the southernmost tip of mainland Greece and legendary entrance to Hades, with nothing but sea between it and Africa. The last part of the walk, along a narrow stony wave-lashed tongue, should not be attempted in the dark. In March 1941 there was a famous battle off the cape in which four Italian ships were sunk or damaged by a British contingent.

On a gloomy moor towards the east of the peninsula lies the gaunt village of **Lagia**. Four families lived here, each with their own settlement, complete with church, and the wrecked state of many of the tower-houses is the result of a 40-year siege which ravaged the village in the 18th century. Inner Mani's only doctor lived here, assured of a steady income from the numerous casualties from Lagia's vendettas, and supplementing it in quiet moments by travelling around to other war-wracked villages. His notebook survives, with details like 'stiletto through foot', 'rock on head', and 'bullets (2) in thigh, straight through', building a vivid picture of life in war-torn Mani. If the place appeals to you, there are very basic rooms above the primitive taverna (the lavatory doubles as outhouse and kennel) and the tourist organisation is in the process of converting tower-houses into a hotel like that at Vathia.

On the east side of the peninsula, **Kotronas** is a moderately attractive fishing village, sheltered by a long headland with a surrounding landscape of olive trees, cypresses and fig trees. The small bay has a pebble beach; though the water is usually clear, it's occasionally marred by oil from the fishing-boats moored at the quay. Its pension can be a useful place for a stop-over if it's too late to drive back across the Taygetos to Areopolis.

Gythion

A small seaside town and port, Gythion, though the nominal capital of the Mani, is a world away from the rest of the peninsula. The glassy harbour is overlooked by elegant pastel-washed town houses, their façades enlivened by iron balconies intricately wrought into flowers, silhouettes and winged horses, giving the sea-front an air of faded romanticism. This is enhanced by the legend that it was on the islet offshore that Paris and Helen spent their first night of illicit passion – or, as Homer more eloquently put it, 'on Kranae lay upon a couch of love'.

Sadly, the romance is only skin deep. Much of the inner town is undistinguished and modern, and the picturesque fish tavernas to the west of the sea-front are punctuated with greasy-windowed kebab shops. Nor is Gythion at its best in mid-summer when the sea-front is invaded by frenetic traffic, although you can escape by climbing up the stepped streets through the old town at the back, up the hill of Koumaro, for views of the bay over the red-tiled rooftops.

The islet, connected to the mainland by a causeway, is at its best at sunset (or sunrise if you can make it) when the white chapel and fairy-tale fortress are suffused with golden light, against the violet sea and the silhouettes of palms, cypresses and black pines. In the harsher light of day it's rather desolate, and distinctly unromantic.

There's a poor public pay beach in town, best avoided in favour of the long, fine gravel beach to the west at **Mavrovounia**: the village itself, on a hill away from the coast, is fairly developed, but quite pretty, with a number of old buildings and tower-houses. To the east of Gythion are more beaches, none of them particularly appealing, and beyond is a series of small coves, reached by tracks from the main road.

Gythion is suitable for a one-night stop, giving you time to wander and spend a long evening in a fish taverna, but not long enough to become disillusioned.

The *Gythion* (A) is a small, smart hotel, with just seven rooms, all overlooking the bay, which offers the rare treat of breakfast with hot toast and coffee. Tke *Kranae* (D) is an elegantly fading almost Italianate *palazzo* with a splendid marble staircase and beautiful tiled halls enhanced by opulent plants. Bedrooms are large and shabby.

Monemvasia

A bald red bulk of rock looms up from the sea, connected to the mainland by a narrow causeway, concealing the medieval town of Monemvasia on its seaward side. Once a Byzantine trading post, it fell to the Venetians, who exported its famous Malmsey wine throughout Europe, and then fell to the Turks. Besieged by the Greeks in the War of Independence – when the inhabitants were said to have eaten rats and, legend has it, even children – the city was eventually invaded, the population brutally massacred, and the town abandoned and left to fall into ruin. Restoration and re-population have recently begun – cafes, tavernas and souvenir shops lurk behind low-arched doors, and there are flats for sale in the carefully rebuilt houses.

Driving across the causeway, you eventually reach the town walls, which climb the rock with stepped turrets. Cars can go no further. The town gate, wide enough for one donkey or a fat tourist, leads on to the barely wider main street. Donkeys and mules are still the only form of transport, and seeing them with their panniers full of sand or cement adds to the medieval atmosphere. Nor do the tourist shops and tavernas jar too much – indeed, the bustle around them makes it easier to picture Monemvasia in its heyday.

Although there are restored and over-enthusiastically whitewashed churches, and a mosque housing a (rarely open) museum, the greatest pleasures come from unexpected discoveries. As you wander through the ruins, you suddenly realise a bulge is an apse, and that behind it there's the shell of a church, or you lose yourself in a steep dark alleyway until you emerge into the sun, with a sudden view over the dappled red roofs to the sea.

The climb up the steep rocky track to the upper town is well worth while. After going through a series of tunnel-like vaults, you emerge on the desolate wind-swept summit. It's dominated by the dome of Agia Sophia, a large church fronted by what looks like part of a Venetian *palazzo*, with Renaissance windows and chunkily vaulted porticoes. Inside, the dome is a swirl of red tiles, and a benign Pantokrator gazes down from above the iconostasis; the wind whistles around, flickering the candles and reminding you of the wild bleakness outside.

A confusion of ruins sprawls across the clifftop and out of sight, giving you an idea of the size of medieval Monemvasia. Identifying most of the ruins is impossible, but if you hunt around you'll find a vast network of water cisterns, and if this doesn't appeal there are dizzying views from the unprotected cliff edge.

Back in the medieval town, the *Malvasia* (A and B) is as yet the only hotel (no advance bookings taken). Accommodation is in traditionally furnished rooms in tastefully restored Byzantine buildings. There are also a few rooms to let (details of these at

Angelo's bar) in restored Byzantine buildings – but these are extremely popular, and you need to arrive early to be sure of finding somewhere.

If you're stuck, the rapidly expanding and wholly unremarkable village of **Gefira** on the mainland has hotels and rooms to rent. By the small fishing harbour, pavement cafes offer breakfast or cocktails; you can turn your back on the resort and look out to sea. Alternatively, you could book an apartment on the beach of **Epidavros Limera**, a few kilometres north: the *Villas Doukas* complex is set in a large garden with views over the bougainvillea and through palm trees to the beach.

Geraki and Mount Parnon

Geraki is an easy 40km drive from Sparta, but the more interesting approach is from Molai in the south, about 25km from Monemvasia. A rarely used but good road passes through a virtually monochromatic landscape of dull-hued bushes, grey rock and mountains so smooth they resemble petrified sand-dunes.

Modern Geraki is a bustling village, its early-20th-century houses stuccoed and balconied; there's no accommodation for tourists. Below it the road crosses a red stony plain, studded with grids of olive trees, and then penetrates a ravine pocked with tiny caves.

About half an hour south-east of modern Geraki (on a rough hill road) are the remains of **medieval Geraki**, its ruined houses and 15 small Byzantine churches clustered beneath the fortified summit of a desolate hill. Some of the churches are mere shells, sheltering traces of frescoed saints, their faces washed away by the rain; others are intact. It's worth obtaining the keys – by asking for the *phylax* (caretaker) at the cafes in modern Geraki. Up an easy path the 13th-century *kastro* has awesome views of the Parnon and Taygetos ranges. One of the main attractions, however, is the rare opportunity of having a site to yourself, and the feeling of discovery as you crawl into the tiny shooting positions in the fortress, or clamber up its walls.

The drive from modern Geraki across sombre **Mount Parnon** to the handsome old town of Leonidion (see page 177) is not for the faint-hearted. Nor is it for anyone concerned about wear and tear on their car.

As the road begins to climb up through severe hills to the summit (1639m), it disintegrates into a rutted track (sections are in the process of being asphalted) before cutting through a forest of fir trees. Often eerily swathed in clouds, its

161

resemblance to the enchanted forests of fairy tales is enhanced by the fact that wolves are said to lurk within it. Beyond the isolated village of Kosmas, the vertiginous descent begins: a seemingly endless series of hairpin bends snakes down what feels like a bottomless ravine dominated by a white limestone crag and a glowering cliff. Stretches of the road are extremely rough, and in places massive chunks of road have simply crumbled away down the gorge. In addition, the ruts and rubble have an alarming tendency to jolt the car towards the sheer, unprotected drops. When you eventually reach the bottom, the road cuts through a long gorge following a seasonal river. The brooding cliffs and crags close in behind you, and, unbelievably, if you look up you'll see a white monastery, guarded by a crucifix, clamped to the lip of the ravine.

Sparta (Sparti) and Mistra

Modern Sparta was laid out on a grid plan in the 19th century, and holds little attraction for tourists other than the fact that there is plentiful accommodation – in simple hotels – and a lively and elegant evening *volta* on the main square. Sparta makes a good base for visiting Mistra, where there is only one hotel.

Ancient Sparta survives only in name and reputation. This is not surprising, because the city-state had no great buildings and wasn't even walled, as the Spartans rightly assumed that no one would dare invade them. The Athenian historian Thucydides conjectured: 'Suppose, for example, that the city of Sparta were to become deserted and that only the temples and foundations of buildings remained. I think that future generations would, as time passed, find it very difficult to believe that the place had really been as powerful as it was represented to be. Yet the Spartans occupy two-fifths of the Peloponnese and stand at the head not only of the whole Peloponnese itself but also of numerous allies beyond its frontiers.'

The reputation of this ruthlessly militaristic civilisation is still chilling – possibly because it isn't difficult to find modern parallels. The society was structured around the determination of a dominant minority of 'true' Spartans to live a purely militaristic life, leaving other labour to a vast population of serfs, known as Helots. Consequently, it was considered vital that true Spartans were strong, disciplined and above all unquestioningly obedient. To this end weak and deformed children were left to die on the Taygetos mountains, and boys sent away to training camp at the age of seven. Here they would stay for 13 years, submitted to harsh discipline, endless drills and brutal competitions. At 20 they would join either the army or the secret police, whose job was to spy on the Helots, killing any they thought might become dangerous. Marriage was permitted, but the men had to spend most of their time at the barracks, eating in a public canteen. One visitor, after dining in Sparta, said that he now understood why the Spartans didn't fear death.

There is one (scant) relic of Sparta's brutality, the **sanctuary of Artemis Orthia**, just off the road to Tripolis. Here boys had to undergo endurance tests, being flogged in honour of Artemis. Pausanias, writer of a guidebook for Roman tourists, reckoned that the goddess was satisfied only when the altar was splashed with blood. In fact, there's no evidence that the Ancient Spartans went to this extreme, although their Roman descendants did, building the gallery, which dominates the site, for blood-thirsty spectators.

Eight kilometres west of Sparta lies the Byzantine city of **Mistra**, enclosed by ramparts and climbing up a steep rocky outcrop of Mount Taygetos. The site is startlingly beautiful, the views from the Frankish castle which crowns it magnificent, and the ruined city itself a wonderfully atmospheric place. But the main reason to visit it is to see some of the finest examples of 14th- and 15th-century Byzantine architecture and wall-paintings in Greece. Mistra was the last outpost of the Byzantine Empire, continuing to flourish as late as the 15th century, while Constantinople was in ruins. It began life not as a Byzantine possession but as a Frankish fortress, built in the early 13th century by William de Villehardouin, Prince of Morea (as the Peloponnese was known). Shortly afterwards he was ousted by the army of the Byzantine emperor and imprisoned for three years until he agreed to hand over Mistra, Monemvasia and the fortress of Maina in the Mani. Mistra then became the seat of Morea, ruled by relatives of the emperor. Under these 'despots', Mistra became a cultural as well as a political centre. Intellectuals and artists flocked here, and Mistran philosophers went as teachers to Italy, where they had a considerable influence on the Renaissance, introducing the works of Plato to the courts of Florence.

In the late 17th century, Mistra enjoyed a second period of prosperity, when its population grew to 42,000. Later, under the Turks, it declined and was largely abandoned. Reconstruction and restoration began late – too late for many of the buildings – and still continues.

Steep overgrown paths wind up and around the maze of ruined houses, palaces and churches to the fortress. The signposting is not very good, and it's advisable to buy a plan at the entrance.

To see it all you'll need at least three hours, but you could easily be seduced into staying a full day. If you go in mid-summer try to make an early start to avoid the worst of the heat and the crowds and be sure to take plenty to drink, as it's a long, steep climb to the top.

Mistra: highlights

• **Metropolitan** This 13th-century church was Mistra's cathedral, and it was here that the last emperor of Byzantium, Constantine XI, is said to have been crowned in 1449. Set into the floor in front of the iconostasis is a marble plaque with the double-headed Byzantine eagle, reputed to be the spot on which Constantine stood during the ceremony.

Of more interest, however, are the frescoes. They are not the loveliest in Mistra, but they clearly show the development of its artists. The scenes from the life and death of Saint Dimitrios in the north aisle are stiff, symmetrical and rather lifeless, whereas those on the opposite wall, illustrating the life of the Virgin and Miracles of Christ, are more delicate and realistic.

The old **Bishop's Palace,** close to the church, now houses a small **museum.** There are fragments of frescoes, icons, jewels and some beautifully carved column capitals.

• **Brontocheion** This monastic complex contains two churches, the most interesting of which is the **Afentiko** or **Odigitria.** The walls of this five-domed basilica were faced with marble, upon which murals were painted. Although they are poorly preserved, enough remains of them for you to be able to see the subtle use of colour, the fluid lines of the bodies and their flowing gowns, and the expressions on the faces. One of the most striking is the Healing of the Paralytic. This elegant monastic church, founded in the 14th century and rebuilt in the 15th, houses some of Mistra's latest frescoes. The best are the scenes from Christ's life, in the vault. They are sophisticated and assured, with the artist using perspective and colour to enhance the drama. In the Annunciation the angel appears to be suspended in mid-air, and in the Raising of Lazarus the yellow background creates an almost surrealistic mood. There's also a nice human touch – for as one attendant prepares to unravel Lazarus's mummy-like winding sheet, another buries his face in his sleeve, as if nauseated by the odour of death.

• **Perivleptos** A tiny 13th-century monastery, altered in the 14th century, whose elongated triple apse and fleur-de-lys decorations show the influence of French Romanesque architecture. Its 14th-century frescoes are subtly coloured and full of movement and details. The best are in the vaults around the dome from which a Christ Pantokrator looks down. The loveliest and most atmospheric of these scenes from the life of Christ is the Nativity, which is actually enhanced by the fact that it has faded. The Virgin reclines, deep in thought in a pale, almost translucent cave, watched by the shadowy figures of angels.

• **Palace of the Despots** Under the Byzantine emperors the area of the Peloponnese over which Mistra held sway was known as the Despotate of the Morea, and it was in this palace that the despots lived. It's not hard to imagine how forbidding it looked, for the L-shaped ruins are massive and extensive, and many of the walls still stand to four storeys.

• **Agia Sophia** This was used as the palace chapel, and its frescoes have been well preserved thanks to the Turks, who daubed them with whitewash when they converted the church into a mosque.

• **Kastro** It's a long, steep climb up to the fortifications of the *kastro*, which crown and guard the town. It is, however, worth it for the bird's-eye view of the town and the surrounding countryside.

Langadha Pass

The highest, wildest road in the Peloponnese traverses the Taygetos ridge between Sparta and Kalamata via the Langadha Pass, constructed in 1940. It's an exhilarating drive in fine weather, perilous in bad; the road is subject to landslides after winter rains.

A few miles from Sparta on the way to the village of Trypi, there is a fine view south across to Mistra; then the road begins to climb, and after Trypi enters the Langadha Gorge. Traditionally, the great fissures in the rocks on the right (called the Kalandes) are where the Spartans hurled down criminals and unwanted infants. The road lies low in the gorge, twisting upwards between towering limestone cliffs, and the river below is hidden in trees and shrubs. Pine forest begins, and somewhere at the summit, over 1500m up, you cross the watershed between the rivers Eurotas and Nedon.

The road stays high as it enters Messenia, with superb views of the Taygetos peaks to the north and south. As the descent begins, convenient bends hold viewpoint car-parks, rustic souvenir stalls and pine-cone picnic-tables. Views west over the fertile plains justify the ages-old descriptions of this region – the garden of Greece, *Graecia felix*. Then the road zigzags down the Nedon valley, a ravine of shrub-scattered limestone, to Kalamata.

Ancient Messene

About 23km north-west of Messini, and an easy day-trip from Pilos, lies the site of Ancient Messene – the great and troublesome rival of Sparta. Unlike its famous enemy, Messene relied on more than the strength and discipline of its army to defend itself: it was surrounded by a 9km circuit of immense walls, whose surviving sections and defensive gates remain its most striking features. The Arcadian Gate (through which the road from Meligala to the village of Mavromati passes) is particularly ingenious, consisting of an outer gate flanked by square towers from which invaders could be shot at, separated from the inner gate by a circular courtyard which would probably have been filled with more soldiers ready to converge on any enemy who managed to get through.

Just outside Mavromati village, a steep path leads down through olive groves to the archaeological dig of a presumed sanctuary to Asklepios, the god of healing, and a small restored theatre. The site is generally uncrowded.

From the Laconian Gate, a path ascends the summit of **Mount Ithome**, where there are the remains of a temple and fortified citadel.

Arcadia and the North

Very few coastal resorts of the northern Peloponnese are worth more than a brief visit. The northern (pebbly) shores along the **Corinthian Gulf** front an almost continuous sprawl of towns, villages and resorts. Although already heavily developed, there's still a lot of new building going on. The scenery, with views over the gulf to the mainland on the other side, is best seen from the fast toll road which avoids the narrow and traffic-laden 'old road' and bypasses the generally unattractive resorts. The eastern side of the gulf is fairly flat; towards the west, the road cuts into the increasingly steep and attractive hills. **Xilokastro** is the nearest to a proper resort of all the gulf towns and villages, and is popular with Athenians; there's a pebbly beach, cafes along the sea-front, and lots of holiday homes.

Patras is the third-largest city in Greece. Set on a wide plain, it's a bustling modern city and port, with straight arcaded streets and several squares, and heavy traffic from tourists coming off the car-ferry from Brindisi. The water-front is lively, there's good shopping and ample accommodation; but most visitors are just passing through.

To the west, the coastal plain continues with little relief; villages and light-industrial towns are often at some distance from the sea, which is reached by numerous slip-roads. There's a lot of market gardening, with vegetables, bamboo and vineyards for both wine and currants – in August you can see grapes for these being spread to dry on specially prepared earth patches.

The vast stretches of soft sand on the west coast, though somewhat exposed, rank among the best beaches of the Peloponnese. Many of the coastal villages are just beginning to develop, with a few rooms to rent or a couple of small hotels. The sea is reasonably clean, but there are few beaches which are not scattered with rubbish – much of it from free-campers. The currents of the open sea are strong, and the sand often shelves steeply.

Kalogria has a good beach – wide, gently shelving sands which stretch for miles. It's popular with Greek holiday-makers, but you can have solitude if you're prepared to walk. Though it's not really a resort, there are a couple of hotels and tavernas. The landscape is flat, but spiced up by two squat and bare limestone cliffs and shady pine groves.

On the western headland of the Peloponnese lies the long, broad sweep of gently shelving fine sand at **Loutra Killinis**. There is no village, just a spa-complex, two ugly Xenia hotels and a campsite set back from the beach among tall, shady pine groves. The southern end – where the campsite meets the beach – gets very crowded, as does the stretch to the north in front of the massive Robinson Club bungalow complex. However, if you're prepared to walk you can find a spot to yourself. Don't confuse the spa with the dingy port of **Killini**, further north, from where ferries go to Zante or Cephalonia.

If you have your own transport, you could take a room in the more genuine Greek surroundings of the village of **Kastro**, 4km north, which is spread below the solitary Frankish fortress of **Chlemoutsi**, also known as Kastel Tornese.

Further south, **Katakalo** is a fishing village with a very commercialised water-front where large cruise-liners disgorge tourists for their excursion to Olympia; it's not an attractive place for an overnight stop. Neither is the resort of **Loutra Kaïafa**, almost equidistant from the ancient site, although this does have a seemingly endless, fine sandy beach (reached by crossing a railway line and scrambling over sand-dunes and through bushes). The beach is exposed, and the currents strong, but it's easy to find solitude; as ever, the beauty is marred by litter. Tucked away behind is an eerie spa-complex, set on a sulphurous lagoon named, like the beach, after the evil high priest of Judah, Caiaphas, who is said to have left the rotten-egg stench behind him after bathing in its waters. You can avoid the smell by staying in one of the houses with rooms to rent along the road.

The **coast of Arcadia**, along the Argolic Gulf, offers more interest than the other northern coasts. Though the beaches are not exceptional – small, narrow and pebbly south of Paralia Tirou, miniature sandy coves to the north – and the high-season crowds overwhelming for their size, out of season they are ideal for a swim and a picnic while touring. The road between Argos and the handsome old town of LEONIDION clings to the coast of the Argolic Gulf, overlooked by hills terraced with olive trees, and with views across the gulf to the Argolid peninsula and the island of Spetses. Behind are the steep mountains of the isolated Parnon range.

The delights of the northern Peloponnese are inland: in the high mountains which encircle Arcadia, and in the remote UPLANDS OF ARCADIA itself – setting for many an English poem, though few poets ever visited it. Despite a recent expensive programme of road-building, many tourists confine their experience of inland Peloponnese to a visit to the famous site of OLYMPIA and perhaps the temple at BASSAE – a pity, as there are plenty of medieval hilltop villages suitable for a one-night stop and the scenery is in places spectacular.

Olympia

Shaded by pines and olive trees, and overlooked by the wooded hill of Kronos, the ruins of Olympia attract over a million visitors each year. Most come because of its modern significance, and indeed it's the remains of the sports facilities – the arena with its running-track, and the ruined colonnades where the athletes practised – which are easiest to imagine peopled with Ancient Greek athletes and spectators. But Ancient Olympia was not only a sports complex: it was also a sanctuary dedicated to Zeus, and it was in his honour that the Olympiads were staged. The centre of the site is scattered with ruined temples, and sitting among the toppled columns of the massive temple of Zeus it's easy to overestimate the spiritual significance of the games. In fact, they were deeply political, for there was no better advertisement of a state's strength than to have a victory at Olympia. Indeed, the king of Sparta used to fight with an olive-crowned Olympic hero by his side. Given the political and social prestige, it's not surprising that some athletes were tempted to cheat. The easiest way to do so was to bribe an opponent to lose, and by 338BC it had become enough of a problem for fines and bans to be introduced. The money collected was used to pay for statues of Zeus, erected at the entrance of the stadium to deter any potential offenders, inscribed with warnings like 'the Olympic victor must win not with money, but with fleetness of foot and strength of body'. Victors were also permitted to erect a statue (with their own features if they'd won three events); these stood in the *altis*, the ground dedicated to Zeus in the centre of the site, and by Roman times there were over 3000.

Under the Christian emperor Theodosius I, the Olympic Games were banned along with all other pagan festivals, and later Christians burned the sanctuary of Zeus and erected a church. The site was further damaged by a series of earthquakes and landslides, and was finally buried in mud and stones when the river overflowed, where it lay until excavations began in the 19th century.

It's advisable to buy a guidebook before going around the site. Those by Yalouris or Photinos are well translated, and have photographs of the museum's reconstructed model of Olympia, as well as clear plans.

Olympia: highlights

• **Gymnasium** A large open-air quadrangle once surrounded by colonnades, of which only the column stumps of two sides have survived. Athletes and runners usually trained in the quadrangle, but when the weather was hot or rainy they would use the covered colonnades.

• **Palaestra** A similar building, used by wrestlers and boxers, but which served also as a meeting-place for philosophers and rhetoricians, who would come to Olympia to entertain the crowds with their verbal athleticism. The columns stand to a greater height, and a plunge-bath and rooms with stone benches and baths survive behind the colonnades. Here the athletes would be massaged with oil for training. Afterwards the oil was removed with sand and they would take a cold bath.

• **Workshop of Pheidias** Here Pheidias, one of the greatest sculptors of classical Greece, created a gold and ivory (chryselephantine) statue of Zeus, one of the Seven Wonders of the Ancient World. The workshop was exactly the same size as the *cella* within the temple of Zeus for which the statue was made, but was destroyed in the mid-5th century by Christians, who built a church in its place, retaining the original proportions. Tools, ivory chips, terracotta moulds used to form the gold parts of the statue, and even a cup with Pheidias's name on it have been discovered, and are now kept in the museum.

• **Temple of Zeus** The stepped platform rises up from a chaos of fractured blocks and column discs toppled like dominoes. There are plans to rebuild it, but even now its size is impressive, and the destruction sobering.

Here the winners were presented with their olive wreaths from a gold and ivory table, watched over by Pheidias's statue of Zeus. Seven times life size, the god sat on a throne of ebony and ivory encrusted with gold and precious stones. Draped in a golden cloak inlaid with lilies and animals, he held a gold and ivory statue of Victory in his right hand and a spray of blossom in his left.

The statue was more than merely magnificent. Cicero thought it had been modelled not on a human but on an ideal beauty visible only to the inner eye. Strabo, however, was less reverent, and reckoned that Pheidias had got the proportions wrong because if the god stood up he would knock the temple roof off with his head. Caligula liked the statue so much he wanted to transport it to Rome and replace Zeus's head with his own, but failed because every time his agents approached the statue it burst out laughing. Theodosius later took it to Constantinople, where it was destroyed in a fire in AD475.

• **Stadium** Walking (or running, if the mood takes you) through a vaulted tunnel, you emerge into the shallow oval arena and the spectacle of tourists playing at being Ancient Greek athletes. Panting along the running-track for the benefit of their camera-clicking mates, they bear little resemblance to athletes, ancient or modern, but fortunately, unlike the Olympian heroes, they usually remain clothed.

• **Museum** A visit to the museum adds considerably to your understanding of Olympia. There are models of how Olympia looked in its prime, and very rich collections from the site assembled chronologically. In the huge central hall the **pediments from the temple of Zeus** have been reconstructed. Though there are many gaps, and the sculptured fragments are held together with struts and wires, they are arranged in their original triangles, and give an idea of the temple's former splendour. On the eastern pediment the central figure is Zeus, flanked by the *dramatis personae* of the Pelops story just before the chariot-race; in the western composition a serene Apollo watches riotous struggles between Lapiths and Centaurs.

THE OLYMPIC GAMES

Origins

For over 1000 years, from 776BC to AD393, the Olympic Games were a four-yearly festival. Greek chronology began at the fixed point of the first official **Olympiad**, *while unofficially the games were much older, and overlapping myth and legend account for their origin. The hero Herakles is credited with clearing a grove for a sanctuary of Zeus, and pacing out the distance of the foot-race, in celebration after his Labour of cleansing the Augean Stables by means of the local river Alpheios. Another sanctuary here belongs to Pelops, whose funeral games may have been the earliest at Olympia. Pelops came to be ruler of some of the area now named after him by marrying Hippodameia, daughter of King Oinamos of Pisa (in Elis). He first had to defeat Oinamos in a chariot-race, and since Oinamos had already killed off a dozen losers, Pelops bribed the king's charioteer. A wheel of the royal chariot duly came off, and Pelops won the race and the bride. He subsequently killed not only Oinamos but also the charioteer – whose dying curse lay on generations of Pelops' descendants, including Agamemnon.*

The truce and the rules

In 776BC, as a means recommended by the Oracle at Delphi of counteracting the constant wars between Greek states, King Iphitos of Elis revived the games; and the half-legendary Lycurgus, lawgiver of Sparta, guaranteed the **Olympic Truce**, *the Ekecheiria. No state participating in the games might for any reason take up arms; the truce, almost universally observed, was extended from a month to two*

Outstanding among other statuary is the famous marble **Hermes** by Praxiteles, epitome of Classical grace, and from the Archaic period the vigorous terracotta figure of **Zeus abducting Ganymede**.

The modern **village of Olympia** exists purely to service the tourists who visit the site. It's very commercialised, but has a range of hotels and is a convenient base, particularly if you wish to visit the site very early in order to avoid the crowds of day-trippers. The *Hotel* SPAP (A), though closed for restoration as we went to press, is a spacious 19th-century establishment with some charm, the *Hercules* (C) a clean and bright little pension. On a hill above the village, next to a campsite, the new *Europa* has gleaming marble floors, tasteful furnishings, a swimming-pool and tennis court, and is an attractive place for those wanting more than a one-night base.

---

and then to three for the protection of visitors coming from increasingly far away to the oldest and greatest Panhellenic athletics festival. Other games followed – the 'circuit' took in the Nemean Games, the Isthmian Games at Corinth, and the Pythian Games at Delphi itself in honour of Apollo.

The Olympics were in the charge of ten important officials *called Hellanodikai (judges of the Greeks). They were umpires and judges in all events, and punished infringements; they supervised the athletes' compulsory month of training in Elis; and as well as fitness to perform they checked credentials. Competitors had to be free men, of Greek (and later Roman) descent. Women, though they had a small separate festival of their own, could not compete at these games. No married woman might even attend them. One who managed it came disguised as her boxing son's trainer: in excitement when he won she leapt across a barrier, revealing all, and after that trainers too had to appear naked to be registered. Athletes of course were naked while training and competing.*

The events

The longest-established events were the **foot-races**, *first short (the length of the stadium), then double-length, then long-distance (24 lengths). The starting position was not the modern crouch but almost the attitude of a diver, with both arms forward and knees slightly bent, toes gripping grooves in the marble starting-sills. (In the earliest years, 'starting from scratch' meant a line in the dust.) A herald's trumpet sounded the off, and after each race a herald proclaimed the name of the victor, his father and his home state. To come second or third meant nothing at all. The victor's reward was a simple crown of*

Bassae (Vasses) and Andritsaena

On a remote mountainside scored with deep ravines, the huge temple of Apollo Epikourios at Bassae, its grey limestone echoing the bleakness of its rocky surroundings, is one of the best-preserved temples in Greece. Built in the Doric style around 450BC as a dedication to Apollo Epikourios (the succourer) after the local population had been saved from a pestilence, it retains an almost complete colonnade. The fine marble internal frieze was removed by a group of archaeologists in the 19th century; the frieze was later sold at auction and acquired by the British government and can now be seen at the British Museum in London.

The precariously balanced cuboid blocks of the *cella* originally

---

THE OLYMPIC GAMES continued

olive; to the winner of the short foot-race went the honour of lending his name to the whole Olympiad. The cross-country 'marathon' run today did not exist at any Greek games; nor did the ancient Olympics include a relay-race with a lighted torch, though it was a curtain-raiser at some other festivals.

The five events of the **pentathlon** *were discus, jumping, javelin, running and wrestling, in that order in a single afternoon. Its versatile athletes were considered rather the inferiors of the specialists, but praised for their particularly supple bodies with no unsightly overdevelopment. Discus throwing was a graceful business, apparently achieving no great distances by modern standards; the javelin had a leather thong around the shaft, which unwound in flight to give spin and steadiness. Jumping was long, not high, and competitors were skilled at swinging 'jumping-weights' to achieve extra impetus.*

Wrestling *had no weight distinctions – the bigger man tended to win. Its most popular hero was Milo from Croton, who won five Olympic victories and twenty-five more around the 'circuit', and whose exploits included downing nine litres of wine for a bet. The* **pankration** *was a form of all-in wrestling, held on ground watered to make it muddy. Gouging and biting were forbidden, but practically everything else was legal – 'Fingertips Sostratos' systematically broke his opponents' fingers – and the event was a great crowd-puller.* **Boxing,** *however, was considered more dangerous; the bloodthirsty contest went on until the loser either admitted defeat or was knocked senseless, and 'gloves' progressed from leather thongs wrapped around the knuckles to the Roman version weighted with iron.*

The hippodrome's **chariot-races** *used teams of two to four horses over distances up to eight miles, with tight turns in each lap. As well as individuals, horse-breeding states might sponsor a chariot for the*

protected a statue of Apollo which faced towards the sunrise, through an opening in the east side. The exceptional length and the north–south orientation of the temple are unusual.

Under restoration at present – work started only in 1975 when the building was in imminent danger of collapse – the temple is covered by a surrealistic white plastic marquee, which hides the classic view of it from the hillside above.

For the temple to have its full impact, you need to see it alone. Until recently this was no problem, but now it's found its way on to the itinerary of excursion organisers, so you may have to wait until a coach-party has had its allotted time at the site.

Bassae can be reached on a good tarmac road from Andritsaena (see below) and incorporated into a round trip with

---

excellent propaganda of a victory. Charioteers were usually employees – though owners received the glory, it was honourable but foolhardy in this hazardous sport to drive your own team. **Horse-races** *followed the chariot-racing over well-rutted ground. Since saddle and stirrups were yet to be invented, jockeys had an even more exciting time than charioteers.*

The Olympic spirit

All Greek athletic activity was a preparation for fitness in battle – leaping rough terrain, physical combat, hurling weapons, managing a war-chariot. When Thermistocles, victor over the Persians at Salamis, attended the 76th Olympiad it is recorded that the crowds were so busy acclaiming him that the athletes were ignored for the whole day. But the suspension of more commonplace civil wars during the Ekecheiria united Athenians, Spartans, Syracusans and the rest in peaceful pursuit of physical excellence, which they dedicated to Zeus in his greatest sanctuary.

Under the Romans the games, though increasingly professional and often corrupt, kept their vitality. Olympia grew even more splendid through the generosity of emperors – for various reasons. Nero just wanted to win, and duly did: he instituted a musical contest for himself, and a chariot-race was laughably rigged. Others had genuine respect for the sanctuary and the festival. After the time of Hadrian, however, there was little left of religious or political significance.

Finally, the Christian emperor Theodosius I prohibited all pagan rites, and the games themselves were celebrated for the last time in AD393. In AD1896 they were re-founded in the stadium at Athens, open to competing nations. The modern Olympic Games have been held in different countries every four years since then except during two world wars.

Olympia (57km north-east). The road to Bassae from the coast at Tholo, via Figalia, is rough in parts and has some vertiginous drops, but is worth tackling for its fine views.

The road passes through peaceful villages of modern and rough-stone houses, their gardens spilling over with flowers, and above a richly wooded valley with glimpses of red-cream rock through the olives, pines and deciduous trees. It then crosses a bridge over a steep and luxuriant gorge. The most nerve-racking stretch is along a rutted road chiselled out of the rock, high above a long, narrow ravine, beyond which there's a turnoff to the isolated village of Dragogi.

When visiting Bassae, it's well worth stopping at **Andritsaena**, 14km north. This lively market town, spread across a hill above an Italianate valley, cypresses spiking its wooded and bushy slopes, is an enchanting place to approach. Seen close up it loses some of the magic, as many of its whitewashed and red-tiled houses are run down.

But Andritsaena's main attraction is its atmosphere: by day it bustles with villagers coming in for shopping and *kafeneion* gossip; at night it's alive with an appealing combination of languor and exuberance, an ideal place for people-watching. The *Hotel Theoxenia* (B) has fairly basic accommodation, but fine views.

Upland villages of Arcadia

A good road from the west coast at Pirgos, via Olympia, follows the green and fertile Alfios and Ladon valleys into the heartland of the Arcadian mountains. The road climbs through increasingly dramatic and barren scenery, roaming ground for goats and solitary goatherds. Hilltops are crowned by villages of honey-coloured stone and terracotta-tiled roofs.

Sixty kilometres east of Olympia, the old village of **Langadia** spills down the steep slopes of a rocky outcrop. Its two tavernas, overlooking a deep ravine, make for a memorable lunch-stop. **Vitina** is a relaxing summer and winter resort in the Arcadian mountains, among whose dark lofty pinewoods and alpine clearings Pan, god of shepherds and goatherds (and drunks) was born. Constantly rejected by women, he worked out his frustration in various acts of hooliganism, terrifying the locals by making the mountains and woods echo with his crazed screams. Vitina today is a sleepy and tranquil village, with a shady square which seems purpose-made for long lazy afternoons of doing nothing but paying homage to Pan with chilled retsina. Seven kilometres away, the *Xenia Motel* (B), with smart traditional-style décor, stands in an isolated position in a mountain clearing, and makes a peaceful base for mountain walks or exploring Arcadia.

South of Langadia, **Dimitsana** is a magnificently sited though slightly scruffy medieval village, its honey-stoned and red-roofed houses clinging to a ridge and scattered over the summit of a hill. It's worth a short stop to wander around the maze of steep lanes and steps, with basic *kafeneions* where the ouzo is served from plastic bottles with cloth stoppers, and to take in the enticing views of the narrow Lousias valley from the platform by the white church on the hill.

Eleven kilometres further on, the mountain village of **Stemnitsa** (or **Ipsounda**) is sprinkled over the gently shelving slopes of a tree-tufted hill. In the centre is an enclosed and shady *plateia* which, with its church, belfry, cafes and huge plane trees, looks like everyone's idea of what a Greek village square should be. With some creeper-covered old stone houses, a bridge over a lush brook and a simple hotel – the *Trikolonian* (c) – in a converted medieval building, you could well be seduced into staying overnight.

About 19km further towards Andritsaena and Bassae, the medieval village of **Karitaena** is so quiet that all you can hear is the sound of birds and distant goats' bells. It's spread in terraces beneath a castle, on an isolated hill guarding the north-west corner of the Megalopolis plain. The austere tall stone houses seem to have been designed to be impenetrable – there are few windows, and the lower storeys appear to have been considered safe only for animals and hay-storage. Some of the houses have been renovated, while others have crumbled into picturesque ruins amid the flopping spiky cactus leaves of prickly pears. Above the small Byzantine church of Agios Nikolaos (with good frescoes; usually locked), a steep and scary path climbs up to the castle. The views are tremendous, but there are unprotected drops and deep cistern holes in the ground. There are rooms in a modern olive-green house on the edge of the village. It overhangs the lip of a hill and the views are good. You'll need to bring your own food as there are no tavernas in the village.

From the Karitaena crossroads the route to Andritsaena twists south and west, crossing the deep gorge of the Alfios just south of the village. There are views into its depths from the bridge and from a lay-by 4km further on. An eastward road goes 14km to the small modern town of **Megalopolis**, which is dominated by a large power-station. The scant remains of the ancient 'Great City' lie just north of the town; its theatre was the largest in Greece and held 21,000 spectators. Ancient plays are again performed here in the summer, though only the first few rows of seats remain on the hill; massive trees shade the top, and though the power-station spoils the view the site still has some magic. The site of Megalopolis was the first to be excavated by British archaeologists; the finds were disappointingly scant.

The Kalavrita Railway

Climbing 2300 feet in 14 miles, at gradients of up to one in seven, the narrow-gauge Kalavrita railway rises through the dark, narrow Vouraikos gorge, crossing vertiginous bridges above the pushing stream and winding through twisting tunnels gouged out of the limestone rock.

It starts at Diakofto, an otherwise unremarkable village on the coast of the Corinthian Gulf, where there's little to do other than join the locals on the station square, sip an ouzo and wait for your train to arrive.

The first stop is Kato Zahlorou, perched on a shady platform above the turbulent stream. It's a lovely peaceful place in which to have a meal or stay at one of the two basic tavernas. A steep track leads up to the monastery of **Mega Spileo** – the views are good, but the building is ugly, having been constructed in the 1930s after a barrel of gunpowder left over from the War of Independence exploded and destroyed the original.

The rail terminus is at **Kalavrita**, a rather forlorn small town in a beautiful setting. Opposite the station is a huge mural, dedicated to the martyred towns of the Second World War. Kalavrita suffered more than any – the entire male population was killed by the Germans in 1943. The clock on the church tower stands at 2.34, the hour of the massacre.

Lake Stymphalia and Kastania

An excellent escape-route from the crowded resorts of the Corinthian Gulf climbs through the Aroania mountains from the old, neglected village of Derveni. A 13km stretch of the road is still unpaved, but it is not seriously rough or steep. With their dense pine woods and lush green pastures, the uplands seem more Swiss than Greek, and even the *Xenia Hotel* (B), isolated and perched on a mountainside outside the scattered old village of **Kastania**, is built like an oversized chalet. It's almost surrounded by impenetrable pine forest, but does have a fine view down the valley.

The main reason for the drive is to see the scene of one of the Labours of Herakles. Hemmed in by close high peaks is a vast reedy lake, **Stymphalia**. Here Herakles frightened away man-eating birds which, brazen-beaked, brazen-clawed and brazen-winged, swooped on passers-by and blighted crops with their poisonous excrement. It's odd and unexpected scenery, eerie or merely impressive according to your mood. You can make it a round trip, returning to the coast at Kiato across fertile slopes of citrus groves and currant vines.

Mantinea

There's not much left of the ancient city of Mantinea, on the flat plain north of the major crossroads town of **Tripolis**, but next to it is Greece's weirdest church – funny or surreal, depending on your taste. It was built in the 1970s by a Greek-American architect who paid homage to his heritage by combining Greek- and Egyptian-style temples with a Byzantine dome, filling it with frescoes, sculptures and mosaics and dedicating the lot to the Virgin, Beethoven and the Muses.

Leonidion

Flanked by burnt red hills and guarded by cylindrical towers at the mouth of a dry valley, Leonidion is a fine town in which to wander, and gets quite crowded in season. There are rough-stone houses with pepperpot chimneys, whitewashed mansions with fancy moulded cornices, and a recently restored semi-fortified house with tapered towers clinging to its walls and an elegant loggia just visible over the walls of its lush garden. Above the garish shops of the main street is a tiny maze of whitewashed cubic houses with narrow streets squeezing between them.

Two kilometres away, across a tiny fertile plain of olive and orange trees, is the sand and shingle **Lakkas** beach; there are no hotels, but there are apartments to rent. More attractive is **Plaka**, Leonidion's tiny harbour village, backed by a sweeping crag-topped hill with a white chapel anchored on top. The beach, of smooth subtly coloured pebbles, is clean and pleasant, and the sea limpid. It also gets quite crowded in season, as the small fishing harbour is used by yachts, flotillas and the Flying Dolphins. However, the village itself has suffered little and development remains low-key. Overlooking the harbour are two restaurants and a hearty taverna, where you sit among a jumble of nautical bric-à-brac or on the terrace, ankle-deep in mewling kittens. The owners run the *Dionysos* (D), a clean and simple hotel close to the beach which has rooms with bathrooms and balconies.

Six kilometres north along the coast, little **Livadi** is a scattering of vine-covered houses among orchards and gardens, with a lane down to a shoreline of rocks and shingle. There's a taverna or two by the water, a few fishing-boats and considerable charm.

CENTRAL GREECE

From the gates of hell to the centre of the world; from the crossroads where Oedipus killed his father to the town in which he married his mother; and from the mountain of the gods to the mountain of the muses – the landscape of Greece's northern mainland is rich with mystery, myth and legend.

The administrative region termed 'Central Greece' does not include Epirus and Thessaly; to a traveller such constraints are of no value, and the region described in this chapter takes no account of the official boundaries. The geographical area we call Central Greece – for it lies between the Peloponnese in the south and Macedonia and Thrace in the north – is flanked by the Ionian and Aegean Seas and stretches from Attica and the Corinthian Gulf to Macedonia and Albania. It is an area largely unknown to tourists. Despite its size – almost twice that of the Peloponnese – only two sights are on the itineraries of whistle-stop coach-tours: the sanctuary of Delphi in the south and the monasteries of the Meteora in the north. And only one coastal resort, Parga, is featured by British tour operators.

The touristic neglect is not entirely justified. What Central Greece lacks in ancient sites it makes up for in fine mountain scenery and the interest of remote settlements. The Pindos Mountains form a central spine which separates rugged Epirus from the rich agricultural plains of Thessaly; the ridge is crossed by the highest road pass in the country. To the north-east lies Greece's highest mountain, Olympos; in the south are the remote peaks of the Parnassos range. Three of the administrative districts of the area have the country's lowest population figures per square mile – with the exception of the monastic republic of Mount Athos.

The greatest attraction of Central Greece is the way in which its ancient sites, monasteries and traditional villages are in total harmony with its landscape. Delphi is ranged down a slope backed by the rocky spurs of Parnassos and looks out to the sea across a vast and ancient grove of olives; the lesser-known site of Dodona

is situated in a remote and silent valley whose slopes echo the
contours of its beautifully preserved theatre; and the fabled
entrance to the Underworld at Ephyra rises above a bleak, dank
plain which was once covered by the hellish waters of the Styx.

Centuries later, the fusion of landscape and architecture
continued. In the northern reaches of the Pindos Mountains,
stone-built villages are terraced on hillsides to leave the few
mountain plateaux free for cultivation; the luxuriant slopes of the
mountainous Pelion peninsula are scattered with diffuse villages of
half-timbered houses which look out over peaceful valleys or the
turquoise Aegean; the mosques and minarets of Ioanina rise above
a lake in the shadow of the barren bulk of Mount Mitsikeli; and
the monasteries of the Meteora are dizzily anchored on surrealistic
stone monoliths.

If you begin your exploration of Central Greece in Athens, the
first region you come across is Boeotia. Though largely
mountainous, it has a vast, intensively cultivated plain in the
centre around the historic city of Thebes, now a prosperous and
dull modern town. Heading north, you enter Thessaly, consisting
of another vast plain, encircled by mountains. In summer this is
one of the hottest places in Europe, and your only comfort may be
the knowledge that the large market towns of Larissa and Trikkala
hold little of interest to tourists and need serve as no more than
pit-stops on your route. The attractions of Thessaly, apart from
the Meteora monasteries, are the villages and beaches of the sea-
fringed Mount Pelion, the lush river banks of the Vale of Tempe,
and the heights of Mount Olympos, home of the gods.

West of Thebes, the most attractive corner of Boeotia is at
Levadia, below Mount Helikon. And off the well-worn tourist
path to Delphi, the Byzantine monastery of Ossios Loukas shelters
some of Greece's finest mosaics. Like western Boeotia,
neighbouring Phokis is dominated by Mount Parnassos. Despite
being small and infertile, the area grew rich because of Delphi,
whose oracular prophecies were central to Greek life for over 1000
years. Generals would come here to seek advice on war,
businessmen on trade and individuals on family matters. City-
states vied with one another in the amount of their offerings,
while all who consulted the oracle were obliged to buy sacred and
over-priced Delphi-raised animals for sacrifice – and doubtless
ended up, like most of Delphi's 20th-century visitors, having to
sleep in its hotels and eat in its tavernas.

West of Phokis, the coastal region of Aitolia and Akarnania
contains little to detain the casual visitor. Its lagoons and marshes,
lakes and islets are more attractive when seen from a boat than
from the shore; and the site of the naval battle of Actium – where
the fleets of Antony and Cleopatra were routed – is at present of

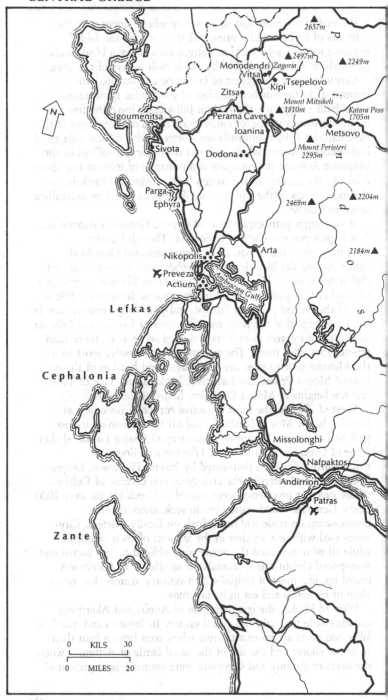

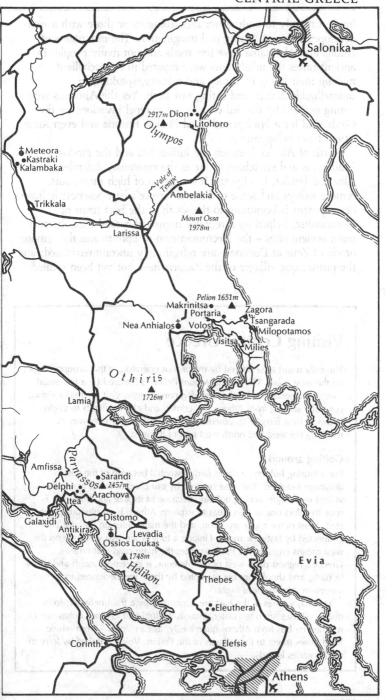

interest mainly to underwater archaeologists or those with a well-developed sense of history and imagination. The mountains of Aitolia and Akarnania have few roads and not many people. In ancient times the inhabitants were reputed to be uncivilised, making their living by piracy and robbery, speaking an unintelligible dialect, and eating raw flesh. Yet the Aitolians were strong enough by the 3rd century BC to repel invasions by the Gauls, and for a brief period ruled Phokis, Boeotia and even some cities of the Peloponnese.

North of Aitolia, between the Ionian Sea and the Pindos Mountains and stretching as far as the rigorously defended Albanian border, lies Epirus. It's a region of high mountains, remote valleys and some of Central Greece's best beaches; holiday development is beginning to the south of the port town of Igoumenitsa, helped by a recently improved coastal road. Its two main ancient sites – the Necromanteion of Ephyra and the remote oracle of Zeus at Dodona – are refreshingly uncommercialised; and the picturesque villages of the Zagoria have not yet been spoiled

Visiting Central Greece

The only resort area offered by major tour operators is that around Parga on the west coast. The area of Mount Pelion is featured by a few small specialist operators. Coach-tours of varying lengths visit the major sights, generally starting from Athens. Scheduled and charter flights to Corfu, followed by a ferry to Igoumenitsa, offer a reasonably easy way of reaching the west and north-west part of the area.

Getting around

For a touring holiday, a car is fairly essential because of the vast distances involved. The area covered by our chapter is not generally visited in a single touring holiday; because of its size and terrain, it is wise to select one or two areas to explore. Athens is an obvious place to start. Most of the roads are good, and the main cities on the east are connected by fast new roads. Linking a tour of the east with one on the west means crossing the Pindos range; the main road that crosses Greece's highest pass, west of the Meteora, is extremely rough and tricky in parts, and should not be attempted by those inexperienced in mountain driving, or at night.

The major cities of the east are connected by a train network; long-distance buses are often faster, though. Delphi and Ossios Loukas can be reached by bus from Athens quite easily, as can Volos – from where local buses travel to the villages of the Pelion. Volos is linked by ferry to the Sporades Islands.

by tourism. The largest town of Epirus is lakeside Ioanina. While largely modern (as indeed are all major towns in mainland Greece) it retains a rambling Turkish citadel whose dilapidated mosques and bath-houses date from the 18th century when it was ruled by the tyrant Ali Pasha.

Just to the west of the Katara pass over the Pindos lies the large mountain village of Metsovo, an enclave of indigenous tradition, in which time-honoured crafts continue to flourish. Many of its inhabitants are Vlachs – nomadic shepherds who still speak a language derived from Latin. Metsovo, along with the similarly remote villages of the Zagoria and Pelion, was one of the few places in Central Greece which enjoyed a degree of freedom during the five centuries of Turkish rule. In fact, its leading families even worked with the Turks, and were granted land in Egypt from which they grew rich by growing cotton. The Zagorians lined their pockets by taking up lucrative positions in Constantinople and eastern Europe, while the inhabitants of the Pelion – many of them also descended from the Vlachs – traded throughout Europe, and were considered so important by the French that a consul was stationed in the area.

A British focus on the area's history is the part played in the War of Independence by the philhellenic Lord Byron. Since *Childe Harold*, the English poet who loved Greece had been urging on its patriots:

> *Hereditary bondsmen! know ye not*
> *Who would be free themselves must strike the blow?*
> *By their right arms the conquest must be wrought.*
> *Will Gaul or Muscovite redress ye? No!*

Philhellenic sentiment in western Europe had greatly strengthened by the beginning of the 19th century as Grand Tourists extended their travels beyond Napoleonic France and Italy. While governments rather deplored the outbreak of Greek revolution, public opinion reacted otherwise: philhellenic committees in England and Scotland, Italy and France, Switzerland and Germany collected funds to add to the money from rich expatriate Greeks; volunteers went to fight. The great Romantic voices raised for Greece – Byron and Shelley, Goethe, Schiller, Victor Hugo – created a moral climate which would in the end ensure some international action.

In 1823 Byron, as emissary and financial agent of the Greek Committee in London, arrived at Missolonghi, the Greek revolutionary headquarters. Four months later he died there of a fever; destiny, as a French heroic poem put it, 'begrudged his fame the honour of falling on a field of victory'. His death produced a shock-wave of support in Europe; it was a catalysing event that

prompted Britain, France and Russia to act in concert. Mourning
at Missolonghi for Byron was followed by his enshrinement as a
national hero, in the ballads of the revolution and the history of
modern Greece.

The East

There are two roads from Athens to Thebes. The quickest route,
along the motorway, has nothing other than speed to recommend
it. Prefabricated factories, brash plastic signs clamped to their
walls, and dusty parking lots where itinerant workers spend their
summers in caravans and under makeshift canopies, combine to
create a shanty town scenario redolent of the Third World. This
eventually gives way to dry brushland, scrub-speckled hills and
sunburnt fields of grass, maize and watermelons – which assume a
surreal aspect as they lie on the dry red earth like abandoned
footballs.

The alternative is a mountain road from Elefsis, west of Athens,
which follows the route of the ancient Sacred Way, the pilgrim
road to Delphi. It winds through a peaceful landscape of grey hills
and pine trees to the narrow pass which separates Attica from
Boeotia. Just after the turnoff to Vilia a path climbs up to the
fortress of **Eleutherai**, built by the Athenians in the 4th century BC
to keep the Boeotians out. Built of regular grey stone blocks, so
well preserved that their edges are still sharp, eight of its sturdy
towers remain, and there are superb views of Attica from the
narrow parapet walk which runs along the northern wall.

Beyond the fortress there are even broader views, north across
the Boeotian plain to the island of Evia, and west to **Mount
Kithairon**. Here Penteus, King of Thebes, was torn to pieces by
Dionysos's female followers, the Maenads, for daring to arrest the
god, and on its slopes the baby Oedipus was pinned by his foot
and left to die. Beyond it the ridge of Mount Helikon stretches
towards Mount Parnassos, whose peaks are often snow-capped
until May or June. From here the road descends to the Boeotian
plain and the city of THEBES, spread across its flat-topped hill.

Beyond Thebes, Mount Spingion rises, stark and forbidding,
to the north of the Levadia road; it was from here that the
furious Sphinx hurled herself, after Oedipus had successfully
answered her riddle. The road skirts Kopaïs, once the largest
lake in Greece – it was drained at the end of the last century,
and is now covered with fields of cotton, cereals, tomatoes and
watermelons. It then rounds the north-east slopes of Mount
Helikon and reaches **Levadia**.

This busy modern town lies at the mouth of the Herkyna

ORACLES

The most famous ancient sites of Central Greece are not palaces, temples or theatres, but oracles. An oracle – from orare, *'to speak' – was the relayed voice of a god, or the source of its transmission. There were several oracles in Greece, but that at Delphi was supreme. According to mythology, Zeus had released two eagles, from each end of the world, and their flights met above Delphi – clearly the centre: there is a stone there called the* omphalos, *'earth's navel'.*

Oracles are as old as religion, and before the pantheon of Greek gods and goddesses was established it was the mother-earth goddess who spoke, in the subterranean rumblings or drifting vapours of certain sites. At Delphi, mother-earth's sacred snake was identified with the Python, a monster sent by Zeus's jealous wife Hera against Leto, mother of Zeus's children Apollo and Artemis. Apollo pursued the Python to its refuge at Delphi, killed it there, and took over the oracle; to appease the anger of mother-earth the Pythian Games were instituted. The priestess who relayed the oracle was called the Pythia.

In response to worshippers' questions the oracles 'spoke' in varying ways: at Dodona in Epirus through the diffuse sounds of a sacred oak wood inhabited by doves and hung with bells and gongs, at Trophonios in Boeotia through echoing whispers in the darkness of an underground cavern. At Delphi tradition has it that the priestess was literally 'inspired' by vapours from a cleft in the earth: she sat over it on a sacred tripod stool, near the omphalos *stone, and the scattered utterings of her trance were interpreted by poet-priests. The Pythia at first had to be a virgin, but this proved so troublesome that instead she became a woman of over 50 and vowed to chastity.*

The consulting worshipper had to purify himself and offer sacrifice; if it was favourably received according to the priests, he put his question. The simplest approach was to request a decision between two courses of action – the lot-casting method. To more complex petitions the answers were often ambiguous. The Delphic Oracle, with a worldwide reputation as the most truthful, could be blandly equivocal: when King Croesus of Lydia asked about the likely success of his invasion of Persia he was told he would destroy a great kingdom, and he did – his own.

gorge and is dominated by the red sandstone tower of a medieval castle. At the southern end of town, two springs of the river Herkyna – memory and forgetfulness – flow into crystal-clear pools shaded by trees and overlooked by a pavement cafe. Now a popular summer Sunday lunch-stop, these were visited until late Roman times by pilgrims seeking to delve into the mysteries of life after death at the **oracle of Trophonios**.

The oracle was an offshoot of the more famous one at Delphi.

It was set up in honour of Trophonios, who, with his twin brother, served Apollo at Delphi. The brothers were told by the Delphic Oracle to enjoy themselves for six days, and that on the seventh they would be granted their heart's desire. On the seventh day, the boys were found dead in their beds, which was thought to mean that their heart's desire had been to die for their god. Trophonios's reward was to preside over his own oracle.

Unlike Delphi, where those consulting the oracle would have the 'truth' revealed to them by a priestess, a visit to the oracle of Trophonios involved 'entering the Underworld' and seeing the truth for oneself. The Greek travel writer Pausanias has left a clear and chilling account of what happened. For several days before descending to the Underworld, pilgrims would have to purify themselves by making sacrifices to various gods, eating only sacrificed meat, abstaining from hot baths, and washing themselves in the waters of the river Herkyna. When deemed fit to consult the oracle, the pilgrim would be led once again to the river, where he would be bathed and anointed. He would then drink from the spring of forgetfulness (Lethe), in order to forget his past, and from the spring of memory (Mnemosyne), so that he might remember his experiences in the Underworld. Dressed in a linen tunic and sturdy country boots, he would walk to the oracular chasm, which Pausanias thought resembled a huge bread-oven. The process of getting into it seems to have been none too dignified: 'The man going down lies on the ground with honey-cakes in his hand and then tries to get his knees in. The rest of his body immediately gets dragged after his knees, as if some extraordinarily deep, fast river was catching a man in a current and sucking him down.' Once inside, the bruised and shaken pilgrim would see or hear visions of the future, before being unceremoniously disgorged feet-first. The experience was understandably terrifying, and each pilgrim would have friends and family at hand to help him recover. As Pausanias poignantly wrote: 'He is still possessed with terror and hardly knows himself or anything round him. Later he comes to his senses . . . and can laugh again.'

Until recently it was thought the actual entrance to the Underworld, a circular pit about 15 minutes' walk beyond the medieval castle, had been discovered, but this has now been proved to be a cistern. Consequently, the only signs of Levadia's mystic history are the rather unexciting niches carved into the rock above the spring of memory (the spring of forgetfulness is now piped off to serve the modern town). In later days the Turkish governor of Levadia found a less than sacred use for the largest niche – he used to sit there for a peaceful smoke after a hard day's work. Though following his example is frowned upon, Levadia remains a pleasant place at which to cool off at midday – but it does get extremely crowded in the holiday season and at weekends.

North-west of Levadia the road cuts through a dramatic valley towards Mount Parnassos and Delphi. The southern turnoff for Distomo and the monastery of Ossios Loukas, known as the Triple Way in ancient times, marks the spot where Oedipus met King Laius, the father who had abandoned him as a child. Not surprisingly, Oedipus didn't recognise him, and when Laius whipped him out of the way of his chariot, the enraged Oedipus attacked and accidentally killed him.

Beyond the undistinguished village of Distomo, a road south winds in hairpin bends through craggy limestone outcrops to the modest seaside resort of **Antikira**. The beach is narrow and pebbly, and the village bland – but it's a convenient place at which to stop for a quick swim while touring.

The eastern road from Distomo leads to the Byzantine monastery of OSSIOS LOUKAS, set on the lower slopes of Mount Helikon and overlooking a gentle valley.

The road west from the Triple Way climbs up below the jagged peaks of Mount Parnassos to **Arachova**, which suddenly comes into sight as you emerge from a short tunnel. Terraced on the steep foothills of Parnassos and overlooking a deep gorge, Arachova is a far more pleasant place in which to stay than modern Delfi, by the ancient site, just 10km west. It too gets its fair share of visitors, lured by the menu board promise of *crêpes, cappuccino* and cocktails, and the woven woollen rainbow of rugs lining the main street. However, though an unashamed tourist trap, Arachova retains its identity. Rubbing shoulders with the fancy colour-coordinated bars are simple bare-floored tavernas and *kafeneions*, and the Arachovans, far from being sated with foreigners, are only too anxious to practise their English.

The village is at its best in the early morning, while the guests in its six hotels are still in bed or lingering over breakfast. Then, with only the Arachovans about – waking themselves up with strong sweet coffees outside the *kafeneions*, sweeping the streets, and watering olive oil cans brimming with flowers – you can explore the steep stepped alleyways alone. The air is still cool, and the light, not yet harsh, finds details of colour, shade and texture in the rough stone walls that you would never otherwise notice. In addition, of course, you will get to Delphi in time to avoid the worst of the crowds. The simple *Apollon* hotel (D) has views into the gorge, as has the *Xenia* (B), which is set back from the road at the Delphi end of the village.

Arachova is worth a visit in itself on 23 April, when St George's Day is celebrated: everyone dresses up in traditional costume for folk dancing, a race between the village's old men, and deliciously excessive feasting.

Eleven kilometres north-east of Arachova lies the ski centre of **Sarandi**, on the slopes of **Mount Parnassos**. The mythological home of Apollo and the muses, and therefore of western arts and poetry, the peaks of Mount Parnassos have been likened to a winged bird. A very tricky climbing route begins at Sarandi; it's advisable to hire a guide, as the mountain is subject to mists. The safest time to tackle it is in July or August: its peak will be free from snow, but you'll have the intense heat to cope with. The rewards on its (rare) clear days, however, are considerable – for the view encompasses most of Greece, taking in Mount Athos, Mount Olympos, the Sporades and the Peloponnese Islands.

Against the backdrop of Mount Parnassos, the ruins of DELPHI are reckoned to be the most beautifully sited in Greece. It is also one of the most popular sites.

Heading north-west from Delphi, the road passes through abundant olive groves. The small town of **Amfissa** is spread over the slopes of two hills and capped by a red stone castle. This is a pleasant place at which to stop for a drink. The climb up to the castle is steep, and the ruins scant, and as there are good views from the road itself, there's little reason to exert yourself.

The castle was built in the 13th century to guard the pass which, like the modern road, cuts between the Parnassos and Gkiona mountains. The road winds through jutting red and grey stone cliffs, above green and golden valleys, and there are fine views of rippling peaks, milky blue in the distance.

Emerging from the mountains, you cross an agricultural plain to the modern sprawling market town of **Lamia**, on the southern border of Thessaly. It's not a pretty place, especially in the heat of summer, but if you're in desperate need of a hotel there are a handful of cheap and basic ones on the main, noisy and mosquito-ridden *plateia*.

A fast modern toll road whips out of Lamia to the narrow coastal strip which skirts the Othris mountains. This is the quickest route to VOLOS, Thessaly's main port and the starting-point for a tour of the villages of Mount Pelion; Larissa, where you turn off for the Meteora; and Salonika. Volos is signposted only as you join the road, and then as you're about to leave it 86km away.

There are a number of resorts along the coast, the most interesting of which is **Nea Anhialos**, 18km west of Volos, which was one of the most important early Christian sites in Greece.

Foundations of five basilicas remain; the site is scattered with intricately carved architectural fragments, and there are mosaics in the tiny museum. The resort has a long shingly beach backed by trees.

There are more beaches between here and Volos, although you may find the proximity of an oil refinery and the fact that Greece's third-largest port is just around the corner a little off-putting.

North-east of Volos, the toll road continues across the Thessalian plain to **Larissa**, capital of the province. The large modern town is situated on the Peneios river; tacky apartment blocks and seedy hotels overlook incongruously pretty *plateias* with cafes shaded by lime and orange trees. If you don't want your drink laced with carbon monoxide, there's a pleasant park with cafes on the far side of the river.

Larissa has a tiny museum, housed in an old mosque with a minaret resembling a factory chimney, on the *plateia* at the end of Odos 31 Avgoustou. Its collection of Greek, Roman and Byzantine funerary sculpture, however, is of interest mainly to enthusiasts.

There's little to detain you along the road from Larissa to Kalambaka, the base for visiting the MONASTERIES OF THE METEORA. If you have your own transport, you can avoid passing through the undistinguished and scruffy market town of **Trikkala**, but if you're travelling by bus you may have to change at its bus station.

Off the Athens–Salonika highway, north-east of Larissa, the village of **Ambelakia** is set on the north-west slope of the conical Mount Ossa, with views across the Vale of Tempe to Mount Olympos. Now a quiet and sleepy place, it was once one of the richest towns in Greece, thanks to red dye from the root of the madder plant which grows on Mount Ossa. At the end of the 18th century its silk and cotton weaving and dyeing workshops combined to form the world's first co-operative. This had 6000 members, traded throughout Europe, and did particularly well out of the Austrian army which had all the fabric for its uniforms dyed in Ambelakia's vats.

The advantages of membership were more than commercial. The benefits for members and their families included free schooling, medical care, performances of Ancient Greek plays and – given that its leader, George Schwarz, was from a Viennese family – opera. But the days of prosperity were short-lived. The bank in Vienna, where the co-operative's money was kept, crashed; business was lost to Manchester's new industrialised mills and artificial dye works; and in 1811 the town was destroyed by Ali Pasha. Less than 50 years after it had been founded, the co-operative was disbanded, and George Schwarz was thrown into a debtor's prison where he later died.

However, the 50 good years were enough for the town's inhabitants to build themselves fine homes. Of the original 600, only around 30 remain – for most were destroyed by the Germans in the Second World War. The surviving houses are built of stone with projecting half-timbered upper storeys; many have been restored. One, right at the entrance to the village, now houses a women's co-operative dedicated to reviving traditional crafts; and the home of George Schwarz has been renovated and is open to the public. With its barred windows, secret escape routes, hidden trap-doors and holes in the floor for pouring molten lead on to the heads of unwanted visitors, the house of George Schwarz sounds like something out of a Gothic horror film. In fact, the interior is at once homely and elegant; Schwartz paid homage to his home town and host country with a combination of Greek folk art and Viennese rococo which is surprisingly easy on the eye. The ground flc r, which was used for business transactions, is relatively plain; its most interesting feature is the strong-room in which a trap-door leads to a secret passage. A creaking wooden staircase, whose treads have worn so thin that they bend as you step on them, leads to the more refined upper floor. Here, important guests could marvel at the excessive rococo fireplace piled with painted porcelain fruit; admire walls decorated with *trompe l'oeil* columns, brimming cornucopias and exotic scenes of harbours like Topkapi and Constantinople used by the co-operative's traders; and then be entertained in the music-room, perhaps with the latest Viennese waltz or Mozartian aria. And, should the performance have been interrupted by marauding bandits, they would have been able to escape down a secret staircase concealed behind a door.

Just beyond the Ambelakia turnoff, the Salonika highway has a toll section, as it passes through the **Vale of Tempe** (Tembi). According to legend the sea god Poseidon split the mountains of Ossa and Olympos with his trident to allow the waters of the vast Larissa Lake to pour through into the sea. Mythology, for once, is not so far from the truth, for in the ice age a cleft did indeed appear between the two mountains, through which the lake gushed to the sea, leaving what is now the Thessalian plain behind it.

More fancifully, Tempe is also supposed to be the scene of the most famous rape-attempt in Greek mythology. It was here that Apollo, after seizing control of the Delphic Oracle by killing its guardian Python, came to purify himself. However, no sooner had he cleansed himself of one crime when he attempted to commit another: spotting his beloved nymph, Daphne, he began to chase her through the woods. She called out to her mother, the earth-goddess, who rescued her by changing her into the world's first laurel tree – still known as *dafni* in Greek.

The vale's beauties are also legendary – thanks to generations of English poets, who waxed lyrically on its loveliness without ever visiting it. However, as they got their information from classical poets who *had* seen it, the descriptions of the 'long divine', 'leaf-fringed' valley, with a 'pleasant shore scattered with flowers' (by, respectively, Tennyson, Keats and Spenser) are not so far from the truth.

What the poets couldn't have known was that the valley would be cut through by a main road and railway. Despite these, the vale, with its sheer creeper-laced crags and luxuriantly wooded banks, remains an extremely popular spot for riverside strolls.

Thebes (Thivai)

There are no visible remains of the ancient seven-gated city that played such an important part in Greek mythology and early history. It was in Thebes that Oedipus and his family lived out their tragedy of patricide and incest. Having been warned by the Delphic Oracle that their son would grow up to kill his father and marry his mother, Oedipus's parents, Laius and Jocasta, left their baby boy to die on the slopes of Mount Kithairon, pinning his feet to the ground to prevent his escape ('oedipus' means 'swollen foot'). He was, however, rescued by a shepherd and grew up to fulfil the oracle's terrible prophecy, beginning by unwittingly murdering his father at the famous Triple Way near Delphi. Continuing on to Thebes, he was stopped by a Sphinx who terrorised all travellers by setting them a riddle – 'What being has sometimes two feet, sometimes three and sometimes four, and is weakest when it has the most?' – and killing all those who failed to give the correct answer. No one had found the solution, so presumably visitors were a rarity in Thebes. Oedipus, however, replied that the being was man, who walked on all fours as a child, on two as a man and with a staff in his old age, and so infuriated the Sphinx that she threw herself off the mountain. Oedipus went on to Thebes, which was in turmoil after the murder of Laius. The Thebans were so relieved at the demise of the Sphinx that they made him king and gave him Jocasta as his wife. After the royal couple had produced four children a seer, Tiresius, arrived at Thebes and revealed the truth; Jocasta then killed herself and Oedipus blinded himself, before leaving Thebes along with his daughter Antigone.

Sadly, the trials of Oedipus's family did not end here. After his death Antigone returned to Thebes, where a quarrel between her brothers Polyneices and Eteocles resulted in the war of the Seven against Thebes, in which Polyneices led seven military heroes and their armies against the city, defended by Eteocles. Predictably, given the family's unfortunate history, they killed each other. Creon, King of Thebes, gave Eteocles an honourable funeral, but ordered that Polyneices's body be left to rot unburied. Antigone objected, and, while attempting to bury her brother, was seized by Creon's army and buried alive.

Ancient Thebes disappeared long ago, partly thanks to Alexander the Great who razed the city to the ground in 336BC after beating the Greeks at the Battle of Chaironeia, which secured his domination of the mainland.

Wandering through the streets of modern Thebes, the only sense of tragedy you're likely to feel is that one of the most famous cities of Ancient Greece has been reduced to a 'could-be-anywhere' grid of apartment and office blocks. The one reason for not bypassing it is the small archaeological museum with a unique collection of painted Mycenaean sarcophagi – but even these are of limited appeal, and are certainly not worth going too far out of your way for.

Thebes: sight

● **Archaeological Museum** The contents of the museum have overspilled into the courtyard, allowing you to relax at a table built of architectural fragments among funerary sculpture in the shade of a vine trellis and pomegranate trees. On one wall are four sections of an early Christian mosaic calendar. Each of the months was represented by a figure engaged in an activity appropriate for the time of year – July, for example, holding a sheaf of corn, and April a lamb. Adjoining what is left of the calendar is a hunting scene oddly dominated by the figure of a hunchback eating a watermelon.

The entrance to the museum is flanked by colossal lions in various states of repair which graced the tombs of prominent Thebans in the 4th century BC. Inside is a good collection of pottery, some terracotta figurines engaged in everyday activities (like grating cheese into a large basin), and a beautiful and well-preserved *kouros* (male statue), in room A, from a sanctuary to Apollo – smiling, as do all the Archaic statues of the 6th century BC.

It is, however, the unique painted Mycenaean sarcophagi that are the museum's highlight. These clay boxes, known as *larnakes*, were found in burial-chambers at Tanagra, to the east of Thebes. They date from the mid-14th to the mid-13th century BC and are painted with scenes of mourning, sacrifice and games in honour of the dead. Such burial-boxes were common in Minoan Crete, but these are the only ones to have been discovered on the mainland, leading some archaeologists to believe that Tanagra was colonised by the Minoans.

The first thing that strikes you about a *larnax* is its size – for most are considerably less than a metre long. Some were indeed used for children, but in most cases the skeletons found inside reveal that the dead bodies were folded up so they would fit in.

The style of the painting is impressionistic – frequently slapdash and in cases almost cartoon-like. Larnax 14 is one of the most appealing, with a caricatured sphinx staring at an equally caricatured priestess, while on Larnax 6 another sphinx suffers the indignity of being tied by the neck to the waist of a female mourner. Of more historical importance, however, are the scenes that show what really happened at funerals. Larnax 1 has a procession of silhouetted women with their arms raised above their heads in mourning. Below them two men wrestle while two others race chariots in honour of the dead. The other side shows the sacrifice of the largest of a herd of goats, while below men fly recklessly over the backs of bulls in a foolhardy version of leapfrog.

Ossios Loukas

The monastery of Ossios Loukas is not only beautifully situated but contains some of Greece's most magnificent mosaics. The monastery was founded not by Saint Luke of gospel fame but by a local hermit, the Blessed Luke, who, attracted by the beauty of the setting, set up home in a simple cell, living only on herbs. He wasn't to be left in peace for long, however, for the word soon spread that he not only had healing powers but was also something of a prophet. Thus, the Christian church's answer to the Delphic Oracle became famous, and Luke was soon joined by so many other monks and visited by so many pilgrims that he decided to found the monastery.

The current monastery dates from some time after Luke's death in AD953. Before dying, he had prophesied that the island of Crete would be liberated from its Arab occupiers; when this event did indeed happen in 961, his fame reached the ears of the rich, who heaped their wealth upon the monastery.

There are two churches: the Katholikon, for the pilgrims, and the Theotikos, for the monks. The mosaics are in the former, and though there are some beautifully carved capitals in the latter it's in the Katholikon that you'll want to spend most of your time. The building is a particularly fine example of the Byzantine style – a Greek-cross plan below a central dome, with rich decorative use of multi-coloured stone, brick and marble.

The narthex is the most sumptuous part of the church, and its gold-backed mosaics are the easiest to see. In Doubting Thomas, tension is created by the worried anticipation on the faces of the disciples, while in The Washing of the Feet every one of the disciples displays a different reaction to Christ's display of humility, creating a mood of awe and incomprehension. In contrast, take a look at the six female saints in the drum of the western arch, in which so little attempt has been made to differentiate between them that they look like three pairs of twins.

In the main part of the church there are more repeated faces of saints in the vaults; but in the squinches the mosaics of the Baptism, Nativity and Presentation in the Temple all use the concavity of the wall to create a sense of perspective. The water in which Christ is baptised really seems to be deep, and the animals peeking over the manger really do appear to be inside the cave. Realism is limited, however, and the convention of showing two separate events as happening simultaneously still holds – consequently, in the same mosaic you can see the Christ child lying in his manger and being bathed by servants.

If the same artist was responsible for the original decorations of the dome, the effect must have been wonderful; sadly, however, these were destroyed in an earthquake and were replaced with unremarkable frescoes in the 17th century.

The crypt is beautifully frescoed and contains the tomb of the Blessed Luke (in which lies his skeleton, clad in black robes).

Delphi

Tumbling down a rugged pine-clad slope flanked by the rose and silver crags of the Phaidriades, the 'Shining Rocks', and overlooking a vast ocean of olive trees smoothly stretching towards the glassy sea, the ruins of Delphi could hardly be in a more beautiful spot. But if you visit them in mid-summer, when the intensity of the heat is matched only by the density of the tourists, it is hard to relax for long enough to appreciate the situation, let alone sense the much-touted mystery with which the site is supposed to be invested.

Delphi, mythical centre of the ancient world and home of the most famous of oracles, has influenced the western imagination for thousands of years, and is still a part of the 20th-century consciousness. For at Delphi it was pronounced that Oedipus would kill his father and marry his mother – thereby giving the world its most tragic hero and Freud his Oedipus Complex.

Before Apollo took it over the oracle belonged to the earth-goddess and over the centuries the fear persisted that the earthquakes that damaged Delphi were expressions of her anger. However, on more than one occasion perfectly timed earthquakes and rockfalls have actually protected the sanctuary.

In 480BC the Persian Xerxes sent an army to plunder the site. The soldiers had just reached the first temple when a tremendous clap of thunder was heard, and two immense crags hurtled down, crushing to death virtually the entire army. Two centuries later, the Gauls attempted to seize Delphi but were thrown into a mysterious frenzy, and instead of ravaging the temples and fighting the Delphians they set about slaughtering one another.

The reason that Delphi attracted the attention of invaders had as much to do with the richness of its treasures as with the prestige of its oracle. Various city-states of Ancient Greece built treasuries in the sanctuary, filling them with opulent objects, war spoils and self-congratulatory statues of war heroes, in order to outdo their rivals, and perhaps hoping to influence the priests who machinated behind the scenes of the oracle. During the Peloponnesian War between Sparta and Athens every oracle was pro-Spartan: either the Spartans' generosity to the oracle outdid that of their rival, or the priests were favourably disposed to their cause.

Despite the fact that to cynical 20th-century ears Delphi sounds fraudulent, it would hardly have continued to have been considered (according to the historian Strabo) 'of all the oracles in the world, the most truthful' for over 1000 years if its advice had not been sound. But its sources were not necessarily supernatural. By the 6th century BC, Delphi was run by the Amphictyonic League of Greek city-states, which had a network of informants throughout the Greek world, supplying it with a wealth of political and economic information that would be the envy of any 20th-century league of nations.

Nevertheless, unequivocal utterances by the oracle were a rarity. Most of those who consulted it on matters of commerce, marriage and childbirth departed none the wiser, though considerably the poorer. Asked what should be done to ensure the birth of a male child, the oracle would recommend the sacrifice of a couple of animals to one god or another. Such a reply thus both shifted the responsibility and ensured some extra income, for the sacrificial beast had to be one raised by the Delphians on the sacred land around the oracle, and, in a monopoly insulated from the influence of market forces, heavily inflated prices could be charged.

In fact, even if the oracle's advice did not include a sacrifice to a god, consulting it was an expensive business. Whoever was in control of Delphi, its priests still lined their pockets. Ridiculous prices were charged for the oracle's own compulsory sacrifice – honey-cakes and a sheep or a goat had to be offered before it would speak. After a morsel of meat had been retained for

Apollo, the rest of the animal would be sold to the shops and hotels of the sanctuary.

Today's shops and hotels are a kilometre away from the site in the village of Delfi, built in 1892 by the French government, who were given permission to demolish the village of Castri that had grown up on the site so that excavations could begin. Since then the village's inhabitants have been able to live off the site – first providing the workers for the French archaeologists, and now accommodation and food for the myriad of tourists. Even if the leftovers from sacrificed goats are not on the menus of modern Delfi's hotels and restaurants, it's some comfort to know that today's hard-sell commercialism is nothing new. Entrance fees may have replaced honey-cakes, and shops of gaudy ceramics the stalls of votive offerings, but as you watch the coaches that jam the road below the site disgorging their loads of tourists, the thought that the Ancient Greeks also visited Delphi in hordes, and that they too were exploited, somehow makes it all a little easier to accept.

Most of Delfi's 30 hotels are on the main street, and in high season you won't have much choice over where to stay. All are of a reasonable standard and more than adequate for a one-night stay.

The main road from Arachova to the modern village of Delfi bisects the hill on which the ruins of the ancient sanctuary are scattered. Surprisingly, given the site's popularity, many of the remains are difficult to make sense of without a plan. To get the most out of what you see, buy a guidebook which has a labelled reconstruction, as well as a ground plan; the book by Themelis has both. The main site, the sanctuary of Apollo, is above the road, below the two precipitous Phaedriades rocks, from which Aesop, of fable fame, was hurled on a manufactured charge of embezzlement – most probably because he had dared to ridicule the oracular priests. To the east of the sanctuary of Apollo is the excellent museum, entrance to which is included in the price of the entrance ticket to the site.

Below the road are the secondary sanctuary of Athena and the remains of the gymnasium where the competitors in the Pythian Games would have trained (the gymnasium is closed to the public while further excavations are carried out). Above the gymnasium, close to the road, is the Castalian Spring, where pilgrims to the site would purify themselves by washing their hair before entering the sacred precinct.

Delphi is a fairly exhausting site, not only because it's ranged over a hill but because the amphitheatrical arrangement of the rocks behind it trap the heat. You can, however, cool off under the trees at the bottom of the site, and around the Castalian

Spring – or, if you have the stamina to pant to the stadium at the top of the site, escape both crowds and heat in the shady pine wood above it.

Delphi: highlights

• **Sanctuary of Apollo** That the Romans, even in the 4th century AD, still considered Delphi to be important is proved by the fact that you enter it through a **Roman agora** (market place). A row of columns remains from the stoa, or colonnade, which sheltered shops where votive offerings could be purchased by those who still believed in the oracle's power. Ironically, it was in this century that Constantine gave Christians the freedom to worship, paving the way for Theodosius the Great, who made Christianity the official religion of the Empire and abolished all pagan sites of worship, including that at Delphi. The temple was closed and later pulled down by Theodosius's son Arcadius.

Four steps lead up from the agora through a gap where the gate to the sanctuary once stood. The **Sacred Way**, paved by the Romans with slabs filched from buildings around the sanctuary, was flanked by treasuries where pilgrims deposited their offerings, and by votive monuments which expressed the wealth and power of the Greek city-states. When the Roman Pliny visited, he counted more than 3000 statutes – and this was after Nero in a huff had carried off 500 because the oracle had condemned his matricide.

The first statue Pliny would have seen was a massive bronze bull erected by the people of Corfu in 490–480BC with a tenth of the proceeds from an immense haul of tunafish. Few of the statues, however, were erected as thanksgiving. One-upmanship at the expense of their rivals was the main motivation behind most of the city-states' monuments and treasuries, as is clear from their arrangement. Beyond a flight of steps is a line of bases on which nine bronze statues of Apollo, Victory and sundry heroes of a successful Arcadian invasion of Spartan Laconia in 369BC were once deliberately placed so that they would glare across at the 37 bronze admirals of the Spartans' monument. This in its turn had been raised by the Spartans to celebrate their victory over the Athenians in 403BC, and had naturally been positioned so that the 37 admirals could sneer down on the heads of the 13 bronze statues of Athenian gods and heroes, erected in 460BC, celebrating the Athenian victory over the Persians at Marathon.

A little further along the Sacred Way are the foundations of the treasuries – mini-temples that would have been stacked with precious objects. The most splendid was the **Treasury of Siphnos**, built by the inhabitants of the Cycladic island of Siphnos, who, according to Pausanias, were commanded by Apollo to donate a tenth of the profits from their gold- and silver-mines to Delphi. They duly built the treasury, which outclassed all others in the opulence of its contents and in the magnificence of its sculptural detail. However, they failed to keep up their yearly tithe payment. This incited Apollo to teach them a lesson by flooding the mines with the sea. Although you can get little idea of the treasury's former glory from the foundations, the beautifully carved frieze and the caryatids that supported it are kept in the museum.

197

The **Treasury of the Athenians** is the best preserved of all the buildings at Delphi. It was built by the Athenians between 490 and 480BC with a tenth of the spoils from the Battle of Marathon, and on the triangular platform in front would have been displayed booty seized from the defeated Persians. During excavations the French archaeologists unearthed virtually all the blocks from which its walls were built. The rebuilding in 1906 was something akin to piecing together a giant three-dimensional jigsaw puzzle, for the blocks were covered with inscriptions, including a hymn to Apollo, complete with musical notation in Greek letters. The columns are modern and the frieze a cast of the original, which is kept in the museum.

Next to the treasury are the foundations of the **Bouleuterion**, where the 15 administrators of Delphi met, and beyond the foundations is a great boulder, which probably toppled from one of the Phaedriades, known as the **Rock of the Sybil**. Here it is believed the first Sybil (prophetess) sat and made divine utterances, in the days before the sanctuary was requisitioned by Apollo. Beyond is a circular threshing floor or **halos**, 15m in diameter, on which every seven years a propitiative play was staged, enacting the death of the Python at the hands of Apollo.

Rising above the halos is an immense crazy-paved wall dating from the 6th century BC, supporting the platform on which the temple of Apollo stands. This method of wall-building is unique, and far more ingenious than at first appears – the irregular blocks are interlocked with curved joints – and the fact that it has withstood all earthquakes is testimony to its strength. Even more interestingly, the walls are covered with inscriptions, most of which have to do with the emancipation of slaves – for Delphi was one of the few places where freedom could be granted, ratified and made public.

It has to be said that the **temple of Apollo**, originally the physical as well as the spiritual focus of Delphi, is disappointing. For this is no gleaming white marble edifice but a platform of blue-grey limestone, with six bulging and weather-worn brown columns re-erected in the 1930s to give some idea of its former magnificence. These are merely the tufa cores of the columns, which would once have been white and gleaming, with a stucco of lime and powdered marble – polished, and in places painted. In fact, the drums from which they were reconstructed do not even date from the same temple, for earthquakes and fires necessitated several rebuildings.

Ignoring the traditional account, that the first temple was a hut made of laurel leaves, the second of beeswax and feathers and the third of bronze, the first temple for which there is archaeological evidence was built in the 7th century BC. This was destroyed by a fire in the following century and replaced with a larger temple, much admired by Aeschylus and Euripides, fragments of which are now in the museum. It was destroyed by an earthquake in 373BC, after which the current temple was built. This in its turn was set on fire by invaders from Thrace, pillaged by the Roman general Sulla and finally, in the Middle Ages, taken apart by locals who appear to have been more interested in the metal clamps inserted as reinforcement against earthquakes than in the stones.

Consequently, it takes something of a leap of the imagination to bring the temple to life. Pilgrims waiting to consult the oracle would shelter in the portico, no doubt killing time by admiring the forest of bronze and gilded statues in front. Though most of these were of Apollo or war heroes, at least one was more controversial – a gilded statue of Phryne, prostitute and lover of the brilliant classical sculptor, Praxiteles. She apparently offended the sensibilities of more than one Ancient Greek pilgrim.

Above the temple of Apollo is the **theatre**, built in the 4th century BC but restructured by the Romans in AD159. It's an impressive place, with most of the stone seats intact and a wonderful view of the sanctuary from the top. There was room for about 5000 spectators, who would come to watch the re-enactment of the battle between Apollo and the Python as well as to hear musical recitals by competitors in the Pythian Games (see below).

● **Stadium** A steep path leads up from the theatre through pine woods to the stadium, where the athletic events in the Pythian Games were held. The games were initially held every eight years, but once the Amphictyonic League had taken control of the sanctuary in 586BC they were held every four years, the league no doubt considering the extra income. In the beginning the games were more of a religious festival, consisting of a hymn in honour of Apollo, but the league widened the appeal by introducing sports events. The first festival of the Amphictyonic regime was held in 582BC, and began with sacrifices to Apollo and the staging of a play about his battle with the Python. Then there were musical contests between musicians and singers in the theatre, followed by athletic competitions in the stadium and a chariot-race on the plain below the sanctuary.

The stadium is oval, like modern stadia, and retains many of the stone seats added in Roman times by the Graecophile emperor, Hadrian. The starting- and finishing-posts are in position, marking each end of a track, a *stade* long (600 Roman feet, 178m), where athletes would have sprinted in the quest for the coveted prize of a laurel wreath. Nowadays the stadium is used every summer, not for athletic events but for the Delphi theatre festival.

● **The Lower Sites** Shaded by pines and plane trees, the two pools of the **Castalian Spring** are filled by water emerging from the ravine which divides the two Phaedriades rocks. It is named after the nymph Castalia, who is supposed to have drowned herself there in order to escape the unwanted attentions of Apollo. Pilgrims to the site would purify themselves by washing their hair, but murderers were required to plunge in. Byron dived in too, convinced by the legend that it fostered poetic powers. There are niches in the rock behind the upper pool into which votive offerings were placed.

The remains of the terraced **gymnasium** are closed to the public, but clearly visible from the road. This is where the athletes in the Pythian Games would train: there were open-air and covered tracks and a circular sunken pool for a cool dip after training. Originally dating from the 4th century BC, most of what you see today is Roman – including the remains of the hot baths which they added.

Beyond the gymnasium is the **sanctuary of Athena**, better known as the Marmaria, or marble quarry – which is what the locals used it as during the Middle Ages. Consequently, the temples to Athena have been reduced to knee-high foundations. Sections of three columns and a curved section of the frieze from the circular Tholos escaped the marble-hungry medieval peasants, and these have been re-erected to form what has become the best-known image of Delphi. No one knows what the Tholos was used for, but, despite the fact that the remaining columns are piebald with modern insertions, this is the most beautiful of all Delphi's temples.

● **Museum** The exhibits are well displayed but are mostly labelled in only French and Greek.

At the top of the steps is a Hellenistic or Roman copy of the **omphalos**, or navel-stone, which marked the legendary centre of the world. It is shaped, as Pindar described it in the Pythian Odes, like half an ostrich egg, and carved with an intertwining network of hanks of wool. The stone would have been anointed with sacred oil every day.

The **Hall of the Siphnian Treasury** contains the sections remaining from the sculpted frieze and pediment of the treasury. Although these are damaged, it is easy to imagine why the historian Herodotus thought it the most striking monument in Delphi: in his day, the hair, clothes and armour would have been brightly painted in red and green, and many of the weapons inlaid with bronze. Two of the most splendid figures would have been the caryatids which supported the west end of the treasury; athough only the upper half of one and the head of the other remains, you can see the holes in their hair where jewels would have been placed.

A sculpted frieze ran all the way around the treasury. The best-preserved sections are from the eastern and northern sides: the east frieze shows the gods sitting and watching the Trojan War, while in the north frieze the gods move from being spectators to participants in a violent battle against the giants.

The hall is dominated by the Winged Sphinx of Naxos, almost 2½m high, standing on the Ionian capital of a column once over 12m. The Delphic priests were so impressed with the Naxians' offering that they granted them *premanteia* (the right to queue-jump when consulting the oracle).

In the **Hall of the Athenian Treasury**, as well as the metopes showing the Labours of Herakles, the Exploits of Theseus and the Battle of the Amazons you can see the text and musical notation (in Greek letters) for two hymns to Apollo which were inscribed on the walls of the treasury. These hymns were sung during a sacrifice at the treasury's altar by a large choir of Athenians accompanied by lyres and flutes.

The **Hall of the Monument of Daochos** contains a very fine marble group of three dancing girls atop a column finely carved with acanthus leaves, and statues from the monument of Daochos, including the slim, slinky runner Agelaios, a victor in the Pythian Games, and his perfectly proportioned brother Agias, who looks far too elegant to have been a famous wrestler and boxer.

One of the finest and most famous statues in the museum is the bronze figure of a victor in the chariot-race of the Pythian Games, in the **Hall of the Charioteer**. It owes its fame partly to its eyes, of black onyx and white enamel, which seem to follow you as you walk around the room. The life-size statue originally formed part of an ambitious group, standing on a chariot pulled by four horses, of which only scant fragments have survived.

In a neighbouring room the marble statue of Antinous appears to epitomise Classical Greek beauty. In fact, the youth was the favourite of the Roman emperor Hadrian, who deified him after his early death by drowning in the Nile.

Volos and Mount Pelion

'Welcome to hell' says the graffito on the earthquake-proof apartment block. An exaggeration maybe, but standing on the sea-front in mid-summer, breathing in rank fishy air thick with dust and exhaust fumes, hell doesn't seem so far away.

Volos is Greece's third port and its newest industrial town; the old town, like all those before it, was destroyed by an earthquake. Its anti-seismic buildings stand in rank and file between the slopes of Mount Pelion and the Gulf of Volos. Beneath the anonymous blocks lie the remains of Iolkos, the port from which Jason and the Argonauts set sail on their quest for the golden fleece; and presumably somewhere below the chaotic lorry-park on the sea-front is the shipyard where the *Argo*, a masterpiece of ancient engineering, was built: a model of the splendid ship sits on a pedestal, shaming its modern descendants – grimy ferries bound for the northern Sporades and, when Middle Eastern politics permit, Syria.

As well as being a ferry port, Volos is also the gateway to the villages of the Pelion. Although most people are only too anxious to leave the town behind, it is worth remaining for long enough to visit the tourist office (on the sea-front) which has bus timetables and lists of hotels and rooms in the area. There is also a surprisingly interesting **archaeological museum**, which contains a superb collection of gravestones and a unique and imaginatively presented display of Neolithic finds.

Many of the marble funerary stones (*stelae*) are painted and show scenes from the lives of the dead (some of them, amazingly, seem three-dimensional). The settings are mostly domestic, with the dead reclining elegantly on curvaceous stools surrounded by their families. The stones were usually erected by the rich, but the modest contents discovered inside some of the tombs from which these were taken suggest that some poorer families also honoured their dead in this way.

Another fine collection is that of Mycenaean pottery

discovered in the nearby palace of ancient Iolkos (full excavation of the site has been held up because it lies under some modern buildings near the Larissa road). Objects include votive figurines with their arms raised in praise of the gods, and a fragment of a pot painted with Jason's *Argo*, most of which has been reconstructed.

Neolithic exhibits include finds from Sesklo, the earliest dated farming settlement in Greece, to the west of Volos, thought to have been founded around 6500BC by pioneers from central Asia. Their houses were built of clay and wattle on stone foundations, and for the first 500 years, as land was plentiful, remained unfortified. Then, as subsequent waves of immigrants led to squabbles over land, the settlements were walled. Objects including fat female figurines, tools, storage pots and carbonised grains are made more meaningful by being displayed along with models, diagrams and designs.

To the east of Volos, the landscape of **Mount Pelion**, curling around like a crooked finger into the Aegean, is unlike any in Greece. Its slopes are covered with apple, walnut and chestnut trees and scented with the aroma of 2000 herbs; roads wind through leafy tunnels and above deep gorges, cutting up to mountain villages or down to beaches; while it's no undiscovered paradise, you can still find villages where the only sounds are the babbling of streams and the hooves of mules thudding on cobbled paths.

The villages are as unique as the landscape. Granted a degree of independence during Turkish rule, they flourished as trading posts, exporting their textiles, silk and wine throughout Europe. The wealthiest traders built themselves beautiful mansions of local stone, crowned by half-timbered upper storeys with stained-glass windows. Some have now been restored by the Greek National Tourist Organisation, and opened as hotels.

Consequently, the Pelion is becoming increasingly popular, and peace can be hard to come by in the better-known villages and on the beaches, especially between mid-July and mid-August. However, on our last visit to Visitsa in late August, we found no one except a couple of agricultural workers returning from their fields on mules. Busier, but by no means overcrowded, were the villages of Portaria and Makrinitsa and the seaside resort of Agios Ioanis.

Starting from Volos, you could see most of the Pelion in two days, but it's likely that you'll want to stay far longer – relaxing on sandy beaches, lazing on plane-shaded *plateias* and getting pleasantly lost in mazes of steep cobbled alleyways. The coast road from Volos passes a series of rather busy pebble beaches; it is only after the turnoff for Milies that you begin to discover the real beauty of the area. (If you do want to stop for a swim, however, there's a sandy beach at Kala Nera.) Leaving the coast, the road cuts through a valley of olive groves, then climbs up alongside a red cliff, looking down to the sea over a green valley spiked with pillars of rock. A dispersed village of largely new houses, **Milies** was a hotbed of the independence movement during Turkish rule, and the headquarters of the Thessalian branch of a secret society that planned and encouraged rebellion. Less violently, it also kept Greek culture alive in the schools – you can visit the library to see bits and pieces of classroom equipment used by the teacher-revolutionaries.

Milies also claims to be the site of a legendary school. In a cave near the old railway station the centaur Chiron, a mythological doctor who gave his name to 'chirurgery' (surgery), is supposed to have trained the god of healing, Asklepios.

At the end of a side road from Milies lies the sleepy village of **Visitsa**, with a large *plateia* shaded by an immense plane tree, and a cluster of traditional mansions. Some have been shattered by earthquakes, others have recently been restored and opened as hotels. Even if you aren't intending to sleep here, it's worth asking to have a look around: the upper, half-timbered storeys are particularly appealing, with beautiful panelled and painted ceilings, and intricately carved shutters opening on to tiny arched and stained-glass windows.

There's more traditional art to be seen in the church behind the plane tree. Outside there are simple frescoes, and, though it is locked because of its collapsed roof, through the windows you can see the carved and gilded wooden iconostasis and stucco decoration.

Wandering along the narrow cobbled alleyways you have to watch your feet, for at intervals runnels, channelling water to the houses, cut across them. There is a taverna where you can eat outside under a trellis heavy with vines, gourds and watermelons, and a cafe with a magnificent view over wooded hills to the sea. If you can't afford to sleep in a mansion, there are rooms to rent.

Just east of Milies, a left turn puts you on the road to Tsangarada, running along the top of a valley and lined with hedgerows and apple trees. The road then zigzags dizzily in and out of a series of sheer rocky gorges which carve their way to the sea. It's worth stopping just before the village of Xorithi for a magnificent view across the Aegean to the islands of Skiathos and Skopelos.

Tsangarada is four villages in one, each with its own church and *plateia*, straggled over luxuriantly wooded slopes which descend towards the sea. The traditional houses are more modest than those in Visitsa, and most of the rooms to rent are in modern buildings. The *plateia* of the Agia Pareskevi quarter is shaded by a gigantic 1000-year-old plane tree, said to be the oldest in Greece.

A road winds down through lush woods to the lovely and fairly popular bay of **Milopotamos**, 8km away. Its coarse sandy beach is backed by rocky cliffs, and a natural archway in the rock leads to a small and quieter pebbly beach. The swimming is good, but the beach shelves quite steeply.

Just off the main road above the village, the *Kantavros* hotel (B) has clean and fresh-smelling rooms with lovely views. Beyond it on the main road are rooms for rent: spotless, with private bathroom, marble floors and pine furniture (the local telephone number is 0423 49228).

Further north along the coast **Agios Ioanis** is a popular resort with a good white sand beach in town and two others within walking distance. The sea-front is lively, with discos, water-sports, tavernas and beach shops; if you want a good night's sleep it's best to choose a room or hotel that is set back from it on the clifftop – such as the new and comfortable *Eftihia* (B).

Scattered among luscious orchards of peach, apple, pear and plum, with views out to the Aegean, **Zagora** is the largest of the Pelion villages. It grew rich from the production of woollen textiles, silk and ribbons, which were exported throughout Europe from the port of Chorefto, 8km away. On the main *plateia*, close to the top of the village, is the church of Agios Giorgios, which shelters an immense iconostasis, gilded and carved so delicately that it resembles gold filigree. **Chorefto** is now a small fishing village with a sweeping golden beach of coarse sand and shingle, backed by wooded slopes. Both villages have rooms to rent.

Back in the direction of Volos (17km away) the inland village of **Makrinitsa** is the most popular village in the Pelion. Its whitewashed houses tumble down a steep mountainside; because of the incline, many have three storeys at the front and just one at the back – which is often the main entrance. No cars are allowed in the village – the cobbled streets are so narrow that even the refuse is collected by horse – so you have to park outside on a shady square.

The Greek National Tourist Organisation has restored and converted several houses into A-category guest-houses; however, there are similar and cheaper private hotels too. The *Diomidi* (B) is a traditional house in a sumptuous garden of fuchsias, clematis and geraniums above the main *plateia*; the *Arhontiko*

Routso is a traditional-style hotel on the main street, with slightly cramped rooms and steep steps. Most of the hotels and tavernas are along the main street, their terraces awash with vines and flowers, and there is also, predictably, a generous sprinkling of souvenir shops. A stall sells sticky cakes of nuts and dried fruit, fruits preserved in honey and many varieties of the medicinal and culinary herbs for which the Pelion is famous – all of them with labels in English detailing the ailments they cure. The main *plateia* is justifiably known as the balcony of the Pelion; from a distance Volos looks like a truncated New York. Here you can shelter from the heat under the spreading branches of a plane tree, eating or drinking at the old taverna, whose neo-classical façade masks a rustic interior decorated with cartwheels and stuffed goats.

Somewhat more tasteful is the décor in the *ouzeri* just behind the church. On its walls are frescoes by the fine local 'primitive' artist Theophilos (1873–1934) of scenes of bucolic boozing, feasting and dancing. Equally naïve are the carvings on the exterior of the small church, the most appealing of which is a dragon with a prettily painted tail.

For the rest, there are steep cobbled streets to explore, some of them winding past neglected and crumbling houses, others leading to churches, and all of them little trodden by tourists. Part of the fun is getting lost, for you never quite know what you'll come across. Below the main *plateia* is a pleasingly eerie church, Agios Assassinassios, which has been abandoned for so long that a tree has grown inside it; below the church clock tower the Theotokou monastery has some lovely carved reliefs in the apse.

Below Makrinitsa, the bustling little village of **Portaria** is a good place at which to stop for lunch, for there's plenty of village life on and around the large *plateia* to keep you entertained while you eat. However, as it's on a main road, and less attractive than Makrinitsa, there's little to detain you.

Below the village, between Anakassia and Ano Volos, in the foothills of the Pelion, is the **Kondos House**, a fine building whose inner walls are completely covered in frescoes by Theophilos. Dressed in traditional costume of woollen hose and a pleated skirt, he moved from place to place, singing as he painted, and asking for no payment beyond the cost of his materials. (He also, apparently, had a penchant for dressing up as Alexander the Great.) There are vividly coloured scenes from the War of Independence, with the occasional mythological event thrown in for good measure, all surrounded by birds, fish, flowers and foliage. The details of background – like the palm-munching giraffe and the fish and ducks bobbing beneath a fountain – and of the rich costumes are frequently more absorbing than the narrative content.

The Meteora monasteries

A chaos of rocky pillars, pinnacles and precipices rises abruptly on the north-west fringe of the Trikkala plain, which lies at the feet of the mighty Pindos Mountains. Many were once crowned by monasteries or hermitages, of which only a handful remain – a few are still inhabited, more are dangerously ruinous or inaccessible. Restoration and tourist interest (the two inextricably linked) has ensured that dereliction has been halted; what is more difficult is to retain some of the feeling of awe at the sight of these extraordinary buildings ('Meteora' means 'in the air') in the face of the broad new road that is now their way of (relatively easy) access, and all the paraphernalia of the tourist trade that attaches itself to such popular sites. While the sale at monasteries of curios like vases or postcards may be questionable, visitors will welcome the sight of cold drinks and ice-cream vendors, particularly after they've struggled, inappropriately shod, up and down the long flights of steps carved into the rocks. Even this is an immeasurable improvement on the methods of access available until the 1920s: a skimpy ladder clamped to an almost vertical rock-face, or a net suspended from a rope which was winched up (the classic reply to a question about how often the rope was renewed was 'only when it breaks').

While the Meteora winters are severe – there have been mists so thick that monks have bumped into one another during mass – in summer it's baking hot, and, though it's tempting to wear as little as possible to cope with the long ascent, the rules for dress are strict. Women in trousers or shorts are not allowed in, and skirts must cover knees; men must wear trousers, not shorts, and the monks at Agios Nikolaos are not keen on long hair unless worn by Orthodox priests; both men and women must have their shoulders and upper arms covered, and a quickly donned scarf is not considered adequate.

The rocks on to which the monasteries cling perilously were formed 25 million years ago, when the sea which covered the whole of Thessaly poured through the Vale of Tempe into the Aegean. It left deposits of silt and sand behind it, which were eroded by water, wind, rain and earthquakes to become today's forest of a thousand stone monoliths.

Streaked by water-deposits and striped with seams of pebbles and sand, they appear creased and folded from a distance, and in the dazzling midday sun you'll begin to see grimacing and distorted faces forming themselves out of the light and shadow.

How the first monk climbed up to build the first monastery, Great Meteoron, on top of a 413m-high pillar of rock, remains a mystery. Legend would have it that in the 14th century its founder, Saint Athanasios, was air-lifted by an angel, while sceptics reckon he used a kite or was given lessons in rock-climbing by the locals. Life on the rocks was severely ascetic, but many monks followed Athanasios to the Meteora, attracted by the opportunity of living a spiritual life uninterrupted by the wars and squabbles which plagued the rest of the country. Some lived as hermits in caves, but most joined together and formed communities, and by the 16th century over 30 monasteries or small communities had been built.

The aim of the Orthodox monastic life was to acquire the Holy Spirit through eternal prayer. The monk passed through a stage of petitioning prayer to a state of spiritual prayer in which he ceased to ask for anything, but gained absolute trust in God. The monk was then thought to step outside himself and to enter a state of spiritual ecstasy. In the monasteries' frescoes, the emphasis is on saints who died for their faith, presumably in a state of ecstasy, rather than on the 'good works' more familiar in western churches.

The monasteries, especially Great Meteoron and Varlaam, are extremely popular with coach-parties as well as independent travellers. Consequently, it's advisable to visit them as early as possible, and then head down to the quieter monasteries which, unlike Great Meteoron and Varlaam, are open at lunchtime.

Meteora: monasteries

• **Great Meteoron** This, the oldest and highest of the Meteora monasteries, is too severe to be beautiful; but the views are formidable and the frescoes memorable.

The martyrdoms frescoed on the walls of the narthex are particularly ghoulish, featuring saints being stabbed, hacked, shot, decapitated, hammered with nails, dragged by a horse, and boiled alive in a cauldron. The ground, not surprisingly, is littered with severed heads, dripping with blood but still retaining their haloes.

In contrast, the inner church is sumptuously decorated with a carved and gilded iconostasis, gold-backed frescoes, and a splendid throne and bible-stand of wood inlaid with marble. The influence of the landscape on the Meteora artists is evident in the Baptism of Christ, which is framed by immense, almost cubist crags. Outside the church is an ancient and heavy wooden plank, beaten instead of a bell to summon the monks to prayer.

In addition, you can visit the kitchen, with its primitive array of clumsy ladles, bowls and a cave-like oven – a nice contrast with the refinement of the icons and illuminated manuscripts in the small treasury, which clearly shows where the monks' priorities lay.

• **Varlaam (Barlaam)** Varlaam, just below Great Meteoron, also has its frescoes of violent martyrdoms, adding to the catalogue of saintly deaths a revolting portrait of a martyr hanging from his ankles while he is skinned alive. Less gory but equally dramatic is the Last Judgement, with the mouth of Hell represented by a curly fanged fish-monster greedily swallowing the damned, while the blessed blissfully float above in cloudy capsules.

When Varlaam's refectory was restored as a museum in the early 1960s, the materials were transported in the time-honoured fashion by a windlass mechanism. As you'll see from the postcards showing black-gowned monks huddled in nets and dangling in mid-air, it wasn't only sand and cement that was transported in this way – even if the monks agreed to take the ride only for the sake of publicity. One look down from the windlass tower is sufficient to terrify most people.

The museum itself has a collection of portable icons, used by monks when they were on the move, and some worn and warped books that look equally well travelled. The strangest exhibit, however, is a tapestry which depicts Christ as if an anatomical drawing from a medical textbook, with his heart, liver and kidneys carefully embroidered on his body.

• **Roussanou** This monastery is fused on to an isolated pillar which is no broader than the monastery itself. To get there you have to cross a narrow but comfortingly sturdy bridge; and best of all, the monastery attracts far fewer visitors than either of the larger ones.

There are some fine frescoes: more martyrdoms, if you can take them, and a magnificent Last Judgement – in the centre the souls are weighed, and the blessed dispatched on clouds to a pretty paradise of flowers and birds, while the damned are sucked down a red 'water-chute' to a hell of vicious beasts feasting on the sinners.

• **Agios Nikolaos** The most remarkable of all the Meteora frescoes are in the monastery of Agios Nikolaos, opposite Roussanou. They are by the 16th-century Cretan artist Theophanis who was famous for painting saints and biblical characters who resemble real individuals rather than lifeless ciphers.

You can stare into the faces of his saints and feel that they are spiritually enlightened, and dally in his gorgeous Paradise in which a vulture, dragon, bear and leopard live in harmony with an elephant, monkey, deer and rabbit. Best of all is the Ride into Jerusalem: Christ is no distant figure, but turns around to talk to the people who are welcoming him.

• **Agios Stephanos** The convent of Agios Stephanos sits on a solitary pillar, joined to the mountain behind by a bridge over a chasm. Its chief glory is the view from the terrace, which takes in the village of Kalambaka below (the actual distance by road to the village is 8½km).

Two villages close to the Meteora monasteries have accommodation. **Kalambaka** is a large and very commercialised village 5km away, with plenty of hotels, rooms to rent, tavernas and souvenir shops. The old village was burnt by the Germans in the Second World War; the one building to escape was the 14th-century cathedral, dedicated to the Dormition of the Virgin, which was built on the site of an ancient temple. You can see fragments of this and of earlier churches in the walls, and inside there are 16th-century frescoes. The modern village is impressively situated, sprawling at the foot of the immense ridged and pocked rocks. Many of the hotels have fine views of the looming Meteora rocks. The *Odissian* (c) on the road out to Kastraki is rather noisy, but has adequate rooms; just beyond lies the similar *Helvetia* (c). In quiet grounds just outside the village above the main road is the *Xenia* hotel (A), whose public rooms are furnished with a tasteful combination of traditional antiques and modern furniture; its bedrooms are spacious and have balconies.

Kastraki is a smaller but equally commercialised village, about 3km from the monasteries. Its position is even more spectacular than that of Kalambaka, for it nestles below an amphitheatre of stone monoliths. But accommodation consists of only a few rooms to rent and just one basic hotel, the *Kastraki* (E), which has clean bedrooms without bathrooms.

Mount Olympos

Mount Olympos forms the border of Thessaly and Macedonia. 'Shaken by no wind, drenched by no showers, and invaded by no snows, it is set in a cloudless sea of limpid air with a white radiance. There the happy gods spend their delightful days' reads Homer's description of the home of the gods. Unfortunately, it appears that many hikers have taken Homer at his word – more of them have died on Mount Olympos than on any other mountain in Greece.

The wooded slopes and rocky peaks of Olympos rise suddenly from a narrow coastal plain – a dramatic setting, but also a hazardous one, for its proximity to the sea means that the mountain, far from being cloudless, is prone to sudden mists and rapid and extreme temperature changes. In addition, it would seem that if Homer ever saw it, it must have been in summer – for between October and March its peaks are capped with snow, making an ascent unwise for any but the most experienced climbers.

Of Olympos's nine peaks, all are above 2600m (8350 feet) and the highest, Mitikas, rises to an awesome 2917m (9186 feet). The nearest village to the starting-points of the trails is **Litohoro**, where there are hotels and rooms to rent.

From Litohoro a rough road leads up to the footpaths. Route 1 (marked with red dots) starts 18km from the village, Route 2 (blue dots) 11km. Between the two you can spend a pretty basic and uncomfortable night at the semi-abandoned monastery of Agios Dimitrios if you want to make an early start.

Most worthwhile hikes take at least two days, but the

mountain is well served with hostels and refuges – some seasonal, some open all year, and others opened by prior arrangement; information is available from the Greek Alpine Club office in Litohoro. The best practical guidebook in English to the Olympos hikes is *Greece on Foot* by Marc Dubin; in the *Flight of Ikaros* Kevin Andrews gives a vivid account of getting lost in an Olympian fog.

Dion

Although little but foundations remain of the ancient Macedonian city of Dion, on the fertile Peiria plain at the foot of Mount Olympos, it played a central role in the religious life of the state. It was the Macedonians' equivalent of Olympia, dedicated to the Olympian Zeus, and with a cultural and athletic festival on the Olympian model, held in honour of the god. Euripides wrote plays for its theatre, and Macedonian kings would come to ask for Zeus's aid before they went to battle, and to offer thanks after a victory. When Macedonia was expanding in the 4th century BC, Dion was considered so vital to the morale of the state that it was fortified, and the Roman *odeions*, baths, houses and public latrine which have been discovered on the site show that it was still important in the 3rd century AD.

Some of the site is closed to the public, as it is still undergoing excavation, and as the ruins are somewhat confusing you should arm yourself with a plan before exploring it. The finds from the site are well displayed in the small museum, and are colour-coded to show which buildings they derive from. There are statues, votive offerings and the remains of animals and humans found in the town's cemetery.

The West

From the site of Delphi, whether you're heading north to Epirus or south to the Peloponnese, you need to take the Corinthian Gulf coast road. This joins the coast at the small ugly port of **Itea** and continues to **Galaxidi**, a quiet water-front town. Its tall stone houses date from the 19th century when the town was home to 50 shipping magnates who traded throughout the Mediterranean.

Beyond Galaxidi there's little to detain you until you reach **Nafpaktos**, a small resort with an oval harbour guarded by towers and dominated by a hilltop Venetian fortress encircled by bands of walls whose crenellations peep through thick woods.

In the Middle Ages Nafpaktos was known as Lepanto, and gave its name to the famous 16th-century battle in which an allied Christian fleet from Italy, Spain and Malta overwhelmingly beat the Turks, thereby proving to the world that the Turks were not invincible.

Beyond Nafpaktos is the small port of **Andirrion**, from which year-round car-ferries make the short crossing to Patras on the Peloponnese.

The road then cuts inland, but before heading north fans of Byron will want to pay homage to the poet and freedom-fighter at **Missolonghi** (Mesolongi), the place of his death. Byron described it as a 'realm of mud', and this town on the edge of a vast and stagnant lagoon is still a dismal and dank place and not somewhere you'll want to linger.

Byron came to Greece in order to help the Greeks in their fight for independence from the Turks. In January 1824 he came to Missolonghi, accompanied by a doctor, nine servants and an extensive and extravagant wardrobe of embroidered uniforms, cocked hats and gilded helmets. He was welcomed by a 21-gun salute and given command of 5000 soldiers. He spent over three months drilling his troops and planning an attack on Nafpaktos, which by then was back in Turkish hands.

That Byron's Missolonghi was as lacking in diversions as is the modern town is obvious from the poet's leisure pursuits – swimming, riding, shooting at bottles and being paddled around the lagoon in a punt, mystifying the boatman with his 'strange western songs'. It was on one of his boating trips that he was caught in a rainstorm, after which he developed the fever that killed him. His request – 'Let not my body be hacked or be sent to England. Here let my bones moulder. Lay me in the first corner without pomp or nonsense' – was ignored. His corpse was dissected, parcelled up in a barrel and sent to England, and though poetic justice might have preferred his heart to have been buried in Missolonghi, it is in fact his lungs which are buried beneath his statue in the town's Garden of Heroes. A small collection of Byron memorabilia is housed in the museum.

From the swampy coastline around Missolonghi, the road heads north into Epirus. Other than a short, dramatic gorge of splintered and jagged cliffs and a couple of bleak glassy lakes, there's little of interest en route until you reach the wide Ambracian Gulf.

On the north-west side, the unremarkable town of **Preveza** lies on one side of a narrow strait which acts as the outlet to the gulf. It is the southern promontory on the strait which is of more interest, albeit mainly to those interested in ancient history or familiar with Shakespearian tragedy – for this is the headland of **Actium** (Aktion), the scene of one of the most famous battles of Roman times, and of one man's downfall for love of a woman. The man was Mark Antony, his lover Cleopatra, Queen of Egypt; and the victor was Antony's rival Octavian, the future Emperor Augustus.

Antony's advisors were agreed that he would do best to conduct a battle with Octavian on land. Not only were his men more experienced in land battles, but his vessels were bulkier and less easy to manoeuvre than those of Octavian, and were seriously undermanned. Antony's foolish insistence to fight at sea was blamed on Cleopatra, whose views were said to have decided the issue. A catalogue of disasters followed. Plutarch relates the story: 'Three or four of Octavian's ships clustered round each one of Antony's and the fighting was carried on with wicker shields, spears, poles and flaming missiles, while Antony's soldiers also shot with catapults from wooden towers.' At the height of battle, 'while neither side had gained a decisive advantage, Cleopatra's squadron of 60 ships was suddenly seen to hoist sail and make off through the very midst of the battle'. The formation was thrown into disorder as they plunged through. 'The enemy watched them with amazement, as they spread their sails before the following wind and shaped their course for the Peloponnese.' It was then that Antony 'revealed to all the world that he was no longer guided by the motives of a commander. No sooner did he see her ships sailing away than every other consideration was blotted out of his mind, and he abandoned and betrayed the men who were fighting and dying for his cause . . . he hurried after the woman who had already ruined him and would soon complete his destruction.' Antony's shame was great; for three days he was unable to speak to Cleopatra.

Antony's men continued to hold out against Octavian for several hours, and finally surrendered; 300 ships were captured, and 5000 men had been killed. His land forces, consisting of 19 legions of infantry and 12,000 cavalry, could not at first believe they had been betrayed by their commander; only when finding themselves cut off from their supplies and deserted by their leaders did they finally surrender to their conqueror, a week after the battle.

Nothing remains on the site of Actium today, although archaeological investigation has found the remains of sunken ships. However, 8km north of Preveza are the ruins of the city of **Nikopolis**, 'Victory City', founded by Octavian as a memorial to his victory. The site is extensive, but very overgrown. The most impressive remaining parts are 6th-century walls built by Justinian, a large theatre and four basilicas, one of which contains one of the finest mosaic floors in Greece.

To the north of the Ambracian Gulf, **Arta** is a largely modern town, in and around which only its remarkable Byzantine churches stand as testimony to its importance in the 13th and 14th centuries, when it was mainland Greece's second city (after Salonika). Set back from the main street, Odos Pyrrou, the churches of Agia Theodora and Agios Vasileos both have elaborately decorated exteriors – the former patterned with intricate brickwork and tiles of turquoise, yellow and white. It's also worth looking inside Agia Theodora if it's open – with its carpets and brass candelabra glinting in the flickering candlelight, the atmosphere is more like that of an opium den than a church.

The most spectacular church is the Panagia Parigoritissa. Grand and palatial, it rises above the central Plateia Skoufa, a massive red and cream brick cube pierced by double-arched windows and crowned with six coolie-hatted domes. The main dome is best seen from inside, as it is supported on a primitive (and cracking) cantilever system which appears to be on the point of collapse.

Leaving Arta by the road to Ioanina you pass its most famous landmark – a multi-humped Turkish bridge which is supposed to have the body of the master-mason's wife incarcerated inside. The story goes that when the bridge was being built in the 17th century, the central pier was swept away by the river every time it was completed. Finally, a proverbial little bird informed the builders that until the master-mason's wife had been bricked up inside the pier it would continue to collapse. So the unfortunate wife was lured to the bridge and, having been told that her husband's ring had fallen inside the pier, climbed down to recover it and immediately found herself being buried alive in a cascade of rubble and stone. Legend would have it that the woman's voice still haunts the bridge.

Igoumenitsa is a useful port town with ferries to Corfu, Italy and Yugoslavia; it's also well served by buses. There is, however, little reason to remain there for any longer than you have to. On the sea-front, to the north of the port, the *El Greco* (C) has extremely clean rooms and a reasonable restaurant.

The main resort in western Greece, and the only one offered as part of a package by British tour operators, is PARGA, 50km south of Igoumenitsa. Holiday-makers who make their way there along the hilly inland main road may never discover the undulating and indented Threspotian coast to the south of Igomenitsa, which shelters some of the most attractive beaches of the Greek mainland – particularly around the small and low-key resort of **Sivota**, about 15 miles from Igoumenitsa. Coastal hills are cloaked with olives, pines, firs and cypresses, and in spring yellow juniper bushes add splashes of colour, and wild herbs scent the air. The beaches are backed by olive groves or architectonic fantasies of fractured rock; some are of soft sand, others of fine subtly coloured shingle or white pebbles, and most are clean, as is the sea. Many are accessible by footpaths from the coast road, but to reach the more out-of-the-way beaches, including those on the maquis-covered offshore islets, you will need to hire a self-drive boat.

Sivota still retains a village atmosphere, despite being popular with Greek, German and Italian holiday-makers in high season. It's a pleasant place, and also makes a convenient base from which to explore Epirus. The focus of life is the tiny harbour, where long evenings can be spent over meals of fresh fish in one of the simple sea-front tavernas (if you want more action there are seasonal discos). The locals measure out their days with cups of syrupy coffee overlooked by shelves of Ajax and packets of biscuits in gloomy *kafeneions* that double as grocers' shops. The pace of life is unhurried, and exchanging money in one of the two tour offices can be a lengthy business, involving traipsing across with the owner to a cafe to check the day's exchange rate in the newspaper.

Excursions can be organised to the sights of Epirus, including Ioanina, Dodona, the Zagoria villages, the Necromanteion of Ephyra, Parga and Paxi, as well as further afield to the Meteora monasteries. If the tour includes lunch it can work out rather expensive, and you may find it more economical to hire a car or motor-bike for a few days.

There are plenty of modest hotels and rooms to rent, and more are being built. The *Hellas* (E) is a clean and simple hotel set back from the main road. The smallish bedrooms have balconies, and the olive-shaded terrace is a pleasant place for breakfast. Five minutes' walk from the port (and ten minutes' from Savgia beach) the *Sivota* (C) is a well-kept hotel on the main coast road which runs through the resort. The bedrooms are of a good size and have balconies; some come with a tiny kitchen. There is a restaurant, but its atmosphere cannot compete with the water-front tavernas. A swimming-pool and tennis court are currently under construction. Reasonably priced excursions to the main sights of Epirus are organised from the hotel.

A more sophisticated base is the *Robinson Club* (B), a hotel complex much used by German, Austrian and Swiss tour operators. It's built in the Epirot style, steeply terraced among well-established gardens on a hill overlooking the island of Bellavraka, and out of sight of the village. The rooms are tastefully furnished, and the simple but elegant restaurant and hilltop disco positioned to make the most of the sea views.

Activities on offer range from sailing, waterskiing and windsurfing from the small beach at the foot of the hotel, to art and silkscreen printing, and there are special activities for children. The steps and pathways which run up and down the hill are rather steep and could be dangerous for young children.

The closest beach to the village is three minutes' walk to the south of the water-front – clean and pebbly, but not very comfortable or attractive. **Mega Amos** is the main, and busiest, beach – 10 to 15 minutes' walk from the village. Facilities include watersports and three taverna-cafes, and it's a popular spot for rough camping. The beach is of coarse sand, fine shingle and rounded pebbles in lovely shades of coral, cream and grey. The sea bed shelves very suddenly, which means the swimming is good, but children will need close supervision.

Closer to Sivota is the small secluded white sand and shingle beach of **Savgia**. The play of light and shadow on the turquoise sea in this sheltered horseshoe bay creates Hockneyesque patterns on the sandy sea bed, dappled by deep inky pools as you swim above rocks. Within swimming distance is a miniature beach of white rocks, which can also be reached by foot from the road along a path overgrown with prickly undergrowth and aromatic wild herbs.

If you are exploring by boat, you could either head south along the coast until you find a beach that appeals, or sail out to one of the three islets. On the islet of Bellavraka, opposite the Robinson Club hotel complex, there are two beaches (with facilities) which can be reached by a sandy causeway in the summer. Far more attractive, however, are the tiny white beaches backed by rocky amphitheatres on the islets of Agios Nikolaos and Mavro Oros. The best are on either side of the straits between the islands.

A slightly quieter base than Sivota in high season is the sleepy inland village of **Perdika**, approached through groves of gnarled olives fringed by juniper bushes. But it's at its most attractive out of season when the silence is disturbed only by the muted susurrus of voices from the *kafeneions* which surround the paved *plateia*. Behind are clusters of faded Epirot houses, but most are modern, red-roofed and whitewashed. Several have rooms to rent. If you are without your own transport you may find it a convenient place at which to stay, as it is connected by bus with Igoumenitsa.

A short drive away is the beach of **Arillas**, a beautiful curve of soft sand backed by maquis, cypresses and juniper bushes. The sand closest to the sea is damp enough for sandcastles, and the seabed is smooth, sandy and level for about 10m, after which it shelves suddenly; to the north are a few rocks where the current can be quite strong. There is a beach bar, fish taverna and a few seasonal rooms to rent; in summer the beach is popular with German, Greek and Italian holiday-makers.

Igoumenitsa is a good starting-point for a tour of inland Greece; you can head east into the mountains to explore the towns of Ioanina and Metsovo and the villages of the Zagoria. Those people who wish to tackle a circular tour of Central Greece should bear in mind the nature of the main-road link between the mountain areas of Epirus and the plains of Thessaly. Although on a map the monasteries of the Meteora may seem deceptively near, the spectacular mountain road that crosses the Pindos Mountains is one of the most awesome in Greece, and not to be undertaken lightly.

As soon as you drive eastwards from Igoumenitsa, the mountains come into view, their smooth bare contours contrasting with the thickly furred slopes of the Thiamis valley. Keen photographers should leave themselves plenty of time, as the textures, colours and forms of the rocks are fascinating – cliffs are scrunched or creased, slopes scarred, gullied and screed by water erosion, and stratas of grey and gold rock tilt at crazy diagonals. In the foreground, bright light intensifies the rust, aubergine, terracotta and creamy hues of the rocks; beyond, in the distance, are the pale blue mountains of Albania.

The road winds up over an immense flat-topped limestone mountain on the border between the regions of Ioanina and Thesprotia and down into a sparer lonely valley. From here you can either continue along the main road to IOANINA or branch off to Zitsa and, further on, to the villages of the ZAGORIA.

Beautifully positioned far above the river Kalamos, the village of **Zitsa** is famous for its fizzy wine and for a visit by Byron. On seeing the river – called the Acheron in ancient times, and supposedly emerging from the Underworld – Byron wrote his famous line 'If this is hell, close shamed Elysium's gates', which can hardly have endeared him to the monks who let him stay in their monastery above the village.

The village itself, though not immediately attractive, has a fascinating main street with an ancient bakery and cavern-like shops in which you can buy the very cheap local wine. There are lovely views from the shady *plateia*, although the peace is sometimes interrupted by the clatter of games machines.

The monastery where Byron stayed is reached by an unmade road at the far end of the village. Attached to the wall is an excerpt from *Childe Harold* which the monks presumably considered more suitable than his praise of hell: 'Monastic Zitsa! from thy shady brow, Thou small but favoured spot of holy ground! Where'er we gaze, around, above, below, What rainbow tints, what magic charms are found!'

Small and shady it certainly is, but its charms have now been discovered by weekend picnickers, and it has been kitted out with barbecue stands and liberally sprinkled with litter. The views on both sides, across valleys and mountains, are some compensation, but the monastery is best avoided at summer weekends.

The road from Ioanina to METSOVO climbs and descends the forbidding Mitsikeli range in great sweeps, then follows a fast-flowing tributary of the Arachtos past the towering crags of Mount Peristeri. The road (which is subject to rock-falls) then ascends a gorge and the scenery of the Pindos Mountains becomes increasingly rugged. Fifteen kilometres beyond the mountain village of Metsovo is the **Pass of Katara**, the highest road pass in Greece (1705m, 5594 feet), which is sometimes closed between mid-October and mid-May. Despite recent improvements, some of the high section of this mountain road stil has poor stretches. Much of it is tortuous, with many sharp bends, blind corners and unmarked edges. It is not advisable to tackle it at night, and even in daylight it requires great care, especially in wet weather.

Parga

Parga is a popular resort in high season, and it shows. The splashes of colour on the traditional whitewashed houses are as likely to be bits of plastic advertising 'English Breakfast' as window-boxes brimming with geraniums; the evening *volta* is less of a stroll than a squeeze through the streets; and any toes you trample on in the process are more likely to be British or German than Greek.

But despite the crowds, and the small modern hotels and villas which have been built to house them, Parga has its attractions. The village has a fine mountainous hinterland and is crowned by a ruined Venetian fortress; it overlooks an islet in a tranquil bay; it's sheltered by promontories green with pines and olives behind which are two long beaches; and it is well placed for trips inland to the Necromanteion of Ephyra (see below) and by caique to the island of Paxos.

Two acceptable hotels are the breakfast-only *Bacoli* (B), in a quiet position above the village, away from the beach and in its own grounds, with sparkling marble floors, a pleasant bar, and a sitting-room with French windows opening on to the shady garden, and the *Paradissos* (D), a basic but clean hotel in the centre.

In town there is just a small and gritty beach; but Valtos Beach to the north, reached along a narrow road winding through olive groves or over the fortress-topped promontory, is a lovely long curve of golden sand sprinkled with pebbles. Three kilometres to the south is Lichnos Beach, a 900-metre sweep of clean, fine shingle. Both beaches have a reasonable selection of watersports. The *Lichnos Beach* (B) is a hotel and bungalow complex used by tour operators, with swimming-pool, tennis and basketball courts, set in a well-established garden of olive and citrus trees, right on the beach. It's slightly worn at the seams, but has lovely views over the garden to the sea from all rooms and the bar.

Parga: sight nearby

- **The Necromanteion of Ephyra** (18km south-east) Of all the oracles in Greece, none has been so clearly exposed as a hoax as that dedicated to the dead – the Necromanteion of Ephyra, just above the small village of Mesopotamo. Far from questioning its authenticity, however, the ancients believed strongly in the oracle, and those brave enough would visit it in order to consult with the ghosts of the departed. Its most famous pilgrim was Odysseus, who visited it in the *Odyssey* in order to have his future revealed to him by the ghost of the prophet Tiresias.

Belief in its authenticity was doubtless aided by its position. Although not mentioned by name in the *Odyssey*, the description of the necromanteion given by Circe to Odysseus clearly refers to Ephyra: '. . . march on into Hades' Kingdom of Decay. There the River of the Flaming Fire and the River of Lamentation, which is a branch of the Waters of Styx, unite around a pinnacle of rock, to pour their thundering streams into Acheron.' The necromanteion does indeed stand on a rocky hill, but the river Acheron, far from Flaming or Lamenting, can be reduced to a trickle, and the lake it formed is a swamp, making it difficult to appreciate the impact they had on the ancients, when their natural mystery was enhanced by superstition. According to mythology, Charon, the ferryman of Hell, would row the ghosts of the dead across the lake and into the Acheron gorge in the distant Suli mountains which plummeted down into the subterranean Kingdom of Hades.

Pilgrims wishing to consult the oracle had to undergo various purification rites: total silence had to be maintained, prayers and ablutions performed, and, according to Homer, offerings of milk, honey, sweet wine and blood were poured into trenches and sprinkled with barley.

Diets were also strictly controlled. Some pilgrims were allowed to eat only walnuts, while others were dosed with expectorants by priests who also deemed it necessary to spit three times into their faces. However, a more thorough manipulation of the senses was yet to come. Excavations have unearthed traces of lupin seeds and Egyptian jonquil which were probably fed to the pilgrims in order to induce hallucinations, giddiness and flatulence – the last possibly an indication of the priests' warped sense of humour.

At the entrance to the site is a plan which is well worth sketching, for although the foundations of the sanctuary are clear, the various parts are not labelled. Though the necromanteion is known to have functioned in the Mycenaean era, and was obviously famous in the 9th century BC, when Homer was writing, the current ruins date only from the 2nd century BC. Opposite the plan is a sunken store-room and next to it the foundations of a series of **ritual dormitories** – square, windowless rooms with walls thick enough to prevent the pilgrims hearing the priests preparing their trickery. In the same row is a **bathroom** in which the outlet and fragments of a runnel remain, and at the far end a **purification room** which the pilgrims would no doubt be made to visit before being sent off along a corridor into the heart of the sanctuary.

At the end of the corridor is a **labyrinth** which would originally have been roofed. It would not only have been totally dark, but would also have been pumped full of hallucinogenic vapours. The pilgrims would have had to grope their way through this to the central room of the **sanctuary**.

From here metal steps lead down into a **subterranean chamber**. This was supposedly the infernal palace of Hades, and the discovery of a windlass mechanism (now in the museum at Ioanina) suggests that either the pilgrims would have been lowered into it, or that the supposed ghosts of the dead would have been raised up to utter their prophesies. If Odysseus's account of his experience at the necromanteion is accurate, it would seem that the latter is more likely: '. . . and now the souls of the dead came swarming up . . . fresh brides, unmarried youths, old men with life's long suffering behind them, tender young girls still nursing this first anguish in their hearts, and a great throng of warriors killed in battle, their spear-wounds gaping yet and all their armour stained with blood . . . from this multitude of souls, as they fluttered to and fro . . . there came a moaning that was horrible to hear. Panic drained the blood from my cheeks.'

Finally, perched above the site are the remains of a 2nd-century church, an indication that the necromanteion's reputation continued for long enough to worry the Christians.

Ioanina

Rising from the shores of a haunted lake, and overlooked by the grim rocky bulk of Mount Mitsikeli, an air of decay hangs over the mosques and minarets of Ioanina's Turkish citadel, the 19th-century capital of southern Albania, ruled by Ali Pasha, a powerful and ruthless tyrant. The ghost that is supposed to haunt Lake Pamvotis is that of his son's mistress, Euphrosine (one of the stories goes that Ali, not satisfied with having a harem of 500 women, set his sights on the hapless girl, who refused his advances, and was bound up, weighted down and thrown into the water).

Ali's cruelties were not confined to women who insulted his manhood. A plane tree outside the citadel once served as the town gallows, from which the severed heads or limbs of anyone unfortunate enough to rouse Ali's dislike were dangled. Consequently, when Byron visited Ioanina in 1809 the first thing he saw was 'a man's arm, with part of the side torn from the body', which, as his companion Hobhouse recorded, made 'Ld B and myself a little sick'. As the two Englishmen were there as Ali's guests, this may have presented something of a dilemma.

Hospitality at the pasha's court was lavish. Another British traveller, C.R. Cockerell, was treated to a banquet of 86 dishes and, no doubt blinded to his host's faults, praised his 'easy familiarity' and 'perfect good humour'. Byron was less enamoured and saw through the façade: as he wrote in a letter to his mother, 'His highness is . . . a remorseless tyrant, guilty of the most horrible cruelties, very brave, etc.'.

Ali Pasha had been placed in Ioanina by the Turks. However, he was not content to remain under their thumb; as a masterful and cunning diplomat, he played off the French, British and Turks against one another, all the time increasing his hold on western Greece. When the fights for independence broke out all over the country, Ali, seeing it as an opportunity to get the whole of Greece for himself, broke off all relations with the sultan. In reply, the sultan sent an army to besiege Ioanina, which it did for 15 months, despite the fact that Ali had most of the town burnt down to reduce its looting value. Ali himself took refuge in the Monastery of Pantaleimon on the lake's island, but was joined on the same day by Turkish troops brandishing a death warrant as well as their guns. The execution was a particularly messy one. Ali was shot and wounded, upon which a Turk attempted to behead him, but missed and stabbed his shoulder. He was eventually killed by a shot fired from the room below.

Modern Ioanina is undistinguished and full of traffic. Although it has some fascinating shops in the souk-like quarter outside the walls of the citadel, and two museums, it is suitable for a stay only because it makes a convenient base for exploring eastern Epirus. On the main street towards the Turkish quarter, the *Britannia* (c) is a convenient, reasonably priced but dingy and functional hotel. Above Plateia Pirou, in the opposite direction to the Turkish quarter, the *Xenia* (B) is a smart modern hotel set back from the road in pretty grounds.

The centre of the modern town is Plateia Pirou, where the tourist office is located. From here the main street (called Yeoryiou as far as Kentriki, or Dimokritos Plateia, and thereafter Averoff) runs down to the citadel. Outside the walls of the citadel is the Turkish quarter, where traditional and now distinctly scruffy whitewashed rough stone houses mingle with gaudy maisonettes. Most of them shelter shops selling the silver filigree jewellery for which Ioanina is famous, as well as hammered copperware, hookah pipes and some rather tacky rugs.

Ioanina: sights

● **Citadel (Frourion)** The walled citadel is entered through a gate decorated with Arabic inscriptions and a bas-relief of a boggle-eyed monster. As Ali Pasha set fire to it during the siege, the houses inside are modern, though fairly attractive – whitewashed, with flowers hanging from their balconies.

All this changes when you enter the inner citadel (Its Kale) at Plateia Katsantani. Desolate and abandoned, the few remaining buildings of Ali Pasha's power-centre rise up from bare scruffy ground pocked with unidentifiable foundations. Inside the gate is a bath-house, crowned with stubby steam outlets, its water runnels visible through a crack in the locked door. Above it, looking out across the lake to the smooth grey slopes of Mount Mitsikeli, is the Fetihe Cami, or Mosque of Victory, still dominated by a rocket-like minaret, but sadly neglected and with its windows smashed. More impressive than either of these is the labyrinthine network of underground passages leading up to the well-preserved walls.

● **Museum of Popular Art** From Plateia Katsantoni a narrow cobbled alleyway climbs up past pyramids of rusting cannonballs to the mosque of Aslan Pasha. Just as the Turks converted Greek churches into mosques, this mosque, in an equally political gesture, has been converted into a museum celebrating the liberation of Epirus from foreign rule in 1913.

If the mosque is the first you've seen from the inside, it will come as something of a disappointment – far from being exotic and sumptuous, it is clumsily decorated with terracotta and bottle-green painted stucco. More appealing are the niches at the entrance where shoes had to be placed before entering.

Wandering around the museum is something akin to rooting around a junk shop, for you are never sure what you will find next. There are heavily embroidered Epirot costumes with tutu-like skirts and pom-pom shoes for the men; the pipe and revolver belonging to the last pasha; faded photographs of Greek freedom-fighters, and cases of the guns they used.

● **Archaeological Museum** Set back from Odos Averoff, in a modern building, the exhibits of the archaeological museum are thoughtfully laid out in light and airy rooms and labelled in English.

The collection is an eclectic one and includes Palaeolithic tools and the bones of a bear, pig and tortoise; a shimmering aquamarine vase from a Bronze Age cemetery; the delicate gold flowers from a 4th-century necklace; local silverware; and ornate 17th-century Evangelariums (Bible covers), gilded, enamelled and studded with gems.

The highlights, however, are the parts of the windlass mechanism used by the priestly hoaxers at the Necromanteion of Ephyra, and the lead tablets from the Oracle of Zeus at Dodona, inscribed with questions to the oracle (translated into English). Perhaps more than anything you'll see in Greece, these bridge the centuries between ancient and modern, revealing the eternal everyday anxieties of ordinary people: there's the pilgrim who asks '. . . about the woman . . . about the wolves and beasts . . . about his desire . . .'; the suspicious one who asks, 'Did not Vostrycha, Dorkon's daughter, steal the money?'; the ambitious businessman who can't decide whether to start trading with the money from his silver-mine; and, above all, the heartfelt cry from the man who fears he has been cuckolded: 'Am I her children's father?'

● **Island of Nissa** Boats across to the wooded island of Nissa leave every hour from the landing-stage below the mosque of Aslan Pasha; the first is at 8a.m., the last returns from the island at 9.30p.m. However, as the lake is prone to sudden storms, boats are often cancelled. If you do get marooned on the island, there are rooms to rent.

Of the island's five monasteries, two are particularly worth visiting. The **Monastery of Pantaleimon**, or rather the ramshackle wooden house next to it, was the scene of Ali Pasha's assassination in 1822. The house now contains a small museum of memorabilia – prints of Ali's life, period costumes and, best of all, the tyrant's hubble-bubble pipe.

The walls of the **Monastery of Nikolaos of the Philanthropini** are daubed with scenes of martyrdom so liberally sprinkled with blood, gore and severed limbs that if they hadn't pre-dated Ali's regime by a century one would assume that he had provided the inspiration. Equally intriguing, if less sensational, are portraits of Plato, Aristotle, Plutarch and Thucydides.

Even if you are not forced to stay on the island because of cancelled boats, you could well be tempted to stay a night – especially given the added attraction of a long evening in one of the fish tavernas, whose menus include trout, eels, frogs' legs and crayfish.

Ioanina: sight nearby

● **Perama Caves** (6km north) Two and a half million years old, the Perama Caves were discovered by accident in the Second World War, when the local people were looking for somewhere to shelter from bomb attacks. The stalactite and stalagmite formations are very fine, their weird shapes enhanced by subtle lighting (aesthetic rather than practical, so you need to watch where you put your feet). Growing at a rate of a centimetre every 80 years, the formations resemble everything from mouldy twiglets and barley-sugar twists to a frozen waterfall and a fairy-tale town of towers and minarets. A leaflet in English giving the names of the most evocative formations is supplied – but you'll have more fun if you make up your own.

Dodona

The theatre of Dodona, cool, elegant and immense (its capacity was 18,000), stands in a remote mountain-fringed valley 22km south-west of Ioanina. The reason for its isolated setting is shrouded in the mists of legend and pre-history.

Dodona is named after an earth-goddess, Dia or Dione, who was thought to deliver prophesies through the rustling leaves of a sacred oak tree. In the second millennium BC Epirus was invaded by patriarchal tribes who, doubtless feeling that their male prowess was threatened by a cult which centred on a woman, seized the shrine and converted it into an oracle sacred to Zeus. Dione, however, was not forgotten, and there are the remains of two temples to her on the site. The oracles continued to be delivered by the rustling of oak leaves, and were interpreted by frenzied priestesses as well as priests who, according to Homer, slept on the ground and never washed their feet.

For centuries Dodona consisted simply of a sacred grove of oak trees around the prophetic tree of Zeus. The god was believed to live inside the tree, his statue was placed in the hollow trunk, and the branches were hung with copper cauldrons which apparently amplified the mantic rustlings. The Dodonian oracle lost much of its custom when Apollo founded a more easily accessible oracle at Delphi. Although poets continued to rate Dodona highly, Delphi, with its worldwide network of informants, soon had the monopoly on political issues. Consequently, Dodona became more of a people's oracle, a sort of clairvoyant agony uncle, dealing with everyday questions like 'Kylon asks whether he will have children from his present wife, Moniska'.

It was not until the 4th century BC, perhaps as an attempt to sharpen up its image in the face of competition from Delphi, that the first temple was built. In the following century, further buildings were added by King Pyrrhus of Epirus. Perhaps as an attempt to make Zeus look on him more favourably, he provided Dodona with temples, a stadium, a meeting-house and the theatre.

Sadly, far from being able to improve Pyrrhus's lot, the oracle proved incapable of foreseeing and thus forearming itself against its own destruction. In 219BC the Aitolians, in their war against the Macedonians, destroyed the new buildings of Dodona and burned the sacred grove of oak trees. There are remains of the temples and stadium; the current theatre is the result of subsequent rebuilding in Roman times (see below).

Dodona: highlights

● **Stadium** Entering the site you can make out the outline of the stadium, with a few tiers of seats remaining on the bank below the immense retaining wall of the theatre.

- **Theatre** Shortly after the Aitolians' destructive visit, Philip v of Macedonia got his revenge by sacking *their* religious capital at Thermon and using the spoils to finance the restoration of Dodona's theatre. Fifty years later it was destroyed again, this time by the Romans, who then remodelled it.

The traces of the Roman conversion are the most interesting aspects of the theatre, for they illustrate the difference between the Greek and Roman notions of entertainment. Dramatic tragedy was not sufficiently violent for the Romans, so they converted the theatre into an arena for their blood-sports. They left the curving rakes of the seating intact, but erected a barrier to protect spectators on the front row from frenzied beasts, and dug a channel around the orchestra to drain off the blood.

- **Bouleuterion** The foundations of the large, rectangular meeting-house are clearly visible, but the outlines of the hotel – where the most important of Pyrrhus's officers would have slept – are difficult to make out.

- **Sanctuary of Zeus** In Pyrrhus's time, the sanctuary, with the sacred oak tree surrounded by a colonnade, must have looked splendid. Today, however, thanks to the marauding Aitolians and Romans, little remains, and what does is frustratingly difficult to make sense of.

- **Temples to Dione and the Basilica** Beyond the sanctuary are the foundations of two temples to the earth-goddess Dione and the remains of a basilica built by early Christians, anxious to stamp out the last vestiges of paganism.

The Zagoria villages

In a region of mountains, high plateaux and deep gorges, spreading north of Ioanina to the Albanian border, are some of the most beautiful villages in Greece. Fine slate-roofed houses of silver-grey limestone or blue-grey granite cling to wooded slopes, tightly clustered along snaking pathways paved with the same mellow stones.

That the villagers of the Zagoria must have been rich to build on such a scale is obvious, but the sources of this wealth are not, for cultivatable land is scarce. Surprisingly, this very infertility proved to be a considerable asset. In the Middle Ages, while the Turks occupied the rest of Epirus and most of Greece, they soon gave up trying to colonise the Zagoria. Its mountains were a natural defence, and as there was so little fertile land, the Turks eventually decided that the struggle wasn't worth it. Fortunately for the landowning Zagorians, many people from outside the Zagoria came to live in the region in order to escape the Turks. The immigrants were not allowed to vote or own land, and were consequently dependent on the Zagorians for employment. Some were put to work in the fields, while others were formed into armed groups to defend the villages, leaving their masters free to concentrate on more lucrative pursuits.

Some Zagorians became merchants exporting goods into central Europe, while others, leaving the immigrants and their wives to work the fields and defend the property, emigrated to Constantinople and eastern Europe, and made their fortunes as merchants, doctors and teachers. On returning home they would build new houses, found schools, have bridges constructed and roads paved. Equally important, because so many Zagorians were in influential positions at Constantinople, the Turks allowed the Zagoria to remain autonomous.

Although Epirus remained in the hands of the Turks until the First Balkan War in 1913, it had long lost its privileges. Ruined by competition from industrialised Europe, the trading lifeline ceased, and many Zagorians either emigrated permanently or turned to banditry – fighting one another over the few fertile fields. As a final blow, those who had deposited their fortunes in the banks of eastern Europe lost them with the drawing of the Iron Curtain. Now the region is still severely depopulated.

Tourism, though low key, is bringing some much-needed income into the villages; but there are very few hotels or rooms to rent. The most popular excursion is up to the village of Monodendri, spectacularly sited above the vertiginous Vikos Gorge; but other villages are equally worth exploring. The following selection is based on ease of access by car or bus from Ioanina.

The square stone houses of **Vitsa** are terraced on a hillside, separated by a gully from the main road. The setting is typical: villages were built on slopes because the level areas were so scarce that they had to be left for farming. In addition, westerly facing slopes were favoured, to make the most of the sun in the frequently chilly mountains.

As bandits were common even in the Zagoria's heyday, defence was essential. The houses were tightly clustered, for the steep and narrow tracks which squeezed between them would slow down invaders. They have no windows on the ground floor, and most have a high-walled courtyard, whose gate was always kept locked.

Almost as soon as you leave Vitsa, there is a view of Monodendri. This is no accident, for each village was built in the sight of at least one other. This formed a visual communication chain along which warnings could be passed by smoke, fire or mirror signals.

In **Monodendri** landscape and architecture combine to create the most memorable of the Zagoria's villages. For behind the village, an enticing maze of steep, stepped streets winding through silvery-grey houses, is the extraordinary **Vikos Gorge**. A narrow street leads out to the gorge, its strata-ed rock cascading 1000m to the bed of the river Voidomatis. Perched on the lip is the Monastery of Agia Pareskevi, with a series of stunning viewpoints and what must rank as Greece's most terrifying WC – a hole in a rock with nothing between it and the bottom of the gorge.

A path runs along a ledge to a hermit's cave, but it soon peters out to become a skimpy track, and is not for the faint-hearted. A degree of sure-footedness and lack of vertigo is also required if you want to do the five-hour hike through the gorge. The trail begins in Monodendri, with a descent so steep and slippery that concentrating on anything other than where you put your feet is out of the question. From the bottom the trail is clearly marked with red blobs, but as there's a rock fall to negotiate, and a steep rocky cliff to climb up, it shouldn't be taken lightly. Nor should it be attempted in spring, as the river overflows. This route, and others in the Zagoria, are described in evocative detail in Marc Dubin's *Greece on Foot*.

In the village the *Pension Vikos* offers rooms in a modern but traditional-style building just above the main *plateia*; breakfast is taken in the courtyard.

Kipi lies to the east of Vitsa, but to get there you need to return to the T-junction with the road that branches up from the main Ioanina road. The road snakes through a valley of strata-ed rock and lush trees, passing a delicate single-spanned bridge, flanked by two immense rocks, built by one of the richer Zagorian emigrés. It's worth parking here and walking under the bridge and up a gorge between red, ochre and grey rocks, to see an even more spectacular three-spanned bridge; the walk takes 25 minutes, and in spring you won't be able to negotiate it without getting your feet wet. An alternative route is to drive along the road above the gorge towards Kipi, and to take a path down to the bridge. Kipi itself is a grimly defensive village spread, as ever, on a slope and is worth a visit if you have time.

Turning off the road to Kipi just after the single-spanned bridge, the road climbs towards the tiny, timeless village of **Kepesovo**. The views *en route* are magnificent – to the right verdant hills ripple towards the distant silhouettes of the Pindos Mountains, and to the left the ochre and silver flanks of the Vikos Gorge gleam like a petrified waterfall in the sun.

When you arrive at Kepesovo you look down from the road, where you have to leave your car, on to a huddle of mottled limestone roofs. Wandering along its narrow streets pocked with animal droppings, you may be carried back in time, as much by the lingering smells of manure and woodsmoke as by the mellow old stone houses.

From Kepesovo take the road marked Vradheto 9km (not that

marked Vradheto 6km). A short way along, a broad brown track
winds down to a single-spanned bridge at the bottom of the
gorge. From the bridge the tiny village of Vradheto (Bradheto)
is reached by an astonishing feat of rustic engineering – the
Kalderimi, resembling a paved python snaking steeply up the
hill. It takes about an hour to reach the village (which has seven
inhabitants), half an hour of which is spent on the Kalderimi.

At the northern end of the Vikos Gorge lie a couple of fine
traditional villages called **Mikri** and **Megalo Papingo**. If not on
foot, you'll need to take a detour south and west via the main
road, and cut back into the mountains (at the road marked
Papingo 23km). As you climb up there are views of the blue
heights along the Albanian border just 20km away. Ahead of
you great peaks loom, snow-capped until spring, creating a
landscape of awesome grandeur. As you pass through the
squalid village of Agios Minai, the immense bulk of rock known
as the Pyrgi ('towers') at the head of the Vikos Gorge comes
into view, shimmering silver in the sun, and resembling a
bastioned fortress of giants.

There is little point in stopping in Aristi, which has as many
modern as traditional houses, unless it's to make use of its
accommodation. Descending from Aristi you pass through a
forest of plane trees to the river Voidomatos, where a pool of
translucent turquoise water with a white pebble bed makes a
pleasant place at which to rest and cool off. Beyond, the road
snakes across a spinal hill between two gorges.

The two Papingo villages are huddled at the foot of the Pyrgi;
there is no access for cars, which have to be parked in the
respective church squares.

Megalo Papingo is a well-kept village of traditional houses,
many of which have been subtly restored. There are a few cafes,
some rooms for rent, and a pretty church with an octagonal
bell-tower.

Mikro Papingo, just above Megalo, is clustered below and
dwarfed by the towering mass of the Pyrgi. A confusing
labyrinth of overgrown paths squeeze and curve their way
between traditional Zagorian houses, making it virtually
impossible not to get lost. There are no cafes, but two simple
hotels. The *Dias* consists of airy rooms in a tastefully restored
traditional house; breakfast and dinner have to be taken at
Megalo Papingo. At the top of the village, the *Agnandi* is a
quirky little hotel in an old restored mansion. The highlight is
the reception area with its low log-beamed ceiling and ancient
embroidered rug. The bedrooms, none of which has a bathroom,
are furnished with a haphazard collection of traditional and
modern furniture; meals are taken in the kitchen.

Metsovo

Terraced on the steep slopes of a ravine, Metsovo, with its traditional stone mansions and narrow cobbled streets, is the most attractive town in Epirus. It is also the only one in which centuries-old traditions continue to flourish. The people wear Epirot costumes every day, and not just for the benefit of camera-clicking tourists; the industries are the traditional ones of cheese-making, wood-carving and textiles; and hotels are furnished with traditional wooden furniture and hand-woven upholstery.

The people of Metsovo are descended from the Vlachs, nomadic shepherds who speak a language which is similar to Romanian and derived from Latin. Until recently it was assumed that they were Slavs, descended from Roman colonisers, and that over the centuries they had wandered westwards through the Balkans in search of pastures. As such, they were discriminated against in the 1930s, when the Greeks felt threatened by Slavic expansion. Slavic names of villages were forcibly changed, and attempts were made to wipe out the Vlach language. However, the latest theory is that the Vlachs are Greek, that they always lived in the remote Pindos Mountains, and that when the Romans colonised Greece they trained them to guard the high mountain passes. Consequently, it is thought they learnt Latin from the Romans, and never lost it because of their isolation from the rest of the country. When the Italians invaded Greece during the Second World War, they found they could communicate quite easily with the Vlachs, for many of their words are similar – Vlach 'pene' for the Italian 'pane' (bread), Vlach 'mulier' for the Italian 'moglie' (woman) are just two examples.

Whichever theory is true – and the second does sound like an attempt to put an end to the insidious racism of the 1930s – the Vlachs of Metsovo have long been settled there, and though many still speak Vlach among themselves they all speak Greek. While you will see the occasional man in baggy trousers and pompom shoes, you are more likely to see women in traditional costume: a long, heavy gathered skirt worn with an embroidered shawl. At festivals (Easter and 24 July) and on wedding days the costumes are richly embroidered, and worn with heavy chains of gold coins. There are weddings on most Sundays in summer, and the celebration always includes a dowry-carrying procession from the bride's to the groom's house and dancing on the main square.

One look at Metsovo's stone and wood mansions makes it clear that Metsovo has had some very rich inhabitants. It owes its wealth to a Turkish vizier of the 17th century who, finding himself temporarily out of favour at the sultan's court, arrived incognito in Metsovo, where the Tositsa family sheltered him for a year. Once reinstated, he returned to Metsovo and told Tositsa that he would give him whatever he wanted. Freedom for Metsovo was requested; and so, independent and tax free, the town flourished. Tositsa's son then amassed a great fortune by growing cotton on land in Egypt granted to him by the Turks.

Metsovo has been able to remain faithful to a traditional lifestyle because of the descendants of the Tositsas and another wealthy family, the Averoffs. In the 1930s, concerned that the population was migrating to the cities in search of work, the national politician Evangelos Averoff decided to do something to save his home town. On discovering that a descendant of the Tositsa family had become a wealthy but childless banker in Italy, he wrote to him in order to persuade him to leave a bequest to Metsovo. At first Tositsa was suspicious, so he tested Averoff's motives by asking him to become his adoptive son (and therefore heir). Averoff, seeing what Tositsa's game was, refused, and so the banker agreed. With his bequest the traditional industries of cheese-making and wood-working were rejuvenated by the founding of small factories. The cheese company is pledged to paying farmers a price above the market rate for their milk, and even provides a bull of exceptional pedigree to improve the quality of their cattle. More picturesquely, the Tositsa family home has been restored as a folk museum.

As for the rest of the town, houses have been renovated and some converted into hotels; a ski-lift has been constructed to attract skiers to Metsovo in the winter; and the shops on the main street and around the *plateia* are full of traditional crafts, generally more tasteful than those you'll find elsewhere.

Not surprisingly, given its architecture, crafts, traditions and mountainous surroundings, Metsovo is an extremely popular holiday base, and if you're going in the high season, or around Christmas, you'll need to book a hotel in advance. The *Flokas* (B) is a traditionally furnished hotel in a restored building beyond the main *plateia*, with wooden floors, woven rugs and upholstery.

On the main *plateia* itself, the *Galaxy* (C) is another traditionally furnished hotel, with friendly owners and a good, cheap and cheerful restaurant much used by locals.

Metsovo: sight

● **Tositsa Museum** The Tositsa family mansion is more than a museum, for it has been laid out just like a traditional (if wealthy) home. The house was fortified against bandits: windows tapering to a slit so that they could serve as shooting positions; stables in the basement to protect the animals; and, most important, its own fountain so that it could hold out if besieged.

On the first floor is the family-room with two large sofa-beds on either side of the fireplace. One was for the man and his wife, and the other for the children and grandparents. Leading off is the larder, positioned so that the owners could keep a watch on the stores and ensure that when the servants went home for the night they didn't take anything with them.

The winter room was a windowless room, furnished with thick carpets, rugs and blankets, where the family would spend most of their time in the severe winter months.

The women worked at their weaving, sewing and embroidery in the 'women's room'. The different traditional patterns are displayed, along with a small exhibition of costumes. The length of red borders on the waistcoats were a sign of class and wealth – the longer the border, the richer the wearer. Likewise, rich men wore all white, the not-so-rich white with a black border, and the poor all black.

On the top floor was the parlour, a huge room used for special occasions such as weddings and feasts. There are sofa-beds of differing heights all the way around the walls: like the costumes, these were also an indication of status, with the highest, by the fireplace, reserved for the patriarchs.

Women were forbidden to enter the 'men's room'. As the collection of pipes includes a hubble-bubble it seems likely that their secret pursuits consisted of more than business and politics (although the Metsovans are adamant that it was used only for tobacco smoking).

MACEDONIA AND THRACE

Though Mount Olympos, legendary home of the gods and one of the religious centres of the Ancient Greek world, lies on the border of Macedonia, it has acted more as a physical boundary than as a spiritual bond between Greece's northernmost provinces and the rest of the country. The greater part of Ancient Macedonia now lies across the mountainous northern border in Albania, Bulgaria and Yugoslavia; and about half of Thrace lies in Turkey. As is to be expected when national boundaries are political rather than geographical, Macedonia and Thrace have as much in common with the Balkans and Asia Minor as with the rest of Greece.

Macedonia and Thrace fell to the Turks in the 14th century and remained under their rule for 500 years; they became part of Greece almost a century after the rest of Greece gained independence in 1830. Macedonia was liberated in 1913, after the Greeks and Balkan nations had allied to drive the Turks out in the First Balkan War. Thrace (after a period of Greek rule before and after a war with Turkey in 1922) lost her eastern territory as a result of the Treaty of Lausanne in 1923, when the region was handed back to Turkey and a population swap ordered – 380,000 Muslims who found themselves on the Greek side of the border were sent back to Turkey, while Greece had to find room for over a million Christian Greeks ousted from Turkish territory.

It's no surprise, therefore, that both regions are scattered with reminders of the five centuries of Turkish rule. Neglected mosques and bath-houses crumble among the brash new buildings of the northern capital and Greece's second city, Salonika; and other towns such as Kavala and Xanthi retain sleepy Turkish quarters. Less picturesquely, as you head east through Thrace towards Turkey you'll pass through strings of flimsy prefab villages built for Greek refugees.

More chillingly, both Macedonia and Thrace have a heavy concentration of military camps, and the existence of airports in the small provincial towns of Kastoria, Kavala and the border town

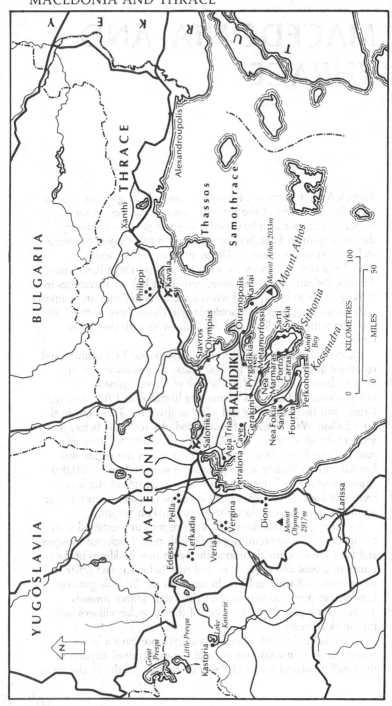

of Alexandroupoli are a constant reminder of the area's vulnerability to the Communist or Turkish bogy, real or imagined. Istanbul is referred to as Constantinople, on roadsigns as well as in conversation; the memory of the Turkish occupation of northern Cyprus in 1973 is still fresh; and rumour has it that when Nato representatives checked out the missiles of Greece and Turkey, they discovered that they had them aimed at each other. The fear of Communist invasion, even in the Gorbachev era, is likewise understandable, given the area's recent history – in the Second World War it was the focus of Communist expansion, and children were abducted from the frontier villages and taken into Albania and Yugoslavia for indoctrination. Not surprisingly, the north-west frontier is still depopulated.

The region's history of invasion and colonisation stretches back thousands of years before the Turks and the Communists. The area was settled by tribes from the Danube in the Neolithic era, invaded by the Dorians in the Iron Age, and eventually became a Roman province. After the fall of Rome it fell prey to a string of power-hungry northerners – Goths, Huns, Ostragoths, Bulgars, Slavs and Serbs – and became part of the Bulgarian empire in the 13th century, before falling to the Turks in 1364.

This saga of subjection, however, ignores Macedonia's golden years of glory. For in the 4th century BC, under Philip II and his son Alexander the Great, Macedonia rocked the world – and ended up by briefly ruling virtually half of it. Having conquered Thrace and the crucial Greek powers of Athens and Thebes, Philip II set his sights on the vast Persian empire, but was murdered before he could do anything about it. The task passed to his son, and by the time Alexander died at the age of 33 the Macedonian Empire stretched right across North Africa and Asia to the Punjab.

Getting off a plane at Salonika airport in mid-summer, you could be forgiven for concluding that you'd landed in one of Alexander's North African colonies rather than in Greece – for the heat in August can be unbearable. While the city isn't particularly appealing at cooler times of the year, it makes a convenient base for exploring western Macedonia. The smaller town of Veria is a more pleasant alternative.

With baking-hot summers and harsh winters, fertile plains and forbidding mountains, both the climate and landscape of northern Greece are more extreme than those of the rest of the country. In Macedonia vast plains, watered by lakes and rivers, blanketed with endless fields of wheat and corn, and cloaked with never-ending groves of apple and peach trees, are fringed by mountains too wild and arid to be beautiful except when snow-capped. The landscape of Macedonia's three-fingered peninsula of Halkidiki is easier on the eye, and its juxtaposition of wooded mountains, sandy beaches and azure sea more familiarly 'Greek'.

Entering Thrace signals a return to a harsh, elemental landscape. The Evros massif on the Turkish border, and the Rhodope mountains which it shares with Bulgaria, account for over three-quarters of its land mass. Thrace's agricultural wealth centres on a coastal plain which stretches from just over the boundary with Macedonia to the Evros foothills. The most important crop is tobacco – ironically enough, the finest Turkish tobacco, Xanthiyaka, is actually grown in the Greek half of Thrace.

It is the Macedonia of Philip and Alexander which has given the region its most interesting sites and archaeological finds. The royal capital of Pella, with its beautifully preserved pebble mosaic floors, is the one ancient site which can compete with those of the Peloponnese, and the astonishingly opulent archaeological pickings from the royal cemetery at Vergina make Salonika's archaeological museum, where they are now housed, second only to the National Archaeological Museum in Athens. Macedonia's other big-name site is the Roman colony of Philippi, notorious from the Bible for imprisoning Saint Paul and from Shakespeare for being the site of

Visiting Macedonia and Thrace

There are no stay-put package holidays on offer to resorts in northern Greece outside the Halkidiki, but a few operators organise extensive touring holidays. Package holidays to the Halkidiki are almost all in A- or B-category hotels; there's a fairly limited range of simpler or self-catering accommodation. Many of the hotels are some distance from the nearest village. Going on a package to a top-category hotel in the Halkidiki can easily be cheaper than arranging the same holiday independently; but if you want to stay in rooms, you can save money by going independently. However, in July and August it can be very difficult for the independent traveller to find accommodation.

In the larger towns there are virtually no rooms to rent, and the D-, E- and even many of the C-class hotels can be fairly basic. There are plenty of campsites, particularly in the Halkidiki, ranging from the small and very simple to large organised sites with watersports, tennis courts, tavernas and bars.

To visit the monastic state of Mount Athos, men (women are excluded) with a serious reason (not simply touristic curiosity) must first obtain a letter of recommendation from the British Consul in Athens or Salonika. The letter has to be presented at the Ministry of Northern Greece, in Salonika, which issues a limited number of the necessary permits for a specified four-day period.

There are direct scheduled and charter flights from the UK to Salonika (Thessaloniki), and several flights a day from Athens. The Halkidiki

the battle which resulted in the defeat and suicides of Caesar's assassins, Brutus and Cassius. The nearby town of Kavala is both a useful base for visiting Philippi and an attractive resort, with some good beaches close by.

Macedonia's most intriguing area, the monastic republic on Mount Athos – the most easterly of the Halkidiki's three prongs – is barred to half the world. Women (and until recently female animals) are forbidden to put a foot on the sacred mountain, and so miss not only some of Greece's most spectacularly sited and beautifully frescoed monasteries, but a unique opportunity to step into an ascetic world in which the rhythms and rules of life have scarcely changed since the Middle Ages.

Ironically enough, the Halkidiki's other two prongs have become an international tourist playground. Indeed, it's to this area that most foreign visitors to northern Greece head, as it has the region's most developed resorts. These are without exception modern and bland, with little to suggest that you're in Greece. If your idea of a Greek holiday includes wandering through a maze

---

resorts are between 1½ and 2 hours' drive from the airport. A bus or coach journey from Athens takes over seven hours.

Northern Greece has a slightly more Continental climate than the rest of the country, with hotter summers and cooler winters. On the coast this is moderated by the sea, and temperatures and hours of sunshine are comparable with the rest of the Mediterranean. There is a rather higher risk of rain, but showers are usually short. The western mountains are cooler and have more rain around Florina and Kastoria. The best time to visit the area is in June or early July, while the land is still green and the hills covered with flowers. The crowds arrive in earnest in mid-July, and throughout August the Halkidiki hotels are packed. September is also a pleasant month to visit, being hot but not oppressive. Most resort hotels are closed from October to May.

Getting around

You can get to most places within northern Greece by bus – although most are old and without air-conditioning and are thus extremely uncomfortable in summer. A railway crosses the region, from Florina near the Yugoslav border through Vergina, Salonika and Xanthi, and continues to Istanbul and Sophia. Charter air tickets may specify that you are not permitted to enter Turkey from Greece.

Car hire is expensive, but well worth it if you want to explore some of the more out-of-the-way sites or beaches in comfort.

Kavala is the ferry port for links to the islands of Thassos, Samothrace, Limnos and Lesbos; less frequent sailings go to Chios, Skiathos, Samos, Ikaria, Kos and Rhodes, and to Piraeus.

of whitewashed cubic houses, you should select an island resort. However, if all you want is sea, sand and the guarantee of skin-sizzling sun, the Halkidiki is fine – though as many of the public beaches are narrow and get overcrowded, it's advisable to select a hotel with its own stretch of beach. The self-sufficient and rather isolated hotel complexes of the Kassandra prong can be ideal for families. Sithonia – the middle prong – is suitable for a quiet and simple holiday, especially if you have a car. Excursions are organised from the Halkidiki resorts to the main sights and to Salonika.

It's worth putting up with the mid-summer heat to visit Salonika's magnificent archaeological museum, but few people are likely to have the energy and will-power to brave the fumy chaos in a tour of its Byzantine churches; and non-experts will need to be selective or ultra-keen if they wish to come away from the scant remains at the archaeological sites of the area with anything more than an impression of having wandered through a bombsite.

Independent travellers visiting Greece for the first time would be better advised to go to the Peloponnese or the islands, whether their priority is ancient sites, good beaches or picturesque villages. Macedonia and Thrace are regions that will appeal mainly to those who know the country already and want to explore a further dimension: for nowhere else does the shadow of foreign subjection loom so poignantly, deepening one's understanding of modern Greece.

The Halkidiki (Chalcidice)

Until relatively recently the Halkidiki peninsula was a little-known area of small farming and fishing communities, rather cut off from the rest of Macedonia. On its southern side – jutting like the claws of a crab into the waters of the Aegean – lie three subsidiary peninsulas whose sheltered sandy beaches and rugged beauty have proved a winning combination for the attraction of tourists. Development began about 20 years ago, mostly on the lowest-lying and most westerly peninsula, Kassandra. Sithonia, the central prong, is still in parts a natural wilderness, with a high wooded interior, steep slopes dropping into the sea, and a series of small sandy bays. Much of the wild and even more mountainous easterly sub-peninsula of Mount Athos is occupied by a self-governing monastic state, generally closed to holiday-makers.

Most of the Halkidiki villages are small; they're not resorts in the usual sense, and tend to be functional rather than picturesque. Much was destroyed in the War of Independence, and few traditional houses remain. Few villages have many tavernas, cafes or bars, those ingredients generally considered essential for the

Greek holiday scene, and the hotels used by package operators are often some distance away from the villages. Many hotels are very large and isolated, and it's especially important to choose one where you're likely to be happy to spend much of your time.

Resort beaches can get very crowded, though if you have a car, or the patience to use the rare buses, there should be little problem in finding somewhere quiet. For a wide choice of watersports your best bet is to select one of the self-contained hotel complexes; elsewhere you may find only surfboards, pedalos and a few windsurfers. Public beaches, even if they seem to be in the middle of nowhere, are often strewn with rubbish – which can be another reason for selecting a hotel with a private beach. Most hotels expect you to pay for the use of a sun-umbrella or sun-lounger – often the only way of securing a place.

In general, the mainland coast of the Halkidiki has much less to offer than the peninsulas. The western headland around **Agia Trias** is popular with day-trippers from Salonika, but the countryside is dreary and the beaches poor. The head of the gulf between Kassandra and Sithonia is also flat and dull, with exposed, shadeless beaches. The village of Gerakini has little charm; **Metamorfossi** is much prettier and more lively. Between Sithonia and Athos a rough road to Pyrgadikia follows some very pleasant stretches of coast. Further north are the attractive bay of **Olympias** and the much larger resort and long sandy beach of **Stavros**.

Inland, about 27km north-east of the head of the Kassandra peninsula, is one of the main excursion sights of the Halkidiki: the **Petralona Cave**. Encased in a forest of garish red-gold stalactites and stalagmites, the oldest skull in Greece was discovered here by local villagers in 1960. Subsequent excavations revealed bones of animals, ranging from horses to hyenas, and the earliest traces of fire. Knobbly reconstructions of ghastly 700,000-year-old archanthropi (they form the link between *Homo erectus* and *Homo sapiens*) squat beneath the rock formations. There's a small anthropological museum.

Kassandra

The east coast of Kassandra is pretty and more sheltered than the west, and its beaches are better cared for and have more facilities. The package hotels are often mini-resort complexes in their own right, usually without much individual style or charm but with ample facilities and spacious grounds. One of the nicest is the *Kassandra Palace* (A), set back from the coast near the quiet village of Kriopigi. It's an attractive low-rise hotel with rustic-style décor in a well-kept, lush garden shaded by palms, weeping willows and olive trees. The pool area is attractive, the taverna has views over the garden to the sea, and the facilities include a good range of watersports, tennis and volleyball courts, children's playground and disco. Built on a human scale, it's relaxed and friendly.

Nea Fokia, in the north of Kassandra, is a small modern village with a tiny beach overlooked by a medieval watchtower; there's a longer stretch of beach to the south. There are summer villas, a pizzeria and a fish restaurant, but no hotels. One kilometre south, above a small sandy bay, there are a few rooms to rent. This area is just beginning to be developed, and there are a number of half-built houses along the road.

With its colour-coordinated cafes and ice-cream parlours, **Kallithea** is a small international resort with little to indicate that it's in Greece. Cycles, Vespas and motorcross bikes can all be hired, and there's a small children's playground and mini-golf course in town. There are rooms to rent and hotels along the narrow, sandy beach, but most British tour operators use the self-contained hotel complex 2km to the south. Opposite the complex is a strip of bars and shops, with a disco and a Doukas Tours office – they not only organise excursions but also have information on rooms to rent and local buses.

The best hotel in Kallithea itself is the *Ammon Zeus* (B), pleasantly situated on a private beach 200m below the town and backed by a green slope on which stand the scant remains of a temple to Zeus and a small Byzantine church. The *Pallini Beach* (A) and *Athos Palace* (A – more attractive, comfortable and expensive) are very large hotels set in extensive grounds with a wide range of facilities and a sandy beach. Shared facilities include indoor and outdoor pools; sauna and massage rooms; children's playground; open-air theatre; cocktail bar and nightclub; and watersports. As you pay extra for all activities, it can work out very expensive. The quality of the food and service reflect the difficulties of catering for 2000 people.

One kilometre south is the *Alexander Beach* (B), a complex of white stucco blocks in pleasant if slightly unkempt grounds on a clifftop, with a funicular and a rough track down to the beach. There's a very small pool, tennis courts and a taverna.

With a couple of discos and Greek dancing laid on for excursion parties in its tavernas, **Haniotis** is a lively resort which gets crowded and very noisy in August. The hotels are on or near the narrow, pale sandy beach, and there's a simple clean campsite, the Kala Nera, outside. The *Pella* (B) is a modest but friendly modern hotel on the outskirts of the resort with a disco, children's playground and pool.

Outside the small sleepy village of **Pefkohori**, with its steep streets and traditional stone and whitewashed houses, is the old-fashioned spa-hotel *Afrodite*, backed by hills on the edge of the peninsula, with some small pebbly beaches nearby. The rooms are large and airy, and each has a balcony at the back and at the front. The food is traditional and home-cooked, and the owner will cook for people on a special diet. The tiny spa caters mainly for people seeking cures for arthritis or rheumatism.

On Kassandra's west coast – wilder, but less attractive and less developed than the east – **Skiviris** has a good sandy beach, a small basic campsite, rooms to rent and a couple of tavernas. Apartments are being built, so its tranquillity may be short-lived.

Fourka is one of the main villages on the west coast; it's scruffy but relaxed and has several large stretches of sandy beach, a couple of hotels and some rooms to rent. Three kilometres from the village there's a newly developing resort, with some smart apartments to rent and a reasonable choice of watersports.

The *Sani Beach* (B) complex lies on an isolated peninsula 10km away from the nearest village (there's a mini-bus service). It's stark, but surprisingly comfortable, with tennis courts, a disco, children's playground and pool.

Sithonia

With its rugged mountainous backbone, dense woods and cliffy promontories, Sithonia is more appealing but less developed than Kassandra. There's a series of sandy bays on the east coast with views across to the austere peaks of Mount Athos, while the west coast has two resorts – a futuristic hotel complex based around a marina at Porto Carras, and the large and lively Nea Marmaras next door.

Despite its position at the foot of a bush-tufted mountain, the inland village of **Sykia** is not particularly scenic. However, as it has restaurants, food stores and souvenir shops it can be useful for stocking up if you're touring.

On a large semi-circular bay with a sandy beach and watersports at Camping Galaros, **Vouvourou** has one good hotel – the *Diaporos* (B) – and plenty of high-quality rooms to rent. Although there's little in the way of nightlife, you can spend lazy evenings at the beachside taverna at the south of the bay. For those with a car, there are more bays to explore between here and the next resort, **Sarti**, which is actually a small town on a large white sandy bay with a couple of inlets. Sarti has a modern motel and a campsite; a more attractive option for campers is to head along the unmade road outside the village to Agios Ioannis, a lovely sandy bay sheltered by rocks. The campsite is tiny and simple; people also camp (illegally) on the beach.

Koufa Bay's wild beauty is unbeatable: a long, silent inlet with a sandy beach, and sheer white rocks plunging into its calm turquoise waters. Camping Nikolas is a tiny, basic campsite right on the bay: if you want more facilities there are rooms, a taverna and the large and more comfortable Camping Porto Koufos nearby.

Porto Carras is known, somewhat misleadingly, as the Greek Marbella; its three hotels stand like stranded ocean liners within a vast estate. Designed as a holiday playground for the rich by the shipping magnate John Carras, they lack real glitterati style and panache, and though they attract the yachting crowd, and are used by British tour operators, the owners have found it difficult to fill the rooms and the atmosphere can be very dull. The beaches near the hotel are narrow, but there are plenty of sandy coves within the grounds, in addition to an 18-hole golf course (bring your handicap card), nine tennis courts (three of which are floodlit), the marina and a casino.

The neighbouring busy resort of **Nea Marmaras** is the place to head for if you want some holiday action. It's a small fishing port with a lively night scene, tavernas and a sandy beach that gets very crowded. There are a couple of hotels, rooms to rent on the sea-front, and campsites outside. *Camping Castello* is aimed at families (facilities include washing machines, kitchen and a tennis court – with a further sports pitch planned). Closer to town is the small beachside *Miramare* complex with 36 apartments and bungalows to rent and a shady campsite next door.

Mount Athos

The village of Ouranopolis is the last place before the frontier of the monastic republic of Athos, which can be visited only by men, with some difficulty (see Visiting Macedonia and Thrace, page 234); women have not been allowed to set foot on Athos for over ten centuries. On the mountainous and wild peninsula are about 20 inhabited Greek Orthodox monasteries; most are on the coast and can easily be seen from a boat. Day cruises around the peninsula are offered, although if you can do without the luxury of a swimming-pool and bar on board it's far cheaper to take a ferry from Ouranopolis.

Ouranopolis itself is an attractive resort with several small hotels, rooms to rent, and a good choice of tavernas, the focus of nightlife. The beaches are sandy but narrow; excursion-boats from the *Eagle's Palace Hotel* (A) go across to Amouliani and other tiny uninhabited islands which have some lovely sandy coves. The Eagle's Palace is the most comfortable place to stay at, set in its own grounds by a sandy beach, with a large swimming-pool and a good range of watersports.

'I would not go again to Mount Athos for any money, so gloomy, so shockingly unnatural, so lonely, so lying, so unatonably odious seems to me all the atmosphere of such monkery. . . .' Edward Lear railed against the monastic community in 1856. Visiting Mount Athos is indeed an uncanny experience; after going through a complex administrative procedure, to arrive there is quite literally to step back in time, for the thousand or so Orthodox monks follow the Julian calendar, 13 days behind that of the rest of Europe. The day begins at sunset, and is divided into unequal 'hours'. Adding to the sense of entering a time-warp, transport on Athos is by mule, on foot or by the occasional boat; apart from a single bus-track up to the main village, Kariai, from the port of Dafni, there are no roads. Architecturally and artistically the 20 functioning monasteries are interesting but not outstanding, and their rich treasuries are rarely open to visitors. The main reason for visiting is for the insight you get into the lives of the monks – some of whom still live as anchorites in mountain caves and shacks. The monasteries all offer hospitality, although only a handful can be said to cater for guests. As a rule the coenobitic monasteries (in which life is led communally) are the most welcoming; in the idiorrhythmic monasteries (where the monks live and pray together but work and eat alone) you'll be dependent on the *archontaris* – or guest-master – to cook for you. Accommodation is basic and food simple – vegetables, beans and the occasional freshly caught fish, with wine served at every meal, even breakfast – so you'd be wise to bring extra provisions to keep you going during the arduous treks from one monastery to another, and some insect repellent to make the nights more comfortable. There is no charge, but you should leave at least enough money to cover what you have eaten.

According to legend, Mount Athos owes its holiness to the Virgin Mary, who spotted it en route to Cyprus to visit Lazarus, declared it her private garden, and is still supposed to haunt the thick forests. At first inhabited only by hermits, the most famous of which was Peter the Athonite who reputedly lived in a cave for 50 years, it was declared a monastic preserve in the 9th century. The hermits began to form themselves into communities, and in the 10th century the first monastery, Lavra, was founded. Two hundred years later there were 40 monasteries, and the population is thought to have been around 20,000. The coenobitic system prevailed until the 16th century when, beset by Turkish taxation, many monasteries switched to the idiorrhythmic system in which monks were responsible for their own food. All monks spend at least eight hours of their days in church, and occasionally services last for 24 hours. Not all monasteries permit non-Orthodox visitors to join in services; one which does is Agios Pantaleimon, whose monks are mostly Russian.

Kariai, the village-capital of Athos, has just a few shops, a couple of cafes and a post office. After completing the administrative business and buying a map, it's worth taking a look at the 14th-century frescoes in the Protaton church – the Nativity is particularly fine.

Mount Athos: monasteries

As there isn't time to visit all 20 monasteries in the four days the permit allows you to stay on Athos, we have selected the following nine – some because of their works of art, some because they are stunningly sited, and others because they are particularly hospitable or convenient for a night's stay. You could either tackle the full circuit or take things easy and concentrate just on one or two that particularly interest you, giving yourself time to enjoy the rare peace and beauty of the mountain. The monasteries are described in clockwise order from the north.

● **Vatopedi** Two hours' walk from Stavronikita (see below), this severe and fortified building is the only Athonite monastery with electricity, and also keeps European time. Though not particularly welcoming, it's artistically rewarding, with Byzantine mosaics, frescoes, and fine bronze doors in the *katholikon*; in the treasury, if the monks can be persuaded to allow you to enter, you can see a girdle said to belong to the Virgin Mary.

● **Stavronikita** A fortress-like building perched on rocks above the sea, this is a small, friendly monastery about one and a half hours' walk from Kariai. It's a good place at which to stay, though there's little of artistic interest, but it gets filled up early in mid-summer. The treasures include a miraculous mosaic icon of Saint Nicholas – it lay under the sea for 500 years, and when it was retrieved had an oyster clinging to the forehead. Its miraculous properties extend beyond its mere survival – when the oyster was removed, blood is said to have poured from the icon.

● **Iviron** About half an hour's walk from Kariai, this is an idiorrhythmic monastery with a rich library and treasury. The monks may be reluctant to show visitors around or to provide accommodation.

● **Grand Lavra** The richest, oldest and most powerful of the monasteries, 10th-century Lavra, encircled by crenellated walls, is one of the few monasteries never to have been rebuilt. At the far end of the east coast, it's accessible by foot (about four hours) from the inland monastery of **Filotheo** (a good place at which to spend the night) or by boat (there are about three a week along the east coast). Many of the frescoes are by the 15th- and 16th-century Cretan artist Theophanes, and are the finest on the peninsula – the Dormition of the Virgin and the colourful Transfiguration are particularly memorable.

• **Agiou Dionisiou** On a fine rocky site, this monastery is also worth visiting for its beautiful frescoes. The most interesting are in the refectory: a Last Judgement and a Ladder of Heaven, with the ladder climbing up from a monster-infested hell. The monks produce what is reckoned to be the best wine on Athos.

• **Simonopetra** The most spectacular of monasteries, fused with the sheer cliff on which it stands, Simonopetra (a tough two-hour walk from Dafni) is approached across a viaduct, and has vertiginous drops on three sides. The dizzy sensation of looking down from its balconies is enhanced by the legend of its construction. The story goes that one Christmas in the 14th century, a hermit, Saint Simon, saw a light on the ridge and decided it was a divine order to build a monastery. Finding that the workers he'd employed to help with the construction were so frightened that they were quitting, he sent his servant with some aquavit to give them Dutch courage. The servant slipped, hurtled down over the cliff, and miraculously landed on his feet without spilling a drop of alcohol. This presumably convinced the workers that they were divinely protected and gave them the confidence to complete the monastery; it has since been rebuilt many times. This is an awesome place in which to wake up in the morning – and you may be given permission to attend a service.

• **Pantaleimon** Better known as the Russian monastery; there were once 1500 Russian monks in Pantaleimon – now there are only 20. Its onion domes offer a rare taste of Russian exotica. The experience is completed by the fact that you are allowed to attend the Russian Orthodox services.

Western Macedonia

Salonika (Thessaloníki)

'Victory-in-Thessaly', the name inflicted on his daughter by Philip of Macedon after one of his conquests, was given by her husband Kassander to the city he founded in 315BC.

When Macedonia became a Roman province Thessaloniki developed rapidly, well situated on the Via Egnatia between Italy and Byzantium. Cicero and Pompey each took refuge here at low points in their fortunes. In the 1st century AD Saint Paul founded a Christian church here, and wrote for it his two Epistles to the Thessalonians. In the 4th century the city acquired its martyr-saint Demetrius (Dimitrios), under the persecution regime of Galerius. Then Constantine the Great transferred the capital of the Roman Empire from Rome to Byzantium, renaming it Constantinople; Thessaloniki became a powerful second city in the Empire, much involved in the high-level hair-splitting of early Christianity's doctrine and government, and bristling with Byzantine churches.

The city survived Goths, Slavs and Saracens to be an intellectual metropolis of the Middle Ages, until in 1430 it was sacked and occupied by the Turks, whose power in this part of Greece was to last almost 500 years (Kemal Ataturk was born in 1881 in Thessaloniki's old Turkish quarter). Some churches became mosques, and synagogues also appeared, for to the depleted Greek population was added a large Jewish colony, encouraged by the Turks to come to Thessaloniki after expulsion from Catholic Spain in 1492. This community – which reached 56,000, the largest in Greece – was exterminated during the Second World War.

That anything of old Thessaloniki has survived at all is something of a miracle. However, despite a drastic fire in 1917 and a severe earthquake in 1978, some fine, well-preserved Byzantine churches – several with beautiful mosaics – remain among the stuccoed concrete blocks of the modern city. Salonika is best avoided in summer, when the combination of throbbing heat and exhaust fumes, spiked with screaming traffic, garish advertising hoardings and the gagging stench from greasy snack bars can be unbearable. But at other times the city is well worth a visit; and its archaeological museum is one of the few that can be unhesitatingly recommended to anyone. The upper city, though squalid by day, looks enticing at night, when the crenellated Byzantine ramparts are floodlit, and the darkness masks the fact that the Turkish houses are mostly abandoned, collapsing and suffocated by modern low-rise flats.

Although Salonika is not a particularly relaxing city, there are islands of elegance – porticoed tree-lined streets and formal gardens – in which to wind down after seeing the sights. In addition, there are classy shops on Tsimiski and Odos Agias Sofias, and smart cafes along the sea-front and on the arcaded square, Ahillion. If you can get there only in the summer, making use of the cheap taxis to see the sights will save time, temper and energy. In cooler seasons, with some comfortable hotels and a lively night scene (focusing on the sea-front cafes and the earthy tavernas of the upper town), Salonika can be a stimulating and vibrant place.

Most of the hotels are conveniently placed along the main street, Monasteriou/Egnatia. The *Capsis* (B), with a roof-garden, swimming-pool and sauna, is cool and comfortable, and its buffet breakfast is hard to beat. The *Vergina* (C) is clean and fairly quiet, and the cheaper *Mandrino* (C) simple and clean, though a little worn at the seams. Prices rise by 20 per cent during the International Trade Fair in September.

Salonika: sights

● **Archaeological Museum** If anything can tempt you to enter the city in mid-summer, this is it. The gorgeous finds from the Macedonian tombs at Vergina (see page 248) and elsewhere in the region are quite simply unsurpassable, and will enthral you even if you know nothing about Macedonian civilisation. Dismissed by the Ancient Greeks as primitive and backward, the Macedonians ended up controlling not only Greece but a massive empire that stretched across North Africa and Asia to the Punjab. Macedonian expansion began in the 4th century BC, when Philip II invaded Greece. Before finalising plans to invade Asia he was assassinated, leaving the task of colonising half the world to his son, Alexander the Great.

The decadence of life at Philip's court is well evoked in items such as the Derveni Krater, a gilded bronze urn used for mixing wines, encrusted with the X-rated erotica of a boozy Dionysian orgy. There are miniature ivory busts of the Macedonian royals – Philip, paunchy and with a grotesquely distorted eye, and Alexander, proud and sneering – but it's the gilded greaves (leg-armour), the golden arrow case decorated with reliefs of the sack of Troy, and the massive gold and ivory shield that really enable one to visualise the magnificence of the Macedonians at war. In sharp contrast, there are breathtakingly beautiful golden wreaths of oak and myrtle leaves, so delicate that they seem to quiver, and a gold chest decorated with the 16-rayed star of the Macedonian dynasty, in which bones thought to belong to Philip II were found wrapped in a purple cloth woven with gold thread.

● **Byzantine churches** The following are the principle surviving examples in the city. Many are undergoing extensive restoration following the 1978 earthquake and may still be closed to visitors.

Agios Georgios is Europe's largest circular building after Rome's Pantheon, the oldest of Salonika's churches and now a national monument. Designed as a mausoleum for the Roman emperor Galerius, it was converted into a church in the 4th century. At the base of the dome and in the recesses, wonderful mosaics create a sumptuous fantasia of exotic temples, peacocks, swans and saints against a glinting gold background; these have been described as the most splendid 5th-century mosaics in existence. Next to Agios Georgios is the city's only surviving minaret – dating from the period when the church was used as a mosque.

On the corner of the formal gardens of Plateia Dikastirion, **Panagia Halkeon** is an 11th-century church which was also used as a mosque. A virtually complete if faded cycle of 11th-century frescoes has survived. **Agia Sophia** is another large church in the throes of restoration, its gold-backed dome mosaics currently invisible behind a shield of scaffolding. The columns of the aisle have huge capitals.

Agios Dimitrios is the largest church in Greece. The basilica was built in the 5th century above the Roman baths in which Saint Dimitrios, Thessaloniki's patron, was imprisoned and later speared to death. Rebuilt after a fire in the 7th century, it was again almost completely destroyed in the 1917 fire, and the current church is almost a total reconstruction. The interior is not particularly attractive, with its green and white marble columns and grotesquely oversized candelabra bathed in an acidic light from the yellow and green windows. There are, however, some exquisite fragments from the original church, most notably the elaborate column capitals with birds snuggling among bunches of grapes, and strange winged animals peeking over lolling acanthus leaves. There are also some fine examples of 7th-century mosaics, among the few in existence (most Byzantine cities were too poor in this period to finance art, as the Persian wars diverted the trade route across central Asia). Several depict Saint Dimitrios: in one he stands benign and rosy-cheeked between two children, in another, gaunt and severe, with two of the church's founders – a treasurer, clutching a purse, and a bishop.

Tucked away in the old upper town, **Ossios David** is an intimate 5th-century church with rough stone walls, traces of frescoes and a memorable mosaic in its apse. Christ, for once clean-shaven and resembling a Romantic portrait of Shelley, stands before a pale rainbow, with the four rivers of paradise flowing from his feet, and the four apocalyptic beasts peering out from behind a symbolic circle of light.

• **Arch of Galerius** The surviving half of a triumphal arch built to celebrate Emperor Galerius's victory over the Persians in AD297, decorated with marble reliefs of battles and processions. The arch is at its most evocative when floodlit at night.

• **The White Tower** A 15th-century tower on the sea-front, once used as a prison and known as the Bloody Tower after a massacre that took place there in the 19th century. It's worth climbing for the view.

Pella

On what was once the mosquito-ridden marshland of Emathia, 38km north-west of Salonika, lie the remains of the ancient capital of Macedonia. The place in which Alexander the Great grew up and planned his world-conquering campaigns, Pella is without doubt the most evocative of the region's ancient sites. The layout of the town is clearly visible, and the white columns and subtle pebble mosaic floors suggest its former elegance. The image of the sophisticated and opulent civilisation of this royal city will be even more complete if you've seen the magnificent collection of Macedonian artefacts in Salonika's archaeological museum.

Though set on a hot and shadeless plain, the site is compact, and you can cool off afterwards in the airy museum in which the most precious of the mosaics are kept for safety. Finding your way around is easy, as the buildings and mosaics are labelled in English as well as Greek. Wandering down the central avenue, lined with clay pipes and stone sewers, you pass the richest of Pella's houses, in which the three best mosaics, now in the museum, were found. To the west, past the foundations of a row of small shops, canopies shelter three more mosaic floors: the Stag Hunt, full of movement, with the hunters' cloaks flying out behind them, and their dog leaping at the deer; the Rape of Helen, in which, although much detail is missing, a sense of violence and fear is successfully evoked by the speed with which Helen appears to draw away, her dress swirling wildly; and a scene with Amazons which is unfortunately difficult to make out.

In the museum the mosaics have been hung upright on the walls – a pity, as the play of shadow and movement, so subtle when they are flat, appears rather obvious and naive. Nevertheless, the soft natural shades of grey, cream, red and ochre blend together beautifully, creating a magnificently maned lion in the Lion Hunt; a languid Dionysos, with tendrils of hair falling on to his exquisite face, lounging on a sleek leaping panther; and a violent Deer Hunt with muscly red-headed hunters about to slash the flecked coat of a stag, which looks as gentle as Bambi, with a heavy axe and glinting knife. Elsewhere in the museum is a bust of Alexander, painted terracotta statuettes in déshabillé, reminiscent of 18th-century porcelain figurines, and the reconstruction of a frescoed wall, the upper section a pale sky blue, adding to the picture of how Pella once looked.

A visit to Pella can be arranged by tour operators, but it is usually included only in a long excursion, much of which will appeal only to enthusiasts.

Veria (Veroia, Beroea)

Spread across a plateau above a dull plain, 75km south-west of Salonika, Veria is a patchwork of old and new, elegance and squalor. Wattle-and-timber churches, and Turkish houses, their upper storeys supported on curving wooden beams, are squeezed into narrow streets behind modern office blocks; Italianate *fin-de-siècle* villas and pavement cafes lead down to the shady garden suburb of Elia; and tucked away behind the main street, Mitropoleos, is the bustling Turkish market quarter, with its ancient barbers' and tailors' establishments, stark *kafeneions* and tawdry souk-like shops. Not all the relics of Turkish rule are as innocent – opposite the old cathedral, abandoned after many years of use as a mosque and still sprouting a chimney-like minaret, is an ancient plane tree from which the town's archbishop was hanged in 1436. In fact, Turkish persecution led the Verians to build most of their churches in concealed courtyards which are still difficult to find.

Veria makes a useful base for people intending to visit the Macedonian tombs at Vergina (11km) and Lefkadia (16km) – see below. However, Veria's archaeological museum is no rival to that of Salonika; it contains chiefly minor finds from Vergina.

The *Hotel Makedonia* (B), in the centre of town, is cool, modern and elegant, with a surprisingly peaceful roof-garden looking out over the bustling streets. It is also excellent value – the price of a double room is about half what you would pay in Salonika.

Veria: sights

• **Neos Christos** One of the churches which is not hidden, this stands right on Mitropoleos. It contains well-preserved and remarkably lively 14th-century frescoes. The Descent into Hell depicts a mass-drowning of martyrs, their haloes falling from heaven like a shower of coconut shells, and a row of saints, many with the same stylised face. Another appealing fresco is the Baptism of Christ in a cascading river surrounded by leaping fish.

• **Bema of Saint Paul** A 1960s reconstruction of the steps from which Saint Paul is thought to have preached to Veria's Jews. They were open to his message, much to the chagrin of the Thessalonian Jews, who entered the town, stirred up the rabble and forced Paul to make a hasty retreat.

• **Folk Museum (Leografico Mouseio)** Agricultural implements, looms with cloth woven to traditional designs and an appealing collection of costumes and embroidered fabrics – the highlight being the magnificent wedding clothes. (If closed, the key is at the office next door.)

Vergina, Lefkadia and Edessa

The Macedonian tombs at Vergina and Lefkadia, together with the waterfalls at Edessa, can usefully be incorporated into a round trip from Veria or from Salonika.

The discovery of the Macedonian royal tombs at **Vergina** ranks as one of the most significant archaeological finds of the century. Vergina has been identified as Aigai, the Macedonian royal residence until the capital was moved to Pella at the end of the 5th century BC, and the small theatre, discovered in 1982 below the palace, is most probably the site of Philip II's assassination at his daughter's wedding. But the hilly site is likely to excite only archaeologists, as the royal tombs are closed to the public, and the massive Palace of Palatitsa is a confusing sprawl of knee-high foundations. There is one (non-royal) tomb which you can visit, but even though you can glimpse a marble throne behind its temple-like façade, there is little to suggest the magnificence of the objects found within the royal burial-chambers, now displayed in the archaeological museum in Salonika.

A small group of Macedonian tombs has been unearthed at **Lefkadia**, among the peach groves of the plain below Edessa. The most impressive, indeed the largest Macedonian temple-tomb yet discovered, is the so-called Tomb of Judgement, with a two-storey façade, whose magnificence is somewhat diminished by its modern protective canopy. This is necessary to protect the fine external frescoes (which depict the tomb's incumbent being conducted by Hermes to the two judges of the Underworld, who would decide, after weighing his soul, whether he could pass to the Isles of the Blessed or be condemned to eternal punishment).

The reason for visiting predominantly modern **Edessa**, stunningly sited along a cliffy ridge, is to gaze at its waterfalls. Though flanked by concrete walkways, the gushing cascades are spectacular, and merit a brief stop. The plains below Edessa produce Greece's best apples, peaches and wine – the fruit is superlative, and the unresinated wine, Boutari, all too easily quaffable.

Kastoria and the Prespa Lakes

Flanked by mountains and spread over a peninsula projecting into a deep lake, the old fur-merchants' town of **Kastoria** sounds unmissable. In fact, the lake is smelly, the streets choked with traffic, and the unappetising surroundings make appreciating its many Byzantine churches difficult. However, the cobbled and tree-shaded Doltso quarter has some fine 18th-century fur-merchants' houses and a folk museum; and despite their unprepossessing surroundings, the intricate brickwork of some of the churches, reminiscent of embroidery-samplers, is extremely attractive. Waterskiing is possible on the lake, but not advisable because of pollution.

Fifty kilometres north-west of Kastoria you can overlook the vast and lonely **Prespa Lakes**. Their bleak mystery is enhanced by the knowledge that parts are in Albania and Yugoslavia. They have been designated a bird sanctuary; Mikri Prespa (Little Prespa), shallow and reedy, is Europe's only nesting-ground for pelicans and the largest for cormorants, while Megali (Great) Prespa, lying mostly in Yugoslavia, is the highest lake in the Balkans.

Eastern Macedonia and Thrace

Kavala

Near Macedonia's eastern border with Thrace, the port town of
Kavala is a good base if you want to punctuate sun-soaking with
sightseeing; although the town beach is poor, there is a series of
picturesque sandy bays to the west – at and near **Kalamitsa**
(4km), which is also the focus of Kavala's nightlife. Overlooking
the ugly port and the white stucco flats and hotels of the
modern town is a sleepy Turkish quarter: a maze of narrow
streets, winding up through pastel-washed houses to the
crenellated Byzantine citadel. This is Kavala's friendliest and
most relaxed part, and is an evocative place in which to wander,
especially in the glow of the late afternoon sun.

Inland sights include Roman Philippi (15km) and Turkish
Xanthi (56km) (see below); the island of Thassos is an easy day-
trip away, and there are ferries each week to Rhodes and Kos
and the islands of the north-east Aegean.

There are comfortable hotels: the *Oceanis*, with roof-garden
and pool, and the *Galaxy*, which has mini-bars in most rooms,
are the nicest of the B-category hotels; the *Esperia* is a good C,
with extremely clean rooms, and has a disco from October to
May.

Kavala: sights

• **Aqueduct** Stretching across the busy modern streets below the
Turkish quarter, the arcaded aqueduct was built by Suleiman the
Magnificent in around 1550 to bring water to the town from the
springs on the opposite mountain. With its stacked layers of arches, it
remains impressive, despite the traffic hurtling underneath.

• **Archaeological Museum** A modest collection, of interest mainly to
devotees of Ancient Greece. The highlight is a reconstructed and
partially frescoed Macedonian tomb-chamber, with a gold wreath and
silver mirror among the objects discovered inside.

• **Imaret** A sadly dilapidated Turkish almshouse with grooved domes
like half gourds sprouting on its roof, this was founded in the 19th
century by Mehmet Ali. There was a charitable boarding-school here
until Turkish rule ended in 1912, but the poor could continue to get a
daily meal of soup, rice and bread (with meat twice a week) until 1923.
It was known in Turkish as *tembel-henneh*, 'place of the lazy', and
appropriately enough there are usually old men sitting outside drinking
leisurely frappés and languidly cleaning fish in plastic buckets.

• **Mehmet Ali's Birthplace** Beyond the Imaret, looking out to sea, is the
half-timbered house in which Mehmet Ali (pasha of Egypt and founder
of the dynasty that ruled it until 1953) was born in 1769. The

caretaker, who speaks a smattering of English, will guide you around, showing you the rooms in which Ali was born and worked.

Far more interesting, however, is the small room with a lattice grille in which his harem of seven women lived, slept and ate, keeping their clothes and quilts in the panelled cupboards. They left it only to entertain Ali or visit the stark bathroom with its primitive sauna and toilet.

● **Kastro** It's worth walking up to the *kastro* for the views from its crumbling crenellated walls. The buildings within the walls are all rather ramshackle, but you can make out a Turkish bath-house with its steam outlets. In summer you may be fortunate to be there for one of the few dance performances which are held within its floodlit walls.

● **Museum of Folk and Modern Art** Housed next door to a tobacco warehouse – it is on shipping local tobacco to the cigarette factories of Athens that most of Kavala's wealth is based – the museum has an appealing display ranging from richly embroidered and appliquéd traditional costumes and ornate tortoiseshell and ivory haircombs to vicious scythe-like swords and cutlasses. There's also a section devoted to the Thassos-born sculptor Polygnotos Vatis, who worked mostly in the USA. The best of his sculptures seem to emerge naturally from the pebble, rock or wood from which they are carved.

Philippi

Fifteen kilometres north-west of Kavala lie the ruins of the ancient city of Philippi, named by Philip II of Macedonia who seized it from the Thracians in 365 BC in order to protect the gold-mines in nearby Mount Panagaeum. Set on a dreary plain with traffic pouring through along the ancient route of the Via Egnatia – which connected the Adriatic with Byzantium – the sprawling foundations and columns are mainly of the later Roman town. It's the historical associations that make Philippi come alive – and if these leave you cold there's little point in visiting. The small museum does not add much to your appreciation of the site, and there's just a basic roadside *kafeneion* in which to cool off afterwards.

It was in 44 BC, after assassinating Julius Caesar, that Brutus and Cassius came to the plains of Philippi, and fought Antony and Octavian. Brutus won his first battle, but Cassius, unnerved by bad omens, was defeated and killed himself. In a second battle Brutus was trapped and overwhelmed, and he too committed suicide. Octavian, after sending Brutus's head to Rome to be thrown at the feet of Caesar's statue, colonised Philippi, aware of its strategic importance, and by the time Saint Paul visited in AD49 it was a completely Roman city in which the worship of pagan deities still flourished.

Saint Paul encountered Lydia (a seller of purple fabric) by a stream outside the town, and converted her and her family; he then exorcised a slave-girl fortune-teller possessed by an oracular spirit. When the girl's owners saw that Paul had deprived them of a valuable source of income, they dragged him before the magistrates, accusing him of introducing an illegal religion. Paul was stripped, flogged and jailed in a cell, but on the first night there was an earthquake and the prison doors burst open. The jailer awoke, and assuming that the prisoners had escaped decided to kill himself, at which point Paul called out: 'Do yourself no harm, we're all here.' The jailer was so impressed that he converted, and took Paul home for a meal, after which the future saint baptised the jailer's family. He then discovered that the magistrates, no doubt wanting to get rid of him before the whole town became Christian, had decided to release him.

Appropriately, the site is dominated by the ruins of an early Christian basilica to the south of the Via Egnatia, which bisects the town. Known as Basilica B, a massive arch and immense cornerstones rise up from a chaos of shattered architectural fragments – most notably the curved chunks of masonry from the dome, whose weight made the east wall collapse shortly after it was constructed, leaving only the narthex, or vestibule, usable for worship. On the other side of the road are the foundations of the short-lived Basilica A. Constructed, like Basilica B, in the 6th century, it was flattened by an earthquake shortly afterwards, and subsequently used as a quarry of ready-cut stone. There are, however, the faded traces of geometrical frescoes and parts of a marble mosaic pavement in the baptistery; and the crypt, thought to be the cell in which Saint Paul was imprisoned, has barely visible frescoes of his life. Beyond Basilica A is a Greek theatre, enlarged by the Romans to make room for gladiatorial shows. It has recently been reconstructed, and is used for an Ancient Drama Festival every summer (mid-July to early August). Ironically, the best-preserved and most memorable part of the site is a 50-seat public lavatory, just behind Basilica B.

Xanthi

Eastwards from Kavala into Thrace, the road passes through tobacco fields and shanty towns of flimsy prefabs built for Greek refugees from Turkey after the border was drawn up in 1923. Greek Thrace still has some Turkish communities, most noticeably at Xanthi. The scruffy but bustling modern town is not particularly appealing, but the atmosphere is unforgettable. You are greeted by the aroma of spices, mingling with cardamom-scented coffee; the fruit market, though housed in what looks like an aircraft hangar, is a riot of colour and activity. While many of the women are veiled, most men have given up their traditional dress and fez. To the east along the main street, shabby souk-like shops and pungent snack bars give way to trendy cafe-pubs and an intriguing antique shop – an Aladdin's cave of hubble-bubble pipes, tea-urns and embroidered traditional costumes. From here the old quarter crawls up a hill, an evocative blend of Turkish houses with their upper storeys projecting out on beams, and mansions with barred windows and wrought-iron balconies. Xanthi has given its name to the finest-quality Turkish tobacco, *Xanthiyaka*, and shops sell locally produced cigarettes, *Kiretsiler*, whose distinctive packet is decorated with a design taken from traditional embroidery.

Samothrace island

From the busy frontier town of Alexandroupolis, it is two hours by ferry to Samothrace, which is attached to Thrace administratively and in terms of practical communications (see also page 595). Occasionally the ferry schedule makes a day-trip possible, but most people stay overnight or longer on the island. Nearly all its accommodation is at the port, a dreary village on the west coast, five kilometres below the island capital of **Chora**, the only village of any size on the island. Samothrace is an island of woods, waterfalls and towering mountains, which rise steep and rocky to a crest of over 5000 feet (Mount Fengari, 1611m), an all-day hike from Therma, a spa on the north coast. There is one long sandy beach on the island's south coast (Ammos), but as a whole it is one of the most beach-deprived of all Greek islands.

The site of the sanctuary of the Great Gods is on the north coast, reached by bus from the port. Founded well before the Hellenisation of the island in about 700BC, and flourishing until the 4th century AD, this was one of the most famous of ancient pilgrimages and the original home of the Louvre's headless statue of Winged Victory (or Nike), from the late 4th century BC. The finer points of the cult of the Great Gods Axierus, Cadmilus, the twin Kabiri, Axiochersa and Axiochersus are not well understood. What is known is well explained in English in the museum near the entrance to the site, as is the role played by the various buildings and altars in the ceremonial processes that initiates underwent. These structures, of which very impressive fragments remain, included the initiation hall, a tile-roofed circular hall used for sacrificial fires, and a large theatre for mystery plays. Beneath an altar in the Hieron (near the theatre), pilgrims were baptised in bulls' blood.

THE ISLANDS

THE ISLANDS

CORFU AND THE IONIAN ISLANDS

Cephalonia, Ithaca, Lefkas, Paxos, Zante

Separated from the Greek islands by Greece itself, the Ionian
Islands are a group apart, with their own climate, their own
history and their own pattern of modern tourism. 'It is the sea
which determines the islands,' wrote Ernle Bradford; 'the Ionian
and Aegean are very different seas. If the Ionian is female then
the Aegean is male. One is soft, enveloped often with that
gauze-like haze which hangs so frequently over the Italian
landscape. The other is clear and precise . . . a carved and
sculptural sea.' Female or not, the Ionian is the deepest part of
the Mediterranean, bottoming out at 4404m somewhere to the
south of Zante. This probably does less to shape its character
than does the wind, which colours the light, brings the rain that
waters the plants, affects the mood, fashions the people.

The Ionian Sea lacks the welcome summer ventilation of the
Aegean's cool north wind. In winter, storms howl down from
the coastal mountains and rain falls for weeks on end. A heavy
moist southern sirocco blows at either end of summer, which
sees long, sluggish spells of flat calm. The atmosphere is often
unconducive to exertion. No sooner had Odysseus been cast
ashore at Corfu than he curled up on the sand, covered himself
with leaves and fell asleep. On the return journey from Corfu
to Ithaca he also slept, so soundly that he even failed to wake
up when being carried ashore and laid gently on the beach.
Odysseus was not the last to sleep heavily on an Ionian beach.
'It is the quality o' th' climate,' remarked Antonio to Sebastian
in *The Tempest*, observing their fellows succumb to sudden
drowsiness. Prospero's enchanted island is usually identified
with Corfu.

The rains fall most heavily on Corfu – 50 inches a year, twice
as much as in London and three times as much as in Corinth.
Not surprisingly, the island is every bit as green and vigorously
overgrown and overcrawled as a reading of Gerald Durrell
suggests. Corfu's fertility is not simply a matter of colour but
one of intense, incessant, sub-tropical growth.

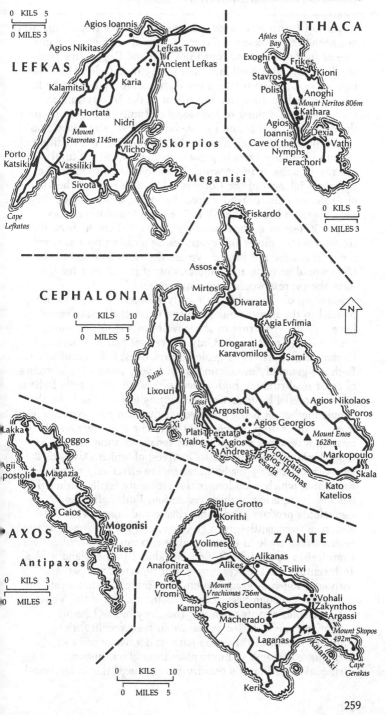

Most of Corfu and Paxos are covered by olive trees. This may not sound remarkable for Greece, where olive trees are about as rare as tulips in Holland, but the Corfu and Paxos olive trees are different, with a wildness and strength that olives elsewhere lack. Here, an olive tree is more than a sturdy pillar of the local economy and an attractive ingredient of the Mediterranean landscape: it is a thing of individual sculptural beauty for which the collective word is not a grove but a forest. The climate no doubt contributes something to this, but so does the tradition of allowing the olive trees to grow unpruned, an agricultural practice of dubious merit which probably has its roots in the notorious idleness of the Corfiots. That, at least, was the view of Professor Ansted, who toured the Ionian Islands when they were about to become Greek in 1863 and found olive trees nearly 30 feet in girth. Ansted also remarked on the beautiful combination of olives and cypresses, as pleasing now as it was then: 'if it were not for the cypress the vast extension of the olive would be tame and monotonous; if it were not for the olive the cypress would be too melancholy.'

Made up of the peaks of a mostly submerged range running parallel to the moutainous mainland coast, the Ionian Islands have a similar structure of sheer west-coast cliffs and much gentler slopes to the east. Only the central pair of Ithaca and Cephalonia, clearly close geological relatives, fail to conform. Both are generally mountainous, with very impressive stretches of coast road running high above the sea. In 1943, 1500 Italians were murdered by their German captors in Cephalonia by the simple method of being marched off the road near Assos, which meant a sheer drop of over 1000 feet. The consequences of missing a bend are no less serious today. In antiquity Cephalonia was famous for its fir trees, of which Odysseus's ships were probably made. Shipbuilding effectively deforested the island, which is no longer conspicuously fertile, although it has low-lying areas of thick vegetation. Both Lefkas and Cephalonia produce good wine, cheese and honey. Zante is almost as luxuriantly green as Corfu, and grew prosperous from international trade in its top-quality currants (the word derives from 'raisin de Corinthe'), first introduced to the island in the 16th century. A 17th-century visitor reported, not perhaps without a touch of exaggeration, that Zante's currants paid for the entire Venetian fleet. Zante was the richest of the Venetian Ionian Islands and its town was the glory of the Levant.

In many ways blessed by nature in their fertility, the southern islands of the group have paid a heavy price in earthquake damage. Commonplace throughout history, earthquakes during this century have reduced the architectural achievements of the islands' foreign occupiers to irrelevance everywhere except on Corfu. Lefkas was destroyed in 1948, the three southern islands – Cephalonia, Ithaca and Zante – in August 1953, when a week of earthquakes began in mid-morning on Sunday the ninth. By the end of the week over 120 tremors had been recorded, 75,000 people were homeless and there was nothing left in the town of Zakynthos to burn. Ithaca and all but the northern tip of Cephalonia suffered devastation on a similar scale, with the result that there are very few old buildings anywhere on these islands, except those that have been reconstructed. On Zante the attempt to re-create something of the elegance of the old town has been surprisingly successful. The architecture on Cephalonia and Ithaca is uniformly dreary.

Throughout history the prevailing influence has been from the west. Unlike the rest of Greece, the Ionian Islands (apart from Lefkas) spent no great length of time under Turkish control and, instead, hosted a familiar Mediterranean roll-call of errant Norman adventurers, Venetians, Napoleon – and the British, unloved protectors for half of the last century. For much of this period (the early 13th century to the late 19th) the island of Kithira counted politically as one of the Ionian Islands. It now has no practical links with the rest of the group and is described in the Peloponnese Islands chapter.

Homeric legend provides the information that Laertes and his son Odysseus, hero of the Trojan War, commanded an Ionian kingdom (probably the islands other than Corfu and Paxos) from a base on Ithaca, a city with a view of three seas, usually identified with a hillside site in northern Ithaca, commanding the main shipping route along the west coast of Greece. After the prophesied 20 years away from home, Odysseus landed to a friendly reception on Corfu, land of Phaeacians under King Alcinous, whose paradise garden of a palace as described by Homer is probably Paleokastritsa. The Phaeacians returned Odysseus to Ithaca, where Penelope had kept herself busy weaving and undoing a shroud for her father-in-law despite many offers of alternative entertainment from her numerous suitors, whom Odysseus did not hesitate to kill on his return.

Despite a lot of digging, most of the evidence confirming the identification of modern and Homeric Ithaca is based on the poet's topographical descriptions rather than the uncovering of any very important archaeological remains. This shows that Homer knew the places he wrote about, but has not brought scholars any closer to a clear understanding of the historical basis of the story. Finds have at least established that Odysseus was revered on Ithaca, albeit many centuries after his time.

Archaeology has also failed to turn up any evidence of Alcinous's palace at Paleokastritsa. Theories that Lefkas was Homer's Ithaca are not viewed sympathetically in academe.

If anything, archaeology points to Cephalonia as the most important of the islands in the Mycenaean period, which is not incompatible with the idea of Ithaca as the regional ruler's power-base. Cephalonia later consisted of four independent city-states, of which the most important was the eastern port of Sami. Corfu enters history as a Corinthian settlement in the 7th century BC, with the ancient town on the peninsula now occupied by the airport. Corfu grew rich and powerful enough to do some colonising of its own in the 4th century BC, and disputed control of a subject town (Durazzo) with Corinth, thereby igniting the long and sapping Peloponnesian War between Athens and Sparta. The 7th century also saw the Corinthians on Lefkas, where they cut the first shipping channel through the muddy isthmus at the northern end of the island/peninsula. Apart from the interest of tracking down Homeric

Visiting the Ionian Islands

The Ionian Islands have much wetter autumns and winters than the Aegean, and visitors between mid-October and mid-March run a high risk of not seeing the sun. April and even May are by no means sure to be fine. Mid-summer, on the other hand, may well be hotter than in the Aegean. The package-holiday season is not short, but local ferry- and excursion-boat services are sharply reduced outside high season. Geographically, the Ionians are the least unsuitable of the Greek islands for those determined to drive out. The Greek National Tourist Organisation in London can supply details of ferries from Brindisi and Bari, which should be booked in advance.

There is a vast range of package holidays to Corfu, Zante and Cephalonia, all of which have a full range of accommodation including big hotels. A few packages are offered to Lefkas and Paxos, mostly featuring simple accommodation in rooms, villas and small hotels. Flotilla holidays feature mainly in the Lefkas/Ithaca/Cephalonia area. Windsurfing and sailing-course packages are available to Lefkas.

Access and ferry connections

Direct charter flights operate from many British airports to Corfu, Zante and Cephalonia. A few direct charters are available to Preveza on the mainland (for Lefkas), and there's a once-weekly scheduled flight to Corfu. Flights go to all these airports from Athens, and there are a few flights a week between Zante and Cephalonia.

sites, there are very few classical remains of interest to the non-specialist on any of the islands.

The medieval history of the Ionians is a dark chronicle of land-grabbing crusaders, the overspill of feudal Europe. Tyrants bought, sold and swapped islands, traded nominal allegiance between emperors, popes and other European powers, and adopted grand titles that clothed no more edifying behaviour than piracy, for which the islands were very handily placed on the trade route between Italy and the eastern Mediterranean. In the tradition of the resourceful and unscrupulous Odysseus, they raided and plundered others, and others did the same to them. Stars in this hardly glittering galaxy are the Tocco dynasty which, by the 15th century, had control of Zante, Cephalonia, Lefkas and Ithaca, as well as large chunks of the mainland. Their rule ended suddenly in 1479 when Leonardo Tocco abandoned the islands by dead of night, with his pockets full, in the face of an impending Turkish raid which few islanders survived. Those that did were mated with Ethiopians

There are lots of boats daily from Corfu to Igoumenitsa on the mainland; and ferries operate most days to Paxos and a few times a week to Cephalonia, Ithaca, Patras (mainland) and Brindisi/Bari (Italy).

The staple connection for Paxos, most days in summer, is with Corfu, on the rusty *Kamelia*, which sometimes calls at Igoumenitsa. Connections between Paxos and the other Ionian Islands are not easy. Ferries on the Italy/Patras beat call in occasionally: when we last visited, this meant sailings to Cephalonia every other night in high season only (until about mid-September). Excursion-boats provide a link with Parga on the mainland, but these are expensive and can be awkward to arrange, as the captains are not supposed to take one-way passengers: some palm-greasing may be called for and luggage should be discreetly smuggled aboard.

The situation for Lefkas is somewhat volatile, and information available on the island (especially in Lefkas town) about its own ferry services is highly unreliable. The soundest principle is to head for Vassiliki for boats to Cephalonia, and to Nidri for Ithaca. The main lines appear to be Vassiliki–Fiskardo (Cephalonia)–Sami (Cephalonia) and back the same way; Nidri–Fiskardo (Cephalonia)–Frikes (Ithaca)–Nidri. But there are also ferries from Vassiliki to Vathi (Ithaca), probably operating a shorter season (July and August only) than the Nidri service. There are several boats a day between Nidri and Meganisi.

Travel between Lefkas and Paxos/Corfu involves a bus, ferry (across the narrow mouth of the gulf of Arta between Preveza and Aktion) and a plod to or from Preveza bus station, which is quite a way from the ferry quay. Room touts patrol the quay at Preveza to accost travellers on their

in Constantinople to produce a strain of half-caste slaves. Zante, Cephalonia and Ithaca had to be repopulated five years later when the Venetians bought back the Ionian Islands from the sultan in exchange for a sizeable annual tribute. Lefkas was excluded from the bargain. Taken by Venice in 1500, it was immediately sold back to the Turks and only retaken by Venice in the late 17th century.

It was much the same story on Corfu. The island, fed up with harsh Angevin rule, had appealed to Venice for protection at the end of the 14th century. In 1402 the king of Naples sold his claim to Corfu to Venice for 30,000 ducats. Far from living a blissful life of uninterrupted peace under the all-protecting wing of Venice, the Corfiots found themselves repeatedly on the sharp end of Turkish aggression. Highly destructive raids

---

Access and ferry connections continued

way to Lefkas. The conventional route is via Igoumenitsa, but Parga is perhaps preferable: a shorter bus-ride, an interesting and amusing place to visit, and excursion-boats most days to Corfu and Paxos. Summer boat-trips (probably only once a week) from Parga to Lefkas add another marginal possibility.

Lefkas being attached to the mainland, there is no need to take a ferry at all. There are daily buses to and from Athens as well as Preveza.

Cephalonia has a variety of services from at least four ports. The most reliable service, with several boats a day, is to Poros/Killini, the Peloponnese port that also serves Zakynthos. Sami is the main port for the international ferries and has connections with Patras, Italy, Corfu and (a few times a week in summer only) Paxos. Sami is also the terminus for the relatively new service to Vassiliki on Lefkas (every day in summer), via Fiskardo. Agia Evfimia is the usual port for Ithaca (Vathi) and mainland Astakos (daily), but there may also be sailings from Sami to Ithaca. A local caique between Fiskardo and Ithaca (Stavros) operates according to demand. The south-coast village of Pesada has a summer ferry link with Zakynthos (morning and afternoon, three days a week), a much shorter connection than the two-leg journey via Killini (which takes about half a day), but not widely advertised. Direct flights between the two islands provide an even quicker link. Reports and advertisements of an Argostoli/Killini ferry service may refer to a bus and ferry journey via Poros rather than direct boats to and from the capital.

Zante has several daily sailings to Killini (Peloponnese) which provide the main link with Poros (Cephalonia). Direct boats to Pesada (Cephalonia) operate a few times a week in summer.

Ithaca has daily services to Astakos (mainland), Lefkas (Nidri and Vassiliki) and Cephalonia (Sami, Agia Evfimia and Fiskardo). Inter-island links are much reduced outside summer season.

---

involved large-scale massacre and the export of women and children to the slave markets of the east: 20,000 were carried off after the siege of Corfu in 1537. The Turks returned in 1571 and 1573, sacking and slaughtering indiscriminately. The Venetians responded to the threat by providing Corfu with ever-stronger fortifications, including a new fortress and a complete system of town walls protecting the area between old and new forts. The Turks attacked again in 1716 and were repulsed thanks only to the miraculous intervention of Saint Spiridon, who brought down a storm of rare violence (and timing, for it was early August) on the besieging army and was himself seen in bishop's robes at the head of a retinue of monks driving off the foe with blazing torches. The delivery is celebrated with a grand procession through the town every 11 August. Spiridon came to the assistance of the Corfiots again during the German bombardment of 1943, when large numbers of townsfolk sought refuge in the saint's church, which was one of the few large public buildings in town to escape damage.

The Venetians subsidised olive planting to the tune of a sequin per tree and also fostered Zante and Cephalonia's vineyards. After the devastations of the 16th century the islands flourished commercially and culturally, benefiting from the links with Italy, where Ionians went to university, and from an influx of refugee artists in the 17th century when the rest of Greece fell under Turkish control. The Cretan-influenced school of Ionian painting is well represented on the islands, with very good icons at Zakynthos (the museum and the Phaneromini and Kyria ton Angelon churches) and Corfu (Platytera monastery). Music and poetry also flourished and continued to do so during the 19th century, with the foundation of various academies, orchestras, opera companies and schools of poetry and fine arts, mainly in Corfu. The period saw the construction of beautiful town houses, arcaded squares and baroque churches in the Venetian style of the time. Zante was the showpiece town, but since 1953 only Corfu town remains to bear witness to the elegance of the Venetian age. There are few more beautiful towns in Greece.

Under Venice, the islands were governed, like the mother city, by closed hereditary local aristocracies. The system bred increasing public resentment as democratic ideas gained currency throughout Europe, and the administration degenerated into corruption and lawlessness. In late 18th century Zakynthos, the freedom to commit a murder could be bought from the Venetian governor for a small fee.

When the Venetian Republic succumbed to Napoleon in 1797, the French were welcomed as liberators in the Ionian, with much gleeful burning of Libri d'Oro (the registers of aristocratic families) in the town squares to celebrate the overthrow of the old social order. French rule turned out to be no more acceptable than Venetian, and was short lived. After Napoleon's defeat in Egypt, a fleet of Russians and Turks in unlikely alliance sailed north through the Ionian Islands in 1798 and took control without difficulty, except at Corfu, where the French resisted for four months. The new rulers established an independent state, the Septinsular Republic, which is always hailed as the first manifestation of the rebirth of the Greek nation. It reverted to the old aristocratic system and was not a success. Cephalonia rapidly sank into civil war, Zante withdrew from the republic and offered itself to Britain, which declined the invitation. By the Treaty of Tilsit in 1806 the islands were returned to Napoleon, but before long the British did move in, expelling the French in 1809. Again, fortress Corfu was the exception: the British did not even bother to attack, and the island remained French until its governor surrendered after the final defeat of Napoleon in 1815. The beautiful, very Parisian arcaded building known as the Liston stands as a fine monument to this second period of Napoleonic rule in Corfu.

Recognising the need to ensure the defence of the islands, Ioannis Capodistrias, an Italian-educated member of the old Corfu aristocracy who had risen to near the top of the Russian foreign office, negotiated the foundation of a new independent United States of the Ionian Islands under British protectorate, with a local assembly to be regulated and directed by a British Lord High Commissioner in Corfu. Instead of acting, as envisaged, like a detached kind of referee and military defender of last resort, the first British Lord High Commissioner, Sir Thomas Maitland, directed and regulated the assembly in such a way that the Ionians effectively played no part in the game at all, and he ruled the islands himself with a heavy hand that did plenty for local prosperity and social conditions but nothing for goodwill towards the British.

In 1823 Lord Byron spent several months at Metaxata on Cephalonia before sailing to Missolonghi. While on the island he received deputations from all the quarrelling Greek factions whom he attempted to reconcile, and made friends with the British Resident (as the Lord High Commissioner's local representatives were known), Charles Napier, who inspired such affection in the Greeks that he was offered command of the revolutionary forces. Napier is remembered as the poor man's champion and cherished a particular love of the fertile valley behind Poros, where he set up a model farm, known as the Colony. With the creation of an independent Greece in 1827, under the presidency of Capodistrias, the Ionians found themselves no longer an outpost of Greek freedom from the Ottomans but an outpost of Greek subjection to the British. Clamours for union with Greece grew in volume, especially after revolutions all over Europe in 1848. They were consistently turned down in Britain, where there appears to have been a general failure to comprehend that any people might not want to be part of the Empire. But the Ionian issue gave Britain plenty of bad publicity in Europe, and eventually it was with some relief that in 1864 the British felt able to conclude that Greece was healthy enough, with a new constitution and a new king (George, a Dane), for the Ionian Islands to be allowed to join it.

Under the British protectorate of the 19th century Corfu was not only the first stop on a traveller's Greek itinerary, it was also a great favourite resort, the capital of the British Ionian Islands with a big expatriate community, good hotels and attractive walks from town along the one-gun (or Kanoni, as it is now known) peninsula, ideal walking ground for women, according to one Victorian visitor. Edward Lear spent a lot of time on Corfu and has left beautiful paintings and descriptions of 'the piggy wiggy island', although he claimed to find the social life of the island even more boring than total solitude. 'As the balls and small monotonous whist or tea parties are wholly out of my line in this very very very small tittletattle place, I decline all visiting.' The British brought parasols, colonnades and gardens to Corfu town, parks and country seats and that uniquely British institution, the picnic, to the island. The mountainous west coast was then, as now, a favourite spot, and if you stumble across any half-buried champagne bottles around Pelekas, the vintage may well be venerable. Corfu had English shops where all the London luxury items could be bought, and one visitor recorded that 'the British even extend patriotism to the votaries of Aphrodite', referring to boatloads of prostitutes imported from London.

Although the Ionians and the British parted company in 1864 without many tears shed on either side, the island did not lose favour with British visitors. Expatriate families included the Durrells, who carried on Edward Lear's work with their writings about the enchanted Corfu of their youth. With its cricket weeks, its country club and its well-tended rose-beds, Corfu town has not lost its genteel colonial atmosphere. Nor are English voices rare on its streets.

The information that Corfu is now, still, the most important British holiday destination in Greece will raise few surprised eyebrows. The style of the island's tourism, no longer genteel, is assessed in more detail in the island description. But what of the rest of the group? The names are not exactly household currency. If asked to rank in order of touristy-ness Mykonos and Santorini, for example, with Zante, most people would place the world-famous Cyclades well ahead of the lesser Ionian. But the truth of the matter can be gleaned by glancing at a few holiday brochures. For summer 1989 two of the main tour operators specialising in Greece, Sunmed and Thomson, offered between them 25 flights a week to Zante (more than to Rhodes), compared with three to Mykonos (also used for holidays on Naxos and Paros) and one to Santorini. Admittedly, Corfu (46 flights a week) and Zante are much larger islands, but the contrast is still striking and real.

It is not just a question of numbers. Ionian island tourism differs from most Aegean island tourism in being overwhelmingly British. There are also quite a few Italians, especially on Corfu and Paxos, which are very easily reached by ferry from Brindisi. The other big difference, inseparable from Britishness, is the preponderance of organised package holidays based in huge hotels or modern self-catering blocks of rooms, rather than the more typical informal village room arrangement. The droves of transient backpacking youth herding on and off ferries, accosted on the quay by local women and children barging and tugging sleeves in the desperate rush to fill rooms, is not an Ionian phenomenon. This makes a profoundly different atmosphere on the islands, and robs them of one of the most characteristic and, up to a point, attractive aspects of Greek island holidays, the mildly bohemian element of the summer population, mingling with the local villagers to the great delight of the tourists and the greater amusement of the local men than their women.

The arrangement of the islands does not suit island-hopping holidays. Strung out along the mainland coast far from Athens, they have simple ferry links to their nearest mainland ports. Inter-island links have been slow to develop for want of any local demand, except between Corfu and its dependency Paxos. Travelling between the islands is now much easier than it used to be, with good summer connections between Lefkas, Ithaca and Cephalonia; but the pattern has been set.

This has its pros and cons. The official Greek line is one of disapproval of penniless travellers who head for Athens on the cheapest charter flight or even the infamous Magic Bus, make for Piraeus and the first boat to some already overcrowded Aegean island where they doss down on the beach and play Robinson Crusoe, eking out a subsistence holiday and contributing nothing but litter and, it is said, the corrosive influence of their behaviour to the local community.

To what extent this is a real problem, rather than an excuse to bash the charter-flight industry, can be debated. In the Ionian Islands it is not a problem at all. Instead, Corfu has discovered that large numbers of young British holiday-makers on rock-bottom self-catering packages are no more of an asset than the great unwashed, although they may spend more money in the bars and do not camp rough on the beaches, except after a particularly heavy night in the pub when they lose their way home.

Identifying and dealing with the problems of playing host to mass tourism are important matters that mercifully are not our concern. For the prospective visitor, it is a question of deciding whether an environment of package tourism is preferable to or worse than an environment of backpacking tourism. Fortunately for those who prefer to shun mass tourism in any of its manifestations, there is still plenty of room in the Ionian Islands, as there is in the Cyclades. There are still some quiet corners of Zante and Corfu, and large empty spaces on Cephalonia. Lefkas is only now beginning to feature prominently in the brochures, Ithaca remains very little visited, and Paxos has evolved its own attractively peaceful and fittingly small-scale, well-heeled style of villa and dinghy tourism. Like the other islands in the group, it is much favoured for flotilla holidays. Given the considerable weaknesses in the Ionian ferry chain, having or renting a yacht of your own is much the best way to get around the islands.

CORFU (KERKYRA)

Corfu knows all about the problems of success. Powerfully promoted by Edward Lear and the brothers Durrell, the greenest and most luxuriantly beautiful of all the Greek islands rode the wave of its own great popularity apparently without thought for the consequences, allowing the proliferation of vast new hotels and coastal resorts to the point where the island now welcomes over half a million British visitors a year. Inevitably, much that was beautiful has been squandered and there has been a reaction.

If anyone wants to illustrate the unacceptable face of Greek tourism – hospitals full of uninsured moped crash victims, once peaceful villages overwhelmed by drunken louts, once lovely stretches of coast littered with the debris of cut-price tourist development, sea pollution – it is to Corfu that they look. Old Corfu hands recoil in horror from the unrecognisable island they once knew and loved, that genteel colony of lotus-eating expatriates who have been powerless to resist the hordes of barbarian invaders. There is a hint of desperation about the rearguard action at the Golf and Country Club, a last bastion: 'Shirts must be worn at all times; each player must have a full set of clubs.'

The bad publicity has had various effects. First, people have been put off: rumour had it that the number of British visiting the island – and Corfu was about 80 per cent dependent on Britain for its tourism – dropped by a third in 1988. Secondly, the authorities are now at least talking seriously about tackling some of the problems, notably the sea pollution that results from the scandalous lack of any sewage treatment. And, last but not least, those who arrive at Corfu in dread are pleasantly surprised to discover that the style of Ipsos, Benitses and the 2000-bed Messonghi Beach Hotel is not the style of the whole

Getting around

Car and motor-bike hire is available at Corfu town and at all the main resort areas. Buses operate to all corners of the island from Corfu town, with three different terminals: the Spianada (town buses and Kanoni); Theotoki Square (a few middle-distance routes in the central section of the island); and just behind the old port (longer journeys to all corners of the island). There are many car hire firms in Corfu town, and a considerable range of prices. It is probably best to disregard the offices prominently placed near the old and new harbours and concentrate on the main street through the new part of town (Alexandras) for your shopping around, bearing in mind that there are no bargains in Greek car hire, merely varying degrees of being ripped off. Out of season, haggling is in order and displaying lots of other firms' leaflets may be enough to elicit some special offer. Suncars, one of the less expensive local operators, gave us good service. With so much choice, it is particularly relevant to scrutinise and compare the small print and the insurance arrangements as well as the prices. (See Information, page 658).

A popular and attractive way of getting around Corfu town and to and from Kanoni is in an open horse-drawn carriage. There are standard fares for various lengths of tour, but be sure to agree on a sum before setting off.

The road network is extensive and lavishly endowed with hazards by no means unique to Corfu: sudden unannounced deterioration in the surface of apparently good roads, big farm vehicles on narrow lanes and a general lack of warning signs. Of the many maps in circulation the rival contenders are Clyde Surveys (which also covers the other Ionian Islands) and the less attractive, generally more up-to-date but not flawless island. Corfu now has such a bad name that, instead of reiterating that much of the island has been ruined, it may be more useful to emphasise that at least as much of it has not.

Of the island's 200km-long coastline, only a stretch of about 40km to the north and south of Corfu town, from Pirgi to Messonghi, has suffered the worst. This part of the coast certainly has lost nearly all its appeal (except to nightclubbers). The resorts form an almost unbroken amorphous straggle of roadside development and, ironically, this most heavily concentrated resort area has the worst beaches of the island – a thin strip of pebble, in many places no wider than a body is long. Ipsos, Gouvia, Kontokali, Kanoni, Perama and Benitses are particularly poor for bathing. The rest of the island has at least its fair share of beautiful beaches large and small and in many cases sandy.

Perhaps the saddest casualty of all is the Kanoni peninsula to

Freytag & Berndt map put out by Efstathiadis. Both can be bought locally, and it is probably worth having both. Maps handed out by car hire firms are no substitute.

The chain of roads around the island is at its weakest in the north-west. Thanks to an improbable-looking rough track through some farms and a bridge over the Melisudi river, driving between Sidari and Karousades/Roda need not involve a huge inland detour as indicated on some maps. The track is signposted from the Karousades end, but for those travelling in the other direction the left turn from the main road out of Sidari (about a mile south of the resort) is not, and nor is the dirt track after the bridge (first left). The bay of Agios Giorgios (north of Paleokastritsa) does break the chain: driving from the northern to southern end of the mile-long beach involves a journey of about an hour. It is not even possible to improvise by driving along the beach itself. If passing through, it is best to use the northern approach, a track down from near Afionas.

Corfu is too large for the usual round-the-island boat-excursions, but there are organised boat-trips and local caique services from most resorts. All the east-coast resorts, from Kassiopi to Kavos, have boats to and from Corfu town. Local services include hops along the bays of the north-east coast, and shuttles between Paleokastritsa and Agios Giorgios, Glifada and Agios Gordis, and around Sidari and Roda in the north. There are also excursions to three offshore islets. Small boats can be hired at Paleokastritsa.

Boat-trips to the islands of Paxos and Antipaxos (one excursion) and the mainland resort of Parga (another) are organised from Corfu town and most of the east-coast resorts. Paxos is really a better place for a stay than a day-trip, its main attractions being peace and quiet. Parga is better equipped (beach, shops, fort) to receive and amuse short-term visitors.

the south of Corfu town, the site of the ancient city and a famous beauty-spot with two monastery islets at the narrow entrance to a vast swampy lagoon. The lagoon has been overlaid with the island's airstrip, and along the peninsula, surveying the runway from very close range, has arisen a succession of huge hotels. Somehow the postcard photographers manage to find gaps between the low-flying jets and point away from the building sites, the tarmac and the ugly concrete causeway across the mouth of the lagoon.

The rest of the island does not lack busy resorts and beautiful bays scarred by big hotel blocks (some of which, incidentally, are among the best hotels of their kind in Greece), but its beauty can still be enjoyed and there are many places on Corfu where peace can be found. The mountain scenery and open sands of the central section of the west coast, where the naked Odysseus was woken from his slumbers on the beach by the lovely Nausicaa throwing a ball around with her handmaidens, are as spectacular as ever.

Separated from the sinister shores of Albania by only a mile or so of water, the north-eastern corner of Corfu has shady coves for idyllic villa holidays. The north and north-west have long stretches of open beach and only a couple of international resorts. In the south-west there is mile upon mile of empty sand without resorts or communities of any kind. Despite the traffic of tourists on hired scooters, the quiet agricultural villages of the island's densely vegetated interior do not seem to be greatly affected by the tourist boom. Locals bump along farm tracks in their Chevrolet pick-ups, with sunbeams filtering through a canopy of magnificent olive trees like shafts of light in the aisles of a Gothic cathedral. Rough tracks lead up bare slopes to the summit of mighty Pantokrator, where a solitary toothless old monk surveys his island realm and waits with coffee to reward his occasional visitors.

Foremost of the island's many remaining attractions is Corfu town, the one coastal community that does not have the atmosphere of a holiday resort, a fascinating historical layer-cake of a town which, unlike the other Ionian island capitals, has come down to us more or less intact. A place of graceful towers and elegant façades, of bandstand and cricket ground and a wonderful seedy backstreet charm, Corfu town is not to be missed. The main drawback to staying in the town itself, apart from the lack of beaches, is the fact that it is a big, busy, noisy place and by no means all old and beautiful.

The island caters for all styles of holiday and all tastes in resort and hotel, from palatial to ethnic primitive via international-airport-style. There are villas (an alluring word that covers a multitude of architectural sins), cheap rooms (usually in purpose-built blocks rather than local people's houses), functional hotels in resorts and self-contained large multiple-amenity holiday-camp hotels out on their own. In general the island is not really geared to independent travellers, although if recent occupancy levels are maintained it should not be too difficult to find a room in hotels normally taken over by tour operators, at a price.

When reading this chapter and holiday brochures, bear in mind that there are two resorts called Agios Giorgios and two called Agios Stefanos.

Corfu town and the North

The main string of modern resorts to the north of CORFU TOWN starts with **Potamos**, a suburb of Corfu town destined to receive the new sewage plant and perhaps the cricket ground if, as has been proposed in what can only be explained as a fit of self-mutilating anglophobia, the existing one is turned into a car-park, and continues through **Kontokali, Gouvia, Dassia, Ipsos** and **Pirgi**, which together account for a large slice of the island's hotel accommodation. None of these places has much of a village centre and this is now an unattractive stretch of coast, although the landscape is undeniably beautiful and thick vegetation does veil much of the ugliness of the recent development. In places (Ipsos, notably) the main road is the water-front, while elsewhere (as at Dassia) it is set well back, which does nothing for the roadside hotels but does allow for some peace and shady tavernas on the long, thin beach. All along the road there are dozens of bars, discos and restaurants, several campsites and plenty of watersports stations along the beaches. Ipsos has few big hotels and is full of young people staying in cheap rooms or camping (probably in greater comfort). The discos are said to stay open all night.

Three promontories break up the long gulf into separate bays and are the attractive setting for a Club Med and some large hotels. The *Astir Palace* (Luxury-category) on **Cape Kommeno** is about the best of these, with lots of greenery, beautiful views, two small beaches, an excursion-boat of its own and good sports facilities.

A hugely popular and easily sniffed-at excursion from resorts in this part of the island is to the stagy **Danilia Folklore Village**, Corfu's Disneyland, out in the country between Corfu town and Paleokastritsa, down the road from an isolated drive-in cinema. The ever-so-quaint arcaded village street is lined by olive wood souvenir carvers' workshops with Special Prices and shavings all over the floor, and a ceramic factory (everything made on the premises and sold at Factory Prices). The small museum is free and has a very interesting collection of agricultural implements, domestic interiors and costumes. The village forum is a disproportionately vast square with enough tables to accommodate the thousands who are bused in nightly from all corners of the island to sample The Corfu Experience with Vassilis the famous tour guide, free wine (orange juice for the kids) until 10.30 and entertainment provided by Alexis the famous *bouzouki* player and by dancers in local costume.

The resort sprawl ends abruptly at Pirgi, where the southern slopes of **Pantokrator** (906m) drop steeply to the sea. The broad grey mountain mass dominates most of the north-east corner of the island. Strange though it may seem, the sub-tropical density of Corfu's vegetation can get a bit claustrophobic; it is a relief to break through the olives and cypresses into a sweeping open landscape, with huge views and cool temperatures. The drive over the western shoulder of the mountain (Pantokrator, Strinilas, Ahavari) is very beautiful and passes through some picturesque rough old villages, notably **Petalia** (which has a taverna) and **Lafki**. From the edge of Petalia a track (very rough for the last mile or so) leads all the way to the summit, crowned by a monastery that would be ugly even without a massive pylon soaring from its main courtyard. The enormous views over the island and mainland coast more than compensate, and the white-bearded, wall-eyed monk is very welcoming. The outwardly promising church has an 18th-century icon screen and a mass of peeling dark paintings covering the low vault.

A much better way to do Pantokrator is on foot. The best starting-point is the lovely tumbledown and overgrown old village of **Perithia**, a place of beehives, nut trees and the music of sheeps' bells and the Capricorn Grill-room's radio mingling as they echo around the steep hillsides. It is no more than an hour's walk from the village to the summit, but the right path is not immediately obvious: ask the man in the Capricorn (there are very few other people in the village to ask) before setting off. Tackling Pantokrator from the south, around Nissaki, is a much more arduous proposition.

The coast road north-east from Pirgi winds its way slowly around through the olives, most of the way well above the sea, with footpaths and a few steep tracks down from the road to small pebble beaches. In a few places the villas and rooming buildings and tavernas almost constitute a resort. **Barbati Beach** has a scattering of accommodation in the groves behind a long stretch of beach and is generally preferable to **Nissaki**, which has the tiniest of beaches and the only big hotels on this stretch of coast. **Kaminaki, Kalami** and **Agios Stefanos** are attractive and very peaceful small seaside communities with villas and apartments for rent, book swaps in the tavernas, watersports on the beach and occasional visits from caiques ferrying tourists up and down the coast. Some of the Agios Stefanos holiday accommodation is very badly located beside the road down to the resort, a long walk from the sea and tavernas. Next to Kalami, it's worth making a short detour to the beautiful little harbour of **Kouloura**: this is the Corfu of the Durrells, only a mile or two from the coast of Albania.

The main resort in this part of the island is KASSIOPI, an old (although not very obviously so) fishing village on a north-facing bay without big package hotels but which has nevertheless grown too big for many tastes. The beaches immediately around Kassiopi are much less good than those further west. Tucked away in the trees near a lagoon on the northern cape of the island, a good area for dispelling ideas of Corfu being overcrowded, is a small and comfortable British-run hotel, the *Saint Spiridon Bay*, with watered lawns, a good swimming-pool and a couple of small sandy beaches near by. A rough track leads across the lagoon mouth and around the deserted cape to link up (on foot, not by car) with the empty end of a huge open beach stretching for several miles westwards as far as Roda. The road across the wide coastal plain now has a lot of shapeless and very unappealing holiday development along it. Much of this area goes by the name of **Acharavi**. **Roda** is not much better, but it does have a more cheerful and villagey sector of tavernas and hotels at the end of the beach. The 700-bed *Roda Beach Hotel* (B) is out on its own cape to the west of the resort and main beach. It is not at all luxurious but has attractive grounds and beach, a good swimming-pool (saltwater) and the usual nightlife package with imported Zorbas to lead the local dancing and a climactic conga around the restaurant.

Signposts from the main road do not make it very easy to find **Astrakeri**, a small beach community between Roda and Sidari; the most direct way is to follow the signs to Sandra's Special Pizza. It is a very modest and somewhat desolate little development with a few cafes and one small hotel, the *Angela Beach*; but there is plenty of space and some more charming small coves, one of them a fishing harbour, near by. More clearly signposted is the *Sidari Beach Hotel* and a few holiday apartments, a few miles to the west. There is no community here, but it is not too far to walk along the beach to the bright lights of Sidari; making the same journey by car involves a long and bumpy detour. This is an unspectacular but attractively rustic stretch of coast, mainly occupied by fertile farmland, with cattle and horses as well as the usual noisy rural congregation of poultry, dogs and donkeys.

SIDARI is the only big resort of the north-west, famous for its beaches framed by low sandy cliffs, the rudely named Canal d'Amour. Like Kassiopi, it has few hotels and consists mainly of rented rooms and apartments spread over a large area of almost sub-tropical luxuriance, with fields full of vegetables and houses built of mud bricks. The north-west corner of the island around Sidari has its own characteristic shoreline of golden cliffs and hard sand beaches. The most beautiful example can be reached

THE BRITISH CONNECTION

The discreet picnics among the olive groves, the memoranda, the protocols, the bustles, sidewhiskers, long top-boots, tea-cosies, mittens, rock-cakes, chutney, bolus, dignity, incompetence, book-keeping, virtue, church bazaars . . .
LAWRENCE DURRELL

For 50 years such attributes of British Empire fortified the rulers of the Ionian Islands: from 1815 to 1864. Britain took the islands from Napoleon and gave them up to independent Greece. Put thus simply, there seems reason for the Ionians' benign memories of the period, and for the good relations ever since between Greece and Britain. Yet it was an uncomfortable half-century; conflicts of temperament, misunderstanding and mutual resentment were escalating to armed enmity by the time Britain broke the deadlock. For a mid-19th-century power to give up sovereign territory was, after all, distinctly unusual.

In 1815, when the Congress of Vienna carved up the Napoleonic Empire, there were several proposals for these islands, thoroughly Italianate after centuries of Venetian rule and (except for Lefkas) never occupied by the Turks though so near to the occupied mainland. Russia wanted them made a principality, under a cousin of the tsarina; Britain would rather see them Austrian – it was, as always, a matter of the balance of power. There was a compromise plea for the Knights of St John, homeless since the loss of Malta, but it was universally rejected. In fact, British military occupation was a fait accompli, and British diplomats won in the end. The seven Ionian Islands were to be a 'single, free and independent state under the exclusive protection of His Britannic Majesty'.

Under their first Lord High Commissioner, Sir Thomas ('King Tom') Maitland, the Ionians acquired a cynical but practical constitution that

by following the numerous signs (as usual, understating the distance) to the Sunset cafe, due west of the farming village of **Peroulades**. The cliffs are higher here than at Sidari and keep the sun off the thin beach for much of the day. Late afternoon and early evening are best. The rest of this corner of the island knows only a small-scale and very informal style of tourism typical of many less developed Greek islands. There are a couple of cheerful small hotels and some apartment accommodation at **Agios Stefanos**, which has a wide hard sand beach, and a scattering of accommodation and campsites along the vast and beautiful sandy beach of **Agios Giorgios**, much visited by excursion-boats from Paleokastritsa. **Arillas**, the wide bay

---

made independence a polite fiction. The autocratic Maitland – described by contemporary critics as insufferably rude, particularly dirty in his person and constantly drunk – ruled until 1824. He saw to law, order and sanitation, and attempted, with singular brutality, to enforce the islands' neutrality during the struggle for Greek independence, outlawing and persecuting members of the patriotic Society of Friends, which was very active on Zante and Cephalonia. One young Zantiot was executed for his part in an attack on a Turkish ship. His body was covered in tar and placed in a cage outside his mother's house, where it took 15 years to decompose. She went mad. Yet the British connection was not entirely negative: education was one of the things the British did better than the Venetians. The picturesque and philhellene Lord Guildford revived the spirit of Ancient Greece in the Ionian Academy, with schools of theology, jurisprudence, medicine and philosophy; and Maitland's successor put a secondary school on each island.

In 1817 Maitland let Ali Pasha of Epirus have the mainland port of Parga, an Ionian outpost inconvenient to defend. Its population promptly evacuated themselves to the islands, but Maitland refused them land for a new town. The nationalistic movement, which came to the boil in 1821, boosted disenchantment with the British. The commissioner dealt with the excitement of the mainland's revolution by declaring in the islands a repressive state of emergency and disarming the population, collecting 13,000 weapons on Corfu alone. By 1823 Maitland had more wisely allowed an influx of mainland Suliote refugees into Cephalonia, and many philhellene volunteers passed through the islands towards the fighting – or in homesick retreat. The British Government, accepting the likelihood of Greek independence, dispatched what was christened The Byron Brigade – the poet and his retinue stayed an agreeable four months before proceeding to Missolonghi.

To the majority of Ionians, once Greece had won her independence

---

between Agios Giorgios and Agios Stefanos, has more new holiday development than either of its neighbours, but both resort and beach are disappointingly unattractive.

Corfu town (Kerkyra)

Corfu is a big town of nearly 40,000 inhabitants, spread around a knobbly joint in the long thin island's east coast. The beautiful old centre, mostly still consisting of tall Venetian 18th-century buildings, occupies the promontory between two impressive systems of fortifications, both basically Venetian constructions of the 16th century but nevertheless referred to as old and new. The main landmark and central feature of the

---

THE BRITISH CONNECTION continued

in 1830 the existence of the British protectorate was simply a frustration of their national urge to unite with Greece. There were no ties of blood, language or religion between Britain and this brief backwater of her empire, and not many financial or trading concessions. When the islands' vital crop of currants failed – a frequent hazard – they received no assistance. Rural life went on unchanged, apart from klephtic rumblings, while the British built roads and aqueducts, promenades and churches, palaces and mansions – an 'English house' was synonymous with one containing a bathroom. A constant stream of cosmopolitan visitors appreciated the picturesque people and the 'gardeny' qualities. Edward Lear, who made affectionate drawings of all the islands, was by turn enchanted and infuriated with 'the drumbeating bothery frivolity' of social life in Corfu town.

Successive Lord High Commissioners from high Tory to Liberal came and went. Many were philhellenes, and some were much loved by the Greeks. Wide-ranging reforms were made and standards of living were improved, so it was hard for the British to comprehend the islanders' lack of gratitude. One of the more liberal of the Lord High Commissioners acknowledged that 'the moral and physical state of the people have not been benefited by the British connection so far as to protect us hereafter from the reproach of having attended less to their interests than to our own'. The reproach was indeed made, and still forms the basis of most assessments of the period, which rarely allow much credit to the British for their positive contributions.

In 1849, as his term of office ended, the well-meaning Lord Seaton reformed the constitution in the islanders' favour. 'In ten days,' said an observer, 'he hurried the wondering Ionians through more political changes than England had undergone in ten generations.' In the same

---

beautiful view of Corfu from the sea is the old fort, separated from the island by a narrow channel and flanked by yacht and fishing harbours. The old fort is open to strollers and has *son et lumière* performances, but the buildings themselves are neither attractive nor interesting.

The most characteristic and delightful part of town is the Spianada (Esplanade), a large area of cricket square and public gardens beside the old fort, surrounded by buildings which handsomely illustrate the island's history. Commanding the ground is the colonnaded Palace of St Michael and St George, built at the beginning of the period of British control in 1819 as the seat of the British High Commissioner. On the inland boundary stands the elegant arcaded block known as the Liston,

---

month meetings, marches and agitation in Cephalonia turned to open revolt beginning with the murder of a British officer; Seaton's successor imposed six weeks' martial law. Throughout the 1850s the British attitude was disillusioned and their reforms fatalistic, while the Ionians grew openly insulting, using their new free press to ventilate their loathing of oppressive British rule. Greek superseded English and Italian as the official language, and British officers had to depend on their Greek-speaking subordinates. The Crimean War saw Britain and Turkey allies against Russia, and the archbishop of Corfu prayed publicly for the tsar. As at the start of the protectorate, so in its disagreeable last years, it was the political balance that mattered; the only island of real importance was Corfu – fortified, lying off Turkish territory – and then only if it belonged to another power.

Gladstone, out of office and philhellene, was sent in 1858 on a mission to resolve the situation. Amid wild excitement it was mistakenly supposed that he came to carry out a recently publicised proposal, that five islands should be ceded to Greece. Corfu and Paxos, not included, were particularly hysterical. But to cede anything to Greece was tantamount to giving it to Russia; Gladstone proposed another reconstruction of government. The Ionians petitioned Queen Victoria. Stalemate prevailed.

In 1862 the face-saving, politically possible opportunity came: a coup d'état deposed King Otto, whom Britain had always distrusted. The bargain was struck. Let Greece refrain from further agitation and take an acceptable new king – not, unfortunately, their first choice of Albert, second son of Queen Victoria, since the Russians would strongly object – and Britain would relinquish her Ionian protectorate. The Danish Prince William duly became George I, King of the Hellenes, and The Times reported: 'Although jealous of everything that may tend to weaken the naval power of England, the public has heard with perfect contentment that the islands are to be ceded.'

erected during the brief period of French control and strongly reminiscent of the rue de Rivoli in Paris. Tourists idle the time away under its arches or the leafy canopy outside sipping their expensive drinks, reading English newspapers and watching the cricket or, more likely, local kids playing football on the square. The quality of the outfield must make ground fielding and even running for a catch decidedly hazardous. The pitch itself is artificial. As well as the cricket ground the Spianada has rose-gardens, fountains, lawns, a bandstand, a classical rotunda commemorating the first British commissioner, Sir Thomas Maitland, and many statues of dignified figures, mostly British.

The walls and tall houses of the old town rise handsomely from the sea between the fortress and the old port, but the waterside walk past the smelly harbour of Mandraki is less attractive than cutting through the heart of the old town via any of the streets leading back from the Liston towards the old harbour. This is an extraordinary, fascinating and at times somewhat disconcerting mixture of busy shopping streets and seedy unmodernised tortuous slumland, an opera set with narrow streets of elegant arcaded and balconied Italian houses, graceful belfries and laundry strung across between the buildings. Considering that the old town area is quite small, it is remarkably easy to get bewilderingly lost, at least briefly. The main streets have an interesting range of shops, not all filled with T-shirts and souvenirs. Of these, olive wood items are a local speciality. There are also lots of jewellers and furriers.

St Spiridon, a late-16th-century church easily identified by its tall belfry standing above the roofs of the old town not far from the Spianada, is the church of the island's revered patron, who is credited with having intervened to protect the island from imminent catastrophe on several occasions (usually plague or the Turks) and whose remains it shelters. Four times a year (Palm Sunday, Easter Saturday, 11 August and the first Sunday in November) they are brought out for a ceremonious procession around the town. Apart from being clearly Italian in style, the interior of the church is not particularly interesting. The ceiling paintings are poor copies of the 18th-century originals.

The more imposing Metropolitan church (late 16th century) stands at the top of the narrow raised square of the same name, overlooking the old port. A picturesque little square just to the north of the Metropolis has a Venetian well dated 1699.

The town hall is an interesting if not outstandingly beautiful 17th-century Venetian building on a lively square to the south side of the main street (Voulgareos) running back from the sharp end of the Liston. The sculptural decoration of the walls includes a splendid swaggering Doge borne by cherubs.

The old port, used by most of the local and inter-island ferries, also has gardens and ranks of horse-drawn cabs, but is only moderately attractive, with a lot of traffic and a very shabby collection of cafes and hotels. Of these, the *Astron* (B) is the least uncomfortable. Connoisseurs of run-down old port hotels with bespectacled old proprietresses swathed in countless layers of shawls and sweaters and long socks regardless of the heat may find the *Akropole*, *Constantinople* and *Mitropolis* (all D) more amusing.

If the old port's charm verges on the seedy, the new port, around a corner to the east, has none at all and is not an area in which to look for accommodation, although there are a couple of hotels. For more comfortable but still modest accommodation in the interesting part of town near the Spianada, there are three C-class hotels near the Liston: the *Arkadion*, *Suisse* and *Splendid*. *Cavalieri* (A) is a more expensive and stylish small hotel at the southern end of the Spianada. The town's big Luxury-category hotel is the large *Corfu Palace*, prominent on the water-front of Garitsa Bay not far to the south. Most of the other big modern hotels and the town's discos are near the airport.

Corfu is very animated in the early evening, with swarms of people parading along the Spianada and the main streets of old town and new, but quietens down surprisingly early – although the Liston bars stay open late. The choice of restaurants is not inspiring. Avoiding the Liston (very expensive), one tends to gravitate to the old port. Even here the main alternatives are credit-card restaurants advertising 'all the Corfu specialities', daunting backstreet cafes where no tourists venture, and some fast-food bars. The simple Nautilus is acceptable and inexpensive.

A large area of Corfu town along the bay of Garitsa to the south of the Spianada and behind the new fort and new harbour is neither old nor beautiful, although trees and broad avenues give it a much more pleasant atmosphere than many Greek towns possess. The tumultuous crossroads of traffic and everyday town life is Theotoki square, whence main roads and busy commercial avenues lead off in various directions. The Paleokastritsa road passes the hospital and the peaceful flower-filled courtyards and attractive small church of the Platytera monastery, which has some good 17th-century icons.

Corfu's beach is Mon Repos, a small patch of sand at the southern end of Garitsa Bay with some swings, a few trees and a cafe. One pays to enter. It is quite a walk from the centre of town, hardly worth the bother. The 19th-century villa and gardens of Mon Repos, where Prince Philip was born, are not open to the public, but there are two interesting Byzantine churches near by. One is the ruined Agia Kerkira opposite the villa gates, the other a beautiful little 12th-century church dedicated to the two bringers of Christianity to Corfu in AD40, Jason and Sosipater. The church is tucked away in the backstreets, invisible from the water-front.

Corfu town: sights

• **Archaeological Museum** Housed in a modern building near the Corfu Palace hotel, this contains interesting information about and finds from the ancient city on the site of the airport, including two outstandingly beautiful pediments. The larger is the famous and arresting Gorgon pediment from the temple of Artemis (early 6th century BC). The grimacing gorgon is shown with snakes around her waist and in her hair and flanked by a pair of handsome hybrid leopard-like beasts and her two offspring, born at the moment she was decapitated by Perseus. Only the hind legs of the winged horse Pegasus (one of the offspring) remain. The other pediment from a slightly later temple shows a bearded Dionysos and a young boy reclining at a feast, but apparently distracted from each other by something, with a dog and a lion under the table. The museum also has some good busts and numerous statuettes of Artemis, usually with deer, bow and arrow.

• **Museum of Asian Art** This is a much more surprising thing to find on a Greek island. Not only is the collection exceptionally interesting, but it also occupies a few of the imposing and richly decorated chambers, including the pompous Throne Room, of the early-19th-century Palace of St Michael and St George, the seat of the British governors. The museum is a tribute to the dedication, discernment and generosity of a Greek diplomat, Gregorios Manos, who spent most of his life and all his fortune amassing a remarkable collection of 10,000 works of Japanese and Chinese art: porcelain, armour, weapons, theatre masks, netsuke and inro (decorative buttons and pouches for seals and medicines). A few other benefactors have recently added to the museum. Follow the sound of giggling to a room of erotic Indian temple sculptures.

• **Kanoni** For the moment there is very little to see of the archaeological zone on the Kanoni peninsula (just south of Corfu town), where the ancient city was located. Thousands of people go there all the same, to visit the two very picturesquely sited and much-photographed churches on tiny offshore islands, one accessible on foot by a causeway below the Hotel Royal, the other (Pontikonissi or **Mouse Island**) reached by one of the caiques that go to and fro very frequently. Bathing is possible but there are no inviting beaches. The Byzantine church on Mouse Island dates from the 13th century. The eastern side of the Kanoni peninsula is the hill of Analypsis, a very tranquil residential outskirt of town with thick stone walls and vegetation reminiscent of rural England. The best viewpoint is near the Top of the Hill restaurant.

Kassiopi

Of all Corfu's well-known resorts, Kassiopi comes closest to most people's idea of what a charming Greek village resort ought to be like. It occupies a small bay clearly defined by low flanking hills, one with a ruined fortress on top, and its centre is a harbour full of fishing-boats, excursion-caiques and yachts. It is bypassed by the main road and not dominated by big hotels; in fact it is hard to find any hotels at all. Drawbacks? Simply that a resort relying predominantly on peaceful village charm for its appeal suffers more as it grows in size than does a beach resort; and Kassiopi has indeed grown. The water-front is a bit of a concrete open space, the bay has no beach and the old village has been all but submerged by the modern resort. It is usually promoted as the island's smart destination, and local villa owners may well include millionaires and a few celebrities. But there is no longer anything very exclusive about Kassiopi, with the cheap self-catering package operators present in force. This is just one among hundreds of cheerful Greek fishing-village resorts, bigger and more lively than most, with plenty of bars and tavernas and a few discos.

The busy beach trail is a path past a few harbourside tavernas and around the western headland, which has some pebble coves and good rocky bathing. There are larger beaches, also mostly pebbles, beside the main road to the west of the headland. Avladi is a more secluded stony beach, with a taverna and windsurfing, about a mile to the east of the resort, reached by a rough track from near the main road junction.

Very little remains to commemorate Kassiopi's importance in the island's history, which was considerable until the Venetians destroyed the fortress on the western headland in the 15th century, after which the town's inhabitants soon dispersed. Roman Kassiopi was the leading settlement on the island and boasted a magnificent temple of Jupiter.

Sidari

Far away in the well-watered and productive farmland of north-west Corfu, Sidari is a recent addition to the list of the island's busy resorts and a good one. The countryside is very attractive, the beaches are good, and the resort, although no beauty in itself, is cheerful without being frenetic. This is a matter of degree and personal taste, of course. A messy modern roadside development entirely devoted to package tourism (and tourism-related building activity) would not be everyone's idyll.

The resort has grown up along the main road where it follows the sandy beach for about half a mile before heading inland and westwards along a river. Fortunately, there is not much through traffic and what there is has little choice but to slow down to walking pace. The gap between the road and the sea is just wide enough to have allowed the erection of a row of shops, bars and restaurants with terraces opening directly on to the beach. Of Sidari's few hotels, the medium-sized *Mimosa* (C) is probably the best choice, well placed at the western end of the main drag, a short walk from the resort centre, such as it is, and from the main beach and the various more secluded small sandy coves around the headland. With their characteristic eroded low sandstone cliffs and headlands, the coves are Sidari's trademark, especially picturesque when photographed with a wide-angle lens: the patches of sand are in reality small and easily crowded. Exploring this beautiful fragmented shoreline gives a welcome purpose to taking out a pedalo.

As well as the usual coach- and boat-trips – which may include visits to the three islands off the north-west coast of Corfu – tour operators organise excursions on horseback. Bicycle hire is also popular and a very practical means of local transport: the surrounding farmland is flat, and holiday rooms are spread widely around the neighbourhood.

The Mid-West

The mountainous central part of the west coast is the most famous and spectacular section of the Corfu coastline, with as many Sunset tavernas up on the hillsides (mainly around Pelekas, where Kaiser Wilhelm habitually came to enjoy the sight of the sun going down) as there are Nausicaa tavernas down by the sea. On this extraordinarily fertile island, even the rocky cliffs seem to be clothed in green velvet, with spiky cypresses silhouetted against the sky. The most celebrated beauty-spot is PALEOKASTRITSA, where a no-through road winds around a serrated mountainous coastline above a series of rocky coves towards an old monastery high on a headland. This is a cramped location for a holiday resort and, with several big hotels tucked into the hillsides and lots of coach traffic, Paleokastritsa is now a bit of a crush.

A particularly beautiful excursion from Paleokastritsa is up into the hills to the villages of **Lakones** and **Krini**. There are superb views of Paleokastritsa, and from Krini it is possible to visit the 13th-century fortress of **Angelokastro**. The road leads on to Vistonas: turn left for the lovely beach of Agios Giorgios. The north-west corner of the island is very peaceful and undeveloped: many of the local women wear traditional costume.

East of Paleokastritsa a steep road descends from **Liapades** to a small stony beach with a hotel beside it and a few holiday villas and tavernas on the way down from the village. This is not a particularly delightful spot, although the cove is relatively peaceful. There is a caique service across the bay to Paleokastritsa.

Further south, there are two magnificent long sandy beaches at the foot of the cliffs, **Glifada** and **Agios Gordis**, both now very busy. Both have a beach hotel complex, a couple of smaller hotels (the B-class *Glifada Beach* is recommended) and some holiday villas, and their steep access roads get choked by day-trippers' cars. But there is much more beach space than at Paleokastritsa, and either place would be a good choice of resort if a beach is your overwhelming priority. **Ermones** is a smaller sandyish bay usually identified as Odysseus's landing-place. Prospective patrons of the Nausicaa taverna or its neighbour should be prepared for an unusually fierce verbal tug-of-war between the rival waitresses who lie in wait on either side of the shared staircase.

There is some simple accommodation beside the road down to the beach, and a luxury bungalow hotel, the *Ermones Beach* (A), high on the hillside above, with its own funicular to the sands, which get very crowded. Ermones is very convenient for the golf course (open to non-members; the British pro will give lessons; renting clubs is possible but expensive, and sharing a set is not allowed; shirts must be worn at all times).

Between Glifada and Ermones is a beautiful small sand and rock beach, **Mirtiotissa**, which has become the main sanctuary of nude bathing on the island. It's reached by a steep and rough track; all but the most determined macho bikers park at the top and walk down. There is a rustic taverna with a few rooms about half-way down, but nothing by the beach except a small monastery tucked away in the trees at the end of the track.

Pelekas Beach is no less beautiful than Glifada and Agios Gordis but much quieter as it can be reached only be caique, by footpath from the touristy hill village of Pelekas (which has rooms), or by a very rough track from near the *Yaliscari Palace* (A), a comfortable and secluded hotel with a good swimming-pool and its own beach steeply below the hotel. Pelekas Beach has all the basic facilities, including windsurfing and rooms for rent at Maria's very cheerful taverna.

The coast south of Agios Gordis is rarely explored olive-growing country with the odd farmhand's cafe beside the rough road. **Paramona** is a very peaceful little resort with a pebble beach and a hotel and some rooms. Unlike most of the island, but like the quiet resorts in the north-west, Paramona's summer season is short.

Paleokastritsa

Arthur Foss, writing about the Ionian Islands 20 years ago and remarking on the changes that had taken place at the famous beauty-spot of Paleokastritsa in the 25 years before that, described 'three hotels and several restaurants' specialising in local crayfish and lobster. 'In addition, there are several recently built villas so that there is now little room for further development.' Well, little room or not, further development there has certainly been, on a considerable scale. Assorted resort buildings – villas, travel agencies, bars, rent-a-bike shops and three very large new hotels – now straggle back along the tortuous coast road from the main cluster of little bays at the foot of the monastery headland (the end of the road) for well over a mile to the Lakones turnoff, and beyond. This has not physically spoilt the celebrated beauty of a coastal landscape of steep wooded hillsides, cliffs and bays fringed by pines and olive trees, but it does mean crowds. The place is choked with coaches queuing up and turning around, and the three small beaches (mostly pebbles) get extremely crowded, as do the beachside tavernas (The Smurfs and Chez Georges), which are more attractive than they sound. Also, staying in the resort almost inevitably involves a lot of walking along the busy road. There is not much of a community at the end of it: a couple of small not-so-modern hotels near the main beach (*Apollo*, c, and *Zefiros*, D, and the original Xenia tourist pavilion, now just a cafe, hogging the prime location). The best of the big new hotels is the *Akrotiri Beach* (A): it has its own beach, and the road does not come between it and the sea. As so often in Greece, the local disco is out of earshot on the edge of the resort, a long walk.

The cave-pitted cliffs framing the beaches provide excellent snorkelling and there is a diving school. Another redeeming feature for keen bathers is the chance to commute by caique to the vast and magnificent sandy beach of Agios Giorgios (tavernas, watersports), a spectacular 10-minute ride to the north. The boats pass beneath the 13th-century Venetian fortress of **Angelokastro**, 425m above the sea.

Tour operators organise donkey rides up into the hills above the resort. Small boats can be hired.

Paleokastritsa: sight

• **Zoodochos Pigi monastery** Tourists queuing up to get into a
monastery is not a common sight in Greece, but it happens after lunch
at Paleokastritsa where the Zoodochos Pigi monastery on top of the
headland is the main sight to be seen apart from the magnificent
landscape, for the appreciation of which it is one of the best vantage-
points. This is a fairly typical Greek monastery, with chicken coops
outside the precinct, an old monk at the gate handing out skirts to
underdressed visitors, dazzling whitewash and beautiful flowers inside,
and a room where the icons are kept and souvenirs sold. Less typically,
the monastery seems to be thriving. This may have something to do
with the stationing of an attendant at the door of the church obliging
visitors to buy a candle before they enter. There has been a monastery
on the site since the Middle Ages, but the present buildings date from
the 18th and 19th centuries. Homer's landscape descriptions have led
many scholars to favour this headland as the site of the palace of
Alcinous, king of the Phaeacians and father of Nausicaa. There is an
offshore rock to fit the story of Poseidon, furious at Odysseus's safe
return to Ithaka, striking the offending Phaeacian ship with the flat of
his hand and turning it to stone as it made its way home.

The South

To the south of the airport lagoon (Lake Halkiopoulou), coastal
development is less dense than to the north of Corfu town, with
three main resorts interspersed by isolated coastal hotels.
Perama is more an area of hotels than a resort, and too close to
the airport for comfort. **Benitses** is full of young people after
what is usually described as a good time, so it's known as the
Benidorm of Greece. The comparison is not very apt, but the
basic message conveyed to those who have not been to
Benidorm is fair enough: if you don't relish the company of
young, lager-swilling Brits, stay away. Benitses has
shortcomings as a beach resort. The busy coast road runs along
the water-front, and there are only token stony pocket-
handkerchief beaches; for want of space sunbathers stretch out
on the concrete pavement. But the charm of the old village has
not been entirely lost.

The big and lively holiday agglomeration of MORAITIKA/
MESSONGHI has grown up on both sides of the mouth of
Corfu's main river, the Messonghi. This stretch of coast is
green and hilly, but not ideal for seaside holidays: the road
follows the shore nearly all the way, and there are few beaches.

A very popular excursion in this area is to the **Achillion**, a
vast palace in a magnificent position on the hills above Perama
and Benitses, built and decorated in a laborious and turgid

heroic classical style in 1890 for Empress Elizabeth of Austria, cousin of Ludwig of Bavaria and King Otto of Greece. After her assassination in 1898 the Achillion was bought by Kaiser Wilhelm II. The best things about the palace are the garden terraces filled with palm trees and statues of Achilles and many other athletes and warriors, and the views they command over the airport lagoon, Corfu town and the nearby coast. By day, when the top-floor casino area is out of bounds, there is very little to see inside the palace except photographs of the kaiser and his enormous yacht, the *Hohenzollern*. It would certainly be more interesting if not necessarily more rewarding to visit the Achillion as an evening player than as a sightseer. The minimum stake is a few hundred drachmas, so the experience need not be ruinous.

As an alternative to the unlovely coast road between Perama and Messonghi, it's worth taking the beautiful hill road through **Agia Deka** and **Strongili**; the former village has splendid views and several tavernas.

South of Messonghi is a lovely stretch of coast which gives a tantalising idea of what much of the east coast must once have been like. Along the rough track which follows the shore there are a few places offering rooms. **Boukari** even has two small hotels. At the end of the road in the far south, KAVOS has grown from nothing into a very large resort and, although one looks in vain for a village core, it is about the best place on the island for those after the simple combination of cheap accommodation, a sandy beach, watersports and lots of nightlife.

The narrow, flat and fertile southern tail of the island has relatively uninteresting scenery, but excellent beaches, mainly on the west coast, which is easily reached by numerous tracks down through bamboo and olives from the main road around Argirades and Perivoli. **Agios Georgios** is an ugly modern package-holiday resort, small but strung out along the shore between huge expanses of sand, and very lifeless outside high season. A much more attractive alternative for *ad hoc* accommodation is further south, at the sandy beach at the bottom of a farming valley below **Marathias** (signposted to 'jetskis'), with a couple of tavernas and rooms to rent.

A mile or so north of Agios Giorgios, **Issos Beach** has a rusty snack cantina, windsurfing and some nude bathing. The best place to go in search of an empty stretch of beach is a little further along to the north, where a long dune bar separates a large lagoon, **Lake Korission**, from the sea. Sandy farm tracks lead down from the Messonghi to Agios Mattheos road to a lakeside taverna (take insect repellent) and the sea at the northern end of the lake, a place marked on some maps as **Mesavrisi**.

Moraitika/Messonghi

This is a big resort zone around the Messonghi river where the main road south turns inland. At the northern end, Moraitika's centre is a row of bars, restaurants and shops along the main road, with a cluster of low-rise modern hotels occupying the space between it and the beach, which is sandy and quite spacious. There are many more non-British tourists than in most Corfu resorts.

To the south of the river, Messonghi has a marginally more villagey shape and atmosphere and is well away from the main road, although some of its holiday accommodation is not: there are apartment buildings in a very undesirable location beside the road towards Agios Mattheos. But most of the hotels and a campsite are very conveniently close to and in some cases just about on the beach, a long and averagely attractive strip of muddy sand and pebbles with a few tavernas. The *Apollo Palace Hotel* (A) is a surprisingly smart new small hotel set back slightly from the beach among olives.

To the south, Messonghi peters out gradually along the rough coastal track, initially passing restaurants and holiday apartment buildings with a few weedy stretches of beach and the occasional villa jetty. This is very attractive strolling territory.

Occupying a large area beside the river between Messonghi and Moraitika is the massive *Messonghi Beach Hotel and Bungalows* (B), a 2000-bed holiday metropolis with its own shopping precinct, ten bars, several tavernas with long queues at mealtimes, lots of wire fencing and lots of jokes about whether this is intended to keep intruders out or inmates in. The scale of the place is enough to inspire feelings of sympathy for battery hens, but there are many nastier factories of tourism than the Messonghi Beach: the beach is not bad, the gardens are well kept, the décor and furniture are less tatty than in many comparable places, the river bank is nicely exploited with its Moorings Pub and excursion-boats, and residents are not stranded in the middle of nowhere – lots of people wander along to the bars of Messonghi at night.

Kavos

Kavos has grown up recently and very rapidly among olive groves behind a very long stretch of sandy beach in the far south of the island, a somewhat isolated location but pleasantly free from through traffic, unlike many of the island's resorts. The place seems to have been conceived to satisfy a simple formula – cheap modern accommodation, a lot of sandy beach, a lot of watersports and a number of bars and discos – and does it well, with no serious drawbacks provided you want these facilities and nothing more. With no big hotel blocks, Kavos seems less like a big resort than a small one that happens to cover a large area. The beach is about ten yards deep and shelves very gently under water.

Most of the accommodation is in small modern rooms, apartments and 'studios' (rooms with basic cooking facilities). Of the hotels, the new *Morfeas* (B), with a swimming-pool, is clean, comfortable and relatively peaceful, on what is for the moment the southern fringe of the resort. Escapists can wander along the empty weed-covered beach southwards to the hills of Cape Asprokavos, the southern tip of the island. Some maps mark a beach on the eastern side of the cape.

CEPHALONIA (KEFALLINIA)

Cephalonia is much the largest of the Ionian Islands and, with Mount Enos rising like a 5000-foot wave above the south coast, much the tallest. Its attractions are numerous and worth emphasising straight away. The small fishing village of Fiskardo, named after the mighty Norman adventurer Robert Guiscard who died there in 1085, is one of the most picturesque and delightful resorts of its kind (yacht people and watercolourists in Breton smocks) in Greece. The fortress headland and village of Assos, the underground Melissani Lake and the beaches of Mirtos and Xi are classic tourist-office poster material and would win places in any hit parade of Greek island beauty-spots.

Unfortunately, these and a few other pros have to be set against a heavily laden con side of the balance. Having lost most of its mantle of fir trees, large areas of the island are now grey and more rugged than immediately attractive, although the broad-shouldered Cephalonian landscape does not lack admirers. Distances are long and the roads, although not bad by Greek standards, slow. Exploring the island is a tiring business, especially if one tries to do it from a single base. A more serious drawback concerns the devastation wrought by the 1953 earthquake (and many before it) and the reconstruction that has followed. Towns and villages rebuilt after complete destruction during this century are rarely attractive, and Cephalonia offers few exceptions, least of all Argostoli, the sprawling low-rise island capital and main resort. Its functional buildings and wide straight streets seem to commemorate and in a sense perpetuate the grim mood of the aftermath of tragedy. Many would consider it among the least charming resorts in Greece, although the competition is fierce.

Of course, one is not obliged to stay in Argostoli or its beach resort suburbs, although very large numbers of holiday-makers do. But there are few good alternatives, which is presumably why the capital has become the surprising focus of the island's tourism. The two main ferry ports, Sami and Poros, are no prettier and are singularly lifeless villages, as is Lixouri, the main village on the island's western limb. Skala, a small resort on the extreme south-eastern tip of the island increasingly favoured by tour operators, is no more than a very long beach. Only Assos and Fiskardo, which escaped the earthquake, stand out, but they too have their drawbacks: not much accommodation and very inconvenient locations (especially Fiskardo) from which to explore the island.

There is no real solution to this. Cephalonia is an island where one looks in vain for cheerful and attractive villages to use as a base or to pause at for a break in a scenic tour. An important ingredient of what most people like about the Greek islands – picturesque village charm – is thus lacking. The best policy is probably to hire a car on arrival and to set off around the island, staying at various places away from the main resorts and being sure not to skimp on the beautiful northern peninsula. When touring the island, it is worth bearing in mind the possibility of using the car-ferry between Sami and Fiskardo (one leg of the link with Lefkas) as a way to save laborious retracing of steps along northern Cephalonia's only road.

To return to the uninspiring subject of **Argostoli**. The island's one big town is set on the sheltered side of a long promontory which creates a subsidiary inlet within the vast Gulf of Argostoli. It is a fine setting, at least when surveyed from above, at a high pass on the Sami road, which begins by crossing the shallow water via a 19th-century causeway, in reality a water-level bridge built by the British. It is no surprise to learn that the head of this sheltered bay was the site of one of the four ancient cities of the island (Krani). There is not much to see *in situ*.

The modern town's unimposing low concrete buildings are laid out on a long grid of indistinguishable wide streets centred on an outsized central square. This well-established anti-seismic town plan is not new: a visitor in 1806 reported that the town's houses had 'only one storey on account of the earthquakes to which the island has the reputation of being more subject than any of the surrounding countries'. There are palm trees, statues (Cephalonia's most famous son was prime minister Metaxas, he of the famous 'Ochi' response to the Italian ultimatum in 1940), cafes and plenty of people milling around in the early evening, but they make little or no impact on the overwhelming impression of unfilled space. The only lively part of town is the busy road along the quay, a noisy morning mêlée of buses, ferries and shoppers.

There are a few hotels on the water-front (including the simple C-class *Tourist*), which are likely to be noisy at dawn, and many more scattered about the town. Of these, the *Castello* (C) is a reasonable choice: clean, small and conveniently placed beside the main square. Argostoli has a small archaeological museum and another devoted to local history and folklore, where any curiosity you may have about what the aftermath of an earthquake looked like will be satisfied. The museum also has good displays of local costumes, crafts and icons recovered from damaged churches.

The road around the **Lassi promontory** passes reconstructions of a 19th-century lighthouse and a water-mill erected to harness the unusual phenomenon of seawater disappearing into the ground. In 1963 the puzzle of where the water goes was solved when dye reappeared on the other side of the island in the Bay of Sami, via the Melissani underground lake.

The western side of the Lassi promontory now has a lot of large-scale holiday development along the main road to the airport, some of it conveniently close to the good sandy beaches of Makri Yialos and Plati Yialos, which serve as Argostoli's local beaches. Unfortunately, they are not large and the number of people, tourists and locals, competing for space on them is very considerable. The *White Rocks* (A) is the most attractive of the big hotels: comfortable, moderately secluded and very convenient for Plati Yialos beach. There is no real resort here, but the area is usually referred to as Lassi. Beyond the airport lies much more peaceful, very fertile fruit-growing country with small prosperous villages where sprightly white-haired men in tropical shirts and shorts wash their cars and water the lawns outside their neat little bungalows. If the scene seems more evocative of Australia than a Greek island, this is no coincidence. Cephalonia has sent many of its children to make their fortune down under, and not a few return to spend their old age at home.

There are several beaches that fill up with locals at weekends and Greek holiday-makers in August, but are otherwise peaceful (**Lourdata, Pesada** and **Agios Thomas**). Pesada has a useful summer ferry service to Zante. These beaches are most easily reached from the main Argostoli to Poros road, and this general area of the south-west coast is good for simple out-of-the-way accommodation (most plentiful at Lourdata).

Near Peratata this road passes a hill crowned by the pine-filled fortress walls of **Agios Georgios**, probably first constructed by the island's Venetian overlords (the Orsini family) in the 13th century. Agios Georgios was the island's main stronghold and official capital until 1757, when the seat of government was moved to Argostoli. Most of the remaining walls, which are well worth inspecting, date from the 16th century. In September 1943 Agios Georgios was the main site of the massacre of thousands of the island's Italian garrison, which had refused to hand the island over to German control. Eight are said to have escaped through an old tunnel, now blocked, to Argostoli. Sources vary on the numbers involved, but the total number of the 'Cephalonia martyrs' exceeded 5000.

The nearby **Agios Andreas** convent's prize relic is the sole of St Andrew's right foot. It also has beautiful 18th-century mural paintings, which are among the few good things to have come out of the earthquake – a covering of whitewash fell off during the upheaval, revealing the previously forgotten paintings.

To the east of the fertile coastal plain, the road continues high above the coast, running beneath the massive wall of Mount Enos, its former cloak of fir trees now reduced to little more than a skull-cap. The main village on this route, **Markopoulo**, is famous throughout Greece for a phenomenon recorded on the yellow church tower beside the road: 'For centuries now, the snakes have come to the bottom of this tower on 6 to 15 August.' The snakes are said to be innocuous, to have black crosses on their heads, to enter the church and pay their serpentine respects to the icon of the Virgin before dispersing, and are considered to be a good omen. They did not appear during the German occupation or in 1953 (the earthquake happened on 12 August). The locals now make their own luck by collecting snakes and releasing them in the village on 15 August.

A rough track from the village joins the road down to **Kato Katelios**, a fine bay with a long sandy beach and a small holiday community and fishing harbour at its western end. There are a couple of large cheerful tavernas, a few campers under the trees behind the beach and, rather surprisingly, British package holiday-makers in rooms. One could do worse.

The main road to Poros cuts the corner of the island, passing through rich farming country and an impressive mountain gateway just outside Poros, one of Cephalonia's numerous ferry ports and its busiest resort after Argostoli/Lassi. There is a much slower but rewarding alternative route along the coast from Kato Katelios, surfaced as far as Skala but rough and beautiful between Skala and Poros, with long stretches of empty beach south of Poros (pebbles) and west of Skala (a vast sandy bay below Ratzakli, reached by an unsignposted rough track). The two routes together make a good round trip excursion from Poros.

Those staying in **Skala** do not need to go anywhere in search of empty beach space, which they have on their doorstep in almost limitless quantity. The beach, a ruined Roman villa with mosaics, and a diminishing but still considerable degree of peace are the attractions of a one-street resort hidden away in the pines behind the beach, which is a mixture of sand and shingle and shelves steeply under water. Skala features in lots of holiday brochures, the most recent of which claim that it now has a disco and some watersports facilities. It also has a couple of small hotels, but the chances of finding an empty room in summer cannot be good. There is plenty of pine shade at the back of the beach, which has some tavernas, and campers cheerfully disregarding the prohibition notices.

Poros is a much more substantial resort, covering about a mile of coast in two or perhaps even three distinct sections: the port, the resort centre and a straggle of off-road beach development to the north of a concrete dry river-bed. It is a busy place in summer but shows few signs of extra-touristic life, and the separation of port from resort by a headland robs the resort of the usual animation that comes and goes with shipping. There is plenty of stony beach immediately below the broad pavement area which passes for the town square, and on for a considerable distance northwards, with an assortment of tavernas and accommodation blocks strung out along it. There are watersports and a tennis court. The central part of the resort, where none of the hotels deserves special mention, is not pretty, but the locals have done what they can to cheer it up with flowers, vines draped over the houses and trees beside the road. One piece of advice will have the ring of authenticity: if arriving by bus from Argostoli and heading for the port, do not get off when the bus stops on the main water-front. It continues to the port, and the headland is steep enough to be hot and bothering if you have bags to carry.

As is obvious from Poros, the coast to the north of it is abruptly mountainous and totally inaccessible, but a rough road running between the massifs of Enos and Kokkini Rachi from Tzanata to Zervata makes the necessary link in a tour of the island, and also provides some very impressive mountain scenery. The surroundings of the southern part of this drive are well watered and fertile, thanks to the small but traditionally bottomless Lake Avithos, which is close to the road near Agios Nikolaos. The region, or rather its livestock population, produces cheese.

Sami, the most important of Cephalonia's four ancient cities and now the island's main port for long-distance ferries, has not developed as a resort to anything like the same extent as Poros. This is not to say that it is any prettier, merely more tranquil – to a fault. It has the double-spaced look so characteristic of the island, as if designed in anticipation of a volume of traffic and evening promenaders which has not materialised. The small hotel *Melissani* (a very good D) is well worth seeking out (set back at the eastern end of the resort) in preference to the more obvious hotels near the ferry quay. Of the two restaurants on the water-front, the Asteria is better than its superior-looking neighbour. Bathing is possible at Sami, but the nearest moderately attractive beach is about a mile along the bay to the west towards Karavomilos, which has shady seaside tavernas convenient for after a visit to **Lake Melissani**, the most celebrated of many caves in this part of the island, its waters fed by the stream that disappears under ground at Argostoli. Visitors are rowed across the lake, which occupies about a third of the cave and is open to the sky like a huge well. On a sunny day, the colour of the water and reflections playing on the walls of the cave are spectacular.

There is a good campsite between Sami and Karavomilos. Sami is a good base for excursions by boat to Fiscardo, Vassiliki on Lefkas, and Ithaca (either via ferries from Agia Evfimia or caique excursions from Sami itself).

In the northern corner of the broad bay of Sami, the small ferry port of **Agia Evfimia** (services to Ithaca and the mainland port of Astakos) has some simple accommodation and a thin strip of stony beach.

The Sami to Argostoli road crosses the rugged scrub-covered mountainous mass of central Cephalonia after passing the other celebrated and much-visited local cave, **Drogarati** (a couple of miles from Sami). A long staircase leads to an impressive and well-lit chamber of stalagmites and stalactites. From the Agrapides pass a 15km road leads all the way along the mountain crest to the 1628m summit of **Mount Enos**, from which point, unsurprisingly, the views are limited only by the weather. The best view down over Argostoli and the fertile south-western corner of the island is from a lower ridge, near the turning to the convent of the island's patron saint, Gerasimos, a busy pilgrimage place on 15 August and 20 October.

The **Lixouri** (or more properly Paliki) peninsula hangs like an open jaw to the west. The main road around the bay of Argostoli is not very interesting, and the best way to get to Lixouri, the only village of any size on the peninsula and the island's largest village after Argostoli, is by ferry from the capital, a trip of about 20 minutes. Lixouri has the by-now familiar featureless building style and logical layout, but benefits from a smaller scale: the palm-filled, cafe-fringed square beside the ferry quay is almost attractive. Lixouri does not have much of a holiday atmosphere, but like Argostoli it is used as a resort, with a couple of hotels to the south of the quay. The nearest beach is **Lepeda**, over a mile to the south of town. These are very sheltered waters, with an attractive mixture of sand and rocks.

There are hills along the west coast, but most of the peninsula is flat cultivation and in places has the unmade look of an earthquake in arrested motion, all whipped-up peaky hillocks and sudden rifts. The main reason to explore this windswept and very dusty part of the island – and the vagueness of maps and signposts means that exploring is what it comes down to – is the beaches, beautiful long stretches of dark orangey sand backed by low earthy cliffs, best reached from the village of Mantzavinata, usually empty and certainly never crowded (although there are organised boat-trips from some resorts). Alternatively, you can walk all the way around the cape from Lepeda, at some length. The locals all know which tracks lead to the sea, where there are a few summer tavernas and a few ramshackle holiday houses among the melon fields, but there is no systematic tourist development apart from the isolated hotel Ionian Sea, a long way from the sea. The main stretch of beach, several miles long, is known as Xi (or simply X), which seems quite appropriate. Not that this is a place reserved for over-18 behaviour: it simply demands no name other than some variant of the Greek for long splendid sandy south-facing beach. The headland to the west is the site of the much-vaunted moving rock **Kounopetra**. Since 1953 it is reliably reported to have been immobile and, if the sign pointing straight on out to sea from the end of the road is anything to go by, it may well have disappeared altogether.

At the northern neck of the peninsula there are good sandy beaches and two attractive little tavernas by a small harbour (**Agios Kiriakis**) below the village of Zola, very peaceful although clearly visible and fairly easily accessible from the main road north from Argostoli. It is a very impressive view northwards along the grim grey cliffs of the island's north-west coast, and the drive along this stretch of coast is no disappointment.

Near the main road junction at Divarata a steep track of about two and a half miles leads down to **Mirtos**, undoubtedly one of the loveliest beaches in Greece: sparkling tiny white pebbles, creamy cliffs and the bluest of water. The nearest taverna is up on the main road.

A few miles further north, a better hairpin road leads steeply and very beautifully down to the village and hammer-headed rocky peninsula of **Assos**, one of those supremely picturesque places that one travels far to visit, only to find that it turns out to look much as it did on the poster and that there isn't a lot to do when you get there except reach for the camera, record it on film, have a drink and go away again. But there are rooms to rent, and ideally one should stay at Assos overnight for a memory that amounts to more than a few snaps in the album. By day there are lots of visiting tour groups.

Assos was the Venetians' main stronghold in northern Cephalonia, and to the natural defensive qualities of the headland they added fortifications which are still impressive although very far from intact. The fortress later served as a prison and was much altered.

On the island side of the narrow isthmus stands the tiny fishing village, with well-kept and colourful houses, flowers, cannon poking decoratively out over the harbour, taverna tables ideally set beneath a plane tree's broad canopy, and splendid cliffs on all sides. A small stony beach can be reached on foot; strong swimmers and those with boats can reach other, more secluded beaches along the cliffs. It is a stiff walk up the hill to the fortress, with a few benches among the pines beside the road ideal for savouring the lovely view down over the village. Hurried or less energetic visitors can drive up to – and indeed through – the fortress.

To the north of Assos the road turns inland and runs through a veritable forest of cypresses before rounding the northern cape (not following its coastline, which is best explored by boat) to the fishing village and pukka little resort of **Fiskardo**.

Arriving at Fiskardo in the late afternoon, it is hard to believe one has not intruded on the filming of an advertisement. The sunbeams slant down through the cypresses on the old harbourside houses and a swaying tangle of massed yacht masts. All hands are on deck for drinks and animated talk of wind strength and other nautical niceties, with the occasional hop ashore for a refill pulled by Tasso, the rough-hewn but friendly seadog who mans the pumps in the Captain's Cabin and sets the mood with some lazy saxophone music.

Fiskardo itself has no good beach, although following the road around past the harbour brings you to a place where swimming is possible. There are better coves in walking distance on the north coast. The village is very small and has little accommodation that the villa operators have not got tabs on. It is a case of asking around in hope.

Fiskardo is a good base for excursions by boat: a caique

Getting around

Excursions are widely organised by tour operators and tour agencies in Poros and Argostoli. The range includes a cruise around Zante; a cruise to Lefkas, Skorpios and Fiskardo; bus-trips to Fiskardo and Assos, and to the caves around Sami; excursions to Ithaca and even Olympia on the mainland. Some of these excursions are very expensive and, before signing up, it is well worth investigating what can be done by public transport, especially since many of the excursions from Argostoli involve long bus-rides to the other ports anyway. Ithaca and Lefkas are the obvious candidates for DIY excursions, given the good ferry services. The same might also apply to Olympia, although the temptation to take a hired car or motor-bike across on the ferry should no doubt be resisted unless the hirer agrees (unlikely). The alternative would be to organise a quorum for a taxi and haggle hard at Killini (it's about 55km from there to Olympia).

Buses radiate from Argostoli. There is a very frequent service to Lassi/Plati Yialos (by day only), several buses a day to Poros and Sami, two a day to Fiskardo. Small villages on the south coast (Skala, Katelios, et al) are also served, and there is a Sami/Agia Evfimia/Divarata bus to connect with the Fiskardo line. The Lefkas ferry service provides a useful local link between Fiskardo and Sami (twice a day each way, summer only). The Argostoli/Lixouri ferries sail about once an hour. Tour operators organise various daytime and evening boat-trips to beaches.

The number of car hire firms in Argostoli is bewildering. If you plan to explore the island it will almost certainly pay off to use one of the firms offering unlimited mileage. The more common arrangement of 100 free kilometres per day does not go far on Cephalonia. Cars and motor-bikes can also be hired at the main ports, Poros and Sami, and at other resorts used by tour operators – Skala, Lixouri, Lassi. The size and mountainous nature of the island do not ideally suit exploration by a typical Greek island Honda 50, although there are masses of them. Bigger bikes are also widely available (mainly in Argostoli) for those competent and qualified to ride them.

service runs across the narrow channel to Stavros on Ithaca, or wherever else people want to be taken, and the ferry schedules allow a full day or afternoon at Vassiliki on Lefkas, recommended for windsurfing and perfectly pleasant for simply sitting around, although there is no reason to leave Fiskardo for the latter.

ITHACA

*Be quite old when you anchor at the island. Rich with all you
have gained on the way. Not expecting Ithaca to give you
riches. Ithaca has given you your lovely journey.*

CONSTANTINE CAVAFY

Ithaca is the wanderer's home, that sense of belonging
somewhere which no amount of good living abroad can
supplant. It is a feeling that has less to do with the place than
with the people left behind, so there is no irony in the fact that
Odysseus's home is no idyllic garden of fertility, nor ever was.

Described by Homer as 'overrun with barren rocks and cliffs'
and less suitable for riding horses than for goats, Ithaca has bred
generations of sailors and travellers of whom Odysseus is the
archetypal ancestor. To this day there are many more Ithacians
abroad (mostly in Australia and North America) than at home,
and many of the old islanders have long and colourful tales of
their life's wanderings to spin, if you let them.

Apart from numerous sites, mostly of no particular intrinsic
interest, which are more or less speculatively identified with
places mentioned in the *Odyssey*, the island has little to offer
the tourist: 80 per cent of its buildings were destroyed by the
1953 earthquake, and the main village of Vathi is an
anonymous little place, although beautifully situated. The island
has almost no good beaches, stony or sandy. Ferry connections
with other islands are, or were until recently, irregular and
somewhat obscure. So not surprisingly Ithaca sees little tourism
apart from day-trip visitors from busier resorts on Cephalonia
and Lefkas, flotilla holiday-makers on an Ionian tour, and
mythomanes who (if they are not to be disappointed) come,
Homer in hand, in a spirit of literary pilgrimage rather than
sightseeing expectation.

A story told by Arthur Foss in *The Ionian Islands* provides an
apt commentary on all this. Foss quotes a boatman claiming to
be Ithaca's official guide, who sounds as if he was in the wrong
job: 'We all know that this is the home of Odysseus. There is
therefore no reason to go scrambling over bad roads in the
burning heat of the summer to look at a trickle of water or the
remains of an old well. Does a gloomy cave in the hillside look
any more interesting by calling it the cave of the nymphs? Does
a little trickle of water become a spring by calling it Arethusa's?
Of course not.' If you share this point of view, don't bother
with Ithaca.

The lack of tourist development has meant the survival of a
peaceful style of life which many more obviously attractive

islands have lost. If you are more interested in people and settling into the cheerful life of a small island than in facilities, beaches, windsurfing, comfortable accommodation or postcard scenes, Ithaca may suit you well. The islanders are very friendly. They have one bus, and if you ask how long and what route it takes for its journey from one end of the island to the other, the driver will shrug and explain that it depends on where his passengers want to go; it might take an hour or it might take two. Like Cephalonia, Ithaca also has one very pretty fishing village in the north, Kioni, much appreciated by sailing holiday-makers.

The island's position is certainly striking. Its west coast rises steep and straight as a stiff back turned on the northern peninsula of Cephalonia. A long windy channel, 14 miles long by little more than a mile wide in the north, separates the two islands. The east coast is little more hospitable but quite different in shape, chewed up in a series of deeply indented bays, notably in the middle where the Gulf of Molos almost divides the island into two. A single narrow mountain ridge, with ruins of an ancient settlement near the summit, links the northern and southern halves of the island.

Sailing into the embrace of this vast and splendid steep-sided central bay, whose deepest and most sheltered recess conceals the port and island capital of **Vathi** ('like travelling down the canals of the inner ear of a giant,' wrote Lawrence Durrell), it is not difficult to imagine something of the joy of the returning traveller. What a shame that Odysseus was asleep at the time.

It is a shame, too, that Vathi does not live up to its splendid setting at the end of the long land-locked inlet, with a tiny former prison island (Lazaretto) lying prettily offshore in the waters where 'well-built ships that once their harbour win, in its calm bosom without anchor rest, safe and unstirred' (Homer). When visiting Ithaca in 1823, Byron began each day with a morning swim out to the island and back. It is easy to think of more unpleasant hangover cures.

Like many other Greek island villages, Vathi was rebuilt after destruction by earthquake in a straightforward functional modern style. Small whitewashed and red-roofed houses and larger public buildings – post office, bank, port authority and so on – line up along the water-front and climb the green hills behind, and that is about all there is to it. Ferries dock at the edge of the village, fishing-boats and caiques in the middle, near the main cluster of cafes and shops. Rooms are advertised but not energetically touted. The village's biggest and best hotel (in a small field, admittedly) is the *Mentor* (B), on the far corner of the water-front from the ferry quay. The choice of restaurants is also very limited.

The road continues past the Mentor along the inlet's northern shore, passing some restaurants and indifferent small beaches, of which the best is at the end of the road. There are other bathing places on the western side of the village, easily seen and reached from the main road along the island, which follows the shore before climbing and spectacularly crossing the narrow ridge at the shoulder of Mount Aetos and continuing along the west coast, high above the sea. Motor-bike riders should be prepared for the full onslaught of the wind as they crest the ridge; this is not a road off which one would want to fall.

Apart from Vathi, the southern half of the island is almost empty. There are a few ruined Byzantine churches dotted around between the new houses at Perachori, on the slopes above Vathi. Walkers can follow paths over the hills to empty coves on the east coast, the southernmost of which has Homeric associations – the fountain of Arethusa, the ravens' crag and the shepherd Eumeus's cave. The cave of the nymphs, with its two entrances (gods to the south, mortals to the north), where Odysseus hid the Phaeacians' gifts, is on a hillside to the west of Vathi, signposted from the road out of the village near the cove known as **Dexia**, often identified as Odysseus's landing-place. Dexia has a small sandy beach with a taverna in summer. The small bay of Piso Aetos can be reached by road but scarcely deserves one.

It is a fine drive north along the flank of Homer's **Mount Neritos**, the island's main peak, looking across at Cephalonia and steeply down to a few small beaches, accessible by track at Agios Ioannis. At **Agros**, also known as the field of Laertes, the 19th-century archaeologist Heinrich Schliemann sat down and read lines 205 to 412 of the 24th book of the *Odyssey* to a congregation of goatherds, translating into contemporary local dialect as he went. At the end of this impressive performance the eyes of all were awash. Men, women and children embraced Schliemann and carried him in triumph back to town.

The corniche road ends at **Stavros**, the unremarkable main village of the much more fertile northern tip of the island, where the hill of Pilicata is now generally accepted as the most likely site of Odysseus's city. The place where the young Homer went to school, signposted from the road near Babi's garage (a corrugated shed), is less convincing. The old mountain village of **Exoghi**, once a safe haven from piracy, has now lost most of its population to a number of scattered communities on the slopes above north-facing Afales bay, where a stony beach can be reached by bumpy track from Platrithias.

From Stavros a road winds steeply down to a small harbour and two pebble beaches at **Polis**, where excavations unearthed 13

Getting around

Motor-bikes can be hired at Vathi and Frikes, outboards at Vathi. There are at least two buses a day (or one bus twice) and a caique service between Vathi and Kioni. The sea route is slightly quicker.

three-legged cauldrons described by Homer. There is a *cantina* caravan and an occasional caique service to and from Fiscardo on Cephalonia. To the east the main road runs down an attractively fertile valley to the fishing village and occasional ferry port of **Frikes**, which has a shady quayside taverna or two and a disco widely advertised on rusting roadside wrecks. The road continues along the shoreline of a few stony coves before crossing a ridge and dropping down to the bay of **Kioni**. There are some old houses at the top of the village near the ridge and ruined windmills on the headland, but most of Kioni is modern. It is a peaceful and secluded village and budding villa/flotilla holiday resort, with comfortable holiday homes spread around the steep hillsides among vines, fruit trees and cypresses. The only focus is the sleepy little port, where a few pedalos and canoes are drawn up on the stones beside the village's excellent main taverna. The only beach worthy of the name is near the graveyard about half a mile to the east of the harbour. Frikes and Kioni have rooms for rent.

It is about two hours' walk from Kioni or a much less arduous drive from Stavros up into the hills to the remote village of **Anoghi**, on a high plateau (500m) destined, so they say, to receive the island's airport, which should give the flagging local economy something of a boost. Anoghi's interesting church and free-standing belfry survived the earthquake. A rough track continues over the mountain through an impressively wild boulder-strewn landscape and passes the magnificently situated **Kathara monastery**, which is no longer inhabited, before rejoining the main road near Agios Ioannis. Eagle sightings are often reported from the vicinity of the monastery, which itself has bird's-eye views over the great bay and southern half of the island.

LEFKAS

'Lefkas' means 'white', after the cliffs of its southward-pointing peninsula, 'Leucadia's far-projecting rock of woe' (Byron). 'Maura', from the island's traditional post-classical name of Santa Maura, means 'black', after a somewhat obscure early Christian martyr. Disappointingly, the subject of such contrasting names does not seem to be a black and white kind of island; in fact, it scarcely seems to be an island at all. The road from the mainland airport at Preveza, which occupies the site of the momentous battle of Actium, to Lefkas town is now unbroken. But an island Lefkas has been for most of history, with a narrow shipping channel having been cut through shifting sandbanks in the 7th century BC, reopened in Roman times and kept open since. Lefkas's close links with the mainland brought it a history different from that of the other Ionian Islands – Turkish control during the 16th and 17th centuries when the others were Venetian – and have retarded its modern tourist development. Not served by any regular ferries and requiring awkward mainland bus journeys of anyone wanting to combine it with visits to other Ionian Islands, Lefkas escaped notice. This has now changed or, rather, is in the process of changing fast. The old chain ferry across the canal has been replaced by a swing bridge, Preveza airport has been opened up to direct charter flights, ferries regularly link the island with Cephalonia, and numerous holiday brochures now proclaim that Lefkas is the undiscovered best-kept secret in the Ionian group, which proves that whatever else it may be it is no longer that. Although the volume of business falls far short of tourism on Corfu, Cephalonia and Zante, Vassiliki and Nidri (the island's two main resorts) are now far from being tranquil undiscovered hideaways.

It is a beautiful and interesting island, with quiet country villages where old women wear traditional costume and sit spinning in their doorways even when there are no coachloads of tourists to watch them. The long, wild mountainous west coast is fringed with wonderful empty beaches. The waters enclosed by its east coast and mainland Acarnania are specially good for sailing, well provided with pretty little islands and secluded inlets. And in Vassiliki and Agios Nikitas, Lefkas has two highly picturesque village resorts.

The island has reached a delicate and in many ways attractive adolescent stage, developed yet uncorrupted. Facilities and roads have been greatly improved, but the advent of tourism has not yet made too profound an impact on the island's life and traditional ways. For the purist, the time to visit Lefkas has no doubt passed. For those who like variety, to observe old-fashioned country life and even escape other people altogether, from a base in a cheerful resort, there are few better islands, and Lefkas should probably go to the top of the list of priorities. Unless Lefkas has the best-kept secret of all, that of eternal youth, this may not last long: once the tourist bandwagon starts rolling, it does not usually take long to transform an island. Having said that, the Lefkadians are very proud of their traditions and folklore, and the scale and style of development may be controlled more carefully than has been done elsewhere, although this is a lot to ask. So far there has been no building of big hotels, even in the busy resorts, which still have a villagey atmosphere. The most popular of them, Vassiliki, has become something of a specialist windsurfing resort, and may be worth avoiding except for that purpose.

There is a certain predictability about the looks and lifestyle of most Greek island villages and ports, but **Lefkas town** is like nowhere else. Professor Ansted remarked in 1863 that it was 'an act of perverse stupidity especially in a maritime people to have selected as the site of the chief town a bare unmeaning unhealthy spot a mile away from any place to which it is possible for a ship to approach'. On the inert waters of its salty lagoon, fishermen in flat-bottomed boats pole about in the perfect stillness at dawn and dusk. Distant conversations and unwelcome smells waft in over the water. The air is heavy and vaguely unhealthy, not like a port, and indeed Lefkas seems more a land than a sea town. Its main water-front is a working area of boatbuilding and yacht chartering but lacks the usual comings and goings and the evening *volta*. Lefkas seems to look inwards on itself. The central square is one focus, but the liveliest area, where most people do their shopping, is the busy division of roads near the bus station at the southern, inland entrance to town.

A single busy street runs the length of town, passing the main square. It is not strikingly picturesque and the ground is flat, so there are no pretty views, but wandering around reveals a fascinating mixture of low grey Venetian churches with beautifully decorated doorways, open metalwork clock-towers designed to withstand earthquakes, and houses built to the same end with timber-framed upper storeys clad with sheets of tin and corrugated iron. The main street provides a succession of mostly pleasant smells – coffee, bread, cheese – and you will probably see some women from the outlying country villages in the island's traditional brown garb.

Most of the hotels are at the northern end of town near the

excursion-boat quay and the causeway that separates lagoon and the narrow waterway at the head of the bay of Drepano where island and mainland coasts converge. The *Byzantio* (D) is a cheap alternative to the comfortable modern *Lefkas* (B) and *Nirikos* (B), and can offer some of its residents a dress circle view from their balcony of the show at one of the town's open-air cinemas at no extra charge. One of the most picturesquely ramshackle old houses is the former hotel Averof (on the main street between the causeway and the square), now closed and probably condemned. The *Santa Mavra* (C) is a bright and cheerful small hotel not far up the main street, mainly used by Scandinavian tour operators.

In August Lefkas hosts a well-attended two-week international folklore festival, a good excuse for dancing in the streets and general uproar. The town also has a local folklore museum, which is open for a couple of hours in the morning and evening.

Lefkas town has no beach: it is about two miles to the long sand bar enclosing the lagoon to the north. The seaward side of the bar has miles of wide sand and pebble beach, with tavernas at the southern end (Agios Ioannis). At the northern end of the lagoon, on the mainland side of the bridge, stand the ruins of the 14th-century fortress of Santa Maura.

The road network now makes a good circuit of the island, although some maps show no road between Agios Nikitas and Kalamitsi. This was practicable without difficulty when we last visited the island, and surfacing work then in progress is probably now complete. The island's main road follows the east coast, passing salt pans, the archaeological site of ancient Lefkas (not very interesting for the non-specialist), several campsites and a variety of small-scale coastal holiday development, including a few new hotels, on its way to Nidri, Lefkas's main resort. It is an attractive drive through green and pleasant country, with good views across the water at the gradually receding mainland hills, followed by a scattering of wooded islands off Nidri.

Nidri has grown up along the main road, which is also the main street, by no means an ideal arrangement. However, the row of shops and tavernas separates the road and the water-front, which turns out to be spacious and relaxing, with overhanging trees and lots of boats – yachts, excursion-boats and ferries serving the small satellite islands and Ithaca. The sailing in and out of the islands is idyllic, and the breeze is rarely too much for debutant windsurfers who have the interest of islands to aim for and the reassurance of not heading out to open water. But the beach is disappointing: no more than a long, very thin strip of pebbles.

The nearest of the little islands is **Madouri**, which has an elegant neo-classical villa facing the shore. A little further from Nidri is the Onassis family's **Skorpios**, where the wedding of Aristotle Onassis and Jacqueline Kennedy took place in 1968. The hilly island bristles with floodlights like a prison camp. Excursion-boats sail past but do not land. **Meganisi** lies to the south, a much larger island with three small hamlets, of which the largest is Vathi, with a beach and rooms to rent. By day Meganisi attracts a number of visitors on excursions from Lefkas and Cephalonia, but very few people stay overnight. One of the sea caves is said to be the second largest in Greece.

The nearest landfall facing the Nidri water-front is not another island but the tip of the **Vlicho** peninsula, which almost makes a lake of a broad yacht-filled inlet. The archaeologist Dorpfeld spent most of his life trying to prove that the peninsula was Homeric Ithaca in the face of plenty of perfectly good evidence in support of the simpler explanation that Ithaca was Ithaca. Dorpfeld is buried beside the pretty waterside church facing Nidri. On the other side of the peninsula, Desimi Bay is a peaceful campsite among olive trees with a thin stony beach, looking out over a narrow channel towards Meganisi. There is another campsite and some holiday bungalows behind the bigger stony beach on Rouda Bay, below the hill village of Poros. The beach has a taverna of sorts, and watersports.

Sivota is a very picturesque, narrow wooded creek with no exit visible from its head. Its tavernas do a very lively evening trade and have rooms to rent, but the place is quiet by day, there being no beach. The main road runs westwards over the hills into the magnificent vast theatre formed by the island's highest peak, **Mount Stavrotas** (1145m), its slopes horribly defaced by quarrying, and the mountainous Lefkatas promontory. These enclose the bay of Vassiliki, which is the main feature of the southern half of the island.

Tucked into the eastern armpit of the bay, **Vassiliki** is a very picturesque little port, with a closely packed and well-patronised row of taverna tables beneath whitewashed eucalyptus and plane trees along the bus-wide quay, looking out over the fishing-fleet and across the bay to the dark hills of the Lefkatas promontory. The quay catches the afternoon sun and is a splendid vantage-point for enjoying the spectacle of expert windsurfers racing up and down the bay at furious speed, with frequent spectacular catapulting partings of company between surfer and board. Surfers fill the bay six days a week (the locals have decreed a windsurfing sabbath).

Vassiliki is said by those in the know to be the best windsurfing beach in the Mediterranean; one specialist magazine recently rated it third in the world. The main reason, believe it or not, is the wind, generated with remarkable consistency by the particular topography of the surrounding mountains. Very gentle in the morning, when apprentices take lessons and practise the basic manoeuvres, it gains strength gradually as the afternoon wears on, reaching a peak at about teatime when the aces and instructors take to the water with their harnesses and tiny sinker boards. The wind blows across the bay, favouring long tacks straight out to sea and back, and the western promontory means you can keep going for about four miles without leaving the bay. Finally, the profile of the beach is ideal, shelving steeply to about thigh depth before levelling out with sand underfoot. This makes a large area where beginners can easily remount after crashing. For sunbathers the beach is adequate, although stony and without shade, but swimming pleasure is certainly compromised by all the boards on the move.

The sport is highly organised, with schools run by tour operators whose clients come for no other reason than to windsurf and who get very disgruntled if the wind proves disappointing, as it can. There is little provision for casual visitors who turn up wanting to rent a board for an hour, but there is no harm in asking around, especially before mid-afternoon. There is at least one dinghy and catamaran sailing-school based on the beach, also mainly offering pre-booked weekly courses via tour operators.

Some accommodation has grown up at the western end of the mile-long beach, a zone sometimes called Ponti, and there is a campsite about half-way along. Considering the longish walk into Vassiliki, Ponti is disappointingly short of bars and shops. Vassiliki itself is still small and seems attractively villagey despite the recent boom (a pun) in its popularity. But non-sailors may well find that watersports people spoil not only the beach but also the evening atmosphere in the village. This is the summer counterpart of a trendy ski resort, with exactly the same mixture of seasonal workers (many of whom spend their winters on the slopes) and madly keen sporty holiday-makers. The ambience is great, provided you share everyone else's microscopically narrow obsession with the sport and their personal battle for mastery. Vassiliki's hotel, the *Lefkatas* (c), is block-booked for most of the season as, no doubt, is much of the room and villa accommodation.

The other platform of Vassiliki's recent expansion is the building of a ferry quay and the creation of regular services to Cephalonia and Ithaca. Not only have these ferries put Lefkas on the island-hopping map, but they also open up the possibility of interesting and cheap day-trip excursions from Vassiliki. Fiskardo on Cephalonia is particularly attractive.

Local boatmen also offer the chance to escape the daily regatta by ferrying tourists to a peaceful beach to the south of the resort (Agiofili) and around Cape Lefkatas to remote and very beautiful west-coast beaches, notably Porto Katsiki, now also accessible by land.

Part of the beauty of Vassiliki's setting (and the excellence of the wind, no doubt) stems from the opposing range of mountains which rise very steeply about 2000 feet above the western end of the beach and extend for nearly six miles southwards to **Cape Lefkatas**, formerly Ducato. On the western side of the cape stood the famous clifftop temple of Apollo from which Sappho hurled herself in lovesick despair over the haughty Phaon, thereby setting an example for unrequited lovers. It seems that criminals were also thrown from the rock (about 200 feet above the water) in a mixture of annual ceremonial sacrifice and trial by ordeal, with feathers and flapping live birds attached to them for buoyancy and fishermen waiting below to pick up the pieces. Priests of Apollo are also reported to have taken the plunge. The precise therapeutic significance of the act is unclear, but there was clearly more to it than suicide. There is a lighthouse on the cape, but very little remains to be seen of the temple. Nor are you likely to see the vultures and eagles reported, or imagined, by Edward Lear.

The easiest way to admire the white cliff scenery is on a boat-trip from Vassiliki, but there is also a rough road along the western flank of the promontory, a long, bumpy and very dusty 20km from the main road turnoff near Hortata, itself a 12km climb (with wonderful views down over the bay) from Vassiliki. So brilliantly white is the dusty earth that beyond Athani, where tarmac ends, the roadside trees could be snow covered. Apart from the interest of inspecting the giddy cape, the road also leads to some spectacularly beautiful beaches, including **Porto Katsiki**. Maps show a little wiggle down from the main track, but in fact reaching the beach involves a detour of several slow miles, certainly worth undertaking. The track ends on a clifftop looking down over a narrow strip of brilliant sand, with some shade from overhanging rock, and water so clear that boats at anchor cast sharply outlined shadows on the sea bed. There are refreshment vans by the car-park, and a steep staircase down to the beach. Other beaches along this stretch of coast are unsignposted and involve more of a scramble.

Continuing northwards from Hortata, a new road leads to the lovely old village of **Kalamitsi** high above the coast, a place of typical, if no longer common, scenes of rural Greek life, with

Getting around

Excursion-boats leave daily from Lefkas town (in front of the Hotel Lefkas) for Ithaca, Cephalonia and the islands off Nidri. It's worth noting that the Greek for p.m. is μ.μ. and for a.m. π.μ., and that the terms are often incorrectly translated as a.m. and p.m., which helps solve the puzzle of an excursion-boat advertising daily trips leaving at 9p.m. and returning at 7a.m. Similar boat-trips are organised from Nidri and Vassiliki, where boatmen also offer excursions to nearby beaches and evening (genuinely, this time) visits to Sivota (taverna evening) and Cape Lefkatas (sunset).

There are buses from Lefkas to all parts of the island (except Cape Lefkatas). Car and motor-bike hire is available at Lefkas, Nidri and Vassiliki. Yachts can be chartered at Lefkas.

old men sitting out under the trees and women spinning and weaving at their looms. This by no means exhausts the delights of Kalamitsi: a rough but perfectly manageable road lurches down the steep hillside of olive terraces below the village to various points along a huge expanse of sandy beach interspersed with a few clumps of rocks where rough campers (the few without Westfalia dormobiles, that is) snuggle down out of sight. There are no facilities on the beach: the nearest cafe is in the village.

Now linked by road to the popular resort village of Agios Nikitas, Kalamitsi is no longer very isolated. The road passes Kathisma beach, not much less beautiful than that at Kalamitsi but much more accessible and much busier, with a big car-park, a cantina, showers and (if the advertising board is to be believed) rooms to rent, although there are no obvious candidate buildings. This is also a popular place for camping rough, or semi-rough (given the showers).

Agios Nikitas is a very pretty village tucked away in the lee of a headland on the north-western shoulder of the island, also isolated until fairly recently but now easily reached by road from Lefkas town and a very popular target for weekenders from Preveza and other mainland towns. A single street of houses thickly overhung and surrounded by vines and fruit trees leads down from the entrance to the village, where cars must be left, to a good coarse sand beach. There are tavernas, rooms to rent and usually lots of people milling about absorbing the village's best-kept charm. A long and exposed beach (Peloukia) extends north of the village, immediately below the road, which climbs a hill before descending beautifully to the plain of dense olive groves behind Lefkas town.

The alternative route between Hortata and Lefkas runs higher along the western flank of the central mountains and offers the chance to visit the biggest of the inland villages and the main centre of the island's needlework cottage industry, **Karia**, which has a beautiful shaded central square. Locally made embroidery is extremely expensive.

PAXOS

Pretty little Paxos, peaceful satellite of teeming Corfu and proud home of a quarter of a million mighty olive trees and the best oil in Greece, is not the smallest of the Ionian Islands. No island ever is: nitpickers can always cite some speck of uninhabited rock of interest only to the passing gull. In this case they need look no further than even littler Antipaxos, satellite of the satellite, and visited by plenty of tourists as well as gulls. But Paxos, whose name might well but probably does not signify peace, is much the smallest of the main Ionians and one of the smallest of all the Greek islands that feature on the tourist map. It is an island in miniature, with miniature beaches, miniature villages and miniature mountains. That is its great charm. It makes you feel big. After a day on Paxos you will have made some local friends and imagine you belong. Initially apprehensive about what you will find to do on so small an island, you will find the days accelerating all too easily by, filled with endless little toings and froings and trivial decision-making agonies. Which little pebble cove today? Which taverna for supper? What to buy for the picnic lunch? The horizon of your preoccupations will shrink to fit.

Tourism on Paxos means Italians, large numbers of day-trip visitors from mainland Parga and various resorts on Corfu, and a few small British villa operators who also specialise in sailing holidays and combine the two by offering their guests the chance to rent dinghies or little outboards for their holiday in the same way that tourists on other islands hire cars and motor-bikes. This is an excellent formula, which many sailing holiday-makers will prefer to the flotilla arrangement. It works especially well on an island no more than six miles long. With a small boat and a willing pair of legs, the visitor has all the necessary equipment for a thorough exploration of the island – and of Antipaxos, for that matter.

Paxos's hotels can be counted on the joints of one finger. It is essentially a villa and 'studio' holiday island, with accommodation scattered along its gentler eastern coast but concentrated in and around the three coastal communities: Gaios, the main port and island capital in the south-east, which is small; Lakka, on a beautiful narrow inlet in the north, which is smaller; and Loggos, which is tiny.

Gaios is the best bet for those arriving at Paxos without pre-booked accommodation, and even here finding a bed may not be easy, with tour operators filling most of the rooms. At least the search is not arduous: Gaios spreads itself not very far along the water-front of a bay which, being almost totally plugged by an island separated from the village by a narrow channel, seems more like a riverside trading station than a sea port. There are in fact two offshore islands, of which the larger has ruined Venetian fortifications, the smaller a church with a very well-attended festival on 15 August. The channel is deep enough for yachts, fishing-boats, most excursion-boats and the incongruously energetic and noisy fleet of Paxos Express speed-boats, which all tie up along the front, where a cafe-fringed square open to the water provides a very pretty focus. The Corfu boat and larger ferries usually use the new quay at the northern entrance to the channel, about half a mile away and out of sight.

With its solid old water-front houses, Gaios has great charm, especially at the beginning and end of the day when not filled with excursion visitors, for whom this is the main stop on the island. The hours to fill and the lack of a beach mean good business for the bars, restaurants and souvenir shops, some of which are surprisingly sophisticated (pottery, jewellery and clothes). There are also local shops and warehouses where local wine and oil are stored in vats and sold in bulk.

The island's only sizeable package hotel, the *Paxos Beach* (B), is out on its own about a mile south of Gaios. It is not a bad little bungalow colony, unobtrusively landscaped, with olives shading the huts and a small beach. The coast road leads on past villas and a few rocky coves to the southern tip of the island, where the island (or peninsula, since it can be reached by a little causeway of stepping-stones) of **Mogonisi** forms a narrow bay. Mogonisi has a small patch of sand, watersports and a restaurant that makes a very popular evening outing: 'music and traditional dancing with Theo and Spiro and lobster, swordfish and souvlaki, nothing frozen' is the alluring promise. The Express boats operate a free evening taxi service from Gaios.

The northern port of **Lakka** is not itself a memorably picturesque village, but the setting is gorgeous: a tight-lipped creek flanked by silver and green hills of olives and cypresses, with keyhole views across a windy strait to the white cliffs of

Corfu. Unfortunately, the village and the inlet are too small to accommodate comfortably the large numbers of visitors ferried in every day: boats queue up at the entrance to the inlet in the peak of the mid-morning rush-hour, foul the clear waters and thoroughly disrupt the morning's activities at the Greek Islands Club's HQ, Rose Cottage, where aspiring windsurfers face a hard task dodging all the traffic as they diligently work on their skills in the sheltered waters of the bay. But the visitors do not stay long, and Lakka soon reverts to its customary state of slumber. There is a medium-sized hotel, the *Iolis* (C), by the harbour and attractive strips of stony beach, with plenty of shade, windsurfing and usually a few campers, on the western side of the inlet. Lakka also has a tennis court.

About half-way between Lakka and Gaios, **Loggos** consists of no more than a cheerful flower-draped cluster of houses, with bars and a taverna of course, overlooking a small fishing harbour. Tables occupy the narrow waterside pavement and have to be uprooted in the great upheaval that accompanies the arrival of the island's bus. With a small stony beach, a tall-chimneyed olive oil refinery and a 'Nick the Greek' watersports rentier lounging in his speed-boat, Loggos is a Greek island microcosm. It suffers less than the other two villages from the influx of day-trippers from Corfu and Parga, but its main fish taverna is used by organised groups on nights out from Gaios. Considering the size of Loggos, it is surprising to learn that the island administration identifies another 40-odd smaller villages tucked away in the olive groves. One suspects that on Paxos there may be some confusion between villas and villages. Certainly there is not much to Magazia, the biggest of these inland communities.

Nearly all the island's hilly interior is covered by olive trees. They are magnificent specimens, often surrounded by plastic matting to collect the fruit as it falls, and make pleasantly shady but somewhat monotonous walking territory. Some of the numerous rough paths westwards from the Gaios to Lakka road lead to spectacular viewpoints over the cliffs of the island's west coast. One of the best of these belvederes is near the old church of Agii Apostoli, reached from near Magazia.

The east coast of the island between Gaios and Lakka has a succession of small pebble beaches with no facilities other than the natural shade of waterside olive and fig trees. In most cases (except to the south of Loggos) they are less easily reached on foot than by boat. For those without one of their own, there are daily excursions from Gaios in the speedy Paxos Express launches, combining a complete tour of the island with a visit and a long beach stop at Antipaxos. This is a splendid excursion,

Getting around

The main organised excursion from Paxos – apart from that to Antipaxos – is to the old mainland town and busy resort of Parga (see page 217). Excursions to Corfu (which is well worth at least an overnight stay) do not need to be organised, since visiting Paxos almost inevitably involves travelling via Corfu. Day-trips to Lefkas may be possible at the height of the season.

Motor-bikes can be hired at Gaios, as can outboards. The island's bus operates a frequent day and evening service between Gaios (terminal on the edge of the village) and Lakka, usually via Loggos. Tour operators will arrange car hire if notified well in advance, but a car is hardly necessary.

with a stop at Lakka and close inspection (which larger boats cannot make) of numerous grottoes and natural rock arches along the west coast, which is cliff scenery all the way.

Only a mile or so south of Paxos, **Antipaxos** is an even smaller and almost uninhabited island with vineyards instead of olive groves but otherwise not dissimilar: cliffs on the west and beaches on the east coast, mostly pebbles but with clear water and sand underfoot. The excursion boats stop at Vrikes, which has a couple of tavernas. Emptier and better beaches to the south can be reached on foot without difficulty.

ZANTE (ZAKYNTHOS)

Fruitful Zante, to give Zakynthos its beautiful old Venetian name, offers itself to the tourist like an artfully balanced and beautifully prepared meal. Not too big and not too small, it has equal portions of fertile plain and rough hill country, of wild cliffs and sweeping sands, and its selection of resorts includes a busy and attractive town, a no-holds-barred modern beach resort and less obtrusive areas of scattered small-scale holiday development ideal for those who like their Greece quiet and countrified. In all departments, except possibly that of mountain scenery, the quality is very high. The beaches, in particular, are among the best in Greece, especially for children. To accompany a meal, Zante proposes the robust Verdea, perhaps the best of Greek table wines.

The great attractions of the island, which was known to our

ancestors as the Flower of the Levant, have not escaped the attention of the British holiday industry. 'There is no other nation but this, thus addicted to that miserable isle,' wrote William Lithgow in 1632, referring to the British passion for Zante's huge output of currants. The remark could still apply today: about 90 per cent of the island's tourists are British. The currants are still produced in great volume, but our modern addiction is to Zante's beaches and green landscape.

The island serves its visitors well. One unusual and attractive feature is the number of tourists pottering around the island's country lanes on bicycles, not scooters. Zante's main drawback is its popularity and the dominance of organised tourism. There is now little room for the independent traveller, who may be given short shrift in the town's hotels (in summer, anyway) and feel that the rough friendly charm of shambolic Greek life has suffered on an island that seems increasingly like a production line. Like Cephalonia, Zante lacks cheerful village resorts.

Also in danger of being squeezed out is a summer visitor more loyal even than the British, the loggerhead turtle *Caretta caretta*, which has the misfortune to share our taste in beaches. Laganas's role as one of the few remaining nesting beaches in the Mediterranean adds a dimension of real importance to debates about the desirability of tourist development. In other places we may feel an essentially selfish sadness at the way the Greeks cheerfully bulldoze their most beautiful landscapes. Distaste may legitimately give way to disgust and outrage at Laganas, where miles of empty sandy beach have been transformed into the island's major resort zone, with monster hotel blocks lining the beach. At last, steps have been taken to protect the small corners of the bay where the turtles still come ashore at night to bury their eggs in the sand, and to limit the use of speed-boats in the bay. British tour operators are said to have behaved responsibly in alerting their clients to the importance of respecting the beaches and staying away from them at night, and in encouraging them not to buy turtle shells. It is probably too little, too late. *Caretta caretta* is a shy reptile, and the prospects for its survival in happy coexistence with the holiday-making hordes at Laganas cannot be good. The Sea Turtle Protection Society, whose campaign to persuade the locals to put the environment before profit is as laudable as it is ambitious, takes a more optimistic view with its motto: 'We can all live together.'

The August 1953 earthquake was every bit as devastating on Zante as it was on Cephalonia. The town of **Zakynthos** had to be completely rebuilt. 'The real Zante has been replaced by a cheap and shoddy provincial town,' wrote Lawrence Durrell who, like few of its visitors today, knew the old Venetian town, a place of graceful arcaded houses, elegant campaniles and richly decorated baroque churches. The harsh verdict is no doubt more a reflection on the beauty of the old town than on the style of the new one, for the task of reconstruction has been lovingly and faithfully carried out. First-time visitors will find modern Zakynthos a stately, lively and agreeable reproduction town, infinitely more attractive than Cephalonia's capital, Argostoli.

Zakynthos is the only sizeable community and port on the island, and home of about half of its 30,000 inhabitants. Its setting is splendid: a wide bay facing the Peloponnese with a fertile central plain running away to the south, flanked on one side by a wooded and fortified hillside rising steeply behind the town, and on the other by the isolated cone of Skopos (492m). The main harbour-front has most of the tourist restaurants (Psaropoula is good but expensive) and shops, which are more interesting than usual thanks to the wide range of local produce on sale: nougat, honey, wine, even a fiery local scent. There is also a good craft shop with locally woven rugs. Tourists riding in horse-drawn and unusual pedal-powered traps give an element of sedate charm, but unfortunately the front is a busy road and Zakynthian youth finds the attraction of roaring up and down it all night on their unsilenced motor-bikes irresistible.

On the northern side of the ferry quay is a fine series of spacious garden squares with hotels, cafes, restaurants and the main public buildings overlooking a statute of the home poet Dionysius Solomos (1798–1857) in declamatory mode. The first significant versifier in demotic Greek and the author of the national anthem, Solomos is much honoured on his native island, for which he appears to have cherished unqualified dislike. He died where he had lived much of his adult life, at Corfu. The Solomos museum occupies one of the arcaded buildings on St Mark's Square and has memorabilia of the poet and other local notables, as well as some evocative photographs of pre-earthquake Zante. The neighbouring building is almost as noteworthy: a bank where they have discovered that in order to cash a traveller's cheque it is not necessary to scrutinise the passport and fill in a huge form before sending you to the back of a half-hour line of Greek shopkeepers banking their fistfuls of takings. Here, they have a special desk for tourists, tap out a receipt on a calculator and give you the cash, all in one go. The town's cathedral (to the north of the square) is much less interesting than its smaller neighbour, Our Lady of the Angels (Kiria ton Angelon), which has well-restored external decoration and good icons inside. Gaining entry is not easy.

The post-Byzantine museum, on Solomos Square, has a good collection of icons recovered from the island's ruined churches. Striking among all the spanking new buildings surrounding Solomos Square is the 16th-century church of St Nicholas, rebuilt using the beautiful unadorned old blocks of sandstone.

The town's main axis, a long arcaded street running parallel to the water-front, has most of the everyday shops and a very good wine/local produce merchant near the Olympic Airways office. Even away from the water-front it is hard to find simple cheap tavernas, most of the locals preferring the *souvlakia* and fish bars. Zochios, on Plateia Metropolitou Alexiou, is good and inexpensive.

Recommended hotels in town are the *Diana* (C), one of the big hotels on the main square, the simple *Kentriko* (D) and the neat and comfortable little *Yria* (B), quietly tucked away in a sidestreet between Solomos Square and the small town beach to the north, which has lawns and changing-huts and charges for admittance. Hotels on the water-front near the ferry quay, such as the rather tatty *Aegli* (C), one of the few central hotels not given over to package business, are likely to be noisy.

The big building at the southern end of the harbour-front is the church of the island's patron saint, Dionysos, one of very few buildings to survive the earthquake, because it was built of concrete in the pre-war period. Externally it is far from beautiful, but the interior is worth a look: the saint's silver reliquary has good relief carving, and the nave of the church is covered by paintings of Old and New Testament scenes. A few blocks inland is the much more beautiful restored 17th-century Phaneromini church.

On the hill immediately above Zakynthos at **Vohali**, the walls and gateways of the Venetian fortress are still discernible although overgrown. They are less of a draw than the views from a picturesque eucalyptus-shaded belvedere surveying the town and bay, with the lights of Killini twinkling in the distance. There are a couple of large tavernas used for organised nights out with dancing and plate smashing.

The triangular eastern half of the island is all very fertile, ascending gradually from the flat central plain to the foot of the western mountain massif, where a row of quiet country villages looks out over what Edward Lear described as 'one unbroken continuance of future currant dumplings and plum puddings'.

The continuance is now broken by the airport, but any of the roads running westwards from town (to Romiri or Macherado, for example) will take you through beautiful and well-tended olive groves, orchards and vineyards where piles of grapes lie drying out, going brown and shrivelling up in the sun, just like all the tourists on **Laganas** beach. The beach occupies the eastern half of the huge Laganas bay (over four miles wide), which forms the entire south-eastern side of the island, framed by two promontories whose mountains are both called Skopos ('look-out'). The resort, which is entirely modern, has grown up at the western end of the beach, thus in the middle of the bay, with shops, pubs and some of the smaller hotels lining the approach road which simply runs out on the beach. Nearby, a picturesquely sited offshore rock, the self-explanatory Disco Island, can be reached by footbridge. Big modern-block hotels have been erected along the back of the beach to the east of the main resort focus. The most modern and comfortable of these are the *Laganas* (B) and *Astir* (B), both with good if somewhat superfluous swimming-pools. The sand on the beach is now hard packed and would probably defeat any nesting turtles that did venture ashore. Apparently, they have not done so for some years, which means that the main Laganas beach is not affected by conservation regulations. The sea bed shelves gently underfoot, and most of the watersports activity takes place well away from the beach, which reduces the nuisance that waterskiers and windsurfers cause to swimmers and vice versa.

Tour operators distinguish between Laganas and what they call Crystal Bay (sometimes marketed as Kalamaki), which is merely the much more peaceful eastern end of the same beach, separated only by some rocks. There are a couple of hotels – *Kalamaki Beach* (B) and *Crystal* (C) – near the beach, which is still used by the turtles despite an increasing amount of new holiday accommodation not far from it. This is presumably one of the zones where speed-boats are forbidden, but there is no objection to exploring the bay on a pedalo in search of turtles, which like to spend their days basking on or near the surface. The females come ashore to bury their eggs (over 100 per brood) at night, between June and August. The eggs remain in the sand for eight weeks before the young turtles hatch. They lie low for a few days before digging themselves out (also by night or in the very early morning) and, provided they are not confused by non-celestial lights, set out on the perilous journey down to the water. So the turtle beaches are effectively out of bounds between sunset and dawn throughout the summer. Not only this: sandcastles and wells and the planting of umbrellas – in fact, any interference with the surface of the sand – are also out. Needless to say, the umbrella and no-bikes-on-the-beach rules are not always strictly observed. Turtles also nest on the small island of Marathonisi, much visited by sunbathers who arrive by pedalo, windsurfer and excursion-boat.

The western half of Laganas bay has less good beaches

(Lithaki beach has tavernas and some accommodation) and a big campsite a long walk from the sea in an olive grove. Pitch springs at (or near) **Keri** beach were known to antiquity and have encouraged locals to drill for oil on a number of occasions. The results have always been disappointing, says the local guidebook, and Keri beach may also disappoint a wider visiting public: the springs are elusive, the beach is thin and stony and the boatmen's offers of outings to see not only turtles (off Marathonisi) but also dolphins and seals sound over-optimistic. There is not much to Keri, a dusty village high up among the pines on the mountainous southern tip of the island, but plenty of hikers and bikers make the journey, simply because it is there, at the end of the road. The church is old and there are good sea and cliff views from the lighthouse at Cape Keri, reached by footpath from the village.

On the other side of Laganas bay, the island's south-eastern promontory extends about ten miles south of Zakynthos and is mostly occupied by **Mount Skopos** (492m), site of an ancient temple of Artemis. This is one of the most beautiful parts of the island, provided you avert your eyes from **Argassi**, a busy so-called resort which is certainly the least attractive on Zante: a cramped straggle, if such a thing is possible, of roadside coastal hotels and rooming/villa accommodation without a village or any good beach. Even the tour operator Sunmed feels it necessary to warn that the beaches 'tend to be on the small side', which should be more than enough to set alarm bells ringing. Admittedly, the resort is quite conveniently located. South of Argassi, the road winds through lovely wooded and rough farming country down to the southern tip of the island, **Cape Gerakas**, with a number of quiet sandy beaches along the eastern side of the promontory and a scattering of holiday accommodation dotted around the fields in an attractively disorganised way, ideal for those in search of peace and rural surroundings. The good beaches are Porto Zorro, Banana Beach, Agios Nikolaos, Mavrantzis (an attractive Caribbean-style campsite, shaded and possibly shady), all with beach tavernas and some watersports. The beach at Porto Roma, which also has tavernas and accommodation, is poor by local standards. The only village on the long promontory is Vassilikos, not much more than a few buildings and a bus-stop. The most beautiful beach of all is at the end, on the western side of the cape, sheltered by low cliffs and variously referred to as Vassiliko or Gerakas, and mercifully spared any buildings. For this we have to thank the turtles, who continue to use the beach for nesting. There is a bamboo refreshment hut, pedalos and windsurfing, and a taverna near the car-park.

A tour of the mountainous western part of the island starts at **Macherado**, which has a popular pilgrimage church with a fine tall belfry on the orange-planted terrace outside. Pride of place inside goes to a miracle-working icon of Saint Maura, heavily weighed down by votive jewellery. The festival is on the first Sunday in June. The church's sumptuous interior decoration mostly dates from the 19th century, but the beautiful gilt screen is original (17th century).

The road across the mountains via Agios Leontas is not signposted and starts from the southern edge of Macherado, not Romiri as marked on maps. To add to the confusion, the village referred to on maps as Agios Nikolaos is called Kiliomeno on the ground. Its belfry is one of the finest of many examples of this characteristic Venetian architectural form on the island.

Kampi is a popular place for sunset coach-tours, and has two competing panoramic tavernas at the top of the cliffs, one offering a fierce sherry-like local wine from the barrel, the other advertising a 'mystery cave – it works' of interest to infertile couples.

Reached by a long and in places very rough track down from Anafonitra, the well-signposted **Porto Vromi** beach turns out to be a narrow steep-sided creek with perfectly clear water and a cafe raft built by some entrepreneurial lads who also run boat-trips to and from the much-photographed Smugglers Wreck beach (a rusting hulk on a brilliant strip of cliff-foot beach), which features in all the round-the-island cruises and holiday brochures. Settle a price before you agree to a boat-trip. Saint Dionysos spent most of his life in the very attractive Anafonitra monastery.

The northern tip of the island is a confusing place to explore, with a lot of new road-building in progress and a shortage of signposts identifying villages or giving directions. From the central of several versions of **Volimes**, which has a weaving centre and roadside stalls offering local produce (honey and cheese), it is not difficult to reach the northernmost coastal settlement, **Agios Nikolaos**, just below Korithi. There is a new hotel and a couple of tavernas, one proudly offering its patrons an Italian kitchen and free parking (thought-provoking, considering the remoteness of the spot), the other promising 'offhand eating', which sounds indistinguishable from the usual taverna experience. Could it mean souvlaki to take away? There is a small sandy beach and boat-trips to the island's finest coastal cave, the Blue Grotto, not far away near Zante's northern cape. From Ano Volimes a road leads down to a seaside hamlet with rocky bathing. The local map and some new tarmac encourage hope of being able to drive along the coast

Getting around

Tour operators offer a fair variety of excursions from the main resorts, including the usual beach barbecues and boat-trips all or part of the way around the island, a long sail of nearly 60 miles. Excursion-boats advertise the next day's cruises from their berths along the main Zakynthos water-front, so there is no need to join a tour operator's group. Bus-tours are offered of Cephalonia (8a.m. to 8p.m.), which sound missable. A visit to Olympia is probably more tempting for sightseers; it might be possible for a group to undercut the excursion price by using taxis from Killini (it's 55km from there to the site).

Bus services from and to Zakynthos are good: several times a day to most corners of the island. The Laganas service is very frequent and runs until early evening. For car and motor-bike hire there is plenty of choice in Zakynthos (offices near the main square). A big fleet of 2CVs means that car hire need not be quite as expensive as usual. Cycling is an attractive way to get around, but fairly energy-consuming: it is about ten miles from Zakynthos to Vassiliko and as far to Alikes. Cycles can also be hired at Laganas and Alikes.

southwards to join the main road on Alikes bay, but this route is at best a hiking path. There are sulphurous springs on the coast somewhere hereabouts.

Alikes means salt-pans, and it is a pleasure to discover that they are operational, giving an interest to a stay in the modern resort, a peaceful although no longer small collection of accommodation (including several hotels) and the usual amenities strung out among the reedy cultivations along a sandy beach, which is overlooked by a row of bamboo birdwatching lookout cabins on stilts. The resort has no identifiable centre, but the beach is good (especially for windsurfing) and the surroundings enjoyably agricultural: vineyards right down to the shore. At the southern end of the beach, the hamlet of **Alikanas** now also has holiday accommodation, as has **Tsilivi**, a similarly peaceful farmyard holiday area with a long thin sandy beach, half-way along the fertile coast between Alikes and Zakynthos. All these places have tavernas and watersports, boat-trips up to the Blue Grotto and hirers of transport, including bicycles. The boatmen at Alikes claim to have the best (in other words the smallest) boat for penetrating deep into the grotto.

THE PELOPONNESE ISLANDS

Aegina, Hydra, Kithira, Poros,
Salamina (Salamis), Spetses

There are various names in circulation for the islands strung out
along the east coast of the Peloponnese, the most conventional
being the Saronic Islands, using the name of the gulf framed by
the coasts of Attica and Argolid. This is unsatisfactory, since
several of the islands lie outside the Saronic Gulf; and the term
Argo-Saronic wouldn't cover the distant island of Kithira. One
thing all the islands do have in common is being close to the
Peloponnese.

   Their position has done much to fashion their history and
present way of life and style of tourism. It is tempting to
summarise this with a simple equation of proximity to Athens,
historical importance and present-day unattractiveness.
Certainly, this seems to work with Salamina, whose glorious
place in the pages of Greek history and its present ghastliness
both result directly from the narrowness of the water separating
the island and the coast of Attica near Athens. And, at the far
end of the line, Kithira is much the most peaceful of the group,
the only one that lies beyond the reach of Athenian weekenders
and day-trip excursion-boats from all the busy resorts around
Athens and in the northern Peloponnese.

   The equation is not all that useful. Salamina was itself never
important, but merely the site of an important event, the
destruction of the Persian fleet in 480BC. It would not now be
very attractive (except to battlefield buffs) even if it were less
full of people, almost none of whom are tourists. Aegina, Hydra
and Spetses, on the other hand, were at different times big
powers in the land (or rather sea) and are in different ways
interesting, beautiful and worth visiting, although often very
crowded. Kithira is peaceful and untouristy, but this begs a big
question to which the answer is that the island is in many ways
rather dreary.

   Commandingly placed in the middle of the Saronic Gulf,
Aegina developed early into a powerful and prosperous trading
island with business all over the eastern Mediterranean from the

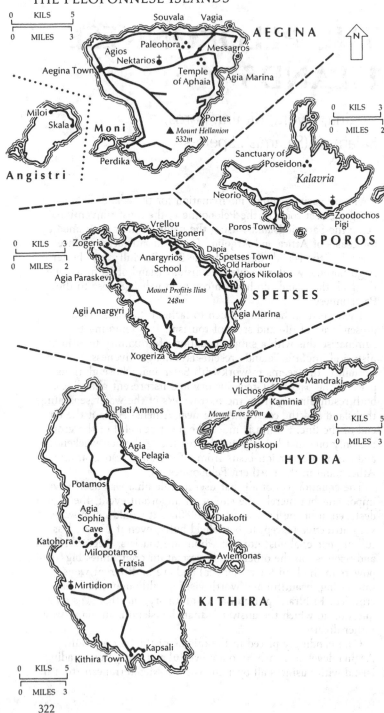

THE PELOPONNESE ISLANDS

AEGINA

Souvala   Vagia

Paleohora
Agios
Nektarios   Messagros

Aegina Town

Temple
of Aphaia   Agia Marina

Portes

Miloi
Skala   **Moni**   ▲ Mount Hellanion
532m

Angistri   Perdika

POROS

Sanctuary of
Poseidon

Kalavria

Neorio

Zoodochos
Pigi

Poros Town

SPETSES

Vrellou
Ligoneri

Zogeria

Dapia
Anargyrios   Spetses Town
School   Old Harbour
Agios Nikolaos

Agia Paraskevi   ▲ *Mount Profitis Ilias
248m*

Agii Anargyri

Agia Marina

Xogeriza

HYDRA

Hydra Town   Mandraki
Vlichos
Kaminia

Mount Eros 590m ▲

Episkopi

Plati Ammos

Agia
Pelagia

Potamos

Agia
Sophia
Cave   ✈   Diakofti

Katohora
Milopotamos
Fratsia   Avlemonas

Mirtidion

KITHIRA

Kapsali
Kithira Town

0 KILS 5
0 MILES 3

Bosporus to the Nile Delta. In the 7th century BC it produced the first Greek coinage, which carried the suitably marine image of a turtle. At the height of its power at the end of the 6th century BC there are said to have been about 40,000 free citizens and 400,000 slaves and aliens on the island. Many of them were no doubt employed in the construction of Aegina's great landmark, the magnificent hilltop temple of Aphaia which was adorned with sculptures to rival those on the Parthenon at Athens.

Rivalry between Aegina and Athens was not confined to art, and often erupted into conflict as the city democracy grew in power and ambition. In the first Persian War (497–490BC) Aegina's trading interests led it to side against Athens and the Greek alliance, but when the Persians returned under Xerxes, overcame heroic Spartan resistance at Thermopylae and occupied Athens, Aegina rallied to the Greek cause and its fleet played a decisive role in the victory at Salamis. The Greeks under the Athenian Themistocles lured the larger Persian fleet into engaging it in the narrow strait now crossed by ferries between Perama, a suburb of Piraeus, and Salamina's main port, Paloukia. With their local knowledge and lighter ships the Greeks outmanoeuvred the far more numerous and unwieldy enemy vessels and routed the few they had not forced into collision, rammed or driven into the shallows. At the end of the day the shores were littered with the wreckage of ships (as much of the coast of Salamina is today, incidentally) and the bodies of the Persian dead. King Xerxes watched the destruction from a throne on the shore and observed gloomily, 'My men have become women and my women men': the only naval commander to serve him with any distinction on the day was Queen Artemisia of Halicarnassus, whose 'brave spirit and manly daring' had sent her to war at the head of five triremes.

With the Persian threat averted, the old quarrel between an increasingly powerful Athens and the island described by Pericles as a sore in the eye of Piraeus soon resurfaced. Aegina was besieged and defeated in 458BC, its population was dispersed and its days of independence and power were over.

More than 2000 years later, another war against the oriental enemy, the Greek struggle for independence from the Ottoman Empire (1821–1829), brought the islands back into play with another heroic performance from a lady sailor of brave spirit and manly daring, this time on the Greek side. Again, the islanders entered the conflict with some reluctance, were largely instrumental in the Greek victory and lost out as a result of it.

The islands in question are not Aegina but Hydra and Spetses, which during the 18th century had established themselves as two of the three leading shipping islands of the Aegean (the other was Psara, near Chios). The islanders, mostly Albanians who spoke no Greek, built the best ships, bred the best sailors and amassed fortunes out of trading and speculation at times of shortage. High-risk, high-reward delivery missions in breach of British blockades during the Napoleonic War proved particularly rewarding. They formed sophisticated companies for the management of their growing fleets. The towns thrived and grew rapidly.

Nominally under Turkish rule, the islands were effectively left alone so long as they paid tax, and were even allowed to do business with and on behalf of the enemy power, Russia, and to arm their boats with cannon to fend off pirate raids. When the Greek insurgents rose up against the Turks in 1821, they had a navy ready: for several years Spetses had been expanding its fleet with war rather than commerce in mind and joined the rebellion immediately, spurred on by the lusty Laskarina Bouboulina, whose new flagship, the *Agamemnon*, was the finest ship in the Greek navy. Bouboulina and the Spetsiots blockaded Peloponnese ports and took Nafplion.

The neighbouring islands were traditional rivals, and the powerful families on Hydra, who found the *status quo* under Turkish rule less than oppressive, responded coolly to the idea of rebellion. However, Spetsiot successes and a popular revolt on the island itself forced Hydra's hand and led to an agreement between the three islands to join forces on the Greek side, under the overall command of the Hydriot captain Andreas Vokas, known as Miaoulis. To start with, the Greeks enjoyed plenty of success, relying, as at Salamis, on daring and superior seamanship to outweigh the enemy's greater numbers. They became particularly adept incendiaries, sailing fireboats packed with gunpowder to the enemy ships and lighting a fuse as they leapt to safety at the last moment.

Unity of the Greek forces proved impossible to maintain, and only the decisive intervention of the allied powers of Russia, France and England at the Battle of Navarino (1827) rescued the Greek cause. In the same year a national assembly bickered for two months in a lemon grove at Troezen (on the Peloponnese near Poros) before appointing as first Greek governor Ioannis Capodistrias, a Corfiot who had served as the tsar's foreign minister. Aegina became the first capital of modern Greece and once again minted coins, this time bearing the image of a phoenix. Capodistrias transformed Aegina with new public buildings appropriate to the town's status, and a new harbour for which he used the stones of the ancient city.

Capodistrias's idea of the new Greek state was not shared by many of the original rebels, whose idea of liberty was freedom from government by anyone. In 1831 he was murdered in church at Aegina by the same men who had welcomed him as a messiah when he arrived on the island two and a half years before. Earlier the same year Hydra had rebelled. Pre-empting an expected blockade of the island, Miaoulis attacked the Greek fleet at anchor off Poros and captured its best frigate, the *Hellas*. Capodistrias brought in Russian help to crush the uprising and Miaoulis made his escape through the strait of Poros in a hail of bullets, having blown up the *Hellas* and another ship before making off. With its huge natural harbour, Poros remained the main naval base and shipyard in Greece until 1878. The island still has its Russian Bay and the national naval academy.

The freedom-fighters and their exploits are the stuff of romantic legend, and the local history books are full of colourful stories: Bouboulina seducing men at gunpoint, the Spetsiots tricking an approaching Turkish naval force by hanging fezzes on the flowers along the water-front, and so on. There is also a certain amount remaining from this period on the islands. The towns of Spetses and Aegina have kept some of their 19th-century buildings and have a sedate charm quite different from the style of most Greek island resorts, partly because they have not grown up in a rush in the last 25 years. But much the most interesting monument to the golden age of sail is the town of Hydra, one of the most beautifully preserved and most commercialised old towns in Europe. Hydra's harbour, so beloved of Romantic painters, is still dominated by the towering mansions of the great sea captains. It is remarkable that an island so barren and with so small and unsheltered a harbour should have become such a formidable sea power. 'What a spot you have chosen for your country!' remarked an American tourist to Hydra's Admiral Tombazi on a visit to the island at the height of its power in the early 1820s. 'It was liberty that chose the spot, not we,' was the patriot's reply; 'and long may liberty preserve and protect a habitation so worthy of her,' wrote the traveller. But it was not to last: as part of independent Greece, Hydra's fortunes declined rapidly and her sailors turned to sponge-fishing.

Officially at least, Kithira was a spectator in the War of Independence. Until 1864 it bore the yoke of British rule, officially known as protection, along with the Ionian Islands whose history it had shared for much of the period since the early 13th century, when the Venetian Marco Venieri successfully claimed the island on the grounds that he was a direct descendant of Venus. Kithira has little in common with the six Ionian Islands and has no transport links with them. It is connected, via a few ferries and hydrofoils each week, with the islands and several mainland towns along the east coast of the Peloponnese, and also has an occasional link with western Crete. Unless, like tens of thousands of Australians, you have family roots in Kithira, the lack of tourist development is the main appeal of the island.

In this it contrasts sharply with the other islands in this chapter, which are among the busiest of all the islands mainly because of the ease and speed of travel to and from Athens. It is sad that between these islands of such noble sailing pedigree the most important means of transport is now the graceless hydrofoil, which has brought Hydra, Poros and Spetses into the

Visiting the Peloponnese Islands

As well as having a busy summer season, the Peloponnese Islands have a pattern of weekend crowds, especially Aegina and Spetses which are favourite places for second-home villas. This can create travel problems as hydrofoils, unlike ferries, have limited capacity. Outward trips to the islands on Friday evening and Saturday morning and those back to Piraeus on Sunday may need to be booked in advance. If you are not in a hurry, using the ferries is probably more enjoyable than being cooped up in the bowels of a Flying Dolphin hydrofoil. It is also cheaper.

Apart from this, the main islands have no particular idiosyncracies. Early and late summer are probably more lively than on many more remote islands. Wind is not the problem it can be in July and August in the open seas of the Aegean, although Hydra's harbour is not at all sheltered: when the wind gets up, tightly parked yachts get squashed. Kithira is one of the many islands to present prospective visitors with the dilemma that its remoteness makes it suitable for peak-season visits, but it has so little holiday accommodation that finding anywhere at which to stay in August is as difficult as on the busiest islands. June, early July and September are probably best.

Holidays to Aegina, Hydra and Poros usually involve hotel accommodation. Spetses has more villas for rent. There are lots of package holidays to Spetses, Aegina and Poros, a few to Hydra and Angistri, almost none to Kithira. Flotilla holidays can be arranged in the area around Spetses, Poros and Hydra.

Access and island connections

Frequent boats and hydrofoils sail from Piraeus to Aegina and Poros, slightly fewer to Hydra and Spetses. Hydrofoils for Aegina use the main ferry port at Piraeus, but those bound for the other islands and mainland

orbit of Athens for day-trips and weekends, a role Aegina has long fulfilled. As well as being convenient places for those wanting to escape from the capital, the island ports, especially Aegina, Poros and Hydra, are highly picturesque and fill up every day with boatloads of tourists based in mainland resorts and on other islands. The waters of the Saronic Gulf are thick with excursion-boats and the water-fronts crammed with day-trippers queuing up to snap the same picturesque view and searching in vain for a souvenir they have not seen before.

Hydrofoils and short hops from mainland ports also make the islands very convenient for tour operators. Palates alert to the nuances of tourism will discern differences of style and extraction of clientele: Hydra is very cosmopolitan, Aegina

---

ports use Zea harbour (only a short walk away provided you find the right road and do not attempt the sea-front route). A few of the Zea hydrofoils call at Aegina.

Other mainland connections, all frequent, are: Perama/Salamina (Paloukia), Galatas/Poros, Ermioni/Hydra, Kosta/Spetses. Hydrofoils also call at Ermioni and Porto Heli, ferries at Methana. Daily ferries run from Piraeus and Aegina to Angistri. Aegina's main port is Aegina town, but Agia Marina and Souvala also have ferries to and from Piraeus.

Access to Kithira consists of daily flights to/from Athens; several ferries a day to/from Neapolis and a few a week to/from Githion. Ferries run twice a week to/from Piraeus via Monemvasia and Neapolis (but none of the other islands), continuing to Crete via Antikithira. In mid-summer there are four hydrofoils a week to/from Piraeus via Poros, Hydra, Spetses and (on the mainland) Leonidion and Monemvasia: two a week at the beginning and tail end of the season. Kithira's main port is Agia Pelagia, but there are also occasional ferries between Plati Ammos and the mainland, and ferries call at Kapsali on their way to Crete.

The summary of all this is that reaching and travelling between the main islands (Aegina, Poros, Hydra and Spetses) is very straightforward. Itineraries do not even need to be planned, unless they include Kithira, whose only frequent ferry connection is with Neapolis on the mainland. The Piraeus/Kithira/Crete ferry (the *Ionion*) is the only connection between this group of islands and the rest of the Aegean. Linking up with this ferry from the other islands involves catching a hydrofoil to Monemvasia or Kithira. The *Ionion*'s recent schedule has been Piraeus to Crete on Tuesday and Thursday, Crete to Piraeus on Wednesday and Friday, but this should not be relied on.

Having to compete with ferries keeps the hydrofoil prices down to reasonable levels for most trips, but tickets for journeys beyond Spetses are very expensive. Travelling from Athens to Kithira by hydrofoil is scarcely cheaper than flying and takes much longer.

distinctly popular (Greeks and Europeans), Spetses very British and very mixed (popular as well as exclusive). The islands are also very popular for flotilla holidays, being relatively sheltered and without stretches of open sea to negotiate.

The islands are very different physically. Poros and Spetses are small and thickly wooded, Hydra larger, more mountainous but barren and empty apart from its town. Aegina is the most varied, with contrasting resorts and landscapes: pine woods, large areas of pistachio cultivation and empty mountains. Unfortunately, its coast is not very beautiful.

Easy access also works in reverse: visits to the mainland can feature prominently in an island holiday and add greatly to its variety. The north-east corner of the Peloponnese has some of the most important classical sites in Greece. Mycenae and Epidavros (which has a summer drama festival) are the most famous but are not the only places worth visiting: Tiryns, Argos, Corinth and Nafplion are all of interest and easily reached on day-trips from Aegina, Poros and Spetses. Athens is also within reach, especially from Aegina; tour operators organise nightlife as well as other excursions. Another reason for visiting the mainland may well be to find a better beach than the islands can offer. Hydra sends daily boatloads across to Hydra Beach on the mainland.

Kithira is an exception to all these generalisations, being relatively inaccessible from the mainland.

Salamina does not appear among the islands described in detail: it's an unattractive place, much of it occupied by a naval and military base (it's the headquarters of the modern Greek navy), with poor beaches and no pleasant resorts.

AEGINA

With all of Greece's islands to choose from, would you stay in sight of Piraeus on an island whose main clientele is Athenians fleeing the capital for their weekend outings and holidays? Probably not. It sounds a bit suburban, and 15 miles a bit too close to the notorious Athenian sea and air pollution for comfort.

If your ideal island is a peaceful hideaway for swimming, slowing down and enjoying the leisured pace and simple charm of Greek village life, you would be right to look elsewhere. But lots of foreign tourists do choose Aegina (drop the 'h' from 'hyena' and you will have pronounced it more or less correctly). Tour operators find the island attractive because of easy transfers from Athens and plentiful hotel accommodation; and presentable thanks to its very photogenic temple and the large number of possible sightseeing excursions – to Athens, to other islands and to the famous classical sites on the Peloponnese.

As a base for a holiday of sightseeing excursions Aegina indeed works well, although if this aspect of Greece is what appeals to you most it may be more sensible to choose a mainland resort or a touring holiday. Aegina also has interesting sights of its own and a very enjoyable resort in its bustling capital, where everyday town and harbour life and an old-fashioned, unsophisticated style of tourism meet in a very cheerful and attractive way.

Thanks to the town, the temple and the pistachio nuts, of which it is the major producer in Greece, Aegina is well worth a visit, if not a prolonged one. It is at its most attractive when you are stuck in Athens or Piraeus with time on your hands and sweat on your brow.

The two main resorts, Aegina town and Agia Marina, are quite different in style. Aegina is a busy town with an overlay of tourism, Agia Marina a much less distinctive, although perfectly satisfactory, big, modern, international resort with the island's only good beach. Other options include simple village accommodation at Souvala and Perdika, small ports of no great beauty, and two self-contained hotel complexes on the west coast. There is a campsite and tents for hire on the small but tall island of Moni, reached by caique from Perdika.

The first capital of modern Greece, **Aegina town** is now a lively little place of about 6000 inhabitants. Everything, unfortunately including traffic, gravitates to the water-front, where tourists ride up and down in traps drawn by horses wearing collars of beads and coloured streamers. Women gossip and bicker in the fish market over trays full of eels, and old men sit in the shadow of the little twin-breasted chapel of St Nicholas on the end of the quay, fingering their beads and watching the incessant comings and goings of yachts, hydrofoils, ferries and excursion-boats. Pistachios are sold (by no means cheaply) from the growers' cooperative stand at the harbour gates, fruit and vegetables from a row of boats that bring their colourful loads daily from the Peloponnese. The various cafes and restaurants between the tourist shops, travel agents and motor-bike shops along the front include a few tourist bars where foreigners have their fresh orange juice and fried eggs. But the general style is more traditionally Greek: a cafe with a fine array of sticky pastries, a simple octopus grill-bar behind the fish market, restaurants with retsina on tap, and the dauntingly local men-only *kafeneion*, a high-ceilinged neo-classical temple of idleness – where, as you would expect, prices are relatively low. A small plateful of pistachios arriving with one's coffee is one of the minor pleasures of being in Aegina.

Considering the number of tourists, Aegina is surprisingly quiet in the evening, once the mass pedestrian parade up and down the water-front has subsided. Dancing in tavernas and discos mostly takes place outside the town, and tour operators organise nights out with Greek dancing.

The colourful mêlée of water-front life is not the sole ingredient of Aegina's appeal. Many of its buildings date from the town's brief moment of prominence in the history of modern Greece, when it became the nation's first capital in 1829. Some of the public buildings (deceptively referred to as public houses in English versions of the tourist literature) from this period still stand, in most cases empty, and some of the water-front houses show signs of having been designed and not merely erected, with balconies and neo-classical embellishments to their walls and roofs. Also of interest is the site of the ancient city and acropolis, on a small hill immediately to the north of the beach, which was the ancient harbour. The hill is called Kolona, after the single column left standing from a temple of Venus; this is surrounded by a considerable extent of semi-overgrown and not easily comprehensible foundations and walls. The island's archaeological museum is now on-site and contains a few good bits of sculpture.

Tourist rooms are not widely advertised or touted, but the travel agencies may be able to help. The main cluster of hotels is immediately north of the harbour (turn left on arrival), a perfectly convenient location between the prom and the town's small and sandy main beach, with the main bus-stop just outside. There is not much to choose between the hotels, but the *Avra* (c) will do. Two hotels in a more peaceful position to the south of the water-front are the *Brown* (c) and *Miranda* (D), an entertainingly run-down mansion beside the road out to Agia Marina. There is another small beach at this end of town.

The port police operate an unusually efficient system of pinning up on a board outside their office a comprehensive daily list of all sailings from Aegina. Having gone to this trouble, they get very upset with people who pester them for information about ferry times.

On the eastern side of the island, **Agia Marina** is a very busy resort on a beautiful bay sheltered by wooded slopes rising steeply to the north and overlooked by the silhouette of the temple of Aphaia. Provided you do not require the slightest vestige of a village community, Agia Marina is not a bad resort; and it has the island's one good beach – gently shelving and well provided with waterside tavernas and renters of windsurfers, pedalos, umbrellas, loungers and so on. There is even a little natural shade from trees along the back of the beach. The bay is ideal for waterskiing and would be good for apprentice windsurfing if the sea were less crowded. Lack of space is also a problem on the beach.

The resort's main street is the last section of the road down to the beach, a long succession of tourist facilities: shops, discos, bars, pubs, restaurants and tourist agencies. Most of the hotels are set back from this axis, on the rocky shoreline to the north of the beach, and some have rocky bathing of their own. A lot of new building is now under way on the southern side of the bay. The beach area and hotel area of the resort are separated by a small headland and Agia Marina's harbour, which consists of little more than a jetty and is not, as so often, a lively focus of activity and idleness.

The flat roads along the island's north and west coasts are popular for cycling outings from Aegina but do not pass many good beaches, especially the north coast where the shore is mainly rocky and littered. **Souvala** has tavernas by the port and a small coarse sand beach nearby.

The **Perdika** road, to the south of Aegina, is more attractive, with pistachio groves and eucalyptus trees, a few weedy bathing places and a cluster of tavernas beside a genuine beach about half-way along. The self-contained hotel complex of *Aegina Maris*, near Perdika, has facilities, open to non-residents, which include tennis and windsurfing.

The sightseeing highlight of the island and the target for numerous excursions from resorts on other islands and the mainland is the **temple of Aphaia**, magnificently located on the high crest of the island above Agia Marina, apparently forming a perfect equilateral triangle with the temple of Poseidon at Cape Sounion and the Parthenon on the Athenian Acropolis. One of the most beautiful aspects of the temple is the rich contrast between golden stone and the dark green of the surrounding pine woods.

As you will read on the admirable explanatory notices on-site, Zeus's daughter Aphaia was worshipped at the site from the 2nd millennium BC. The legend is that the beautiful Aphaia fled Crete to escape the attentions of King Minos only to find that the fishermen whose help she had enlisted were no less pressing. In desperation she jumped overboard near Aegina, swam ashore and disappeared in the woods ('Aphaia' means 'disappearance'). An earlier temple burnt down before a second, or even third, was erected at the beginning of the 5th century BC, when Aegina was at the height of its power as an independent state. The temple's excavators and their successors have re-erected enough of the temple to give a very good impression of its structure, including a section of the internal two-storey colonnade, a unique feature. The superb pediment sculptures, which included 17 complete figures, were removed and bought by Ludwig I of Bavaria; they are now in Munich, the subject of rather less controversy than the Parthenon marbles in London.

Several things may detract from the pleasure of a visit to the site: there is nothing you can do about the wireless mast beside the temple or the rope surrounding it, but by arriving on the dot of ten you can avoid the worst of the crowds.

Paleohora is the site, on a steep hillside to the north of the Aegina to Agia Marina road, of what was the island's capital from the end of the 9th century until the early 19th. The story of looting of coastal towns by pirates forcing islanders to retreat to the relative safety of inland hill citadels is a familiar one in the Mediterranean. Even at Paleohora the inhabitants of the island, who were themselves not beyond the occasional piratical wreaking of havoc on others, were not safe from attack. The height of their misfortunes was a visit in 1537 from the sabre-rattling Khaireddin Barbarossa, who slaughtered all the men and carried off 6000 women and children into slavery. A French traveller soon afterwards found the island uninhabited.

The remaining buildings are a fascinating collection of over 20 small medieval churches, many with frescoed interiors, scattered across the steep stony hillside, with ruins of 17th-century Venetian fortifications on top. In the morning there is usually someone around to open locked doors and point out the most interesting churches. Even without the interest provided by all the churches, the walk up the hill would be worth while.

Beside the main road immediately below Paleohora is an impressive and much-visited pilgrimage site, the **monastery of Agios Nektarios**. The present monastery was built by and is named after a bishop who lived in retreat there for 13 years before his death in 1920. When his body was disinterred some 20 years later it was found to have defied the natural processes of decomposition. With many miraculous healings to his credit, Nektarios was canonised in 1961, the most recent Orthodox saint. His crowned skull is now on display above a casket of relics.

Moni is a large rocky lump of an islet reached by a short water-taxi ride from Perdika. The island is owned by the Touring Club of Greece, which levies a small charge on all visitors and runs a campsite on the single flattish strip of pine-covered land behind the beach on the north side of the island.

Getting around

Organised excursions are widely offered to the other Peloponnese Islands (Poros and Hydra combine to make a very picturesque day-trip), to the Peloponnese (Mycenae, Epidavros and the Corinth Canal) and to Athens. There are also organised evening outings to Athens and Epidavros. For day-trips to Poros, Hydra and Athens, going on an organised excursion is not really necessary.

Frequent buses run from Aegina along north-coast villages; to Agia Marina via the Nektarios Monastery and the temple of Aphaia; and to Perdika. Motor-bikes, bicycles and possibly cars can be hired in Aegina and Agia Marina. There are frequent caiques between Perdika and Moni, Aegina and Angistri.

Bicycles are fine for pottering along the coast from Aegina – it is about five miles to Perdika – but not for going to Agia Maria and/or the temple unless you are seriously into hill cycling. There are links between the three main roads (those used by the buses) so it is possible to explore the island without having to retrace steps, although maps are unhelpful and signposts lacking. These links include at least one road up from the north coast at Vagia to the inland route across the island near the temple; a rough road around the mountain from Agia Marina to Messaros; and a more serious explorer's trail across the wild southern mountain massif, between Aegina and Portes, a small (and not very attractive) fishing village south of Agia Marina. For this route, which gives magnificent views over the island and the entire Saronic Gulf and from which a path leads to the summit of Mount Hellanion (532m), it is worth referring to Anne Yannoulis's useful guide to the island, widely available locally in comprehensible English (which is more than can be said for Mr Karides's sometimes hilarious, sometimes plain baffling *History of Aegina*).

Moni's inhabitants are elusive wild goats, and peacocks which are all too friendly if there is any chance of food.

The small island of **Angistri** can be reached by boat in about 20 minutes from Aegina (boats leave from the fruit-sellers' quay about four times a day) or directly from Piraeus. The small island is known and marketed for its thick covering of pine trees and its beaches, which sounds lovely. It is not. Coming from Aegina, the first port of call is Skala, a scruffy little modern resort with a sandy beach exceptional only for the time it takes to wade out to knee-deep water. There are surfboards for rent, and the shallow water suits beginners well. Drab as it is, Skala is paradise compared with Miloi, where boats also call and which now has some hotels. A couple of minutes' walk above Miloi is the island's very sleepy main village, Angistri, now with a sizeable summer population of foreign tourists, mostly British. There are motor-bikes for hire and, more to the point on an island such as this, a book swap agency. It takes about half an hour to walk from Skala to Miloi, and about an hour and a half from Miloi to Limenaria, a small village on the south side of the island with tavernas and a small beach nearby. Angistri has a bus, which runs between Skala and Limenaria via Miloi village.

HYDRA

The port of Hydra (sometimes written Idra, and pronounced 'eedra') is one of the more remarkable sights in Greece. Cannon guard the narrow entrance to a harbour surrounded by grim grey hills. The port is dominated by a collection of massive grey square buildings, as dauntingly sombre in tone and mood as the island landscape. These imposing edifices are not arsenals or fortresses but homes built by the most successful of Hydra's sea captains, who by a combination of nautical, diplomatic and commercial skill made fortunes for themselves and brought their island great prosperity and independent power, both of which it soon lost after the successful conclusion of the war to free Greece from Turkish rule in the early 19th century. Ironically, the Hydriot naval commanders had contributed more to this victory than anyone else.

After more than a century spent making a meagre living out of sponge-fishing, the resourceful Hydriots have transformed their unproductive island into a money-spinning business via tourism. The barren and almost beachless island was understandably neglected in the early years of Greek tourism, but artists and film-makers appreciated the beauty of the port and fashionable Athenians followed them. Trendy French and Italians soon discovered the island, and now the whole world visits Hydra: Americans and Japanese on once-in-a-lifetime Mediterranean cruises; students doing Europe in a summer; flotilla holiday-makers, who have to double park in the crowded harbour; package tourists; and day-trippers from Athens, other islands and all over the Peloponnese.

The revival in Hydra's fortunes has left its gaunt beauty in many ways wonderfully intact. No new building has been allowed except in a strictly traditional local style. Old houses have been meticulously restored. The island has no cars or motor-bikes. Hydra still looks magnificent from the water and is still a fascinating place to explore on foot.

In other ways it is less delightful. The water-front is full of smooth-talking multilingual salesmen of jewellery, carpets and expensive paintings of donkeys and windmills. The resort is no longer very exclusive, although there are a few handsomely furnished hotels, a French restaurant and plenty of rich people on their cruisers. Restaurants deal in set menus translated into several languages, water-front cafes charge double the usual rate and hoteliers charge far more than anywhere else for a simple hotel room, to visitors who don't know they're being overcharged.

The forbidding martial aspect of the port and resort of **Hydra town** is only a first impression. The rocks below the cannon and windmill stumps are draped with sunbathing beauties, the houses are not all grey and the water-front is a colourful throng of tourists window-shopping, yacht-spotting and fending off the attentions of all the boatmen, waiters and shopkeepers competing for their custom. Donkeys stand around, patiently photogenic. Predictable elements of the water-front are the cafe terraces and the knick-knack shops and jewellers who do not close for a siesta for fear of missing an excursion-boat. More surprising is the presence of a couple of old-fashioned, unmodernised hotels, the *Argo* (D) and *Sophia* (D). One reason why the Sophia has resisted progress may be its close proximity to the graceful but loud belfries of the beautiful Panagia monastery, built in the late 18th century using stones brought from the temple of Poseidon on Poros. The monastery's marble courtyards are a welcome calm refuge from the front, and the church has a beautiful carved marble iconostasis. The slender western belfry was built to replace one demolished in 1806 by a winter flood, apparently a common phenomenon on the island; it is no coincidence that one of the main streets (Kouloura) leading up the hill out of town looks like a dry river bed.

The most impressive mansions, for which the correct singular term is *archontiko*, were built in the early 19th century by the leading families (whose names will be well known to the small number of visitors well versed in the early history of modern Greece: Miaoulis, Kondouriotis, Kriezis, Tombazis, Voulgaris *et al*). The architectural style is said to have been inspired by visits to Italy, where many Hydriot ships were commissioned, and there are a few Italianate open loggias, notably beside the splendid Tombazis house which rises proudly above the western side of the harbour. But in general the buildings are more dominant than decorative, as was doubtless intended, and only a little less sober inside than out. The two least difficult to enter are the Tombazis house, now used as lodgings for students of an art school, and the Tsamados house on the eastern side of the harbour, now a naval academy with a restaurant (Laikon) on the ground floor. Some of the *archontika* are still owned and inhabited by the founding families. One of the earliest and architecturally most interesting is the house built in 1780 by Lazaros Kondouriotis (just to the west of Lignou street, not far from the Hotel Hydroussa).

Wandering around town reveals many other fine houses with first-floor terraces and walled gardens. Most of these were built towards the end of the 18th century, when the island's population was inflated by refugees from the Peloponnese and is estimated to have grown from about 3000 in 1770 to 11,000 in 1794 and an astonishing 28,000 at the outbreak of the revolution in 1821. Within a generation of the end of the war, the head-count fell back to little above its 1770 level, which is roughly what it remains today. The sudden spurt of house-building activity no doubt accounts for the town's very harmonious appearance. The socio-historical background is well evoked in the new museum beside the ferry quay.

It is worth following the main street, Miaoulis (beginning between the Hotel Sofia and the monastery), all the way up to a beautiful square known as Kala Pigadia, a reference to the two capped wells that provide most of Hydra's water. The large house just below the square is the oldest of the big mansions, dating from 1763. This hillside, known as Kiafa, was the main settlement until the period of expansion and new building around the harbour in the 18th century. A path winds around through Kiafa's mostly ruined houses and along the top of the town and eventually leads to Kaminia (see below), passing not far above the small church of St John the Baptist (Prodromos), which is reliably reported to contain beautiful murals. The church is not at all easy to find.

Shops, restaurants and bars line the lower reaches of the streets leading back from the water-front. The most trendy bars and discos are on the slopes to the west of the harbour and are easily identified. Finding Greek music or tavernas serving a recognisably Greek style of meal is much more difficult. Hotels are widely spread around the town. The *Hydroussa* (B, formerly Xenia) is nicely placed on a flowery square behind the monastery, but is expensive, as is its close neighbour, the beautifully restored *Orloff* guest-house. The *Amaryllis* (B) is also attractive, less expensive and quietly tucked away not far from the harbour on Tombazi street. The *Delfini* (B) is simple, relatively cheap and very convenient for the ferries. All the hotels are small and rooms are often very hard to come by.

The beaches on Hydra are very poor. All the port has to offer, on the western side of the harbour below Disco Heaven and a few cannon, are bare slabs of rock with a concrete bathing platform. Any flattish patches of rock are taken early.

Getting around

There are two sorts of water-taxi. One sort, rather like a bus, waits at the quay until full and chugs slowly along the coast, either to Kaminia and Vlichos or to Miramare, at very low cost; comings and goings are frequent in the morning but the flow tends to dry up in the afternoon. The others are speed-boats that await your bidding and charge a lot. Weather permitting, there is a daily boat-trip around the island, with a long stop at a stony beach on the south-western tip of the island.

Donkeys can be hired for excursions into the hills, substituting financial for physical pain. Somewhat surprisingly, one agency near the water-front advertises car hire. This can refer only to the mainland, and might be useful for sightseeing day-trips – though Hydra is less suitable than Poros, Aegina or Spetses for these.

For exploring the town a street plan is essential. The Lycabettus Press guide to the island, by Catherine Vanderpool, has a detailed description of the town and its old houses, and also an excellent summary of the relevant bits of the island's history.

The island's only easily accessible beach is at **Mandraki**, often known as Miramare beach, about half an hour's walk east from the harbour entrance or a few minutes by boat. The wall of the *Miramare Hotel* (A) seems to enclose the beach, but the doors are not locked and the various watersports facilities are not reserved for hotel guests. The beach, pride of the island, is small and stony and the hotel's bar and restaurant are expensive.

About half an hour's walk to the west of the port is **Kaminia**, a little fishing harbour with a taverna and a very small beach. An obvious path follows the coast, passing an impressive old family property about half-way along, and a number of secluded places for sunbathing on and swimming from the rocks. There are several other ways around to Kaminia from the upper part of Hydra (the two communities merge on the inland side of the coastal spur): the easiest route to follow is Kriezis street, but it is also possible to take a longer route via Kiafa hill. The coastal track continues from Kaminia to **Vlichos** (about a quarter of an hour further on foot), which has a small and little-visited stony beach with a couple of simple tavernas. The track continues for several miles over the mountain to some pine woods and houses collectively known as **Episkopi**.

There are about half a dozen monasteries dotted along the hilly island, with an aggregate population of about half a dozen monks and nuns. None of the monasteries is less than an hour's walk from the port, and the furthest is four hours away. Given

337

the barren and mountainous nature of the landscape, visits to these places come into the category of penance rather than tourism. For an alternative point of view, see Marc Dubin's *Greece on Foot*: 'Hydra is conceivably the best for walking (out of peak season) because of its ample size . . .'.

KITHIRA

For the seasoned Greek island traveller there are few more seductive destinations than Kithira, birthplace (or first landfall, to be strictly accurate) of Aphrodite and, if Pausanias is to be believed, site of the oldest, most beautiful and most venerated sanctuary in Ancient Greece. One big attraction today is its remoteness similar to that of distant Karpathos (see page 562), the other minor link in the chain of islands sweeping around the southern Aegean from the Peloponnese to Turkey via Crete and Rhodes. Both islands have large expatriate populations. In Kithira's post office you can consult the diaspora telephone directory, a fat volume which includes Athens and a very large section of Sydney, home of some 45,000 Kitherians. The island itself now has fewer than 3000 inhabitants. They are a very friendly lot, especially those who have retired here after a life in Australia. They love a chat and will have the family snaps out of the wallet at the slightest excuse.

Kithira's main line of communication is with the southern Peloponnese, which is itself off the beaten track of tourism. The island is even more so, despite having its own airport with daily flights to and from Athens. There are half a dozen sizeable villages, some decent beaches and a good road from one end of the island to the other, yet Kithira sees very little tourism apart from visits from returning expatriates. There are only two or three hotels.

One reason for this is a simple lack of interest on the part of the inhabitants, and especially the expatriates, who retain their stake in family property and veto development. A similar situation has prevailed on Karpathos and yet there the tourist bandwagon is well and truly rolling. On Kithira it is not, which suggests that there may be another reason, namely that tourism is as uninterested in Kithira as Kithira is in it, for the good reason that Aphrodite's island is actually not very attractive. Its villages are nearly all inland (the old story of retreat from sea raids) and are neither colourful nor appealingly primitive. The landscape of scrub-covered hills is a bit featureless and the coastline is mostly rocky and inaccessible.

The irony of this was not lost on well-versed antiquarian romantics who slogged out to the island of love confident that their pilgrimage would bring them to a green and pleasant arcadian picnic land of lazy dalliance as depicted by the painters and poets. What they found contrasted sadly with Watteau's celebrated vision, which owed more to the rustic playgrounds of Versailles than to Greek reality. ' . . . instead of Venus, half-wild Greek women; and instead of beautiful lawns enamelled with flowers, naked and rugged rocks or valleys grown over with brushwood,' recorded a disappointed M. Pouqueville at the beginning of the 19th century. Gerard de Nerval was equally disappointed: 'not a tree on the coast, not a rose, not a shell on the shore where the Nereids chose a conch for Aphrodite.'

Modern Kithira is a very peaceful island which, although scenically dull as a whole, has one great redeeming feature, a blue and white hill village sheltering under the wing of a mighty Venetian fortress and overlooking a shapely pair of curling sandy bays divided by a small port and holiday village. The hill village is the capital, **Kithira**, the port **Kapsali**. They complement each other perfectly in a classically lovely Greek island landscape composition, a fitting welcome for Aphrodite. This small corner of the island seems to have been painted by a completely different hand.

Kithira and Kapsali are separated by a stiff 20-minute walk. Both places have simple accommodation in rooms (Kapsali's are more modern) and matters are uncomplicated: if you want to be close to the beach you stay in Kapsali; if you prefer to be based in an old village you stay in Kithira. If you can't make up your mind and budget permits, you might try the smart new tourist lodgings beside the road about half-way between the two. Whichever way, you will probably do a fair amount of walking uphill and down between village and beach. In summer Kapsali is the livelier of the two, but it closes down almost completely out of season. Finding rooms in either village is said to be very difficult in high season. Kapsali has a campsite.

Kithira is not the liveliest hill village in Greece, but it has the right ingredients: small whitewashed and blue-shuttered houses strung along a ridge looking out over the twin bays of Kapsali immediately to the east; a central square with palm trees and beautiful sunset views from the terrace on its open seaward side; and an impressively dominant fort. All the village (especially the main square) seems to lack is much animation – cheerful tavernas and cafes, for example. Traffic squeezing down the narrow village street detracts a little from the pleasure of wandering around.

There is a two-room museum at the top of the village, but

the main sight is the Venetian fortress occupying the spur at the south-eastern end of the village. Built in the early 16th century, it contains a variety of not particularly beautiful ruined buildings ancient and modern, numerous cannon, a few pine trees and a surprising exhortation not to camp – which scarcely seems necessary, especially in view of the number of snakes around. The fort looks magnificent when viewed from the bay and, conversely, the terrace at the top of the fort gives a lovely view down over dozens of old church roofs to the graceful bays below.

Kapsali village, like the fort, is rather less beautiful from close range than from a distance: no more than a small collection of modern buildings on a thin strip of land dividing the two bays, with a church and quay on the rocky headland at the end. There is very much a front and a back to Kapsali, with all the activity – ferries, yachts, beach, cafe tables – on and around the western bay below the hill village and a ring of rocky hills to which cling the whitewashed buildings of an old monastery. Only fishermen use the almost landlocked eastern bay.

Kapsali has a very sheltered gently shelving beach and some sand; it also has pedalos and waterskiing and some windsurfing. Pedalos are a popular way to reach the small pebble beaches on the western side of the bay, which are also accessible by footpath.

There are three tavernas along the village's street; the nearest to the quay is the most fun and the only one likely to be open out of season. The management of the nearby supermarket can provide reasonable rooms. Ferries visit Kapsali only about twice a week, and then in the small hours. The place does not exactly bustle. Nor can either village offer any significant nightlife except for one disco on the hillside between the two. In Kapsali chairs are stacked on tables and lights go out early.

It is a beautiful, albeit steep walk up from the port to Kithira, with a couple of welcome roadside bars near the top. The other notable landmark on this walk is the resplendent Harbour View House, adorned and surrounded by seafaring knick-knacks, a mariner's gnome garden.

The main alternative to staying in Kithira or Kapsali is **Agia Pelagia**, the island's main ferry and only hydrofoil port. It is a desolate, windswept spot, neither a resort nor a village, with just a few facilities – a simple hotel, shop and taverna by the jetty and a new hotel on the hillside at the western end of the beach. This is no place for a prolonged stay but, given the limitations of Kithira's public transport, Agia Pelagia can be useful, indeed unavoidable, for an overnight stay. The partly sandy beach is long, open and gently shelving; it also has showers that work.

For escapism the most fruitful line of exploration is the
mostly well-surfaced road east from Fratsia to Avlemonas,
passing Paliopolis, the site of the ancient city and temple, of
which there is very little to be seen. In a broad agricultural
landscape that seems to belong to a much larger island, the road
passes a vast expanse of wide open, mostly stony beach,
sometimes with a few rough campers. The bungalow
community of **Avlemonas** lies beyond the beach, straggling along
the last half-mile or so of road before a tight little fishing creek.
There is a taverna or two. On the northern side of the same
cape, **Diakofti**, reached with some difficulty past the airport, is a
similarly desolate little village with a sandy beach and a couple
of tavernas. Like many villages on the island, it manages to give
the impression of being simultaneously run down and
unfinished. In the north there is a small beach and a couple of
tavernas at **Plati Ammos**, a small fishing village and occasional
ferry port.

Until the late 17th century **Elafonisos** was linked to the
Peloponnese. Now it is an island with a small community on its
northern side and a splendid sandy beach to the south. There
are boats from Neapolis (on the mainland) and from Agia
Pelagia.

Touring the island is not very exciting, although there is
plenty of slow-moving agricultural activity to observe. Like
many other islands Kithira claims to produce the best honey in
Greece thanks to the quality of the thyme that covers much of
its surface. Honey is the third-biggest industry on the island,
occupying 160 people.

Kithira is also proud of its caves, especially the **Agia Sophia
cave**, whose natural architecture of limestone concretions has
been supplemented by the erection of an icon screen near the
cave entrance. There are guided visits a few times a week,
starting from the very welcoming Platanos cafe in the verdant
and well-watered village of **Milopotamos**, the most attractive of
the inland villages. Information about the timing of these visits
may be forthcoming in Kithira if you ask around.

A visit to the cave can be combined with the ruined fortress
village of **Katohora** on the hillside below Milopotamos, entered
by a rough arched gateway surmounted by the winged Venetian
lion holding between its paws an open book inscribed (in Latin)
'Peace be with you, Mark my Evangelist'. The buildings are
overgrown and dilapidated, but a few churches and houses
(mostly 16th century) are now being restored, which gives one
the chance to peer in.

In a more spectacular and less easily accessible position on the
side of a steep gorge east of Potamos stand the ruins of the

Getting around

There's a daily bus between Agia Pelagia and Kithira/Kapsali, not connecting with ferries or hydrofoils. Motor-bike hire is possible in Kithira and Kapsali and is also advertised, not very convincingly, in Agia Pelagia. Car hire is advertised in Kithira.

The bus is not timed to suit tourists' needs, and most people travel by taxi; it is worth reserving in advance if you have a plane, boat or hydrofoil to catch. The motor-bike hirers can be elusive as they dash up and down between their shops in Kithira and Kapsali. In a fiercely competitive environment, Panayiotis offers special incentive rates for watersports to those who rent their wheels from him, while Mike's Bikes offers free petrol.

On its way from Piraeus to Crete the *Ionion* calls in at both Agia Pelagia and Kapsali, but unfortunately does not represent an attractive way to travel from one end of the island to the other: the journey takes about eight hours, via the mainland port of Githion.

The main road along the island is good and impressively signposted. However, further exploration is likely to involve plenty of trial and error. The Toubi's island map is, as usual, richly detailed and frequently misleading.

---

medieval island capital, **Paleohora**, sacked by Barbarossa and never inhabited since. The villagers are said to have thrown themselves from the village walls into the gorge rather than be butchered by the Turks.

The island's main pilgrimage venue (24 September) is the **Mirtidion monastery** on a wooded coastal hillside below Kalokerines. Its black virgin icon, which was discovered in a myrtle bush, was reputed to turn approaching pirate ships to stone; the nearby rocky islets in question are not, however, particularly ship-shape. The monastery buildings are neither very old nor architecturally interesting, but the setting is splendid, the gardens immaculate and the peacocks noisy. Pilgrims are accommodated in the rough barracks outside the monastery precinct.

The one event that regularly succeeds in bringing the island to life is market day: Saturday at Kalamos and Sunday at Potamos, the island's main farming village.

POROS

'To sail slowly through the streets of Poros is to recapture the joy of passing through the neck of the womb,' wrote Henry Miller, putting a questionable gloss on what every visitor feels about the village of Poros: instant uplifting infatuation.

Two extremities of the small island almost touch the Peloponnese mainland and enclose a broad expanse of sheltered water, a magnificent natural harbour which has ensured Poros a prominent role in the naval history of Greece. One extremity is a promontory occupied by the village of Poros town, a red and white hillside of houses reflected in the busy waters of a strait no more than a few hundred yards wide, which seems to link rather than separate Poros and the mainland village of Galatas. Excursion-boats and ferries on their way up and down the Peloponnese coast and islands queue up for a berth. Hydrofoils zoom up, subside and settle briefly before speeding off again. Sluggish car-ferries lumber across the strait, and hundreds of little craft buzz to and fro among the heavy traffic.

The strait is indeed Poros's main street, and the boats tie up not at some concrete quay projecting out to sea – there is no room for that – but on the pavement, a few feet from the cafe terrace, and well within range of the village balconies for an exchange of cheerful banter between sailors and locals.

Unless you have an unlimited capacity to absorb the same picturesque scene, a long acquaintance with Poros is unlikely to make the heart grow fonder. A constant throughput of day-trippers has inevitably turned the village into a bit of a tourist trap, and the rest of the island has little to offer except a thick mantle of pine trees and one very pretty monastery. Were it not for the supreme beauty of the view as the sun descends behind the dark hills of the Peloponnese, Poros would be ideal for the day-trip treatment. As it is, the island is worth at least an overnight stop.

Just about every house on the island faces the mainland, and a longer than one-night holiday on Poros is best considered as a holiday on the Peloponnese. Looked at this way, it is possible to ignore the limitations of the island and concentrate instead on how much nicer the village is than its more dreary mainland counterpart, Galatas. The contrast between the two seems to illustrate neatly the special charm of the Greek islands.

Once you set foot ashore, the best is over: like so many Greek villages, Poros shows its best profile to those afloat and, in this case, the mainland. Poros town occupies about half of a rocky, hilly promontory only fairly recently joined to the more fertile body of the island by a narrow isthmus. Pausanias records two separate islands, one (the promontory) called Spheria, the other Kalavria.

Poros town climbs a small hill to an elegant blue-domed belfry. Its staircase streets are attractive in an ordinary and residential way, in striking contrast to the commercial and very touristy water-front, which stretches for a long way around two sides of the promontory, facing south and west, the western sweep (to the left as you disembark) having most of the agencies, bike hirers, hotels and smarter restaurants. The more picturesque area lies in the other direction, with a couple of squares open to the sea and a succession of tavernas and bars beside the fishing-boat and yacht moorings. Net menders and taverna customers share space on the pavement. Although many of the houses in this part of town are still fully occupied by local people, the bars and restaurants are thoroughly international: the Ship advertises Guinness and draught Stella, another bar offers 78 different cocktails, and in the cheerful Lucas taverna you may have the rare experience of being served your starter before the main course, a sure sign of foreign influence. Lots of the tourists are flotilla holiday-makers.

The main disadvantage of staying in Poros village, apart from its lack of beaches, is the noise on the water-front, which sleeps for no more than a few hours between its late nights and early mornings. Yet this is where most of the hotels are, including the tatty *Aktaion* (c) and the slightly smarter *Seven Brothers* (B), both absolutely central. At the end of the west-facing promenade (turn left on arrival), the *Latsi* (B) is quieter.

Poros has a small archaeological museum on a square near the fishing-boat quay, next door to the Three Brothers taverna. A more prominent monument is the naval base occupying the narrow strip of land that links the two sections of the island. This was the chief base for the operations of the Greek fleet until 1877, when Salamina took over, and is now the country's naval academy.

It is only a short walk along the water-front from the centre to the naval base, and the stroller's natural inclination may well be to complete a circuit of the promontory by returning along the eastern side. Be warned: this side is much longer than the other, and its main feature is a pungent rubbish dump which must detract more than somewhat from the pleasure of a spot of open-air *sirtaki* at the disco Sirocco. This side of the hill is uninhabited and the road unlit except by candles in the numerous shrines where Poros's drivers have missed a corner or pushed pedestrians over the edge. It is quite a relief to round the final corner and confront the beautiful sight (if it is still light by this time) of the strait, the villages on either side and the land-locked gulf beyond. In fact, it is well worth walking from the village centre past the fishing and yacht harbours to this corner just for the view.

There are no other resorts on the island, but holiday accommodation and tavernas are strung out most of the way along the road that follows the south coast of the main part of the island (**Kalavria**) for a couple of miles to the east and west of Poros. The west side is preferable for views of the village and across the water, and the small hotel *Theano* (B) is in a good compromise location, far enough from Poros to be quiet, but no more than 15 minutes' walk from the village centre. If being near a beach is more important than being near the village, the best choices are at either end of the road: in the east, the large hotel *Sirene* (B); in the west, Neorio, a small community with one of the island's two good beaches, some tavernas and a couple of hotels, *Pavlo* (B) and *Angyra* (C).

Beaches are not Poros's strong point. The road along the southern shore of the island passes numerous thin and usually very crowded strips of grey beach, mostly pebbles and/or very coarse sand, and stony under water. Windsurfers, waterskiing and pedalos are available in several places. West of Neorio the coast road deteriorates promisingly but passes only a few quiet stony coves before petering out on the shore of a bay among the ruined buildings of an old naval base used by the Russian fleet at the time of the Revolution. Yachtsmen seem to like the bay, but for the earthbound it is not particularly attractive for bathing. There is an overland route to a beach on the northern side of the island, but it is not worth the trouble. Beaches on

Getting around

There's plenty of scope for excursions on the mainland and to other islands (Hydra and Aegina are the obvious targets). Evenings out in Athens and at the Epidavros theatre are organised.

Bicycle, motor-bike, car and boat hire is available in Poros. There are frequent buses from Poros west to Neorio and east to the monastery. Water-taxis ply along the island coast and across to Galatas. Bicycles are perfectly adequate for all travel on Poros except the only moderately interesting excursion up into the hills. If car hire prices seem surprisingly reasonable there is probably a catch: you are not allowed to take the car off Poros, which is to say the least limiting. Hiring a little boat is definitely the most attractive way to explore the immediate surroundings and may not be prohibitively expensive.

the mainland served by boat-trips from Poros are not much of an improvement on the island beaches.

At the end of the eastern branch of road lies the 18th-century **Zoodochos Pigi monastery**, often simply known as the Kalavria monastery, a typically pretty spick-and-span whitewashed and tiled establishment, thickly embedded among pines, olives and cypresses, and looking out to sea over a small stony beach. Gravestones commemorate some distinguished Greek sailors of the revolutionary period, plus Brudnell J. Bruce, an ensign of the British Foot who died 'unhappily' at Poros on 8 October 1828, having accompanied His Majesty's ambassador.

The hilly interior of the island was the site in antiquity of an important shrine, a temple of Poseidon, but very little now remains to be seen: some foundation stones and column bases from the 6th century BC. The site is reached by road from a signposted fork about half-way between Poros and the monastery. The temple is where Demosthenes took refuge from his Macedonian creditors in 322BC and bit his poisoned pen nib rather than face captivity.

SPETSES (SPETSAE)

Traditional arch-rivals and neighbouring superpowers in the maritime affairs of pre-revolutionary Greece, Hydra and Spetses could scarcely be more different in aspect. Spetses is as gentle, fragrant and self-effacing as Hydra is rugged and confrontational. From a coastline of small wooded coves rise green hills, their contours veiled by a covering of Aleppo pines, from which the island takes its name. The one village lies largely unseen behind a long water-front of buildings straggling for miles along the shore.

The Spetsiots claim to have been the first of all the islanders to espouse the cause of freedom in 1821, thanks to the dynamic leadership and fiery patriotism of their lady admiral, Laskarina Bouboulina. They were also the first to espouse the cause of tourism, thanks to the forward-looking Sotirios Anargyros who, having made his fortune abroad, returned home to build the palatial Hotel Posidonion on the front in 1914, reforest the island with pines and open a college modelled on an English public school. Pre-war Spetses was the height of fashion.

In those days the clientele was mostly British and it still is, although the tone is somewhat lower now. The pianist on the drinks terrace in front of the Hotel Posidonion is less in tune with the style of the modern resort than the barman with a heavy hand on the volume control in the Anchor pub.

In no way spectacular, the island so beautifully evoked by John Fowles in *The Magus* caters fairly well for just about every style of Greek holiday. The landscape is attractive and the island small enough to explore on foot or bicycle. Though the town beaches are small, often crowded and rarely clean, and the island has no sand, the many stony coves around the coast make an attractive selection. Spetses has its own interesting history and many reminders of its former wealth and elegance – gracious old villas, working boatyards and single-horse-power taxi-carriages which, in the long and more or less car-free village, are as useful as they are picturesque. Heavyweight classical sightseeing lies within easy reach on the mainland.

The agglomeration of greater Spetses town stretches for several miles, about a fifth of the entire coastline of the island from the drab Xenia hotel and the former Anargyrios school (at which John Fowles taught) in the west to the livelier beach suburb of Agia Marina in the east. It is an unusually diffuse place, with a series of little harbours and various different sectors with their own character. This has its disadvantages: very long walks from accommodation presented as being 'on the outskirts of the village' and a lack of any immediate picturesque charm. Visually, it does not help that most of the handsome old buildings are not on the water-front. But the layout does mean that one can choose between several different Spetses according to taste. Despite its size, Spetses is not at all towny. There are very few cars and no main roads.

The resort cannot be pigeonholed: as well as plenty of very loud and ugly junk tourism it has some interesting off-beat shops and quiet residential areas with luxurious private villas and civilised holiday flats; it has hotels of all styles and nightlife that extends the usual range at both top and bottom of the scale, from genuinely sophisticated restaurants all the way down to burgers and the Hotel Myrtoon's Cock and Pussy bar. The cinema has an up-to-date programme of films in English.

The most public area of **Spetses town** is the central section around the small ferry, hydrofoil and excursion-boat harbour, the **Dapia**, guarded by a row of cannon on a terrace of shaded cafe tables. To the west is a broad and usually empty esplanade with Spetses' statue of liberty, the striding figure of Bouboulina, in front of the Hotel Posidonion's pompous façade. Bouboulina's house is on a square behind the Star Hotel, not far from the grand wedding-cake villa built for Sotirios Anargyros in 1904. On the other side of the harbour is an attractive group of buildings where village life goes on regardless of tourists – the cab rank, the locals' cafe, the barber's shop, the creaky old Hotel Saronikos and the fish market – followed by a row of modern buildings ending at the town's small beach, which has a disco behind it and is consequently heavily littered with rubbish and broken glass. Set back from this dreary water-front are the main shopping streets and the equally unlovely Clocktower Square, the main focus of tourist life. Behind this lies a confusing and extensive network of narrow streets with some beautiful old houses among many more concrete new ones. This hinterland zone suffers from a lack of views (from street level, anyway) out over the town and sea.

Agencies on the Dapia control most of the tourist rooms available. The two hotels on the Dapia terrace, *Roumani* (B) and *Star* (C), are very convenient and far enough from Clocktower Square to be fairly peaceful, especially the Star, whose proprietor claims to have nothing to do with tour operators. On the evidence of a visit at the end of June, the *Posidonion* (A) does not have a lot to do with visitors of any kind, perhaps not

FLOTILLA SAILING

Many be the summer mornings
When with what pleasure, what delight,
You enter harbours never seen before. C. P. CAVAFY, *Ithaka*

Sailing among the archipelagos of Greece – once a privilege of the yacht-owning classes – caught on in the 1970s as a style of package holiday, affordable by many. Coming in between yacht charter and mere day sailing, the flotilla is a group of six to twelve boats which sail roughly together for a fortnight, stopping at a different place each night. There is a lead boat with highly qualified crew, considerable freedom to sail off by yourself, and plenty of socialising in the evenings.

The yachts range from four to eight berths, and the more of the party with some sailing ability the better. If you're used to British waters the Mediterranean, though not hazard-free, will be relaxing luxury. For complete beginners there's the villa-flotilla option – land-based for the first week, when you can be taught sailing techniques on the spot – or the three-day preliminary sailing courses in Britain offered by some of the operators.

In Greek waters the Ionian Islands and the Saronic Gulf are the gentler sailing areas; the Aegean, fully exposed to the prevailing brisk north winds of summer, is more demanding. Wind and sun become a reliable combination by late May and June. In July and August you need to be able to cope with high activity in very intense heat.

The skipper in the lead boat is in overall charge and sets the day's

surprising in view of the terms: compulsory and expensive half-board. At the other end of the scale of cost and comfort, the harbourside *Saronikos* (D) is fun but very basic.

Most of the tourist restaurants are on and around Clocktower Square, offering anything from fast food to fillet steak and Mateus Rosé (in the Verandah, which claims unconvincingly to offer the best food in town). For simple Greek taverna food in the centre of town, the Stelios, on the water-front near the Hotel Soleil, is recommended, although its cramped terrace is not very inviting. *Amigdalota*, an almond and honey sweet, is a local speciality and available from several of the village cafes.

One of the finest old mansions, built at the end of the 18th century, now houses the island museum (open every morning except Tuesday) which is mainly devoted to the events, ships and personalities of the War of Independence and whose prize exhibit is Bouboulina's bones. It is surprising, on such an anglo-

---

course, the engineer copes with breakdowns of everything from engines to lavatories, while the hostess organises social events and advises on shopping, eating out and so forth. You stock up your galley (when the port has a shop) for breakfast and lunch, and spend evenings at a taverna or a barbecue. In between you receive instruction and spend the day at sea, in contact by sight and by radio; you anchor to picnic and swim, or take the dinghy to explore a new cove. On the built-in days of 'free sailing' you can be more adventurous or quite lazy.

Although it's a simple lifestyle, yachts are sophisticated and flotilla holidays no cheaper than those on land – and generally more expensive. The cost depends on when you go, what yacht you have, and how many people you share it with. What in addition you spend on daily living depends on where you go. Couples who want a boat to themselves will pay considerably more, but for couples and singles there are yacht-share arrangements.

To enjoy a flotilla holiday you need to be reasonably fit and love the sea; and you'll have to get on with your crew in cramped quarters and the inevitable stressful moments. Essential packing includes high-protection suntan lotions; sunhats and glasses; light cover-all clothing (to protect against wind-chill in spray) and old shoes (for rocky bathing); insect repellent and sea-sickness pills. To find out more, it's worth not only reading the comprehensive brochures but visiting the Boat Show in London in January, to talk to the operators and see the boats. Much depends on choosing the right flotilla.

Specialist operators offering flotilla sailing in Greece include **Falcon Sailing** *(tel 01-727 0232),* **Flotilla Sailing Holidays** *(tel 01-969 5423) and* **Island Sailing** *(tel Waterlooville (0705) 210345).*

influenced island, that there are no explanatory notices in English; the Lycabettus Press guidebook to the island has a good detailed description of the contents.

It is a very attractive walk or cab-ride east from the town beach along the water-front past comfortable villas and gardens to the **Old Harbour (Paleo Limani)**, which itself has separate areas for yachts, fishing-boats and shipbuilding. This eastern part of town is a quiet, well-heeled area with French and Italian restaurant terraces looking out over the water and bars full of yachting folk. Just above the cluster of cafes at the entrance to Paleo Limani is the **Agios Nikolaos monastery**, where the flag of independence was first raised on Palm Sunday 1821. The congregation marched to the Dapia and ordered the Turkish bey off the island. The event is celebrated every year and commemorated in front of the monastery by one of the town's many pebble mosaics, featuring the figure of Bouboulina and the freedom-fighters' flag, a Greek cross above the Ottoman crescent with an anchor and a snake on one side, a spear and an owl on the other, and the motto 'freedom or death'. A plaque inside the church records the death in 1827 of Napoleon's nephew Paul-Marie Bonaparte, in the cause of Greek freedom, and the conservation of his mortal remains in a barrel of rum in the monastery until 1832.

A number of new villas are under construction around Paleo Limani, but the rocky cape on the far side of the harbour is still empty, and swimming from the rocks is possible. The built-up area extends eastwards along the road out of town (which skirts Paleo Limani) as far as **Agia Marina**, a small beach community with tavernas, watersports, a disco and holiday accommodation.

The western part of Spetses town lies to the west of the Dapia and the Hotel Posidonion just past a vast disused cotton-mill. Villas and restaurants are strung out along the water-front as far as the big modern *Hotel Spetses* (A), which flies flags and has a small patch of lawn, as every self-respecting A-class hotel should. There are a few strips of stony beach beside the road and below the hotel, various watersports facilities and a few jetties where boatmen on the daily beach shuttle stop to take on passengers. Just west of the town hall (*dimarcheion*) is the house where Bouboulina, who had at least as many houses as husbands, was murdered in 1825; the courtyard has good pebble mosaics. The waterside road is relatively new and suffers from the fact that the old villas face south, turning their backs to the sea. The town runs out at a thin strip of stony beach, with tavernas and windsurfing, below the bungalows of the Hotel Kastelli/Xenia, just beyond the Anargyrios school. Beyond this is a surprising modern hillside estate of bungalows and flats known as Blueberry Hill.

Dotted around the coast are several attractive stony coves; some are accessible from the coast road without great difficulty. Boats from the Dapia take daily loads to and from the splendid bay of **Agii Anargyri**, much the biggest and busiest of the out-of-town beaches and a small farming and holiday community in its own right, with several tavernas, two watersports operators, accommodation in rooms and a good hotel, the fairly expensive *Akrogiali* (A) – not a bad base for a beach holiday, provided you don't mind the daily invasion of boatloads and weekly evening beach parties. Tasos's taverna, set back slightly from the beach behind a big snack bar, is also recommended. One of the advantages of hiring a bike is being able to enjoy Agii Anargyri when it is empty, early and late in the day.

A few boats also go to **Agia Paraskevi**, which has a cantina, windsurfing, more shade and fewer people than neighbouring Agii Anargyri; and to **Zogeria**, a particularly beautiful pair of coves on the north-western tip of the island (reaching the beach here from the coast road demands perseverance). There are a couple of old churches, ruined hospital buildings and a cheerful taverna behind the western beach, properly known as Lazaretto. Unfortunately, the sea itself is less attractive than the shoreline: sea urchins and litter in the water are a problem on both bays. In general, bathing is more inviting on the other side of the island.

Beaches without any facilities include Vrellou and Ligoneri, both small and well shaded, not far west of Spetses town, and a couple of larger beaches below the road at Xogeriza, mainly used by the few people in nearby villas. Access to the east coast, where a series of rubbish dumps look out over a narrow strait to Stavros Niarchos's island of Spetsopoula, is not possible in many places.

There is not much to see outside the town. Rather than plod around the coast road, walkers should strike out for the hills, or rather hill, which climbs steadily behind the town to a ridge about 250m above sea level. There are two small churches and a few ruined houses on the crest of the island, but the main reward is the simple pleasure of walking through the woods and the broad panorama from the top. A rough track leads down to the cultivated bay of Agii Anargyri and the welcome prospect of a swim, a drink and a bus- or boat-ride back to town.

One of the island's more famous houses is the **Villa Yasemia**, the Bourani of John Fowles's *The Magus*, prominently located high above the sea between the bays of Agii Anargyri and Agia Paraskevi, and best seen from a boat or a windsurfer.

The Lycabettus Press guide to the island, by Andrew Thomas, is recommended for its detailed description of the sights to be

Getting around

Sightseeing excursions to the mainland (Epidavros, Mycenae, Nafplion, Corinth) are easy to arrange via Porto Heli, and are also offered as all-in excursions from Spetses, as are trips to Hydra and Poros. If schedules allow, it is usually possible to undercut excursion prices by travelling independently. A rare exception might be boat-trips to Hydra if the alternative is hydrofoil travel. Dinghy sailing outings from town can be arranged, and excursion-boats cross the two-mile strait to the sandy beach at Kosta on the mainland.

A few buses a day travel from Spetses (by the beach) to Agii Anargyri via Agia Marina, and more frequently from the Hotel Posidonion to Ligoneri via the Hotel Spetses. The excursion-boats from the Dapia to Agii Anargyri are infinitely preferable to the bus service, which stops early and is often very crowded. In town there are horse-drawn taxi-carriages (*monippa*) and water-taxis. Bicycle and motor-bike hire is available from several establishments near the main town beach, east of the Dapia. Outboard hire is available from the so-called Yacht Club (on the Dapia).

There are very few cars on the island (a special permit is needed) and motor-bikes are banned from the water-front area from 2p.m. to 7a.m. Finding one's way around the town through the high-walled maze of back streets is not at all easy and caution is, as always, needed: the lack of cars does not mean a lack of hazards and obstacles such as construction vehicles. The horse-drawn taxi-carriages will not go beyond Ligoneri and Agia Marina.

The road around the island (about 15 miles) is not what a Dutchman would call flat but nor is it seriously hilly: cycling is an attractive way to explore the coast. Only the eastern sections of the road are tarmac, from Spetses to Ligoneri and Xogeriza (a few miles east of Agii Anargyri). The track over the crest of the island to Agii Anargyri is practicable by motor-bike but not well signposted from town and is in places very rough.

seen and the historical background, and also has a useful section on town restaurants and walking routes across the island.

EVIA AND
THE SPORADES

Alonnisos, Skiathos, Skyros, Skopelos

In the beginning there were only two groups of Aegean islands: those circling sacred Delos (the Cyclades), and the rest, not unreasonably referred to as the Sporades, or 'scattered islands'. Over time, divergence of local history and the demands of administration have forged new partitions in the waters, not always of great importance (except to writers of guidebooks) and not always clearly defined. Some one-time Sporades have joined the new enlarged Greater Cyclades group, while others participate in the unimaginative post-war arithmetic of the Dodecanese, and the islands in the north-east Aegean are now usually called nothing more controversial than the North-East Aegean Islands. The ancient name of Sporades survives only on a close-knit archipelago of small islands just off the mainland coast of Thessaly between Athens and Salonika. Oddly enough, they are not scattered at all.

The archipelago extends eastwards from the tip of the Pelion peninsula far out into the Aegean – if you count Kira Panagia, Gioura, Psathoura and Piperi, which can muster a collective population of a handful of lighthouse-keepers and monks, and goats and seals in greater numbers. The islands that count are the three nearest the mainland, reading west to east on the map and in order of tourist development: little Skiathos, which like Mykonos is famous for its sandy beaches and has made the transition from very fashionable to very popular; Skopelos, the largest of the three, now busy but with a firmer grip on the reins of development; and Alonnisos, the least beautiful of the three unless the beauty you seek is that of silence, with which peaceful Alonnisos is well endowed. The islands are separated by straits of only a few miles, as is Skiathos from the mainland; these are ideal flotilla holiday waters.

The great loveliness of the Sporades is their evergreen vegetation, with pine woods covering the hills and an attractive variety of small-scale cultivation in and around the villages: fig trees, nut trees, plum trees, and berries to pick as you ramble.

EVIA AND THE SPORADES

Pefki
Agios
Georgios
Neopirgos
Loutra
Edipsos
Ilia
Vassilika
Rovies
Limni
Kria Vrisi
Galataki
Mantoudi
Prokopi
Pili
Makri Yialos
Dafni
EVIA
Politikon
Mount Dirfis
1743m
Hiliadou
ATTICA
Nea Artaki
Lamari
Chalkis
Steni
Stropones
Mount Olympos 1172m
Manikia
Kimi
Euripus Channel
Eretria
Makrihori
Vrissi
Kimi port
Amarinthos
Aliveri
Paralia
Murteri
Neohori
Avlonari
Perivoli
Lake
Distos
Kalamos
Agii Apostoli
Panagia
Athens
Nea Stira
Stira
Marmari
Kalergi
Cape Kafireas
Karistos
Mount Ohi 1398m
Platanistos
Potami

KILOMETRES		30
0		
0	MILES	20

354

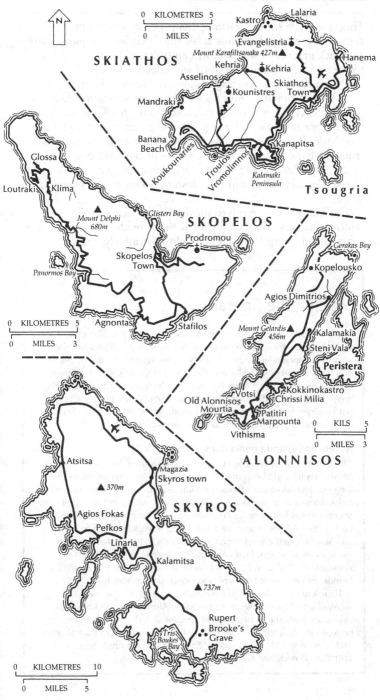

EVIA AND THE SPORADES

N

0 KILOMETRES 5
0 MILES 3

SKIATHOS

Lalaria
Kastro
Evangelistria †
Mount Karafiltsanaka 427m ▲
Hanema
Kehria
Kehria †
Asselinos
Skiathos
Town
Kounistres †
Mandraki
Kanapitsa
Banana
Beach
Koukounaries
Troulos
Vromolimnos
*Kalamaki
Peninsula*

Tsougria

Glossa
Loutraki
Klima
*Mount Delphi
680m*
Glisteri Bay

SKOPELOS

Prodromou
Skopelos
Town
Panormos Bay
Agnontas
Stafilos

Gerakas Bay
Kopelousko
Agios Dimitrios
Mount Gelardis ▲
456m
Kalamakia
Steni Vala

Peristera

0 KILOMETRES 5
0 MILES 3

Votsi
Kokkinokastro
Old Alonnisos
Chrissi Milia
Mourtia
Patitiri
Marpounta
Vithisma

0 KILS 5
0 MILES 3

ALONNISOS

Atsitsa
Magazia
Skyros town
▲ 370m

SKYROS

Agios Fokas
Pefkos
Linaria
Kalamitsa
▲ 737m

Rupert
Brooke's
Grave
*Tris
Boukes
Bay*

0 KILOMETRES 10
0 MILES 5

355

This is a much softer landscape than the dry stony hills of the typical Greek island – if one takes the Cyclades as typical, that is. Thick greenery can transform an ordinary village, such as Skiathos, into a thing of beauty and effectively veils the unpleasantness of a downright ugly one, such as Patitiri, port and modern capital of Alonnisos. Abundant vegetation also has practical advantages, casting valuable shade on villa terraces, water-front tavernas, hillside paths and beaches. It has one big drawback: flying insects. The village architecture also differs from the basic whitewashed-cube style of the Cyclades. Houses in the Sporades are larger and more elaborate, and pitched roofs of red tiles add an unfamiliar splash of colour to the village scene.

The contrasts are resolved on the lonely island of Skyros, which is usually considered part of the Sporades for want of any other island group to join, but is administratively and in

Visiting the Sporades

There are package holidays galore to Skiathos, plenty to Skopelos, a few to Alonnisos, very few to Skyros, and flotilla sailing holidays to Evia/Skiathos/Skopelos/Alonnisos. Skiathos is best avoided in August unless you have a pre-booked villa and car; people fight to get on the buses and the normally lively town becomes pandemonium. The remarkably green landscape of the Sporades testifies to abundant rainfall, which is not confined to the winter months. Finding accommodation on Skyros in high season is even more difficult than on most islands.

Access and island connections

Charter flights are available to Skiathos. Flights from Athens to Skiathos (several daily) and Skyros (daily) are recommended alternatives to the long bus journeys from Athens (Liossion terminal) to the relevant ports – Agios Konstantinos (for Skiathos, Skopelos and Alonnisos) and Kimi (for Skyros). Volos has more sailings than Agios Konstantinos but is much further from Athens. There are a few flights a week between Salonika and Skiathos, and a weekly boat from Kavala to the Sporades, a very roundabout approach. Hydrofoils operate frequently from Agios Konstantinos, Volos and Salonika (via Moudania) to the three main islands, twice a week from Volos to Skyros (a four-hour marathon).

There are lots of boats and hydrofoils up and down the main archipelago of three – Skiathos, Skopelos, Alonnisos – but links with Skyros are limited to a twice-weekly hydrofoil and a few boats a week between the Sporades (Skopelos and Alonnisos more often than Skiathos) and Kimi. A weekly ferry links the Sporades and the north Aegean (Agios Efstratios, Limnos and Kavala).

practical terms of ferry connections more closely linked to Evia and the mainland. Skyros has the rare and very attractive combination of a whitewashed hill village as picturesque as any in the Cyclades and a green and fertile landscape. In the north, anyway: Skyros is an island of two remarkably dissimilar halves, with only bare rocky mountainsides south of the central valley that separates the two. This is not the end of the island's appeal, for few Greek islands have a stronger or more individual cultural identity. The Skyrians are craftsmen and artists who take great pride in their skills and local traditions. Theirs is a fascinating island at a delicate stage of development: well known, trendy and now with an airport of its own, but with very few other tourist facilities (hotels, for example). This has kept the big tour operators at bay, but it can create problems for visitors.

Evia is something else again, and belongs to the mainland

Visiting Evia

Evia is a better bet than most islands for a visit in high season, with its coastal resorts at their most cheerful and summer tavernas on many of the more remote beaches. The main resort, Edipsos, would no doubt be very dreary when empty of visitors. But it is an island which more or less demands a motoring tour, and long August hours at the wheel may not be everyone's idea of fun. It is possible to travel along and across Evia by bus, but journeys are very long – Chalkis to Edipsos takes over four hours – and the freedom to explore remote parts of the island lies at the heart of enjoying a visit.

Access and island connections
From Athens (Liossion terminal) there are buses to Chalkis and Kimi, and trains to Chalkis. Ferries operate from the mainland: several daily from Rafina to Karistos, Marmari and Nea Stira (different boats), from Agia Marina to Nea Stira (or, occasionally, Almiropotamos beach), from Glifa to Agiokampos; very frequently from Oropou to Eretria, Arkitsa to Edipsos; weekly from Volos to Kimi (on Evia's east coast) via the Sporades.

Ferries go to/from Kimi: daily to Skyros; a few times a week to Skopelos, Alonnisos and (occasionally) Skiathos; weekly to Limnos, Agios Efstratios, Kavala. A short bus- or taxi-ride between the two neighbouring mainland ports of Arkitsa and Agios Konstantinos makes it possible to make a fairly straightforward connection between northern Evia and Skiathos, Skopelos and Alonnisos. It is also possible to link up with the Cyclades from southern Evia via the mainland port of Rafina.

rather than to any group of islands. An island it is, though, and the second largest of them all: about twice as big as Lesbos and half the size of Crete. Long and mountainous and lacking any fast roads, it is, at least in terms of the time taken to drive from one end to the other, the largest Greek island by an uncomfortable margin of several hours. Shaken loose by some tremendous upheaval vaguely alluded to in mythology, Evia faces mainland Greece across the Evian Gulf, which narrows to less than two miles in the north and to only 100 feet at Chalkis – the Euripus Channel – where it is bridged. As well as the bridge, there are ferry shuttle services to the mainland from various points along the island. For the main towns these are more important lines of communication than the road along the island, which may explain the lack of any clear island identity. Evia's towns and villages are not strikingly picturesque, nor obvious choices for beach resort or sleepy fishing-village holidays. But the island does have great beauty, which mainly lies in its many landscapes of woods and mountains and farms. In places, Evia almost demands the use of that tired and devalued adjective, undiscovered. It is an island to explore. Given its size and the state of its roads and maps, exploration takes some perseverance.

The open east coast of Evia was so notoriously stormy and short of safe havens that the Evian Gulf was the ancient sea route along the east coast of Greece. This gave enormous strategic importance to the Euripus Channel and explains the early emergence of Chalkis as one of the great powers of Greece, along with its close neighbour and frequent enemy, Eretria. The great period of Chalkidian power climaxed with the defeat of Eretria in the late 8th century BC after a long and sapping war between the cities. Chalkidians founded colonies on Sicily and the Italian peninsula and gave their name to land owned in northern Greece, the area still known as Halkidiki. The city's golden age came to an end when it fell under Athenian control in 506BC. From then on, Evia became provincial, albeit a rich and strategically important source of timber, marble and meat (the island's classical name, Euboea, means 'cattle-rich'), with Chalkis a fortress town guarding the Euripus.

In common with much of Greece, Evia was ruled for much of three centuries after the fourth Crusade in 1204 by the French, Genoese and Venetians, who called the island Negroponte, probably a corruption of Euripus rather than a reference to any black bridge. After a month-long siege and a scarcely credible reported toll of over 70,000 Turkish and 30,000 Evian lives lost, Chalkis opened its gates to Sultan Muhammad II in July 1470.

The 1821 revolution started a long period of intermittent fighting on the island, and Turkish control did not formally end until 1833, when Chalkis was handed over to Greece in exchange for the island of Lemnos and a guarantee of freedom of religious observance for Muslims in the city.

Of the Sporades, Skyros alone features prominently in myth, as the ancestral home of Theseus and King Lykomedes, who pushed the former king of Athens to his death from the acropolis and in whose palace Achilles misspent his youth dressed as a woman, until found out by Odysseus and dragged off to Troy and his mortal destiny. Skyros has its Achilli Bay, from which the heroes sailed for Troy, and impressive fortress ruins, mostly Byzantine and Venetian, on the site of the ancient acropolis.

The ancient history of the other islands is obscure, to the point that even their names are uncertain. The confusion has concerned the old island names of Halonesus, Peparethus and Icus. In line with the general policy of renaming islands by their ancient names, the island known until this century as Hilidromia has become Alonnisos, on the assumption that it was ancient Halonesus. Few scholars now believe this to be correct. Some maintain that modern Skopelos was ancient Halonesus (as well as being ancient Scopelos, cited by Ptolemy and Hierocles) and that modern Alonnisos was ancient Peparethus and/or conceivably ancient Icus, which might otherwise be modern Panagia Kira. Alternatively, modern Skopelos may be ancient Peparethus, although the fact that Ptolemy and Hierocles mention both Scopelos and Peparethus implies that they are different islands. Part of the reason there is so much doubt is that the ancient writers do little more than name the islands and that little of antiquarian interest remains on them, which makes the whole subject somewhat arid.

Skiathos was a favourite refuge for the revolutionaries of 1821, and it is said that the Greek flag had been first raised outside the Evangelistra monastery in 1807 when the oath to free Greece from the Turks was taken. Its inhabitants also played a big and, from their point of view, very dangerous part in the operation of smuggling Allied troops from Greece to Turkey in 1941, although the island was under Italian occupation at the time.

EVIA (EUBOEA)

Evia (Euboea to classicists) hugs the coast of Boeotia and other unpronounceable bits of the Greek mainland like a loose piece of jigsaw puzzle, so closely and for such a long way that it seems no more of an island than the Peloponnese. Its capital, Chalkis, a big town only an hour's drive from Athens, spreads itself over both mainland and island sides of the narrow Euripus Channel, which was first bridged in 411BC. A visit to Chalkis will fill few travellers with the desire to explore further, and the bus-ride across the island to Kimi, the port for Skiros, is little more encouraging.

These impressions are deceptive. Evia may not have the simple, picturesque, nicely rounded, fishermen's backwater charm of a typical Greek island, but there are ample rewards in its magnificent changing landscapes of high mountains, rich rolling farmlands, lush river valleys and long tracts of wild uncharted coast, and in a few coastal resorts that differ refreshingly from the Greek norm in attracting hardly any foreign tourists. This is not necessarily an advantage: many people would find the resorts a bit dull without the usual entrepreneurs offering boat-trips and renting out cars, motorbikes and windsurfers. But it is certainly different. Unfortunately, the one part of the island that is used by lots of tour operators (a few of them British) – the coast around Eretria and Amarinthos – is very dreary indeed.

'The scenery is perhaps the most beautiful in Greece owing to varied combinations of rock, wood and water,' declared the forthright Encyclopaedia Britannica (eleventh edition, 1911). 'However, no part of Greece is so destitute of interesting remains of antiquity.' Some overstatement on both counts perhaps, but the gist is correct. Neither is Evia really a beach holiday island: it is almost devoid of watersports (except at the big hotels around Eretria) and most of the good beaches are on the east coast, which involves long diversions from the main road and often some slow, bumpy driving. But the island is nevertheless a popular spot for holidays and weekend escapes with Athenians and the islanders themselves.

Evia cannot be seen from one or even two bases. The main resort for stay-put holidays is Loutra Edipsos in the extreme north-west, the biggest spa in Greece, with 80 hot springs, as many hotels and lashings of old-fashioned charm.

The North

The existence of a road, absent from most maps, between LOUTRA EDIPSOS and Limni makes possible a circuit of the north of the island. Between the two resorts are long stretches of easily accessible beach, and some accommodation and stony beaches at the peaceful villages of **Robies** and **Ilia**; there's a good campsite just north of Robies. There is little of specific interest apart from the scenery, nowhere finer than on the long descent from Mirtias to Limni, which in Ancient Greece was Elymnion where Zeus and Hera were married. Ruins of an early Christian basilica include an interesting mosaic pavement.

Modern **Limni** is the most attractive alternative to Loutra Edipsos, indeed much the prettiest coastal village on the whole island. It's a peaceful old port on a very sheltered south-facing bay, with narrow streets of handsome white houses and cafe tables under the canopy of a huge plane tree on the sea-front. Limni has a few simple hotels, but only poor beaches.

It is worth diverting to vist the **Galataki monastery** at the end of a rough road 8km south of Limni. The first monastery on the site is thought to have been founded during the 8th century. After destruction at Turkish hands the monastery was abandoned for nearly a century until a ship's captain, having narrowly escaped disaster in a storm nearby, rebuilt it in 1547 (as an inscription over the door relates). Twenty years later another sailor enjoyed the same good fortune and commissioned the decoration of the church with beautiful frescoes. Some of these remain, including a Last Judgement and the portraits of the two benefactors. The premises are now a convent.

On the tip of the island west of Edipsos, **Agios Georgios** is an attractively peaceful, straggling fishing community and resort, with tavernas and rooms for rent. This is a busy stretch of coast in summer, with tourist-boats between Edipsos and Kamena Vourla (a big spa on the mainland) stopping at Agios Georgios. The big modern beach hotel at **Gregolimano**, east of Agios Georgios, is now a Club Med.

The main road around the north of the island passes beaches at **Neopirgos** and **Pefki**, a small beach resort with a campsite and simple hotels. The road runs along the sea-front, and Pefki does not have much village atmosphere.

Some of the island's loveliest scenery is the rich farmland and wooded river valley between **Prokopi** and **Mantoudi**, a genuine leafy glen with flocks of goats paddling in the shallow water. Goats apart, this is ideal picnic territory. Pilgrims by the thousand visit the very ugly church of St John the Russian in

Prokopi, a large village that received relic-bearing refugees from an earthquake in Turkey in 1923 and took its present name from their home town. The bus from Chalkis to Edipsos usually stops for five or ten minutes beside the church. Local farm produce (including nuts and very good honey) is sold from market stalls outside the church. The saint's day festival is 27 May.

Many of the remote east-coast beaches are popular for rough camping; some have freshwater streams running down from the hills. From the hill village of **Vassilika**, north of Limni, there's an obvious road down to a long beach. The coast near Mantoudi is mostly spoilt by the local mining industry, but there is a small beach community at **Kria Vrisi**. Prokopi's local beach is at **Pili**, a big strip of dark sand with some scruffy holiday develoment (including a taverna) near by. A rough road continues along the coast for another ten miles or so, passing Vlahia, where a track follows a river down through woods to a very pretty stony beach (**Makri Yialos**), a popular camping spot with a ramshackle taverna.

Loutra Edipsos

A beautiful setting on a sweeping, sheltered bay would have brought Edipsos good business as a resort even without the sulphurous local waters which are said to rank fourth in Europe for effectiveness in combating various ailments from rheumatism to gunshot wounds and what are politely termed female disorders. The spa was well known in antiquity: Herakles came here to recuperate whenever he suffered serious injury, and the Roman general Sulla came for his gout. Plutarch records that as well as valetudinarians, Edipsos attracted many healthy Greeks who came to discuss literature and philosophy, go to the theatre and bathe in pools. The level of discussions and evening entertainment is less elevated these days – moussaka westerns in the open-air cinemas are the big attraction – but Edipsos retains a much broader appeal than most spas, and is heaps of fun for all the family.

The resort faces westwards across a wide bay on what looks like an inland sea, with mountainous coasts of island and mainland apparently merging to the north-west. Pines and eucalyptus trees shade the broad promenade, where in summer the world parades from early evening until 10.30 sharp. Fishermen bring their catch for sale on the sea-front, old men grill corn-on-the-cob, children ride up and down on bicycles or in pony-traps and skim stones from the beach into the last reflected rays of the sun before it goes down in flames behind the dark hills across the water. The scene is perfectly viewed from the cafe Klima, an exotic little pavilion projecting over the water on stilts. Fairy-lit ferries glide silently in and out until late.

There are very few non-Greek visitors (just a few sickly French) and the atmosphere is quite different from that of most busy Greek resorts: no motor-bikes or windsurfers for rent, no topless sunbathing, no shops full of 'No Problem' T-shirts, no cocktail bars. Shops along the front specialise in gluey sweets and liqueurs, with excellent *loukoumia* and *baclava* sold by the kilo and Evian honey straight from the barrel. Many of the hotels predate the Greek tourism boom, and the two largest of them (*Avra* and *Aegli*, both A) are sedate, comfortable institutions on the sea-front. The *Agapi* (B) is one of the few modern hotels: small, clean, comfortable and fairly expensive, a few minutes from the front. Curiously, the resort lacks tavernas, and there are few alternatives to *souvlakia* bars and cafes. One exception is the Hotel Istiaia's restaurant on the promenade, a very friendly place but no palace of gastronomy.

At one end of the promenade is the ferry harbour and beyond it a long thin sandyish beach. Around a corner at the other (eastern) end is the spa zone, with a huge thermal pool and bathing establishment. There are boat-trips across the bay to other beaches and villages on Evia's wooded north-west cape.

The Centre

Chalkis, a town of some 40,000 inhabitants, is no place for a holiday, but is the usual gateway to the island. There are smart hotels and restaurants on the wide car-free esplanade immediately north of the Euripus Channel, on the island side. The *Paliria* (B) is comfortable and much less expensive than the Luxury-category *Lucy*, which is expense-account territory. The most useful places in town are car hire offices (near the Euripus bridge on the island side), the bus station (walk up Kotsou from the bridge) and the railway station (on the mainland side of the bridge).

The main sight of Chalkis is the famous **Euripus Channel**, a mere 100 feet of often fast-flowing water separating island and mainland. The irregular tides were one of the great brain teasers of antiquity – the current changes direction between once and seven times a day. The search for an explanation is said (unreliably) to have driven Aristotle to such a degree of frustration that he threw himself into the Euripus declaring this to be the only way to get to the bottom of the unfathomable problem. The Euripus phenomenon and various influences of sun, moon, wind and the earth's rotation are still not completely understood, but there are thought to be two separate currents, often running in opposite directions. It is all, or most of it, a question of syzygy.

The best view of the channel, city and converging coastlines is from the ramparts of the splendid 17th-century **Karababa fort** on the mainland side of the water. With the archaeological museum closed until further notice, the main points of interest in the town centre are the old mosque, a fine 16th-century building which is also closed, and **Agia Paraskevi**, a vast Byzantine basilica with a surprising gothicised interior, the work of the island's Venetian rulers in the 14th century. There is a section of Roman aqueduct beside the road out to Nea Artaki and the north.

The coast near Chalkis is best avoided or at least passed through as rapidly as safety will allow. To the north, **Nea Artaki** and **Politikon** are outlets for Chalkidian weekenders, with little accommodation and crowded beaches which are popular for rough camping. The coast road runs out at **Dafni**, a popular leafy beauty-spot beneath impressive cliffs. A stream runs down past a shady taverna to a small stony beach; out of season, it must be delightful.

A number of big package hotels have sprung up along the coast road south of Chalkis, but the beaches are not good and the very busy coast road is a nuisance. **Eretria** is the main resort on this stretch of coast, for foreign tourists anyway. Blank modern-block buildings on a widely spread flat grid of streets make a very dreary village, but the area of tourist shops, tavernas and holiday accommodation beside the ferry harbour is certainly peaceful. There is a surprisingly pleasant little beach (with a shower, sunshades and a watered lawn) beside a wooded promontory, the grandly named island of dreams, occupied by a bungalow hotel.

The **ancient city of Eretria** rivalled Chalkis and disputed the fertile plain that separates the two cities. A large area of excavations, the acclaimed archaeological highlight of a visit to Evia, is on the inland edge of the modern village and includes a theatre (4th century BC), now overgrown and enclosed by fencing, and the foundations of several temples. There is not much in the museum.

East of Eretria the main road continues to follow the shore most of the way to the power station at Aliveri and reveals few beaches worthy of the name, although there are lots of seaside, roadside hotels. **Amarinthos** is much livelier than Eretria but has a major traffic problem: with the main road separating sea-front tavernas from their dining-terraces, Amarinthos waiters cannot find it easy to get life insurance. The simple *Artemis* (D) is one of the few quiet water-front hotels.

The road between Aliveri and Kimi runs across a fertile plain with a ruined Venetian watchtower on the flanking hills and a beautiful Byzantine church beside the road at Chania. A well-preserved tower stands at the top of the old hill village of Avlonari and provides a focus for a wander. North of Avlonari the road forks, with a coastal route to Kimi port and a high road through a series of remarkably verdant hill villages to Kimi. Shortly after the fork (on the high road), the church at Agia Thekla has good frescoes. The sprawling hill town of **Kimi** is nearly 300m above the sea, and has a couple of old hotels and an excellent folklore museum (open morning and evening) at the bottom of the village beside the road up from the port. As well as displays of old costumes, uniforms, domestic interiors, lace, rugs and all sorts of rustic utensils, the collection includes a small display devoted to the memory of the celebrated cancer doctor George Papanikoloau, a native of Kimi and inventor of the so-called Pap test. One of the most striking coastal landmarks near Kimi is an abrupt church-topped peak of obvious volcanic origin above Oxilithos. There is a rough road up to the top (414m), and wonderful views in all directions. Five kilometres of hairpin bends later, the **port of Kimi** is the only community of any size on the east coast. It's a natural stop-over point, although not really a resort. There are a few shops, tavernas and a shabby modern hotel beside the ferry harbour, and beaches to the north and south. Those to the south have easier access: the vast expanse of exposed beach between **Paralia** and **Murteri** (although the villages are not well signposted from the main road) and good beaches on either side of the rocky headland at **Kalamos**, reached without much difficulty via **Neohori** and **Perivoli**.

The glory of the thick central section of the island is the mountain scenery of the **Dirfis range**, which peaks at 1743m above **Steni**, an old village and modest hill station with at least one hotel, in attractive woodland country. The road continues to a high pass commanding superb views of the mountains and both coasts of the island: fertile and inhabited to the west; wild, wooded and enticing to the east. From the pass it is possible to drive, albeit very slowly and uncomfortably, down to the east coast at Hiliadou (below Lamari) and from there to follow the mountainous coast all the way around to Kimi without retracing steps to Stropones. **Hiliadou** and **Metohi** have beautiful stony beaches, summer tavernas and colonies of campers and gypsies.

The scenery on the southern side of the range is no less

beautiful and no better represented on maps. The road up a wide canyon of rust-coloured rock from Vrissi to Manikia and Makrihori is recommended, for scenery if not surface. It is no doubt possible to continue to Amarinthos, making a slow alternative to the main road across the island. Do not expect signposts, even to identify villages as you come to them.

The South

The two biggest villages, Karistos and Marmari (a lively port famous, as the name suggests, for its local marble), both have direct ferries to and from the mainland near Athens, which means lots of Greeks fleeing the capital at weekends and in high season. In all respects **Karistos** is the more attractive of the two. It's a cheerful small town and resort on a huge bay facing the open sea (a very rare attribute for a resort on Evia) and dominated by the towering mass of Ohi (1398m), Evia's second-highest peak. Hotels include the friendly *Karistion* (c), well placed near a small sandy beach and only a short walk from the main shopping streets and wide sea-front promenade of restaurants, bars and ice-cream parlours. Everyone congregates here in the evening, and by day the port is busy with yachts, ferries and fishing-boats. The main beach (coarse sand) is at the end of the promenade. Karistos has been an important settlement for thousands of years but, apart from the single tower remaining from the 13th-century Venetian harbour fortifications, it has the logical look of a planned town: wide straight streets, regulation-sized gardens and a surfeit of empty space, for all of which we have to thank a Bavarian architect of the mid 19th century. Although it is by no means just a holiday resort, Karistos might be a bit depressing out of season.

At **Marmari** a rough road leads southwards along the shore to two lovely secluded beaches (without tavernas) about a mile or so from the port. The beaches face the wooded Petali islands, which also have beaches; boat-trips are advertised at Marmari. **Nea Stira** is another resort with a ferry link with the mainland, and is more of a resort and less of a community than Marmari or Karistos, thanks to its sandy beach beside the dock, where the road runs out in front of a group of hotels.

Two small weekend resorts with a much more tranquil hideaway atmosphere are the beach community below Almiropotamos, sometimes identified as **Panagia**, and **Agii Apostoli**, a fishing-harbour and expanding holiday-home village on a sheltered bay, one of very few anchorages on the notoriously inhospitable east coast. Its main street is the beach

Getting around

The hub of the bus system is Chalkis, with daily services to and from Kimi, Karistos and Edipsos. Car hire is essential for exploring the island and can be arranged at Chalkis and Eretria (which also has motor-bike hire). Using the ferry services from Eretria, Nea Stira, Marmari and Karistos, tour operators organise sightseeing trips to Athens and Cape Sounion.

Planning a tour of the island is by no means straightforward. If you have your own transport or hire a car in Athens, it makes sense to disregard Chalkis and plan an itinerary from one end of the island to the other, using the ferries that link mainland and island at Karistos and Edipsos, the obvious termini. If you intend to combine Evia with a visit to other islands, you will probably have to start at Chalkis or Eretria, assuming you plan to hire a car.

Perhaps the greatest impediment to exploration is the poor quality of local maps, which fail to take account of some new road-building and are very inaccurate in what they do show. Modern road maps of the whole country are more useful than larger-scale but older and imaginative island maps. The road between Limni and Edipsos exists, has at worst a couple of miles of very rough surface, and cuts about 25 miles off the Edipsos/Chalkis drive. There is a new rough road (without signposts, naturally) along the coast linking Kimi and the road across the mountains from Nea Artaki to Steni and Stropones. This is a spectacularly beautiful drive but not a short cut across the island. Take an extra spare tyre or a puncture repair kit.

of muddy sand, where cars are parked, boats beached and the world put to rights in a row of tavernas. The only hotel is *Rudy's Xenon*, which is run by the man himself, an enthusiastic raconteur.

The main road does not follow the coast in this area. From Lepoura it is a beautiful drive south to Karistos, with much of the traffic consisting of donkeys and farm carts, a welcome change after the heavy traffic on the Chalkis to Aliveri stretch. After Lake Distos, a lush green vegetable patch in summer, the road twists this way and that along the mountainous spine of the narrowest part of the island, with sea views on both sides. The main road ends at Karistos, no less than 270km from Edipsos in the north-west. It is possible to add considerably to this total by tackling the rough road that circumnavigates the great mass of Ohi and the south-eastern tip of the island as far as Kallergi on the northern side of Cape Kafireas. Our experience of this remote corner of the island runs out at **Platanistos**, a pretty village and popular outing from Karistos, with a track down a fertile valley to the sea at **Potami**.

From Karistos it is well worth hiking or driving (via Mili) up to the magnificent medieval fortress known as **Castello Rosso**. Those who scale **Mount Ohi** will find on top an ancient chamber made of huge flat slabs of rock. It is not known whether this was a place of worship or a beacon.

ALONNISOS

Alonnisos is the most tranquil of the Sporades, consisting of no more than a small modern port, Patitiri, a picturesque, partly ruined old village on the hill above Alonnisos, and a secluded bungalow holiday complex on the coast at Votsi. These three settlements are within easy walking distance of each other at the southern end of a long, narrow, hilly island, the rest of which is quite empty except for a few beach tavernas and a colony in the far north dedicated to the protection of the rare and reclusive Mediterranean seal, which still basks in these unfrequented waters.

The little port of Patitiri, built in a rush to accommodate the islanders after an earthquake destroyed their old hill village in 1965, is drab by comparison with other village resorts in the Sporades. But in other ways the island has a similar green and pleasant charm, and dozens of small beaches (mostly pebbles) dotted along its eastern and southern shores. The reasons for a singular lack of modernisation and almost no attempt to exploit the island's tourist potential lie in the intricacies of local politics, which are subject to the usual jealous guarding of control (there are only 1000 voters) and some resentment of the foreigners, mostly German, who bought up the ruins of old Alonnisos for next to nothing and made them into holiday homes. For whatever reason, the island's all-weather road network adds up to about a mile, electricity has only very recently reached the hill village and running water is still to come. In a delightfully eccentric flight of fancy, some maps mark an airport, an ambitious project whose realisation is not to be expected imminently. For the moment Alonnisos is an island for wandering the fertile hills, taking little boats to little beaches and sitting around on the water-front at Patitiri engaged in no more strenuous activity than watching the ferries, hydrofoils and yacht flotillas on manoeuvre. Many visitors would find it far too peaceful, but for others this case of retarded development is just about ideal.

Greek architecture of the 1960s and 1970s wins few merit awards, and that of **Patitiri** is no exception. Considering the circumstances of its creation, this is hardly surprising. It consists of little more than two parallel streets climbing the hill from each end of the concrete quay, which is no larger than it needs to be to accommodate a small fishing fleet and visiting ferries and hydrofoils. The houses are dull blocks, the variety of shops, cafes and restaurants is not great, but Patitiri does not lack an intimate, lazy charm with occasional eruptions of frenetic activity when ferries arrive to disgorge and take on their cargo of cars, trucks and building materials in the usual mêlée of shoving humanity and livestock. There are lots of flowers to brighten the buildings, and walking along the front involves picking your way between vine-shaded cafe tables occupying the very limited space between the houses and a little stony beach where fishermen pull up their boats and children play late into the evening.

The best thing about the village is the beauty of the sheltered bay, with low golden cliffs tightly enclosing the port, and wooded hills all around. Some of the nicest hotels look down on the village and bay from the clifftops on either side. They include, on its own at the beach end of the bay, the bright, clean and comfortable *Galaxy* (C) and, among several hotels on the opposing rocky promontory, the *Kavos* (E, but by no means primitive). The idea of a cliff may sound unnecessarily daunting; distances are not great and it is only a matter of a couple of minutes up from the Muses pub at the end of the water-front to the Galaxy. There are also a few hotels down by the quay, and room touts greet ferry arrivals.

Small and quiet as it is, Patitiri is on the flotilla holiday itineraries and now sees a fair volume of package-holiday business, with a peaceable clientele attracted by the idea of an island where very little happens. There are a couple of discos and several water-front bars with rock music, but the evening atmosphere is pretty quiet. Evening boat-trips and beach barbecue parties are often organised.

As well as hotels and rooms in Patitiri, tour operators and locals greeting ferries offer rooms and self-catering accommodation in **Votsi**, a dreary suburban community which spreads around the two small bays immediately north of Patitiri. Votsi proper is the further of the two from the port, at least 20 minutes on foot. Both bays have tavernas and stony beaches but lack any village atmosphere.

Alonnisos has lots of beaches dotted along the southern half of the east coast (more sheltered than the west). Although mostly small and stony, they are peaceful and fairly attractive, with wooded and cultivated hillsides dropping down to the water. Some beaches can be reached by car or bike, but the

Getting around

Motor-bike and caique hire is available in Patitiri. Car hire can be arranged given a day or two's notice. All the roads, except the one between Patitiri and Votsi, are dirt tracks and may be impracticable after rain, as was the case when we visited the island (in July). The network consists of a single spinal road from Patitiri/Votsi to Gerakas Bay in the north, with numerous tracks leading down to east-coast beaches. Despite the abundance of placenames on the map, there are very few habitations, and nowhere resembling a village, north of Patitiri. On the subject of beach names, the island map is very unreliable, diverging in many places from common usage.

Day-trips to Skopelos are advertised, but it is quite straightforward to organise your own excursion there (or to Skiathos or Skyros) using the ordinary ferry and hydrofoil services. Boat-trips to the uninhabited islands beyond Alonnisos – Kira Panagia, Gioura et al – may be possible to arrange, but are not organised on a regular basis.

usual and most convenient transport is provided by the caiques which sail up and down between Patitiri and Agios Dimitrios a few times a day, calling in at the main beaches (Chrissi Milia, Kokkinokastro, Steni Vala and Kalamakia) on the way. Boats also serve Marpounta, Vithisma and Mourtia beaches on the southern tip of the island. All these beaches have tavernas or cantinas; there's accommodation at Club Marpounta, a large and decidedly unluxurious bungalow holiday camp, and a more recent bungalow hotel (the *Alonnisos Beach*, c) between Chrissi Milia and Kokkinokastro beaches. The biggest of the beach/fishing communities is at **Steni Vala**, where several tavernas, rooms for rent and a campsite almost constitute a hamlet. The west coast is good for snorkelling but notorious for dangerous currents. Kopelousko, in the north-west, is said to be safe for swimming and worth the walk, which may well be a scramble, from the road. In the interests of the seals, entrance to Gerakas Bay by land or sea is forbidden.

The main activities on the island are excursions to other islands; boat-trips to beaches on Alonnisos itself and the almost uninhabited islet of Peristera; and the beautiful $\frac{3}{4}$-hour walk to the old village of Alonnisos, preferably by the old donkey path which winds its way up through orchards and nut groves from the port, rather than by the longer and less attractive road route.

Old Alonnisos enjoys a magnificent hilltop setting looking steeply down over the south and west coasts of the island, and makes a splendid sight for passing yachtsmen and ferry passengers on their way to or from Skopelos. Some handsome old houses survived the earthquake, and lots of noisy rebuilding and restoration work is now in progress. The new colonists are an arty lot who are taking every care to restore the village authentically, with rough stone and the right materials. Galleries and home-made jewellery shops are springing up among the ruins, and the first macrobiotic restaurant cannot be long delayed. The main taverna has a terrace with a beautiful view; it is well worth arriving early for lunch.

From near old Alonnisos there is a rough road down to one of the southern beaches (Mourtia), from where it is possible to return to Patitiri by boat.

SKIATHOS

Skiathos is the smallest, prettiest and busiest of the Sporades and one of the most inviting of all the Greek islands. It has green hills and pine woods, a very colourful and picturesque port, and a scalloped south coast where one sheltered sandy beach follows another. The islanders have not been reluctant to cash in on their blessings, and large-scale tourist development came relatively early: a road along the beach coast, big hotels beside the much-hyped sands of Koukounaries bay, and an airport. The south coast is now punctuated by a series of big hotels, each with its own slice of sandy beach and its tennis court, swimming-pool and watersports club. More and more holiday villas are springing up to fill the space between them, and Skiathos town itself is dominated by foreign tourism for a long summer season. By Greek standards, accommodation and meals are expensive.

But if Skiathos is an undisguised holiday playground it is a good one. The town has been spared modern-block buildings, and the development of the coast has been better managed than on most islands that have opted for mass tourism. Even on a busy island less than ten miles long there is still plenty of room for explorers and walkers to get away from other people and find peace in beautiful, unspoilt surroundings.

There is just one community, the town and port of Skiathos itself, and one main road along the south coast between the bays of Skiathos and Koukounaries in the south-west. Most of the interior is wooded and deserted, as is almost the entire length of the more rugged north coast, except when boatloads of round-the-island trippers descend on some remote beach for

371

their statutory half-hour. The north coast takes the full assault of the prevailing winds; the cliff scenery is impressive and the beaches often littered with washed-up debris, including jellyfish. The sheltered south coast has a much softer complexion: green and gold beaches of fine sand and pine trees, as seen on all the posters. In all respects the contrast between one side of the island and the other is remarkable.

Skiathos has something for everyone except sightseers and those wanting to hide away in a peaceful Greek fishing village. In general, however, there is not much hotel accommodation for those who have not pre-booked a package, and not much accommodation of any description (except a couple of campsites) left for independent travellers in high season. Skiathos is best avoided in mid-summer when the number of tourists strains the little island to the limit. Skiathos town itself has surprisingly few hotels and no beach; most people are accommodated in one of the isolated big hotels along the coast, expensive and mostly block-booked by tour operators, or in rented villas, mostly out of town on the Kalamaki peninsula about half-way along the south coast.

Skiathos town is a small town of some 4000 inhabitants, always lively and often bedlam, set on a splendid wide bay and spread over two shapely hillocks overlooking two harbours separated by a wooded promontory (Bourtzi) where a disco has replaced an old fortress. The island road bypasses the town, so the water-front hubbub does not include traffic, except when a ferry is loading or unloading. Skiathos looks particularly lovely from the sea, with trees and graceful belfries standing out from colourful tiers of red roofs, blue shutters and whitewash, and green hills behind. The disco promontory has trees and benches and is a popular location for early evening strolling and later assignations; it also serves as the town 'beach', despite having only a mediocre concrete pavement on the rocks.

The traffic-free, tree-lined western quay is always very animated, with all the excursion-boatmen loudly touting for custom in the morning and an assortment of pavement artists and knick-knack salesmen working late in the evenings. A wide staircase leads up from the quay past the busiest tavernas, their leafy terraces looking out over the boats and the bay. The main shopping street is not free from traffic and is much less attractive, running straight back from the middle of the water-front between the two hills. The higher ground is peaceful and residential, with well-kept churches and balconies full of flowers.

Although Skiathos is a full-blown international resort teeming with noisy young people swilling pints in the Admiral

Benbow Inn and other similarly anonymous places, its style is not uniformly trashy. As island capital it has everyday needs to cater for, and there are plenty of reminders that before it became very popular Skiathos was very fashionable. Wandering the streets you will come across a shop dispensing wine and brandy from the cask, another with good cheap home-made sandals, and a number of classy galleries and antique shops (rugs, jewellery and costumes), one of which (Archipelago) is more of a museum than a shop and well worth a visit. Even in the more routine aspects of tourist shopping – jerseys, jokey T-shirts and leather goods – the range and quality are high.

Accommodation in the town centre consists mainly of rooms; local women greet ferries. The new *Morfo* (B), back a bit and right a bit, is one of the few central hotels, and claims to keep some rooms for independent travellers. There are a few basic old hotels on the street running parallel to the eastern (ferry) quay. The main recent growth of the town (including most of its hotel accommodation) has taken place in the direction of the airport. Quite apart from the considerable nuisance of the planes, this is the least attractive part of town. The road runs along the messy shore and there is no bathing. As well as hotels, restaurants and new rooming houses, there are discos in this neighbourhood, where no one (else) notices the noise.

Sightseeing in Skiathos town consists of the museum in the humble dwelling where the journalist and short story writer Alexandros Papadiamantis, a native of the island, spent his last years and died, in 1911. There is not much to see.

The fame and fortune of the island of Skiathos is founded quite literally on sand. The claimed tally of over 60 beaches leaves little of the coastline unaccounted for; most of it is fringed with beautiful fine sand. Ironically, an exception is the whole of the main harbour bay in Skiathos town. Most of the main beaches along the road have tavernas, windsurfing and waterskiing.

The beaches between the edge of town and the **Kalamaki peninsula** (to the south-west) are sandy but not particularly attractive. The peninsula itself is a pretty part of the island with some semi-private bathing places for those prepared to scramble down to the sea. This is where most of the island's villa accommodation is. Convenience for the shop, tavernas, beaches and the bus-stop varies considerably (from about two to fifteen minutes on foot), as does seclusion.

On the town side of the peninsula is the pick of the out-of-town hotels, the *Nostos* (A), a relatively secluded and attractive bungalow hotel with a good swimming-pool and a small beach. Next to the hotel, **Kanapitsa** is a peaceful little beach with a cheerful taverna and, usually, a better windsurfing breeze than the other beaches. In a quiet position behind the beach is the *Plaza* (B), a straightforward new package hotel.

On the other side of the peninsula, **Vromolimnos** is perhaps the greenest and most golden of all Skiathos beaches, with pines sheltering (and in places shading) the sand. The name means stinky pool, and there is one. One taverna is open in the evening. A mile or so further on, **Troulos** has some holiday bungalows and a larger and slightly less secluded beach, also very pretty.

In the crook of the south-west corner of the island is **Koukounaries**, the much-vaunted 'most beautiful beach' in Greece, almost inevitably a disappointment. Never mind: it must have been wonderful before hotels were built on the hills at either end, before the peace was shattered by the incessant drone of waterski boats, and while it was still possible to find room to lie down on the sand. And although the beach is overcrowded (and surprisingly undercatered and unhygienic), the sweeping bay is still a magnificent sight. The name refers to tall umbrella pines behind the long stretch of sand. As always, No Camping signs and warnings of fire risk act as more of an invitation than a deterrent. Behind the trees is a marshy lagoon and lawns (well, grass anyway) where the construction of a golf course has apparently come to a halt.

The prime location is the headland at the western end of Koukounaries occupied by the typically drab former *Xenia* hotel, now run by a British tour operator. There are some newer, smaller hotels along the road behind Koukounaries in easy walking range of the beach; the *Mandraki* (B) and the *Jupiter* will do nicely, provided a beach is all you require: there is no community.

The narrow west end of the island has two similar very pretty sand and pine beaches facing the mainland, both with snack cantinas and windsurfer hire. A path from near the terminal bus-stop by the Xenia hotel leads down through a grove of olives, figs, sheep and goats to **Krassas**, universally known as Banana Beach, the island's official sanctuary of nudism, which gets very crowded with serious-minded naturists.

People who prefer to bathe and sunbathe naked also tend to head for some of the more remote beaches on the north coast. Those that are easily accessible are **Hanema**, past the airport, littered and unlovely, and **Asselinos**, reached by rough road from Troulos through fertile farming country. The latter beach is coarse sand and has showers and a taverna; there's a campsite here, with a shop and delightful rustic surroundings (it's on a farm). There are buses into town a few times a day. Near

---

Getting around

No one does anything much on Skiathos except go to the beach or take boat-trips, of which there are countless permutations: shuttles along the south-coast beaches provide a welcome alternative to the bus service; trips to neighbouring Tsougria island (a beach and taverna); along the north coast and back or all around the island. In the unlikely event that you can't find a trip that suits you, caiques can be chartered from town and outboards rented by the hour or day from several beaches (including Koukounaries).

There are also organised day-trips to Skopelos and Alonnisos with stops of a couple of hours on each island. Ferry services make it possible to visit either island for the day much more cheaply, as does the hydrofoil service to Skyros. Mainland excursions to Athens, Delphi and the Meteora monasteries are also advertised, but are very expensive and involve a disproportionate amount of travelling.

There are frequent buses between Skiathos and Koukounaries until about 11p.m., and three buses a day to Asselinos. In high season demand for bus space far exceeds supply, making life very difficult for those not staying in town. There are numerous motor-bike and car hire firms (and one bicycle hirer) in town, at the big hotels and from several establishments along the main road. If hiring a car, beware the small print – conditions stipulate no departure from the main road.

If you intend to do much exploring on foot, it is well worth buying the island guidebook edited by Rita and Dietrich Harkort.

Asselinos, a temptingly good road and official-looking signposts lead to the **Kounistres monastery**. It is a pretty spot with fine views northwards, and drinks are served on the terrace. The road continues down to the coast, but does not lead anywhere rewarding.

For those wanting to get off the beaten track, there are the two long stretches of sand known as **Mandraki**, reached by a beautiful 15-minute walk through the pine woods from the road behind Koukounaries (near the Hotel Jupiter). There is no shade on the beaches, but plenty of driftwood ideal for making shelters, which give a Crusoe-esque desert island look to the empty shore; nude bathers add to the exotic effect. The admirable local landowner fells trees to make sure motor-bikes can't get through and has erected no signs. The easterly of the two beaches has a taverna.

Kehria also consists of two beaches, both pebbly. The easterly one is particularly delightful, a small stony beach where a cool stream runs down between grassy banks to the sea. An enterprising and very obliging islander has set up a little cantina and some tables on the grass, and has even diverted the stream to make a shower, using a perforated gourd as the shower head. He has also posted makeshift signs at most of the numerous forks in the rough roads across the island (from near the Esperides Hotel), making it relatively straightforward to find Kehria. It's possible to go on a donkey or hiking excursion to the beach, and to the beautiful **Kehria monastery** church tucked away on a hillside above, about 20 minutes' walk from the eastern beach. There is a refreshing fountain outside the church, dark 18th-century frescoes and a colony of bats inside.

Lalaria is about the most spectacular beach on the island: a narrow band of very fine silver pebbles beneath a cliff wall, accessible only by boat.

At the northern tip of the island is the old citadel town of **Kastro**, which is much more easily reached by sea than overland. Abandoned 150 years ago when the islanders felt safe enough to move back to town, it is now a magnificently sited ruin, with only a few churches that have been maintained. Kastro was used as a hiding-place and secret ferry port for Allied troops being smuggled from Greece to Turkey in 1941.

Determined overlanders can reach Kastro on foot or muleback and combine it with a visit to the **Evangelistria monastery**, high up in the hills behind Skiathos town, a longish, in places steepish and decidedly hottish hour's walk. Most people go by donkey, a very popular excursion, usually including a picnic. There is also a road up to the monastery, but at least half the fun of the trip is the journey, which gives beautiful views down over the town and bay. The monastery (closed from noon to four o'clock) is spendidly set, with an old cannon pointing out to sea northwards over a narrow wooded gorge, a reminder of the monastery's proud role in the movement for national liberation. It was in this remote spot that the Greek flag was first raised, in 1807, when a group of nationalists came together and swore to free their country from Turkish rule. The flower-filled monastery courtyard contains a delightful old rough-stone church, with cats, bees and doves completing the picturesque scene. Outhouses include a fine ruined kitchen, its octagonal chimneys now serving as dovecotes. If you want to have the place to yourself, arrive before ten.

SKYROS

Wasp-waisted Skyros is the odd one out of the Sporades, separated from the archipelago of little green islands by plenty of water and a lack of ferry connections. It is an island of great fascination, whose marginal location seems to be reflected in the landscape – one half is green, wooded and productive like the rest of the group, the other Cycladic grey, barren and uninhabited. The town of Skyros, along with just about everything on the island except the grave of Rupert Brooke (who died of fever on a troop ship there in 1915), is in the green northern half of the island yet seems also to belong in the Cyclades. In a classically picturesque hill village arrangement, staircase streets of whitewashed, flat-roofed houses climb steeply to the old walls of a hilltop acropolis where Theseus, King of Athens, was pushed to his death.

Skyros has long been famous for its highly individual local art and crafts, and the beautiful local pottery is now on sale at a high price throughout Greece. Islanders still fill their houses with elaborately carved furniture and decorate their walls with plates, copper pans and embroidery. Old men still wear their traditional baggy pantaloons, furry caps and uniquely elaborate many-thonged sandals, and open doorways still reveal an island of working craftsmen. The Lent carnival celebrations are among the most famous in Greece, and include a complicated fancy dress ritual with a surprising amount of transvestism, perhaps something to do with the Achilles legend.

With a magnificent long sandy beach – one of the best in Greece – completing its great attractions, Skyros town has all the required ingredients of a Greek island idyll and has yet to be developed for mass tourism. It is, however, well established as one of the most trendy off-beat destinations in the Aegean, popular with arty Athenians, people into growth (there are two holistic holiday centres on the island) and such summer residents as Stan Graf, who coaches 'holotrophic breathing: an adventure journey to unknown realms of your soul facilitated by breathing to provocative music'.

Improved communications can only fuel the island's popularity. There are now daily flights to and from Athens, and a new hydrofoil link with the other Sporades has put Skyros on the island-hopping map and brings day-trippers to the town from resorts on the other islands. There are motor-bikes for hire, London glossies on the bookstalls and fast food, cocktails, *crêpes* and *gelati* advertised along the high street.

Even when it was less well known, Skyros suffered from a

shortage of beds in high season. As so often happens, access has improved without much provision for more visitors. There are very few hotels, and accommodation in private rooms is relatively expensive and often hard to come by; it makes sense to take up any sleeve-tugging offers of a room, at least for the first night.

Skyros town is unquestionably one of the most beautiful hill villages in the Aegean. It climbs up and around the sheltered inland shoulder of a sharp coastal spur to a hilltop fortress, with a very steep drop down to the sea on its north-eastern side. With its flat-roofed white houses, packed far too tightly to admit any cars, Skyros is immediately reminiscent of a Cycladic village although the architecture is more elaborate.

The axis is one main street, a succession of shops, cafes and restaurants made picturesque by the clientele outside them, but lacking the usual attractive focus of a spacious central square. The street meanders up to a fork: up and right for the most interesting old houses (many with small gardens and wells), the fortified monastery of St George and finally the windswept acropolis ruins which command wonderful views, not least over the splayed pattern of the village roofs; half-left for a panoramic terrace with a nude male statue commemorating Rupert Brooke and the spirit of eternal poetry (following signs to *ΜΠΡΟΥΚ* – the Greek for Brooke). A Belgian work of the 1930s, this is no eternal masterpiece, but it is well sited, the figure's feet hovering on the horizon where empty sea and sky converge. The long staircase which descends from the terrace passes the island's excellent popular art and folklore museum in a beautiful old house near the top, and one of Skyros's two discos about half-way down.

Evenings are pretty lively, at first along the main street, later in the discos. The keen seeker after ethnic Greek truth may well be disgusted by the pubs and cocktail bars at the bottom end of town. Beyond this zone, the village remains satisfyingly traditional in style, as does the dress of many of the villagers. Houses are used as workshops by carpenters and cobblers. Skyros sandals, with heavy-duty cross-ply tyre soles, are sold, as is Skyros pottery, though little cheaper than it is anywhere else.

At the foot of the village is a fine long sweeping sandy beach. The straggle of holiday accommodation along the back is known as **Magazia** – reached either by the long staircase from the top of the village or by road from the bus-stop; about ten minutes' walk either way. Magazia is quieter and less claustrophobic than Skyros town, and has the island's main hotel, a typically unlovely *Xenia* (B) in a typically perfect position, a campsite,

Getting around

Buses between Linaria and Skyros town operate to coincide with ferries. Motor-bike hire is available in Skyros.

The road from Linaria to Atsitsa via Skyros/Magazia is good but does not give access to any of the north coast. The road across the southern half of the island to Tris Boukes is very rough, as is the north-west coastal road between Atsitsa and Linaria, especially between Agios Fokas and Pefkos. Dead-end quarrying roads add considerably to navigational problems, and the local map (in the Welcome series) is much more often a hindrance than a help.

windsurfing and pottery workshops. It is well worth walking up to the northern end of Magazia beach where sand becomes abrasive rock which has been quarried, carved and worn into unusual shapes. A church and a few houses have been cut from the rock.

Kalamitsa, signposted from the main road south of Skyros but also accessible over the hill from **Linaria**, is a long stretch of stones (sand at the Linaria end) with a taverna, rooms and windsurfing. There are stony beaches further south, but no facilities.

North of Linaria there is a small beach with a taverna in walking distance of the port. Further off the beaten track, on the coast, there are peaceful beaches with tavernas and rooms at **Pefkos**, a beautiful wooded bay, and **Agios Fokas**, which is more remote and slightly less picturesque. **Atsitsa**, a peaceful wooded bay on the north-western side of the island, is the site of a British-run holistic health and fitness holiday centre (bookings through 1 Fawley Road, London NW6; tel 01-431 0867). There's some rough camping under the pines here, but not much of a beach – although swimming is possible, as is windsurfing (though available only to people staying at the centre).

The main sightseeing interest on the island is **Rupert Brooke's grave** at Tris Boukes. This can be visited either by boat-trip, details of which are advertised in Skyros town, or overland – a long hike or a not-so-long bumpy motor-bike ride from Linaria across the rocky barren southern half of the island. The route is pretty obvious but unsignposted except by the occasional ΜΠΡΟΥΚ with an arrow splashed on a roadside rock. The bay is easily identified from the two islands at its entrance ('Tris Boukes' means 'three mouths'), but it is easy to miss the grave itself, tucked away beneath a few olive trees to the left of the track down to the sea. The clean white marble tomb is inscribed with the whole of 'If I should die. . .', and a tireless choir of cicadas grinds out an unflagging shrill lament in the overhanging branches, an oasis in an utterly dead landscape.

One great advantage of not taking the organised boat-trip is that you will almost certainly have this lonely spot to yourself, which is just as it should be. The southern half of the island is said to be the home of a unique race of miniature ponies, but goats and hawks are the main inhabitants.

Apart from the sentimental pilgrimage to Tris Boukes Bay, exploring the island beyond the immediate vicinity of Skyros town is not particularly rewarding. The island is a big military base and uniformed personnel keep the village cocktail shakers busy in the evening. The north coast is reserved for war games, a sure sign that the beaches are excellent.

The guidebook by Manos Faltailtz, whose house and collection constitute the folk museum, is available in English and contains lots of interesting background information on the history and culture of the island.

SKOPELOS

Everything about Skopelos invites comparison with its smaller and busier neighbour, Skiathos. To many minds the quieter of the two is preferable for that reason alone. Its port and island capital is even more picturesque than Skiathos town – in fact it's one of the most beautiful villages in all the islands; and the countryside is a similar lovely mixture of pine woods and fruitful hillsides dotted with the domes and cloisters of scores of quiet monasteries. Skopelos cannot match Skiathos for quantity of beaches and proliferation of watersports facilities, but there is nothing (except overcrowding in mid-summer) wrong with the beaches that there are, and the beauty of the coastal scenery is not marred by big hotel blocks. And, unlike Skiathos, the town has a beach of its own. This is a very alluring island, peaceful but far from primitive.

It is also an increasingly popular one, with a rapid recent growth of package-holiday hotels on the edge of town. The standard of this accommodation is exceptional, and the buildings themselves are mostly attractive. To use the jargon of tourism, this is higher-quality business than most Greek resorts attract. Prices are correspondingly high, and the atmosphere in the resort correspondingly civilised, or bland, depending on your point of view. Governments may disapprove of young and independent travellers, but Greek island resorts are duller without them.

Skopelos is the only island of its group with more than one sizeable community; in addition to Skopelos town there's Glossa, an untouristy village in a beautiful position high above the sea in the north-west. Most ferries on their way to and from Skiathos call in, and a few peace-seeking tourists stay, at Glossa's sleepy little port, Loutraki.

Nearly all the island's accommodation is in and around **Skopelos town**, which has a mixture of village rooms and medium-sized, mostly fairly expensive package hotels. Seekers of Greece at its postcard prettiest need look no further than Skopelos town, a labyrinth of staircase alleys scaling the steep western flank of a splendid deep, sand-fringed bay on the island's north coast. This is an unusually exposed location for an Aegean island port, and the natural beauty of the setting is often lent a note of drama by rough seas lashing the harbour wall and rocks at the foot of the village. In very rough weather, ferries have to divert to the more sheltered waters of Agnontas on the other side of the island. In normal, calm conditions the incoming sailor confronts a typically picturesque scene: tourists and villagers idling on the leafy water-front and yacht masts swaying against a red and white wall of tile-roofed houses interrupted by the turrets and towers of over 100 churches. On its northern side the village terminates abruptly with a cliff wall where a series of beautiful chapels is perched above the sea like battlements along the ramparts.

The effort of exploring the heights of the village is rewarded with splendid views. The older houses themselves are interesting, with elaborate balconies and overhanging upper storeys. Unfortunately, much of the village had to be rebuilt after earthquake damage. The red roof-tiles are a cheap modern substitute for the traditional and very handsome rough hewn grey-green slates brought over from the mainland, still evident on some of the older houses and most of the churches. At the top of the town are scant remains of an old Venetian *kastro*, a couple of tavernas and a disco. A path leads down to a stony beach with a taverna. The sea is usually much cleaner than on the main town beach near the harbour.

The focus of village life is the wide water-front promenade, an attractive tree-shaded area for strolling and lounging around (there is even room for a few swings and seesaws), with restaurants, cocktail bars, travel agents and tourist shops, some of them quite sophisticated and expensive, although most of the village is uncommercial. If staying in the old part of the village,

---

Getting around

Boat-trips on offer include sailing on a crewed yacht and sunset trips to west-facing Panormos Bay. Ferry and hydrofoil services make day-trips to Skiathos and Alonnisos straightforward, with no need to go on an expensive organised excursion.

Beach boat-trips are organised to the empty islands of Tsougria (off Skiathos) and those north of Alonnisos (Peristera and Kira Panagia) as well as around Skopelos.

There are buses between Skopelos and Loutraki, and car and motor-bike hire is available in Skopelos. The single main road, from Skopelos to Loutraki, is well surfaced and very beautiful. There are rough roads to some of the monasteries in the hills around Skopelos Bay, but most of the island's interior is accessible only on foot. The road branching off northwards just before Glossa leads only to a military air base. Hiring transport does not add greatly to the number of accessible places.

---

you may need to memorise your route home carefully: navigation is unusually tricky after a relaxed evening on the water-front.

Hotels line the road that runs inland from the end of the water-front, not a very picturesque location, but convenient for the long sandy town beach, which looks better from a distance (and in brochures) than it turns out to be: a lot of rubbish and worse is blown in by the north wind and drifts around from the harbour. Relatively unobtrusive hotel development now extends most of the way along the back of the beach, the furthest hotels at least 15 minutes' walk from the port, of which they have a lovely view across the bay. Among the more comfortable hotels, the *Prince Stafilos* (B), *Agnanti* (C) and *Aeolus* (C) are recommended but probably not relevant to independent travellers, except out of season. The older *Stella* (E) and *Akti* (D) offer more basic accommodation closer to the village. There are also modern hotels in an unattractive location beside the road that runs around the back of the village up to the *kastro*. At all levels of comfort, hotel accommodation is relatively expensive.

A kiosk on the quay serves as a clearing house for room accommodation. This makes it easier to communicate with the old ladies who greet the ferries, but does not solve the problem of knowing whether the rooms on offer are near or far – an important point, given the height and steepness of Skopelos town.

The island's single road, 32km from Skopelos to Glossa, passes the main beaches, along the beautiful south-west coast, which is mostly hilly and wooded.

The most popular beach is **Stafilos**, 4km from Skopelos, at the limit of what moderately energetic tourists are prepared to walk – a beautiful narrow fringe of sand and pebble at the foot of low scrub-covered cliffs. The main drawback is the lack of space, with lots of people stepping over prostrate bodies on their way to the wider and emptier beach of Velanio, separated from Stafilos by a narrow headland. Both beaches have windsurfing and cantinas; Velanio has nudism.

The main road runs past stony beaches at **Agnontas** and **Panormos**, a fine wide sheltered bay ideal for safe windsurfing; there are quite a few campers here, both on the main beach and on more secluded coves around the bay (there's no official campsite). **Limnonari** and **Milia** are sandy, more peaceful and easily reached by rough tracks from the main road. There is a caique service between Agnontas and Limnonari. All these beaches have tavernas or cantinas and some watersports. For empty beaches, the best bet is to walk down through the woods from the road north of Panormos. Parked motor-bikes are a giveaway. There are two villages on the road which are worth exploring, and which have some fine old houses: **Klima**, which has stood abandoned since the 1965 earthquake, and **Glossa**, which has plenty of picturesque rustic human and animal life. Glossa's port, **Loutraki**, has a small stony beach and trees shading taverna tables.

Very little of the north-east coast is accessible overland, except **Glisteri** bay, about an hour's walk from Skopelos town. There is a small stony beach and perhaps a taverna in summer.

The main activities on Skopelos are visits to monasteries and villages. Both are offered as organised bus-excursions by agents and tour operators in Skopelos, and both are probably best viewed as ways to enjoy the lovely island scenery. The monasteries most often visited are a group of four on the hills to the east of Skopelos, with a rough road up through groves of fruit trees and cypresses to the mostly 18th-century **Prodromou**, the biggest and most interesting of the monasteries, high up on the eastern cape of the island. The contents are fairly typical: an icon-filled church and a brightly whitewashed courtyard and cloister with vines and flowers. A path continues around the hill and gives a fine view across the strait to Alonnisos. The nuns insist that visitors are decorously dressed and can provide the necessary drapery. Prodromou is about five miles from Skopelos, and these monasteries make a good day's hike. The two occupied ones close for several hours at mid-day.

THE CYCLADES

Andros, Ios, Kea, Kythnos, Milos, Mykonos and
Delos, Naxos, Paros, Santorini, Serifos, Sifnos,
Syros, Tinos, The Remote Islands

The Cyclades are so named (from *Kyklos*, a ring) because they
circle the sacred island of Delos – birthplace of Apollo,
pilgrimage centre of the ancient Aegean world and, in
Hellenistic and Roman times, also the cosmopolitan hub of its
commerce, a Babel populated by Greeks, Italians, Egyptians and
Syrians. But glance at a map and you will find that they don't:
the bull's-eye of the whole group is the appropriately round
island of Paros. If one wants to identify a ring of islands around
Delos, it is an inner circle formed by Mykonos, Tinos, Syros,
Paros and Naxos. Andros sticks out on its own to the north,
Amorgos to the east, and a long chain of many islands, from
Kea to the lonely outpost of Anafi via Milos and Santorini,
frames the group to the west and south. Ferry schedules
roughly reflect these sub-groupings and, obeying the logic of
the map, Paros is now the hub of all the ferry routes, the island
where most aimless travellers, who arrive at Piraeus and get on
the first ferry they see, disembark for their first taste of the
Greek islands. It is a typically picturesque place to start, and the
quayside windmill that has been converted into a tourist office
neatly summarises the last 20 years of Cycladic history.

Ferry connections feature strongly in the Cyclades, a group of
over 30 small islands which are the favourite playground for
travellers who use the ferries for a week or a whole summer of
island-hopping, moving on after a few days to change the
context of an unchanging style of holiday whose basic
ingredients are a small village, a cheap room or a campsite, a
friendly taverna or two, and a beach. It is the ideal pick 'n' mix
group, with all sorts of permutations of itinerary made possible
by the interlinking ferry services, and islands for all tastes:
spectacular volcanic scenery, busy resorts with frenzied disco life
and beaches ideal for sleeping it off, and untroubled desert
island idylls, their waters undisturbed by windsurfers and
waterski speedboats, perfect for escapists in full flight from
comfort, facilities, leisure activities and other trappings of
modern life. Part of the fun of travelling in the Cyclades lies in

sampling the remarkable contrast between the islands and their modern summer lifestyles.

Archaeologists of the future will distinguish between various styles of Cyclades tourism. The most famous beauty-spots, Mykonos and Santorini, feature on many cruise liners' itineraries, which means a daily throughput of tourists weighed down by expensive cameras and fistfuls of credit cards. Inevitably, there is no shortage of shops encouraging them to make the most of their credit limits, with jewellery, carpets and reproduction Greek vases (often very well made) at sky-high prices. These islands are famous enough to attract long-haul travellers who do not confine themselves to the June to September period: Mykonos town and Fira (the capital of Santorini) have an unusually long season, with life in the bars and organised excursions operating from Easter to the end of October.

The same islands, Mykonos and Santorini, also have international airports and lots of mainstream package holiday-makers staying in village rooms and a few new out-of-town hotels and all-modern beach resorts, although these are a much less dominant part of the island scene than on Corfu, Crete or Rhodes. Compared with the busiest resorts there, Mykonos and Santorini have come through the great tourist boom with their famous beauty, if not their traditional way of life, relatively unimpaired. Do not let talk of mass tourism put you off visiting them.

The lack of direct flights to the other islands, and the awkwardness of organising ferry or internal flight connections with charter flights arriving in the small hours or 12 hours late, keep most of the big tour operators at bay. Elsewhere in the Cyclades tourism is less organised but not always less noticeable. Paros has become the island-hoppers' capital, a natural consequence of the enormous number of ferries that call there. Naxos is almost as popular with young independent travellers and campers, and also has plenty of package tourism, mostly non-British. Sifnos is a discreetly charming favourite of discerning Greek and Italian holiday-makers. Ios became a favourite dropout place for the flower-power generation of the late 1960s and has not altogether lost the free-and-easy atmosphere and the ear-splitting noise levels of the time, although its clientele is now extracted from a fairly conventional stratum of international disco-dancing, daiquiri-sipping, moped-riding youth.

Free spirits of the present generation look further afield for an unspoilt idyll. A fair gauge of development and credibility among serious-minded island cognoscenti is whether or not

THE CYCLADES

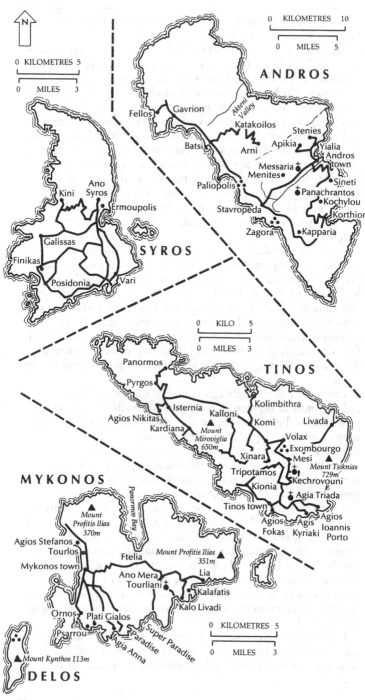

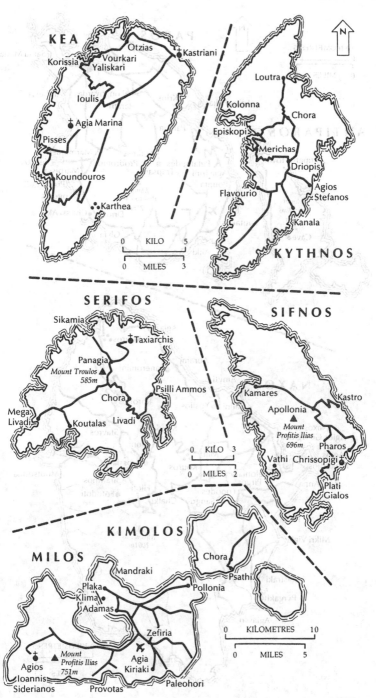

THE CYCLADES

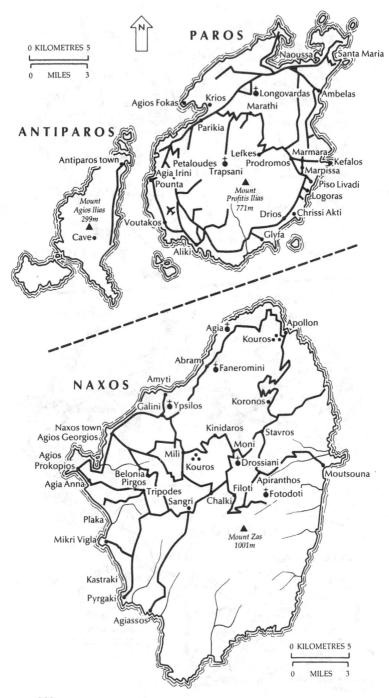

0 KILOMETRES 5

0 MILES 3

PAROS

Naoussa · Santa Maria

Agios Fokas · Krios · Longovardas · Ambelas

Marathi

ANTIPAROS

Parikia

Antiparos town

Lefkes · Marmara

Petaloudes · Prodromos · Kefalos

Agia Irini · Trapsani · Marpissa

Pounta · Piso Livadi

Mount Agios Ilias 299m · *Mount Profitis Ilias 771m* · Logoras

Cave · Voutakos · Drios · Chrissi Akti

Glyfa

Aliki

NAXOS

Agia · Apollon

Kouros

Abram · Faneromini

Amyti

Galini · Ypsilos · Koronos

Kinidaros · Stavros

Naxos town
Agios Georgios · Mili · Moni

Kouros · Drossiani

Agios Prokopios

Belonia · Apiranthos · Moutsouna

Agia Anna · Pirgos · Filoti · Fotodoti

Tripodes · Sangri · Chalki

Plaka

Mikri Vigla

Mount Zas 1001m

Kastraki

Pyrgaki

Agiassos

0 KILOMETRES 5

0 MILES 3

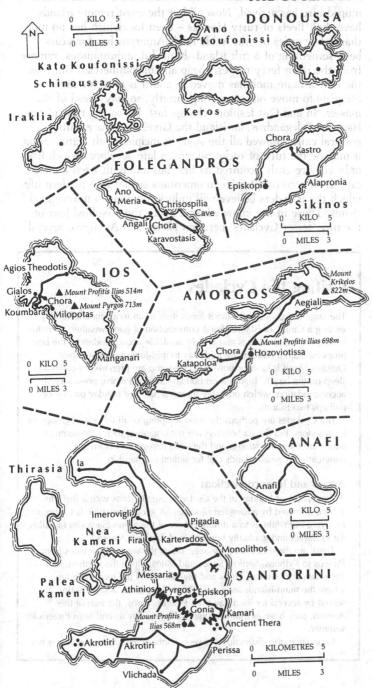

THE CYCLADES

DONOUSSA

Ano Koufonissi

Kato Koufonissi

Schinoussa

Iraklia

Keros

FOLEGANDROS

Chora
Kastro

Episkopi

Alapronia

Sikinos

Ano Meria
Chrisospilia Cave
Angali Chora
Karavostasis

0 KILO 5
0 MILES 3

Agios Theodotis
IOS
Gialos
▲ Mount Profitis Ilias 514m
Chora ▲ Mount Pyrgos 713m
Koumbara
Milopotas

Manganari

Mount Krikelos 822m

AMORGOS

Aegiali

▲ *Mount Profitis Ilias 698m*
Chora ● Hozoviotissa
Katapoloa

0 KILO 5
0 MILES 3

0 KILO 5
0 MILES 3

ANAFI

Thirasia
Ia
Anafi

Imerovigli
Pigadia
Nea Kameni
Fira Karterados
Monolithos
Messaria
Palea Kameni
Athinios Pyrgos ✛ Episkopi
Gonia **SANTORINI**
▲ *Mount Profitis Ilias 568m* Kamari
Ancient Thera
Akrotiri
Akrotiri
Perissa
Vlichada

0 KILO 5
0 MILES 3

0 KILOMETRES 5
0 MILES 3

moped hire has arrived. Now all but the most remote islands have their fleets of rusty Hondas – even Ios, which has no more than a few miles of practicable road. Amorgos has for years been something of a cult island: beautiful, mountainous, remote from the main ferry routes, cheap and uncommercial. But now the rent-a-moto mob has moved in and it is time for the escapists to move on, grumbling bitterly, to stay ahead of the masses. In and Out fashions change fast, but at the time of our last visit Folegandros, an island the Greeks associate with political exile, showed all the signs of incipient cult status. Soon it may be the turn of rocky Sikinos, a late developer which has only very recently acquired its first bus and built itself a quay capable of receiving ferries, momentous strides into modern life which the islanders believe will unlock the door to unimagined riches. Those in the know whisper about the unsullied joys of the tiny 'lesser Cyclades' between Naxos and Amorgos, several

Visiting the Cyclades

The large group of small islands lends itself to an independent holiday visiting a variety of islands. For a combination of good weather, plentiful ferries, animated villages and widely available accommodation, the best times for such a holiday are mid-May to mid-July, and September/October. April is best for flowers. Unless you are prepared to camp and sleep on the beach, high-season holidays should involve pre-reserved accommodation, which probably means a package holiday on one or perhaps two islands.

The Cyclades are perhaps the most tempting of all the island groups for keen sailors. But flotilla holidays are not organised there: the summer winds are often too strong, and the wide expanses of open sea punctuated by small islands call for skilled seamanship.

Access and ferry connections

An independent holiday in the Cyclades usually starts with a flight to Athens followed by a long ferry journey. A good alternative is to begin by flying from Athens to a distant corner of the group (Santorini or Milos, for example) and gradually hopping back towards Athens.

There are three distinct ferry axes: down the western Cyclades from Piraeus to Kythnos, Serifos, Sifnos and Milos; along the northern arm from Rafina to Andros, Tinos and Mykonos; and the remaining area, where the main islands are Syros, Paros, Naxos, Ios and Santorini, all served by several ferries a day from Piraeus. Paros, the hub of the Aegean, may have as many as eight sailings a day to and from Piraeus in summer.

In practice, the distinction between northern and central islands is not

of which have yet to receive electricity. One of the last to win a place in the island-hopper's itinerary will surely be Anafi, a remote and desolate island to the east of Santorini. Anafi features nobly in the sunrise view from the hills of Santorini, and is probably best left at that.

Tourism apart, the islands have much in common, an instantly recognisable Cycladic-ness. These are the islands of postcards and calendars, the ones that match up to what people who do not know Greece expect all Greek islands to be like. The most familiar element is the village architecture of huddled little white cube houses, their flat roofs designed to ensure that not a drop of precious rain evades capture. Individually, the houses are quite unremarkable, but when gathered together in a maze of alleys smothering a steep hillside suspended between the sea and sky they make wonderfully picturesque and harmonious villages. The islanders whitewash everything, not stopping at

important: there are daily ferries from Piraeus to Syros, Tinos and Mykonos; lots of connections between Mykonos and Paros/Ios/Santorini; and an increasing number of sailings from Rafina to the central Cyclades (Syros, Paros, Naxos and occasionally beyond, on the classless *Delos* which still has its cross-Channel duty-free prices advertised on the wall and SNCF ashtrays in the lavatories). Thus, of the northern Cyclades, only Andros cannot be reached directly from Piraeus or the central Cyclades. Even this rule is not without exceptions: some of the ferries from Syros to Rafina call at Andros.

The western islands, however, are separate and much less busy as a result. Their simplest link with the central islands is the daily Sifnos/Paros connection, a tourist boat that operates a long summer season. There are also infrequent connections with Syros and several sailings a week along the southern arc, linking Milos and Santorini via Kimolos, Folegandros and Sikinos. The *Kimolos* and *Milos Express* compete fiercely for this out-of-the-way business, operating ridiculously similar schedules and racing each other. In a scenario familiar to users of London buses, 'twice a week' in the southern Cyclades tends to mean twice in the morning followed by a gap of six and a half days. The *Golden Vergina* also visits these remote southern islands on its long journey to Rhodes via Milos, Santorini, Crete and Karpathos. Officially Kea is one of the western Cyclades, but for travel purposes it is isolated.

With so many ferries to choose from, it can be worth asking about journey times, as the ferries do not all travel at the same speed; the first to leave may not be the first to arrive.

As well as all the big ferries, there are more and more summer tourist boats based on islands and rarely mentioned in the official schedules. The *Megalohari* makes a daily round from Tinos to Mykonos, Paros, Ios, Santorini and back. The *Nearchos* jet-boat makes even longer journeys from Crete to Santorini, Ios, Paros, Mykonos and back.

walls but painting decorative patterns on the paving-stones of their streets, ships and flowers on their doorsteps, and even whitewashing tree trunks. Scores of blue or red church domes (colour conventions vary from island to island) add curves and colour to the island roofscape, and rows of tumbledown windmills line the hilltops, tribute to the cooling, sail-filling *meltemi*, economic life force of the Aegean in the days before steamships and tourism. On Mykonos it is said that the wind is strong enough to drive the mills for 300 days a year. The Cyclades are the windy islands.

Once thickly wooded, the Cyclades have been deforested, like so much of Greece, by the combined appetites of ship-builders and goats. With a few exceptions, notably Naxos, the islands are now virtually treeless apart from scatterings of olive cultivation and beach tamarisks lining the shore, casting valuable shade on the sand as the tall plane tree's canopy does over the village square, which is often simply known as O Platanos. Briefly

---

Access and ferry connections continued

The following suggestions for access to minor islands and connections with other groups are not exhaustive: for example, Naxos is not the only island with sailings to Amorgos (nor Santorini to Crete), but it has the most frequent sailings. The best island for connections with other groups is Paros, which has two boats a week to Samos and Ikaria, and a similar number to Kalymnos, Kos and Rhodes via Amorgos and Astypalaia. Tinos and Syros have occasional connections with Patmos and the Dodecanese, as Mykonos has with Ikaria and Samos.

Amorgos and the lesser Cyclades (Iraklia, Schinoussa, Koufounissia, Keros) are best approached from Naxos; Delos from Mykonos; Astypalaia and the Dodecanese (Kalymnos, Kos, Rhodes) from Paros; Ikaria and Samos from Paros; Crete from Santorini; Kimolos from Milos (caique service from Pollonia as well as ferries from Adamas); Folegandros and Sikinos from Milos, Ios or Santorini; Anafi from Santorini.

Kea's only direct connections are with the mainland. There are usually two sailings a day to/from Lavrion, served by frequent buses from Athens (via the West Airport). Connections with other islands are provided by sailings three or four times a week from Lavrion to Kythnos, once a week from Kea to Rafina, once a week from Lavrion to Andros. If you don't coincide with any of these, the best bet would be a taxi or two-leg bus journey from Lavrion to Rafina. Buses follow the coast road on the way from Athens to Lavrion but return via an inland route. Annoyingly, the Kea boat does not sail at the same times every day, despite its uncomplicated shuttling schedule. Lavrion is not a place at which to spend more time than is absolutely necessary, and it has no hotels, so try to check ferry times before turning up there. The Lavrion/Kythnos ferries

colourful in April, the Cyclades soon become parched and dusty brown for a long summer. Theirs is a harsh stony landscape, with contrasts of light as sharp as in a snow scene. The sky is unclouded, the views uncluttered, the breeze invigorating, the light famous for its binding brilliance and clarity.

'Sentimentality and woolly thinking are impossible,' wrote Ernle Bradford, contrasting the Aegean islands with the misty, green and altogether more romantic islands of the Ionian.

The Cyclades are mostly small – the largest, Naxos, is less than 20 miles long – and have very little industry, except mining, now in decline if not altogether abandoned. The islanders make a simple living from farming or fishing. Methods are no longer as simple as they were, and are even quite modern on a productive island such as Naxos, which exports a lot of food; but there are still plenty of donkeys around, carting building materials up and down the narrow village staircases, and even a few working windmills, although it is more often

do not sail on down the western route to Serifos, etc.

Rafina is a useful and increasingly busy alternative port to Piraeus. It is less intimidating for the inexperienced ferry traveller and much less unpleasant, with a number of acceptable hotels, a decent beach and excellent fish restaurants at the port. As well as the services to the northern and central Cyclades, there are several sailings daily to Evia (Marmari and Karistos).

One ferry, the *Kythnos*, divides her time between the Andros/Rafina area and the Kea/Lavrion/Kythnos area and is the main hope for connections between Kea and other islands. Unusual items on her schedule not already mentioned under Kea include one sailing a week from Rafina to Kythnos, returning via Lavrion and Kea; and one from Rafina to Kimi (Evia), Agios Efstratios, Limnos and Kavala, and back the same way.

The Rafina bus terminal in Athens is Plateia Egyptou, near the National Archaeological Museum.

Flights

Direct charter flights are possible from the UK to Mykonos and Santorini. There are flights from Athens to Milos, Mykonos, Paros and Santorini (Thira) several times a day. Airports on Naxos and Syros are promised for 1990 or 1991.

Inter-island flights operate from: Mykonos to Santorini, Crete (Heraklion) and Rhodes daily, and to Chios, Lesbos and Samos a few times a week; from Paros to Crete (Heraklion) and Rhodes a few times a week; and from Santorini to Mykonos daily, and to Crete and Rhodes a few times a week.

pride than economic logic that keeps them turning and grinding. On the smaller islands farming amounts to little more than subsistence – a few chickens running around the yard waiting for the knife, some goats, perhaps a cow, a vegetable patch and a plot of olives, all thrown together in typical Greek chaos. The island's fleet of little caiques sets off at night from the port, returning in time to send the best of the night's catch to Athens on the morning boat, while the rest is sold to early-rising taverna keepers on the quay. This job done, the fishermen sit down to the laborious task of darning their nets.

There are still farmers and fishermen on Mykonos and plenty of vignerons on Santorini, whose rich volcanic earth produces some of the best of Aegean wines. Many of the islanders persist in their traditional way of life regardless of tourism, out of a mixture of pride and mistrust of a living that has its foundations in the sand in more ways than one. The tourists arrived in a rush, bringing easy money with them. Who is to say they won't vanish just as suddenly? Besides, in many places tourist development is controlled and staffed by outsiders and the islanders see little of the action, a situation that is bound to fuel resentment. If local antagonism to tourism is as widespread as many who know the islands well maintain, most of the islanders are too polite to let it show.

Many of the islands are small enough to have only a single main village, usually set in a defensive hilltop position, where the islanders retreated from their coastal settlements during the long centuries when all the Aegean islands lived in the constant fear of attack by pirates, a period of maritime lawlessness which lasted with a few interruptions from the early Middle Ages until Greek independence in 1830. Usually these inland villages are called Chora, the village, and may be referred to in English by the name of the island followed by 'town', which should not be taken to imply anything larger than a village. In the Cyclades only Ermoupolis (on Syros) and Naxos qualify as towns. If fortified, the village may be called Kastro, for obvious reasons, but more often the *chora* has an inner *kastro* sector in it. Some of these fortress villages are fascinating and beautifully preserved – Sifnos and Folegandros are perhaps the most interesting examples of them all from a purely architectural point of view, but there are dozens of other highly picturesque old whitewashed Cycladic hill villages.

Most of the ports have been resettled and rebuilt relatively recently and can rarely match the hill villages for beauty, although whitewash, flowers and a fishing harbour can go a long way to lend charm to the most ordinary modern village. There are exceptions, like Mykonos, which was itself one of the main corsair headquarters in the Ottoman period. As on other powerful shipping islands of the Aegean, the rich captains of Mykonos built themselves houses grander than the usual basic Cycladic cubes. At Syros and Naxos the old hill villages are close to the port, which has subsequently grown to swallow them up. Many of the ports have become the main resorts on their islands by virtue of being by the sea and obviously convenient for travellers. This creates a kind of segregation, with the more reclusive islanders re-enacting history by sheltering in their old hill villages and leaving the coastal settlements to the invaders.

If the Cyclades are the essential Greek islands, it is entirely appropriate that they should have given birth to the first flowering of Greek civilisation, known as Cycladic. Stepping-stones across the sea, the islands were settled by Carians, who came from some ill-defined part of the Turkish coast. Their civilisation flourished during the third millennium BC before the region came increasingly under the influence of Minoan Crete. Important Minoan sites have been excavated on Milos and most recently Santorini, where the discovery of the buried city of Akrotiri in 1967 shook the archaeological world as violently as the eruption that buried it and shattered the island in about 1500 BC. The scale of the eruption is hard to imagine without visiting Santorini, a large fragment of volcanic crater rim which is a more graphic illustration than any eyewitness could have left. Pumice has been found at an altitude of 800 feet on the nearby island of Anafi, suggesting a tidal wave of at least that height. Volcanic ash landed on a fall-out zone of 100,000 square miles, including eastern Crete.

After the great eruption and the subsequent rapid decline of Minoan civilisation, the Cyclades came under Mycenaean, Athenian, Roman, Byzantine, Venetian and Ottoman rule before Greek independence in 1830. These are the broad and greatly oversimplified lines of the history of Greece, in which the Cyclades did not feature prominently, once the great days of Delos had come to an abrupt end in the 1st century BC, when the defenceless little island was sacked and abandoned for good. Apart from Santorini and Delos, the group is not a great area for historical sightseeing.

In terms of local history, the dominant member of the group from the Bronze Age to the War of Independence was Naxos, the largest and most fertile of the Cyclades, now one of the islands with the most to offer travellers in search of more than pretty villages, sea views and beaches. Its varied attractions include the best collection of ancient Cycladic art outside the National Archaeological Museum in Athens and the British

Museum (where the presentation of Cycladic civilisation is excellent). Naxos and Paros provided marble and sculptors to Delos and many more distant corners of the Ancient Greek world, and both islands were rich and outward-looking enough to colonise abroad; Naxos in Sicily was one of the first Greek settlements in Italy (734 BC) and, until it unsuccessfully challenged Athenian power by withdrawing from the alliance known as the Delian League in 470 BC, Naxos was one of the big independent powers of the Aegean.

When self-interest hijacked the Fourth Crusade in 1204 and western Christians sacked Constantinople and divided up its empire among themselves, most of the Greek islands fell to Venice. The Doge's nephew Marco Sanudo took control of the Cyclades, where only Naxos offered any resistance. Sanudo overcame it, bravely burning his boats on landing to inject a sense of urgency into his soldiers, and established himself and his successors as rulers of most of the Cyclades, with Naxos their well-fortified power base and Dukes of the Archipelago their sonorous title. The islands withstood Ottoman raids in the 14th and 15th centuries, but only Tinos managed to hold out against the infamous Khaireddin Barbarossa in his terrible 1537 raid. Having observed the devastation visited upon nearby Paros, the duke of Naxos of the day decided on negotiation and succeeded in buying off Barbarossa and hanging on to his ducal title for a few more years.

Even after the extinction of the Venetian duchy, many of the old Latin families kept their estates and effective feudal control of Naxos and other Cyclades, with the Ottoman overlords content not to interfere in exchange for an annual tribute. None of the Cyclades has mosques or other Turkish buildings: these are the islands of cruciform chapels with cross-topped domes. In a less characteristically Greek vein, many of the Cyclades have large Catholic minorities as a legacy of the centuries of Venetian occupation. Naxos has a western cathedral, and a very common sight is the twin-aisled, twin-domed church where Catholic and Orthodox Christians worshipped side by side in a rare spirit of harmony.

The two biggest Catholic communities are on Syros and Tinos. Syros's Catholics appealed to France for protection against piracy which arm's-length Ottoman rule could not provide. The French involvement kept Syros out of the War of Independence, and its population was rapidly inflated by an influx of refugees from war-torn islands. The new town of Ermoupolis became the busiest trading port and cultural capital of independent Greece in its infancy, and remains the only big town and industrial port in the Cyclades.

Tinos was a direct dependency of Venice and had an impregnable mountain fortress which no raiders bothered to attack. Its Venetian garrison survived until 1715, but offered little protection to the islanders, who suffered repeated raids and understandably drifted away to more peaceful homes. Nor was the island of more than symbolic value to decadent Venice. A French traveller in 1700 found a ragged garrison of 14 badly dressed soldiers of whom seven were French deserters. In Venice, Tinos was regarded as 'a place of mortification'. Its last governor got fed up and went home, where he was rewarded with the chance to ponder at length the relative merits of life on Tinos and life imprisonment in Venice.

Apart from Naxos, the other consistently prominent member of the group is Milos, a mineral-rich island half-way between Crete and the Peloponnese, with the biggest and best natural harbour in the Aegean. The prehistoric city (or cities, for there are several layers superimposed) of Filakopi has yielded some of the best of all Minoan and Mycenaean works of art, and the island capital in the archaic and later classical periods has proved no less fertile ground for the treasure-hunter. The Louvre's Venus de Milo, found by a local farmer in 1820, is only one among many great masterpieces of classical art unearthed from the hillsides above Klima and now gracing museums in Athens, Berlin, Paris and London. Of all the local treasures, not one has remained on Milos, the most impoverished of all Greek islands in this respect. All you see on the spot are shops full of cheap plastic replicas.

ANDROS

Andros is a lovely, if unspectacular, island with an unlikely combination of easy accessibility, good beaches and only a modest amount of tourist development, which is mainly confined to one busy resort. Like Kea, it is a popular place for Athenian weekenders and holiday-makers. Unlike Kea, it is in no sense a dead-end for island travellers: daily boats to Tinos and Mykonos provide a perfectly good link with the mainstream of Cycladic travel.

Apart from the beaches, the main charm of Andros is its peaceful, green and well-watered landscape, with springs and rivers that do not run dry in summer, mulberry woods, fertile valleys flanked by steep terraced hillsides, pretty dovecotes and dry-stone walls constructed in a very decorative local style, with big flat slabs of stone set into the fabric of the wall at regular intervals, creating an effect like blind arcading. Similar walls exist on other islands (Kea, for example) but nowhere to the same extent as on Andros, where they do not merely divide up the landscape but, like the terraces, positively decorate it.

Wealthy from silk production in the period of Ottoman control, which meant an unbridled feudal local aristocracy of old families who paid the necessary taxes in exchange for non-interference, Andros became a wealthy ship-owning island in the 18th and 19th centuries. There still seems to be plenty of money around, especially in the town of Andros, which fills up with huge yachts and rich kids in summer. It is said that the Andriots prefer to keep their island to themselves, and the capital, a splendidly sited village with good beaches but little tourist accommodation, seems to confirm the story. But on the other side of the island lies Batsi, a busy little resort whose summer population is as foreign (that is to say, predominantly British) as Andros's is Greek. It is an acceptable segregation, for Batsi is an excellent resort of its kind. All visitors to the island can appreciate the benefits of local wealth in the form of a good new museum endowed by a local family, which achieved a rare victory in securing the return from Athens to its island home of a minor masterpiece of classical sculpture, the Andros Hermes.

Andros is the northernmost of the Cyclades and the largest after Naxos, separated from the southern tip of Evia by a notoriously stormy six-mile strait and from the northern tip of Tinos by no more than half a mile of clear water. The island consists of a chain of mountains in four distinct masses, reaching a top height of 1000m (plus or minus a few) above the bay of Paliopolis, site of the ancient capital. At first sight, Andros does not seem impressively mountainous, but its summit is not much lower than the top of Naxos, the highest point in the Cyclades, and may even be higher; sources vary on the precise height of both peaks and suggest that they may be the subject of some local rivalry and statistical inflation. The hills drop steeply down to the sheltered south-west-facing coast, but between the mountains three fertile valleys descend more gently to the exposed north-east-facing coast. Most of the islanders live in two of these valleys and the coastal villages of Andros and Korthion at the bottom of them.

The modern ferry port is **Gavrion**, in a sheltered south-facing bay in the north-west. It is an unprepossessing place, with a wide open concrete water-front, a mess of modern buildings and just a hint of untreated sewage in the air (and more than a hint in the harbour). However, it has its advantages as a base on the island, especially for independent travellers in high season, when rooms in Batsi or Andros town are likely to be very hard to find. The clean and orderly *Gavrion Beach Hotel* (c) is run by a returned expatriate; his family are the hosts of an excellent taverna – whose menu extends the usual Greek island repertoire considerably – set back from the road out of town towards Batsi. Gavrion's shops stay open late, and there is a very good sticky-pastry cafe near the ferry quay. The existence of a campsite on the edge of the village brings Gavrion a lively young summer clientele.

The Gavrion Beach Hotel lives up to its name, for the water-front does not extend far beyond it, giving way to a long, little-used muddy sand beach with a boat-builder and a few houses, including a very attractive waterside taverna. The beach is not perfect, but fine for a peaceful morning dip.

A steep road leads up from the campsite to an impressive and very intriguing monument, the **Agios Petros tower**, unsignposted but clearly visible as you approach. Both date and function of the isolated 65-foot-tall round tower are uncertain. The beautifully cut massive unbonded blocks of masonry suggest to some experts the Hellenistic period, but the rougher stone of the bottom section of the tower, a single domed chamber, recalls Mycenaean tomb architecture and raises the possibility of a much earlier date for the original structure, later heightened to create a watchtower/beacon. An internal spiral staircase is clearly visible above first-floor level, but is not practicable.

The main road south from Gavrion passes a succession of splendid sandy beaches, with a couple of roadside discothèques and tavernas. Agios Petros beach and its Marabout disco are in reasonable walking range of Gavrion and the campsite. Much more secluded and equally sandy is **Fellos** beach, reached without great difficulty by turning left from the only road leading north from Gavrion, shortly after the surface becomes rough (Kato Fellos is signposted right). There is a colony of holiday villas emitting English voices by the beach, but neither taverna nor shade. A second sandy Fellos beach, popular with rough campers, can be reached by pursuing the track past the main beach and over the hill. Beyond Fellos, the far north of the island is rough country with a few small hill villages linked by an unsignposted network of tracks and still inhabited by Albanians, whose ancestors settled in this part of the island in the 17th century. Access to the coast and an empty beach below Ano Fellos is possible but not easy and hardly worth the bother.

The fact that the main road bypasses **Batsi** is not the least of the island's main package-holiday resort's attractions. As a small beach resort it works extremely well, with a good wide stretch of sand next to a picturesque little harbourside village on a south-facing bay, and quiet villas and good medium-sized hotels well placed for beach and village centre. The beach has tree shade and the island's only watersports, including windsurfing.

The close-knit centre has an attractive selection of bars and shops, including a sandal-maker, and steps lead up from the water-front to a street filled with taverna tables, which also encroach on the road around the harbour. There is some accommodation in this part of the village, including the original old-fashioned *Avra* (D), but most of the hotels and modern holiday villas are spread out in the area behind the beach. The *Scouna* (C) is clean and friendly and about the best of the hotels, at the far end of the beach from the village (which means a walk of no more than a few minutes). Batsi is gradually overflowing this central area, with new building on the headland opposite the village – a fine viewpoint – and up on the hill near the main road, which is also the site of the resort's discos. Some of this accommodation is a stiff walk from the village. There is a new hotel (the *Anerousa Beach*, C) along a rough track to the south of Batsi, about 20 minutes on foot. The hotel is an unusual collection of pastel-coloured, marble-floored villas and has a couple of small beaches below it, one with a bar. Caiques in Batsi harbour offer transport to these and other beaches in the vicinity.

Batsi is the starting-point for beautiful excursions across the island, either by hired car or bike, or, for those prepared to undertake long hikes, on foot. From the crest of the island near Katakoilos you can either follow the lovely terraced **Ateni valley** down to two small sandy north-facing beaches, passing a few farms, livestock and fine examples of Andros walling; or branch off right for the hill villages high up on the slopes of the island's highest mountain, Profitis Ilias. The rough road climbs as far as **Arni** (about 700m), a cool and very leafy village sprawling across the steep hillside. The road does not continue over the mountain to Andros town. There are several tavernas in **Katakoilos**, a popular place for evening outings from Batsi. Not far north of Batsi (near the Pell Mell disco), a rough road leads up to the **Zoodochos Pigi monastery**, one of the few monasteries on the island accessible by road. A few nuns inhabit the place, whose looks were not improved by extensive alterations earlier this century. The holy spring water from which it takes its name is on tap in the courtyard.

Continuing south from Batsi, the main road runs high above the sea, a magnificent stretch of coastal scenery, with distant outlines of islands to the south; the nearest is empty Giaros. A few roadside tavernas mark the point where a long series of stairs and garden paths (over 1000 steps) lead down to the site of the island's ancient capital, **Paliopolis**. Streams run and must often rush down the steep hillside; they and time have washed away all but the most fragmentary remains of the ancient city, but it is a pretty walk and there is a small beach at the bottom.

From a high crossroads not far south of Paliopolis the main road to Andros passes a number of villages as it descends. There are mineral springs at **Menites**, with tavernas under a canopy of plane trees, and **Messaria** has the two most interesting of the island's churches, Taxiarchis and Agios Nikolaos. The Taxiarchis is dated by an inscription 6666 after the Creation, which by our reckoning is AD 1158, in the time of the Byzantine emperor Manuel Comnenos. High on the south side of the valley stands the rugged **Panachrantos monastery**, said to have been founded by the 10th-century Byzantine emperor Nicephorus II. The monastery is accessible only on foot, by a steep unsignposted path.

Andros (or Chora) is a large village in an unusual and striking situation, around and on a long low rocky promontory jutting out into a wide bay on the exposed eastern coast. Despite the setting, it is not the most picturesque nor the liveliest village in the Cyclades, although the traffic-free main street running most of the length of the village is busy and colourful in an untouristy way. The most attractive of the few hotels is the old-fashioned *Aegli* (c), to the south of the main street not far from Kairis square. Few houses advertise rooms to rent.

The street ends at Kairis square at the near end of the promontory. There are cafes around an old marble fountain and staircases lead down to beaches on either side of the village. The island's extremely smart **archaeological museum** is on the northern side of the square, with piped classical music, soft lighting and explanatory notices in Greek and English; the quality of the presentation flatters the contents, which are elevated above standard local museum fare by the splendid marble Hermes (a 2nd-century-BC copy of a Praxitelean bronze) found by a farmer at Paliopolis. The museum explains and sets in its wider context the ancient history of the island and its two cities, Zagora and Paliopolis, as well as displaying objects unearthed. There are also good examples of stone carving from the Byzantine and Venetian periods. Nearby is a modern art museum.

From the square a gateway gives access to the old part of town, on the promontory itself, now a comfortable and secluded residential zone. At the end is a broad terrace with a statue of a striding figure with a bag slung over his shoulder, a monument not to the unknown island-hopping backpacker but to the unknown soldier, or sailor. A single arch of an old bridge spans the gap between the terrace and the rock where once stood the

---

Getting around

Andros is not an island where many excursions are organised, even from the busy resort of Batsi, where boat-trips are limited to visits to nearby beaches. Island bus-tours are offered, as are evenings out in tavernas with live music and dancing at Katakoilos or Paliopolis. Day-trips to Tinos can be made by using the standard ferry services from Gavrion, which allow a few hours on Tinos. Visiting Mykonos and Delos involves an overnight stay.

Bus services are based at Andros town. There are frequent services to Gavrion via Batsi, and less frequent ones to Korthion, Sineti, Stenies and Apikia.

Motor-bike hire is available in Gavrion and Batsi, car hire in Batsi and Andros (Aegli hotel). The fleet of cars for hire on the island is not large, and in July or August you will probably need to book a few days ahead. George's Bikes in Batsi (in the beach hinterland zone) make a smart and comfortable contrast to the fleet commanded by the Gavrion George, who is apt to sport a highly appropriate Rent-a-Rek T-shirt.

A Practical Guide to Andros by Alexandra Britton is on sale locally and recommended, especially to hikers for route finding.

13th-century Venetian fortress, of which little remains. Local boys egg each other on to make the daring plunge from the rocks beside the terrace.

Swimming need not involve the high dive. The southern beach is sandy and bigger but less popular than the northern beach, which has a road behind it and extends around the more sheltered side of the bay as far as the yacht club, fashionable hub of summer life in Andros, and the local disco. The southern beach and surroundings are not built up, and campers unworried by the wind and surf inhabit the rough ground behind the beach. The staircase from Kairis square is the simplest but not the only way to the beach, which can also be reached by following signs to Psestaria Paraporti, and indeed should be, for the valley floor is delightful. The Psestaria in question is a restaurant by the beach, which also boasts a shower.

The road along the back of Andros's northern beach leads on past the yacht club to **Yialia**, an attractive spot where a river runs down to a thin stony beach with a popular taverna in the shade of a tall eucalyptus. You can swim around or walk over the next headland (up the staircase past the church and down the other side through a cowfield) to a much better and emptier sandy beach. On the hill above Yialia, **Stenies** is said to be the wealthiest village on the island. Do not expect Cadillacs and swimming-pools: Stenies is a neat and tidy red-roofed hill village, attractive enough to explore on foot (motorised traffic is not allowed in), but not outstandingly interesting. Nor is **Apikia**, which has the island's main mineral water springs and a big bottling plant (Sariza). Lots of people bring their empty flagons for a fill-up at the Sariza spring and there are several restaurants, rooms to rent and hotels.

As it were one block beyond the Andros valley, the Korthion road makes a similar descent from a high western ridge to a wide eastern bay, with lush valley floor and coastal village. From a few hundred yards south of the main road junction (Stavropeda) an unsignposted path leads down to the naturally fortified cliff-girt promontory site of ancient **Zagora**, the island capital progressively abandoned (probably because of the lack of a water supply) in favour of Paliopolis after about 700 BC. Zagora has been of considerable interest to archaeologists and is well illustrated and explained in the Andros museum, an advisable preparation for a visit to the site.

Few tourists bother with Korthion, but it is a fine drive down, and the village of **Kapparia** stands among the best collection of intricate turreted dovecotes on the island, with plenty of birds fluttering prettily around. **Korthion** itself is a somnolent and depressed port with a long sand and pebble beach and an uninviting grey concrete hotel at the end of it. Most of the new buildings are unfinished and the old ones deserted, but there is one very picturesque little cafe on the water-front, where a few old men sit in the shade watching the world go by, not a very stimulating pastime in Korthion.

Visits to Andros and Korthion can be combined in a round trip by using the tortuous road around the eastern end of the Gerakonas mountain between Korthion and Andros, via Sineti. The coast is not accessible, but the road gives fine views out over the sea, especially from the lofty site of an old Venetian castle near Kochylou, which commands both Andros and Korthion bays. Very little remains of the castle.

IOS

Ios is a marvellously uncomplicated place. A steeply pitched, whitewashed, windmill-crowned hill village looks down over two bays separated by a rocky headland. One bay, an excellent natural harbour, has the island's small port, a typical functional service community. The other is filled by a mile-long, beautiful broad crescent of bright sand. It is no more than a quarter of an hour's walk up the donkey track from port to village, and no further down the other side from village to beach. A few rough tracks lead over the empty hills to empty bays and the empty northern cape, where over two centuries ago a Dutch sailor claimed to have found and opened Homer's grave and watched the poet's remains decompose before his eyes. But really there is no more to Ios than the port, the village and the beach. It is the classic picturesque small Greek island.

If you want to appreciate its simple beauty, be sure to avoid the four-month period from June to September, for there is no denying that the classic small island has now become a grotesque caricature of small-island tourism. On a summer evening the narrow village street, just about wide enough for a laden donkey, is ear-splitting, claustrophobic mayhem. No question of an evening stroll: you barge your way up and down, bracing yourself for the din as you run the gauntlet of open pub and disco doorways. This sequence of non-stop noise factories is punctuated by T-shirt merchants specialising in extra-lewd slogans and extra-explicit graphics. Queues for the tavernas and hamburger joints fill the street and add to the congestion. Down by the water, the loudspeakers of the Far Out Cafe boom out over the sands of Milopotas beach from dawn to dusk. Thousands of young backpackers pour into Ios for the summer, sleeping-bags carpet the quay and fill the campsites at the back of the beach. Vast as it is, Milopotas beach is crammed with bodies.

Ios simply cannot cope with large numbers of visitors and, with several ferries now arriving every day instead of one or two a week, there is no way to keep the numbers down. Belatedly, a certain amount has been done to create an infrastructure, but there are still nothing like enough beds, lavatories, restaurants or water to go round. Ios seems nicely full in May and October, when there are a few hundred tourists around. May is certainly preferable, not only because spring is always prettier than autumn in Greece, but because in October the locals are in a near-catatonic state resembling shell-shock after the trials of the tourist season. If nerves seem frayed, you have to be sympathetic. The island was heading for depopulation before the tourists moved in, and now depends almost entirely on tourism. From November to April it recharges its batteries in almost complete hibernation. A winter visit is not recommended.

Looking back to the descriptions of earlier travellers and contrasting them with present-day reality is an entertaining if often poignant game to play. In the case of Ios one does not have to look back far. In the 1960s Ernle Bradford could write of a peaceful, spotlessly clean backwater idyll with a unique warmth of welcome and with windmills still in use. More recently still, Lawrence Durrell wrote of calm poetry, felicitous silences and the full sleep of early childhood.

Times have changed. The great influx started in the late 1960s, and although the current visitors are mostly very young there is still something uniquely hippiefied about Ios: people with long hair play the guitar on the beach, and the air is thick with Bob Marley and ganja. Most of the time, the atmosphere is very relaxed and good-humoured, and the old men in their furry caps and baggy knickerbockers sit outside their traditional cafes in the middle of the cacophony that is an evening at the village (Chora), evidently unworried by the turn of events and revelling in the attention they attract. But there are also persistent reports of thieving and vandalism, as well as the inevitable sanitary problems that thousands of people sleeping rough create.

The port of **Gialos** is a better base than the *chora*, although it lacks charm or beauty of its own. The collection of buildings clustered around the quay and bus-stop includes a small selection of quite acceptable hotels, including the good, clean *Fragaki* (c), a tourist agency or two and a few bars and restaurants. You are much more likely to get some sleep at Gialos than up in the village, although the port does have a disco of its own. It also has a long strip of beach, nothing to compare with Milopotas but, again, quite acceptable. There is an unusually well-equipped windsurfing school on the beach and a campsite on the other side of the bay. A track along the back of the beach continues over a stony hill to a series of coves around a long rocky promontory, no more than 20 minutes on foot from the port. These collectively are **Koumbara**, Ios's so-called official nude bathing zone, although by no means the only topless and bottomless place on the island. There is a taverna and quite a few beach-sleepers. Koumbara faces west and is a good target for a sunset stroll from Gialos.

The summer lifestyle of **Chora** is its Why Not? Pub, 69 Disco, Down Under Toast Club (10 different sorts of hamburger to choose from), I Like Donkey Work T-shirts and lots more in the same vein. The village, essentially very picturesque, is perfectly viewed from an approaching boat, splashed across the steep hillside above the bay in a single brushstroke. Unless it is very hot and you are heavily weighed down, it is much nicer to walk up from the port than to take the bus, minding the broken bottles and the previous night's vomit which are now more frequent hazards than donkey droppings. The path, now flanked by holiday apartments most of the way, soon emerges on a square at the bottom of the main village street. The square has the island's bank and a hotel right in the thick of things, which

---

Getting around

There are frequent buses between Gialos and Milopotas via Chora, and a (red) bus twice a day in summer to Agios Theodotis. Daily boat-trips are available to Manganari bay, and there is motor-bike hire at Gialos.

The Ios road network is extremely limited: tarmac from Gialos to Chora to Milopotas and rough roads to Koumbara and over the island to Agios Theodotis. Not surprisingly, there is scant local demand for maps and those that do exist are extremely crude. The route to Kalamos bay in the south-east is not practicable by motor-bike and, given the comprehensive coverage of the modest bus system, the recent arrival of the rented motor-bike is pretty superfluous. The firm does good business, needless to say.

---

is probably not ideal. The narrow street winds its tortuous way up through the throbbing heart of the *chora*, widening in a couple of places to allow space for a few cafe tables to be set out of doors, but without anywhere qualifying as a spacious relaxing square. The Spyros Antonis taverna is cheap, simple and good. At the top of the village stands a collection of old windmills in an advancing state of dilapidation. There are always a few old men in traditional island costume out and about in the village by day, and staunchly occupying their traditional drinking tables at night, and the quiet streets at the top end of the village are full of donkeys. No village is more photogenic for amusing snaps to illustrate the well-worn theme of continuity and change in contemporary Greece.

The road up from the port skirts the village on its way over to Milopotas, with a town bus-stop on a rough open space, the municipal basketball pitch. As well as the No Problem cocktail bar and pension, this area has the *chora*'s best and relatively secluded hotels, the *Parthenon* (E), and *Aphrodite* (D), both clean and modern. Prices are relatively high for the category. Just off the road near the top of the path up from Gialos, the Ios disco commands a spectacular view over Gialos; the sun goes down over Sikinos to the accompaniment of classical music.

Milopotas is one of the best and most famous of Greek beaches – long, wide, sandy and carving an elegant sweeping crescent between the rocky headlands framing its bay. There is now a cluster of hotels and bars at the head of the beach, where the road arrives and buses turn; and a smaller cluster far away at the southern end of the beach. But the bay is certainly not dominated or defaced by the new buildings and, when not overcrowded, Milopotas is as lovely as ever. The bus-stop zone is now a self-contained mini-resort in its own right, with a supermarket as well as several restaurants and rooms to rent at the back of the beach, two campsites and two watersports operators. The *Ios Palace* is a smart and attractive new bungalow hotel looking down over the bay, with a handsome but scarcely necessary seawater pool. There are several simpler and cheaper hotels quietly set back in the rough cultivations behind the beach, about the most fertile part of the island.

The hub of Milopotas life is the smooth-running Far Out Cafe, with its video evenings, self-service restaurant and non-stop beach music broadcast loud and clear for all to enjoy – or not. Fortunately, the beach is long enough to escape the din and, usually, the crowds. The farm tracks lead around to the emptier southern end of the beach, preferred by unclothed members of the beach community. There is a scruffy taverna and simple accommodation.

The route to **Agios Theodotis** bay is not signposted but easy enough to follow once you find the road: turn left at the discos on the way out of town towards Milopotas, then right and left through the ruined windmills. The road runs through a beautiful landscape of rough farmland, with low walls and a scattering of olive and fig trees, and lovely views back over the hill town and sea behind. Explore this part of the island on foot and you will get some idea of what Lawrence Durrell was on about. In much wilder country to the east side of the island's spine, the track descends obviously to a good wide sandy beach with a taverna and a collection of bamboo beach huts, more picturesque than comfortable accommodation.

In the extreme south of the island, **Manganari** bay has an excellent, very sheltered beach and, a few minutes' boat-ride away on a secluded rocky cove of its own, an isolated bungalow hotel village which trades, fairly enough, on escapism: no TV or newspapers, as promised by the blurb, making a virtue out of deprivation, and certainly no exhaust fumes. There is, however, a disco. Manganari can be reached on foot overland, but it is a very long walk from Chora – at least five hours – and most people prefer to go by boat.

KEA

A Greek island holiday often gets off to a less than ideal start, with a stuffy night in Athens or a squalid one at Piraeus. One way to beat the system is to head for Kea. Instead of catching the Piraeus bus from the airport or the 133 into town, cross the road outside the West Airport and hop on the orange bus which will trundle you along the grandly named Apollo Coast through resort suburbs, smart marinas and eventually open country before depositing you beneath the famous temple of Poseidon at Cape Sounion, which overlooks a sheltered beach, a clutch of tavernas and a straightforward, adequate hotel. What better setting for a first night in Greece? A few miles north of the cape lies the port of Lavrion, home of the *Royal Daffodil of Merseyside*, which made the long journey to the Aegean in 1977 to become Kea's very own ferry under the name of *Ioulis Kea II*.

There is one big snag to this strategy: once you get to Kea it is very difficult to go anywhere else except back to Lavrion and Athens. Although it is the closest of the Cyclades to mainland Attica, Kea is isolated from the rest of the group. The problem is not insuperable (see ferry details in Visiting the Cyclades, page 000), but, if you want to combine Kea with other islands, timetables need to be researched carefully.

The ferry arrangements are both symptom and cause of the fact that Kea's visitors consist mainly of Athenians, some of whom have converted windmills into holiday homes, an admirably picturesque arrangement. At weekends and in August Kea is reported to be 100 per cent full of Athenians, but even when full it is certainly never crowded, for the island is rural, with only a handful of small villages and a very limited tourist capacity. Hotels can be counted on the fingers of one hand, and only one of them is large. Although neither overwhelmingly picturesque nor varied enough to keep many visitors amused for more than a few days, it is a very attractive little island (about ten miles by five), mountainous but much more fertile than it looks from a distance, with fig, almond and oak trees and lots of cattle on its steep terraced hillsides. No less engaging an inhabitant of the grassy slopes is a very cheerful 2500-year-old granite lion, itself well worth the journey to the island.

Most of the time the island is extremely peaceful, and it is hard to remember that ancient Kea supported four powerful city-states, which between them played an important role at Salamis, produced a number of celebrated poets and philosophers but were most famous for their suicidal habits: Keans over 70 who could no longer usefully serve the community drank hemlock.

Nor did the island's glory perish with the ancients. Writing about a hundred years ago, James Theodore Bent described how, when Piraeus was in ruins in the late 18th century, all the Turkish government and merchant ships doing business with Greece laid up at Kea, sailing up the Saronic Gulf only when summoned by beacons on the spurs of Mount Hymettus. All nations had consuls on the island. But when refugees from

Chios wanted to settle there after the massacres on their island in 1822, the Keans would not have them, and Syros, which did, took over as the 'emporium of the Cyclades'. The unambitious Keans were apparently quite happy about this, and watched without regret as the steamers sailed past without stopping; they had their acorns, milk and honey in more than sufficient quantity. They seem to take a similarly relaxed attitude to being bypassed by ferry-loads of tourists, who glide past the southern cape of the island on their way to Mykonos.

On the north-west corner of the island a narrow-mouthed but broad and very sheltered inlet, unseen from approaching boats, conceals two villages, one of which is the island's port, **Korissia**. This is an unpicturesque but cheerful little place which suffers from being hidden from the open sea and the sunset by a steep ridge. A famous 6th-century *kouros* (in the National Archaeological Museum, Athens) was unearthed near the village, but there is now nothing much to be seen of ancient Korissia. The modern village consists of little more than its concrete quay, which has cafe tables by the capstans and the necessary facilities: a few shops, tavernas and a hotel, the *Karthea* (c), modern and quite adequate. There are rooms to rent in various houses near the quay and more accommodation, including another hotel, in the building zone which is beginning to overwhelm the cultivations behind the beach; at peak times this is the only accommodation to be had. The beach is long and mostly sandy but not clean and not very inviting.

A road follows the shore of the bay past a small beach (Yaliskari) with alluring shady terraces of gum trees and a taverna. At the northern end of the bay, **Vourkari** is a colourful and very well-to-do little yacht harbour with a few tavernas. Excavations on the promontory opposite Vourkari (Agia Irini) have unearthed a Bronze Age settlement inhabited as early as 3000 BC and, in later centuries, home of Minoans and Mycenaeans. It is an attractive location, with a small chapel standing above the ruins, but not easy to interpret.

The road continues northwards through delightful cultivations of almond groves, orchards and vineyards to **Otzias** (6km from Korissia), a pretty north-facing horseshoe beach, of muddy sand and tamarisks, at the head of a long narrow inlet. Here, as at Yaliskari, there are Strictly No Camping signs on the trees, and tents beneath most of them. The community is no more than a cluster of buildings around a church overlooking the bay. Windsurfing and pedaloing are possible in high season and there is a taverna. A rough road continues along the empty and much more rugged north coast as far as the **Kastriani monastery**, which is finely set on a lofty spur but is not otherwise remarkable.

Getting around

Motor-bike hire is available at Korissia, on the way out of town towards Ioulis. There are lots of buses between Korissia and Ioulis, fewer to Otzias. Organised excursions are not a feature of Kea's tourism, except possibly from the Kea Beach Hotel. Day-trips to Sounion and Athens are possible by ferry and bus.

The island as a whole is excellent for hiking, with Ioulis a very attractive and well-placed base. Given the familiar shortcomings of the island map and the lack of signposts, some local guidance is vital, unless you are prepared to stick to the roads. Bear in mind that there are no shops or tavernas other than at Otzias. Vourkari, Korissia, Pisses, Koundouros and Ioulis. But there is plenty of pathside fruit for those walking at the right time of year.

The road cuts a red scar across the rocky hillside and there are signs of ancient quarries: red ochre was exported to Athens via Otzias and used for vase painting.

Rather than retrace steps to Korissia, it is possible to follow a rough road up over the hills to the upper reaches of the steeply pitched island capital of Ioulis, though it is more directly and simply reached by a 5km hairpin road from Korissia. **Ioulis** (or Chora) is a red-roofed old village of great charm, beautifully spread on terraced slopes over 1000 feet above the sea and commanding magnificent westward views over island coast, sea and the bare island of Makronissos. Every house has a view, and the main street could be named 'panorama walk'. The road from the port ends on a square at the bottom end of the village, which is as far as cars can go. Passing through an old gateway, a left turn leads up on to a spur with some dilapidated remains of the medieval *kastro* and, in prime panoramic position, the simple, very friendly *Hotel Ioulis* (B), which is well worth the walk up from the bus-stop and village centre. The village's one street climbs the hill in the other direction from the gate, passing a few tavernas and shops, another small hotel (the *Filoxenia*, E) and a very attractive central square with a neo-classical town hall occupied at ground-floor level by the old men's *kafeneion*. At the top of the village the street dwindles to a path, which leads on around the hillside past a cemetery to a grassy terrace, where the grey stone lion, thought to date from the 6th century BC, lies curled up among a family of goats.

The island's only other surfaced road leads southwards from just below Ioulis through oaky hill country and down to the sea at **Pisses**. Despite its unpromising name, this is one of the most pleasant places on the island, with a thick green carpet of fruit trees, olives and cypresses at the foot of the valley behind a grey sand beach, which has a few rooms to rent, a new campsite and a good taverna (beside the road several hundred yards before the beach). There are no obvious remains of the ancient city of Poiessa. About half-way between Ioulis and Pisses a track branches off right (west) to the small monastery church of **Agia Marina**, over which tower the massive walls of a ruined Hellenistic watchtower (2nd century BC).

From Pisses an unmade road continues southwards along the coast to **Koundouros**, where the *Kea Beach Hotel* (B) dominates an otherwise handsome rocky coastal landscape from a promontory. Its dreary modern block and surrounding mini-bungalows contrast with smart windmill conversions on the other side of the rocky cove. The hotel has its own sports facilities, a good swimming-pool, its own bus (which it needs) and its own very small patch of sandy beach. There are other beaches to the south of the hotel promontory, with some holiday rooms which, lacking the hotel's facilities, must be seriously isolated, although there is a taverna.

As in the north it is possible to make a circuit, returning to Ioulis by an inland route: a rough road through peaceful oak groves and farming country generally known as Kato Meria. Unsignposted paths lead down to empty east-coast coves, one of which has the scanty ruins of Karthea, the least accessible of the four cities of ancient Kea unless you have your own boat.

KYTHNOS

Of all the Aegean Islands, Kythnos must be one of the most often viewed – almost all ferries sail past on their way to or from Piraeus – yet least often visited. If few of those who pass by on their way somewhere else feel the urge to return for a closer inspection, it is no wonder: Kythnos is a dull-looking brown lump which does not improve much when set foot upon. The Romans, King Otto and Metaxas all used the island as a place of exile for undesirables. It is best known for its hot springs and was called Thermia until this century.

The waters of Loutra still pull in the sickly trade in mid-summer, and the little spa, which trebles up as small fishing-port and an increasingly popular yacht harbour, has the old-fashioned charm of a seasonal watering-place, with enormous old ladies basking in the sea in their wide-brimmed sunhats. The ferry port of Merichas is the main resort for foreign visitors and is much less attractive. The hill village capital is pleasant enough but unremarkable, and the rest of the island is empty and unspectacular, with rough tracks across scrub-covered hills leading nowhere in particular.

The standard line about Kythnos is that it can be a very rewarding place to visit if you have the equipment (fluent Greek) and the time necessary to get to know local people. This may be true. Its traditional unhurried way of life is more agricultural than maritime – the island is particularly proud of its cheese and honey – and its festivals are notoriously boisterous. One attractive feature (not unique to Kythnos) that anyone can enjoy is the islanders' habit of not only whitewashing the houses but painting whitewash ships, flowers and geometric patterns on the doorsteps and flagstones of the narrow streets.

Life on Kythnos is certainly slow, but the island can no longer be presented as unsullied by tourism. In what might be termed the Kythnos (or possibly the Leros) syndrome, Greek island tourism has reached the stage where tour operators, having opened up all the obviously interesting and beautiful islands, are now turning their attention to the uninteresting and ugly ones simply to be able to present a 'totally unspoilt new discovery' to a clientele they assume to be ever hungry for novelty. The island's single attraction, that of being too dull for tourists, has itself become a selling point.

Until fairly recently there was no more to the west-coast port of **Merichas** than a few buildings at the bottom of the Chora road, which drops steeply down to the end of the quay. Merichas has now grown into something resembling an international package-holiday resort, with an area of very ordinary small modern buildings (including cocktail bars, the Sunshine Pub, shops and tourist rooms) behind the beach and the Posidonion hotel, a big modern block already seriously down at heel, at the southern end of it. The beach is mostly pebbles and scruffy, but has an attractive arrangement of whitewashed tamarisks shading the tables of the Restaurant Breakfast, a very pleasant place at which to sit gazing out to sea while waiting for your boat to steam into the bay. The buildings lining the road immediately above the quay include the cheerful blue and white *Hotel Kythnos*, a much better bet than the Posidonion.

Before heading up into the hills to Chora, the main road passes the next bay to the north, **Episkopi**, which has a good little beach (sand and flat rock) with some shade, a taverna, windsurfing and campers. Episkopi is no more than 15 minutes' walk from Merichas. Easily visible along the coast to the north is a more unusual beach, formed by a thin spit of sand linking

Getting around

There are four or five (red) buses a day between Merichas and Loutra via Chora, and two or three (green) buses a day between Merichas and Kanala via Driopis. Motor-bike hire is available in Merichas (there's a curfew at 8p.m.). Water-taxis operate from Merichas to Kolonna beach. Tour operators in Merichas organise excursions to Serifos.

the islet (or, strictly, peninsula) of Agios Loukas to the coast of the mother island. The track shown on the island map is no more than a path; **Kolonna** beach, as the spit is known, is a good hour's walk from the road, but is usually reached by caique from Merichas. The beach has neither shade nor facilities of any kind. If you plan to walk one or both ways, take good shoes and socks: Kythnos is a very scratchy island to explore on foot.

The island capital, **Chora** or **Kythnos town** (7km from Merichas), occupies a gently rolling upland plateau in the middle of the island, not spectacular but attractively (and surprisingly, in view of the barren coastal landscape) fertile, with waving cornfields, and inquisitive cows leaning over the rough stone walls. This totally exposed saddle of land has been chosen for the establishment of modern wind and sun 'parks' – power stations of a kind, although without the monstrous generating buildings associated with the term. As well as all the little propellers turning in the wind, there are a few working old windmills. The village itself is a simple little whitewashed place with a few cafes along the main street and no lack of picturesque islanders, but little else to detain the visitor.

Chora is in walking range (5km) of **Loutra**, the island's traditional resort and, if the wind is wrong for Merichas, occasional alternative ferry port. In summer Loutra is usually the more windy of the two for it faces north-east; work is in progress to extend breakwaters, and there is a general air of messy activity, with the village's dominant institution, the sprawling spa-hotel *Xenia*, also enjoying some long-overdue refurbishment. The hotel has thermal baths, and hot sulphurous spa-water (said to be particularly beneficial for circulation disorders, arthritis, rheumatism and 'women's problems') flows out of the hotel and down to the resort's pebble beach in an open drain.

Beyond the hotel, Loutra's small harbour is tucked into the northern corner of the bay, an attractive arrangement of water-front tavernas, yachts and fishing-boats. A street climbing steeply from the fishing end of the harbour has more attractive accommodation (the *Porto Klaras* rooms, for example) than the wide main street, which leads straight back from the harbour. Dominated by the spa trade and Greek tourism, Loutra alternates between being 100 per cent full in high season, when rooms are booked far in advance, to being excessively peaceful the rest of the time. Motorised traffic is barred from the track that leads north along the coast past a series of small bays to a quiet beach at Agios Sostis, a popular walk. Less far in the other direction, there is a small fishing harbour and a littered stony beach at Agia Irini.

If the northern half of Kythnos is quiet, the south is as silent as the grave. The road across the island from Merichas passes **Driopis**, a hill village once known for its potters and roofed with un-Cycladic red tiles, before crossing the crest of the island and descending, with fine sea views (Serifos is the island in sight) to **Kanala**, a curiously soulless little modern village strung out along a rocky promontory with beaches on either side and a monastery among some pines. The main beach is on the western side (to the right as you approach) and has a taverna. Kanala comes to life for festivals on 15 August and 8 September.

Between Kanala and Driopis, on top of the island, a rough track southwards leads all the way along the hills to the bay of **Agios Dimitris**: a long and not very interesting journey with no great reward in prospect. There is no need to go all the way to the end: not shown on the island map, a manageable but very rough road leads down to the bay of **Flavourio**, which has beehives and a few cultivations at the back of its twin beaches. The bathing is better than at Agios Dimitris, but there is no taverna on either bay. Branching off the main road near Driopis, a new rough road has made it possible to reach the beaches north of Kanala, in the area marked on the map as Agios Stefanos. There are a few houses, but no shade and no taverna.

MILOS

Milos is the biggest of the western Cyclades, a useful place for travel connections, with flights to Athens from its airstrip and ferries to Santorini, Ios and Crete via the more remote islands of the southern Aegean. If that seems a prosaic way to introduce the island, so be it: there are not many other good reasons to include Milos in an itinerary than its usefulness as a staging-point. It is an island without charm, and this impression will probably last longer than the memory of a few individually interesting places and beautiful views.

Devoting a single sentence to the island, Lawrence Durrell wrote of it as 'a damnably dull hole', harsh but characteristically well chosen words, for holes are a recurrent theme. The main feature of the coastline is a vast bay which almost divides Milos into two. The coastline of sharp volcanic rock is riddled with caves like a fossilised loaf, and the hills are scarred by abandoned open mines.

If you do find yourself on Milos with time to kill, there is no need to despair, for exploration of Milos has its rewards, and not only for geologists and enthusiasts of prehistoric archaeology, although these are the groups likely to appreciate it most. Typically if unspectacularly volcanic, it has hot springs and sulphurous smells and rocks of surprising colours and formations.

Much of the ugliness of Milos stems from its mining industry, which brought the island wealth and considerable importance in antiquity, especially when obsidian, a volcanic glass of which Milos was the main source in the Aegean, was used to make weapons and sharp tools. The island was strategically placed between Crete and the Peloponnese and has a magnificent natural harbour. With Naxos, it appears to have been one of the most populous of the islands in pre-Minoan times, and its prosperity obviously continued, to judge from the very high quality of Minoan and Mycenaean pottery and frescoes and classical statues found on Milos. The Cycladic/Minoan/Mycenaean site of Filakopi was abandoned in about 1100 BC and is mainly of interest to the specialist, but the scattered vestiges of the later island capital on the steep slopes above the old harbour of Klima are beautifully situated and well worth visiting.

The mining (sulphur, alum and many other more obscure-sounding minerals) still goes on in a desultory way, but Milos is no longer the economic power it was until quite recently. The population has shrunk to a few thousand, most of whom live in the port, Adamas, and the confusing collection of villages on the hills above it. There is a small second port and growing resort in the north-east, Pollonia, but the rest of the island is empty of people and short, if not quite devoid, of interest. Milos is not a very touristy island, but lots of Greeks come home for August. Some of them may come from Soho, for Greek Street was named after a colony of refugees from Milos and Samos who made their home there in the 17th century.

The great central bay often sheltered entire navies, most

recently during the First World War. In earlier centuries it was a notorious pirate base and, according to a local guide, the largest market place in the Mediterranean for dealing in stolen goods. The overall landscape is undeniably handsome, but does not improve on closer inspection: the shoreline is littered with rusting cranes and assorted industrial installations.

The island's port, **Adamas**, is set on the north-eastern side of the bay in a very sheltered position from which the bay seems entirely land-locked. Apart from its fine views out over the calm waters of the bay, Adamas is a decidedly unpicturesque large modern village, with concrete streets, ordinary modern houses and run-down, semi-industrial outskirts, especially to the south, where the road follows the shore past a few strips of beach. About a mile from the port, these have campers, a taverna and windsurfing.

The most cheerful part of town is the harbour-front itself, traffic nuisance notwithstanding. There are several good restaurants (not including the *ouzeria* advertising Hellenic Tidbits) in the main cluster to the south of the ferry quay; the blue and white Kynigos fish restaurant is recommended and a good place for lobster, for which you should arrive early. There are hotels at both ends of town, the best locations being by the main town beach and disco to the west of the harbour (turn left on disembarking). The small sandy beach is dominated by the *Venus Village Hotel* (B), an unappealing but in some circumstances useful collection of semi-public low buildings with a swimming-pool and bar, tennis courts and watersports. There are several small and more attractive hotels near by, including the *Delfini* (a good D). Perhaps the best of an uninspiring bunch of hotels is the most convenient, the *Adamas* (B), on a bluff immediately above the quay. But in general Adamas is one of those ports where it is worth resisting the temptation to plant one's roots and discard impedimenta immediately on landing: there are several better alternatives on the island, namely Pollonia, Paleohori and Klima.

The road to Pollonia follows the rocky north coast and passes a couple of surf-pounded beaches at Agios Konstantinos, some impressive rock erosion and grottoes at Papafrangas (best seen by boat) and the site of ancient **Filakopi**, spread over a low hill overlooking the sea: there is not a great deal for the lay visitor to see on-site, although the walls and layout of three different settlements are clear enough to confirm that you have indeed found the right place. **Pollonia** is set on a fine small curving bay facing north-east across the narrow strait dividing Milos and Kimolos, a busy shipping lane with caiques and windsurfers dodging the big steamers passing through and freighters on their way to the quarries at Voudia, just around the headland to the east. The bay has a good wide stretch of sandy beach, with tree shade and even some playground swings and slides. A sprawl of residential resort development is spreading across the northern headland, whose western shore is very inhospitable jagged rock. There is not a lot to the village proper at the south-eastern end of the beach – a few small hotels and restaurants where the road runs out near the fishing-jetty. Cafe terraces overlook the bay, but Pollonia seems almost to turn its back to the sea, for the good reason that this is a very exposed place when the *meltemi* is in full cry; for much of the summer the terraces must be untenable. One restaurant has taken the unusual step of building a wall between its dining area and the sea.

The windy strait and the target of Kimolos less than a mile away has its appeal for hotshot windsurfers, and the beach has its colony of campers and Dormobiles piled high with boards and rigs for extreme conditions. There is also windsurf rental, but the place is scarcely ideal for the less accomplished, who should stick to the more spacious and safer waters of the island's main bay. Pollonia is quiet in the evening: about the only nightspot is the well-named 8 Bofort bar, a forum for gybing talk well into the small hours. Landlubbers may need reminding that Beaufort is to wind what Richter is to earthquakes. In windy weather Greeks are apt to greet tourists with a 'Bofor!' by way of conversation.

One attractive traditional aspect of the little port is provided by the comings and goings of the ferry *Tria Adelphia*, a caique based on Kimolos that makes the crossing four or five times a day, quickly tackling the choppy waters of the strait before hugging the sheltered waters of the south coast of Kimolos on its way round to the port of Psathi. This coastline is a popular place for latter-day Crusoes, who pitch tents on its small rocky coves and patches of sand. The boatman (who is quite happy for rented motor-bikes to be hauled on board) keeps an eye out as he potters along and pulls in to any of half a dozen makeshift rocky harbours if anyone gives him a wave. In calm conditions there are boat-trips from Pollonia to a cluster of remarkable rocky outcrops known as Glaronissia ('gull islands') and the Papafrangas caves.

Paleohori is a splendid series of coarse sand and pebble beaches interrupted by richly coloured low crumbling cliffs on the south coast, reached by rough road across the low central strip of the island. This is attractive, tranquil farming country and would make very enjoyable walking (it is about five miles to the sea from the village of Zefiria). There is no village at Paleohori, just two tavernas and some rooms to rent in the middle of the bay where the road arrives. There are hot sulphur springs under water at the western end: with the wind in the wrong quarter the whole bay may get a bit smelly. The name of Paleohori applies more properly to the village of Zefiria, the main settlement on the island until it was abandoned in the 18th century because of epidemics, earthquakes and poisonous fumes emanating from the ground, which killed livestock. In the circumstances, Zefiria seems a less than appropriate name. The village has been resurrected on a modest scale and its few inhabitants now look healthy enough.

Paleohori is not the only lovely beach on the long and uninhabited south coast of the island. The bay immediately to the west, **Agia Kiriaki**, can also be reached by rough road (not shown on the island map) from Zefiria and has a very basic taverna with rooms. Route finding in the agricultural hinterland is not always easy, with lots of unsignposted and identical-looking farm tracks. A wrong turning on the way back from Agia Kiriaki may bring you abruptly on to the tarmac airstrip, a disconcerting experience. Only a couple of flights a day come in and out of Milos, so you would be very unlucky to coincide with one. Further west, the place marked as Provatas has fine empty beaches, accessible with no great difficulty from the road round the main bay after the salt-pans and the turning to the airport. The mountain between Provatas and Agia Kiriaki, Tsigrados (219m), is reported by the local guide to have a crater 2km round, 'vapour wisps and hot-spots'. The road down to Provatas passes another hot-spot, a steamy cave greatly appreciated by local arthritics, apparently at its most torrid and beneficial when the wind is in the north.

The mountainous western half of the island, dominated by the considerable mass of Profitis Ilias (748m), is empty except for a few lonely farms and monasteries. The most distant of these, **Agios Ioannis Siderianos** (the 'iron-maker'), has a turbulent history. The saint intervened to reinforce the church to protect a group of islanders surprised by pirates while visiting it on festival day. A woman's skirt got caught in the door and torn off, and a pirate blew off his own hand trying to shoot people through a hole in the dome; both hand and skirt were ('until recently') preserved as holy relics in memory of this miraculous deliverance. There still remains lodged in the framework of the south window an unexploded British shell aimed at a German gun battery near by.

Exploring the west coast overland takes time and considerable determination: the main interest is the rock formations of the coastline, especially in the extreme south-west, and a boat-trip

Getting around

The island's two excursion-boats, based in Adamas, offer a similar programme of excursions around Milos and Kimolos five days a week in summer, with separate excursions to Paros and Sifnos on the other days. The long round-the-island trip takes nine hours and is much the best way to inspect the rocky coastal scenery and grottoes. Short-haul boat-trips to nearby caves and islets can be arranged from Pollonia. The caique ferry from Pollonia can be used for a day or half-day excursion to Kimolos, but the port of Psathi is of no great appeal.

Motor-bike hire is available in Adamas and Pollonia, bicycle hire in Adamas. There are frequent buses from Adamas to Plaka and nearby hill villages, to Pollonia, and a few times a day to Zefiria and Paleohori. Caiques go across the bay from Adamas to Emborio (ask around at the port).

is much the best way to see them. The main road passes a sandy beach at Hivadolimni before running out at the foot of Profitis Ilias near the very pretty monastery church of **Agia Marina**, from which point it is a pleasant walk or a very bumpy ride down to the shore of the main bay at Rivari, a lagoon sheltered by a long sand bar. The map gives hope of a cafe at Emborio, at the northern end of this long beach. A simpler way to reach these parts is by caique across the bay from Adamas.

The broad hilly promontory forming the north-eastern arm of the main bay is the home of most of the islanders. The various modern villages which almost merge on top of the hill are dull and confusing to navigate, but worth visiting. **Plaka** (or Milos) is the main centre and commands magnificent views over the bay from the terrace of its main church (Korfiatissa). The steep climb up to the chapel on top of the old fortress is rewarded with an even better 360-degree panorama. This rocky peak (280m) was probably the ancient acropolis. There is an excellent little folk museum in a restored old house near the church, and a small archaeological museum with disappointingly undistinguished works of art from all periods of the island's history, a very modest tribute to its one-time cultural fertility. The collection includes a cast of the Venus de Milo.

Tripiti is the other village worth finding; it looks steeply down over Klima. The steep terraced hillsides between Tripiti and the sea were the site of the ancient capital, whose inhabitants must have been very fit. At first glance the slopes seem empty, but the closer you look the more you find – rough ruins (including a beautifully situated theatre), rock-cut tombs and a series of early Christian catacombs (usually open in the morning, and free). A sharp-eyed farmer spotted the Venus de Milo lying half concealed under a loose stone near the theatre.

From the eastern end of Tripiti a narrow road leads steeply down to **Klima**, which in ancient times was the island's port. This little fishing hamlet has a wonderfully picturesque row of balconied houses lining the weedy shore, their ground-floor boathouses lapped by the water. Donkeys paddle their way along a narrow cobbled path to empty the village dustbins. There are a couple of patches of sand just big enough to sunbathe on and swim from, but bathing at Klima seems almost an invasion of privacy. A staircase between the houses leads up to a simple hotel and restaurant, the *Panorama* (D), after which pleasure you will never again voice the opinion that Milos is an island to avoid, except possibly in an attempt to prolong the world's ignorance of Klima and the Panorama.

The northern cape of this central part of the coast has some good beaches and spectacular rocky scenery, especially on the bay side around **Fourkovouni**, a waterside hamlet similar to Klima but without hotel or restaurant. Hikers can follow the signposted path from Plaka down to Fourkovouni and on over the hills to **Platiena**, a splendid coarse sand beach between rocky headlands (no taverna). Platiena and Fourkovouni can also be reached by rough road from the other direction, signposted to Firopotamos from the outskirts of Plaka. The far northern beach of Nerodafni is a desolate quarrying zone. On the north-facing coast, **Mandraki** is worth visiting in preference to Firopotamos, with a small beach to the east of a lovely white rocky headland. There is a village, but no shops or cafes, and no sign down from the main road.

MYKONOS and DELOS

The Aegean is a world of hard contrasts, but even by Aegean standards Mykonos is an island of extremes. The light is at its most brilliant and most dazzling reflected in the whitest and most labyrinthine of Cycladic villages; the *meltemi* is at its most fierce, powering windmills as it howls unimpeded across the low island; the landscape is dry, treeless and scattered with blocks of granite. Even the sand on the famous beaches is as harsh and abrasive as ground glass. There is also the style of the island's tourism, which is utterly immoderate, as is the local cost of living. Mykonos is young, noisy, trendy, narcissistic, gay – an intense experience for the eyes, ears and rashly exposed skin.

The basic ingredients of the small infertile island's huge popularity are an outstandingly beautiful village port, a succession of superb sandy beaches along the south coast and, perhaps, the close proximity of Delos, sacred island at the heart of the Ancient Greek world and one of the great sightseeing attractions of the Aegean. There are now a few other resorts, more peaceful than Mykonos town but dull by comparison, no more than concentrations of modern accommodation. And there is a rural interior with farms and a few monasteries; but no one goes to Mykonos for a holiday of tranquil rustication. It is the town and the beaches and the human spectacle that count.

Mykonos does not feature much in the history of Ancient Greece, but in the 17th and 18th centuries the islanders prospered greatly from trade and piracy, and established a reputation for expert seamanship. In the antiquity of Greek tourism, a full 30 years ago and more, their beautiful town attracted artists, and the notoriously canny islanders did not object to artistic behaviour and the development of their homeland into a liberated haunt of a wealthy élite, with many famous names among the clientele of Galatis, a flamboyant local couturier. Mykonos is a very different place now, needless to say: although Galatis is still in town, his famous clients have moved on to more secluded playgrounds as Mykonos has become a hugely popular package-holiday resort. The cool jazz has given way to loud disco music, but Mykonos still flatters its visitors into believing they are somewhere smart and a bit different – self-styled bistros, art galleries, much more varied and sophisticated shops than usual – and charges accordingly: prices are about double the Greek island average.

If no longer conspicuously rich, famous or arty, Mykonos people are still colourful, young and beautiful. Single-sex couples are much in evidence, but the gay aspect of the island's tourism is not particularly loud or dominant. The beauty of the village has been carefully and successfully preserved: traffic (including motor-bikes) is banned from the village centre, and there has been almost no new building. In fact, there is quite a shortage of accommodation in the centre.

Mykonos town is gathered around its harbour in the middle of a wide bay that accounts for much of the island's west coast. Fishing-boats are beached on the sand along the main promenade, and there is even a small sandy beach between the fishing and ferry sectors of the harbour, where many a weary traveller has dropped his bags for the night. In the crook of the water-front, the heart of the village is a small open square with a statue of a local heroine of the War of Independence. Restaurants and the trendiest disco-bars fill the handsome buildings overlooking this space, and their big upstairs balcony-terraces lend themselves admirably to the purpose. One upstairs restaurant, Cleopatra's, has its own swimming-pool (not filled with asses' milk).

The water-front promenade is idling territory with cafe terraces and shops including an oriental carpet merchant ('We ship everywhere') and two convincingly local *kafeneions* underneath the arches of the handsome town hall. Fishermen mend nets beside a tiny little waterside chapel where the senior of the island's two mascot pelicans now spends most of its time, pestered by children and tourists who want a flap of its wings for their snapshot. The more itinerant younger bird, sometimes to be seen as far afield as the ferry quay, is much more photogenic. The original Mykonos pelican, Petros, occasioned a famous tug-of-love lawsuit by migrating to Tinos. In a manner reminiscent of some tale from mythology, the Mykonian claim to the bird, which the Tiniots disputed on the grounds that it might be a different pelican, was solved when the visiting judge from Syros staged a mock attack on a Mykonos fisherman who had forged a special relationship with Petros. True to its name and the legendary selfless character of its species, the bird came to the defence of its friend and thus proved itself to be the said Petros. Tinos now has a pelican of its own.

Throngs of people mill around until late at night, but the water-front is marvellously peaceful in the early morning, until people start to arrive for a late breakfast and the daily exodus of excursion-boats. Local farmers, of whom there are still a few, bring their donkeys to the water-front laden with basketfuls of vegetables and flowers. On the once-fortified promontory closing the harbour to the west stands the Paraportiani, the most photographed Greek island church of them all, a cluster of chapels that seem to have melted together like ice-cream left in the sun. This organic masterpiece of accidental architecture, from which the straight line is completely absent, seems to change shape as sun and moon paint endlessly varied patterns of light and shadow on all its planes and swellings.

The jumble of streets behind the harbour is utterly confusing, tortuous and uniformly whiter than white. It is said that the whitewash is for hygiene, and the apparently random twists and turns of the street plan are designed to defeat the wind. Most of the streets are filled with shops, often on two levels, exploiting the local architecture: typical Mykonos houses have separate flats with outdoor staircases up to the first floor, their painted banisters adding some colour. Sooner or later you will emerge on a little seaside terrace between the houses, filled with *ouzerie* tables, a very wet place for a snack if the sea is anything but flat calm. To one side, inevitably known as Little Venice, wooden galleries of the finest old houses lean out over the waves. To the other, the equally famous row of loosely thatched windmills surveys the port, one of them often rigged and turning. Windmill hill, or Kato Myli ('lower mills'), is a splendid place for an evening stroll to watch the sunset. There are tavernas by the small beach below, also ideally placed for meals in the last rays, a shaft of silvery water that singles you out like a theatre spotlight. In Mykonos you will search in vain for an untouristy cheap local backstreet taverna, and may as well settle for somewhere with a view. From the southern side of the windmill ridge the modern bungalows of the *Xenia* hotel look out over a stretch of rocky coast (Korfos bay) and the main town beach (Megali Ammos), which is not particularly attractive although it too has sunset tavernas by the water.

Brightly coloured woven smocks, jerseys and bags are a local speciality, and there was a time when 'le look Mykonos' was all the rage. Old cuttings from the glossies are on display outside Galatis's shop near the harbourside square, and from them you will recognise the man himself, reclining in gorgeous finery, probably more interested in showing himself off than making a sale, unless you look very rich. In a familiar cycle, the charm of the local weave fuelled tourism, tourism gave Mykonians an easier living than they could make from weaving, and the looms were forsaken. But products that are Mykonos inspired, if not Mykonos made, still fill the shops.

The town has several museums worth visiting. The **archaeological museum** (beside the sea between the town centre and the ferry quay) has a lot of funerary sculpture from Rheneia, the burial ground of Delos, and a splendid vase (7th century BC) decorated with reliefs illustrating the Trojan War, including a horse full of ill-concealed soldiers peering out of portholes. There is an excellent local **craft and folklore museum** (furniture, costumes, textiles, musical instruments, household utensils) in one of the old houses between the town hall and Paraportiani and an equally good **maritime museum** near Tria Pigadia square, whose three wells are the traditional source of the island's water. Model ships of all periods, old maps, engravings and navigation instruments provide a fascinating insight into the nautical history of the Aegean world. A 19th-century house near the maritime museum, **Lena's house**, has been restored and furnished in period style and is open to the public under the aegis of the folklore museum, as is a windmill beside the road around the back of the town.

Most of the accommodation used by tour operators is in modern hotels and small apartment buildings (small buildings, small apartments) that have grown up around the hills behind Mykonos, whose built-up residential area now covers a large expanse, northwards to the resort of Agios Stefanos and southwards over the hill to Plati Gialos. Many of the places have lovely views and the considerable advantage of peace at night, but the small print about walking distances deserves careful scrutiny. 'Only 15 minutes' walk to the town and nearest beach' may mean stuck out half-way along the road between one and the other. For passers through, the ideal location is the middle of town looking out over the harbour, where there are three hotels, a nice trio of local names: the discreetly low-slung, expensive but somewhat styleless *Leto* (A), one of the few modern buildings in town; the *Delos*, a simple D near the Olympic Airways office; and, a miraculous survival, the old-fashioned, eccentrically run *Apollon*, surely the most expensive D-class hotel in Greece and worth every drachma.

To the north of Mykonos town, **Tourlos** is no more than a couple of small roadside beaches. **Agios Stefanos** is a more developed resort, with a handful of hotels near its beach, which is sandy and has watersports as well as an acclaimed mini-golf course. A rough road continues over the hill to an unattractive stony beach, worth visiting only for its taverna, which has a swimming-pool. The end of the road is a lighthouse in the far north-west, surveying the very windy strait between Mykonos and Tinos.

South of town, the west-coast road crosses a thin strip of land to the relatively sheltered and peaceful bay of **Ornos**. There are tavernas and expensive hotel colonies on and around the beach, which has watersports and a sub-aqua school. Boats make trips to the south-coast beaches.

Plati Gialos was the original Mykonos beach resort, a short bus-ride or a long and not very interesting walk from town. Now it is a busy resort with a long sandy beach whose only serious drawback is crowds. A lot of accommodation is crammed in along the road as it descends to the head of the beach, and there is a row of tavernas with terraces on the sand. Such is the frequency and lateness of the bus service between Mykonos and Plati Gialos that one could stay there without renouncing the delights of Mykonos by night, and it is the ideal base for excursions to the best beaches. **Psarrou** is separated from it by a small headland and is a more secluded little beach colony, bypassed by the masses who stream through Plati Gialos on the way to the beaches. Sub-aqua is advertised at Plati Gialos and Psarrou.

The classic routine for Mykonos beachcombers is to head for Plati Gialos on the bus and from there to walk along the south

Getting around

There are good bus services from Mykonos to beaches and outlying resorts. The last buses to Ornos, Plati Gialos and Agios Stefanos leave at 2a.m., to Kalafatis at midnight. Taxis operate from the central square on Mykonos water-front, where standard fares for set journeys are displayed. Lots of boats shuttle along the south-coast beaches as far as Elia from Plati Gialos, with some connections to Ornos and Mykonos.

Car and motor-bike hire is available at Mykonos (there are lots of establishments along the road running around the back of the town), Agios Stefanos and Paradise beach. Old-style Suzuki jeeps are very much the local trend.

Several boats go to Delos every day, weather permitting, all leaving at about 9 to 10a.m. Launches can be rented at Plati Gialos for excursions to Delos, cave inspections and picnic outings.

coast to the beach of their choice, metaphorically and perhaps literally shedding clothing as they go. Like an army on the march, they file along the coastal path in their hundreds every morning and file back again in late afternoon. For those who prefer not to walk, there are lots of little boats providing a taxi service from Plati Gialos, and a few from Mykonos and Ornos. In geographical order from west to east, the beaches are Agia Anna, Paradise, Super Paradise, Agrari and Elia. They all have splendid clean coarse golden sand and all have tavernas. Paradise is the best for watersports and is much the busiest of these beaches, with a good campsite, and tavernas competing loudly via style and volume of musical output, not food. There is lots of nudism on this and other beaches to the east. Super Paradise is as good a beach and much less crowded.

Agia Anna has small beaches on either side of a narrow isthmus, a small hotel and a few rooms to rent; this is a beautiful quiet beachside location only a short walk from Agios Stefanos (for buses to Mykonos) in one direction and, in the other, Paradise.

These beaches can also be reached, with some difficulty except in the case of Paradise, which is well signposted, by a series of tracks that branch off from a rough road through very attractive farming country between the airport and the island's single inland village, **Ano Mera**. This is an uninteresting place with a surprising (in being inland) big modern A-class hotel, the *Ano Mera*. The nearby **Tourliani monastery** can be visited and has an interesting display of icons and treasures. Like many Mykonos churches, its domes and roofs are not blue but rust red.

The main feature of the north coast is the fine wide bay of Panormos, fully exposed to the *meltemi*, which sends rollers crashing on to the sands of **Ftelia** beach, obvious and easily reached from the main Mykonos–Ano Mera road. For the real experts and wave-jumpers this is the prestige place on the island for windsurfing, but there are no boards for hire and just a single taverna set prudently back from the beach. The map shows roads to beaches on the north-eastern corner of the island, and these places are accessible, but the beaches are littered and stony and the roads to reach them unsignposted.

The south-eastern coast is much more rewarding, a continuation of Paradise and the other beaches of the south-west. **Kalafatis** is a lovely bay, with beaches on either side of a narrow-neck rocky headland, **Diakofti**, with a big new package hotel (the *Aphrodite*, B) dominating the main stretch of sand and a bungalow hotel above the smaller cove, another Agia Anna. Both beaches have watersports. Diakofti looks much too good a site for the founders of ancient cities to have missed, but awaits excavation. Lia is a beautiful little beach of coarse sand turning to pebbles under water, with miraculously clear water. Bamboo windbreaks have thoughtfully been set up on the beach, no doubt by the management of the excellent and unusually soigné fish taverna, who also put flowers on the tables and assemble elaborate salads. Kalo Livadi is another very attractive beach, little visited and with a pastoral accent – small cultivations behind the sand, and a few ducks and goats. There is a small taverna and windsurfing.

Delos

Conventional wisdom applauds the Ancient Greeks for choosing the most beautiful sites for their great sanctuaries. But objectively viewed, the birthplace of Apollo is disappointing, a small and unspectacular thin island (about one kilometre by five) two and a half nautical miles to the south-west of Mykonos. Legend speaks of the river Inopus as if it were the Nile; it turns out to be little more than a winter trickle. Legend speaks of Leto clinging to the boughs of a palm tree during labour; the only one there now was planted by archaeologists half a century ago. Legend speaks of the island bursting into flower when Apollo was born; even the local guidebook has to admit that 'the flora is poor'. Mount Kynthos climbs to the modest elevation of 113m. A large area of the island is covered by archaeological excavations, but there are no imposing temples erect, nothing as striking as the Parthenon or Cape Sounion.

In short, Delos does not take the breath away. Although there is plenty to see, including a good museum, it demands an effort of the imagination and, of course, a basic interest in what it represents.

To make a coherent story out of all the versions of the legends surrounding the island and the birth of Apollo is quite impossible. Delos was Asteria, a woman who took to the sea to escape the attentions of Zeus and drifted with the current before stopping to take on board another refugee mistress of Zeus, the pregnant Leto, who was fleeing the wrath of Hera in the form of a quail, according to some sources. Poseidon anchored Delos to the sea bed and made it 'visible to all' ('Delos' means 'visible') – there is some suggestion that Asteria had hitherto drifted just below the surface like a jellyfish, and had thus been invisible. Leto promised that her child would honour the island afterwards. She gave birth to Artemis on the nearby larger island of Rheneia (traditionally known as Greater Delos) and then, on Delos itself, to Apollo.

Entering the realm of fact, Delos is known to have been inhabited during the early Cycladic period (3rd millennium BC) and archaeologists have found evidence of Mycenaean settlement in the same area of the sanctuary of Apollo, whose worship and famous festivals (the Delia) started with the Ionians in about 1000 BC. Homer refers to 'the long-robed Ionians' gathering with their children and their noble wives and celebrating Apollo with boxing, dancing and song.

The sanctuary flourished in the 7th and 6th centuries BC, initially under the control of Naxos, which was the main source of statues and other works of art. The earliest of the three temples to Apollo dates from the 6th century BC. Athens later came to dominate the island, and in 540 BC the tyrant Peisistratos carried out the first purification of the island, transferring graves to Rheneia. A second purification took place in 426 BC, when it became a rule that neither birth nor death should be allowed to take place on the sacred island. Pregnant women and the dying were transported to Rheneia, the Delians' hospital, graveyard and lying-in home.

Delos was the nominal centre of political alliances between Greek states and became an increasingly important commercial centre; its festivals brought people together, its sanctity gave it some protection against attack, and it was well placed on trade routes. According to a most experienced sailor, Ernle Bradford, 'Delos is the last and best anchorage between Europe and Asia'. In 166 BC the Romans gave it to Athens as a free port, and after the destruction of Corinth in 146 BC Delos prospered as never before, with 25,000 inhabitants from all corners of the

Mediterranean, bringing many different cults with them. Strabo reports that 10,000 slaves changed hands in a day. Delos was the busiest trading centre in the eastern Mediterranean, in Lawrence Durrell's words 'the Wall Street of the ancient world'. Many houses survive from this period of great wealth, along with their lavish mosaic pavements. The good living came to an abrupt end when Delos was destroyed in 88 BC and again in 69 BC, during the war between Rome and Mithridates, King of Pontus. The island never recovered, although it remained sparsely inhabited for a few centuries and supported a small Christian community in the early Middle Ages.

Well placed though it may have been, Delos is surprisingly short of good harbours for so busy a trading place. The sacred harbour, now used by excursion-boats, is an unimpressive landing in the middle of the west coast of the island immediately to the north of the commercial harbour area, where vestiges of dockyard buildings can be identified by the water. As you enter the site, the excavation zone extends to the left and right, covering much of the northern half of the island. The main houses and monuments are identified with signs in Greek and French.

Most groups set off to the left along the Sacred Way to the heart of the sanctuary zone and on to the mud-coloured modern buildings (museum and restaurant). It may be better, if you are unguided, to start by heading right and going up **Mount Kynthos**, for this is the energetic part of the tour and gives a splendid overview of the whole site and surrounding seas. The route up the hill takes you past the theatre (3rd century BC) and houses with mosaics, mostly from the 2nd century BC. In geographical order, look for the **House of Dionysos** (beautiful images of Dionysos riding a leopard and a tiger), the **House of Cleopatra** (whose cistern is still in use), the **House of the Trident**, the **theatre** (with a large vaulted cistern in front of it, where all the precious rainfall was drained from the theatre), the **House of the Masks** and the **House of the Dolphins**. Above this area are remains of **temples** (2nd century BC) to various Egyptian and Syrian gods, the latter with its own theatre built in, and a temple of Hera (6th century BC). There are scattered ruins around the summit of Kynthos itself, and a grotto sanctuary just below it on the northern side.

Follow the path down past the Egyptian and Syrian temples to the **museum** and restaurant for a mid-visit pause. Most of the finest works of art found on Delos are in Athens, but the museum has a good selection of archaic statues and vases illustrating the evolving styles, Mycenaean ivories, a few mosaics and wall-paintings. There is not much background explanation.

Near the museum a **shrine of Dionysos** (4th century BC) is flanked by massive broken phalluses. To the north of a vast rectangular open space (the *Agora* of the Italians) lies the now-dry **Sacred Lake**, with its solitary palm tree, overlooked by the famous row of lean and hungry roaring marble lions (7th century BC) squatting on their haunches. Five out of an original sixteen are in place. The walk back to the harbour takes you through the heart of the **sanctuary** and **market area**, with extensive and confusing ground-level ruins of temples, stoas, shrines and market squares. Several shrines have been identified as the Keraton, where Theseus and Athenian youths danced the crane dance on their way back from slaying the Minotaur. The main temple of Apollo shows no sign of the huge bronze palm tree erected in 417 BC, and only the base survives of the great Apollo *kouros*, with an inscription boasting that statue and base were all one block of marble. The palm tree was blown down in a storm and brought the statue down with it, but Apollo was re-erected and a visitor in the late 17th century reported that it had been standing until a few years before his visit, when a British ship's captain, unable to carry it off, had contented himself with breaking it up and carrying off the head and other extremities. Fragments are now widely dispersed, with a hand in the island museum, a foot in the British Museum and bits of thigh and torso *in situ*.

How best to tackle a visit to Delos? The danger is that either you stroll around not bothering with the detail of what exactly each pavement or fragment of wall represents, generally hoping to absorb the spirit of the place, which you probably won't (although the lions are magnificent and the phalluses fun) or that you stumble about, nose deep in a ground plan and a dense archaeologist's guide, wondering whether the block of stone before you is the Propylaeum, the Thesmorphion or the Artemision, and failing to look at anything or give your imagination a chance to work.

Up to a point, all this applies to archaeological sites in general; usually, the objects on view are not works of art of abstract beauty, but fragments of history, clues. They need interpretation, and the site at Delos has no guides. The simplest solution is to join a group with a guide. A Delos excursion-boat ticket bought at Mykonos covers only the transport; for a guided tour go to a travel agent or tour operater.

It is a sound policy not to arrange a visit to Delos the night before: in strong winds all excursions may be cancelled. The boat-ride from Mykonos is short but can be very rough, and you should be prepared for a dousing. Trips usually allow about three hours on the island, which is about right for a leisurely tour, although the local guidebook warns that 'a closer study of

the monuments requires a stay of at least seven to ten days'!
But there is no accommodation for the general public on Delos,
and as a rule tourists have to be off the island by three in the
afternoon.

There is a good self-service restaurant on the site. Tramping
around in the sun for hours at midday can be quite gruelling:
take a hat. Also wear shoes, not sandals. There are said to be
poisonous snakes on the island, but you are more likely to
confront lizards. There is no good beach in the immediate
vicinity of the excavations, but bathing is possible near the
quay. Although Mykonos is the main base for visits to the
island, excursions are organised from a number of other nearby
islands (Syros, Tinos, Paros, Naxos), usually including visits to
Mykonos.

NAXOS

Naxos, island of Ariadne and Dionysos, is not only the largest
but also reputedly the most beautiful of the Cyclades: high
praise indeed, in one of the most famously beautiful corners of
the world. Far be it from us to dispute the wisdom of
Herodotus, Byron and James Theodore Bent, 19th-century
traveller and hero of bookish Cycladophiles. But first-time
visitors should be warned that Naxos wears its beauty modestly:
the port and island capital is no picturesque sleepy whitewashed
Cycladic charmer but a messy and often noisy market town,
with a one-way system and lorries rattling and impatiently
hooting their way along the water-front. Most of the islanders
live inland, and the main road across the island does not follow
the coast, much of which is inaccessible or scarred by mining.
The island is much too big to potter round on foot or on a small
hired motor-bike.

But the beauty is no romantic fiction. It lies in the
exceptional variety and richness of the island's landscapes, way
of life and historical interest, which add up to a deeply
satisfying holiday. There is also a vast stretch of sweeping
sandy beaches to the south of town, with real dunes and a thin
covering of tourists, many of whom are themselves entirely
uncovered. While the beauty of Mykonos is immediately and
dazzlingly obvious and can be fully enjoyed in an hour, Naxos
is an island that grows on you and to which you will return. It
is a popular island for camping, and is also an excellent place for
an out-of-season visit, not only to avoid the campers but
because it has attractions other than bathing and idling in the

sun and does not close down out of season. In many ways Naxos resembles a small Crete.

For historical interest Naxos cannot rival Minoan Crete, needless to say. But its various minor attractions give a purpose to exploring the island and are themselves unusual and fascinating. There are little Byzantine churches hidden in the olive groves; tall watchtower-houses (*pirgoi*) usually referred to as Venetian but mostly dating from the 17th and 18th centuries, when the island was under Ottoman rule, which was not intrusive; and a speciality offering of half-formed reclining marble male statues (*kouroi*) emerging from the open hillsides where they were abandoned, presumably because the stone split. Like neighbouring Paros, Naxos was much used in antiquity as a source of marble. The famous Delos lions came from Naxos, but so far no half-carved ones have been uncovered on their native island.

The landscape is a splendid tiered mixture of bare grey mountain slopes, notably the great mass at Zas, at 1001m the highest peak in the Cyclades; deep-pile dense green inland valleys of citrus and olive groves; and a wide and very fertile coastal plain extending southwards from Naxos town. Farming landscapes are not always beautiful, but this one is variegated, rolling, productive and handsome, with lovely views of the sandy coastline and the distant town set on its seaside hillock.

Naxos represents a very nice balance between work and pleasure. In town, the shops are full of everyday items, local cheeses, wines and fruit liqueurs; the standard tourist clothes, souvenirs and items of so-called popular art tend to be pushed into a corner of the store. The little bay of Agia Anna is a quiet beach resort and rural harbour used for the export of the island's prized potatoes. Heading back to town from the beach at the end of the day, on the bamboo-vaulted farm tracks, you may have to wait for stubborn cows to move out of the way, and pass farmworkers' *kafeneions*, donkeys tethered to the rail. Any tourism is too much for some tastes, of course, and there will soon be much more of it: completion of the airport is said to be imminent and no doubt will do more to the island than rupture the tranquillity of a few campsites.

Messy and noisy as it is, **Naxos town** (sometimes called Chora) makes a very good resort, with a satisfactory division between the port and fortress-topped old-town hill on the one hand and a large area of medium-sized modern package-holiday hotels on the other, out of sight but in easy walking distance of the port. Resort is encroaching on town, however: a sprawling new holiday complex (Mathiassos Village) has been erected at the back of the hill, a singularly dreary location.

Town and island's great landmark is a massive marble doorframe, all that remains erect of a 6th-century BC temple of Apollo, like a huge goalmouth on a small promontory sheltering the harbour. This promontory, once an island and traditionally held to be the place where Ariadne was abandoned by the stony-hearted Theseus, is a popular place for a sunset stroll, waiting for a ferry – and for sleeping under the stars to the strains of the latest disco sounds until shortly before dawn. Near the disco is a small bathing platform – the swimming isn't very delightful but it's shallow and sandy under water.

The water-front is a lively mixture of styles, with a cluster of tourist agencies and bars near the ferry quay, followed (in a southward progression) by a small square open to the front and a number of establishments with a more local atmosphere; some of these have first-floor restaurants with balconies looking out over the harbour, entered from the street that climbs from the square past the back of the houses on its way up into the old town.

Naxos shopping is less predictable than in most island villages, where the usual rule is tourist shops or nothing. There are shops selling farm produce, a specialist wine shop, a second-hand bookshop (greatly valued by long-stay visitors), Naxos liqueur sold on tap by the water-front petrol pump attendant, and a number of replicas of the typical ancient Cycladic figurines on sale in the souvenir shops. Originals of the genre – very engaging minimalist cross-armed figures gazing hopefully upward, perhaps at the sun – can be seen in great number in the **town museum** (closed on Tuesday), the main focal point of exploration of the **kastro**, a peaceful area of handsome old buildings at the top of the hill. The fortress walls, which date from the early 13th century, when the Venetian Marco Sanudo took over the island and founded the duchy of Naxos, are still clearly visible in many places: some of the streets pass through old vaulted and beamed gateways. Considering that Naxos is now quite a busy island, it comes as a surprise that the narrow alleys and the streets inside the *kastro* precinct itself have almost no shops and restaurants. It is a fascinating area to explore, and there are fine views from the museum terrace. There is also a medieval cathedral, very western in style, and a number of Venetian escutcheons above the doorways of the old houses, some of which are still owned by descendants of the Venetian ruling families.

Provided you don't mind a short walk uphill to your hotel, the most attractive accommodation is in the old town, which is quiet and panoramic. Just outside the *kastro* walls, the *Panorama* (c) is widely although not consistently signposted on alley walls and is close to the very well-kept *Anixis* (D), which has a small garden and leafy terrace. The *Pantheon* (D) is another friendly little hotel in the old town. It may be simpler to settle for accommodation on the water-front: the basic *Okeanis* (D) is convenient for the harbour and will usually take small-hours arrivals. At the southern end of the water-front, the *Hermes* (C) is a comfortable establishment run with old-fashioned charm and great courtesy. Unfortunately, its position is rather noisy.

The package-hotel zone at the southern edge of town is a fairly anonymous grid of streets, and the hotels are much of a muchness, all close to the long curve of **Agios Georgios** beach, which is good: hard sand, tree shade, sheltered and very gently shelving under water. There are tavernas at the northern end of the beach and various watersports. The *Glaros* (B) and *Nissaki* (C) are the most attractive of the Agios Georgios hotels.

Continuing past Agios Georgios beach, a rough road crosses the neck of a rocky promontory (Stelida) and passes the site of the airport-to-be and several campsites, considerably further from town than the 1500m indicated on signs at the port. Naxos Camping is the nearest and has bamboo shelters for those without tents. **Agios Prokopios** is a busy beach popular with the campers and has some simple accommodation of its own. The track continues southwards to **Agia Anna**, which is similar, apart from its ramshackle harbour installations. As well as the freighter traffic, in high summer there is a frequent caique service to Naxos town and to Paros (Piso Livadi). Both bays have windsurfing, and Agia Anna has a couple of small new hotels, either of which would be a good choice for those seeking a peaceful out-of-town base well placed for the island's best beaches. Building development is under way, however: not on a very major scale, but enough to make a noise and a mess.

The beaches in question are reached by sandy track over the headland that closes Agia Anna bay to the south. The coast opens out into a huge wide beach of white sand and sparkling clear water, extending southwards for over two miles to the headland of Mikri Vigla. The beach is generally known as **Plaka** and has a few tavernas and another campsite or two, ideal for those who want to be close to nature and naturism; the number of people declines and the proportion of naked increases the further south you go, and the track runs out about half-way along at a taverna in the dunes. To reach the more-or-less deserted southern end of the beach, known as **Kara**, the best way is not to approach via Agia Anna but by the main road south from Naxos to Pirgaki, turning off at the entrance to the farming village of **Vivlos**, confusingly marked on the island map as Tripodes. The road descends steeply from Vivlos, giving beautiful views, before deteriorating into rough walled farm tracks. There are occasional signposts (including one to Plaka at the main-road turnoff), but plenty of scope for going wrong. Once down among the cultivations at sea level, the bamboo and the walls conspire to make route-finding surprisingly difficult, considering the amount of beach available. Following the tracks northwards eventually brings you to the less minor farm road leading down to Agia Anna from near Agios Arsenios. This is the more conventional approach to Agia Anna from Naxos, used by the bus.

South of Vivlos/Tripodes, finding the coast is much more straightforward, as the main road runs down towards it and the farmland is much more open. The headland of **Mikri Vigla** has a rather desolate village and beaches with tavernas on both north- and south-facing sides. The first is very popular with windsurfers and rough campers, with an ideal grassy platform and some scrub trees beside one of two tavernas. By now, the escapist idyll has probably been terminated by the completion of a bungalow hotel complex that was under construction when we visited. The southern beach is more sheltered and peaceful, and continues southwards with a series of beautiful sandy coves known as **Kastraki**, the shore track here and there interrupted by farmland and bamboo screens running right down to the beach. There are a few rough tavernas and a scattering of holiday rooms (alas, no longer including Zorba's Place of Independent Feelings, now a melancholy ruin), but the coast remains in a semi-virginal state, which is pleasantly surprising and cannot be expected to last. The main road runs out on a pine-covered headland scarred by the ugly shell of what must have been an ambitious new building project, abandoned unfinished long ago. There are paths down to tiny secluded coves on the headland, and a sand track continues along a wide open sandy beach as far as a bungalow hotel that has been finished, although not to any high degree of sophistication. This is **Pyrgaki**.

The island's main road winds its tortuous way round, up and over the hills from Naxos town to Apollon, a slow, beautiful and in places demanding 54km drive, a good two hours even without stops, with full concentration required all the way. The coast road is much shorter and empty of traffic, but rough to very rough for most of the way, so not much quicker, if at all. It has its wild beauty, however, especially in wild weather, and those not averse to rough driving can make a fine round trip of the Apollon excursion.

Climbing from the bamboo-curtained coastal farming plain, the road passes the **Belonia Pirgos** – crudely restored but a fine

example of the tower-house genre. The main purpose was not
armed defence – the prickly battlements are no more than
ornament – but as beacons; the occupants could watch for the
approach of pirates and give the alert to neighbours by lighting
a fire on the roof, to be repeated across the island in a visual
chain warning. This tower-house has a commanding view of the
coast around town and also has a twin-aisled chapel in the
garden: one aisle for Orthodox, the other for Catholics.

Agiassos is signposted south from the main road (initially, at
least) after Sangri. Ten kilometres or so of rough road leads to a
quiet sandy beach with a taverna and, surprisingly, a bus, which
spends the afternoon by the beach before returning to Naxos
town in the early evening. Agiassos is a peaceful and
attractively remote spot, but somehow disappointing: the
beaches between Pyrgaki and Naxos are so splendid and
uncrowded that long excursions to this and other more distant
corners of the south and east coasts are hardly worth the
bother. From Agiassos it is possible to drive across the hills to
Pyrgaki and return to Naxos town that way. Identifying the
track is not difficult at Agiassos, but would not be at all easy if
you tried to make the link in the other direction, starting at
Pyrgaki.

The area of the **Tragea** is the most celebrated of the inland
landscapes of Naxos, a magnificent theatre of mountains
framing a basin full of olive groves, with villages pitched in a
balcony position on the slopes above the trees. Looking down on
the scene, you can pick out the domes of little churches among
the trees, but tantalisingly they disappear from view as you
approach: here, as in Plaka's rural hinterland, you can spend a
long time hopelessly lost in a labyrinth of dark farm tracks.

The biggest of the Tragea villages is Filoti, but **Chalki** is much
more attractive, with the finest of the island's tower-houses (the
Grazia Pirgos) and a handsome Byzantine church beside the road,
which skirts the peaceful old village centre. The church has good
murals (11th to 13th century) but is often closed. It is well
worth wandering briefly around the village centre, which has
fine old vine-draped houses and a cafe with a pretty, shaded
terrace.

The most easily found of the Tragea churches is the **Panagia
Drossiani**: take the left fork at the northern edge of Chalki, and
follow the Moni road for a few kilometres. The church is
signposted from the road but easily missed as you climb steeply
up the olive-covered hillside to the village of Moni, high up on
the rim of the Tragea basin; if you reach the village, you have
gone too far. Drossiani is a gorgeous and very ancient (6th- to
10th-century) little grey church, with a splendid view out over

the Tragea, and a welcome cooling tap. Pull the bell rope to summon the priest's wife, custodian of the key; if she manages to distinguish between the church bell and the sound of all the goats' bells echoing around the hills and responds, you will be able to admire (once eyes have adjusted) a mass of dark wall-paintings.

If not bound for Apollon (or if returning from there), you can continue over the hill from Moni, with a remarkably sudden change of landscape from fertile to barren rock-strewn grey, and return to Naxos via Kinidaros and the Melanes Kouros (see below).

Filoti is strung out along the road with a number of cafes and tavernas and a massive whitewashed plane tree shading tables and marking the heart of town. Filoti is the scene of exuberant festivities on 14 August but is otherwise of no great interest. There tend to be more people around than in Chalki, so this might be a better source of directions for church and tower excursions. One such target is the beautiful fortified **Fotodoti monastery**, reached by footpath from the Danakos road (signposted from the main road a couple of miles west of Filoti). The same road is the best starting-point for the ascent of the island's great peak, **Zas**. The hike is neither exceedingly long nor arduous, but the route is not wholly obvious. Unless you are guided by someone who knows the way, get as precise directions as possible. The writings of John Freely, in a guide to the island available locally and in the *Travellers' Guide to the Cyclades*, do not solve all problems, although they certainly bring one closer to places than do any available maps.

Leaving the Tragea, the road leads north through increasingly wild mountain country, passing **Apiranthos**, the third of the main inland villages. The people of Apiranthos are famous improvising versifiers, of Cretan descent. Their village, topped by a well-restored tower-house, has streets paved with marble slabs, and a small museum – but few cafes, and an even more serious lack of public sanitation.

North of Apiranthos, the road gives fine views down over the east coast of the island and passes quarries and rusty cables and pylons of lifts connected with the now-extinct emery mining industry. The old emery port is **Moutsouna**, reached by road from near Apiranthos. It is a depressing place, not really worth the long drive down from the mountains, although a rough track can be pursued for miles southwards along the east coast. The various deserted sandy beaches in this area may be appreciated by the most determined escapists, but there are no facilities and the road is a dead-end. Lionas, reached from Koronos or Skado, has a similarly desolate and abandoned air about it.

After passing a few more remote mountain villages surrounded by vineyard terraces, the road makes a long and beautiful but very poorly surfaced descent from Koronida (sometimes Komiaki) to the northern bay of **Apollon**. Somehow one expects more than a small collection of bars and restaurants waiting for the daily coachloads to be poured into them at midday, but this is more or less what Apollon amounts to, although there are some signs of fishing activity. There are also a couple of small hotels and some rooms, and a sandy strip of beach near the cafes.

Looking back from the beach, the prone form of the famous **Apollon kouros** is clearly visible on the hillside, only a few minutes' walk up from the village. The massive weathered figure, over 10m long, dates from the end of the 7th century BC, which makes it a very early *kouros*. In archaic style, the bearded figure gives just a hint of marching stiffly forward with forearms outstretched in a tray-carrying gesture. Concrete steps have been built alongside, allowing close-range inspection of the statue, which has a big crack across the face, perhaps the reason for abandonment. The intended destination for such a monumental sculpture is unknown, but Delos is an obvious candidate.

Returning to Naxos town gives the choice of either varying the interior route to compare *kouroi* or braving the bumps of the coast road. The first option diverges from the main road already described at the magnificent windswept pass and five-way junction of **Stavros**, not far south of Koronos. Naxos is signposted via Moni, a more direct route than via Apiranthos and Filoti. The route is intended to be via Moni and Chalki but, to visit the **Melanes kouros**, keep right at Moni for Kinidaros. The road runs through impressively wild boulder-strewn country, once the main marble-quarrying area of the island. After Kinidaros the road is rough; provided you are on the right road ('Kouro?' will do, or, failing that, 'Naxo?') you will eventually reach a signposted track left to the *kouros*. If approaching from Naxos, matters are much simpler: Melanes and/or *kouros* are signposted fairly consistently from the main road out of town. The only confusion lies in the fact that Melanes, marked on the map as a village, is in fact the name of a valley with several hamlets. Mili is the nearest of these to the *kouros*, which lies in a family's delightful, meticulously tended and very lush gardens near a river. They welcome visitors, sell drinks and may well hand round some fruit; this enchanted setting, at the end of a dark bamboo avenue, gives a unique charm to visiting the Melanes *kouros*.

The recumbent statue is smaller than the Apollon figure, a

Getting around

Excursion-buses tour the island daily and include stops at Chalki,
Apiranthos, Apollon and Moni. This is not a bad way to see the interior
for those not wanting the expense and hazards of hiring transport, but
hardly ideal. Apollon gets very crowded with coachloads for a few hours
at midday.

Ordinary buses (to and from Naxos town) include lots to Agia Anna;
several a day to Chalki, Filoti, Apiranthos, Apollon, Pyrgaki, Melanes,
Mikri Vigla and Agios Prokopios; and occasional services to nearly all
the remote villages. Many of these services, especially for the remote
villages, are timed to bring villagers to town for the morning rather than
to take tourists out into the country for the day, but the bus system now
well serves the west-coast beaches. If intending to use the bus to visit the
Melanes *kouros*, make sure to inform the driver who will let you know
when to get off. The so-called Tourist Information Centre (an agent) near
the ferry quay has a bus timetable on display, but the most reliable one
is at the grand-sounding bus organisation office, near the Hotel
Okeanis.

Caiques operate between Naxos town and Agia Anna hourly, and from
Agia Anna to Piso Livadi (on the island of Paros) three days a week in

---

mere 6m or so, and is thought to be about 50 years younger
(mid-6th century BC). The figure does not give as strong an
impression of emerging from the rock, being more finished and
much more mobile in the legs, one of which is broken. The
arms, however, are held tight in to the body, which has led
some experts to speculate that this may have been a funerary
sculpture, although there is nothing exceptional about
the pose.

For a fee, the son of the family will don his gumboots and a
hat and guide you up the stony hill, which is not wet but very
scratchy, to another very similar *kouros* lying on the open
hillside. The route is not at all obvious. Given any
encouragement, he will expound (in Greek) his theories about
the hill having been an ancient fortress and point out remains of
houses and boulders he identifies as *kouros* fragments.
Recognising the rare value of the treasure they have lying in
the back garden, these people seem to see *kouroi* in the most
natural-looking boulders.

The coastal route from Apollon to Naxos town is slow, wild
and largely deserted north of the village of Galini, which lies in
a beautiful citrus-growing valley, no less beautiful than the
Tragea. Apart from this landscape, the undoubted highlight of

midsummer. Boat excursions are available to the islands of Delos, Mykonos, Ios, Santorini and Paros.

Car, jeep, beach buggy, motor-bike (including some big-engined machines) and bicycle hire is available in Naxos. The Naxos beach buggy fleet is sizeable. The buggies (converted *VW* beetles) are a bit less expensive to hire than other open cars and are attractive, but should be driven cautiously: they do not handle well. Hired bicycles are cheap and useful for the immediate neighbourhood of Naxos town and the camping/beach zone around Agia Anna.

The Naxos renters place great emphasis on how dangerously the islanders drive, and do not overstate matters. In addition, the roads are in places in a very bad state: potholes; signs lacking, hidden or faded into blankness; blind corners (bamboo); unannounced narrow bridges on otherwise good stretches of road; exposed drops; and lots of buses, lorries and tractors on the main Naxos to Apollon road. There are not many petrol stations outside Naxos town: the station between Chalki and Filoti is the most northerly.

As indicated in the main text, route-finding on Naxos presents lots of problems and often consists of trial and error rather than map-reading. Fortunately, error tends to be as interesting as success.

The island guide by John Freely, available locally, is recommended. It has invaluable details on excursions (mostly hikes) to the more remote monuments.

the drive is the wonderfully romantic fortified **monastery of Agia**, not easily distinguishable from the characteristic tower-house genre, set among olive terraces between sea and mountains, with rooks circling and, often, clouds gathering over the dark hills. At such a place it is easy to understand Byron's fascination for the island. Further south, there is another empty monastery (Faneromini) and several accessible small coves, one of which, **Abram**, has a small hotel at the back of a weedy beach. There are one or two other isolated tavernas by the road, and tracks down to cultivations and the sea, but the best bathing on this coast is at **Amyti**, signposted from Galini. The beach faces north and does not lack wind-blown rubbish, but the sand is lovely and there are often genuine waves crashing in. The fortified tower/**monastery of Ypsilos** is unsignposted and invisible from the main Galini to Naxos road, but worth finding and more or less where it is indicated on the island map: explore cart tracks leading uphill not far out of Galini. There are some fairly unfriendly farm dogs in the vicinity, adding to the somewhat piratical wildness of the scene. The road returns to Naxos town along a bare stretch of mountainous coast where, according to one version of legend, Ariadne is said to have thrown herself from the cliffs rather than bear the children of Dionysos or having borne the child of Theseus.

PAROS

Paros and Mykonos were the first of the Cyclades to win exclusivity – and the sobriquet of artists' islands – and both have now evolved into very busy holiday destinations. Paros attracts a young crowd of visitors including lots of campers who swarm in on the ferries – up to 30 a day in summer. Its port of Parikia is highly picturesque. When it became too busy for the taste of the island's habitués they did not have to decamp far, for the smaller northern fishing port of Naoussa is if anything even more delightful, in fact one of the prettiest ports in Greece. Inevitably, Naoussa is also a busy little resort now, but that is the way of the Cycladic world. Neither of the two villages has lost its charm: there may be a lot of tourism, but it remains on a human scale, with caique-rides to sandy beaches, and accommodation in campsites, village rooms and small hotels, not huge blocks. Like a muted Mykonos, Parikia has wine bars with *courgettes au gratin* and piped Vivaldi, and even a Mai Thai restaurant. All (or most, anyway) is tasteful, an alluring if somewhat sugared blend of charm, quite different from the rougher magic of big brother Naxos.

Apart from the charm of the two main ports, the main attraction of the island is its dozens of sandy beaches, dotted all the way round the island but particularly good in the north and east. The landscape, if not memorably spectacular, has a tranquil agricultural beauty. Paros is a fruitful island producing good wine (not the ubiquitous Naoussa wines, which are from northern Greece) and famous in antiquity for the superlative quality of its marble, the raw material for countless masterpieces of ancient sculpture including the Venus de Milo and, more recently, Napoleon's tomb in Paris. As Theodore Bent wrote: 'Paros is but one huge block of marble covered with a thin coating of soil.' The most celebrated stone is called Lychnites, mined from deep underground shafts ('Lychnites' means 'extracted by torchlight') near Marathi. Its great quality is translucence up to a thickness of 3.5mm, compared with 2.5mm for Carrara marble. Marble brought Paros great wealth in antiquity, as did the gold-rich island of Thassos, which was colonised by Paros in the 7th century BC. Under Rome, the island's population may have been as large as 150,000, mostly slaves employed in the marble-mines (which are no longer exploited).

The island's pear-shaped outline has two chunks bitten out of it – wide bays in the north-west, occupied by Parikia and

Naoussa. A single mountain mass, Profitis Ilias, fills most of the island, climbing evenly to twin peaks (775m and 630m), visible from all corners. A road crosses the northern slopes from Parikia to a small village and beach resort on the east coast, Piso Livadi, passing the marble-mines and the old village of Lefkes, which was for many centuries the islanders' main settlement and refuge from pirates. Apart from this, the main road is a complete circuit of the island, running some distance inland except where there are villages on the sea. The surface is extremely rough in the south-west, between Aliki and Drios, a peaceful corner of the island where few tourists venture.

Parikia, a small town of 2000 inhabitants, is strung out for a long way round the southern side of its bay and is not the most immediately picturesque of Greek island villages, quayside windmill (now a tourist information centre) and blue-domed church notwithstanding. The main reason is that the water-front itself has no great charm: bare concrete promenade, loud cocktail bars and fast-food restaurants on one side (south-west) of the ferry quay, and a messy zone of garages and fishing harbour on the other, where the road leads round to sandy beaches at the eastern end of the bay. This edge of town has now seen the development of an anonymous modern beach resort (hotels, restaurants and shops) on a small grid of streets, and also has the town's main campsite.

Matters improve greatly once you head away from the sea back into the heart of the old village, which is lovely. The main shopping street heads off from the back of a small square and skirts the inner side of the old *kastro*, which occupies what guidebooks traditionally describe as a low eminence, looking out over the nightlife zone of the water-front to the west of the ferry harbour. The pleasures of exploring old Parikia are manifold: an interesting mixture of shops, handsome old houses with flower-filled balconies, old fountains at street corners, kittens playing on toy-sized chapel domes, and the pleasant surprise, just when you are beginning to tire and think yourself utterly lost, of emerging once more on the water-front near a small beach complete with shading tamarisks. The Venetian *kastro* has kept many of its old buildings and walls, including a section where ancient masonry has been used in a very decorative way, with column drums set on their sides – 'an everlasting monument to the vandalism of the Frankish lords of Paros,' wrote Bent. 'To the archaeologist who here sees temples, public buildings and theatres destroyed and turned to so base a use, the sight is one of extreme anguish.' The columns formed part of a temple on the acropolis, now occupied by the *kastro*'s main church. Ancient stonework is also visible in its walls and others near by.

Bent held no such reservations about the famous **cathedral of Ekatontapiliani**, and posterity has in general upheld his view that this is 'by far the finest church in the Aegean – in all Greece, I believe.' The name implies that the church has a hundred doors, which it certainly does not, but may be a corruption of Katopoliani ('in the lower town'). This is a fair description of its location, set back from the harbour on the north-eastern edge of the old village. Follow the road back past the hotels Kontes and Oasis, car hire offices and post office, and you will find the church, enclosed by a cloister of monastic buildings.

Ekatontapiliani is traditionally associated with a vow made by Saint Helena, mother of Constantine the Great, which came to fruition in the mid-6th century, when the emperor Justinian ordered the construction of the church under Isidorus of Miletus (one of the architects of Hagia Sophia, in Constantinople). According to legend, Isidorus left the work to a local, Ignatius, and was so provoked to jealousy by the excellence of the result that he tried to push Ignatius from the roof; the pupil hung on and both men crashed to their death. The story is alluded to in reliefs (which are not old) at the foot of the columns framing the north entrance to the church.

The church was reconstructed after earthquake in the 10th century and again in the 18th, and was described by Bent as a Babel of architecture. It now looks much more harmonious, having been thoroughly revamped in an attempt to restore its original Byzantine appearance. The interior, a haven of freshness and peace, has many beautiful old and restored pillars and capitals in the main aisle. The chapel to the left of the main sanctuary is the oldest part of the church, a Roman building coverted into a Christian church possibly as early as the 4th century, thus at the time of Saint Helena. Some Doric columns are still in place, and a Roman pavement uncovered in the chapel during the recent restoration is on display in the nearby **archaeological museum**. As well as a variety of ancient statuary, the museum also has a fragment of the so-called Parian Chronicle, an inscription detailing the history of Greece in the 4th century BC, found in the walls of the *kastro* in 1897. A larger fragment of the Chronicle, tracing the history back to the 16th century BC, was found in 1627 and is now at the Ashmolean in Oxford.

There are rooms to rent and a few small hotels in the old town, but for harbourside convenience there is no beating the *Oasis* (c) and *Kontes* (D), both of which are clean and adequately comfortable. Rattling chains and other assorted ferry-related noise might be a bit of a problem. Another obvious choice is the *Georgy* (c), which overlooks the shapeless open square occupied by a dry river bed and some gardens, set back only a few paces from the windmill. The square has some simple restaurants, but the most animated dining area is the water-front to the west, among the bars and ice-cream parlours. The Hibiscus (a restaurant) is recommended. Staircase streets lead up to the *kastro* from this part of the water-front, and the most select bars look out across the bay where the sun goes down to the accompaniment of opera, chamber music or jazz, depending on which bar terrace you chose. Simple everyday tavernas are not over-abundant in Parikia.

There are sandy beaches and an increasing amount of villa development on the northern side of the bay of Parikia, reached either by rough road or more simply by the caique that shuttles bathers across the bay. The caiques usually go to **Krios**, an attractive small beach with tavernas, watersports and a nearby campsite. For greater seclusion, wander along the shore to other sandy coves between Krios and the headland of Agios Fokas, which closes the bay.

The main road to Naoussa runs inland over low hills, passing the thriving 17th-century **monastery of Longovardas**, which commands a splendid view over the north of the island. Women are not allowed into the monastery. The buildings are less interesting than the sight of an industrious monastery in full swing: the monks work in the fields, make wine, shoes and books, paint icons and presumably find some time for contemplation.

Naoussa sits in the middle of an even wider, very serrated bay open to the north, its western shores littered with weirdly eroded boulders interspersed by small sandy beaches. As at Parikia, a frequent caique shuttle takes bathers across from the port to this beach area (Kolimbithres), where there are several tavernas, rooms and watersports. A rough road goes all the way round the western side of the bay as far as a boatyard and monastery on the northern cape, passing a campsite not far out of Naoussa. The beaches get very full, but this is an idyllic place for a walk late in the day, or for a beach stop at any time of day out of season. A chapel-capped islet sits prettily off shore, and the view across the bay is marred only by Naoussa's ugly oversized main church.

Naoussa itself has grown considerably over the last 10 years, with areas of anonymous if not outstandingly ugly resort development on both sides. But the heart of the village is wonderfully pretty, a huddle of vaulted alleys around a narrow and very congested fishing harbour, where everything seems to be on a Lilliputian scale – boats, houses, cafes and the harbour itself are all diminutive. Even the National Bank occupies a

typical little Cycladic cube house. The main congregation and
taverna area is at the back of the village, a broad bus-turning
and car-parking square redeemed by a splendid canopy of
eucalyptus. The best-located hotels are near the bridge over a
dry river bed immediately to the west of the harbour: the
Atlantis (a smart and fairly expensive C) and *Galini* (also C, but
simpler). The small town beaches are not at all inviting.

Immediately to the east of the village, a series of very shallow
lagoons offers poor bathing, but there are good beaches further
down the bay (Lageri) and even better ones (known as Santa
Maria or Chrissi Akti) on the open sea, looking across an often
windswept channel to the town and mountains of Naxos. This
dune-backed bay, which can be reached in several places by
rough farm tracks, is a favourite nesting ground for that
common summer migrant visitor to the Aegean, the all-over-
tanned German windsurfer in camper van. Signs on the beach
attempt to segregate bathers and windsurfers, and nude bathing
is forbidden.

The main road does not follow the coast on its way south
from Naoussa but runs through flat farming country. There is a
rough road alternative via the coast and **Ambellas**, a small
fishing hamlet-cum-resort with a couple of hotels, some rooms
to rent and a small sandy beach. Although most island maps do
not show them, there are drivable rough tracks along the coast
north and south of Ambellas, and a succession of very peaceful
sandy beaches between Ambellas and Piso Livadi.

About half-way down the east coast is the third concentration
of population on the island, a slightly confusing collection of
villages, of which **Prodromos**, **Marmara** and **Marpissa** are the
hillock-set originals, **Piso Livadi** and **Logaras** the seaside holiday
communities. Logaras is little more than a small sandy beach
with a couple of tavernas, one hotel and windsurfing; Piso
Livadi a lively little resort that has grown up around an
attractive fishing harbour. As well as rooms to rent and several
small hotels, Piso Livadi has a campsite, not very well placed
some way back from the port. There is a caique service to
Naxos (Agia Anna) in summer.

Piso Livadi has some sand of its own, but there are much
bigger and better beaches to north and south, easily reached by
tracks from the main road or on foot along the coastal paths. A
rough road leads down from Marmara to **Molos**, a splendidly
situated beach between two headlands, with several tavernas.
The southern headland, **Kefalos**, is crowned by the ruins of the
main Venetian stronghold on Paros, where the duke of Paros
put up his last stand against Khaireddin Barbarossa in 1536, in
full view of Naxos. Having seen what happened to their fellows

on Paros, the Naxiots decided on a negotiated settlement which cost them a lot of money but saved thousands of lives.

The most popular of the east-coast beaches is another **Chrissi Akti** (which means golden beach), easily reached by rough track down from the main road just north of Drios. The beach has two hotels, tavernas and watersports; and lots of people in season – it is the usual beach stop on island bus-tours. **Drios** itself has recently sprouted an unappealing scattering of modern holiday buildings, including a couple of small hotels. The beach is not special, but there is a very pretty old village between the road and the sea. South of Drios the coast road degenerates into rough track as far as Aliki, and it is no coincidence that there are tyre repair specialists at both places. A number of peaceful coves are visible from the road but the sea is not easily reached, except at **Glyfa** (about half a mile south of Drios), which has a cantina on the beach in summer.

Aliki is a small fishing village and straggling holiday community, busy in midsummer but with no animation at all out of season, when you may not even find a cafe open. There is a lot of small-scale new building work in progress and more important work under way to enlarge the island airport, which is very close. When large jets can be accommodated, Aliki will not be a conspicuously peaceful place for a holiday. At present the small shaded sandy beach where the road runs down to the harbour is not unattractive: you can imagine worse places for an enforced halt while a puncture is repaired. Should you wish or be obliged to prolong the halt overnight, the newly refurbished harbourside *Hotel Angelika* (c) awaits.

As usual on the island, the main road does not follow the coast between Aliki and Pounta, but there is a rough farm track nearer to the sea, running through some of the most fertile country on the island. **Voutakos** is a very secluded and smart colony of private villas which do not quite preclude access to a thin sandy beach looking across the channel at the hills of Antiparos. There is no taverna. The channel is at its narrowest, less than a mile, at its northern end, where caiques shuttle to and fro between Antiparos port and the small village of Pounta, which has a big modern hotel complex but no great merit as a resort.

Of the beaches accessible from the Parikia/Pounta road, much the prettiest are the two adjacent sandy coves collectively known as **Agia Irini**, which between them can boast palm trees, watersports, a summer taverna, a makeshift campsite and fine views out over Antiparos. The other main beach on this stretch of coast is **Parasporos**, only about a mile and a half from Parikia. The beach has good sand and is a popular place for nude

---

Getting around

Paros: Roads, Trails and Beaches by Jeffrey Carson and James Clark is available locally and very useful, delivering what it promises admirably: a meticulous catalogue of just about every rough track and patch of beach on the island. It also has the only reliable map of the island (and of Antiparos, described in the section on the Remote Islands; see page 479).

Car and motor-bike hire is possible at Parikia, Naoussa and Drios. There are frequent buses from Paros (near the ferry quay) to Naoussa and to Drios via Lefkes, Piso Livadi and nearby villages; and a few a day to Aliki and to Pounta (separate buses).

Excursions are organised from Parikia and Naoussa: bus-tours of the island, including visits to Lefkes, the marble quarries, Petaloudes and Chrissi Akti beach; donkey rides to Petaloudes; fishing trips from Parikia; and boat-trips to Antiparos, Santorini, Naxos, Delos and Mykonos.

---

bathing. There is a campsite a few minutes' walk from the beach.

Like Rhodes, Paros has its Butterfly (more accurately moth) Valley (**Petaloudes**), a luxuriantly vegetated hillside looking out over Pounta and Antiparos. The moths, which are attracted by the presence of running water, are likely to be in residence from May to August. The site, a beautifully kept private garden, is signposted from the main road between Pounta and Aliki, but can also be reached by minor road over the hills from Parikia. It features prominently on organised excursions from Parikia, both as part of a round-the-island bus-tour and as a target for a donkey ride.

The road across the island is not only the quickest way from Parikia to the busiest east-coast beaches; it also runs through very attractive and fertile hill country and passes the old marble quarries, three deep shafts at the base of a hillside just outside Marathi, not signposted. The miners worked with lamps to extract the raw material for many of the greatest masterpieces of Ancient Greek sculpture and if you want to inspect the shafts you should take a torch. Some ancient relief carving can still be made out.

Lefkes, the highest village on the island and its capital during the period of Ottoman rule, has now regained some of its former glory as the standard picturesque hill village stop on an island tour, and even boasts a comfortable hotel. The village has lashings of leafy charm and fine views over the east coast, which is about an hour and a half's walk from Lefkes by the old road.

Panorama collectors will be tempted by the ascent of Profitis Ilias (771m), a not unduly arduous hike of about half an hour from a point near a quarry above the Trapsana monastery. The monastery is signposted from the main road, but the path is not. The thrill of conquest and all-embracing views is compromised by the presence of an army communications system on the summit.

SANTORINI (THERA)

Santorini is one of the wonders of the world, a breathtakingly spectacular fragment of gigantic volcanic crater that lies at the heart of one of the great riddles of history. Did the great eruption of Santorini destroy the Minoan civilisation of Crete? Was Crete, or even Santorini itself, the lost Atlantis? Neither a visit to the island nor prolonged study of all the voluminous scholarship surrounding it will answer these questions, but the clues and the arguments are fascinating. Here, at least, no one could complain that ancient history, geology and archaeology are dry subjects.

Santorini has busy beach resorts with the usual range of nightlife and watersports of a very popular Mediterranean holiday spot, but it is not the most obvious choice for a cheerful relaxing island holiday, even if you are not put off by the inevitable consequences of fame (swarms of tourists and high prices). Volcanoes have their fascination, and it is interesting to observe and participate in the paradox of man's perverse determination to inhabit places where nature seems so profoundly hostile. But the sight on view is destruction, and the island could not be described as attractive. The rock wears the satanic red and black colours of fire and darkness. Even the beaches are black. It is easy to sense a hint of desperation in the nightly revelry at Fira, the island's capital and main resort, which sits precariously on the very rim of the crater nearly

---

Place-names are a matter of some confusion on the island, which picked up the name Santorini, a corruption of Saint Irene, in the early Middle Ages. The ancient name of Thera or Thira has now officially been reinstated: don't expect to find Santorini on any flight schedules. To add to the muddle the town is called Fira (or Phira). Ancient Thera refers to the archaeological site in the south-east of the island. The northern village of Ia is often written Oia.

1000 feet above the sea. Whether because of the thoughts provoked or the sulphur in the air, Santorini is not a place for sound sleep and sweet dreams.

When an eruption split the island in 1500 BC, water flooded in to fill the *caldera*, as the crater is properly termed, to a depth of 1250 feet. The tidal waves resulting from this tremendous displacement devastated a much wider area than the deluge of huge basalt rocks and volcanic ash which covered the island. The ash, over 100 feet thick in places, set into pumice and pozzuolana, a rock much used for underwater and waterside building. In the days before tourism, this rock was one of the mainstays of Santorini's economy. It was quarrying at the time of the building of the Suez Canal that first revealed evidence of prehistoric settlements.

Earthquake and eruption are not confined to prehistory. Santorini erupted many times before the great cataclysm, and has erupted violently many times since. A long period of eruptions in the early 18th century first threw up the small island of Nea Kameni in the middle of the *caldera*. The rock of this island is still raw, black and hot, bits of pumice float in the water, and green sulphurous deposits in its own little crater still smell and smoke. In 1956 severe earthquakes shattered Santorini's two main towns, Fira and Ia, and killed 48 of the few inhabitants who had not fled at the first tremors. Many of the ruined houses remain as the earthquake left them, broken shells that give the steep upper slopes of the *caldera* wall the look of a smashed honeycomb.

After the great eruption, what remained above the water was the eastern half of the outside of the cone, a crescent with cliffs of up to 1000 feet on its inner side. The cliff face is an extraordinary sight, with strata of black, red, chocolate and sandy brown from all the different eras of volcanic activity. On top stand two brilliant white villages, blobs of cream topping on the chocolate cake: Ia, on the extreme north-western tip of the island, and Fira, in the middle. Along most of its longer eastern coast, the island slopes more gently down to the sea, with terraces of vines, figs and vegetable cultivation. There is very little water, but the rich volcanic earth is extremely fertile. On the western side of the *caldera* the island of Thirasia is another much smaller fragment of cone, with a similar arrangement of inner cliff wall facing Fira and a village on top, reached by a steep path from the sea.

Most holiday-makers now arrive at Santorini by air. As so often, the traditional way of doing things is infinitely preferable, sailing in to the *caldera* between Ia and Thirasia, ideally at sunset, which brings out the full splendour of the rock colours. Unfortunately, Santorini's position, a good 12 hours' sail from Piraeus, means that most ferries arrive by night; nor do many of them pause at the foot of the cliffs below Fira in the time-honoured way to transfer passengers into little bumboats which shuttle them to the old port, where donkey teams wait for the hairpin path up to the town. The more usual modern procedure is an ordinary docking a few miles to the south at the new port of Athinios, a few miles to the south of Fira, followed by an uncomfortable bus-ride up the hairpin road to a messy square without a view at the back end of town.

If you do get the chance to stop at the old port, you will certainly be accosted by donkey drivers ('Muli? Muli?') in much the same way that room touts hustle for business on other islands. The donkey drivers of Santorini have a reputation for extortion, but their position has been greatly weakened by the installation of a telecabin, which makes the journey from port to town much more quickly and comfortably and infinitely less picturesquely than by mule. Check the price of the lift before opening negotiations with a mule driver, who can probably be beaten down to a price not much higher than the lift fare. Any temptation to walk up the 600-odd stairs is best resisted: not only is it a steep and long climb, but the drivers have ways of punishing pedestrians, encouraging their beasts to harass and brush them aside. The staircase is also inches deep in donkey droppings in some places, which does not add to the pleasure of a walk. The donkeys stop and turn at about stair 500, where the malodorous carpet is exceptionally thick; most people dismount here, but it is possible to continue on up along the narrow and more extreme track that forks left past Zorba's taverna to the telecabin station. Prices for going down by donkey are attractive, but the ride is much more uncomfortable and possibly alarming, with the donkeys swinging wide at every hairpin to give their riders a plunging view of the sheer drop down to the sea.

Most of the building of **Fira**, and its imposing cathedral, post-date the 1956 earthquake. But such is the beauty of the town's location that any shortcomings of its architecture go unnoticed. Besides, the style of the building is typical Cycladic and the village nicely huddled and car-free. At sunset, everyone gathers on the panoramic street that runs along the top of the cliffs to watch the sun drop neatly down to the sea between the two islands on the other side of the *caldera*. The cliffs do not drop away sheer from this street, and the town is built into the steep slopes below, with church domes and cube houses and threading staircases falling away. Outlined against the sea and sky, this sight of the town is about the most familiar of all Greek views, a well-worn cover shot. Many of the houses are hotels and restaurants with roof terraces and even swimming-pools, and all have the same fantastic view. Prices for the hotels with a view are unsurprisingly very high in season, but probably worth incurring if you get the chance. The *Lucas* (D) and *Cavalari* (C) are recommended. The town's top hotel, the *Atlantis* (A) has the best position of all but is ridiculously overpriced, even by local standards, for no great luxury. The slopes below the Atlantis at the southern end of Fira are relatively tranquil, very picturesque wandering territory and a good area for inexpensive panoramic accommodation, like the simple *Keti* (E) and *Villa Renos* rooms.

The heart of the village is strung out along the crater rim, no more than a few alleys wide. The main centre is between the top of the staircase and the bus-stop square at the back; this is the main tourist shopping area, with a couple of streets running off northwards from the central thoroughfare. Not surprisingly, since this is the traditional way into town for those decanted from ferries and cruise liners, all the expensive shops flank this main axis and the upper reaches of the staircase itself. Goods include lace, expensive clothes, carpets, leather, jewellery and volcanic stones, paintings and, of course, reproduction 'Greek art'. Some of this is good and very expensive, and includes reproductions of the Minoan wall-paintings from Akrotiri. Nor is it hard to find the usual run-of-the-mill junk items – orgiastic painted vases and thrusting satyrs. Apart from the local stone, the most interesting local product is wine, some of which is very strong. Despite the attractions of such predictable brand names as Vulcan and Inferno, the best is simple Santorini white. There is one very picturesque backstreet shop where local wines can be tasted and bought quite cheaply. The proprietor of one of the wine firms, Halaris, also runs the best restaurant in town, the Galaxy. On the main everyday shopping street, Nikolaos is about the cheapest place and always very busy. At the other end of the scale, there are various expensive credit-card restaurants for steak, lobster, French wine, uniformed waiters and Richard Clayderman on tape; Kastro, near the lift station, is about the smartest of these.

The liveliest nightlife resides in the bars pitched on the steep slopes beside the main staircase: beautiful places to drink at and look out from, but heaving and impossibly loud late in the evening. Here too are some of the most popular tavernas – like Volcano at stair 555.

The northern end of the village, around the lift station and beyond, is relatively peaceful and well worth exploring both for the simple pleasure of wandering around and to visit the local museum (closed Tuesdays). The collection of vases from

Akrotiri and Ancient Thera is excellent, but there are only postcards of the Akrotiri wall-paintings, now in Athens. Immediately north of the museum are the Catholic cathedral and a convent where local girls are trained to weave. Rugs and embroidery are on sale.

Most of the cheap accommodation, including a youth hostel, is on the outskirts of the town looking out over the east coast. This is a somewhat underprivileged location, but it may be some consolation that sunrise over Anafi is almost as beautiful as sunset over the *caldera*. Walking distances are generally manageable, but beware hotel touts who greet flights and bus arrivals at the town's main square with mini-buses of their own. This is usually a sure sign of a very isolated location – there are hotels dotted along the road between town and airport, where the gum tree crossroads outside Mesaria is almost a resort in its own right. The village of Karterados, which also has hotels (and tennis courts, surprisingly enough), is marginally preferable, but not recommended. People with private rooms to rent may greet arrivals on the main square at the back of Fira, but may not: on one off-season visit to the island we found all the private rooms closed by police order to keep the hotels in business.

A beautiful road follows the crater rim northwards from Fira to Ia, winding this way and that and giving alternating views along the cliffs and down over the terraced cultivations to the east and north. Not far north of Fira the road bypasses the village of Imerovigli and the clifftop site of a ruined fortress (Skaros) which the Venetians made their capital on the island. Another splendid viewpoint is the chapel at the highest point of the entire crater wall (Mavro Vouno, 330m), reached by rough track. Lots of people hike from Fira to Ia, and for most of the way there is a panoramic path away from the road. It is a bit like walking along a clinker heap, best not attempted in sandals.

Ia's position is very like Fira's, with equally spectacular views from the panorama street, a similar mixture of new and abandoned broken houses, and a staircase down to the sea, where a small port is also an occasional drop-off point for ferry passengers. As at Fira, tourists lean over walls and ignore the signs of 'Verboten' on every roof in their anxiety to get the best snap of the village and cliffscape. But the atmosphere in the village is quite different. At Ia the signs of 1956 destruction are much more obvious, and the village is only now beginning to shake off desolation. As a resort it has a slightly alternative atmosphere, with more art galleries than souvenir shops, and accommodation in Greek National Tourist Organisation-run 'ethnic rooms'. There are also two simple hotels in the village centre, the *Fregata* (D) and *Anemone* (E), neighbours in prime panoramic position. Ia has a small maritime museum.

In contrast to the situation at Fira, a rough road leads down to the shore at the north-western tip of the island, and from here you can walk (and paddle) round to one of Ia's two small harbours (Ammoudi), which has a taverna and small red pebble beach among a lot of ruined buildings. Viewed from here, the clifftop village looks almost completely abandoned and ruinous. There is a staircase up from Ammoudi as there is from the more sheltered main harbour. Nudism is advertised (and practised) at Katharos beach, the stony cove immediately to the north of Ammoudi.

From Ia it is possible to return to Fira along the outside of the island, by a rough road that follows the shore most of the way. It is a very peaceful and empty cultivated landscape, not particularly beautiful but a welcome change from the tumultuous scenery on the other side of the island. Gaps in the low cliffs give access to dark stony beaches before the road heads inland, climbing gently back towards Fira. As it reaches the lower outskirts there is a fork down a dry river valley to a point on the coast marked on the map as **Pigadia**, which has a small beach and the beginnings of a new resort. Another track leads eastwards to the coast from Karterados. Just south of this is **Monolithos**, a dreary little seaside village with a vegetable canning factory, at the northern end of the airfield which, by Greek island standards, is busy and noisy. Monolithos has a beach with some shade, tavernas and rooms, but is a pretty desolate spot. A rough track (drivable) runs southwards, sandwiched between the airport's perimeter fence and the shore, which is uninterrupted, unremarkable beach all the way to Kamari.

Kamari is Santorini's main beach resort, a collection of modern hotels aligned along the stony beach immediately beneath the great mass of Profitis Ilias (566m), which fills the south-eastern corner of the island and drops into the sea between Kamari and Perissa no less abruptly than the crater wall on the western coast. Kamari is not a bad place to use as a base if you want a modern hotel, beach and resort facilities (nightlife, watersports, excursions), but suffers from airport noise and has no charm at all, although there is a small village area set back slightly from the beach hotels. Very few independent travellers stay at the resort, whose season is much shorter than Fira's. There is a campsite.

In season or out, it is worth going to Kamari for a visit to **Ancient Thera**, the site of the main post-Minoan settlement on the island, which was recolonised by Dorians from Sparta (including a certain Thiras) a few centuries after the great eruption of 1500 BC. A 4km hairpin road climbs from Kamari to a col near the entrance to the site, also accessible by an equally steep path from Perissa, to the south. There are donkeys for hire at Kamari, the going rate being significantly more than the cost of a ride up to Fira, but still a very worthwhile alternative to slogging up on foot, especially as there is plenty of walking left after you reach the top of the road, where a caravan sells drinks. The donkey track takes a more direct line than the road, and the more vigorous beasts get up the hill almost as quickly as labouring scooters.

The site of the old city is the spur of Mesa Vouno (369m), a subsidiary peak of Profitis Ilias projecting high above the sea. The wind and limitless views of sea and sky make a visit to Ancient Thera an exhilarating experience, which lots of tourists omit on the grounds that Akrotiri is the main archaeological sight to be seen on the island, and one is enough. The two places could not be more different – one still half buried, the other suspended in mid-air. Nowhere dispels the gloom that seems to hang over Santorini more effectively than Ancient Thera.

Not that there is nothing to see. The rough path through the long narrow site passes an early Christian basilica, foundations of private houses and temples, a theatre, and (on the inland side of the peak and *agora*) a rock-cut sanctuary from the 3rd century BC with relief carvings on the rock of an eagle (symbolising Zeus), a lion (Apollo), a dolphin (Poseidon), a phallus (Priapus) and a portrait of the founder of the sanctuary, Artemidorus of Perge, an admiral of the Ptolemaic fleet who was visited by these deities in a dream. The square at the extreme eastern end of the site is where naked boys danced and sang hymns to Apollo at the annual summer festival, or *Karneia*. In inscriptions on the rocks, spectators recorded their enthusiasm for this display and such remarkable feats as the lifting of a 480-kilogramme stone by Eumastas, son of Kristobolos.

Most of the visible structures date from the Hellenistic and Roman periods, but many older items have been recovered, mainly vases and sculptures from the burial area near the top of the road. This saddle commands a magnificent view down over Perissa and its vast black beach, and one of the advantages of visiting Ancient Thera by donkey or on foot is the chance to make a round trip, walking down to Perissa, bathing and returning to Fira by bus from there. The really energetic can make a more ambitious round trip by tackling the rough path between the saddle and the summit of Profitis Ilias.

Getting around

Car and motor-bike hire is available from Fira, Kamari and Ia. There are several other motor-bike hire places, including Akrotiri, Perissa, Messaria and Karterados.

Frequent bus services operate between Fira and Kamari; Athinios; Perissa; Ia; Akrotiri; the airport. There are also direct services from Kamari to Athinios and the airport. Early-morning buses from Fira more or less tie in with the ferry departures from Athinios. There are no buses after about 9 p.m., except from Athinios when ferries arrive.

Fira has a long season, and a full range of excursions is likely to be on offer from May to October inclusive. Bus-trips from Fira and Kamari usually include visits to the monastery (Profitis Ilias), wine-tasting, Akrotiri and Perissa. A few include Ia and Ancient Thera.

Boat-trips are organised by agencies in Fira and Kamari: be sure to check which port the boat uses. If possible, select a trip using the old port, especially if you have not arrived via the old port and donkey route. The agencies say ferry and excursion tickets cannot be

The Kamari to Fira road passes a few points of interest, including a good wine-tasting (and selling) establishment near Mesa (or Episkopi) Gonia, open every afternoon. The rough road past the winery continues to a lovely 11th-century Byzantine church, the **Panagia Episkopi**, on a shaded terrace looking out over Kamari. There are frescoes inside, for a sight of which you will be charmingly but firmly invited to offer a donation to the lady at the door. Of several inland villages on the northern slopes of Profitis Ilias, the most picturesque is **Pyrgos**, well worth a pause on the way up to the pylon-crowned summit of Profitis Ilias, a popular excursion thanks to the good road, the huge views and the 18th-century monastery near the top. The monastery has a small museum, with various religious treasures and items of local historical interest on display.

If driving, riding or hiking south from Fira or returning there from the south, take the rough road through the vineyards along the cliffs in preference to the main road via Mesaria: it is more direct and gives beautiful views.

Shortly south of the turning to the new port (Athinios), which is a facility not a community, the southern road divides. Heading left, the road crosses a mountain ridge lined with old windmills before descending to a triangular plain bounded by the steep slopes of Profitis Ilias and a vast extent of black sand beach. The two converge and the road reaches the sea at **Perissa**, which has a less planned look about it than Kamari and seems

bought at the ports. This seems unlikely, but the risk is not worth taking.

The main excursion target is the volcanic islet of Nea Kameni, usually called Volcano. It is a stiff walk of about 20 minutes up from the mooring over bare black rock to the crater of the island (124m), into and around which you can walk, sniffing the sulphurous exhalations from various hot rocks encrusted with green and orange crystals. Boats often include a swimming stop at the hot springs between Nea Kameni and the older islet of Palea Kameni: these are disappointing – a muddy lagoon where the murky water is not very hot. It does, however, leave a metallic taste in the mouth.

Longer boat-trips from Fira also include a visit to Ia, to the island of Thirasia, and to Akrotiri. Thirasia is a mirror-image of Santorini, with a small beach and a couple of tavernas at the harbour, and a long staircase up to a white village on the clifftop; from here paths lead across and along the island, much of which is quarried. Rooms can be rented at the harbour and in the village. Daily boat-trips operate from Ia to Nea Kameni and Thirasia.

In midsummer Fira and Kamari agencies also organise boat-trips to Anafi; Ios; Folegandros and Sikinos; and Amorgos.

to be the more popular commuting beach for tourists based in Fira. Compared with passengers on the late afternoon bus back to town, tinned sardines are spoilt for space. As a resort, Perissa's main drawback is the location of its new hotels, which extend a long way back along the road, in some cases quite a walk from the beach and such resort centre as there is. This has all the necessary resort trappings, including discos and a youth hostel ('no curfew'). The beach has no shade and, being black, gets very hot. It shelves steeply under water and extends southwards for several miles.

Back at the windmill-lined ridge, a rough road is signposted south to **Vlichada**, perhaps the best beach on the island, sheltered by low golden cliffs and overlooked by old factory chimneys and a very peaceful and beautifully situated hotel.

The reason for a visit to the southern branch of the island is the archaeological site of **Akrotiri**, a short distance from the south coast and about a mile below the old hill village of Akrotiri, which is of no great interest, although it has good views northwards across the *caldera*, some simple tourist accommodation and shops (including wine-tasting).

Akrotiri is the city that lay untouched from 1500BC, when it was buried by volcanic ash, until 1967 when Professor Marinatos began excavation, which is still very much in progress without him. As at Pompeii, much of the settlement has been found in a very good state of preservation, notably a superlative collection of wall-paintings which, apart from their outstanding value as works of art, have provided a wealth of information about the local civilisation. All the paintings are now in Athens. In contrast to Pompeii, the archaeologists have found no human remains and few movable valuables, so it is clear that the inhabitants had time to evacuate before disaster struck. From the buildings already excavated it is also clear that Akrotiri was a highly sophisticated community with close cultural links with Crete and trading connections with Egypt and the eastern Mediterranean. It was not, however, a Minoan town, and its layout resembles a typical Cycladic village more closely than it does a Minoan palace community as seen on Crete.

The position of the site is not at all spectacular, and the excavations are covered by corrugated iron roofing with meccano-like support. Visitors follow a roped itinerary through the streets of the town, between houses of two and three storeys, their walls and rooms intact. All the houses had storage rooms or shops downstairs and large-windowed living-rooms above, in some cases adorned with wall-paintings. There is very little in the rooms except some beautiful tall *pithoi* (storage jars) and, in D16, wreaths in memory of Professor Marinatos who died on-site in 1974. Apart from this, you pass signs saying things like 'In this room the famous painting of the Akrotiri boxers was found', which may be slightly frustrating. To make the most of Akrotiri, it is best to visit the site on an organised tour with a guide, who will give a vivid exposition of the layout, the domestic architecture and the way of life of the people.

Of the books available locally, *Santorini* by Professor Christos Doumas is recommended: beautiful glossy souvenir photographs of the island and many of the works of art now in Athens, ground plans of the archaeological sites and good background information about Akrotiri. Professor Doumas describes Akrotiri as 'a station for Minoan agents' who established a presence in an already thriving Cycladic community; a bourgeois society wealthy from commerce and shipping, in which farmers and artisans continued to have their place. One thought-provoking inference from the detail of the paintings is the presence of Mycenaeans in this part of the world before their time. Professor Doumas concludes that Cretan power was well on the wane in the eastern Mediterranean before the eruption.

There is a hotel and taverna by the sea near the archaeological site. This is not a very tempting bathing place, but there are boat-trips along the south coast of the island as far as the lighthouse at the western end. The first stop on the trip,

Red Beach taverna, can be reached by rough track from the excavations. The name is no exaggeration: the rock colours are as spectacular as anywhere on the island, despite the fact that this is not the inside wall of the *caldera*. For the full effect and the good beach you must walk over the black rock headland to the west of the taverna.

SERIFOS

Iron-stained Serifos speaks of poverty and silence, and its drear reaches of rock induce a mood very different from the heart-lifting ones induced by Rhodes or Mykonos.

In any light it is one of the loveliest sights in the Kyklades and could well represent the ideal Greek island.

Thus wrote Lawrence Durrell and Ernle Bradford in the two best recent books on the Greek islands, showing just how personal reactions and judgements of island mood inevitably are. Or perhaps not; it could be that the difference is one of time. For a modest degree of very informal and small-scale tourist development has turned Serifos from a very depressed island into a cheerful one, where one can sit back and enjoy the beauty of the views without feeling too guilty about the barely submerged poverty of an island of redundant iron miners, with its rust-coloured rock and rusty industrial machinery littering the bays.

We certainly incline towards the (second) Bradford view of the island, and notice in retrospect that the attempt to paint a word picture of the typical charm of a small Greek island in the introduction to this guide bears a close resemblance to Serifos. In its present state it is a very alluring place, the best answer to questions about what Ios must have been like 20 years ago. If you are setting out on a Greek island odyssey of your own and want to start with love at first sight, board the *Ionion*, the *Kimolos* or the *Milos Express* at Piraeus, avert your eyes from Kythnos and alight at Serifos. It would probably be stretching a point to plan a stay of more than a few days, unless you take relaxation very seriously indeed. Sample the irresistible prettiness of the overall bay, beach and hill village scene, go for a few hikes and you will have done the island.

An increasing number of young people do choose to linger on Serifos, for the word has gone round on the sleeping-baggers' grapevine that it is an ideal place for their kind of a holiday: tolerant (if not exuberantly outgoing or entrepreneurial) people, a very pretty sandy beach with shading trees, others in easy walking distance where no one minds if you strip off, a small resort (the island port) just along the beach where a few laid-back bars play Californian beach music, and the necessary shops. This style of tourism is liable to sudden change if the local authorities decide they have had enough of it, for the law is on their side. But beach campers and Serifos have been getting along fine for quite a few years now, and it is hardly a mass invasion. As always, a hard line is much more likely to be taken out of season, when the hotels and tourist rooms are unfilled, than in July and August, when the only alternative to sleeping on the beach is catching the next ferry and sleeping on that.

The island where Danae and the infant Perseus were washed up in a box and where Perseus returned to save his mother by turning the evil king Polydectes and his entire retinue to stone by showing them the head of Medusa is an appropriately boulderous place; the hills give plenty of scope for speculative identification of petrified retainers. The ferries from Piraeus follow the east coast of the barren-looking island – 'Serifos' means 'dry' – giving a side-on view of the hill village before turning into a long south-facing bay and confronting it in a perfect composition: steep-sided bay with beaches and harbour tucked into one side, and a long fringe of tamarisks and sand curling away to the right. Far above the sea, the white village spills like froth over both sides of a high spur, sharply outlined against a theatre of much higher wild grey-brown mountains. As the ferry manoeuvres its way into port there is plenty of time to study little details of the island's life, picking out the donkeys on the long winding staircase up to the village, selecting the shaded cafe terrace for the first iced coffee, the tree under which to doze or plant a tent. Even before setting foot ashore, you know your way around and feel at home.

There is indeed very little more to the port of **Livadi** (and Serifos, for that matter) than meets the incoming eye. Holiday rooms and a few small hotels are strung out along the beach, which curves round the head of the bay from the harbour. The best of the hotels are the *Maistrali* (c) and *Serifos Beach* (c), but both annoyingly insist on half board in midsummer. Rather quaintly, a grand roadsign to the Serifos Beach advertises 0 per cent reductions for foreigners: a number has been conveniently painted out, presumably indicating that foreigners no longer need special inducements. The main beach is a mixture of stones and sand, an acceptable dormitory, with the prospect of a warm awakening in the morning sun. With all the young people around, the evening atmosphere in Livadi is now quite lively,

Getting around

There are no advertised excursions. A frequent bus service operates between Livadi and Chora. Motor-bike hire is available in Livadi. The island map is a very crude tool. The roads marked in yellow are, at best, donkey trails, possibly relevant to hikers.

with several discos and rock music in the bars. The village is expanding fast, with messy new building above Livadakia beach, but it is all on a small scale and Livadi still looks and sounds like a rustic village, with a strip of mixed cultivation behind the beach and an assortment of goats and chickens wandering around among the tavernas where before long they will be served up on plates. Donkeys, cockerels and dogs do their cacophonous best to ruin sleep.

Campers seem to prefer, or are perhaps sent to, the relative seclusion of Livadakia beach, immediately south of the ridge by the huge ferry quay and no more than a few minutes' walk from the harbour. The beach is coarse sand and has shade and the only windsurfing (among other watersports) on the island. The nearest taverna is on the ridge, where there are also rooms and a small hotel (the *Areti*, в). From the southern end of the beach a sandy path leads over a hill to another broader and emptier sandy beach (Karavi), with no shade, fewer campers and more nudism; in all, no more than half an hour's walk from downtown Livadi.

The island's best beach, with the softest, whitest sand and the most people, is **Psilli Ammos**, on the east coast of the island, reached by a 2km rough track (unsignposted) from the eastern end of Livadi bay, near one of several bridges over dry river beds. There are two tavernas. The track continues northwards for a few hundred yards before running out above a much emptier sandy beach. Walk down over some rocks past a small church.

From Livadi it is a stiff 40-minute walk up to the hill village (**Chora**) by road, then staircase, which cuts a lot of hairpins out of the 5km journey by road. On the lower fringe of the village the path passes a token folk museum. There is not much to see inside, but entrance is free and it breaks the journey. In town, the main square is the buses' turning area on the ridge, a windy and not very delightful spot, with a few cafes and restaurants on and around the square. The rest of the village has nothing specific to offer except lovely views out over the bay and terraced hills, and the pleasure of wandering through the tumble-down whitewashed streets to the fortress ruins at the very top of the village. There are few shops in Chora and no accommodation is advertised. The form on Serifos is that if you can't find a room at Livadi, you sleep on the beach.

From Chora, a road continues over the hills to the north of the island. The main target is the **Taxiarchis monastery** in the north-east, looked after by a very welcoming monk who introduces himself as Makari and offers water and *loukoumia*. It is a pretty place in a fine setting above the sea, with farm animals outside, a few trees and icons inside, and a date of 1447 on the church doorframe. Finding the monastery presents no problems: simply follow the road until you get there. From a roadside chapel near the village of **Panagia** a very rough track leads down to Sikamia, a windy (north-facing) sand and pebble beach with a few scattered buildings but no taverna. There are signs forbidding camping and nudism, with illustrations to make sure the message gets through. High up in the mountainous middle of the island, the main fork in the island's uncomplicated road system offers the chance to descend by rough road to two bays in the south-west, both littered with ruined buildings and other debris of the old iron-mining industry. **Mega Livadi** is the more cheerful of the two, with fishing-boats, eucalyptus trees, a couple of tavernas and a small beach of hard sand. There is more scope for exploring various beaches on the wider bay of Koutalas, but there is no shade and the one cafe does not appear to welcome business.

SIFNOS

Sifnos is a relatively green and even more uncharacteristically neat and well-kept member of the western Cyclades, and the most touristy of the sub-group, which is not saying much. The island has a few good beaches, pretty villages and a lot of quiet charm, especially now that its port, Kamares, has grown into a lively little beach resort, a role it plays well. This nicely complements the island's main resort, a sprawling agglomeration of several whitewashed villages widely spread across the pastoral rolling hills of the island's interior. None of these is the original island capital, which survives neglected but still inhabited on a rocky and exposed stretch of the east coast. This old fortress village, Kastro, is one of the most beautiful and best preserved of its kind in the Cyclades. Sifnos is an excellent island for medium-range hikers – about the right size for half-day walks, with a very pretty variegated landscape and a suitably underdeveloped road system.

Sifnos is something of a connoisseur's island, a fashionable holiday spot among well-to-do Athenians which claims proudly to produce the best cooks in Greece. It also has a discerning French and Italian clientele, which lends an unaccustomed stylish note to island life and may also have something to do with the generally high standard of restaurant food and accommodation. The Greeks take over the place (especially the hill villages) in August, when finding a room is impossible.

The island has been famous for its pottery for over 2000 years, and the cottage industry survives in several coastal villages (Kamares, Vathi and Plati Gialos). Sifnos ware is better known for its fireproof properties than for any great decorative beauty, but painted plates inlaid in village walls, potters at the wheel and trayfuls of newly made pots drying in the sun all contribute to the island's homespun charm, a far cry from the rough magic one usually associates with small Greek islands.

The port of **Kamares** is set on a rather grim, steep-sided, barren mountainous inlet, its flanking summits crowned, as so often in Greece, by highly improbable chapels. The resort has grown up in a bit of a squash between the steep bare hillside on the southern side of the bay and the waters of the harbour, and its main drawback is traffic to and from the boats, on the only village street; buses and trucks nose past the cafe tables in a manner unlikely to commend itself to parents of small children or anyone enjoying a quiet drink. Apart from this it is a cheerful and sophisticated little place, with tamarisk-shaded bars and restaurants strung out along the waterside and, in the case of the Captain's bar and restaurant, with tables on the sand where harbour gives way to beach. Kamares also boasts an Italian restaurant with an espresso machine, an exotic *gelateria* and a number of places advertising mouth-watering breakfasts. The *Stavros* (c) is the obvious central hotel, attractive and well kept, the *Voulis* (B) a smart and expensive little package hotel in a secluded position behind the beach, a few minutes' walk from the village. There are rooms to rent, but you are unlikely to be greeted at the quay by the familiar reassuring gaggle of locals jostling for the chance to take you in.

Kamares is beginning to spread up the hill beside the road out of town, where there is a cheap dormitory hotel, doss-house of second-last resort. The sandy beach stretches across the full width of the bay (about half a mile) and has tree shade, a campsite and a watersports outfit whose most popular facility is a shower block, much appreciated by the campers. The bay is not ideal for windsurfing, for the mountains do very odd things

461

to the wind, and the comings and goings of ferries are a further hazard. At the northern end of the beach a smaller collection of waterside buildings – as on the other side, sandwiched between water and steep orange mountainside – includes some tourist rooms, an excellent taverna and a disco. Disco noise notwithstanding, this is a lovely place to make one's base, as it is for a starlit dine and dance looking across the water at the not very distant lights of Kamares. Mister Kostas (the title means a lot to him) is the man to seek out for rooms or even a bed on the roof.

The stiff climb up from Kamares to the island's modern capital, **Apollonia**, follows an increasingly fertile valley, with neat olive terraces and dovecotes, almond trees and figs on the lower outskirts of town. Apollonia is the central, most commercial and resort-like of the collection of hill villages loosely gathered on the rounded crest of the island. The road runs briefly through the middle of it before a confusing parting of the ways at the top of the town. As at Kamares, traffic compromises the charm of the main square, where buses stop, taxis linger and horns blare angrily. The square has a small and moderately interesting local museum and a very good restaurant with a garden looking out over the valley. Most of the few small hotels are also on or near the square: the *Sofia* (c) and *Sifnos* (c) are fine, but the *Anthoussa* (c) has a better position, with lovely views out over the green and pleasant chapel-spotted hills on the eastern side of the island. On either side of the road, an extensive network of highly picturesque whitewashed alleys and paths makes pleasant strolling territory, especially the main shopping street (Stylianou Prokou) which climbs to the right (north) of the square and has jewellers, pottery galleries and what can only be called fashion boutiques. In the other direction, an up-to-date path leads very prettily from the square to Artemonas via Pano Petali. Out of season, it would not be difficult to rent a room in the houses along this route, although Sifniots rarely stoop to advertising rooms. Artemonas has some fine old houses but is mostly residential and not very animated.

It is a lovely walk down from Apollonia to **Kastro**, but a long haul back up the hill: ideally, time a visit to coincide with the bus back. The old village, which was the island's capital from the 14th to the mid-19th centuries, occupies a naturally defensible coastal spur dominating a rocky stretch of the east coast below Apollonia. It now has a population of about 100; the inhabitants must spend much of their time with a brush and tub of whitewash, for the village is spotlessly clean. There are a few modern tourist rooming buildings beside the road down to Kastro and a taverna at its gates, but the village proper shows

Getting around

Round-the-island boat-trips operate once a week from Kamares. Walking tours are organised by tourist agencies in Kamares and Apollonia. There are buses about every hour between Kamares and Apollonia; they often continue to Plati Gialos or Kastro or Pharos. In summer there are four or five boats a day from Kamares to Vathi. Motor-bike and car hire is available at Kamares, motor-bike hire at Apollonia (turn left at the crossroads). At Kamares, Sifnos Car is recommended (even for bikes) in preference to Dia's Bikes (when we visited, Dia took casualness beyond a joke, rarely turning up for more than a few hours in the morning).

few signs of the 20th century (apart from telephone wires) or distractions from pure Cycladic architecture, of which Kastro is a fascinating example. In the unusual split-level streets, terraces at *piano nobile* level are linked by bridges spanning the narrow vaulted alleys below. The backs of the village houses form the outer walls of the community which is turned inwards on itself like a monastery, or indeed a fortress. Most of the big houses at the top of the town are now abandoned and semi-ruined.

Kastro probably occupies the site of one of the ancient cities of Sifnos, which prospered from gold- and silver-mining until the islanders tried to cheat on their annual tribute to Apollo at Delphi by sending a gilt instead of a golden egg. They were rumbled, and the mines destroyed by the wrathful god. It seems likely that the legend relates to earthquake damage. At Kastro bits of antique masonry can be seen in the village houses, and outside one of the village gates stands a beautiful ram's head sarcophagus, apparently used as a tub. There is a small harbour with stony beach and taverna below the village.

The main road south from Apollonia leads to the island's most popular beaches, on the sheltered south-east coast. **Pharos** is a very peaceful little rural hamlet gathered around a small beach of muddy sand, with a few rooms to rent and a couple of tavernas. The Gorgona bar offers an exceptional combination of fresh orange juice, piped Beethoven and Luxury-class sanitation, but most of the village's amenities are less sophisticated. People camp in an olive patch behind one of three small beaches, and it is they, one suspects, who have provoked the polite notice requesting that anyone wishing to bathe naked should 'withdraw to isolated places'.

On the far western end of Pharos bay, the very prettily sited and much photographed monastery church of **Chrissopigi**, on a small rocky promontory, sports a similar request, although the rocks are not the most tempting place for a swim. The church has a miracle-working icon and an Ascension Day festival. There is a long beach near by, with a shaded taverna.

Plati Gialos is the island's original beach resort, not so much a village as a scattering of accommodation (rooms and two small hotels), tavernas and potteries strung out between the road and a good long beach, which is mostly pebbles. The road runs out at the *Hotel Xenia* (B), typically past its prime but beautifully situated at the southern end of the bay. Plati Gialos has a campsite in a hillside olive grove, quite a walk from the beach.

Vathi is an idyll – a beautiful sheltered horseshoe bay in the south-west, surrounded by tall hills and accessible only on foot (tracks from Apollonia and Plati Gialos) or, for the less energetic, by boat from Kamares. Fishing-boats are beached on the sand, and caiques tie up beside a lovely twin-domed church. The community is strung out along the thin sandy beach, its single street. Comforts include a couple of tavernas, a shop, a pottery and a tap – all you need, in fact. A few tents are pitched on and around the beach in summer.

SYROS

Unlike many island capitals, Syros's is not simply called Syros or Chora. Ermoupolis, the city of Hermes, sounds like a town to be reckoned with and indeed it is, the thoroughly urban capital city of the Cyclades, with a population of about 15,000. The town is not merely the focus of the life of the island; here the small island seems little more than the appendage of the town.

The town's prosperity began in the 17th century. From their hill settlement, now known as Ano Syros, the island's Catholics appealed successfully to the king of France for protection, which brought Syros a rare degree of relative safety from piracy and immunity from Turkish interference in its affairs. The French founded missions to make sure the spiritual life of the island did not suffer, and Syros remains to this day one of the main strongholds (along with neighbouring Tinos) of the western creed in Greece.

The French connection kept Syros officially neutral during the War of Independence, when it welcomed large numbers of refugees from all corners of the Greek world, notably from Chios and Psara. The newcomers settled the area around the harbour and brought their shipping and trading skills to establish the busiest trading port in the Aegean and the foremost commercial and cultural city of independent Greece in

the early decades of its existence; they named their town after
the divine patron of trade, Hermes. The surprisingly grand scale
and neo-classical style of its central square and public buildings
are a legacy from this period of great wealth and elegance.
Decline set in towards the end of the 19th century, when the
use of oil instead of coal did away with the need for a refuelling
port in mid-Aegean, and the opening of the Corinth Canal in
1893 consolidated the superiority of Piraeus.

With its twin hills, homes of the island's Orthodox and
Catholic communities, climbing from the broad and very busy
harbour area, **Ermoupolis** is a splendid sight from the sea. It still
has a big shipyard and a lot of sailors (merchant and military)
in port; lining the working half of the harbour is an area of
warehouses and assorted dingy industrial buildings. It is in
many ways a fascinating place, an unselfconscious living
monument to a period of Greek history, which makes towns like
Hydra and Symi seem stagy and hollow; the fact that it is now
a bit seedy and a far from obvious choice for a summer holiday
in no way diminishes its curiosity value to those with an eye
for an offbeat style of Greek island. But its appeal as a place for
a prolonged stay can easily be exaggerated. In midsummer,
Greek holiday-makers add a cheerful and leisured note to the
life of town and animate its suburban beach resorts. But, even
on this least touristy of the main Cyclades, finding
accommodation in high season can be very difficult.

Ferries arrive at the northern entrance to the harbour and are
greeted by bearers of the island's specialities, nougat and
Turkish Delight (which in Greece must always be called
Loukoumia for fear of causing offence). They beat back the
passengers waiting to disembark and briskly hawk their sticky
trayfuls round the ferry before hopping ashore at the last
moment. Although no longer the hub of the Aegean ferry
network, as it was until recently, Ermoupolis is still a very busy
port of call, and the nougat-seller's job is no sinecure. There are
shops in town specialising in the sweets, which are not at all
expensive.

The ferry quay is as good a part of town as any to look for
accommodation, especially if you propose only a brief visit, in
which case simple convenience of location weighs heavily in the
balance. The *Hermes* (B) is the best hotel in town and
immediately obvious – an imposing place with spacious halls. Its
neighbour, the *Kymata*, is a more modest establishment, but
recently revamped and attractive. A bit further along the water-
front (near the office of the tourist agency, Teamwork), the
Hotel Syrii (B) looks seedy and poky but turns out to be clean,
reasonable and friendly. Teamwork is a big if not wholly

appropriate name in the small world of Syros tourism, with its finger in a lot of local pies. They will probably be able to see you right if you're stuck for somewhere to stay, at a price, and may be able to arrange out-of-town villas to rent.

The long sweep of harbour-front has a cheerful central section of moorings for fishing-boats, excursion-boats and private yachts, with streets leading back into the elegant, marble-paved, balconied heart of the 19th-century town. The water-front itself is less beautiful, but animated late into the night in summer, with crab grilled on the barbecue outside the Delfini Ouzeri and various bars pumping out rock music. The southern half of the harbour is industrial and very shabby.

Venizelou street leads from the harbour to the vast and splendid arcaded main square, named after the national hero of the War of Independence, Miaoulis. A statue of the great sailor stands, hand on the tiller and flanked by cannon and flags, in the middle of the square. There are palm trees, shady cafe terraces and creaky old hotels of dubious repute on the square, which is dominated by the stately neo-classical town hall. Next door to it is a small archaeological museum. It is worth exploring the area to the north-east of the square (in other words, beyond its far right-hand corner if viewed from Venizelou street) passing a theatre built in 1862 and modelled on La Scala in Milan, on the way to an area of many beautiful houses overlooking the sea, around the church of Agios Nikolaos. There is no town beach worthy of the name.

The more interesting of the two hills is **Ano Syros**, on the left when viewed from the sea. This is the original town, inhabited and fortified by the Venetians in the 13th century and the traditional home of the town's Catholic community. French Capuchin monks established themselves on the hill in 1633, and it was they who appealed to King Louis XIII for the protection that was largely responsible for the town's subsequent growth and prosperity.

It is a long walk up to Ano Syros from the lower town via Plateia Metamorphosis and the Orthodox cathedral (to the west of the main square), Omirou street and a lot of stairs. The journey can be broken to inspect a British military cemetery, where lie the victims of a troopship sunk in the Aegean in 1917, and an Orthodox cemetery with grand monuments to the wealthy bourgeoisie of 19th-century Ermoupolis. Alternatively, you can take a bus, taxi or drive yourself up around the hill to a point from which it is only a few minutes' walk up through the narrow alleys of the old town to the 13th-century Catholic Cathedral of St George on the summit and the Capuchin monastery (or Moni Kapoutsino) near by. There is not much

Getting around

The Teamwork tourist agency arranges a variety of mostly very expensive excursions to other islands. Their most tempting offer is a round-the-island boat-trip, visiting (among other places) Grammaton bay in the north-west, which often served mariners well as a port in a storm. Inscriptions on the cliffs recording thanks and supplication for deliverance are said to date back to Roman and Byzantine times. Mykonos-by-night excursions are also advertised at the harbour, as are day-trips to Mykonos and Delos (with or without Tinos) and weekly ones to Serifos and Sifnos.

Motor-bike hire is available in Ermoupolis (several places on the water-front) and Finikas. There are frequent buses from Ermoupolis to Ano Syros and all villages in southern Syros, mostly on a circuit excluding Kini, which has a separate, less frequent service (a few buses a day). The town bus terminal is on the main water-front.

commercial life in Ano Syros, and it is easy to lose the thread of narrow stepped alleys.

The Orthodox hill town of **Vrontado** dates from the 19th and 20th centuries and is much less picturesque, although its big domed Church of the Anastasis is a handsome landmark, at least when viewed from afar.

The north of the island is mountainous, sparsely inhabited, poorly provided with roads and best explored by boat. The broader southern part of the island is much tamer country, with well-irrigated farm cultivations and comfortable out-of-town villas dotted around the coast, and a number of small peaceful beach resorts which offer an alternative, very low-key style of holiday base to Ermoupolis and are mainly the realm of Greek holiday-makers. Southern Syros can be toured in a round trip from Ermoupolis of no more than 30km on mostly good roads, comfortably accomplished in half a day. The only good reason for the tour is to find a quiet beach on which to settle: there is nothing very interesting or beautiful to see.

Taking the circuit anti-clockwise, the first beach place is Azolimnos, a scruffy little beach with a taverna or two, not really worth the detour from the main road. The bay below **Vari** is more attractive, with a cheerful cluster of simple hotels and taverna terraces beside a short but wide patch of sandy beach. The road follows the coast, passing a small sandy beach just before the village of Giaros, where it cuts across the southern cape of the island to the main resort area of **Posidonia** and **Finikas**, which now more or less merge along the shore of a wide bay in the south-west. But there is quite a difference of style between the places. Posidonia, also known as Dellagrazia, is the island's main community of moderately grand 19th-century villas built for a life of gracious *villeggiatura*. Posidonia lacks a focus, but there is accommodation and tavernas on a rocky promontory, with beaches on either side. The main hotel is the *Posidonion* (c) and the best of the beaches is to the south of the headland, a location marked on the island map as Agathopes. Finikas has more international tourism, with the tell-tale presence of motor-bike hire and watersports. The resort is a bit of a roadside, beachside straggle and the beach itself is not very inviting, although there is some sand and trees. Other facilities include a concrete helipad jutting out into the water half-way along the beach. Comings and goings must present an interesting challenge to windsurfers.

Galissas is something different again, a small and casual studenty holiday development that has grown up in the secluded reedy cultivations at the head of a steep-sided rocky inlet with a good sandy beach, the best on the island of those easily accessible by land. On the south side of the bay some caves are inhabited by a summer colony of latter-day troglodytes. For those in search of more sophisticated accommodation, there are two campsites and a couple of hotels (including the clean new *Francoise*, a c) near the beach, which has watersports and some disco life. There is also some accommodation in Galissas village, which is beside the road about half a mile inland.

It is a splendid drive over the hills from Galissas to **Kini**, approached by a steep hairpin road down to the sea with signs announcing a speed limit of 80, a terrifying tribute to the lunacy of Greeks at the wheel. This is the only hint of frenetic pace at Kini, an attractively peaceful Sunday resort for Ermoupolitans, with two small beaches, a small fishing harbour, a few tavernas and some simple holiday accommodation (a hotel and some rooms), all close to the shore. From Kini the road back to Ermoupolis crosses the high and bare central mountain ridge; by keeping left at the crossroads it is possible to descend via Ano Syros.

TINOS

Tinos is the most famous place of pilgrimage in Greece, known understandably but rather misleadingly as the Lourdes of the Aegean – understandably, because on and around the feasts of Annunciation and Assumption, 25 March and 15 August, Orthodox pilgrims hoping for a cure for themselves or their loved ones come in their tens of thousands to the miracle-working icon of the Panagia Evangelistria in the island's port, capital and only resort, also called Tinos, and misleadingly, because the pilgrimage trade does not dominate the town all the time, or the whole island any of the time.

The town itself lacks the casual villagey charm of most small-island ports. But it does at least have plentiful hotel accommodation (provided you don't choose festival time, or any time in August, when you will have to join the multitudes sleeping in the streets). There are good beaches not far away and the rest of the island is delightful, not dissimilar to Andros in its rural charm, only less rugged, with lots of farming villages high up in the hills, fat cows and windmills that are not yet all abandoned.

Tinos was the most enduring Venetian possession in the Aegean thanks to its impregnable mountain citadel of Exombourgo, and was taken by the Turks in 1715 only after the Venetian governor had gone home, fed up with presiding over an island abandoned by most of its population – frequent Turkish raids were responsible for this – and thus not at all lucrative. It has a sizeable Catholic community (about a third of the population) and an Italianate architectural note in the elegant open-framed belfries which are a characteristic and attractive feature of the landscape. But the real hallmark of Tinos is the dovecote, a turret with pigeon-hole walls in an intricate house-of-cards design, seen all over the island. A dovecote style of decoration has inspired much of the recent new building, even the archaeological museum. The domes and belfries of 800 churches and chapels combine with 1300 dovecotes (with innumerable doves in residence) to give Tinos a tranquil atmosphere appropriate to its holy status, officially declared in 1971. At the time this meant strict control over behaviour and dress on the island; matters have since been relaxed. Tinos is also well known for its marble carving; the marble is quarried on the island, mostly in the north, where Pyrgos is the main sculptors' village. All the churches give the sculptors plenty to decorate, but their work is also exported throughout Greece.

A pear-shaped island on the same north-west/south-east axis as Andros, from which it is separated by a very narrow strait, Tinos is generally mountainous, highest and broadest in the south-east, where its tallest peak, Tsiknias (729m), legendary home of the god of the north wind, drops steeply to the sea.

Like many pilgrimage places, **Tinos town** seems overwhelmingly commercial except at festival time, when it is the scene of spectacular demonstrations of mass piety about which there is nothing false. Modern hotels are lined up all round the harbour, and two parallel streets run up the hill towards the imposing complex of church buildings at the top of the town. One of the streets is a narrow teeming bazaar of tourist souvenir shops giving way to religious souvenir shops as it ascends; the other a wide road which many a pilgrim climbs on all fours. The archaeological museum is beside this road and worth a visit. Local finds include a sundial from the 1st century BC, relief-decorated vases of the Geometric period from a site near Exombourgo, and objects from the sanctuary of Poseidon and Amphitrite at Kionia, which made Tinos as famous a pilgrimage island (for the sick) in antiquity as it is now.

The grand ice-cream-coloured church of **Evangelistria** or Megalohari, approached by red-carpeted flights of marble stairs, was built soon after the discovery there in January 1823 of a miraculous icon painted by Saint Luke, whose existence and location had been revealed in dreams to a local nun called Pelagia six months earlier. The event, which was soon followed by reports of miraculous cures, came as a sign of encouragement to inspire the Greeks at the beginning of the War of Independence.

On festival day 15 August 1940, before the official outbreak of war between Greece and the Axis powers, a well-aimed but ill-calculated Italian torpedo sank the Greek warship *Elli* in Tinos harbour, outraging the Greek nation and hardening its will to resist, as was soon to be demonstrated. Metaxas's famous 'No' to Mussolini followed at the end of October.

The main church is entered through the upper of the two elegant colonnades. Pilgrims queue at the icon to write their message or plant a kiss on the glass, either of which an attendant will immediately erase. The work of Saint Luke is not easily assessed, the painted image being almost totally obscured by encrustations of precious metal and jewellery. Hanging ex-votos fill the church, all related to specific instances of miraculous intervention, some more obvious than others. As well as parts of the body and pairs of spectacles, there are several houses, a bunch of grapes, a fork and a monkey wrench. The lower colonnade fronts the crypt, which commemorates the exact place where the holy icon was found beneath a pile of stones visible near by. In the neighbouring chapel a bit of the Italian torpedo is preserved. The buildings surrounding the handsome courtyard include a very mediocre picture gallery and a first aid room, which must be kept busy when 15,000 pilgrims are in town for 15 August, many of them sleeping in the church courtyard, on the road and water-front. They must wish the icon had come to light somewhere nearer to a beach.

The most cheerful part of town and the main taverna and bar area is around the corner to the north of the main harbour. The Pigeon House restaurant is recommended, down an alley to the left of the main road up towards the big church. The best of the hotels are the *Avra* (c) and *Tinion* (b), respectively on and set back slightly from the main drag of the water-front (turn right on disembarking). There are also some cheap rooms (*Ogiannis*) and a cheap old-fashioned hotel, the *Thalia* (e), well placed on the quiet south side of the harbour; and a campsite beyond the Tinion, on the way out to **Agios Fokas** beach and the disco zone. Only about 1km from the harbour at its near end, Agios Fokas extends for another two and improves markedly the further you go from Tinos, with plenty of empty sand at the eastern end. The town end of the beach is thin, crowded and stony.

Ancient pilgrims to the sanctuary of Poseidon and Amphitrite, which flourished at **Kionia** from the 3rd century BC until Roman times, can have had no complaint about sleeping arrangements, for the ruins, now overgrown and fenced in, occupy a prime beach location about 4km north-west of town. Poseidon was here worshipped as the god of healing and is credited with having cleared the island of its infestation of snakes. Quite a few have since returned. It is recorded that, like the modern pilgrimage church, the sanctuary had numerous statues dedicated to the two divinities by those who had been healed.

The site's neighbour is the *Tinos Beach* (a), a big package hotel with watered lawns, a good swimming-pool, a tennis court, windsurfing and waterskiing. Surprisingly, there are no other watersports on the island: these and the hotel's other sports facilities are open to non-residents and the beach is public. Poseidon as sea-god is treated with due respect on Tinos, and, if in doubt, the Tinos Beach keeps its boards locked up. The beach stretches along much of the coast between Tinos town and the hotel, but is a longer walk from the centre than Agios Fokas. Here too, the best part of the beach is the furthest from town.

The road to the south-eastern tip of the island passes through very attractive dovecote and farm country on its way to two neighbouring beaches, **Agia Kyriaki** (or Agios Sostis) and **Agios Ioannis Porto**, the first of which (nearer Tinos) is preferable, with better sand and fewer people. Agios Ioannis has a complex of new holiday bungalows (*Porto Raphael*). About half-way between Tinos and the beaches is the **monastery of Agia Triada**, which has a display of folk art, mainly carved marble decoration, seen all over the island above doors and windows on chapels, dovecotes and private houses. The monastery was one of many in Greece with a secret school during the Ottoman period. The monastery and beach make a good walk from Tinos, less than five miles each way and not seriously hilly. Catering facilities at or near the beaches are at best well hidden and possibly non-existent, so take a picnic.

The rest of the island falls into two distinct excursions. One is the trip to **Pyrgos**, a very picturesque artists' village in the far north-west, easily accomplished by bus, since there is not much to be seen, except coastal scenery, on the way; the other is less specifically targeted exploration of the numerous villages in the hills of the eastern half of the island, possibly including the ascent of Exombourgo. Both start by climbing the main road up into the hills behind town; you are invited to inspect a restored windmill beside the road.

Touring the inland villages is not always easy, especially if too much reliance is placed on the island map. Several of the villages are gathered round the slopes of the old fortress mountain of **Exombourgo** (the 'E' is often dropped), which has a big cross on top and dominates Xinara (seat of the Catholic archbishop of the Cyclades) and Tripotamos. The ascent of Exombourgo is no stroll, and it is less surprising that the fortress resisted capture for so long than that the mountaintop was ever the site of a fortified town, as it was for five centuries. Ask locally for directions if you want to walk up.

The **Kechrovouni monastery**, founded in the 12th century, is a rare thriving religious community and looks like an entire Cycladic village on the hill, with a magnificent view out over the sea. It is a very popular outing from Tinos, and the spiritual hush is compromised by buses hooting an angry summons to members of their flock. The monastery is beautifully kept and several churches can be visited, as well as the cell inhabited by Saint Pelagia, of the momentous dreams.

Connoisseurs of wild and remote wind-lashed beaches should not miss **Livada**: turn right at the crossroads just outside Mesi, go through Steni and turn right down a dirt road just before the village of Myrsini. The road leads at some length down a splendid valley of goats and oak trees to the sea about five miles from Steni, the nearest taverna and bus-stop. The Livada valley is an oddly unbalanced landscape, with a remarkable chaos of loose boulders on one side but not the other, where the slopes climb to the summit of Tsiknias. There is the same contrast down by the sea, with a mixture of sand and big orangey-grey boulders, many of them weirdly eroded.

Possible explanations of the loose boulder phenomenon, which is strictly localized to one mountain mass, include volcanic eruption and a meteorite landing. The rocks are at their most other-worldly and impressive on the other side of the mountain around the village of **Volax**, where some of the boulders are bigger than the houses. There is some evidence of the basket weaving for which the village is said to be famous, and of a colony of French summer residents among the energetic restorers of the old grey houses; but no tavernas or shops. There is so little flat ground that the villagers use a wide bend in the road, itself hardly a bowling-green, for their football pitch. At the next village, Skalados, it is basketball that spans the road.

The wide valley to the north-west of these mountains is the most fertile part of the island and presents a very different landscape. **Kalloni**'s long narrow whitewashed main street leads up to a surprisingly grand 19th-century Catholic church, with a lovely view from the terrace over lemon groves, dovecotes and belfries to the distant and very alluring bay of **Kolimbithra**. This is easily reached by rough road through dense bamboo growth from Komi, and is no disappointment: two beautiful uncrowded sandy beaches with a couple of tavernas and rooms. Here, as at Livada, the sea can be quite rough. From Kalloni a rough road continues all the way up to the top of the valley, where it joins the main Tinos–Pyrgos road approximately as indicated on the local map (for once). This is fine country and the track is a good, if bumpy, way to save retracing of steps.

The Pyrgos road runs beautifully along the western side of the island's mountain spine, passing a creaking, working windmill just outside Kampos and giving splendid views over the coast and open seas to the south, before crossing the island at a high pass and descending to Pyrgos. The track mentioned above, to Kalloni and Kolimbithra, is unsignposted but not difficult to spot, heading off northwards by a dovecote-like roadside shrine just after you get a long view from the main road down the valley to the sea on the far side of the island. There are roads down to beaches below the handsome balcony villages of Kardiani and Isternia, both of which are set back from the road and worth exploring on foot. Quarrying roads complicate finding the way down to the sea from Kardiani (branching off about 1km east of the village); **Agios Nikitas** (or Isternia harbour, as it is signposted) has a very pretty sandy beach around the corner from the port, where there are a few tavernas. The good beach is clearly visible from the road on the way down.

Pyrgos, the main village of northern Tinos, is almost suspiciously picturesque, its narrow streets paved with marble and full of flowers. Near the bus-stop on the edge of the village are two museums, one devoted to the congregation of Tinos

---

Getting around

There are bus-trips from Tinos town to Pyrgos and Kechrovouni; and daily boat-trips to Mykonos/Delos.

Car and motor-bike hire is available in Tinos (most offices are on the main road out of town, running back from the harbour near Hotel Avra). Several buses a day operate from Tinos to Pyrgos, Kalloni, Steni, Kampos, Agios Ioannis Porto, and the Tinos Beach hotel (Kionia).

---

artists, the other to their high priest, Ianoulis Chalepa, leading Greek sculptor of the 19th century, who lived and worked at Pyrgos and drew other artists to the village. Both museums are free and open briefly in mid-morning and late afternoon. Pyrgos is still a village of working artists and craftsmen, with big slabs of uncut marble lying around in village gardens awaiting the hammer and chisel. Sculptors open the doors of their studios to tourists strolling through the village and, of course, sell their work, much of which is conveniently souvenir-sized. Many doors and windows are embellished with decorative carvings (there's a particularly fine double-headed Byzantine eagle at the back of Chalepa's house) and the plane-shaded small central square is delightful, with a graceful 18th-century marble fountain. Rooms are advertised near by.

It is a pleasant stroll of about 20 minutes down the road from Pyrgos to its marble-exporting port, **Panormos**. This is not a conspicuously beautiful little village, but there are tavernas on the water-front, a strip of sand and pebbles to swim from and trees to sleep beneath. Caiques shuttle bathers to a much better beach on the far side of the vast rocky bay. The only accommodation is in rented rooms.

THE REMOTE ISLANDS
Amorgos, Anafi, Antiparos, Donoussa, Folegandros, Iraklia, Kimolos, Koufounissia, Schinoussa, Sikinos

More than any other group of islands, the Cyclades has minor islands that deserve more than a place on a list of remote bolt-holes for the most determined escapists, if only because they are not all alike. The islands in question are covered here. Naturally, some of them will be of great interest to a minority of visitors to Greece, whose main interest is not sun and sand but observing and, up to a point, sharing the traditional life of the insular Greeks. Others like these islands simply because they are peaceful and infinitely relaxing.

Much the most important of these remote minor islands is **Amorgos**, a long and impressively mountainous hammer-headed island to the east of Naxos, its east and north coast almost unbroken cliff scenery. For some years Amorgos has been one of the chosen islands among the more imaginative backpacking contingent, which has not been unreservedly welcomed. The anti-tourist mentality is exemplified if not very clearly articulated in a response to a recent description of the island in *Holiday Which?*. 'You do the island a great disservice,' wrote our reader, a resident of Amorgos of 11 years' standing, 'since it means it is overrun by people who wish to spend no money while those who do [wish to spend money] stay away because of the others. Tourists are hated by the islanders because of the large numbers of them who walk almost naked through the streets. . . . This [the hatred] is disguised because they want their money but it is none the less there.' This depressing dirge, which reflects no better on the locals than it does on the tourists, will soon become familiar if you get chatting to people on Greek islands or, still more likely, about them in pubs at home. Our own visits to Amorgos have not left an impression of an island overrun, nor one of stony-faced hostility between visitors and locals, many of whom were positively friendly. On the most recent occasion the Greek National Tourist Organisation was making a promotional film about local traditions, so presumably we will not be universally condemned for joining in the quiet chorus of approval.

It is interesting and perhaps reassuring to note that over a century ago Theodore Bent wrote of his concern about the frequency of the weekly steamer, 'a dangerous enemy to primaeval customs'. Already the young women of Amorgos were scorning their ancestral costume, which included a very unwieldy head-dress called a *tourlos* (tower). Their scorn is understandable: the *tourlos* was so cumbersome to remove and install that the ladies of the island left it in place for weeks until they could no longer bear the itching from all the trapped vermin. Bent also remarked on the seriousness of the islanders. There was no dancing after the Easter festival, for example. So if a local does not smile at you, it may not mean he wishes you would go away.

Amorgos has two ports on its more sheltered and hospitable west coast, Aegiali and Katapola. Ferries often call at both ports, but the southern port of Katapola is the more important of the two and the island's main resort, and above it stands the island capital, Chora or Amorgos or Chora Amorgou, about an hour on foot or a short bus-ride from the port. Katapola extends round its bay in several sections, and is a cheerful and relaxing place with ducks waddling around under the gum trees in the dry river beds. There are cafes and tavernas on the water-front, several small hotels and pensions (the *Hotel Minoa* and pensions *Tasia* and *Amorgos* are recommended) and a campsite. The beach is shingle and not particularly good. Two new hotels on the far side of the bay from the ferry quay may do something to relieve the shortage of beds in high season for which Amorgos is notorious.

The *chora* is a typically beautiful whitewashed old village clustered around a massive fortified rock, with the statutory row of windmills and plunging sea views. Not many tourists stay at Chora, but there are rooms to rent as well as a few tavernas and arty shops, and the village comes to life in the evening when the whole population (a few hundred) seems to be out on the plane-shaded squares.

Amorgos is most famous for the astonishing monastery of Hozoviotissa (life-saving Virgin), founded by the 11th-century Byzantine emperor Alexis Comnenus and built into the cliff face of the island's east coast hundreds of feet above the sea, like a white drawer in a grey-brown chest, as de Tournefort wrote. After the War of Independence Hozoviotissa was quite literally the eastern bulwark of Greece, Astypalaia and points east remaining in Turkish hands. This came about quite by accident, according to Bent's source: when the boundary line was drawn at a conference of the great powers, they had such a bad map that Astypalaia was assigned to Turkey by mistake. At the time the monastery owned all the richest land on Amorgos and also the islands of Schinoussa and Keros. Like other monasteries it was dispossessed at the beginning of this century; it now has only a handful of monks. Hozoviotissa is about half an hour on foot from the *chora*.

A visit to the monastery can be combined with the magnificent walk along the mountainous spine of the island from Chora to the northern port of Aegiali, about four or five hours along the beautiful old donkey track, which has only recently been replaced by a rough road and is still in good condition. For those who don't object to a very early start, a good way to do the trip is to catch the dawn boat from Katapola to Aegiali and walk back. Aegiali has better beaches than Katapola and a more off-beat, studenty atmosphere, with young campers whiling away the hours and weeks playing backgammon in the waterside cafes. There are rooms to rent, and a few craft shops. While motor-bikes are now available for hire at Katapola, at Aegiali a rented donkey is the preferred mode of transport. There are rooms to rent.

One of two main stepping-stones in the little-visited southern waters between Ios and Milos, **Folegandros** (the emphasis falls on the 'leg' syllable, not the 'and') is a long and mountainous island, rising almost sheer on its windy northern side. The island is best known as a place of exile in both ancient and modern times, and its port of Karavostasis, at the south-eastern end of the island, is not in the least inviting, surrounded by boulder-strewn hills of unrelieved barrenness with no alluring white hill village in view. There are rooms, bars and tavernas and a stony beach at the port, and a seaside campsite a mile or so away, but Karavostasis is less appealing as a base than the *chora*, which is magnificently and very breezily situated on the cliffs in a position recalling that of Fira on Santorini. Chora is reached by bus (or a little under an hour on foot) from the port.

This Chora is one of the most beautiful villages of its kind, with a perfectly preserved inner precinct, walled on three sides by the backs of its houses. The fourth side needs no fortification, consisting of a very steep 700-foot waste disposal chute to the sea. Bent saw little evidence of its use – the streets were impassable for mire of pigs. Inner (Meso) Chora is now a very neat and tidy place, whitewashed and full of flowers and creepers in its vaulted courtyards. Some of the old houses inside the walls are occupied by the *Hotel Danassi* (E). There is an equally delightful shaded square outside the main gate, filled with taverna tables under the eye of a very busy and switched-on local, who knows all about the contemporary young Aegean traveller's taste for fruit juices, cocktails and what are advertised as 'yoghurt combinations', and even lends out backgammon boards. Folegandros attracts a young and trendy set these days.

From Chora it is a lovely walk northwards along the clifftop road, flanked by the handsome greenish dry-stone walls typical of the island. After about 40 minutes' walk, a donkey track leads steeply down to Angali (or Vathi), a beautiful narrow bay on the south coast with two good tavernas at the back of a sandy beach. There are rooms by the beach and a rough-camping area on a beach (Agios Nikolaos) not far to the north, reached by coastal path or caique from Angali. A team of donkeys is usually available to take the sweat out of the climb back up to the road, and a mini-bus stops at the halt a few times a day on its way between Chora and the northern village of Ano Meria. Angali and Agios Nikolaos can also be reached on boat-trips from Karavostasis, as can the island's most famous sight, the Chrisospilia, or golden cave, named after the colour of its stalagmites and stalactites. The cave's aperture is just above water level in the north-coast cliffs and is accessible only in calm weather.

Sikinos is an even more forbidding tall mountainous mass with no good anchorage, famous for its undiluted ethnic stock, which is still clearly visible in the islanders' faces: Sikinos was deserted before the arrival in the 16th century of a few hundred refugees from Ottoman-controlled Crete, who built the hill village and remained there, 'pure unadulterated Greeks . . . never likely to be disturbed by the advent of steamer or telegraph' (Theodore Bent). Never is a dangerous word. These days Sikinos can be dialled direct from Britain and cannot even claim to be undisturbed by steamers, now that the islanders have built themselves a proper quay. No longer does a visit involve the traditional adventure of throwing your bags and leaping from the ferry's lowered ramp into a launch tossing around on the waves below.

Somehow, the islanders managed to land a bus before they built their ferry quay. This prized vehicle spends most of its time at rest by the sea, occasionally making the bumpy journey up from the port to two adjacent villages, Chora and Kastro, about 4km away. Surprisingly enough, Kastro is the lower of the two. The island also now has a few cars, one of which is owned by the proprietors of a very smart (and not underpriced) set of new holiday rooms on the slopes above the port. The port, Alapronia (commonly referred to as Skala), consists of two clumps of houses like book-ends, with a scruffy beach and some rough ground between them, no longer occupied by a summer colony of rough campers who have been moved on. Like many of the island's concerns, the new rooms are run by a member of the Loukas clan, as is a good fish restaurant in the northern bit of village. The village centre and jetty is at the other end of the beach. There is a picturesque fishermen's cafe by the water and tucked away around the corner, the island emporium (Kontouris), which combines the roles of restaurant, shop, travel agent and provider of accommodation. This is one of the few places left where the extremely strong local wine, celebrated since antiquity, is on tap. There is an occasional disco on the outskirts of the village and boat-trips to a beach are advertised.

The fortress hill village (Kastro) is less impressively set but in itself scarcely less picturesque than Folegandros, in a much rougher and tumble-down way. Not far away to the south (about an hour's hard walking) lies the island's main curiosity, Episkopi, a Roman temple-like building transformed into a Christian church in the 7th century and into a monastery in the 17th. Traditionally assumed to have been a temple dedicated to Apollo (because of an inscription found near by), a mausoleum is now considered the most likely explanation of the original building's function. Who chose this magnificent spot for the family vault is unknown. It was less isolated than it is now, for the mountain was the site of the island's ancient capital.

Kimolos is probably best visited as a brief excursion from Milos, using the caique that crosses the strait several times a day in all but very rough weather. Like Milos, it is a much-quarried island, its prized mineral being fuller's earth. The old hill village is finely situated (about 15 minutes on foot from the port, Psathi) and guarded by a row of windmills on the ridge. But there is not much to see, and the port itself lacks charm. Psathi has a couple of tavernas by the harbour and a block of modern holiday rooms beside the road up to the *chora*. A rough road forking left by these buildings leads over a ridge to a considerable extent of beach (Aliki), with a few tavernas and holiday rooms and, further west, small sandy coves along a more rocky stretch of shore, popular places for camping rough. The great attraction is being right away from it all and yet able to wave down the caique as it passes for shopping or lunch excursions to Psathi or, preferably, Pollonia on the Milos side of the strait.

Antiparos may seem a surprising inclusion in this chapter, being no more than a short hop from its mother island and a popular target for excursions from there (frequent boats from Parikia and Pounta). However, it is a destination in its own right and has a similar appeal to that of the small islands between Naxos and Amorgos: a peaceful little port with a few simple hotels, and a series of excellent sandy beaches much favoured for camping and nude bathing. Antiparos has been on the Greek tourist circuit for many centuries thanks to its great cave, the finest in the Aegean. The cave entrance lies up in the hills in the south of the island, about an hour and a half on foot from the port, or half an hour from a jetty used by excursion-boats. The cave is often locked, so make enquiries before setting off if you plan to visit it other than on an organised tour.

Rock pillars frame a chapel at the entrance and a long 400-step staircase leads down to a magnificent chamber 720 feet long by 678 wide by 360 high, according to Bent who, like all visitors until recently, had to be lowered down by rope. Bent is not at his most reliable on the subject of altitudes (he estimated the height of the cave entrance at 1000 feet, whereas in reality it is less than half that) and he had only the flickering light of burning brushwood by which to assess the size of the cave; but it is certainly vast. A 17th-century French ambassador to Turkey, M. de Nointel, three times brought a retinue of 500 people down into the cave in this way to celebrate Christmas. One of many graffiti in the cave marks the stalagmite that served as an altar on Christmas Day 1673.

In an exceedingly superstitious nation, the people of Antiparos are particularly known for their superstitious nature: the Pariotes called them crows, after their habit of taking oracles from birds. A crow sitting in the south side of a tree meant the corsairs were coming, and the Antipariotes shut themselves away in their village. A crow in the northern branches meant no danger, and the islanders settled down to an untroubled siesta. To put it more simply, pirates sailed on a north wind. The island is now virtually treeless, but is not without a few portentous crows.

In Cycladic terms **Anafi** is the far east: to a Greek the name conveys isolation and poverty. Covered in volcanic rock from Santorini's eruptions, Anafi has very little to offer the visitor apart from the good humour of its inhabitants, which is as famous as it is inexplicable. There are no beaches to speak of, and no village at the port; just a hill village about a mile away, which does not exactly hum with commerce. As on Santorini, its houses tend to have barrel-vaulted roofs as a defence against earthquake, and windows in only one wall, above and beside the door. The landscape was concisely characterised by de Tournefort, who reported that there was not enough wood to cook the partridges that abound.

Between Naxos and Amorgos lies a series of small islands usually known as the Lesser Cyclades, with a collective population of about 500: the inhabited ones are **Donoussa**, **Ano Koufounissi** (there is also a **Kato Koufounissi**), **Keros**, **Schinoussa** and **Iraklia**, not to be confused on ferry timetables with the capital city of Crete. All have yielded evidence of thriving ancient Cycladic settlements. But they are not sightseeing islands: people visit them to enjoy the very simple life to be had on their quiet bays, camping or staying in basic rooms in the harbour communities and nearby hill villages, spurning such things as hotels, discos, watersports, rented motor-bikes and

other trappings of tourism to be found on most islands.
Koufounissi is the only one with electricity and most often
visited: its port on a south-facing bay has grown into a small
tourist resort. Perhaps the most picturesque is Schinoussa,
where a typical old white Cycladic village looks down over a
narrow bay. Donoussa is a long way north of the rest of the
sub-group and is served by different boats. Naxos and Amorgos
are the best platforms for visits to the islands, but some ferries
on their way to and from Piraeus call in for a glimpse of the
Lesser Cyclades, and day-trips are organised from Naxos.

CRETE

Crete is Megalonissos, The Great Island, and its legends begin
with the greatest Greek god: Zeus was born in its Dikte
mountains, used its little offshore island Dia as his private retreat
from Olympos and is even rumoured to have returned at last to
Mount Ida to die. This is the largest Greek island by far – 160
miles long and up to 38 miles wide, many times bigger than Corfu
or Rhodes. Its size alone makes it a different experience: if you
hire a car and drive 1000 miles in a week, you won't have seen
half of it. Yet, more perhaps than any other island in the
Mediterranean, Crete demands to be explored. A touring holiday
of the island can be an intense, mentally and physically exhausting
experience, but also profoundly rewarding. If you merely spend
your time in an indolent progression from hotel to beach to
taverna and back, with perhaps an excursion or two to the island's
(extraordinarily fine) archaeological museum and the famous
Minoan palace of Knossos, you may have had a surfeit of
sightseeing but you will not have done the island justice.

Saki, writer of short stories, remarked that 'the people of Crete
unfortunately make more history than they can consume locally':
many strands of an eventful past have left in abundance things of
interest for the visitor. Crete is exceptionally rich, not only in
history and archaeology but in sheer visual pleasure – scenery,
wild flowers, frescoed churches. Early travellers in quest of
legendary beauty were not all favourably impressed: French
botanist de Tournefort (clearly a pioneer of the Picturesque)
reported in 1700, 'This celebrated Mt Ida exhibits nothing but a
huge overgrown, ugly, sharp-rais'd, bald-pated eminence; not the
least shadow of a landskip, no delightful grotto, no bubbling
spring, nor purling rivulet to be seen: there is one poor sorry well
with a bucket, to keep the sheep and horses from perishing with
thirst'. But the spirit of Crete is that of the mountains; and
increasing numbers of travellers sought out remote villages
reached by mountain tracks. Crete was one of the first places in
Greece to graduate from travellers to tourists *en masse*.

In the 1960s young hard-up Americans and Scandinavians over-wintered on the south coast and formed what were to become hippie colonies, living in caves on yoghurt and honey. Now new generations of backpackers continue to live cheaply off the land and make forays into serious cultural tourism, while the erstwhile hippies who stayed have children and lead an established life-style. All of these are heavily outnumbered by straightforward package holiday-makers who come to sit in the sun, acquire the taste for *tsatsiki* and find their feet on a windsurfing board.

Because of Crete's early development as a package-holiday destination, many of its resorts grew up in an uncontrolled sprawl of concrete, making much of the north coast outside and between Crete's cities a continuous suburban ribbon. Many buildings still stand unfinished, their owners putting off paying taxes on a completed project; and more appear in every gap, edging up behind the towns and resorts. The north-east stretch – between the capital Heraklion and Malia, and around Agios Nikolaos – is the most heavily developed; and the north-west coast is built up around Chania and Rethymnon. While the resorts aren't very beautiful, they do provide a lively beach holiday with plenty of sightseeing interest (provided you don't mind long excursion bus-rides). In contrast the south coast is largely unspoilt, and the far east and west completely wild.

The development of Crete has been dictated by its geography, which has played the most influential part in shaping the island's history, mythology and climate. Dominating all is its great mountain backbone, with peaks over 8000 feet described by Patrick Leigh Fermor as 'rising like a clenched fist'. In the east are the Sitia mountains, craggy but slight by Cretan standards; further west are the Dikte and Ida (or Psiloritis) massifs, which dominate Central Crete; and in the west lies the finest range, the White Mountains (Lefka Ori), where eagles soar over gorge and chasm, and uninhabited heights became for centuries the stronghold of brigandage and revolution. Throughout the ages, the rough and rugged nature of the landscape has been quoted as matching that of the people, an inescapable truism from observers and a source of pride to the Cretans themselves. The mountains effectively divide the island into two parts, as abundant old songs illustrate:

> Fie on the young men down on the plains
> Who taste the good things of the world, the choicest foods,
> And are base to look at, like the creeping lizard.
> Joy to the young men up in the hills
> Who eat the snow and the dew-fresh air
> And are fine to look at like the orange tree.

On Crete's northern side the gentler slopes have allowed space

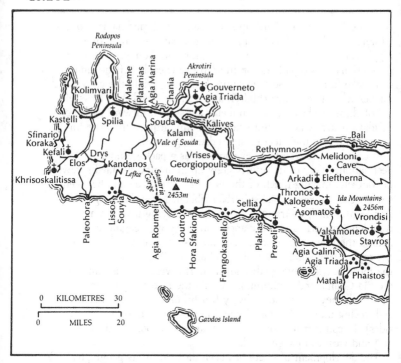

for the concentration of large towns; in the south the mountains drop sharply into the sea. Between them, only a few roads have until recently connected both halves of the island, and the southern coast still supports relatively few people; but a new road link from the south-eastern resort of Ierapetra to the Messara plain (and thus improved access to the capital Heraklion) will mean a major shift in emphasis for travel on the island.

North and south enjoy different climates. The Aegean winds which brought traders from mainland Greece and the Balkans to enrich the earliest Cretan civilisations still blow relentlessly on the northern beaches, particularly in August, while the mountains attract a summer cover of cloud. The protected south is free from clouds, and enjoys high winter temperatures which have attracted colonies of year-round long-term visitors. As in ancient days the sailors looked to Egypt and the Nile Delta for their trading route, now countless Hotel Livikons look across the Libyan sea towards Africa, only 186 miles away. Crete lies further south than Algiers or Tunis, and the nearby tiny island of Gavdhos is the southernmost point of Europe.

Crete's climate has long been favourable for cultivation, though it's no longer Homer's 'fair and fertile Crete' or the granary of Roman and Venetian times. As on many other Greek islands, the

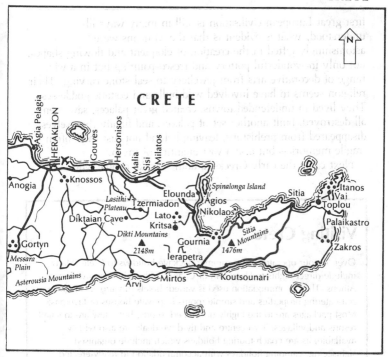

ancient coverings of forest have been largely destroyed by man, and flocks of goats continue the damage. Mount Ida, described by the 17th-century traveller William Lithgow as 'overclad even to the top with cypress trees', is now bare and rocky, and much of the island's interior is covered by a sweet-smelling herb scrub. But southern Crete has become Athens' greenhouse: acres of ugly plastic 'glasshouses' shelter winter vegetables, and there are olive, citrus and banana groves, vineyards, and fields of melons and apricots. Crops flourish on the high upland plains, a characteristic of the landscape of central Crete; and figs, almonds, pomegranates and quinces grow everywhere. The island's climate and position close to Asia have encouraged a wonderful variety of wild plants and flowers. Crete has more than 2000 plant species, almost as many as Britain, including many rarities; guided botanical tours are popular.

While the landscape of Crete deserves exploration for its diversity and scenic splendour, the island's sightseeing opportunities are the attraction for most holiday-makers. Crete is a sightseer's paradise, with an extraordinary range of art and architecture, historic and prehistoric. The period that generates the most interest is Crete's fascinating Bronze Age of settlers who became known as Minoan, after the legendary King Minos. This first great European civilisation is still in many ways ill-understood; what is evident is that the Minoans were astonishingly gifted in the creation of eloquent and flowing shapes, not only in wonderful pottery and fresco-painting but in a wide range of decorative arts from jewellery to seal-stone carving. Their religion seems to have involved wild bulls and ecstatic goddesses. They lived in undefended towns, created great palaces, saw them all destroyed, built another set of palaces, and finally themselves disappeared from prehistory, leaving behind not just their often fragile memorials but also a vast quantity of myth.

Next came the early Greeks, a dour warlike people who built

Visiting Crete

Over 50 tour operators offer summer package holidays to Crete. Many include direct flights to Heraklion or Chania, although some fly via Athens. The accommodation used is varied: hotels in various categories, self-catering properties and simple rooms in private houses or tavernas. Most packages are to the highly developed resorts, but a few are to small resorts and villages. Two-centre and fly-drive deals are also widely available, as are coach-touring holidays which include organised sightseeing, camping holidays with accommodation in ready-erected tents, and walking and nature tours.

For independent travellers accommodation is easy to find on the spot, even in peak season. Plenty of direct charter flights are available.

Hotels in Crete fall into two main types. Beach hotels (which may be some distance from the nearest town or village) are usually large, modern, low-rise buildings with extensive gardens, a swimming-pool and lots of sports and entertainment facilities. Town hotels (outside Heraklion) are usually smaller and cheaper with few public rooms or facilities. Although many of the hotels are well equipped and reasonably comfortable, there is little variety of architecture or character, and the most comfortable hotels are usually large and impersonal.

Simple rooms, either in private houses or tavernas, can be rented for one or more nights in all the main resorts and large villages. Some have private bathrooms.

There's a good range of self-catering properties to choose from. In and around the main resorts – especially Agios Nikolaos – there are lots of simply furnished apartments, often in quite small buildings, and without communal facilities like a swimming-pool, bar or reception desk. Cooking facilities are often quite limited (but tavernas are so cheap that there's little incentive to cook for yourself).

There are lots of modest 'villas', usually plain concrete buildings, although some are more attractively designed or are well restored older buildings; the more expensive villas can be quite isolated, making car

cities of their own pattern, strong and massively walled for defensive purposes. The ruins of some of these may still be seen, often in remote places, and are among the most impressive monuments of Crete. Through the classical era, Cretan Greeks contributed in artistic spheres but were too preoccupied with internal quarrels to take political part in the mainland's major wars. Later, they became valued mercenaries among the Hellenistic kingdoms. Independence in soldiery and seafaring predisposed them to the outright piracy which the Romans used as justification for occupying the island in 69BC. Large new cities soon arose, with the island now used as a base for the Roman

hire essential. Filling a modest villa with a party of four to eight people may be cheaper than taking a budget apartment for two.

Spring is a good time to visit Crete: the island is carpeted in wild flowers in March and April, and the weather is warm. From June to September it can get very hot, particularly on the south coast. Cooler, wetter weather in October and November brings back some green to the landscape. Crete is not a major winter sun destination for package holidays, but is well worth considering for a winter break. Temperatures are generally high (20°C–23°C December to February, warmer in November and March), although occasionally it can be cold and stormy for short spells.

Getting around

There are half- and full-day coach-excursions to the main sights from all the major resorts (although some involve very long journeys). Most of the excursions can be made by public bus for well under half the price.

The island is covered by a comprehensive bus network – even some small villages only reached by unmade roads have a daily service. Buses are generally quite frequent, clean and reliable, but on occasions may be too full to get on. Two systems run in tandem. Each nome or prefecture – Heraklion, Chania, Rethymnon and Lasithi (based on Agios Nikolaos) – has its own internal services, generally connecting the villages with the main town. These buses tend to come into town in the morning and leave again in the afternoon (the wrong way round for town-based tourists). Connections between bigger places in the same nome – between Paleohora and Chania, say – are considerably more frequent. There are inter-nome services, running mainly along the north coast and connecting all the main towns to one another. It is worth understanding this system because it explains the considerable number of different bus stations in each town (Heraklion has four). In some outlying districts there is a special class of rural taxi to supplement the bus service.

Taxis are plentiful in the larger towns and very cheap, particularly when shared by three or four people.

You can hire a car through your tour operator before you go, or on the

administration of considerable portions of North Africa. When the Roman Empire split into western and eastern halves, Crete formed part of the great eastern complex, passing naturally into a Byzantine period based on Orthodox Christianity. In the 9th century Arabs conquered Crete and held it for 150 years, after which there was a second Byzantine period, which lasted until the aftermath of the Fourth Crusade (1204). Each of these stages in Cretan life, with the sole exception of the Arab, left its own memorials.

In the 13th century a still richer period for monuments began. After a brief episode of domination by Genoa, Crete passed into the hands of Venice. Venetian architecture now flourished, mainly in military and religious buildings; still splendid, these are one of the great features of the island. Meanwhile, native Cretan artists and sometimes Greeks from Constantinople were painting the interiors of country chapels and churches in a rich resurgence of Byzantine fresco work; many of these survive today, though often in bad condition. These churches and chapels are frequently remote, and not uncommonly locked; but to enthusiasts the search for an elusive key is a challenge and the final reward of the paintings – however dark, confused or fragmentary – a great pleasure. Cretan-school painters later went far afield – most famous among them Domenikos Theotokopoulos, El Greco – and

---

Getting around continued

spot from a local firm. It is important to compare carefully the conditions of hire and insurance arrangements as well as the prices (see Information at the end of the book). All the norms of driving in Greece apply to Crete: drivers don't use their rear mirrors, expect you to hoot when overtaking, come round the corner on the wrong side and generally behave with spirit and enterprise of a kind which those from northern Europe may find disconcerting. Roads can deteriorate very suddenly or even, in winter, fall off the sides of hills. Generally, though, road surfaces are good. Most dirt roads are easily passable and the New Road along the north coast is a fast, modern highway. As elsewhere in Greece, the available local maps tend to take an optimistic view of many road surfaces. One exception to this rule is the new road which links Ierapetra to the Messara plain and Phaistos, Agia Triada, Matala and Agia Galini, as well as providing improved access to Heraklion.

Motor-bikes are available almost everywhere, but it's worth bearing in mind that a long Cretan journey, as well as being subject to the hazards described above, can be made very tiring by the hilly and mountainous nature of the terrain.

Day-excursions to the island of Santorini by hydrofoil or by boat are possible, as is a two-night 'mini-cruise' to Egypt.

in a parallel renaissance of Cretan literature the high point was a prodigious epic by the poet Cornaros.

Though it fostered such creativity, the regime of imperial Venice was more generally exacting and oppressive, its approach indicated by the administrator who declared Cretans wild beasts fit only for the bastinado. There were many uprisings: a revolutionary tradition took root. But from 1646, Cretans and Venetians together fought off the Turks for almost a quarter of a century, watched (but unassisted until too late) by the rest of Christendom.

In 1669 Heraklion fell to the Turks, who proceeded to rule with a heavy hand – suppressing some 400 revolts – until 1898. Many Cretans converted to Islam; others endured a repression which made the earlier Venetians appear easy masters. The Cretan Christians – calling themselves 'captains', or *palikares* – fought back when they could in a series of revolts, ever more ferocious and ever more noted by the outside world, right through the 18th and 19th centuries. But the Great Powers which helped establish modern Greece as an independent nation in 1832 were content to let Crete linger on in Turkish hands. It was only in 1913, after a brief international wardship, that Crete became a part of Greece. In that year the Greek national flag was first raised officially – among the Venetian defences of Chania.

Crete's modern history is one of struggle against poverty, followed by struggle against the Germans. In May 1941 Allies and Greeks were defeated in the Battle of Crete and four years of fresh repression began. The Cretans are rightly honoured for a resistance as bitter and hopeless as any in their past. Memorials of the war are an almost inescapable and often very moving element of a visit to the island.

One aspect of Crete that separates it from other Greek islands is its towns. While they may not be entirely appealing as a summer holiday base, Chania and Rethymnon are two of the most beautiful and fascinating old towns in Greece and offer a very attractive mixture of town life and tourism. The biggest town of all, the island's capital, is not included in this recommendation – Heraklion is a very ugly modern city, like a big chunk of Athens with the redeeming feature of being on the sea. But it offers a handful of sights well worth a visit, in particular the exceptionally rich Archaeological Museum, which houses the finds from the Minoan sites of the island.

Recent improvements to Crete's roads make it possible if rather tiring to reach Heraklion and the palace of Knossos, and even the popular natural sight of the Gorge of Samaria (in the far south-west), on a day-trip from almost any part of the island. But the best way to sample the island's variety is on a touring holiday, using a hired car, and preferably out of high season.

The Centre

Central Crete possesses a disproportionate share of Crete's main monuments. HERAKLION, the island's capital, is not a place where one would choose to spend a holiday; but its Archaeological Museum is of international renown and contains the best of Minoan art and artefacts. Just outside lies the great Minoan palace of KNOSSOS; in the south are two more major sites, PHAISTOS and AGIA TRIADA, as well as the large Graeco/Roman/Byzantine site of GORTYN.

Most of the resorts are situated along the north coast, mainly to the east of Heraklion; there are some more isolated centres in the south. One or two are either attractive or unusual enough to be worth considering seriously, but others will score low on any list of good holiday bases.

Travelling west from Heraklion and as close as possible to the coast (that is to say, for the time being avoiding the large modern highway that runs along just inland) the first resort area is Amoudara and neighbouring Linoperamata. The beach is good, but views are considerably interrupted by a large power station. After this, to continue along the coast, you have to join the New Road, as it is generally called. This climbs north around a rocky cape, with side turnings down to **Agia Pelagia**, a series of coves with a rapidly growing resort village along the back of the best beach. It's a popular place for Heraklion weekenders and, increasingly, foreign tourists. There's a cheerful arrangement of tavernas lined up along the back of the beach, and the promontory at the end is occupied by the *Capsis Beach* (A), a big package-holiday hotel with a good swimming-pool but no beach of its own. In a more secluded position away from the resort are a few smaller hotels, above small sandy beaches. The *Peninsula* (A) is the best of these.

Further west, the New Road cuts through impressive mountain coastline to pass **Bali**, reached by its own side-road and consisting of a series of east-facing coves strung out along a bay. The furthest cove is a pretty, sleepy little fishing-harbour. There are fruit trees, rooms to rent and villas, a choice of beaches and a choice of medium-sized hotels, among them the *Bali Beach* (B). A few miles further comes the somewhat bedraggled settlement of Panormos. After this, the coast belongs more clearly to Rethymnon and the west (see below).

Travelling east from Heraklion, one passes first the airport and then Heraklion's town beach. There now begins an ugly, hastily assembled, unfinished strip of bars, hotels and apartment blocks lying behind a good sandy beach. The names of the tiny straggling villages are used to locate the often isolated hotels – Amnissos, Karteros, Hani Kokkini. Lower or 'Kato' **Gouves**, just past the American military airbase of Gournes, is a strange little open peninsula with hotels along its coast – notably the *Creta Sun* (A), an attractive package hotel.

Next comes **Limani Hersonisou**, the Port of Hersonisos. Despite a shortage of beaches (mainly scraps of pebble and sand to the east) this small town now qualifies as a resort. Its busy little front rises above a picturesque sea wall, crammed with restaurants and fashionable, expensive boutiques. The drawback is the main road that cuts through town about a block behind the shoreline. This is the main throughway for holiday-making pedestrians returning to their hotels as well as for traffic roaring through, an unhappy combination. The huge *Creta Maris Hotel* (Luxury-category) at the western edge of the resort has the best beach (large and sandy), agreeable gardens and architecture that pays attention to Cretan vernacular. Hersonisos definitely has its good points.

Malia, the next major resort along the coast, has the beaches Hersonisos lacks (though you need to walk about half a mile from the resort to reach them and they become very crowded). The main beach is good and sandy, with a small island offshore. The resort itself is a mixture of the festive and the depressing, with a throng of discos and gaggle of tavernas, supermarkets, small hotels and abundant quantities of genuinely cheap building. Malia also has many plastic-covered greenhouses, mostly used for growing bananas. Just to the east, close to the main road, are the extensive remains of the Minoan palace of MALIA.

The last places on this strip of coast (before the main road cuts up inland to re-emerge at Agios Nikolaos) are the villages of **Sisi** and **Milatos**. Sisi, backed by the same gauntly theatrical mountains as Malia, is beginning to emerge as a holiday venue, though only a small one at this stage; there's a pretty cove of sand and pebbles over the hill to the east of Sisi.

A moderately fast main road crosses Crete diagonally south-west from Heraklion. It rises through vineyards over the centre of the island and drops down into the broad **Plain of the Messara**, rich in agriculture generally and olives in particular. The sites of PHAISTOS, AGIA TRIADA and GORTYN are on this plain.

Continuing the diagonal progression, though finally by minor roads, one arrives eventually at the former hippie colony and resort of MATALA, on the west-facing coast of the Messara. Or, by crossing the Messara at first due west and then north-west, one arrives, through a host of plastic greenhouses and bypassing the dismal resort of Kokkinos Pirgos, at the bustling resort village of AGIA GALINI.

Heraklion (Iraklion)

Heraklion is a convenient place for an overnight stop on first
arrival, but hardly ideal for a holiday base. It is large and noisy,
with that special concrete atmosphere which visitors may
recognise from Athens. But like Athens during the course of
mainland or inter-island travels, Heraklion is a useful
administrative centre for a stay in Crete, with many worthwhile
things to see concealed beneath the charmless surface. While
there's no beach in the town itself (though several quite good
ones within a few miles), little nightlife and few exceptional
restaurants (though many are very popular), Heraklion
possesses in its Archaeological Museum the best of Minoan art
and artefacts and is only three miles from the major site of
Knossos.

The city is best seen at dusk when the streets are teeming
with people, the food market has come to life after a long
slumber and the gardens are full of strollers. People congregate
in two of the main squares: Eleftherias, where waiters dodge the
cars to serve the tables on large tree-filled traffic islands, and
little Venizelou Square, known to all foreigners as Fountain
Square, with its 17th-century Venetian Morosini fountain which
incorporates marine motifs and 14th-century lions. In the
immediate vicinity there are several restored or reconstructed
Venetian buildings – St Mark's right on Fountain Square, the
Venetian Loggia just beyond (now used as the city hall) and
behind the two the church of St Titus, Paul's emissary to Crete
and patron saint of the island. In the old harbour the 16th-
century Venetian fortress, which held out against the Turks
before falling in 1669 after a 24-year siege, is much restored.

There are a fair number of hotels in every category. A
generally safe stand-by is the *Astoria* (A) in Eleftherias Square
(though on a recent winter stay its hot water proved
inadequate). The newer *Galaxy* (A) is further from the centre,
but its swimming-pool is very welcome.

Heraklion: sights

• **Archaeological Museum** The Heraklion Museum is one of the great
shrines to the Minoans, as high on the list of essential viewing as the
palace of Knossos itself and probably outranking even the delectably
sited palace of Phaistos. Its unique collection, consisting of the best of
everything Minoan which can be brought indoors, offers two principal
perspectives on a rich and delightful civilisation. First, the museum
invites us quite simply to take pleasure in the beauty of Minoan art.
Then there comes the game, at least as intriguing for beginners as for
scholars, of trying to imagine Minoan life on the basis of the surviving
art and artefacts of this mysterious people.

The collection, which is disappointingly housed, includes finds from the fourth great palace at Kato Zakros (the most recently excavated), Minoan sarcophagi, a major gallery of Minoan frescoes, and a private collection of Minoan art donated to the museum; there are also Greek and Roman antiquities.

The main art forms represented, developing and changing over the full 1200 years or so of Minoan exuberance, are pottery, seal-stone engraving, stone-carved vases and utensils, miniature sculpture, relief carving in stone, jewellery and various kinds of metalwork. Fresco-painting, in which the Minoans were to excel, came later than the other arts and lasted until the end. The emphasis in all the arts appears to be on grace and flow, and there is a far greater degree of naturalism than was evident anywhere else in early Middle Eastern and Mediterranean civilisations.

Visitors will no doubt follow their own noses, but it is certainly worth looking out for some of the best known (and most frequently reproduced) Minoan masterpieces.

Selected highlights include: Gallery One: Agios Onouphrios and Vassiliki ware pottery; wonderful early stone-carved jars, boxes and box-lid from Mokhlos in the east; early seal-stones. Gallery Three: Kamares ware pottery (Old Palace period), mainly from Knossos and Phaistos (this includes infinitely delicate eggshell ware and huge polychrome vessels frequently encrusted with ornament); the Phaistos disc (see page 503). Gallery Four (New Palace period): the two miniature faience snake goddesses from the sacral area of Knossos (both bare-breasted, one with her arms entwined with snakes, the other holding out snakes in her hands); the bull's head vessel (rhyton) for pouring libations, from the Little Palace of Knossos (this majestic effigy in serpentine stone has one surviving eye in jasper and rock crystal); a miniature acrobat in ivory; a ceremonial sword from Malia and an astonishing piece of a sword handle, a pierced disc showing an athlete in gold foil bending his body backwards, toes to mop of curly hair. Gallery Five: New Palace-style amphoras and some vessels with marine decoration, notably octopi. Gallery Seven: three relief-carved serpentine vases from Agia Triada (one, the unreservedly wonderful Harvester Vase, showing a celebratory procession on its shoulder, all that survives of the original); also gold jewellery, including the very famous pendant of bees or hornets holding a honeycomb. Gallery Eight: finds from Zakros (mainly New Palace period) including some of the finest of all rhytons, one of rock crystal, one in the form of a bull's head. Gallery Thirteen: Minoan sarcophagi, painted clay, some in the form of chests, others perhaps having also seen service as baths, including the most celebrated of all Minoan sarcophagi, a magnificent plastered and fresco-painted chest from Agia Triada. There is also a wooden model of Knossos in its glory, useful if you can retain the detail in your head. Galleries Fourteen and Fifteen: frescoes, all worth close attention, mainly for content and treatment but also for reconstruction (it is from the images portrayed in seal-stones, signet rings and frescoes that some of our clearest notions of the Minoans may be derived). Few can pass by the bull-leaping fresco from Knossos without amazement, both at the grace of it and at the possibility that something of the sort actually took place; but there are many other pleasures too, like the lumpy-nosed and large-eyed lady known as la Parisienne.

● **Historical and Ethnographical Museum** (just behind the front, west of the Venetian castle) This has an interesting early-Christian collection, largely from Gortyn (see page 501); good icons; memorials of the struggle for Cretan independence, with portraits of moustachioed Cretan 'captains' bristling with weapons; a reproduction of the study of the Cretan novelist Nikos Kazantzakis (author of *Zorba the Greek* and *Freedom and Death*, both set in Crete); moving 20th-century photographs; and, perhaps most engaging of all, a display of Cretan weaving and textiles.

● **St Katherine's Sinaiite Church** (Agia Ekaterini) The church contains a set of icon paintings by Michael Damaskinos. This Cretan-born and Cretan-trained painter (a contemporary and probably a fellow-student of El Greco) returned from Italy in the later years of his life and progressively abandoned Renaissance perspective in favour of the old Byzantine style, formal and hierarchical.

Knossos

The great Minoan palace of Knossos (5km south of Heraklion) is accessible either direct from the city or by turning off the New Road and driving a short distance south.

Knossos ranks with Delphi and Mycenae as one of the trinity of outstanding Greek sites where ruins, myth and even some fragments of surviving memory are deeply intertwined, compelling our awe and astonishment.

Knossos is older than the other two by centuries, and the many legends associated with it even more amazing. Was there any basis in reality for the stories of its king, Minos, who consulted every nine years with almighty Zeus deep in a cavern? What of his wife Pasiphaë, 'lewd and luxurious', who fell in love with a bull and produced the monstrous Minotaur, half-man, half-beast, living off human flesh? Was there really a labyrinth of some sort to contain this monster? Were wild bulls really confined at Knossos? Were there 'bull-leaping' rituals? Did Theseus really come from Athens as part of a human tribute to be devoured by the Minotaur? Did he ally himself with Ariadne, daughter of Minos, and somehow put a stop to this periodic sacrifice? The story has Theseus entering the labyrinth and step by step unwinding a ball of thread given him by Ariadne so that after slaying the monster he can make his escape. Perhaps these tales are as deliberately symbolic as that of Daedalus and Icaros, father and son. Implicated in the death of the Minotaur, they escaped by flying away from Crete on home-made wings – except that Icaros, perpetual symbol of heedless pride, everybody's wild boy on a motor-bike, flew higher until the sun melted the wax and he plunged into the sea.

What is so astonishing about Knossos is that while archaeology has not provided positive backing for any of the tales, it has revealed a host of parallels and associations – fascinating hints which challenge you to tease out a version of Minoan reality. If ever a palace looked like a labyrinth, that palace is Knossos. Bull themes are overwhelmingly plentiful: the bull's head libation vessels now in the Archaeological Museum at Heraklion, the horns of consecration which once adorned the walls around the palace courtyard, and above all the extraordinary bull-leaping fresco, also in the museum.

Another aspect of Knossos is the manner of its restoration, which is unique. Sir Arthur Evans, its original excavator, who worked there in the early years of this century, was not content merely with digging and recording but actually restored large areas to what he believed to have been their original condition. You are thus offered a version, in places a somewhat over-imaginative version and certainly in decorative terms a rather crude one, of a full-blown Minoan palace, looking as if only recently destroyed. Some find this acceptable, some off-putting; but the stimulus here certainly helps to start up the imagination on later visits to other sites, left just as they were after excavation.

Knossos is the best known of Crete's archaeological sites, and is on the itinerary of every tourist, whether as an organised excursion or an independent visit. It consequently gets very crowded. The best time to visit is very early in the morning or late afternoon. Visitors enter Knossos from the car-park, following a raised stone 'causeway' across a paved area and passing various pits and wells, to reach the west entrance of the New Palace.

Knossos: highlights

- **Corridor of the Procession** The west entrance leads to this ceremonial corridor, once ornamented with a fresco believed to have contained hundreds of figures. The most famous is the cup-bearer, a broad-shouldered and wasp-waisted figure typical of Minoan portrayals of young males. The corridor leads round eventually to the southern entrance to the palace, a handsome structure with pillars and frescoes (the original frescoes are in Heraklion's Archaeological Museum but replicas are displayed here, most *in situ*).
- **Central Court** The southern entrance gives access to this large space, a dominant feature of all the Minoan palaces. The palaces seem in fact to have been built outwards from the courtyards, always with a sacred area of crypts and shrines on the western side of the court. The sacred area was in turn associated with store-rooms for oil and grain. To the

THE MINOANS

The Minoan civilisation flourished on Crete between about 2600BC and the destruction of almost all the major sites in some ill-understood disaster in approximately 1450BC. Knossos seems to have lasted, damaged but reoccupied, for another two generations and more. This time-scale means that the Minoans emerged on the very heels of the Neolithic period and that the long Minoan phase of high achievement ran through most of the Bronze Age of the eastern Mediterranean. The Minoan civilisation fell, probably not by pure coincidence, just as the Bronze Age Achaian/Mycenaean civilisation of the mainland arose. Classical Greece came almost 1000 years after the high point of the Minoans. They were, in short, astonishingly early, the first major civilisation to arise on what is now European soil.

Compared with related but differing developments in Egypt and the Middle East, the Minoan progression appears extraordinarily attractive, at least to the many who visit Crete and become Minoan enthusiasts. To take one important theme, it seems the Minoans lived in peace: their towns, and later their palaces, were undefended. This may not have been due to innate peacefulness, but because of their great strength as a commercial and a maritime power – they traded widely and were perhaps so successful that they did not need to fear attack. Another aspect of Minoan life about which we have some information is their fondness for play; the term 'ludic' is sometimes applied to their civilisation. Among archaeological finds there are gaming-boards that look like ancestors of chess sets and frescoes showing Minoan crowds in pleasant animation, as if at some form of entertainment. Men are represented as athletic, balletic even, women as lively and unrepressed. This is often taken as a sign that women enjoyed high status. Few would dispute that the Minoans excelled in each of the visual arts they practised.

All this, it must be said, refers to those who inhabited the great Minoan palaces. The evidence suggests that theirs was a completely stratified society, with a wealthy palatial group at the upper extreme and a humbler population, probably a very large one, living in crowded circumstances in towns and villages. The ruler, whether controlling merely a locality or the whole of the island as a single

east or north, depending on the site, 'royal' apartments were placed; at Knossos they were on the east side of the court (entrance two-thirds of the way along on the right-hand side if you come in from the south).

• **Royal apartments** There was one floor at courtyard level and one above, with a further two below, cut into the steep slope of the hill and reached by what Evans dubbed the 'Grand Staircase'. In large part this still exists today, a genuine survival, and is widely regarded as one of the most notable of Minoan architectural achievements. Descending the

entity, was most probably a priest-king, presiding over both religious and economic life.

Wealth seems to have consisted, just as one might expect in the Mediterranean, of olive oil and grain. There was no currency but gold was much appreciated. As for the nature of Minoan religion, this may best be felt in the dark and secretive-seeming shrines that were to be found on the western side of the central court of each of the great palaces. A goddess seems to have been central to the cult; she and her priestesses were closely involved with snakes, probably associated with immortality and healing. The Minoans may also have worshipped bulls, which figure large in Minoan art – sometimes being hunted with net, noose and stave, sometimes in bull-leaping rituals where athletes somersault along their charging backs. Altars sometimes had horns; sculpted pairs of horns, described by archaeologists as horns of consecration, were used to decorate the tops of walls in houses and palace courtyards.

*Four great Minoan palaces are known: at **Knossos** near Heraklion, at **Phaistos** in the south of the centre, at **Malia** on the northern plain and at **Zakros** in the extreme east. There may well be another great palace, ancient Kydonia, still to be discovered in Chania, or somewhere near by. There is a secondary palace at **Agia Triada**, just near Phaistos; a number of manor houses have been located and explored; and there are many known townships of a more artisan and domestic nature. In addition, there are many shrines and caves where the Minoans worshipped, leaving behind gifts for the gods and little statues of themselves in attitudes of worship.*

Many visitors to Crete experience difficulty with the chronology. This is partly because the early archaeologists themselves found it difficult and expressed their findings in ways that were far from simple. The easiest place to start is with the dating of the palaces. All the known palaces were built in an early version round about 1900BC. They were then destroyed in about 1700BC in a catastrophe, perhaps an earthquake, which scarcely disrupted the Minoan progression. The palaces were soon rebuilt, but these 'new' palaces were themselves destroyed, with the partial exception of Knossos, in about 1450BC. We know that in their final stages, a form of early Greek was used for keeping records, suggesting that the Minoan civilisation had been taken over by the Achaian (Mycenaean). The reason for the final destruction, even its nature, remains totally mysterious, though

staircase, visitors will notice a plentiful array of the large inverted pillars the Minoans used (they seem to be everywhere in the Evans reconstruction). There are remnants of grand chambers and reproduction frescoes of figure-of-eight ox-hide shields. The ground floor is the most rewarding and contains, among other important rooms, the Queen's Hall or Megaron (south of the stairway – you have to wiggle round to find it) with a fresco of dolphins and a delightful glimpse of a girl dancer. Nearby is a closet with a clay bath, described

burning seems to have figured. One theory, closely related to
speculation over dating, suggested that Cretan civilisation was virtually
obliterated by a tidal wave spreading out from the dramatic eruption
of the island of Santorini to the north. It is beyond dispute that
Santorini did erupt, in the greatest known seismic disturbance of the
ancient world and with climatic consequences felt as far away as
California; but archaeologists today have recently returned, again via
arguments over dating, to the original 'classical' belief that the palaces
perished in some kind of military conflagration.

The Greeks themselves did not get much of a look-in in early
excavation, though Greek scholars are making up for this today.
Phaistos was excavated mainly by Italians, Malia by the French and
Knossos under the autocratic but brilliant Englishman Sir Arthur
Evans. Evans proposed a dating scheme which has broadly stuck, which
divides the whole Minoan period into four – 'Before the Palaces',
2600–2000; 'Old Palaces', 2000–1700; 'New Palaces', 1700–1400; and
'After the Palaces', 1400–1150.

From the early Minoan periods, the most plentiful finds are pottery.
There are several types: Pyrgos ware, Agios Onouphrios ware and
Vassiliki ware, each named after the site where examples of what
proved a particular style were first uncovered. Of this early pottery,
newcomers to the Minoans generally get most fun out of Vassiliki
ware, with its teapot-shaped vases ending in impossibly long spouts
and with deliberately uneven, oddly mottled firing. There were also
beautiful stone jars from the early period, probably hollowed out with

as the Queen's Bathroom (and in this area there was even a flushing
lavatory). It is these rooms more than most others in the palace which
seem to evoke the people who lived in them.

• **Sanctuary** This sacred area lies on the west side of the central
courtyard. The main places in this series of dark and numinous
chambers are fairly easy to find, but for the identification of each
individual room a ground-plan is necessary. Starting from the northern
end of the courtyard and working southwards at ground level (there is
a partially restored *piano nobile* above), one first enters an outer
chamber with a replica throne and then, behind it, a strange and
impressive throne room containing its original throne (perhaps intended
for a priestess). This is flanked by fresco griffins and is close to a lustral
basin reached by descending six stone steps.

A short way to the south, past a set of stairs to the first floor,
visitors can look into a little warren where sacred temple goods,
including the two snake goddesses, were discovered buried in
rectangular cysts beneath the floor. In the same complex but further
behind are the Pillar Crypts, dark little shrines where the sacred
symbol of the double axe (*labrys*) was scrawled into the rock. This, one
feels, was the very heart of Minoan religious life.

*reed drills and infinite patience. Miniature carving on sealstones
flourished, along with the miniature sculpture of religious shrines.*

*All these arts were carried forward into the period of the early
palaces. Wonderful golden jewellery now came to the fore –
extraordinary examples were recovered from Malia – along with fine
ceremonial weapons and a new type of pottery, Kamares ware, named
after a cave high on the mountains above Phaistos. Some Kamares
ware is astoundingly fine and delicate, other examples grander and
more elaborately decorated. This is an incomparable period in Minoan
pottery.*

*In the time of the new palaces, perhaps it is architecture we should
most admire. This was inventive and certainly decorative from within.
The Minoans seem to have invented the world's first flush toilets.
Equally, though, one must admire the frescoes (most now gathered in
the Heraklion Archaeological Museum). These are heavily restored –
sometimes to the point of incredibility – but cumulatively they seem to
show in larger and more cursive form the joy in naturalism and love
of natural beauty revealed on the tiny scale of Minoan seal-carving
and in Minoan miniature sculpture. Other Minoan artefacts from the
new palace period, including the finds of the Greek archaeologist
Nicholas Platon at Zakros in the 1960s, are too numerous to mention
but will surprise and delight the receptive visitor.*

*The Minoan legacy is by any reckoning an extraordinary thing.
Perhaps, at base, we admire the Minoans because they held artistic
values and explored artistic perceptions which still seem relevant – and
beautiful – today.*

In this general area are examples of the giant pottery storage jars
Minoans used for storing oil and grain. Other examples, often
exceedingly elaborate, can be found at all the other palaces.

• **Northern Portico and Royal Road** Leaving the courtyard by the
northern entrance, one passes a portico with a splendid relief fresco of a
charging bull, a fearsome guardian. And then one is out again, strolling
across typical wide Minoan paving to a spot where a road running in
from the north-west terminates in a set of beautiful but somewhat
wonky steps. This corner forms what is usually called the Theatral
Area, clearly well adapted for performance or ceremony. After some of
the more threatening aspects of the palace interior, this sun-soaked
spot, today set among pines, seems by contrast open and delightful in
atmosphere.

Malia

The Minoan site of Malia is close to the main road some 3km
east of the resort of Malia. It consists of a flattish set of ruins
looking up to the mountains behind. Here, as at the palaces of

Knossos and Phaistos, there is a central court with sacred chambers to the west, and, in this case, a large hall on the same side. There are storage pits, once roofed, in the south-west corner of the site. Just behind the south-west corner of the court itself, a round limestone slab is set into the floor; it has a depression at its centre and 34 smaller hollows around its edge, like a giant roulette wheel. This strange object is generally taken as some kind of table for votive offerings. The east side of the court was probably less impressive than the two-storeyed west, with a series of storage chambers. The 'royal' apartments were to the north of the court.

This is a much less emphatic site than those at Knossos, Phaistos or Agia Triada (see below), pleasant to wander through but not a knockout. Many magnificent art objects and weapons came from Malia, however, as well as the brooch of the pair of bees holding a honeycomb, excavated from a tomb area some minutes' walk away (now in the Archaeological Museum, Heraklion).

Anogia and the Idaian Cave

On the northern slopes of Mount Psiloritis (or Ida), 30km west of Heraklion, Anogia is a large and active village which was destroyed by the Germans in the Second World War in reprisal for sheltering the group who abducted the German commander-in-chief, General Kreipe, and smuggled him off the island in a spectacular episode of derring-do. Anogia has since repaired its fortunes by attention to the tourist trade and is a favourite spot for weaving and organised 'Cretan evenings'. It is also the starting-point for expeditions to the **Idaian Cave**, rival contender to the Diktaian Cave above the Lasithi Plateau (see below) as the birthplace of Zeus. Legend links Zeus's youth and upbringing quite specifically with this cave, and it was a place of pilgrimage during classical Greek times. The cave is a long trek on a rough road from Anogia; as we went to press it was closed for excavations.

Melidoni Cave

Near the north-coast resort of Bali, and 4km east of the village of Perama, this is another spot for a torch and non-slip shoes. The entrance-way leads down into a grotto of stalactites where altars commemorate the massacre by the Turks of 300 local people who had taken refuge here during the wars of the 1820s. The scholar and indefatigable traveller Robert Pashley – his great two-volume work *Travels in Crete* is a bible for lovers of

the island – visited the cave in 1834 and found it strewn with
the bones of the victims, asphyxiated by fires set at the mouth
of the cave. 'Alas,' he wrote, 'the passages through which they
rushed suffered the destroying vapour to follow them . . . the
bones and skulls of the poor Christians are so thickly scattered
it is impossible to avoid crushing them as we pick our way
along.'

Lasithi Plateau and Diktaian Cave

This area may be reached from the north coast (33km from
Hersonisos) or from Agios Nikolaos (42km). The Lasithi Plateau
will soon become familiar to visitors on Crete as one of the
island's most popular picture-postcard subjects. The stock shot
shows great numbers of tiny windmills, triangular canvas sails
stretched tight on little metal frames, busily whirring away to
irrigate a high flat plain, with mountains in the background.
Petrol pumps have thinned the windmills over recent years but
the scene is still a very pretty one in early summer, certainly
most unusual, and the drive up through rugged country is also
enjoyable.

Crete has a number of these high, flat valleys cupped by
mountains. Lasithi is the biggest and, agriculturally, the richest.
Because it was remote, it became a centre of resistance under
the Venetians, who accordingly prohibited cultivation here for
centuries. Today, it is vigorously farmed, and produces good
crops of apples and potatoes. An extra feature is the **Diktaian
Cave**, just a few minutes' walk from the village of Psykhro. This
is the major of the two candidates for the legendary birthplace
of Zeus (the other is the Idaian Cave; see above). The cave,
which was certainly sacred to the Minoans, is damp and slippery
underfoot, and gets very crowded in high season.

The villages of **Psihro** and **Tzermiadon** cater for the many
tourists who visit this area.

Gortyn

On the fertile Messara plain, a little west of the large village of
Agii Deka, this extensive site – Graeco-Roman, with important
early Christian contributions – is one of the most pleasing in
Crete. Most of the remains, including a magnificent fragment of
early Christian basilica, are enclosed in the main site, but
others, well worth exploring, are scattered around the olive
groves on the other side of the main road, a few hundred yards
towards Heraklion. Visitors can have the delightful sensation of
strolling unrestrained and unregarded through profuse remnants

of antiquity, like 18th-century savants recovering a lost world. Some of the major ruins are very fine and handsome.

Gortyn rose to eminence at the end of the Minoan period – long before the discovery of Knossos it was traditionally held to be the city of King Minos, because of a presentably labyrinthine cave system in the nearby hills – and became an important early Greek city-state. The chief of its Greek remains are the temple of Pythian Apollo (south of the through road) and the large stone blocks magnificently inscribed with a text known as the Code of Gortyn, Europe's first known legal code. The script is in an archaic form of Greek, and the letters of every second line are inscribed back to front so that you read from left to right and then from right to left – a form of writing called *boustrephedon*, the Greek for ploughing with oxen.

Gortyn became an extremely large and important city during the Roman period, ruling over Roman territory in North Africa. The handsome Praetorium (south of the through road) was the seat of the Roman administrator. The Odeion (north) was used for theatrical performances.

There is a good small museum on-site, with sculptures and lots of photographs of excavations in progress (including Italians supervising armies of traditionally-costumed Cretans), but the best local finds are in the Historical and Ethnographical Museum in Heraklion.

Phaistos

Ranking second only to Knossos in size and interest, the Minoan palace of Phaistos occupies an outstandingly beautiful site on a low hill in the plain of the Messara, looking up to the slopes of Psiloritis. Here, in sharp distinction to Knossos, there has been no reconstruction and the excavated palace stands in beautiful if somewhat complex purity. Many of the objects found here during the excavations are now in the Archaeological Museum in Heraklion, including the particularly fine Kamares ware items, special even by Minoan standards.

Visitors enter in the north-west corner of the site, crossing a paved open space, the Upper Court. Built up against its southern side, though not reaching the full height of the wall, there is a set of steps like those in the theatral area of Knossos. It seems probable that these, whether used by performers or audience, must have fulfilled the same function as at Knossos. The west court lies at the bottom of the theatral steps, with the front wall of the original Old Palace running across it. The main difficulty in understanding Phaistos is that remains of the old palace (destroyed around 1700 BC) are interlaced with those of

the New (destroyed around 1450 BC). Turning left (eastwards) at
the theatral steps, the New Palace is entered by its own
handsome flight of stairs. Just to the right of these steps there
are extensive store-rooms, some with giant storage jars.
Beyond, to the east, lies the large central courtyard, which was
common to both Old and New Palaces. As at Knossos, the
sacred chamber lay on the western side (half-way down the
court). Here, though, the 'royal' apartments are on the extreme
northern edge of the site (covered with modern roofing). They
are notable for the quality of their materials rather than for
frescoes or other decoration and must have offered fine views of
Mount Psiloritis (ancient Ida). In the ruins of the Old Palace,
just a few paces to the east of the royal apartments, the Phaistos
disc (now in the Heraklion Archaeological Museum) was
discovered. This mysterious baked clay tablet is inscribed with
241 characters which have so far eluded all attempts at
deciphering.

A couple of miles north of Phaistos, in the village of **Vori**, is
an **ethnology museum**. This excellent new museum is well
presented, and contains a refreshingly accessible collection of
local crafts that will appeal to many visitors frustrated by the
obscurities of archaeological sightseeing. There are shepherds'
crooks, bagpipes, pottery, threshing sledges, and lots of
basketwork including fish traps.

Agia Triada

This is a far smaller and considerably less visited Minoan site
than Phaistos (3km to the east), though it's even more
beautifully situated – around the foot of a small hill on the
Messara plain, looking west towards the sea (which in Minoan
times came right up close to it) and up towards Psiloritis. Why
there was any need for a second palace so close to Phaistos
remains a minor mystery; what is certain is that some of the
most remarkable of all Minoan objects came from here. The
carved steatite vases now displayed in the Archaeological
Museum at Heraklion (including the Harvester Vase in Gallery
Seven) came from Agia Triada; and two frescoes in Gallery
Thirteen originated here. The much-admired fresco sarcophagus
shown in the same gallery came from just a stone's throw
away. Many visitors will probably wish to enjoy the site
without bothering themselves excessively over details of
archaeology, although it's probably worth noting that the main
palatial site is in the south-west corner. Extending to the north
are the remains of a town, including what appears to have been
a row of shops.

Matala

Matala is a small port and seaside village whose excellent sandy beach is flanked by cliffs of soft and sandy rock. Into these, over the centuries, great numbers of small caves have been carved, some perhaps initially as tombs. Many have clearly been used, at one time or another, as quite comfortable little dwellings. During the 1960s, after long abandonment by local people, they were taken over by full-time hippie occupants. Nowadays, the caves are closed off at night by the police, but the hippie memories live on – helped by graffiti slogans ('Life is today') scrawled over the harbour wall. But the image is deceptive, for this is now a fairly regular little package-holiday resort, lively and still quite trendy, with concrete hotels, tavernas and coach-parties of bathers having a breather from their organised sightseeing excursion. The most beautiful resident colonists climb up to the rocky ledges to sunbathe naked, coldly surveying the crowded beach like leopards draped over the branches of a tree.

Agia Galini

This is the pick of the popular package-holiday resorts of Crete – with a picturesque setting and a compact, villagey layout clustered around a small harbour with very narrow, animated, traffic-free lanes climbing the hill behind. Tavernas line the harbour and back alleys, and there are several discos. A row of attractive medium-sized hotels looks out over the bay. The *Soulia* (C) is well placed in the thick of things by the harbour; good hotels in a quieter position on the hill include the old-fashioned *Minos* (D) and *Akteon* (E). The village beach is narrow and confined; a concrete causeway leads round the base of low cliffs to a long but uncomfortably stony beach (about a quarter of an hour's walk).

Agia Galina generally provides a very attractive contrast to the sprawling north-coast resorts, and is very well placed for sightseeing excursions to all parts of the island – from Knossos to the Samaria Gorge.

Valsamonero and Vrondisi Monasteries

The journey to these two monasteries in fine mountainous settings near the quiet and prosperous village of **Zaros** is half the pleasure, taking the traveller up on the southern side of Mount Psiloritis through a deeply rural Cretan landscape with olives and vineyards. From the village of Vorizia (7km north-west of

Zaros) a track leads south (2½km) to the abandoned-seeming little church, all that remains of the once-important monastery of Valsamonero. It is a delightfully irregular little building, with ornate doorway, tiny belfry and two naves running east to west, with a third tacked on at right-angles at the western end. The interior contains a rich display of frescoes of various periods. The nave the visitor first enters dates from the early 15th century and has frescoes depicting scenes associated with John the Baptist. The cross-wise nave to the left is fractionally later and contains the unfamiliar scene of the Communion of the Angels (Christ offers them the sacrament). The nave furthest away from the entrance is early 14th century, with frescoes of the Life of the Virgin.

Another rough track north of the Agia Galini to Zaros road leads to the attractive monastery of Vrondisi, noted for its fine 15th-century Venetian fountain.

The East

Agios Nikolaos, regarded as the main tourist resort on Crete, and long a favourite with British holiday-makers, lies only a short way over the invisible border that divides the centre from the east. But the fact that it is separated by a sizeable cape from the long sprawl of the north coast helps to establish it as different in feeling from the west and centre. Visitors sometimes report that eastern Crete is sweeter in temper than other parts of the island. The east has the widest range in type and standard of accommodation, a lofty but slightly less rugged landscape than the west, and a reasonable number of good objectives for the culturally inclined. The most important of these is ZAKROS, the fourth and most recently discovered of the great Minoan palaces, in a remote site in the furthest east.

AGIOS NIKOLAOS lies on the Bay of Mirabello, bubbling with summer visitors. Sometimes it is rather loud, with sights and sounds that may annoy the more fastidious of locals; but unquestionably the town is having a good time. The Bay of Mirabello is itself one of the finest of Crete's many fine natural phenomena. The line of coast leading north to the attractive resort of ELOUNDA is only moderately dramatic; that running south from Agios Nikolaos is a little arid, even disappointing. But the views across to the Ornon mountains opposite are exhilarating, making it seem as if the wall of rock is vertical. And the views back again over distant Agios Nikolaos are equally appealing.

Away from the resorts of Agios Nikolaos and Elounda, there

are only a few isolated hotels and villas on the Mirabello coast (among them the *Istron Beach Hotel*, 13km from Agios Nikolaos). A simple, not to say crude tourist encampment is now growing up at Pahia Ammos at the southernmost point of the bay. From here, a quick road cuts across the island at its narrowest point to reach the sprawling town of **Ierapetra** on the southern coast. The main attraction of Ierapetra, and the only possible justification for the considerable number of package-holiday hotels and campsites which lie just to the east of town, is the long, grey-coloured, southerly facing beach. Ierapetra has its complement of tourist facilities – discos, tavernas, even a scrap of Venetian castle and some fallen columns and other fragments from the days when it was a Roman throughway to Africa – but it is a confusing and muddled sort of town, very short indeed on charm.

The coast road west from Ierapetra is unattractive to start with, messily built and lined with plastic greenhouses. A short turn down off the main road leads to **Mirtos**, a quiet little resort with a small beach, some old houses, but not much of a village focus or life outside tourism. From Mirtos a rough but practicable road follows the coast, running through an area of rough cultivations (mostly bananas). There is a stony beach and a simple, very peaceful hotel (the *Ariadne*, c) at **Arvi**.

From Ierapetra and the little coastal area to its west, a new road makes it possible to cross direct to the Messara plain, a route leading direct to Phaistos, Agia Triada, Matala and Agia Galini and also providing improved access to Heraklion.

From Ierapetra eastwards, considerable development has taken place, with hotels and small resorts proliferating along a fairly promising stretch of coast. On the beach side of the road, at **Koutsounari**, the Luxury-category *Lyktos Beach Hotel* has just been built, while on the inland side an ambitious attempt to resurrect the once-deserted village of Agios Ioanni Koutsounari has led to a dismal outgrowth of assorted 'villas'.

SITIA, isolated on the north coast, can be approached in two ways: from the valley route which links it with the south coast east of Ierapetra, or, more dramatically, from the north-coast road from the Bay of Mirabello via Pahia Ammos. The road curves and buckets through spectacular scenery before cruising more gently downwards to make an unfortunate rear entry to the large and charming town.

To the east, near the Minoan cemetery at Agia Photia, there is a rather sparse scattering of villas which are rather distant from town for those without transport.

In the far east is the very beautiful, wide, coarse-sand, palm-fringed **Vaï beach**, one of the best on the island. Vaï has long been famous for its grove of rare palm trees – a type of inedible date – which is now fenced in, in a protected area officially referred to as an 'aesthetic forest' with its own 'park rangers'. Despite its relative inaccessibility, it gets very crowded and littered (it's a favourite with the young and topless, and there's nude bathing on the other side of a rocky headland). To see Vaï at its best, you need to get there very early or late in the afternoon. Just up the road, the few scattered remains of ancient **Itanos** guard a beautiful small rocky bay. Inland in wild hills is the fortified monastery of TOPLOÚ. South of Vaï, **Palaikastro** has a nice peaceful beach with thick olive groves between it and a small village; there are tavernas and some accommodation. There is also a hotel at Apano (Upper) Zakros and the possibility of rooms, at least in summer, on the beach by the palace of Zakros.

Agios Nikolaos

The success of Agios Nikolaos must be due to something other than its beaches; few summer spots with such poor swimming have achieved equal popularity. The key, undoubtedly, is Lake Voulismeni, a small, deep pool of water, fed by an underground river, with a high theatre of naked rock behind it right at the centre of the town. This semi-circle of rock and lake was originally divided from the sea by just a tiny spit of land; on the other side of the spit lay the harbour, tucked in neatly under a sheltering promontory. Some time during the 19th century, the spit was pierced and bridged, so that now there is a harbour with larger boats on the seaward side, while craft of rowing-boat dimension creep underneath the bridge into Lake Voulismeni. The scale of the whole scene is petite to say the least.

From the bridge, a growing town now radiates: up and over the promontory to a small town bay on the east side; back up west behind the lake on to higher ground (the Archaeological Museum, second only to Heraklion's for Minoan treasures, is here); and southwards from the bridge, up a pair of sloping main streets, full of jewellery shops and boutiques, to a town square with a war memorial.

The centres of activity are the harbour-front (restaurants and discos), the street leading over to the town bay and little roads off this (more restaurants and lots of bars), the two main streets (for shopping), and round the front to the north-west where a line of hotels follows the sea-front; typical are the large *Hermes* (A) or the smaller, family-run *Mirsini* (C). A little further out, still going northwards, are the charming Luxury-category *Minos*

Beach complex, with lovely gardens and swimming-pool area on a rocky beach, and the new and smart *Minos Palace* (also Luxury) on the crest of a promontory, with excellent views from its swimming-pool over Mirabello and inshore islands.

Apart from the comparative seclusion of the smarter hotels, Agios Nikolaos is active, populous and jolly, with an atmosphere more that of a town than a resort. But its bathing facilities are very poor: a couple of small (and unappealing) shingle beaches in town, some rock and concrete bathing-platforms and, just out of town, a tiny, crowded sand beach. On the hilly coastline south of the town are fast developing villa communities, in clusters all the way to, and beyond, the hillside village of Kalo Chorio and the little bay of Istron.

Elounda

The road from Agios Nikolaos rises high (with magnificent views backwards and out over the bay of Mirabello), then drops, some way before the village, to a spot where a series of hotels has begun to congregate, each in its own grounds, beside the sea. The first of the best is the *Elounda Beach* (Luxury-category), with bungalows set in attractive gardens around a large and well-appointed central block. There is one small sandy beach and swimming from ladders fixed to the rocks. This was one of the first hotels to use aspects of Cretan village architecture, and it remains quite possibly the best hotel on Crete. The smart *Elounda Mare* (also Luxury-category), just above, is less attractive, but well situated, with attractive swimming-pools; more fetching is the *Astir Palace* (Luxury-category), just beyond, with a very pretty lawn.

A spit of land (with a channel cut through it and remains of ancient Olous, mostly under water) runs out just nearby to join mainland Crete to the promontory of Spinalonga (distinct from the island of Spinalonga to the north). This spit and promontory form the outer part of a bay, with the village of Elounda on its western, mainland side. The newly built approaches to Elounda straggle along the road in a style that is commonplace on the island. But the large village square opening on the sea is far more attractive, with harbour atmosphere and cafes under awnings, agreeable views over the water and impressive if rather barren hills rising behind. There are a number of small hotels, among them the *Kalypso* (C), looking out on to the harbour, and plenty of rooms to rent. But there is a considerable shortage of beaches – patches of sand and pebble to the north, or rock bathing on **Spinalonga** island (reached by a causeway). This is a major destination for caique trips from Agios Nikolaos and for briefer expeditions from Elounda. Its main feature is another of those grand Venetian fortresses, impressive in a general sense, but in practice less interesting the closer you get. This one, like the fortress in Souda Bay, near Chania, continued to resist the Turks for decades after Heraklion and the mainland had fallen. More recently, it has been used as a leper colony, closed only in 1955.

Sitia

The town of Sitia is isolated on the north-east coast; it's a two-hour journey from Agios Nikolaos. The best of Sitia is to be found along its harbour-front and on the hill which rises up above, airy and bright with terraces of white cubic houses, and a peaceful atmosphere. The busy tree-lined harbour has tavernas, tourists and a pier at the far end where small ships come to collect locally produced sultanas. East of the harbour there's a long coarse sand beach. Some remnants of a Venetian castle can be seen, though they are not a central feature. The Turks let the town lie in ruins for centuries, and it began to come to life again only about a century ago. There is a variety of B-, C- and D-class hotels and rooms in town and behind the beach. The valley behind the town features a settlement of plastic greenhouses.

Kritsa and the Panagia Kera

Kritsa, a hill village 10km south-west of Agios Nikolaos, is a popular place for outings and is particularly well known for its weaving. Cretan weavers use strong colours and bold patterns; their work seems entirely appropriate to both the island's scenery and its climate and can be bought more cheaply here than in the resorts. Busloads of fellow visitors will compete with you for the most attractive pieces.

Kritsa is larger than it first appears, with village streets winding along the slopes and good views down from the occasional little balcony on to the exposed, rear side of shops and cafes.

The Panagia Kera is a little whitewashed church of rustic and Byzantine aspect, set among cypresses, a short way before Kritsa, on the right. Like the village, the church is very popular; but it is well worth visiting, since the interior contains Crete's best-preserved Byzantine frescoes. There are three aisles. In order of subject-matter, the first (entered by the side door) shows scenes from the story of Mary's mother Anne, and of Mary's pregnancy and Joseph's tribulations. The central nave shows other gospel scenes (the tableware in the Last Supper arouses much comment), and the third has an impressive

Second Coming. The punishments of sinners, here and in the central nave, look less than agreeable. These are just a few incidents among many.

A dirt road to the right just after the Panagia Kera leads to the impressive rugged ruins of the Dorian city-state of **Lato**, comparatively unfrequented and in an outstandingly beautiful hilltop position giving some of the most splendid views in Crete.

Gournia

The attractive site of Gournia is near the southernmost point of the Bay of Mirabello, 20km south-east of Agios Nikolaos. This was a Minoan township, whose close-packed and domestic-seeming ruins tell a very different story from those of Knossos and Phaistos – or at least a very different part of the same story. It lies just in behind the sea, easily visible to the landward side of the coast road, on a small hill climbing up inside a slightly larger valley. Visitors will see at first glance that the township was made up of small houses packed around tiny cobbled lanes. Tools and artisan dwellings have been found here, creating an impression of business and manufacture. Near the top of the hill were larger buildings, probably associated with a governor or person of authority. These include a modest court; a larger, public court is also visible.

Toplou Monastery

The fortified Venetian monastery of Toplou, 15km east of Sitia, is one of the most famous spots in eastern Crete. Its main features are strong defensive walls, a distinctive domed bell tower, and an engaging inner courtyard with cells on various levels. In the church there are 14th-century frescoes and a particularly important 18th-century icon containing 61 separate small scenes, each rendered in the most exact detail. One shows a ploughing scene, for instance, another a castle spanning a river. The monastery was strongly associated with the Cretan independence movement; during the Second World War its abbot ran a resistance radio station and was executed by the German occupation forces.

Zakros

In a sheltered bay on Crete's extreme east coast, 43km beyond Sitia, lie the remains of the Minoan palace of Zakros. This is a lovely spot but it is unquestionably remote. Visitors who have not developed a good eye for the Minoans may find the ruins disappointing after so long a journey. Minoan enthusiasts, by contrast, generally enjoy it deeply – not least because excavations began here only in the 1960s and are still continuing. An aura of discovery, much enhanced if one has already seen the major Zakros finds in the Heraklion Archaeological Museum, still attaches to the site. Because of changes in sea level, some of its eastern side is quite often submerged or at least awash, and local agricultural efforts have also proved unhelpful. But there is still plenty for enthusiasts to see. As at the other main palatial sites, there is a central courtyard with sacred and cult areas to the west. One feature on the eastern side of the court is a large round cistern. The most spectacular Zakros finds, including a bull's head rhyton to rival that of Knossos and an astonishing conical rhyton in rock crystal, came from the west side of the court.

The great beauty of the site of Zakros is its spectacular setting, and the best way to enjoy it is to walk down from the upper village of Ano Zakros, via a superb rocky canyon (about one hour). Below the site is a good pebble beach with a couple of tavernas.

The West

Thanks to its rugged mountains and a rugged friendliness among the local population, western Crete is unforgettable. The White Mountains (Lefka Ori) of the far west, 2450m at their highest point, seem actually awesome (Psiloritis, south-east of Rethymnon, is fractionally higher, though softer contours give it an almost gentle look). The area has splendid landscape for exploration by road or on foot, and to traverse the GORGE OF SAMARIA, cutting through the southern half of the White Mountains, can be a memorable experience. There are isolated villages where the visitor is likely to have friendly encounters with local inhabitants, and the island's two most outstanding towns, Rethymnon and Chania. While there are not as many Minoan sites as in the east or centre, Byzantine chapels and Venetian and Turkish memorials abound (so, sadly, do memorials of the Second World War).

If all this sounds like a paean of praise for western Crete – so be it. For what it has to offer in terms of people, sea and mountains, the west certainly makes a good area in which to stay. And while it can be reached from the centre or even from the east on long day-trips, the reverse is just as true.

As in central Crete, the main towns and resorts are along the northern coast (although one or two places in the south are beginning to grow quite swiftly). The New Road west from Heraklion comes tearing in from rocky hills and valleys behind Agia Pelayia and Bali to run across a plain as it approaches Rethymnon. Very soon, hotels begin to appear, followed progressively by an outbreak of tourist tat which establishes this stretch of coast as a strong entrant in the competition for the ugliest development in Crete. Amid all this, the principal hotel of the area is doing very nicely – the large *Rethimnon Beach Hotel* (A) is used as a conference venue as well as by holiday-makers. The attractive bungalow village lies right on the beach, has pretty gardens and swimming-pool, good facilities for children and is popular with families. It provides, in fact, a complete environment.

Entering RETHYMNON itself (7km further west) one passes through drear outskirts to reach a jewel of a town.

Beyond, the coastal plain resumes, rocky and bleak at first and then consisting of just one endless sandy beach, backed by the road, exposed to wind and weather and with only a few scattered holiday and hotel developments, generally rather desolate in appearance. At the end of this stretch, the coast turns north to form the headland of Drapano, while the New Road goes straight on for Chania. The small resort of **Georgiopoulis** nestles in the corner, just at the parting of the ways. It's a lively, modern little place with a rather scattered centre under the shade of tall eucalyptus trees, perhaps the most striking feature of the resort. There are one or two shops and cafes, a reasonable beach (sandy, with some rock under water) and a disappointing harbour by the river mouth. The *Hotel Gorgona* (C), definitely an improvement on the ubiquitous Ariadne as far as names are concerned, stands on the beach a few hundred yards from the resort centre.

As the New Road proceeds across the base of the Drapano peninsula, fine views of the Lefka Ori begin to open up. There is a left turn from Vrises which leads up high over the mountainous centre of the island and down through the rugged region of Sfakia to Hora Sfakion. Keeping to the north-west, the New Road reaches the sea again at **Kalami**, a little place with views across the mouth of **Souda Bay**, the deep-water inlet and anchorage which has always featured large in Cretan maritime affairs. The island (also called Souda) in the mouth of the bay, heavily fortified by the Venetians, held out against the Turks for many years after mainland Crete had fallen.

A right turn along the northern shore here leads to **Kalives**, a village of no particular interest, but offering rooms, one or two hotels and sandy beaches as it straggles unemphatically along the road. The beach and countryside just west of Kalives are splendid, in part because the road itself runs a little inland. The fertile **Vale of Souda** was described by the 17th-century traveller William Lithgow as 'the combat of Bacchus and Ceres; no region or valley more hospitable in regard of the sea, having such a noble haven cut through its bosom, being as it were the resting place of Neptune'. This is attractive, rolling agricultural landscape, with bamboos, olives and fruit trees. A little further east is Almirida, smaller and jollier than Kalives, but also a quiet seaside village with tavernas, simple rooming accommodation and windsurfing.

Returning to Kalami and proceeding westwards along the shore of Souda Bay, one soon arrives at **Souda**, ferry port and sensitive naval base (photography is definitely prohibited). There are small hotels here to serve the ferries, but it is no place at which to stay for pleasure. Nearby, in the direction of Chania airport, in a superb position at the head of the bay, the **Commonwealth War Cemetery** contains the graves of British, New Zealand, Australian and other Commonwealth soldiers who died in the Battle of Crete in 1941.

To the north, connected by a neck of land between Souda and Chania, the **Akrotiri** (literally, the 'peninsula') juts out. The landscape is a little bizarre – generally flattish and scrub-covered, with an impressive row of mountains on its north-eastern edge. It offers a few small resorts, several beaches and monasteries. On the peninsula **Stavros**, an almost circular bay blocked off to the north by a tall and stony mountain, has acquired at least a certain local fame, featuring in the final scene of the film *Zorba the Greek* and now attracting a number of visitors. Little white block-like villas are dotted about, lending it a slightly desolate air; but there is a crescent of good sandy beach and an agreeable taverna.

If touring, most people will probably visit CHANIA first and then backtrack to Akrotiri. This would be logical, since Chania is the geographical and psychological focus of the area, and is reckoned by many to be the finest town in Crete. It is also the easiest starting-point for expeditions to the Gorge of Samaria, virtually due south.

To the west of Chania, one passes through another of those coastal strips, dreary in looks but lively in season, which have become so characteristic of Crete's northern coast. A ribbon of haphazard low-rise seaside development, making use of the long stretches of sand, is slowly connecting the villages of **Agia Marina**, on an attractive bay, and **Platanias**. 'Villas' and hotels of varying categories abound, one or two stuck up on little knolls and offering good views; these appear to be outnumbered by tavernas, small grocery stores and purveyors of gaudy pottery, sunglasses, water-melons and postcards. Towards the small resort of **Maleme** the hotels get larger, culminating in the *Claudius Crete* (A). At Maleme, a signposted turn south from the coast road leads to the **German War Cemetery**. The Germans who fell in the Battle of Crete in 1941 are buried in a specially dramatic site, the scene of one of the most bitter engagements in that bitter contest. This was the struggle for the small landing-strip at Maleme between newly landed German paratroopers and the defensive Allied forces. The eventual loss of the airstrip by the Allies was the turning-point of the whole battle and signalled the loss of Crete. The cemetery, neat and verdant, overlooks the airstrip and modern Greek airbase.

Soon after Maleme, an interesting road strikes down (or rather up, at first) towards the south-west corner of Crete and the distant resort of PALEOHORA. The north-coast road continues some distance behind the beach, offering increasingly impressive views of the gaunt Rodopos peninsula stretching to the north. **Kolimvari**, with a prominent monastery, is tucked in just at the base of the peninsula; it's a seaside village which has developed into a summer tourist spot. There are rooms and tavernas and a long, thin, mostly pebble beach, growing sandier towards the east. Kolimvari has a disco and motor-bikes to rent, but its moustached old men still favour baggy breeches and knee-high leather boots. There is a distinct sensation that one is approaching deep country.

The sensation is only partly accurate. As the road rises to cross the base of the Rodopos peninsula, a fine view opens out, revealing in front and to the left a wide valley with olives and orange trees, and to the right the spectacular Gulf of Kissamos, backed in turn by another rugged peninsula, Gramvousa. This is all extremely rural and ruggedly delightful, just like the old men of Kolimvari. But **Kastelli**, or Kastelli Kissamos, the town and ferry port lying on the southern shore of the bay, is dull, lacking either a lively central square or a picturesque harbour-front. There's some basic accommodation in town and along the beach to the west; the ferry port (boats to Santorini, Kithira and the Peloponnese, and Piraeus) is a very desolate spot a couple of miles away.

South of the Rodopos peninsula (10km south-west of Kolimvari) is the **Church of the Archangel Michael** at Episkopi. The road from Kolimvari leads first to Spilia, a pretty farming settlement in a vale with olives and tangerines and with several frescoed churches in the immediate area. Then, 2km before the village of Episkopi, is the church, one of many which, while not totally extraordinary in itself, illustrates the kind of unexpected find one may make in almost any part of Crete. It is a beautifully restored, golden church with a most distinctive stepped dome, built on the site of an early Christian basilica. The basilica mosaic still in part survives, though it has lately been hidden by builders' protective plastic sheeting.

It is possible to travel on beyond Kastelli into the extreme west. The attraction is the magnificent scenery, wild beaches, small monasteries and Byzantine village churches, and the sense of escape; but there are fewer places at which to stay. **Platanos** has some accommodation, and very fine views as you crest the hill in the direction of the archaeological site of Phalasarna. At the neighbouring splendid sandy beach of Livadi there are rooms, tavernas and plastic greenhouses.

Dropping south from Platanos along this handsome coast, one first reaches **Sfinario**, a pretty agricultural village in a bay under wild and rocky mountains. A modest hotel and tavernas are on offer, but the beach is stony, steep and grey. The west-coast road surface is generally good – mostly asphalt. Between Sfinario and Kefali there are pretty, leafy villages with farmyard clutter, and rooms and tavernas advertised in English.

Kefali, an important little crossroads, lies inland, proffering rest to weary travellers, with rooms to rent and several cafes. A small, winding, rough road descends southwards to the isolated **monastery of Khrisoskalitissa** – with dramatic views and a sandy beach nearby – and about 7km further the little island of Elafonisi, a wade across shallow water. Here there is a summer taverna and an increasing number of day-trippers (both Khrisoskalitissa and Elafonisi can be reached by boat from Paleohora, a less fatiguing prospect).

Equally, it is possible to retreat inland from Kefali, through the very pretty village of **Elos**: a stream goes rushing through, providing water for a fountain, while plane and eucalyptus trees in the village compete with chestnuts round about. This is a good village for cafes, eating places and rugged-looking old men in Cretan costume.

Shortly north-east of Elos a turning leads southwards to Kandanos and continues down to PALEOHORA. The road is reasonable, with only a few unmade miles between Drys and Kandanos (where the main road joins). There's a lot of road-building going on. The drive down, through a rocky defile before a wide coastal plain, is splendid, particularly thrilling if the final sight of the Libyan sea is your first experience of the south coast.

About half-way between Chania and Rethymnon, on the New Road, is the inland village of Vrises. South of this, a mountainous road leads to the region of Sfakia, economically battered today but once the most strongly independent part of Crete. Its capital is Sfakia or **Hora Sfakion** on the south coast, reached by a snaking and precipitous descent. It was by this route, high over the island ridge then steeply down again, that the defeated Allies retreated during the latter stages of the Battle of Crete in 1941. Many were taken off the island by the British navy; several thousand were left behind. Of these, some were captured by the advancing Germans, others rescued by Cretans and smuggled out later.

Today, thousands of people a day make a more peaceable trek down the Gorge of Samaria; many are then fetched by boat from Agia Roumeli at the mouth of the gorge and deposited at Hora Sfakion. (There is also a boat service westwards from Agia Roumeli to Paleohora). While it's a perfectly reasonable place at which to stay overnight, most walkers are simply passing through; the tiny town is no more than a shadow of its former self. In the evening, buses leave in great shoals.

A short boat-trip (or a long hike) to the west lies the charming village of **Loutro**, behind an almost circular bay at the base of a line of mountain. Loutro has as yet no road and, though populous in summer, retains a pleasantly out-of-the-way feeling. Rooms are available but fill up quickly. East of Hora Sfakion, the castle of **Frangokastello** is a notable feature, though impressive mainly in its general aspect – grey and orange stone on a brown plain under grey-brown mountains to the north. The castle itself is now merely an enclosure of battlemented walls containing ruins. But just below there is a wide and sandy beach, gently shelving, with a shady taverna. It is a peaceful-seeming place. East of Frangokastello the road becomes rough around Argoules, but returns quite soon to asphalt. From Rodakino it is easy to descend (2km down a good road) to the thoroughly peaceful little beaches of **Koraka**. On the way to Sellia, the next village of note, the mountainsides are bare and strewn with rock and scrub. From Sellia itself there are magnificent views downwards. **Plakias**, a small but rapidly expanding package-holiday resort, lies below in its own bay, reached from various directions by impressive orangey-grey gorges. The setting is particularly fine, with mountain behind and a rocky eminence at the eastern end of the bay. The resort has many hotels, none exceptional: the *Livikon* (c) and *Atlantis* (b) are the biggest and smartest; several are situated further out. There are tavernas and rooms for rent, cocktail bars, newspaper shops and watersports, and the beach is huge. Though Plakias appears geographically isolated, it has good bus services, and boat-trips round to Preveli beach, with palms and a taverna, from which it's a stiff walk up to the MONASTERY OF PREVELI.

From Plakias, one can cross north again to Rethymnon or, after reaching the Rethymnon road, turn east for Spili and Agia Galini. It is also easy to make the trip by road from Plakias to the Preveli monastery.

Rethymnon

Rethymnon is a town of mosque and minaret, Turkish inscriptions, Venetian fortress, crumbling fountains and sleepy harbourside. Its fine old houses, with arched doorways and small wooden balconies – though often the worse for wear and sometimes damaged by repairs done out of style – lend a pleasing air to the old town. But the newer town to the east and west ranges from scruffy to slum-like.

The centre of tourist affairs is a little square in the old quarter, the Plateia Petitikhaki. To reach it from the landward side, you pass one of the town's several minarets. In Petitikhaki there are restaurants and old-fashioned *kafeneions*, just the place for a glass of *tzikoudia* (also known as *raki* – a fierce spirit made from grapes, served in tiny glasses, and quite distinct from aniseed-flavoured ouzo). After this, the adjacent Arimondi fountain, bequeathed by the Venetians, will look all the more agreeable in its gentle and roofless dilapidation. There is a small archaeological museum near by. A wander across the neck of the peninsula, working one's way along with glimpses of the fortress on the seaward side, will prove the most rewarding exercise of all. The little circular fishing harbour to the east of the fortress is one of the prettiest places in Crete. All the old houses here have been made over into restaurants; the air is rich with the smell of frying squid. Most people sit at the outdoor tables; for winter-time the Taverna Vassilis has the most interesting interior. There are more restaurants and cafes round to the right on the gentle curve behind the town beach.

Many of Rethymnon's visitors stay in the coastal strip to the east (the A-category *Rethimnon Beach Hotel* itself accounts for several hundred), which has a long stretch of sandy beach. There are also various package hotels in town: the *Kyma Beach* (c), right behind the town beach, is the smartest and newest in its area. The *Ideon* (B) is on the front by the Venetian fortress. People passing through would probably do best to stay in one of the cluster of hotels around the two bus stations. Among these are the B-category *Olympic* and *Regency*, each modern and comfortable. It's not a pretty part of town, however; although the hotels are only a few minutes' walk from the old town, there's a busy road between. But they offer a very different perspective on Rethymnon – more workaday perhaps, but more a part of the real world.

Arkadi Monastery

In a wild setting among low barren hills 21km south-east of
Rethymnon, reached by a rocky, orange-coloured gorge, lies the
monastery of Arkadi. The name is a byword for heroism in the
long struggle for Cretan independence: the monastery was
blown up by its own defenders on 9 November 1866 in
preference to capture by the Turks. In point of fact, a good deal
of the complex survived the blast – though it killed literally
hundreds both of besiegers and of besieged, men, women and
children – and it is no surprise that it is much visited today.
Seen from outside, the low two-storey enclosure appears
moderately unpromising, and the main gateway into the
courtyard has been reconstructed. But, within, the original
golden-coloured late-16th-century church survives, the chief
glory of Arkadi. It has perhaps the most handsome façade in
Crete, with elegant circular windows, twinned composite pillars
and capitals, and an elegant belfry above.

Those who are fond of fearsome portraits of Cretan *palikares*
with guns and daggers in their belts will no doubt enjoy
Arkadi's small museum. What seems to matter most here is the
spirit of the place, coupled with the ornate beauty of the church.

Eleftherna

A signposted dirt road from Arkadi (or a better one from
Perama and Prines) leads to the site of Eleftherna, about 35km
south-east of Rethymnon. The site of the ancient fortress city is
a narrow rocky promontory projecting from an escarpment near
Prines, with steep slopes dropping down to rivers on both sides,
a natural moat. From a remarkable network of caves carved out
of the hillside and used as cisterns, a bewildering number of
farm paths lead down to the river bed or, more often, peter out
in an olive field. If you do make it down to the overgrown,
boulder-strewn river bed, clamber along it as far as a splendid
Hellenistic bridge in a remarkably clean chiselled state of
preservation. An alluring farm track leading uphill from near
the bridge does not bring you back to Prines, but to the main
road several miles to the east of it. There is a friendly cafe in
Prines and it may well be worth asking around for someone to
show you the way to the bridge.

Amari Valley

Starting some 30km south of Rethymnon, this high valley runs
in a south-easterly direction under the mass of Mount Psiloritis
rising immediately to its east. The valley is outstandingly

beautiful, even by the high standards of Cretan landscape, and fragrant in spring with almond blossom against the snowy bulk of the mountain. It is a particularly good place for the pursuit of Byzantine chapels and frescoes. In **Thronos**, for example, at the head of the valley, there are dark and sombre frescoes in a small church built on top of a far older mosaic, much bigger than the church and running out beyond its walls. Near the **Kalogeros** turning is another church, in this case in the middle of a field and hardly big enough to provide shade for a donkey. (The walk to find it is very scratchy – shorts not advised.) At **Asomatos**, there are kumquats, a huge plane tree and a former monastery now incorporated into an agricultural college. These are only some of the pleasures of Amari. It is above all a place for slow discovery and individual exploration.

Preveli Monastery

On the south coast, almost due south of Rethymnon and some 14km east of Plakias, lies Preveli, reached by descending one or other of two fine gorges (Kotsiphou or Kourtaliotiko). The final leg of the journey is also very beautiful, leading through a valley tucked in under mountains and hidden from the sea by hills. The road passes a graceful 19th-century bridge and the ruins of an earlier monastery. Finally, it emerges on the coast, curling round to the west to reach the present (17th-century) monastery, high above the sea. Preveli has few monks today but, like Arkadi and Toplou, has a splendid history of independence and resistance. It took part in the rebellion of 1866, and in the Second World War it became the point where the Allied troops who had escaped capture after the Battle of Crete were concentrated and secretly embarked on submarines from the beach below. A memorial in the monastery courtyard testifies to the ferocious reprisals that followed. The buildings are of old and weathered grey stone, well sited but rather sad in feeling; the church itself is 19th century.

To drive down to the beach, follow the signs to the taverna, then to Amoudia; the road is very rough, as is the scramble over the rocks to Palm Beach – a river-mouth, lagoon-style beach which really does have palms. You can also reach the beach by boat-trips from Plakias.

Chania

Chania is the second largest town in Crete. It's a fine, assertive place with busy backstreets and a beautiful old port, which seems to catch much of the atmosphere of the west. To the south are the White Mountains, and much of Chania's hinterland is deeply rural. Yet at the same time it can seem 'towny' in quite a disobliging way – hot and noisy, with rather too many soldiers, sailors and airmen, and more than its fair share of backpackers, young and old. At times it can get to feel quite rough.

Parts of the city are visually more elegant than anywhere else in Crete; but much was destroyed during the war and has since been rebuilt without great sense of style, giving large areas a fairly utilitarian atmosphere. The old harbour – in fact, it is an outer harbour with a fishing harbour tucked within – is obviously the leading attraction. Facing the lighthouse opposite, handsome old mansions line a semi-circular water-front, with busy restaurants in their lower storeys. One or two of these buildings are hotels or pensions, among them the attractive *Amphora* (A), more restful in winter when the music-booming bars have closed. It occupies an old house with Greek, Venetian and Turkish elements, and all its few rooms are elegantly decorated. The fine red block of the *Hotel Plaza* (C) has big rooms looking out over the water; it's an old hotel which has recently been done up.

The harbour-front is the main meeting-place for those at leisure – both tourists and locals – and there is a lively evening *volta*, especially on Sundays.

Directly opposite the Hotel Plaza across the harbour, the **Nautical Museum** offers model ships and naval pictures, as well as access to the fortifications where the Greek flag was raised in 1913. Just before the museum, a very handsome small street, Angelou, leads up to a little road running back from the sea, the beautiful Theotokopoulou, named after Domenikos Theotokopoulos, the Cretan painter more generally known as El Greco. Wrought-iron balconies, pointed chimneys with slits, and other intriguing architectural features compete for attention with boutiques. Behind the Nautical Museum are two other recommended hotels: the small and stylish new *Palazzo* (A) and, just opposite, the simpler and cheaper *El Greco* (B).

The hill on the Plaza Hotel side of the bay is Kastelli, site of the first Venetian fortifications, possibly also of a lost Minoan palace. It is very tumble-down, but retains Venetian echoes. Beyond, dropping down first to the fishing harbour and a series of Venetian *arsenali* or warehouses, one passes a tightly packed little district of churches and old and quirky streets, to arrive, after quite a while, at a neo-classical area occupied from the end of the last century to 1913 by diplomats and the island's governors.

Straight up behind the harbour, the little street of Halidon leads to Plateia 1866. On your right, ascending, is the **Archaeological Museum**, worth visiting for its setting alone, in the nave of a Venetian church; there is also a very pretty Turkish fountain in the garden. The museum contains a small and beautifully presented collection of clay sarcophagi with familiar Minoan motifs of double-headed axes and horns of consecration.

Halidon is a tourist street with cafes and souvenir shops, masses of foreign newspapers and lots of hustling and haggling; busy Skridlof, leading off to the left as you ascend, has leather goods. Nearby is the large cruciform market, popular and perhaps a little overrated but with squid and octopus to admire. Just across from it is the *Kydon* (A). Another hotel, the *Dorna* (B), once home of Britain's diplomatic representative to Crete, is an unexpected pleasure – a neo-classical building furnished with antiques and ornaments, overlooking the sea (and a fairly busy road) on the western side of town. Visitors passing through may find it more convenient to stay at one of the group of hotels around the bus station and Plateia 1866; these include the *Samarias* (B), the *Omalos* (C) and the *Canea* (C).

To the east of Chania, a newer and rather dreary part of town spreads east above a moderately unappealing beach. To the west there is a more definitive new town actually called the Neo Hora; this has livelier beaches and a cluster of restaurants.

Chania: sights nearby

● **Akrotiri Peninsula** North-east of Chania, the Akrotiri peninsula is the site of one of the island's two airports, and a large military base. Elsewhere there is little sign of development. On the hill of Profitis Ilias, which gives splendid views of Chania, is the simple tomb of Eleutherios Venizelos, Crete's great modern statesman (1864–1936), for a long period prime minister of Greece; he is buried with his son Sophocles. The **monastery of Agia Triada** was founded by Venetian converts to Orthodoxy, and bears a distinctively Venetian look. It has a large, orange-coloured, many-domed church dating from 1632, and tangerine trees in the courtyard. A little further along the road is the **monastery of Gouverneto**; and down by the coast are the romantic ruins of another monastery. There are several beaches dotted around the rugged coastline, notably at Stavros.

Gorge of Samaria

This is the most spectacular and challenging of the popular excursions on Crete. Over 10 miles of rocky pathway lead between cliffs which are over a thousand feet high in places and less than 10 feet apart at the narrowest point (the 'Iron Gates'). Waterfalls, wild flowers, streams and trees enliven the rocky scenery, and the air hangs heavy with the scent of herbs.

The descent begins in the heart of the White Mountains, 4km south of Omalos. None of the walk is uphill, but it takes about five hours on average and requires stout shoes and a stout heart. Nevertheless, at the height of the season several thousand people pass through each day; and however you may plot and plan to avoid your fellow men, the experience is one of togetherness rather than solitude. In summer it's hard to stop and take a look without the person behind you cannoning into your back. In addition, the going is so rough for much of the way that you spend a great deal of time looking at your feet rather than at the splendours rising all around. Despite advice about the need for good footwear, some people persist in going down in flip-flops, an experience that always ends in tears.

The walk begins with a steep descent down a well-made zigzag path with wooden railings. This is the Xyloskalo or Wooden Staircase; it drops down many hundreds of feet, with a splendid rockface opposite, positively dolomitic in appearance. Pine and cypress stand about the Xyloskalo, proffering their heady, resinous scent. Finally, the walker reaches the valley floor and the traverse of the gorge proper begins. The track still runs basically downhill but now through an ever-narrowing cleft with views upwards of birds and rocks and trees perched on perfectly impossible spots on the precipice. There is an old church on the way down and then, once on the near-flat, the ruins of the former village of Samaria. This was as isolated a settlement as it is possible to imagine; now it's packed each day with hikers who rest for a while and wonder whether their feet will stand the strain. Samaria is about one third of the full distance of the walk. At about two-thirds of the distance, the rock walls on either side, now almost frighteningly high, converge until they are just a few feet apart – the Iron Gates. You feel you can practically touch both sides; a cooling stream, sometimes a dangerous torrent, goes hurrying through. The last part of the walk is less attractive, hot and rough and much of it over open land, leading down finally to Agia Roumeli, the increasingly busy point of arrival on the coast. This is the place for a swim, a beer and, when one has recovered sufficiently, a meal in one of the beach-front tavernas.

All of the Gorge of Samaria walk, except the rather dreary seaward end, lies within a national park – home for 100 Cretan ibex, wild goats with splendid heads of horns, 51 species of birds including the bald vulture, and 12 species of mammal, including the wildcat, hare and badger, The park rules, intended to preserve the area despite its popularity, are strict: no camping, no smoking, no swimming, no straying far from the path, no picking of flowers or other plants. There are plenty of wcs and

water-points *en route*, and plenty of fairly tasteful waste bins –
helping along the seditious feeling, which must occasionally
strike all walkers here, that but for the wild views one might as
well be in suburbia. The park is open from May to October
inclusive, but even this is rather marginal, since rain can bring
exceedingly fierce flooding with virtually no notice. There have
been drownings in recent years as well as heart attacks and
broken legs. Despite its populousness, it really is worth thinking
of the gorge as a fairly serious undertaking.

Many organised excursions visit the gorge. Holiday-makers
are ferried by coach to the high flat plain of Omalos as early as
possible in the morning (the earlier the cooler), then decanted
over the lip of the gorge. They walk down under the loose
charge of a tour guide and are taken off by boat in the
afternoon, almost always to Hora Sfakion where a bus waits to
carry them back to the starting-point. Those who start at points
west of Omalos are likely to be taken back via Paleohora.

This is reasonably satisfactory but is likely to mean that you
go down at a crowded time. The alternative is to make an
independent trip. For this, the starting-point is Chania, whence
a series of buses starts off reasonably early (6.15, 7.30, 8.30 –
taking about one and a half hours), with a return offered via
Hora Sfakion. The trouble is that plenty of others are trying the
same thing, so you wind up going down at an hour which may
be earlier than the organised excursions, but is also crowded.

There are two lazy ways of seeing some of the gorge. One is
to take the boat to Agia Roumeli and walk across the flat to the
Iron Gates and back again. This may be better than nothing but
is a poor substitute for the walk down. (Some people, the kind
with thickly knotted muscles in their calves, actually walk up.)
A better way is to arrive at the top of the gorge after all the
crowds have left (mid-afternoon) and descend the steep steps to
the first viewing platform (about 15 minutes), which gives you a
sufficient impression of the awesome scenery and a good
measure of solitude in which to enjoy it. You will need to
retrace your steps afterwards.

Paleohora

The village of Paleohora is reached by descending a rocky gorge
and then crossing a little plain through an avenue of eucalyptus
trees. It is not what you might call a pretty place, but it gains
by its position, far distant from the major resorts and as yet
untroubled by large hotels. This is not to suggest it is anything
other than busy – in summer it fairly teems with life. Families
with children form much of its clientele, many from mainland

Greece. And there are backpackers, and travellers who, shunning even this obviously touristic paraphernalia, assert a greater authenticity by carrying their possessions in a blanket.

Paleohora has one particularly good coarse sand beach with lively windsurfing, sometimes too demanding for beginners; a very pleasant main street set out with tables in the evening; and an outdoor cinema in summer. This sheltered spot seems to have its own microclimate, and the winters are warm.

The village lies across the base of a promontory which is itself surmounted by the ruins of a Venetian *kastro*. Just under the castle on the eastern side are a few pretty little lanes of some antiquity, and cafes on the water. Then there's a little harbour where local excursion-boats put in, and a stretch of water-front with blocks of stone piled up as a breakwater, with restaurants behind them. This is followed by a stony beach, not much patronised, with a campsite well out beyond the edge of town. The sandy beach is on the opposite, western side of the promontory. It offers views to the *kastro* and along a curving coast backed by mountains with a gentle plume of smoke from the spot where municipal rubbish is burnt.

There are villas, apartments and many rooms to rent. The *Aris* (B) is a modern hotel, reasonably attractive. The *Polydoros* (C), in the middle of the village, is clean and almost smart. The *Libikon* (D) is about the only old building of any size, and perhaps the most promising of a rather ordinary selection.

Coach-trips to the Gorge of Samaria are on offer, with a local boat making a daily trip to Agia Roumeli, a splendid journey along Crete's most imposing stretch of coast. The boat calls at **Souyia**, another spot very popular with young travellers, with some modest accommodation and a fine tamarisk-shaded beach. Nearby (15 minutes by boat or 1½ hours on foot) is the Graeco-Roman site of Lissos, where there's a temple of Asklepios.

The countryside east of Paleohora offers fine opportunities for hiking; the scenery is particularly fine, and much of the area is still very remote.

Boat-trips run daily, wind permitting, to the beach-island of Elafonisi round the south-western corner of Crete, and caique sailings to the island of Gavdos, 50km to the south, the southernmost point in Europe.

RHODES AND THE DODECANESE

Astypalaia, Chalki, Kalymnos, Karpathos,
Kasos, Kastellorizo, Kos, Leros, Nisyros,
Patmos, Symi, Tilos

The region that gave birth to that dazzling tapestry of numeric symbolism, the Apocalypse of St John the Divine, itself bears the sacred number 12. 'The twelve islands' may sound a straightforward enough name for a group, but in fact it is a bit of a puzzle: which exactly are the designated 12? There is no doubt about ten of them: Patmos, Leros, Kalymnos, Kos, Nisyros, Tilos, Rhodes, Symi, Kastellorizo and Karpathos. Include all the inhabited minor islands of the group and the lonely outpost of Astypalaia, stuck out on its own between the Cyclades and mainstream Dodecanese, and you reach a total of anywhere between 15 and 20. With the help of some arbitrary selection one reaches a satisfactory group of Rhodes and its 12 apostles, including Astypalaia, Kasos and Chalki but letting the rest of the small fry – Pserimos, Lipsi, Arki, Agathonisi and other plankton – slip through the net back into the waters of the Aegean.

The Dodecanese occupy the south-east corner of the Aegean, tucked up along the very jagged Turkish coast. Rhodes and Kos have their mosques, but Turkish influence is no more pronounced than on many of the other Aegean islands and is a less distinctive feature of the group than the legacy of Italian rule for most of the first half of this century. Under Turkey the Dodecanese enjoyed various tax exemptions and were known as the Privileged Islands. When in dispute with Turkey over North African matters, Italy took advantage of local discontent about the threatened removal of these privileges to intervene as liberators of the Dodecanese in 1912. Under the Fascist regime all ideas of giving the islands to Greece were forgotten and the Italian Aegean Islands, as they were known, did not join the modern Greek state until March 1948. Many tax exemptions were restored, and duty-free status is one of the minor tourist attractions in some of the Dodecanese.

The Italians' attempts to suppress Greek language, education and even religion were greatly resented, and no Greeks celebrate

Ochi Day (28 October, to commemorate Metaxas's one-word response to Mussolini's ultimatum in 1940) with more enthusiasm than the islanders of the Dodecanese. All the same, you will still come across old people whose second language is Italian. The islands owe a certain amount to the Italians, who replanted forests (especially on Rhodes), modernised harbours, built roads, restored ruins and excavated extensively on Rhodes and Kos, where they took advantage of terrible earthquake damage to the town in 1933 to unearth large areas of its ancient predecessor. But the most striking legacy is the style of the public buildings left by the Italians, which still set the tone on many a Dodecanese water-front. Typical examples of totalitarian architecture, they are leaden and pretentious buildings, inflated with empty rhetoric. The port police stations and banks wear battlements about as imposing as a party hat on an overweight civil servant. Once seen, the style that proclaims Mussolini Was Here is not forgotten.

The ancient and modern history of the Dodecanese is dominated by Rhodes and Kos, large and fertile islands close to the coast of Asia Minor. Both islands were prosperous and important cultural centres in antiquity, key bases of the crusader Knights of St John in the 14th and 15th centuries, and are now mass tourist destinations with good beaches and much more to see than on most Greek islands. The other group members, although by no means similar to one another, are of limited historical interest and have only a modest amount of tourism. Patmos and Symi are the exceptions, attracting large numbers of visitors, mostly on day-trips, to see the 900-year-old Patmos monastery and Symi's beautiful old mansions from the days of its great wealth as an island of ship-builders.

In mythology Rhodes rose from the sea (and fossilised shells give support to the story) as a gift to the sun god Helios, who had missed out on a division of the spoils after Zeus conquered the world. Helios liked the island and smiled on it. Rhodes was settled by Phoenicians, Minoans, Mycenaeans and Dorians, whose three cities on the island (Kamiros, Ialysos and Lindos) united with Kos and the Asian mainland cities of Knidos and Halicarnassus to form a federal league, the Dorian hexapolis. The Rhodians (especially the Lindians, who had the largest but least fertile part of the island) were great sailors, thrived on trade with Egypt, Asia, Greece and even the western Mediterranean, and founded their own colonies as far afield as Sicily, Spain (Rosas) and France. Even when subject to Athens or other Greek powers, Rhodes was important and distant enough to maintain its own independent civilisation. At the beginning of the 5th century BC under the leadership of an

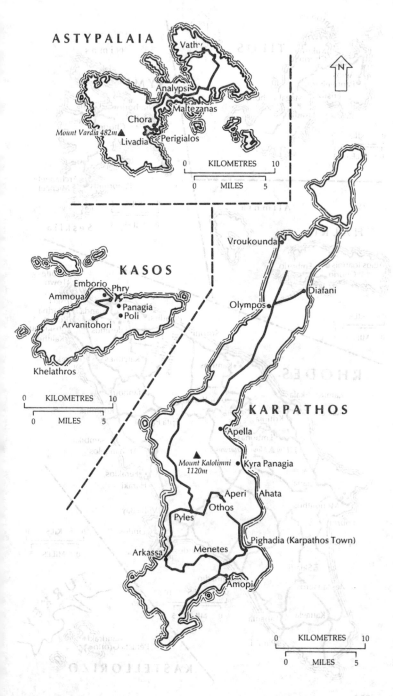

RHODES AND THE DODECANESE

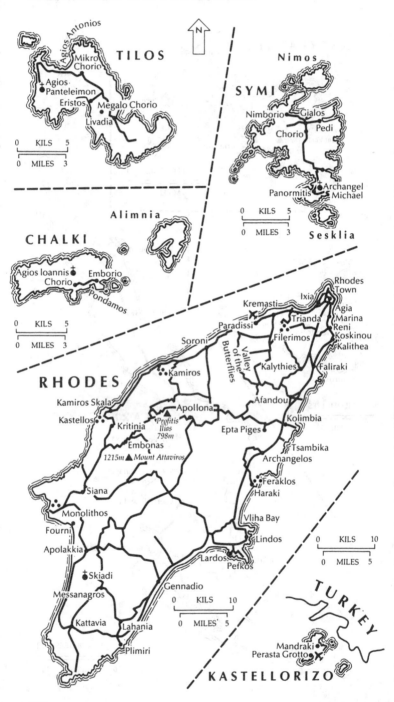

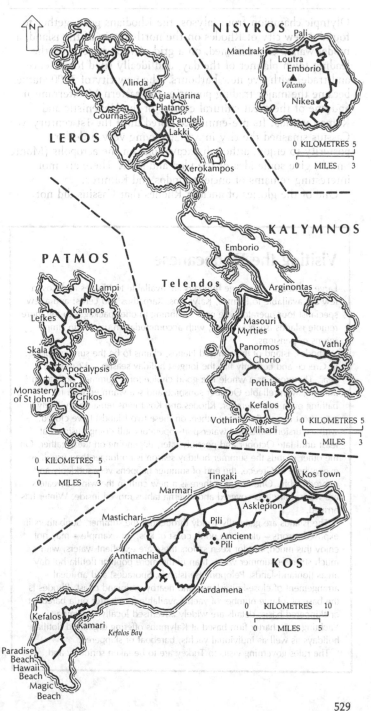

NISYROS

Pali
Mandraki
Loutra
Emborio
▲ *Volcano*
Nikea

0 KILOMETRES 5
0 MILES 3

LEROS

Alinda
Agia Marina
Platanos
Gournas
Pandeli
Lakki
Xerokampos

KALYMNOS

Emborio

PATMOS

Lampi
Kampos
Lefkes
Skala
Apocalypsis
Monastery
of St John
Chora
Grikos

Telendos

Arginontas
Masouri
Myrties
Panormos
Chorio
Pothia
Kefalos
Vothini
Vlihadi

Vathi

0 KILOMETRES 5
0 MILES 3

0 KILOMETRES 5
0 MILES 3

Tingaki
Marmari
Mastichari
Pili
Asklepion
Ancient
Pili
Antimachia

Kos Town

KOS

Kardamena

0 KILOMETRES 10
0 MILES 5

Kefalos
Kamari
Kefalos Bay
Paradise
Beach
Hawaii
Beach
Magic
Beach

Olympic champion from Ialysos, the Rhodians got together to found a new city of Rhodes on the northern tip of the island, a model walled city designed, on a grid of wide streets, by the leading town planner of the day, and ideally sited for defence and trade, with five new harbours. The new city of 3000 statues became the major trading power in the eastern Mediterranean and one of the great cultural centres of the Hellenistic and Roman worlds. Its pre-eminence lasted until the 1st century AD: Cassius smashed the city in AD42, leaving very little for posterity to enjoy, although excavations on the acropolis (Monte Smith) give some idea of the plan and scale. There are more interesting remains of ancient Lindos and Kamiros.

One of the glories of ancient Rhodes that Cassius did not

Visiting the Dodecanese

Large numbers of package holidays are available to Rhodes and Kos; a few are available to Patmos, Kalymnos, Karpathos and Leros; and a few specialist tour operators are now beginning to offer packages to the more remote islands (such as Tilos), with accommodation usually in simple rooms or pensions.

Rhodes, island of the sun god Helios, claims to be the sunniest place in Greece and certainly has the longest holiday season – 12 months a year. The group as a whole is a good choice for a 'summer' holiday in autumn, with reliable October sunshine and sea warm enough for bathing even in November. Rhodes and Kos towns remain very lively after most resorts (including others on these two islands) have closed, with excursion-boats and watersports operators still doing business at least until late October and possibly later, depending on the weather. On the other islands the summer holiday season is no longer than usual. As everywhere in Greece, the end of summer happens very suddenly and unpredictably. One morning there is a new chill in the wind. Sweaters are worn, bare legs covered and taverna tables moved inside. Winter has arrived.

The islands are generally windy throughout the summer. Sunbathers in exposed resorts – along the north coast of Kos, for example – may not enjoy this much, but for keen sailors these are excellent waters, with much stronger summer winds than in the more popular flotilla holiday areas (Ionian Islands, Peloponnese Islands, Sporades) and an ideal arrangement of close-knit islands and nearby mainland coast. Rhodes is the base of a large number of yachts available for charter on a bareboat or skippered basis; details are widely advertised locally. Kalymna Yachting is a charter firm based at Kalymnos offering organised flotilla holidays as well as individual yachts, bareboat or skippered.

The rules governing visits to Turkey are to be taken seriously and

have to destroy was the Colossus, a 100-foot bronze statue of Helios erected after an unsuccessful Macedonian siege in 306BC in accordance with the terms on which the siege leader Demetrius agreed to leave. The statue took Chares of Lindos 12 years to complete and stood for little more than 60 years before being felled by earthquake in 226. The rubble lay untouched for nine centuries until raiding Saracens carted it off on 900 camels and sold it for scrap. Whether the statue stood, as it is always portrayed, astride the entrance to the harbour is doubtful on both technical and aesthetic grounds, although we should probably not be in too much of a hurry to draw conclusions on the basis of our ideas of good taste. Masterpieces of Rhodian sculpture that have come down to us include the Louvre's

always worth checking. At the time of writing the position was that if you travel to and from Greece on a charter flight (which includes almost all package holidays), you are not allowed to leave the country during your visit except on a day-trip. Day-trips to Turkey from Kos have been stopped. If you charter a yacht you must check in to three Greek ports before visiting Turkey. Breaking the rules may involve not being allowed on to the flight home, which risks making your Turkish rug rather expensive.

Some of the Dodecanese are duty-free islands and the big resorts are full of booze-dominated supermarkets, where prices are lower than at airport duty-free shops. So ignore all in-flight propaganda along the lines of 'Duty-free facilities at Rhodes airport are poor and we may have only limited stocks available on your return flight, so you are advised to buy now any duty-free goods you may want to take home,' which shocking piece of disinformation was directed at us on a recent charter flight to Rhodes. No less shocking is the quality of some of the alcohol on sale very cheaply in the local stores, often very cleverly packaged: 'Napoleon French Brandy *VSOP*' you wouldn't wish on a Christmas pudding and 'Caribbean' rum for under £2 a litre which turns out to be Greek. Well-known brands of the real thing are also widely available.

Access and ferry connections

The basic Dodecanese ferry route is Piraeus to Patmos, Leros, Kalymnos, Kos, Rhodes, and back the same way. Because of the distance involved, the timetable is even less reliable than usual, and late-afternoon boats tend to become late-night ones and small-hour boats to involve all-night vigils. Of course, there is no guarantee that a ferry will not arrive and depart ahead of schedule. Local shipping agents often know or claim to know roughly how late a ferry is running (it only takes a phone call to another island, after all) but it is a brave traveller who sets the alarm on the basis of such information. Even when on time, the Dodecanese boats generally keep very anti-social hours, especially for those travelling down

Winged Victory of Samothrace, the Laocoön in the Vatican museum, and two lovely statues of Aphrodite in the Rhodes museum.

Although less powerful than Rhodes, Kos was an equally prosperous and civilised island, much visited for its sacred sanatorium or Asklepion, which may well have been founded by, or in memory of, Hippocrates (460–356BC), a native of the island and, if the dates are correct, a fine advertisement for his own teaching. Hippocrates was the first to depart from a purely supernatural approach to medicine, emphasising the importance of analysing symptoms and regulating diet. He wrote

---

Access and ferry connections continued

the line towards Rhodes. All in all, it is well worth making the initial journey to the Dodecanese by air, from Athens if not by direct charter.

The main ferries sail through the Cyclades but rarely stop at any of them. The few connections (once or twice a week each) are with Paros and Syros.

Other big ferries on more varied itineraries include the *Papadiamantis*, *Alkeos*, *Nereus*, *Kyklades* and *G. Vergina*. *Papadiamantis* rarely leaves Dodecanese waters except to visit Samos once a week, and calls in at the major and minor islands of the chain (including those south of Rhodes) once or twice a week. This is the staple ferry for Kastellorizo (twice a week from Rhodes). The other ships between them create regular but infrequent links between the Dodecanese and Crete, the Cyclades and northern Aegean islands. There are now fairly frequent sailings along the Piraeus, Paros, Astypalaia, Kalymnos, Kos, Rhodes route, usually via a number of minor islands on the way. If in doubt, approach Nisyros and Pserimos from Kos; Tilos, Symi, Chalki, Karpathos, Kasos and Kastellorizo from Rhodes; Astypalaia either from Piraeus/Paros or Kos/Kalymnos; Lipsi and neighbours from Patmos.

If travelling to Karpathos by ferry, make sure you get off at the right port: some ferries call at Diafani as well as the island capital Pigadi.

Because it has so much to offer on its own, Crete is rarely considered as an island to include in a hopping holiday. It can be a useful link: in addition to the wanderings of the *G. Vergina*, which directly connects the southern Cyclades (Milos, Folegandros, Sikinos, Santorini, Anafi) and southern Dodecanese (Kasos, Karpathos, Chalki and Rhodes) via Crete, there are indirect connections: sailings most days in summer between Crete (Heraklion or Rethymnon) and Santorini; less often between Crete (Sitia and Agios Nikolaos) and Karpathos/Rhodes, and between western Crete (Kastelli) and the Peloponnese via Kithira. Inter-island flights should also be considered when planning itineraries, especially if they include Karpathos (see flight information below).

Hydrofoils beat up and down between Rhodes and Patmos, often

---

extensively about science and the ethics of medicine, although the wording of the Hippocratic Oath cannot be traced all the way back. The Kos Asklepion had a painting by the celebrated Apelles, also local, of Aphrodite emerging from the waves, and sculptures by the son of Praxiteles. One of the presiding physicians was the Xenophon who poisoned Emperor Claudius.

Strabo reported that Kos produced more food than did Egypt. Its wealth was founded on milk and honey, fruit, corn and cattle rather than on trade or conquest. The Koans felt no need to leave their homeland and still do not – refreshing news, after so many depressing stories of mass emigration from the Greek

---

calling at Kos and occasionally at Leros. These add little to what can be achieved by ferry, except in opening up the possibility of very long-distance, very expensive day-trips.

For those content to hop from one island to the next rather than make long leaps, small local ferries usefully supplement the big ferry schedules in summer and are indeed generally preferable: they sail by day and usually on time. On the other hand, in windy weather the small boats may be very uncomfortable or not sail at all.

For a journey between Kalymnos and Kos, bad sailors would do well to consider using the speedy little launch that connects Kalymnos and Kos airport, crossing twice a day to Mastihari. This is a much shorter and usually calmer ride (only about half an hour) than the more obvious link between Kalymnos and Kos town, which can be a gut-churning two hours of rock and roll, as the captain has no choice but to sail across the prevailing swell.

Other useful local services include Patmos/Samos (Pithagorion) at least three times a week in summer, the main link between the Dodecanese and northern Aegean islands; Kalymnos (Myrties)/Leros (Xerocampos); Rhodes (Kamiros Skala)/Chalki.

Many more links are made possible by excursion-boats, which do not or should not sell one-way tickets. Patmos, Kalymnos, Nisyros, Symi and Pserimos are very popular excursion targets from busy islands within striking range. There are excursions to Astypalaia from Kalymnos.

Because of the duty-free status of some islands there are customs formalities involved in travelling to Piraeus. These are usually cursory, but do involve filing through customs sheds rather than the usual stampede.

Direct charter flights are available from the UK to Rhodes, Kos and Karpathos. Daily flights operate from Athens to Rhodes, Kos, Leros. Inter-island flights operate from Rhodes to Karpathos, Kastellorizo, Crete, Santorini, Kos, Mykonos, Paros, Lesbos and Kassos; from Karpathos to Crete; and from Kos to Leros. Some are as frequent as twice a day, others only twice a week.

islands. Although tourism has now taken over as the great provider, Kos is still a very productive island – cheese, honey and excellent melons – and its landscape has traditionally been celebrated in the most glowing terms. This may seem puzzling today, when we look for other things in a landscape than its yield. We tend to find the Highlands more beautiful than Leicestershire and Greek fishing villages more attractive than Greek farming villages, and may find many less fertile Greek islands more beautiful than Kos. The flourishing crop of big hotel blocks sprouting up all along the coast does not help.

The episode of the Knights of St John began with the expulsion of all Christian crusading forces from the Holy Land in 1291. The company of knights negotiated the purchase of Rhodes and some of the other Dodecanese islands from their Genoese rulers and continued the Holy War by means of targeted piracy. They armed their HQ town of Rhodes, the eastern bulwark of Christendom, with walls over 40 feet thick, and added to its defences by erecting a series of outlying fortresses and beacons around the island and on Kos (which has two knights' forts), Leros, Kalymnos and Tilos, among others. In the 15th century Islam took the offensive. The Knights of Rhodes resisted two sieges during the 15th century before succumbing in 1522 after a long and brave defence. The victorious sultan, Suleiman the Magnificent, let the 180 surviving knights go free and apologised nicely for evicting the 70-year-old Grand Master Villiers de L'Isle Adam from his home at such an age. The reasonable Turks did not destroy the walled town of the knights, but merely banished Greeks, who were not allowed inside the walls after dark, and converted the churches to mosques.

All the fortresses are impressive, but it is to Rhodes that one goes in search of the knights, walking the two miles of battlements, imagining the clatter of hooves outside the national Inns on the steep Odos Ippoton (Street of the Knights) and enjoying the sober magnificence of the 15th-century hospital buildings as much as their contents, the island's excellent archaeological museum. The old town of Rhodes may seem a trifle over-restored by the diligent Italians (and the Palace of the Grand Masters more than a trifle), and the whole place teems with tourists, but never mind: there is no finer fortified city in Europe. And there is more to it: a few paces from the main axis of tourist shops bring you deep into the old Turkish quarter, still very much alive and in its own way at least as picturesque as the knights' half of town.

Undoubtedly, the amount and the style of tourism on Rhodes detracts a lot from the pleasure of a visit to the island. Dense and in places high-rise development now covers a large area of the north of the island. The problem is most acute at Lindos, although the beautiful old village of rich sea captains' houses has been preserved from any new buildings and looks as good as ever. Once exclusive, Lindos is now what is known as a lively young people's resort, which makes it a deafening place in the evening and a difficult place at which to sleep. By day it is no better, such is the crush of visitors pushing through the narrow alleys of the village on their way up to the knights' fortress and ancient acropolis. Rhodes's population of 70,000 swells to ten times that in summer, on top of which come all the day-trip visitors from other islands and cruise visitors. On a busy day, which is any day in summer, it seems that all three-quarters of a million people are in Lindos.

Much the same is true of Kos, although the numbers are smaller and the danger of claustrophobia less acute. Naturally, if you come into the lively category, these islands may well be ideal. Both have excellent sandy beaches and plenty of wind for the keen windsurfer, as well as the gale-force Madonna.

If your requirements of a Greek island include neither sightseeing nor nightlife nor watersports, you will no doubt be more tempted by the smaller Dodecanese islands. Patmos combines a degree of peace with the considerable interest of its great monastery, which is as impressive a fortress as any built by the Knights of St John. More serious anti-tourists may prefer Leros, which is nothing if not peaceful; or silent Tilos, or even little Lipsi, no more than a cheerful little port with a few rooms to rent and a couple of beaches with the clearest of water. But perhaps the most beautiful of all the Dodecanese lies far from the mainstream of history and modern travel between Rhodes and Crete. This is rugged, mountainous Karpathos, second in size to Rhodes and as rewarding for the hiker as it is for the connoisseur of uncrowded beaches and time-warped villages. For many years Karpathos has been an island spoken about between friends in a whisper. Now it has an airstrip, and a few tour operators have introduced it to a wider audience. Great change is afoot and the town is dancing to the merry tune of sledgehammer and bulldozer. All the more reason for a visit before the road system is improved, which will usher in the next phase of development.

The outsiders of the group are Astypalaia, a Cycladic island in all but name, dusty brown and brilliant white; and Kastellorizo, the Aegean island that isn't. Out on a limb 70 miles east of Rhodes, Kastellorizo is one of those awkward islands that feature in insets or are simply left off the map altogether. Only a mile or so from the Turkish coast, it has a Falklands-like quality and has remained inhabited only thanks to government subsidy.

The Dodecanese make a fascinating and admirably varied group of islands to tour. Patmos, Kos, Rhodes and Symi have sights not to be missed. Kalymnos has its sponge-fishing and Nisyros has the spectacular smelly cauldron of its volcano. Chalki has elegant mansions to rival those on Symi, and, in Olympos, Karpathos has one of the most interesting old hill villages in all Greece.

RHODES

Rhodes Town

The town of Rhodes divides neatly into two: the Old Town, the fortified City of the Knights, and the New Town, which includes the medieval naval base of Mandraki Harbour. North and west of the harbour the New Town is almost entirely taken over by hotel blocks. Below the dominating Castle of the Grand Masters and its palm-fringed gardens, the area throbs in high summer to the sounds of disco beat and the revving of motor-bikes. Labels are everywhere, not just the 'No Problem' T-shirts of the tourist shops. The style is Italian and smart, with designer shops, Benetton and Gucci; strangely, in this island of year-round sun, fur coats and monogrammed umbrellas are big business too. Pizzerias, spaghetti houses and *gelaterias* are as common as tavernas, and *capuccino* coffee is more popular in the corner cafes than Greek coffee. The daytime haunt for seeing and being seen is the Dolce Italia on the corner opposite the Municipal Gardens.

Rhodes's legacy from her period of Italian occupation (1912–1943) is not as attractive. Facing the harbour is a row of large and pompous buildings which include the post office, court-house, town hall, police station and national theatre (featuring Rhodian character plays). The Aliens Bureau or Ministry of Public Order is behind the post office. A less controversial Italian contribution to the city is the large number of public gardens and parks.

Mandraki Harbour is the hub of life. This is where the Municipal Tourist Office is (in Plateia Rimini), and where the taxis and buses stop (at the back of the New Market, or Nea Agora). The shops backing on to the market sell olives and nuts, and duty-free drinks – much cheaper than at the airport. Most people sit and watch the world go by at one of the many cafes underneath the market arches opposite the harbour; it's touristy and a bit expensive, but very atmospheric. Others watch the boatmen go about their business from a free park bench on the promenade, surrounded by oleander bushes.

For a taste of real Greece it's best to go into the market itself. Here nautical types stock up for their boats, housewives look for bargains, old men do nothing in particular over coffee and worry-beads. Stalls are packed with fruit and vegetables, slabs teem with fresh fish and butchers prepare their meat. You can buy freshly baked *psomakia* (bread rolls), *koulouria* (biscuit rings) or doughnuts from the bakery, freshly squeezed orange juice, *souvlakia* and pitta; or a good-value continental breakfast from a market stall. And in the little *kafeneions*, which are named after their owners' homes – like the Symi or Chalki bars – and are the haunt of fellow islanders passing through, you can sit over a cheap coffee or ouzo. Mandraki buzzes night and day with artists, popcorn vendors, sponge-sellers and agents plying tickets for their boat-trips. Morning boats leave for the island of Symi and its Panormitis monastery – a popular excursion – or Lindos, down the east coast. You can go on barbecue cruises, disco boats, or catch the hydrofoil to Kos (the big inter-island ferries go from the commercial harbour a short walk away).

The harbour, guarded by twin bronze deer where the Colossus once stood, is packed with strollers in the evening as the world and his wife take a pre-dinner turn past the picturesque medieval windmills (in which grain for the cargo-ships used to be milled) down to the old fortress of St Nicholas, now a lighthouse. At the northern end, the picturesque Governor's House, with its Venetian Gothic arches, is always popular with photographers. Next door is the Bishop's Palace and Church of the Annunciation (Evangelismou), a 1925 replica of the old church of the knights – well worth a visit.

A stroll towards Elli beach takes you to the grandly named Hydrobiological Institute at the northern tip of town, which contains supposedly the only aquarium of its kind in Greece. It boasts 39 tanks of regional fish, and a female seal from Britain called Katerina; a small museum houses assorted freaks of nature, including a seven-legged calf.

At night, especially in August, the New Town pulsates with nightlife. Young tourists spill out on to the pavements and into the road from the many bars and British-style pubs. Chic Rhodians or those in the know head for quieter, more ritzy cocktail bars or Italian restaurants. For late-night owls, Rhodes has *bouzouki* clubs, and some good discos just out of town towards Ixia; and the Grand Astir Palace has one of Greece's few casinos (smart dress and passport essential).

In the Municipal Gardens beneath the Palace of the Grand

Masters there are English *son et lumière* performances every evening, delivered in pukka accents reminiscent of wartime newsreels. If you seek a more genuinely Greek experience, head for the Old Town.

Just out of town to the east lies **Rodini Park**, home of the ancient school of rhetoric and now the venue of a wine festival every evening from July to September (entrance and wine tasting are free). In high summer the park provides welcome shade; there are rose-gardens, lakes with rustic bridges and a Hellenistic tomb.

To the west, **Monte Smith**, the hill of Agios Stephanos, is the site of the ancient city. Some (restored or reconstructed) parts survive: temples, stadium and theatre. The hill was named after

THE KNIGHTS HOSPITALLERS OF ST JOHN

This remarkable body of religious soldiers originated early in the 11th century at Jerusalem. Christian pilgrimage was a hazardous business, and the nursing monks at the Hospice of St John extended their services to providing armed escort. Then, after the first Crusade, they formed a military order, sworn to make war on the infidel as well as tend the sick. But they were driven out of the Holy Land – not only by the forces of Saladin but through bitter rivalry with the Knights Templar: the latter were much the most powerful organisation to emerge from the Crusades, but they over-reached themselves and were suppressed in 1312.

The order of St John transferred itself first to Cyprus, then, in 1309 – with the help of the Pope and after a two-year siege – to Rhodes. There they undertook to keep the Turks from dominating the Mediterranean; they built wonderful fortifications on Rhodes, annexed outlying islands in the Dodecanese and built up a powerful fleet of war galleys. Their flagship was the Great Carrack of Rhodes – a carrack was a merchant ship modified for war; this was an eight-decker, equipped to accommodate a small army for six months at sea. The power and reputation of the 'Knights of Rhodes' increased steadily, and so did their wealth. They derived income from estates all over Europe, and they inherited considerably from the Templars.

Within the order, a maximum of 600 Military Knights were recruited from the nobility. So honourable was a career in this aristocratic foreign legion that it became the practice to put younger sons' names down at birth; their lineage was thoroughly vetted and their dowries had to be large. In addition to vows of chastity, poverty and obedience they took others relating to battle: never to fight against

Admiral Sir Sydney Smith who kept watch from there for the Napoleonic Fleet in 1802, and offers fine views over Rhodes; it's also a favourite spot for courting couples.

Rhodes town's beaches, with their regimented rows of umbrellas laid sideways against the prevailing winds, get impossibly crowded. Both consist mainly of coarse sand, but that on the east side of town is wider and sandier than that on the west, which has a very busy main road running behind. Hotels used by tour operators may be five minutes' walk from a beach, and you may have to cross several roads to get there. None of the hotels is directly on a beach. The quieter areas of town are the side streets off Mandraki, behind the municipal buildings or at the north-east tip. For a night's stay when

---

a Christian nation, never to retreat, surrender or lower the order's white cross. Blue-blooded, high-minded and backed by divine right, they were a formidable force. It was also possible to be made a Knight of Grace, honorary membership of the order, conferred on those who rendered it great service. Other ranks, less exclusively recruited, included chaplains, sergeants and serving soldier-brothers.

According to their nationality, the knights belonged to one of eight langues *(tongues): France, Provence, Auvergne; Aragon, Castile; Italy, Germany, England. The head of each* langue *was called its* pilier *(prior), and each had particular responsibilities: the* pilier *of France directed all the order's hospitals, that of Italy was Grand Admiral, and the English office of Turcopilier, commanding light cavalry, was a leftover from the early days in the Holy Land. The Knights had commanderies all over Europe administering their affairs and ambassadors at every court; their services were available for hire to Christian princes at war with non-Christians. Head of it all was the Grand Master, appointed for life, in theory subject to the Chapter General – a council, which in practice he seldom summoned. In the 213 years in Rhodes, 14 out of 19 Grand Masters were French; Latin and French were the official languages of the Order.*

Rhodes survived two Muslim sieges in 1444 and 1480; in 1522, under Grand Master Villiers de L'Isle Adam, 7000 knights and islanders held out for six months before defeat by Suleiman's army of 200,000. The knights left Rhodes – but under astonishingly generous terms, with a safe conduct for men, ships, movable property and Rhodian followers. De L'Isle Adam negotiated for seven years before they next found a permanent, sovereign home as the Knights of Malta. From here they kept the Turks out of the western Mediterranean for three decades before their finest hour – the great siege of Malta in 1565. Under another heroic Grand Master, de la Valette, they held out against massive attack for four months while relief forces were assembled in sufficient strength to make the Turks retreat. All

passing through before visiting other islands, the *Spartalis* (B) is handy for all ticket agencies, friendly, a bit shabby, but with a nice breakfast terrace and views over the harbour. The *Constantinos* (B) is simple and quiet; the *Kamiros* (A), near Mandraki, is well kept, quiet, and has a roof-garden; the simple and cheerful *Maris* (C) is near the eastern beach and has a small swimming-pool; and the *Siravast* (A), across the road from the town beach, is stylish. The grandest hotel of the New Town is the *Grand Astir Palace* (Luxury-category), which houses the island's casino.

Rhodes town: sights

● **Old Town** The fortified, medieval city was divided into two parts, which retain quite different characters: the citadel (which contained the administrative and religious headquarters of the knights) and the rest of the town, where Greeks and Jews lived. In the 16th century, when the

---

THE KNIGHTS HOSPITALLERS OF ST JOHN continued

Christendom prayed for Malta – in England, whose langue *had died out after the Reformation, Queen Elizabeth ordered prayers to be read in the Protestant churches.*

In 1571 an alliance of European powers assisted by the Order trounced the Turks at sea in the Battle of Lepanto. For the Knights it was the beginning of redundancy as a fighting force. New World and Far East trading routes supplanted the Mediterranean as the arena of interest, and the great powers left the order far behind in building fleets of sailing vessels. On Malta, the fine new town of Valetta took shape; work on fortifications never to be tested went on for a century and a half. The Knights kept house with a pomp and circumstance increasingly perceived as ridiculous in the European Mediterranean of the 17th and 18th centuries.

After her revolution, France rejected her knights and confiscated the Order's French assets. In 1798 Napoleon, on his way to Egypt, annexed Malta with little trouble: confronted with a fleet and an ultimatum, the Grand Master surrendered promptly and ignominiously. Within four days, the Knights of St John had removed themselves from their last domain.

In Britain the St John Ambulance Association revived the traditions of the Order in 1877; its Ambulance Brigade branch was formed ten years later. Seeking a link with the original home of the original Order, the Association founded the St John Ophthalmic Hospital in Jerusalem (eye disease was found to be an urgent problem there) – and its full title is The Venerable Order of the Hospital of St John of Jerusalem.

Turks arrived, the Greeks were turned out to live in the New Town, which started to develop outside the walls.

The city can be reached through any of 11 historic gates. Once inside, its cobbled streets, turrets, ramparts and fine buildings are so well preserved you feel you might bump into a crusader. Head from Papagou Street, past the Tourist Office and the taxi-rank beneath the Palace of the Grand Masters and you can't go wrong. Climb any of the stairs into the gardens on the right and you're up on the Great Wall looking down into the moat, now filled with palm trees and deer. For a bird's-eye view over the fine mixture of Byzantine, Frankish and Turkish architecture, you can walk around part of the 5km circuit of the city walls (Mondays and Saturdays, tour starts outside the palace at 4p.m.).

Probably the best-known gate into the Old Town is the Pili Eleftherias (Freedom Gate), a narrow gap busy with traffic and tourists. Through here you step into Plateia Symis, where you are immediately confronted by the remains of the 3rd-century BC temple of Aphrodite, behind which is the Inn of the Order of Auvergne, completed in 1507. There is a giant map of the Old Town at this point on a splendid new mosaic pavement; it's worth stopping to get your bearings and plan your route, as it's easy to get lost in the maze of alleys, especially at night.

The first stop from here is one of the town's oldest buildings, thought to be the original 14th-century Knights' Hospital, now the Archaeological Institute (not to be confused with the Archaeological Museum). Swathed in bougainvillea and overlooking a lovely fountain, it has been captured by millions of tourist cameras. Next door is the Museum of Decorative Arts (see below) and opposite is the Byzantine Museum, situated in the former cathedral of the knights, later a mosque. Heading past Plateia Moussiou (Museum Place), the next stop is the 15th-century Knights' Hospital, now the Archaeological Museum (see below). The courtyard was used to store goods for the Infirmary above, and the cells were for contagious cases. Opposite is the Inn of England, a 1919 replica of the 1493 original.

The most splendid Inns are to be found on the narrow and cobbled Odos Ippoton, known as the Street of the Knights – the Old Town's most famous sight. At the top is the Palace of the Grand Master, the leader of the knights (see below). Because the street is mainly flanked by institutions and there are no shops at all, the atmosphere is very sober and lifeless, and the appearance very preserved. The restored medieval buildings are so perfect that it's difficult to believe you are not on a film set. The Gothic inns are embellished with sculpted decoration and coats of arms. On the right-hand side is the Inn of Italy, followed by the palace of Grand Master de L'Isle Adam. The beautiful Inn of France is the most elaborate, with seven coats of arms and crocodile gargoyles; it provides a venue for exhibitions, and has quiet gardens. Along the way are also small churches, a Turkish school, the French Chapel, the Inns of Spain and Provence, and sundry piles of cannonballs.

Turning south inside the ramparts you come to the Clock Tower of the Mosque of Suleiman the Magnificent, which marks the end of the knights' quarter; beyond lies the Turkish quarter, with Orfeos Street lined with plane trees and thronged with portrait artists. You can have your likeness – and your cash – captured instantly here and tourist shops abound. The main street is Socratous, the Golden Mile, a giant bazaar with jewellery shops, lace and embroidery stalls, ceramic stores and tourist paraphernalia. Here you can see carpets being woven – rugs are good buys – and you can also pick up cheap bedcovers, table linen, pottery and gold (don't forget to haggle). In this area are also the Mosque of the Agha, the Mosque of Ibrahim Pasha, and the old Turkish baths (*hammam*) which still operate (Arheiaou Street, daily from 5a.m. to 7p.m.).

There are twisty, narrow alleys where houses have flying buttresses (acting as support against earthquakes) and wooden balconies with trellises, leading into leafy squares with cafes and tavernas. And there are some fine fountains, particularly the ornate Seahorse Fountain on the Square of the Jewish Martyrs (Platia Evreon). The deeper you go into the heart of the Old Town, the more Greek it becomes, as well as cheaper and less touristy. Within the city walls there are several good pensions and small simple hotels, such as *Lia's House* on Pythagoras Street. The area naturally has its tourist traps, and visitors may be lured into restaurants with free ouzo. However, if you want to see Greek national dance at its best, it's worth going to the Nelly Dimogiou Theatre, behind the baths on Adronicou and Antiothiou Streets; the gardens are open all day for refreshments, and there are nightly (except Saturday) folk dance performances at 9.15p.m.

● **Palace of the Grand Master** The turreted building is a lavish Italian reconstruction of the former palace, which was used as a prison in Turkish times and destroyed when an arms store in the nearby Church of St John exploded in 1856. It became the summer residence of King Victor Emmanuel III and Mussolini. Recently given a facelift for the 1988 EEC Summit, about 14 rooms are open to the public. There are marble floors and staircases, but it's all fairly bare; however, it's well worth visiting for the many Roman and early-Christian mosaics brought from the island of Kos.

● **Archaeological Museum** Housed in their former hospital, this fine museum is full of relics and memorabilia of the knights, including tombstones (some bearing the skull and crossbones of the plague). There are also ceramics, coins and ornaments from Mycenaean graves at Ialyssos, and Hellenistic and Roman sculpture, including the famous life-size Aphrodite known as the Marine Venus, and the marble head of the sun god Helios.

● **Museum of Decorative Arts** Displays of folk art, including local pottery, carpets, costumes and interiors of Rhodian houses.

The West Coast

The fast west-coast road which links Rhodes to the airport is Leoforos Triandon – noisy night and day. The first resort just out of Rhodes Town is **Ixia**, which consists mainly of high-rise or bizarrely shaped hotel or apartment blocks set in their own grounds or with high hedges to muffle the sound of traffic. Here are the international 'de-luxe' hotels, conference centres out of season, such as the huge *Rodos Palace Hotel and Bungalows* (Luxury-category), with an array of facilities including sauna and masseuse, and the *Miramare Beach and Bungalows* (Luxury-category). Tributes to concrete and rivals to a Dallas soap set, the circular *Olympic Palace* (A) is like a vast flying saucer, the *Metropolitan Capsis* (A) two sweeping curves. The *Rodos Bay* (A) is set amid pines with a private beach; the *Blue Bay* complex (A) also has a private beach, together with swimming-pools, sports facilities and disco.

Many hotels are over the road from the long narrow shingle beach which is a haunt for early-morning joggers and becomes very crowded in high summer. There are beachside restaurants, a children's playground and plenty of watersports from skiing to windsurfing. The wind can get very fresh, so parasols are needed (available to rent, with sun-loungers, on the beach).

In the evening crowds of people stroll from the hotels into town. After dark the string of hotels, bars and nighteries on the main road are lit up like a golden mile. Neon signs invite you to partake of *smorgasbord* and burgers as well as *moussaka* and *souvlakia*; and there is a Kentacky (*sic*) bar. Surprisingly, there are still a few tavernas offering authentic Greek food and music. But the locals are more likely to be found in the village of Tris (left at the crossroads beyond the Miramare Hotel).

There are supermarkets and shops for self-caterers, and a couple of quieter roads alongside the beach or into the village of Ixia, where you can still see small farmsteads with cattle in the fields.

Ixia merges with **Trianda** (9km from Rhodes), which is similarly commercialised as a package-hotel resort but has a large and bustling village which retains some local atmosphere and charm. High above the resort on the plateau of **Filerimos** lies the ancient Acropolis of Ialysos, one of Rhodes's most outstanding beauty-spots. The hill is studded with cypresses and pines and was the site of one of three ancient cities of Rhodes. In 1522 Sultan Suleiman used Ialysos for his assault on the knights.

There are ruins of the great temple of Athena Ialysia and a

reconstructed Doric fountain with lion-head water spouts. But Filerimos is visited more for the heavily restored church of the Virgin Mary built by the knights on the site of a Byzantine basilica; and the monastery, an Italian restoration of the original. Reached by a flight of steps bordered by cypresses, the monastery and its domed chapels feature the coat of arms of the Grand Master d'Aubusson. Beneath the ruins of a small Byzantine church is a tiny underground chapel with 14th-century wall-paintings. The monks sell their own liqueur known as Sette, made from seven local herbs. Modest dress is essential for a visit here – no shorts, plunging tops or swimwear. From the monastery there's an uphill path to the south-west of the hill, along which are 14 icons representing the stations of the cross. Stunning views and a riot of flowers make it popular with photographers.

Kremasti, a little further along the coast road, is hardly a resort but a busy village with rooms and self-catering apartments and a few package hotels such as the *Blue Bay* (A) and *Electra Palace* (A). There is a wide pebbly beach with the usual sun-loungers, parasols and watersports. The village is famous for its *panayieri* or Festival of the Virgin Mary on 15 August. There is a giant street market, fiesta and funfair; and the Panhellenic Craft Fair is held here on 22 August. Kremasti is otherwise distinguished as a Greek army base and has a few jolly tavernas. Neighbouring villages are Pastida, another army centre, and Maritsa.

Only 2km further on is Rhodes Airport, frenetic on Wednesdays and Saturdays, the main transfer days for package tours. The village of **Paradissi**, on the flight path, is hardly heaven, but has a nice central square, quaint little backstreets and friendly tavernas. It's a good place for rooms if you're travelling independently and have just arrived on the island, and it's not even as noisy as you would imagine. On the slopes of Mount Paradissi, opposite the little village of Damatria, there is a cave with a church inside.

About 7km from the coast road is the island's number one tourist attraction, the **Valley of the Butterflies** (Petaloudes). Despite heavy high-season crowds, it is well worth the trip. The narrow leafy village with its gentle stream is criss-crossed by rickety rustic bridges. Cool and captivatingly pretty, the valley teems with butterflies from June to September. Dull, spotty greyish-brown at rest, in camouflage on the trees, the Quadrina (*Callimorpha quadripuntaria*) rise in clouds of vermilion as you pass. They are attracted to the valley by the resin of the storax trees which smells like vanilla and is used for incense. Notices along the stony way warn you not to disturb the butterflies, but there's a natural inclination to clap hands to set those wings in motion – sad, as every flight weakens the resting creatures. In high summer it must seem as if they are constantly taking a bow as clapping reaches a crescendo with every coach-trip.

Although organised excursions head to Petaloudes thick and fast, you can go independently by bus from Mandraki (it's best to go early in the morning to avoid the worst of the crowds). The bus stops in the middle of the valley; turn right for the restaurant and public conveniences, turn left past the gift and souvenir stalls and continue upwards through the woods to the charming **Monastery of the Virgin Mary of Kalopetra**, a tranquil resting-place with fine views over the plains. The church, built in 1782 by Alexander Ypsilantis, the grandfather of the leader of the Greek national uprising, is well worth the uphill trek. Meals are provided at rough benches in the grounds.

There are some good walks in this area, including a wooded trail which leads to the **Monastery of Agios Soulas**, about 4km from the main west-coast road. Here the village of **Soroni** has a giant fiesta on 30 July with folk dancing and donkey races, made famous in Lawrence Durrell's *Reflections on a Marine Venus*.

Down the west coast road Theologos or **Tholos** is not so much a resort as a collection of roadside tavernas, shops and a British-run supermarket. The main hotel is the comfortable *Doreta Beach* (A), popular with families but half an hour by bus from Rhodes town.

The other big tourist attraction off the west-coast road is the hillside site of **Kamiros**, the second of the three ancient cities of Rhodes. The extensive remains of the flourishing but mysteriously abandoned city were discovered in 1859. The layout of the city is clearly visible, and it is relatively easy to imagine how it looked in its heyday. Unlike other Rhodian sites, Kamiros is devoid of the hand of Byzantium or knightly influences, as it was undisturbed in the Middle Ages. There are remains of temples, an ancient water basin which supplied 400 families, ruined Hellenistic houses and shops, and an altar to Helios the sun god. The city was never fortified and had no acropolis.

Plenty of organised excursions feature Kamiros, but you can go independently by bus from Mandraki. There's a taverna down at New Kamiros on the main road for after-site refreshments.

High above ancient Kamiros rises the pine-clad peak of **Profitis Ilias** (798m). At the top are a hotel and lodge, the Elafos and Elafina (stag and doe), built appropriately in chalet-style. There's also a monastery of the Prophet Elijah (Profitis Ilias). It's a wonderfully peaceful spot.

Back on the coast road, **Kamiros Skala** is a pretty fishing harbour which has recently been enlarged to take bigger ferries. There are some excellent fish tavernas from which you can see your choice being unloaded from the caiques. The small ferry *Chalki* and caique *Aphrodite* leave daily at 3p.m. for the unspoilt island of Chalki opposite. If you want to linger longer, one of the tavernas offers rooms, handy if you miss the boat. Kamiros Skala is popular with Greek families at weekends, and is a staging-post for Chalki housewives and schoolchildren heading home from Rhodes. Otherwise it's a restful place for a leisurely lunch before exploring the castle which guards the headland above.

The majestic ruins of the former knights' stronghold of **Kastellos** are reached through lemon groves and pine woods; there are breathtaking views over the sea and nearby islands, or over the rugged vineyards of this agricultural area.

About 5km away, the village of **Kritinia**, founded by refugees from Crete, is a cluster of white houses clinging to the hillside. The landscape gets wilder and the road more winding here as you climb the foothills of **Mount Attaviros** (1215m). On its slopes, the village of **Embonas** acts as base camp for a climb up the mountain (about four hours return), and is famous for its fruit, especially watermelons and grapes; the country around abounds with vineyards, olive groves and tobacco fields. Many of the villagers still wear colourful national costume with long boots, and are renowned for their dancing.

By now you have left the well-worn tourist trail behind you, as the road winds through sparsely populated herb-scented hills. The pretty village of **Siana** is famous for its honey and fiery Suma, a kind of *schnapps*. You can sample both at the roadside cafes in the village, where the oldest houses have clay roofs. The church of Agios Panteleimon has basil at the doorway and a lovely interior.

From Siana, a newly resurfaced road and a steep track wind up to the crusader castle of **Monolithos**, perched on a vast and precipitous single rock which offers one of the most impressive views in Greece. The castle surrounds a tiny chapel reached by precarious steps. The uphill toil is worth it for the scenic reward, but extreme care must be taken as there's a sheer 800-foot drop on the other side.

The winds that batter the west coast have kept mass tourism at bay, and there are miles of unspoilt beaches, such as the sweeping bay of Apolakkia further south.

At the northern end of the bay, **Fourni**, quite a long drive down from Monolithos, is a lovely little sandy beach, with low rocky headlands closing off the cove, some pine trees and a cantina. The water is clear, with pebbles underfoot.

The unexceptional village of Apolakkia is pleasant enough, and has rooms. A more interesting halt is the **Skiadi Monastery** (7km away), which enjoys a fine setting looking out over pine-covered hills and eroded soil to the sea beyond. There's a patterned pebble floor, an elaborately carved screen and a collection of icons. The monks will put you up, for a donation.

The roads begin to deteriorate as you head south, but there is a decent road from Apolakkia across the island to Gennadio, connecting with the main east-coast road up to Lindos.

Kattavia is the southernmost village of the island, on a dusty plain populated by very healthy cattle. There's a church with frescoes and niches with sculptures, and – perhaps of more importance to visitors – a petrol station. From here it's 8km down a rough road to the tiny peninsula at the tip of the island – Prassonissi, or Leak Island – attached by a narrow neck of sandy beach (one side windy, the other calm). It's a splendid place for bathing, and has a jolly taverna. From Kattavia there's a real road through the mountains (with very fine views) via Mesanagros, and a track along the coast.

The East Coast

Although far more developed for mass tourism than the west, the east coast still has deserted beaches and beauty-spots to be discovered – particularly near Haraki and south of Lindos.

Just out of Rhodes town (past the British and Italian cemeteries) there are beach-hotel developments at **Agia Marina** and **Reni Koskinou**, with self-contained and impersonal hotel complexes which have much in common with Spanish holiday resorts. The sand and pebble beaches here get very crowded. The village of Koskinou itself is well worth stopping at: its houses have intricate mosaic pebble courtyards, a speciality of the area.

The former spa of **Kalithea**, built in the 1920s by the Italians, was once busy with tourists taking the healing waters. Now sadly abandoned, the splendid domed pavilions with pink marbled pillars and Moorish archways set in beautiful gardens are reminiscent of a film set (and are indeed used by film-makers), but it's still popular with sun-seekers. While there's only a tiny area of beach, there's a lido area beneath the palm trees with sun-loungers and a refreshment bar. Kalithea's secluded rocky coves are popular with nudists and snorkellers – the seawater is crystal-clear and the scuba-diving school boat regularly calls in.

Along the bay of Kalithea, in the direction of Faliraki, the

Eden Rock Hotel (A), on a rocky stretch of beach, is comfortable, and its small bungalows are ideal for families. It shares its beach with the *Paradise Beach* (A), which has a swimming-pool and children's playground. Both are well placed for Kalithea, and there are regular buses to Rhodes.

Wall-to-wall hotels lead to the busy resort of **Faliraki**, bursting with the young, free and single. It's also a good base for families who like a lively holiday: there are plenty of facilities including a variety of bars, fast-food places, mini-golf and a swinging night scene. The long beach of coarse grey sand offers para-gliding and all kinds of watersports; it gets very crowded. Some accommodation is across the busy main road from the beach. Three hotels which are on the beach and comfortable are the *Apollo Beach* (A), well appointed if a bit impersonal, set in its own grounds, the similar neighbouring *Faliraki Beach* (A) and the large and modern *Esperides* (A), 2km north.

For a cultural injection, move swiftly on to the village of **Kalythies** and the **Monastery of Agia Eleoussa** which has some frescoes. Back on the coast road past the quaintly named Anthony Queen (*sic*) coves – where *The Guns of Navarone* was filmed – you come to the quieter and more select resort of Afandou.

Site of the 18-hole Rhodes golf course, **Afandou** is set among apricot orchards and is known for carpet weaving. The beach is long, coarse sand and shingle, with secluded rocky inlets; it's popular with barbecue-boats, but there is still plenty of room for seclusion. The *Xenia Golf* (B) is an attractive hotel in the golf course grounds and bordering the beach, with three swimming-pools. The landscape along the bay of Afandou is made rather unattractive by the many wide, stony and dry river beds.

If you have transport it's easy to go inland 'over the top' via the village of Psinthos to the butterfly valley of Petaloudes and the west coast (see above). **Kolimbia** beach is worth visiting just for the splendid avenue of eucalyptus trees which leads down from the village. There are several big hotels and quite a lot of new building going on here, but the beach is rather ordinary, a greyish strip of sand and pebble, backed by rocky hills.

A little past Kolimbia, you can head inland to **Epta Piges** (Seven Springs), another of the island's beauty-spots and popular excursion-places. Peacocks strut beside babbling streams and waterfalls in the leafy glades, and the seven springs in question feed a central lake. You can either take a woodland trail to the lake or shuffle ankle-deep in water down a narrow, pitch-black tunnel. The traffic is two-way and chaotic, quite scary at times, and it's not for the tall or claustrophobic. After that ordeal you can relax over retsina and a charcoal grill at the restaurant.

Back on the coast, the **Tsambika Monastery** is perched high on a hilltop, overlooking a popular, golden sandy beach. The Greek answer to fertility drugs, the tiny white Byzantine church is a place of pilgrimage for childless women who walk up barefoot to pray for a family at the festival on 8 September. If blessed, they pledge to name the child Tsambikos or Tsambika – names unique to Rhodes – in gratitude to the Virgin Mary.

Archangelos, the island's largest village, is worth a visit. Villagers make soft leather peasant boots and hand-thrown ceramics; there are excursions to the potteries, and plates are a good buy. There are lots of tavernas, bars and restaurants, and two B-class hotels – the *Archangelos* and the *Fivos* – set in large peaceful gardens on the edge of the village.

Above sandy Agathi Bay the castle of **Feraklos**, one of the strongholds built by the knights, was the last to fall to the Turks in 1523. It looks down over **Haraki**, a fishing village now burgeoning as a resort, with good beach tavernas and self-catering accommodation. It's still peaceful and atmospheric, and has lovely views down the sweeping unspoilt beach to Lindos. This stretch is largely deserted, and you can pick your way off the main road down through vineyards and olive groves for secluded sun-soaking.

Vliha Bay, further along and 5km around the headland from Lindos, is a stop on round-island coach-tours. It has bustling tavernas and a tree-framed beach with watersports. The chic *Steps of Lindos* hotel complex (A) clings to the hillside about ten minutes' walk from the coarse sand beach. There are bars, coffee shop, children's playground, swimming-pool, even a church; and there's a mini-bus service into Lindos. Down on the beach, the *Lindos Bay* (A) is comfortable if rather more conventional.

South of LINDOS, Pefkos makes a quiet alternative base. Less frenetic than its famous neighbour (a three-mile walk away), it's fringed by pines and has a long coarse sand beach with neat *cantinas* and watersports. There are several good tavernas and self-catering studios, sporadic taxis and a bus service.

Five kilometres inland, the village of **Lardos** is also featured in some tour operator brochures; it's a smart place, with plenty of local atmosphere in the bustling square. One of the island's two campsites is here, and the bay below has miles of shingle and sand-dunes. The area has, not surprisingly, been earmarked for development.

Heading south from the crowds, the beaches near the few

villages – Gennadio, Plimiri – are usually frequented by Greek holiday-makers, and prices are more reasonable and food more ethnic than in the north. There are buses to the southern villages of **Lahania, Katavia** and **Messanagros**. The main road goes to Katavia, from where rough tracks lead to the peninsula of Prassonissi.

Lindos

Lindos was the most important Rhodian city in ancient times. Its position – at the foot of a tall, sheer, rocky headland with a natural harbour on each side – and its fairly barren surroundings encouraged the development of a seafaring people. They built ships, and developed trade with colonies in other countries such as Italy, France and Spain.

There was a temple on the headland at least as far back as the 10th century BC and, over the centuries, the temple evolved into an acropolis; the village below is now only a quarter the size it once was. The setting is startlingly beautiful: dazzling white houses like sugarcubes tumbling down the honey-coloured hill.

Getting around

Rhodes has excellent public transport. The city buses, as well as cross-town services to Monte Smith and Rodini Park and the round-the-city tours, depart from in front of the New Market. Buses for east-coast resorts and villages go from Rimini Square, outside the tourist office, and for west-coast places from up the road a little, opposite the New Market. There's an information kiosk, and stops for island sights such as the Butterfly Valley and Ancient Kamiros are suitably illustrated with butterflies and ruins so you can't go wrong. In general, buses are cheap and frequent, and even remote villages are served. It's worth checking times of last returns from villages, especially on holidays and festivals.

Coach-excursions are available to all the main sights and beauty-spots. They're bookable through tour operators or agents in Mandraki. Triton in Plastira Street is particularly helpful for all tickets from air to boat trips.

Car and motor-bike hire is widely available. Make sure that the small print on the conditions of hire does not stipulate that you're not allowed on rough roads. The main coast roads and bus routes are good, and so are some links across the interior. But in the south roads are little more than tracks and can be dangerous. New roads are scheduled to be built from the airport to Faliraki, and another between Katavia and Apolakkia in the south.

Taxis are a cheap alternative to car hire. Prices are fixed, but it's

There are Byzantine churches, quiet alleys and courtyards set with intricate patterns of black and white pebbles, and beautifully restored 17th-century houses with fine sculpted doorways. Hotels and high-rise buildings are banned, and the village is traffic-free – the steep streets are often no wider than a donkey and basket. The curved beach, with its splendid views towards the acropolis, is wide and sandy.

If all this sounds like a dream come true, it would be giving the wrong impression, for it takes no account of the effect that tourists have had on Lindos. Here, almost more than in any other place in Greece, the evolution of tourism has finally reduced the beautiful village to a caricature of itself, and has destroyed its charm; cute, grossly over-commercialised and packed to the point of bursting at the seams in high season, it has the island's highest prices and the most world-weary service.

It is hard to imagine that 20 years ago half the houses were derelict. It was only then that Lindos was discovered by tourists, and the wealth that they have contributed has meant that houses could be restored and that most of the population of 650

sensible to check the prices before you go, particularly if your journey is to far-flung places. It's common to share a taxi to keep the cost down. You can flag down taxis anywhere, and it's normal to yell your destination at the driver.

There are daily boat-trips from Mandraki down the east coast to Lindos, Afandou and Anthony Queen, plus barbecue and disco cruises at night. It's worth shopping around along the harbour for the best deal.

Boats leave daily at 9a.m. for the island of Symi and its Panormitis Monastery. There are hydrofoils to Kos and excursions to Nisyros and Patmos. You can go to the island of Chalki from Kamiros Skala (the bus links with the small ferry which leaves at 3p.m.).

Inter-island ferries can take you throughout the Dodecanese and beyond, to Crete, Lesbos, Turkey, Israel and Egypt from the main commercial harbour. Free crossings are offered to Kastellorizo in a bid to encourage visitors. Check departures with agents – each boat has a different one and information can vary. Rhodes Tourist Office in Mandraki has timetables.

Rhodes offers some splendid scenery for serious hikers. The free English newspaper *The Rhodes Gazette* is compiling a list of walks for keen ramblers.

The maps of the island by Freytag & Berndt and Clyde Surveys are reasonably clear (though the information on roads is not always correct) and show locations of tourist facilities; they also have plans of main towns and sights. Local maps are available from the Greek National Tourist Organisation.

people have been able to find work in the new industry. Bars, restaurants, tavernas and boutiques followed. Long the haunt of artists and lotus-eaters because of its extraordinary light, Lindos became super-smart and famous; assorted Britons from rock stars to academics bought homes there, and its atmosphere became very 'Hampstead-on-Sea'. *Holiday Which?* reported in 1974 that Lindos was 'good for a relaxing holiday, but has virtually no organised nightlife'.

Now Lindos is second only to Rhodes town as a package-holiday resort. Pulsating music echoes over the village until the early hours, there are burger bars and a cafe selling fish fingers, the beach is an international playground offering everything from windsurfing to wet-biking, and the place teems with tripper-laden donkeys nose-to-tail up to the acropolis. A magnet for young people, Lindos has become a shrine to sun, sand and sea, dedicated to tourism.

The Lindos formula hinges on the fact that there are no hotels. Accommodation offered by tour operators is in the form of rooms, studios or apartments in Lindian houses. Often rooms lead off central mosaic courtyards entered by communal front doorways; kitchens and bathrooms are often shared. As self-catering is the norm, there are plenty of supermarkets and shops.

The village is an uphill trek from the large, sheltered and sandy beach (donkey service available), and in high summer the temperature soars well into the hundreds; the streets are choked with day-trippers disgorged at the top of the village from the many coaches; and the low buildings – sheltered, too – tend to become airless in the absence of a cool breeze. There are very few places, apart from the acropolis, from which there is a view towards the sea.

At night, the village swings. There are all kinds of bars, with particular favourites for early evening, après-dinner and extra-late sessions, and two discothèques. Some of the bars and restaurants are in attractive Lindian houses with fine courtyards. The tavernas offer anglicised menus which include puddings.

A pleasant walk from the village takes you to the cove of **St Paul's Bay**, almost enclosed by rocks, where the apostle is said to have landed. There's a tiny white chapel where on 28 and 29 June a festival is held. The beach here is less crowded than its neighbour.

Lindos: sights

• **Acropolis** Whether you go by donkey or on foot, the acropolis is well worth the trip, particularly for the fine views. The medieval fortress of the Knights of St John surrounds the acropolis, with hundreds of steps leading up to the entrance. The pathway is full of scuttling donkeys and women selling lace and embroidery. The first thing you come to after passing through the outer gate of the stronghold is a remarkable relief carving of a trireme ship chiselled into the rock face; then steep steps lead to the ruins of the fortress itself and a Byzantine chapel. There are monumental stairs and terrace, and several pillars which convey the immense height of the former portico or arcade.

The remains of a small temple of Athena stand on the site of a Doric temple built by Cleovoulos and destroyed by fire, which in turn replaced an original temple built in the sanctified grove around the 10th century BC – according to legend by Danaos, in gratitude to the Lindians who extended warm hospitality to him *en route* to Argos with his 50 daughters.

The statue of Athena, renowned throughout the ancient world, was taken to Constantinople by a Byzantine emperor. Other statues were looted by Cassius when Rhodes sided with Mark Antony after the murder of Julius Caesar. Their bases remain, inscribed with the names of the sculptors.

• **Church of the Panaghia** Just off the main square, the beautiful domed 15th-century Byzantine church has a very rich, dark interior with a black and white pebble floor and 18th-century frescoes by Gregory of Symi – saints line the walls, men on the right, women on the left, and St Francis is shown with the head of an ass.

• **Lindian houses** In the village are many fine houses dating from the 15th to 17th centuries, some built in Gothic style with Byzantine or oriental decoration. The Houses of the Captains – with a small room perched above the house for the owner to have a view of his ships in the harbour – have been restored and their interiors preserved as folk museums. Many houses have balconies and rooms resting on pillars in Arab and Byzantine style; others have ornately carved door and window surrounds, or courtyards paved with patterned pebbles. Hanging on the walls may be bright Lindos plates – some families have valuable collections of 16th-century ones.

• **Tomb of Cleovoulos** Near the north-east end of the Great Harbour, looking down over the village, is a giant circular chamber made from square stone slabs, which has become known as the tomb of the 6th-century tyrant king.

ASTYPALAIA

Butterfly-shaped Astypalaia is the most westerly of the Dodecanese. It has a deeply indented coastline with high cliffs, and a hilly interior which is fertile in parts with cornfields and citrus groves. At first glance it seems that the island would be more at home in the Cyclades – cubic, dazzling whitewashed houses tumble down the steep alleys from the fortress and

Getting around

There are plenty of boat-trips to beaches, around the island, to Vathy and to other islets.

A bus links Livadia with Chora, Perigialos and Maltezanas. There are three taxis. Motor-bikes can be hired in Perigialos.

Astypalaia has recently been included in a ferry route from Athens to Kalymnos. There are passing ferries to Kos, Nisyros, Symi and Rhodes.

upper town. But closer inspection reveals a more haphazard mingling of styles – Turkish-style wooden balconies, and strong Italian overtones in the arcades and peeling stucco of the harbourside buildings. Astypalaia was ruled by a Venetian family, the Quirini, for three centuries; and after a long period of Turkish occupation it was the first of the Dodecanese to be taken by the Italians in 1912.

The island is remote, and has only recently started to be developed for tourism. Smart Athenians are building holiday homes, there are boutiques and bars, a disco and a *bouzouki* club which attracts the odd star from Athens. And there are excellent fish tavernas – being so far from any big centres, the fishermen sell their catch at home.

The boats dock at **Perigialos**, or Skala, which has a town beach, some rooms to rent and three small harbourside hotels – the *Astynea* (D), *Paradissos* (C) and *Aegon* (C). Most of the accommodation offered by the couple of specialist tour operators which feature the island is in self-catering studios or the new *Hotel Vengelis*. The port is the setting of the evening *volta*.

The old upper village of **Chora** lies just above the port and is reached by a steep flight of steps. A line of windmills stretches along the ridge to one side; above are the ruins of the huge castle of the Quirini. Over the entrance is the restored monastery church of Panagia Portaitissa.

The best beach on the island lies at **Livadia**, south-west of Chora, a 20-minute walk up and over the ridge from the port. There's a long stretch of shingle fringed by tamarisk trees and tavernas, rooms for rent, a beach bungalow and watersports. There are more beaches both to the south and north accessible by boat. On the 50-metre-wide stretch of land where the two 'wings' join, there's a beach on each side (you can choose whether to sizzle or cool off in the breeze). About 7km out of town the fertile plain of **Maltezanas**, the former lair of Maltese pirates, gives way to the pretty cove of **Analypsi**, which has two tavernas and is popular with nudists. Contrary to what is marked on the local map, the road peters out here, and the 'lost lagoon' of **Vathy** in the north of the island is accessible mainly by boat. It's a sleepy fishing village, hidden in a deep and narrow fjord-like bay.

CHALKI

Tiny Chalki, ten miles west of Rhodes, is being reborn. After the inevitable pattern of depopulation and decay after the decline of the sponge-fishing industry, a government plan in 1987 to boost the economy has given the kiss of life to the community. The island was designated Island of Peace and Friendship, and the once-grand neo-classical mansions which had fallen into decay have been restored (under a UNESCO-funded scheme) by skilled craftsmen as well as shepherds and fishermen, and repainted inside and out in traditional Dodecanese colours – vanilla, ochre and strawberry. The old olive-oil factory has been turned into a government-owned Xenia hotel, originally for Greek youth and political groups, conferences and UNESCO visitors. Happily, the project has spurred Chalkians to return and do up their family homes. New tavernas have opened, and young people are staying instead of going to work in Rhodes.

Barren and rocky, the island has no fresh water and relies on the water-boat for supplies. The houses have wells, which have to be filled regularly, and the tapwater is brackish and undrinkable. If you don't relish washing in saltwater or need several showers a day, Chalki isn't for you.

The harbour and only settlement is **Emborio**, an idyllic little place with a backdrop of windmills and, high on a hill a mile inland, the ruins of a knights' castle. Fishing-boats bob in front of the handful of bars and tavernas, there are a few little shops, and the lovely church of Agios Nikolaos has a distinctive pebble mosaic courtyard and supposedly the highest bell tower in the Dodecanese. Nightlife revolves around the tavernas and bars, where you are likely to see impromptu dancing; sometimes local musicians are laid on for a *bouzouki* night and the whole village joins in.

You can swim from several little pebbly coves behind the Xenia, over the headland near the windmills and army post. The island's main beach is at **Pondamos**, a sandy bay on the road out of the village (a ten-minute walk along rather slippery paths). This is gradually being developed: there are sun-loungers and

Getting around

You either walk, take a boat or rely on a lift. The island's ferry, *The Chalki*, runs a regular early-morning service to Kamiros Skala on Rhodes, connecting with the bus into Rhodes town, and returns at 3p.m. There's also a caique to Rhodes, and excursions to Alimnia and Tilos islands. Inter-island ferries call on the way to Karpathos, Kasos and Crete.

umbrellas, an excellent daytime taverna with rooms, and studios for rent. The beach gets busy at weekends, when there are trips from Rhodes, and in August.

Other easily accessible beaches include the small pebble beach at Kania, which has fig trees and sheep, and the little bay of Arous. Stalwarts can pick their way down a difficult path from the castle to Trachea, a narrow neck of beach, sandy in places and windy on one side; or tackle the long hike up past Chorio and down the other side to Lali, where the sea crashes on to white pebbles and rushes into caves (this walk shouldn't be attempted in full sun).

Fishermen will take you to far-flung beaches – Areta, Agios Giorgos, Trachea – and pick you up later. Backed by steep cliffs, these beaches are in shade by mid-afternoon. Fishing trips can also be organised, though much depends on the *meltemi* which can whip up quickly and disrupt all plans.

Weekend barbecue-trips are offered to the uninhabited island of **Alimnia**. Green, and with plenty of fresh water, Alimnia has deserted beaches, a little white chapel and the remains of Italian barracks, complete with bullet holes. During the war British commandos were caught there on a sabotage raid (Italian submarines were based in the deep harbour), and the villagers were forced to leave, never to return.

Chalki has a few olive groves, almond trees struggling without water, plenty of figs, and wild herbs – including thyme, from which the excellent local honey is made. The only sounds you are likely to hear on a walk through the interior are the goats' bells and hawks wheeling overhead; there is little traffic (apart from dumper trucks and pick-ups as there is nowhere to go apart from the ruined high town of **Chorio**, where a church clings to the side of the cliff, and the **castle** ruins, which include late-Byzantine frescoes in its chapel. A new road – the grandly named Tarpoon Springs Boulevard, named by its Florida-based Chalkian donators – links the port to Chorio, and is being extended to the monastery of **Agios Ioannis** on the west of the island, reached only by a three-hour walk along a donkey track. It's best to go in the early morning, have a siesta and a coffee, and tackle the descent at dusk when it's cool. It's also possible to stay overnight. At the annual festival of St John the Baptist on 29 August, a mule train takes up all the essentials. Another festival, on 15 August, takes place in Chorio; celebrations include local music and dance, the fast and furious Chalki *sousta*.

In August, when Chalkiots return home for their holidays, it can be very difficult to find a room on the island if you haven't pre-booked. Small tour operators organise packages to Chalki homes or restored houses, with self-catering facilities, and to the *Xenia* hotel, which sometimes has rooms for independent travellers between groups. Towards Pondamos the *Hotel Argyrenia* has new self-contained studios, and *The Captain's Pension*, a beautiful old Chalki mansion, offers rooms and B&B. Some families offer accommodation to independent travellers.

KALYMNOS

Kalymnos, island of contrasts: uncompromising grey rocky mountains confront the approaching sailor and suggest an altogether barren island, but the massifs are divided by dark green valleys of pines, eucalyptus and citrus groves, and at sea level and on the beach Kalymnos has more vegetation and shade than many more fertile islands. There is also quite a contrast in style between the town (Pothia), where tourists seem incidental to the conduct of everyday life, and the rapidly growing international holiday-resort area (Myrties and Masouri) on the other side of the island. This holiday zone is not at all special; but the town has great vitality and is the most distinctive and attractive aspect of the island, although it is not the most peaceful place for a holiday.

Although not a small island, Kalymnos consists mainly of inhospitable and more or less inaccessible rocky land, and the island presents a rather limited range of possibilities for a stay-put holiday. A brief visit is probably a better bet. Its beaches are indifferent; its archaeology is largely unexcavated (and under water, in the case of the ancient city) and hard to find; and only one community (Emborio) comes into the category of charming peaceful coastal village. In short, the island lacks most of the usual ingredients of Greek island charm. In this and its urban character, it resembles Syros in the Cyclades.

Kalymnos is best known as the last centre of the Greek

sponge-fishing industry, which is said to be the island's main source of income, although tourism must be catching up fast. There is no need to go to Kalymnos to buy a natural Greek sponge, however, and prices are not significantly lower on the island, although it is possible to buy very cheap runt sponges and off-cuts that are not worth exporting. Nor is there anything to be seen of the fishing, which takes place in far-flung parts of the Mediterranean, the Aegean beds having been exhausted long ago. Sponge tourism should ideally be timed to coincide with the festivities that mark the days preceding the departure of the annual sponge-culling expedition or following its return, although this may not be easy to arrange since both events depend on the weather. The fleet usually sets sail during the week after Easter and may return any time in late September or October.

Sponges are animals, which feed by sucking and filtering seawater through their fibrous bodies. Prised from the sea bed by divers armed with axes, the sponges are dark grey before the process of having stones and other foreign bodies shaken, rinsed, trampled and beaten out of them, being bleached in a sulphuric acid solution and clipped into shape by sponge topiarists. When shopping for sponges, bear in mind that the value depends not only on size but also on consistency of texture and especially the bore of the tissue. A dense small-bore sponge is much more durable and more expensive than a broad-veined floppy sponge of the same size. In contrast to the usual practice of selling sponges wrapped, size-graded and labelled, Kalymnos sponge sellers (some of whom set up stalls on Kos and other Dodecanese Islands and show off their antiquated diving suits) have trays of loose sponges at different prices. Haggling can be fruitful, especially if you are prepared to buy several sponges.

The town of **Pothia** (sometimes referred to as Kalymnos) is sandwiched between steep grey mountainsides in the south-east corner of the island. Its considerable size (a population of over 10,000) is surprising on such an island and recalls the old days when others similarly unfruitful, such as Hydra, supported large populations living from the sea. The rest of the island has only a few thousand inhabitants. The town dates only from the mid-19th century; previously the village of Chorio, on the hills a couple of miles up the valley, was the main settlement.

It is a colourful and lively place and makes a fine sight from the sea, blue and white like the Greek flag. This is said to be deliberate, houses having been painted blue as a gesture of Greek patriotic defiance to Italian rule and attempts to impose Italian language and culture on the population. An amusing centrepiece to the water-front is a complex of public buildings, half-fortress and half-harem-like palace, housing the police, customs, town hall, a gleaming church and the food market.

This complex divides the water-front into two. In the usual contraflow of evening strollers, local people tend to hang around in the posh area (the southern end, near the ferry quay and the sponge export warehouse) of hotels, western-style bars, souvenir shops and the excursion-boat and yacht moorings; while discerning tourists gravitate to the teeming popular zone of rough local fish restaurants to the north of the police palace and market. Shops include several big duty-free liquor supermarkets. Oddly enough, cheap umbrellas are another local speciality.

An unusual feature of the water-front is an impressive collection of modern bronze sculptures, the work of a local father and daughter team: a winged nymph, a naked sponge diver carrying his helmet like a heroic warrior of legend, Jupiter enthroned, and many others. More familiar is the Muses cafe, once a reading-room, with a grand façade of Ionic columns and interior decoration of sponge-related panels of relief sculpture. Pothia seems to have an even larger population of idle cafe-based males than most Greek towns. This may be less obvious when the fleet is at sea.

The sponge warehouse near the ferry quay is full of sponges at various stages of treatment. The doors are flung open whenever a boat lands, and sponges are for sale.

The town's hotels are clustered around the southern section of the water-front. The prominent *Olympic* (c) is the biggest and most comfortable, although nothing special, and well placed for ferries. Others close by include the basic, inexpensive *Alma* and the *Pension Patmos*, set back slightly in the angle of the port and relatively quiet (nowhere is *very* quiet in Pothia, even if building-works are not in progress at six in the morning outside the bedroom window). The latter's friendly proprietor waits up for the small-hours ferries if he has vacancies, and the rooms are good.

The backstreets are a maze of billiard halls and motor-bike garages, with no more specific points of interest than the fun of wandering around a foreign town. The local archaeology museum is on the northern hillside.

Kalymnos's main valley crosses the island like a cutting, climbing from Pothia to a central ridge where Chorio stands beneath the clifftop fortress ruins (Pera Kastro) and dropping down to the west coast at Kantouni (otherwise known as Panormos or Linaria). Several roads lead up the valley out of town, all ending up at Chorio and passing another fortress

(Hrisoheria, with windmills) dominating the southern side of the valley on the way out of town. This was the main island base of the Knights of St John, who built a chapel into the walls of the castle.

The ruins of **Pera Kastro** can be reached by concrete staircase signposted from the centre of Chorio, leading up the cliff to a belfry in the walls. On top very little remains except a few whitewashed chapels, circling crows and a lot of sheep, which will come running if you are unable to resist the temptation of the bell rope. The view from this wild and boulderous spot is very fine, well worth the steep trudge up. The local guidebook does not contain the information that from these grey heights local men and women hurled themselves rather than yield to the Turks.

From Chorio down to Kantouni the road passes (on its left) a ruined Byzantine church built from the stones of a Hellenistic temple and with a number of inscriptions still visible. The eastern Emperor Arcadius sponsored the church after finding at Kalymnos a safe haven from a storm.

Kantouni is the local beach resort for the town, with a single ugly large hotel surrounded by citrus groves and holiday homes, and grey sand beaches on either side of a rocky headland. A track from the same main road turning leads to Plati Gialos, another dark sand beach with a taverna, but little other development and fewer people than most of the beaches on this, the bathing zone of the island.

The main tourist area has grown up to the north, where a narrow channel separates Kalymnos from the imposing mountain island of **Telendos**, which sits like a tall hat thrown from the shore. The channel dates only from AD554, when the ancient city (also called Pothia) was submerged after a mighty earthquake lasting a fortnight. Ruined buildings are said to be visible on the sea bed. Telendos has a small village facing the mother island and a quiet beach facing open sea, only a short walk over the hill from the village.

This is a lovely stretch of coast, but the resort development (**Myrties** and **Masouri**) suffers from being strung out along the road, which runs through thick greenery steeply above the sea. Paths and staircases lead down to beaches, which are mostly pebbles and have some tree shade and the only watersports on the island. The *Hotel Plaza* is best placed for bathing. At Myrties a bit of a resort centre has grown up beside the quay, which is used by excursion-boats and ferries to Telendos (on demand) and Leros (daily). Most of the new hotel-building has taken place and is still going on at the northern end of Masouri, which is gradually growing along the road northwards, further and further from the beach.

Getting around

Kalymnos is said to have over 6000 motor-bikes, and Pothia, Myrties and Masouri have plenty of hirers. Those on the Pothia water-front are polished exponents of the art of luring clients with a display of impressive new machines and keeping the fleet of tatty old ones they actually rent out well out of sight until you have signed, or at least psychologically committed yourself. Car hire is advertised in Pothia and short-term yacht charter can also be arranged. As well as being a good way to explore the island and its neighbours, this is a legal way for those on a package or charter-flight holiday to visit Turkey, and may not be expensive if you fill a small (skippered) yacht with a number of people for a day-trip. Boat-trips from Pothia go to Pserimos (a peaceful little island between Kalymnos and Kos, with a beach and a taverna), Kos, Leros, Patmos and Astypalaia. The last is a long and expensive jet-boat ride. There are also round-the-island boat-trips.

Conventional wisdom restricts the bus system to an occasional service between Vathi and Pothia but, having observed bus-stops along the main road and a bus in Kantouni destined for Masouri, we are confident that the network has now grown to embrace the west-coast resorts as well. Whether any buses continue as far as Emborio is less certain, but they may well do, now that the road has been surfaced. In common with many small islands relatively unused to tourism, Kalymnos lacks signposts; local people do not need them. This, combined with the problem of numerous cases of divergence between common usage, placenames marked on the map and those described in books, makes travelling around the island something of a mystery tour, and seeking out its less-prominent monuments distinctly tricky. Fortunately, the road network is not extensive, so the scope for getting lost is not great.

It is a splended drive along the new road north from Masouri around the narrow head of **Arginontas** bay (which has a quiet, shaded beach and tavernas) and along the coast of the island's long mountainous northern peninsula as far as the sheltered and very peaceful south-facing village of **Emborio**, which is just beginning to discover its role as a resort. It performs very well: the pebble beaches have an admirable row of tamarisks for shade, there are a couple of tavernas and a few rooms to rent; and the view of the offshore islands and along the west coast is delightful, like that of a lake bounded by empty mountains on all sides. Locals tend to take the direct sea route across to Myrties, and you may be able to hitch a ride on a caique full of goats.

Sturdy hikers may tackle what must be an arduous but amply rewarding crossing of the mountain ridge from Arginontas over into the northerly of Kalymnos's two great transverse valleys, which runs down through a remarkable dark green vale of mandarin groves to the small port and very narrow inlet of **Vathi**, passing a couple of quiet villages and a considerable extent of unexcavated archaeology and Byzantine chapels on the northern slopes of the valley. The best of these are near the village with the big plane tree, probably called Platanos. Most tourists go no further than Vathi, arriving by road from Pothia – an uninteresting drive along the rocky, quarried coast, redeemed by the beautiful discovery of the fertile valley – or by boat. If driving up or down the valley, take care in the surprising one-way system of high-walled roads, because the locals are unlikely to do so, and tend to treat the one-way signs as optional.

Vathi, little more than a narrow concrete quay, now has a hotel as well as tavernas, a shop specialising in charming (and very cheap) rugs and cloth woven by local nuns and schoolchildren, and a small boatyard. The sides of the inlet are steep and rocky and there is no beach. Boat-trips include a grotto visit here, as they do in the extreme south of the island, where the vast **Kefalos cave**, rich in impressive stalagmites and stalactites, is more easily reached by walking up from the sea than over the hills from the village in this corner of the island, **Vothini**.

Vothini can be reached from Pothia by the road that scales the town's pine-covered southern flanking hillside. The bay below the village (**Vlihadi**) has two small beaches and a taverna in summer. The coast road south from Pothia passes a disco and a few small stony beaches (the nearest to town) on its way to an old waterside thermal establishment, apparently disused and overrun by hens.

KARPATHOS

Dramatically beautiful Karpathos is the second-largest island in the Dodecanese, but one of the least known – largely because until very recently the island was awkward to get to and difficult to get around. Things are unlikely to remain this way much longer: the island has fine and varied mountain scenery and glorious remote sandy beaches. The newly enlarged airstrip now receives a weekly charter flight from Britain, and extensive holiday development is under way in some parts.

South of the mountains that divide the island, Karpathos is surprisingly populous and prosperous, thanks to a large expatriate community. Local tradition demanded that property be handed down the female line; as men were unable to marry before their sisters, hundreds went to America to seek their fortunes and many have returned to Karpathos, living on US pensions. In Karpathos you are as likely to hear 'Have a nice day' when you go shopping as 'Kalimera'. In the villages expensive cars stand outside well-maintained villas with distinctive wrought-iron work (with family initials worked into garden gateways).

The red-grey crags in the centre and south of the island loom over the pine forests on the lower slopes, with the scent of resin filling the fertile valleys; the dry river beds glow with the brilliant pink of blooming oleander. The mountainous northern spine is linked to the rest of the island only by a long, rough, very spectacular road, or by boat. It's remote and rugged, with clouds hanging around the high peaks and a chill wind blowing up the cliffs; the mountainsides are covered in a bleak, grey scree and support only a few olive groves. Near the far north is a spectacular mountain village, Olympos, until very recently isolated in a time warp; it now receives regular busloads of visitors from the northern port of Diafani. In the east, dramatic gorges and awesome rock formations around Apella are the legendary site of the Clash of the Titans.

Like most of the Dodecanese, Karpathos has a Roman and Byzantine history. It was under the rule of the Knights of St John for only two years; after a period under the Genoese and the Venetians, it was taken for the Turks by the pirate Barbarossa, and came under Italian occupation again from 1912 to 1944. The island's medieval Italian name of Scarpanta is still used.

The island has twelve main villages and six small hamlets, most in the southern part of the island. The main harbour is at **Pighadia**, or Karpathos town, a plain and workaday modern community on one side of the wide and sandy Vrontis Bay, with a skyline of mountains. Small and compact, it slopes up from the harbour in a mix of red-tiled roofs, balconied apartments and the occasional villa with painted shutters. There has been a recent building boom; holiday studios are springing up, and the town has had a facelift – the long promenade is now adorned with smart black streetlamps. There are pavement cafes on the harbour-front, a couple of bars with disco music, plenty of rooms for independent travellers, some good tavernas and a few small hotels. The *Atlantis* (c), on the edge of town, overlooks a small swimming bay with an excellent taverna; the *Anesis* (D) is cheap and cheerful. The town beach is a ten-minute walk from the centre – long, with greyish-white sand

and some rocks, backed by several new hotels. The *Seven Stars* (B) is good for families; so is the *Romantica* (C), a smart, family-run hotel with self-catering studios in its lemon grove, over the road from the beach.

Over the headland south of Karpathos town (about a 15-minute drive, or a tricky walk and climb through olive groves and pines) is the growing resort of **Amopi**, which has three lovely sandy beaches (one for nudists), with a white chapel perched above. There are pensions and tavernas and the new *Hotel Helios*. On the slopes north-west of Amopi, **Menetes** has quaint vine-covered streets and courtyards, a church with a beautifully carved icon and a small folk museum. You can walk back from here to Vrontis Bay through fields and lemon groves.

The road north from Karpathos town leads to the island's most prosperous village, **Aperi**, seat of the Archbishop of Karpathos and Kassos. The village spring has an inscription: 'Washes away sins, not just what you see.' There are fountains, fine houses and the remains of a Byzantine cemetery where the cathedral now stands. The village of **Othos** is the starting-point of the rough overland route to the north; it too has traditional Karpathian houses, one of which has been preserved as a craft museum. Neighbouring **Pyles** has picturesque narrow streets and wonderful views. The road down from Pyles towards the west coast is particularly rough and hair-raising.

On the wild and often windswept western coast, **Arkassa** (reached via Menetes) has new self-catering studios with a swimming-pool; on the headland are the remains of the ancient capital, and traces of mosaic pavement from several Byzantine churches. Many consider remote **Lefkos** as the jewel of the island – three horseshoe bays of pure white sand, a few apartments and a taverna which offers home-grown vegetables.

The east coast has pretty coves, more easily accessible by boat than by road, all the way to the port of Diafani. **Ahata**, **Kyra Panagia** – with a pink-domed church, a pension and villas – and **Apella** all have fine, quiet beaches.

The rugged north of the island is accessible by a rough road, with steep drops to the side, dangerous in windy weather. Even this is relatively recent; previously, an even rougher mule track was the only land route linking the south with the northern communities. There are few springs, and water gets very scarce; the pine forests on the way still bear the black scars of forest fires in 1983. In the north-west of the island, on the slopes of Profitis Ilias, dotted with windmills, the large mountain village of **Olympos** is spectacularly sited below barren peaks. Cut off from the rest of the world until a road was pushed through from the port of Diafani a few years ago, Olympos still seems

Getting around

Organised excursions are available from agencies in Pighadia, and boats go daily up the east coast to beaches and the port of Diafani.

There's an infrequent bus service to the southern villages of Aperi, Othos and Piles, and to Amopi and Menetes; if you go to Arkassa, you should expect to stay overnight. Taxis will take you to less remote villages; and there are taxi and mini-bus services from Diafani to Olympos.

Cars and motor-bikes can be hired in Pighadia. The two so-called main roads are very rough in places, with sheer drops to the sea in the north; on the wind-buffeted west coast, a motor-bike can be dangerous.

The island is popular with serious hikers, and there are good walks from Aperi, or from Spoa (above the tiny east-coast harbour of Agios Nikolaos) to Olympos – with stunning views of Crete. Possi Travel on Pighadia water-front has maps and details of walks.

in a time warp; the inhabitants speak an ancient form of Dorian Greek, wear traditional costume (high leather boots, intricately embroidered clothes and special collars of gold coins for festivals) and bake their weekly bread in communal ovens from flour ground in their medieval windmills. The place seems bleak at first glance, particularly when the wind whistles down the narrow streets; the stone houses, painted with pastel washes, blend with the hillsides. Even modern houses follow the traditional pattern – one divided room, built around a central pole or pillar which is covered with embroideries and wedding photographs. On a raised platform behind a carved rail are rolled mattresses and a dowry chest of clothes and linen. The room is usually crammed with items gathered by seafaring relatives – plates, lace, crochet and knick-knacks, in an explosion of fairground colours. The inevitable television serves as a shrine for icons.

Despite the fact that the villagers are used to visitors (and welcome them into their houses), and receive regular busloads from Diafani, life continues largely unchanged; people carry faggots on their heads, and herd goats up the hill from the port. On 15 August at the well-attended festival of the Virgin Mary, the villagers play goatskin bagpipes. There are a couple of cheap but comfortable pensions in the village: *Anixi* and *Olympos* are recommended.

In order to explore some of the north of the island, it's worth staying at Olympos, or at a harbourside taverna at **Diafani**. Here, the water is too shallow for the inter-island ferries, so you go ashore by caique. You can take a mini-bus or taxi up to Olympos, or walk up through the woods. At the island's northernmost point, **Vroukounda**, there are some ruins, a castle, graves hewn into the cliffs and a shrine to St John in a cave.

KASOS

Kasos, just six miles from Karpathos, is the most southerly island of the Dodecanese. It's gaunt, mountainous and remote, with precipitous and inaccessible coasts; and it is yet another example of depopulation and the consequent abandoned and crumbling houses. In Kasos the final decline started with a savage raid by Egyptians (then allies of the Turks) in 1824; the men were killed, women and children carried off as slaves, and the island razed. The event is still referred to as the 'Holocaust', and makes it all the more difficult to understand why a large part of the male population left for Egypt voluntarily only three decades later in order to help construct the Suez Canal. Skills acquired there laid the foundation for generations of Suez pilots; ship-owning then became an activity with which Kasos was associated, and which was responsible for the building of many fine houses.

Kasos, unlike many other islands, has not yet witnessed a change in fortune with the onset of tourism, despite an air link with Rhodes and Karpathos. There are rugged coves, but few proper beaches; and there's little of interest to visit. Perhaps because visitors are relatively rare, they are welcomed with great friendliness by the local people.

The capital, **Phry**, is a charming fishing port set against a mountainous backdrop, with a clutch of tavernas, pensions, rooms and a couple of hotels – the c-class *Anagenissis* and *Anessis*. Across the bay is the small port of **Emborio**, also picturesque with fishing-boats, tavernas and cafes. Just outside Phry is the village of **Panagia**, where the dilapidated old houses of the former sea captains and ship-owners testify to the island's former wealth.

Rough roads lead to the village of **Arvanitohori**, with a church hewn out of the rock, and to the former capital, Agia Marina, 3km from Phry. **Poli**, almost 3km from Phry in another direction, is the site of the acropolis of the ancient city, and has a Byzantine church.

Kasos is very peaceful, and good for walkers; there are sheltered gardens, orange and lemon trees and olive groves. Near the tiny airstrip, there's a beach at Ammoua, and several

Getting around

Kasos has one bus and two taxis, so unless you can persuade a friendly local to act as chaffeur by land or sea, you're likely to have to walk most of the time. Flights are available from Rhodes and Karpathos, caiques from Finiki and Karpathos, and inter-island ferries stop on the way to Crete or Piraeus. If the sea is rough, you have to go into Phry harbour by small boat as the ferries can't dock safely.

caves with fine stalactites. Across the island there's a small sandy beach at Khelathros; and boats cross to the islet of Armathia which has a fine sandy beach.

KASTELLORIZO (MEGISTI)

Kastellorizo, the Italian Castelrosso, is the most far-flung Greek island and the last – or first – in Europe; it's 70 miles east of Rhodes, and only a mile from Turkey, where the locals go shopping. Though it's the smallest of the Dodecanese islands ($3\frac{1}{2}$ square miles), Megisti (meaning 'the biggest') is in fact the largest island in an archipelago of 12 islets. Once, like Symi, it was rich and populous, with 17,000 inhabitants; during the Second World War the people were sent to the Middle East, and homes were looted and burnt. A further tragedy struck at the end of the war when returning islanders were drowned in a shipwreck. Many emigrated, mainly to Perth, Australia, and the island fell into decline; its population is now only about 200 people. Like many other islands, Kastellorizo is largely supported by overseas funds and by retired folk who have returned to restore their old family homes or open tavernas; recent government subsidies have encouraged tourism.

Although the natives are fiercely Greek, there's an eastern flavour to the red-tiled houses with their narrow windows and wooden balconies. The old Turkish mosque has been turned into a small folk museum. The lovely harbour, **Mandraki**, is topped by the ruins of the red medieval Castle of the Knights, destroyed and rebuilt several times. There are a few pensions and rooms to let, and the small and smart *Hotel Megisti* (B), offered as part of a package by some specialist British tour operators. Nightlife is minimal – a new disco bar at the end of the harbour, and some good fish tavernas.

> ## Getting around
>
> There are no roads on Kastellorizo, so you either walk or take a boat. Ferries are infrequent, and the summer flights from Rhodes may be disrupted by bad weather. There may be a dumper truck to take your luggage from the tiny hilltop airstrip, and a transfer bus is on the cards; but you'll probably have to make the 30-minute walk into town.
>
> You can take a boat-trip across to Turkey – but you're not permitted to stay overnight.

The island has a craggy coastline and no beaches; swimming is from the hotel steps, or from rocks. Boats go to beaches on some of the other islets, some of which are within swimming distance. All are uninhabited (though two have lighthouse keepers).

There's little to do on Kastellorizo apart from visiting its beauty-spot, the **Blue Grotto of Perasta**, a rival to that at Capri. The cave is reached by a three-hour round trip by boat, and is renowned for the colour of the water, opaline in the sun's rays.

KOS

Kos, island of the eponymous lettuce, has everything: a fascinating and colourful town of minarets, palm trees, archaeological sites, a knights' castle and a bustling harbour; a varied landscape of mountains and wide fertile coastal plain; and mile upon mile of sandy beach, as empty or jam-packed as you like.

If the combination of sand and sightseeing interest gives Kos an unusually broad appeal, there is no doubt that most of the island's visitors are more interested in the beaches than the history: Kos has gone for mass-market tourism in a big way. The town itself pounds out disco music as loud and as late as does Rhodes, and there are more and more big new hotel complexes lining the coast. These isolated hotels are a more characteristic feature than resorts, of which there are only two of any size – Kos town and Kardamena. For a holiday in a totally self-contained modern hotel with a good beach, Kos is perhaps the best of all Greek islands.

The popular game of likening the shape of islands to bits of anatomy, animals, cigars, hour-glasses and so on is not very illuminating, but Kos's outline is irresistibly fishy, perhaps even whale-like, for it is a big beast, over 40 miles from nose to tail. There is still lots of open space: even where large-scale hotel development has taken place, it is comfortably spaced out rather than densely packed, as similar development tends to be on Rhodes or Crete. The Kos style is not necessarily preferable: hotel dwellers without independent transport may feel very isolated and face few alternatives to the hotel's so-called international cuisine. Fortunately, Kos is also a very good island for organised excursions. Seekers of solitude might wish the developers would stick to one corner of the island and leave other areas untouched. While Kos as a whole certainly does not seem overcrowded, empty areas of coast are a dwindling commodity. Beautiful Kefalos bay has been parcelled up and built upon, and there are signs of a programme of road-building all around the still-deserted mountainous western tail of the island, its last wilderness.

In general, the scenery is not outstanding by Greek island standards. Much of the mountainous south coast is inaccessible by land or sea; and the north is decidedly featureless, a wide unkempt rural plain and a monotonous windswept sandy coastline. The main road runs through unattractive sprawling villages set well back from the sea, which makes the hotel clusters that pass for resorts all the more peaceful but does not make interesting scenic driving. Only those who head up into the mountains are likely to come away with a memory of Kos as a beautiful island. The smaller and emptier western half of the island has a different complexion of low sandy hills, unproductive and also rather featureless, apart from Kefalos bay, the one undeniably beautiful stretch of the island's coastline.

The island of Hippocrates was synonymous with fertility, culture, health and hygiene and a generally enviable quality of life in former centuries. Describing the island in a famous passage from the *Idylls*, Theocritus wrote of the loaded branches of plum trees kissing the ground. A generation ago Kardamena (see page 574), a fishing village with its feet in the sand, summed up all that was most appealing about Greece – an escape to the quiet life of sun, sea, a simple diet and a simple billet, with the magical extra Greek ingredient of friendliness sincerely and spontaneously offered. Sad to say, Kardamena has lost all its fragile charm, although it still has its feet in the sand. It now seems no different from scores of other shoddy modern building-site resorts where lots of young people get very drunk and very sunburnt. The appeal of a place such as Kardamena cannot survive growth. It depends a lot on the local people, and their attitude has inevitably hardened and become more exploitative since the tour operators moved in to block-book not only the hotels but also most of the village rooms. You may read that Kardamena is still a village of potters and fishermen where bartenders cannot be bothered to tot up the drinks, but this was not our experience.

For those not interested in the big beach hotel experience, this really leaves only **Kos town** which, fortunately, is not only picturesque and historically interesting but also has a vigorous life of its own which shines through the impersonal influence of tourism. It is a town of stark contrast between old and new, summarised by the street of bars and discos flashing their strobe lights over the mosaic pavements and re-erected columns of the ancient forum. The integration of archaeological zones and modern town is part of Kos's casual charm: people use the rutted ancient high street as a short cut through town and, if the music is too deafening, there is nothing to stop you taking your Metaxa out on to a bench of antique masonry and doing some moonlit sightseeing. There seems to be no bridge between ancient and modern. The reason is that Kos was flattened by earthquake in 1933, which prompted the Italians to excavate large areas of the ancient city which would otherwise still lie buried. The rest of town has been rebuilt in a drab functional style, redeemed by a profusion of flowers and trees for which the town has been famous since antiquity.

The immediate surroundings of the narrow-mouthed harbour have all the picturesque ingredients: cafe terraces, palm trees, excursion-boats, yachts, sellers of herbs and sponges, tourists on bicycles, fishermen selling their catch from trays in the morning before settling down to repair nets in the shadow of the massive walls of the knights' fortress. The harbour entrance is too narrow for ferries, which have to use an exposed jetty at the end of the fort. This can lead to problems in windy conditions and also means that ferries come and go unseen from the water-front cafes. The fortress walls are the best vantage-point.

There is no need to look further than the harbour for accommodation: the old *Kalimnos* (E) is a classic port hotel, its door always open to late arrivals, its aged proprietress happy to be roused from the sofa where she spends her days and nights in fitful dozing. The Kalimnos is not the height of luxury and noise may be a problem, but Camay, a fresh towel and a bottle of water in the bedroom are more than many an A-class hotel can boast. The *Astron* (B) is a convenient big modern hotel, used by tour operators, on the northern side of the harbour. The Limnos is a good simple restaurant on the harbour-front.

A short walk up from the harbour, the town's main square (Eleftherias) has a mosque and an expensive French restaurant;

but it's a busy cross-roads flanked by ugly public buildings including the food market and the museum. This last contains an excellent small collection of sculptures and mosaics from the 3rd century BC to the 2nd century AD. A mosaic in the main hall shows the god Asklepios with the medical attribute of a snake around his stick arriving at Kos, greeted by Hippocrates. The surrounding area is the commercial heart of the town, with lots of duty-free supermarkets. Signs identify an Old Town zone where the streets are indeed narrower and the houses whitewashed. The main attraction is not the buildings but their contents: leather, jewellery and expensive pottery as well as the usual souvenir clothes. Just beyond this popular strolling zone, and also signposted, a 16th-century Turkish bath has been converted into an unusual and inexpensive restaurant.

The pleasure of a visit to the **knights' fortress** mainly consists of wandering around the low but nonetheless imposing battlements surveying the town and harbour, the Turkish coast and shipping ploughing through the often choppy waters between, a channel the fortress was designed to guard in defence of Rhodes. The grassy compound inside has a large number of broken antique sculptures and pillars and an inner set of walls. The fortress was originally built in the 14th century and later reinforced in the face of Turkish threat. The impressive gateway dates from the beginning of the 16th century.

The fortress is entered by a bridge spanning a splendid avenue of palm trees from the cobbled Platanos square, named after the enormous tree under which Hippocrates, a 5th-century BC native of Kos, is said to have taught and Saint Paul to have preached. The vast and venerable (but not that venerable) tree is propped up by an extensive framework of crutches and flanked by a handsome 18th-century mosque, a Turkish fountain and various other ancient fragments, as well as another expensive restaurant and a genteel tea-room. The main avenue of palms, which has replaced the fort's moat, leads around to a thin pebble beach, the hydrofoil quay and a few hotels among, and in, pre-war Italian buildings between the sea and the port zone of excavations. The beach is not good, but this is a peaceful and densely vegetated part of town, an attractive alternative to staying in a hotel on the port; the *Iviscos* (c) is large and old-fashioned, one of the few comfortable hotels in town predating the recent tourist boom.

The town's main beach, a mixture of sand and pebbles, extends north from the harbour all the way to Cape Skandari (or simply Faros), and is interrupted here only by an encampment of soldiers, who scan the three-mile strait between Kos and the Turkish Bodrum peninsula, ancient Halicarnassus.

At the town end the beach is narrow and usually very crowded, and is backed by some factories and a dreary all-tourist area of new hotels, rooming blocks and restaurants. The northern half of the beach is more spacious and attractive, with picturesque converted windmills as well as big hotels, several of which are a very long walk from the town centre. By the cape is a small area of north-facing beach favoured by windsurfers, who should watch out for shipping – Greek ferry captains are unlikely to be troubled by the etiquette of sail before steam. There are numerous watersports operators and tavernas dotted along the main beach.

Of the two main excavated areas of the ancient city, which are both unfenced, the port zone (near the harbour and Platanos square) is attractive to wander around but less interesting than the western zone, bounded by one of the town's perimeter boulevards. Buildings here include a restored bath-house (closed, but you can see in), streets with cart ruts, colonnades of an ancient gymnasium and a partly restored house with a mosaic (3rd century AD) showing a generously proportioned Europa being abducted by a bull. This and other precious mosaics are displayed under shelters; others are left unprotected except by a layer of sandy dirt, which those who know where to look sweep away. On the other side of the boulevard, a beautiful avenue of cypresses leads to a small theatre (odeion). To the east of this, an ugly low modern block is the reconstruction of a huge 3rd-century Roman villa, the Casa Romana, with three courtyards, swimming-pools and a few mosaics. The excavations outside the house are thermal baths.

South of town, a road follows the coast around the eastern tip of the island for about ten miles, running out at the shoulder of the mountains near a point where hot spring water runs into the sea in a steaming little lagoon. For much of the way the road is flanked by a succession of big self-contained hotels next to the sea, mostly with swimming-pools and their own buses and sports facilities; the best of these hotels is the Oceanis (A), new and smartly decorated. There are beaches, or rather a beach, all the way along the coast and, as in the north, an army station on the cape.

The island's most famous monument is the **Asklepion**, the most celebrated of several hundred similar medical sanctuaries in Ancient Greece, dedicated to the god of healing, Asklepios, who learned about herbal and other miraculous cures from a centaur. The site, set among pines and cypresses on a hillside 4km from town, consists of a monumental staircase and three terraces commanding a wonderful view of the town and Turkish coast. All the buildings now identifiable – various temples, wards for patients, lodgings for doctor/priests and Roman baths – date from after the time of Hippocrates (5th century BC), but the father of the medical profession is traditionally held to have founded the Asklepion, a combination of spa, pilgrimage resort and medical research centre. The presence of mineral-rich springs probably decided the choice of location.

The main road charts a dull course across the fertile plain from Kos town to the airport at Antimachia, nearly 20 miles to the west. The interminable sands of the north coast are easily accessible by road or farm track in a number of places, and it is just about possible to find a minor cart track alternative to the main road for most of the way along. This is well worth doing, especially if you are on a bicycle: the main road has a lot of bus and lorry traffic and driving manners are, as ever in Greece, appalling.

The two all-modern resorts on this northern stretch of coast are **Tingaki** and **Marmari**, separated by an area of salt-pans. Tingaki is within cycling range of Kos town and has a more villagey atmosphere, with several small hotels as well as the vast *Tingaki Beach* (A), and some cheerful tavernas on the beach with terraces facing inland – sheltered from the prevailing north wind, which must render these resorts all but uninhabitable at times. Apart from this, the beach is fine: sandy for as far as you can be bothered to trudge, and with some shade. Tingaki's regular visitors include a pair of nesting storks. Marmari is no more than a loose gathering of big new hotels, of which the *Marmari Beach* bungalow colony is a good example of its kind, with lots of flowers, well-tended lawns and attractive swimming-pools.

Mastichari is a simple little village with a fishing harbour and a twice-daily ferry link with Kalymnos, timed to tie in with Kos/Athens flights. Mastichari has no great charm, but would certainly be a peaceful place for a holiday. There are rooms to rent and a small hotel, and sandy beaches on both sides of the harbour, with some dunes to the east. Here, too, there is no shelter from the wind.

There are much more rewarding diversions to the north of the main road, up into the foothills of the island's mountain massif, Dikeos (846m). From the main road at Zipari a road climbs rapidly through a changing landscape, with groves of fruit trees and olives beneath a higher band of almost Alpine woods, mountain streams and refreshing temperatures. **Zia** is the most picturesque and leafy of the hill villages and a good base for hikes up to the craggy peaks. There is at least one taverna and a few tourist shops, with local honey much in evidence. The road continues eastwards along the mountainside, giving magnificent views and passing semi-deserted villages (Agios Giorgios and Agios Dimitrios) whose residents are still surprised to see tourists, which is certainly not the case in Zia. Heading west from Asfendiou (a three-way junction below Zia), a rough road through Lagoudi and Amaniou, both of which have tavernas, joins up with one of the roads to Kardamena at **Pili**. From Amaniou a road leads left (north) to the beautiful site of **ancient Pili**, a ruined medieval village beneath a remarkably perched rocktop fortress. A leafy river gully makes a delightful picnic-spot. Lagoudi and Zia are the usual targets for organised coach-trips.

The village of Antimachia and nearby airport occupy a low sandy saddle of land, a vast scrub-covered, petrified dune. This is the style of much of the western end of the island, which has few inhabitants other than the military, who are omnipresent in these parts. The triangular fortress of **Antimachia**, reached by track from the main road on the Kos side of the main Antimachia roundabout, suggests that this is nothing new. It is well worth visiting, an impressive ruin in a wild situation overlooking Kardamena and the south coast. Like the fortress in Kos town, Antimachia was built by the Knights of St John. The outer walls and gatehouse (dated 1495 on a coat of arms) are well preserved, as are a couple of small chapels inside. One of these is dated 1520, only a few years before the island fell to the Turks.

The fort would make a good half-day's walking excursion from **Kardamena**, but such exploration scarcely fits in with the style of the resort, whose visitors rarely feel the urge to hike further than the bar. The village consists of a long and uniform grid of modern streets, nowhere far from the sea. Some of the accommodation buildings and a central row of bars and tavernas open directly on to the sand – the most attractive feature of the resort. There is no natural inlet, but moles enclose a small harbour. The caiques do less fishing than ferrying of tourists. Most of the accommodation in the resort is in basic modern rooms and self-catering studios, but there are half a dozen hotels, none worth singling out.

Beaches stretch for several miles to west and east, giving a total sweep of about six miles, not so much a bay as a long open expanse of coast. Much of the eastern half is dominated by an army camp, beyond which stands a huge new hotel complex and all-in-one resort, the 1000-bed *Norida Beach* (A), out on its own beneath the mountains. There is also a scattering of beach hotels and tavernas to the east of Kardamena, where an increasingly rough track runs along the shore before expiring near Cape Helona, about three miles from the resort. With so

Getting around

There are buses between Kos town and Asfendiou, Pili, Kardamena, Kefalos, Antimachia, Mastichari, Tingaki and Dimitra Beach (serving the coastal hotels south of Kos town). Many of the big beach hotels have their own mini-bus services into Kos or Kardamena, usually with some evening service.

Car, motor-bike and bicycle hire is possible in Kos, Kardamena, Tingaki and many other places: most of the big beach hotels can also arrange hired transport. Cycling is popular, cheap and very practical for those in hotels at the eastern end of the island. The main road leading west from Kos town is not recommended to cyclists. Whatever transport you pilot, beware the dangerous intersections in and around Kos town.

Hydrofoil and/or boat-excursions are offered from Kos town to the islands of Pserimos, Patmos, Leros, Kalymnos, Rhodes and Nisyros (individually or in permutations of several islands); boat-trips to Nisyros are also available direct from Kardamena and Kamari. Tour operators organise sightseeing and beach bus-trips on the island and 'meet the locals' evenings at a taverna in one of the hill villages, as well as beach and barbecue boat-trips. Day-trips to Turkey (Bodrum) have been stopped.

Pserimos is a small island between Kos and Kalymnos with a sandy beach and a few tavernas. The number of excursions from Kos and Kalymnos suggest that the island may not always be a haven of tranquillity.

much space it is not difficult to escape crowds, although at Kardamena itself the sands are packed.

From Antimachia it is a dull ten miles to Kamari on **Kefalos Bay**. Army manoeuvres relieve the monotony and tracks lead left (south) to a series of beautiful sandy beaches, the best on the island: Paradise, Hawaii and Magic Beach. As usual on Kos, they are really only sections of the same beach, but the dunes climb steeply (the track down to Hawaii is particularly sporting), giving some shelter and the impression of individual bays. Paradise Beach has a taverna in the dunes; Magic Beach has a cantina on the beach. All have umbrellas and windsurfing in season.

Sweeping Kefalos Bay is split into two by a rocky promontory which features mosaic floors and a few re-erected columns of two 5th-century Byzantine churches, probably on the site of an earlier temple. This eloquent ruin is also a practical division, separating the watered lawns and bungalows of a handsome Club Med camp, to the east of the point, from a more typically Greek scruffy beachside straggle of small hotels, rooming houses, tavernas and a quay. This is **Kamari**, more a bus-stop with buildings than a resort. One bus has come to a full stop on the beach, where it wears a shroud of whitewash. Much of the Kamari half of the bay is pebbles, but Club Med has sand. At this point the island is only about a mile wide, and the low neck of land does little to shelter the south-facing bay from the wind, which usually blows (and sometimes howls) offshore, making windsurfing a dangerous game for the inexpert. A rocky offshore islet opposite the ruins offers some reassurance. On a sandy escarpment above the western end of the bay stands the only village in western Kos, **Kefalos**, near the site of the original island capital, which is known to history confusingly as Astypalaia and was abandoned in the 4th century BC. Kefalos is a quiet and dusty place with some working windmills but little else to entertain or interest the visitor. Rooms are advertised.

The tail of the island is wild, empty and extensively burnt out by forest fires. Exploration is quite straightforward as far as the ruined monastery of Agios Ioannis, which gives a splendid view of the south-western tip of the island. From here on, it is possible although not exactly easy to make a bumpy clockwise circuit of the western end of the island, passing another monastery (Agios Theologos) and a number of empty coves (sand and rocks) before returning to Kefalos.

West of Mastichari, the north coast of the island is accessible in a few places, but the effort is hardly worthwhile: the most likely reward for perseverance is a beach as full of wind-blown rubbish as it is empty of people.

LEROS

An island of asylums, political exile (under the Colonels), war graves and peeling monuments to Mussolini's cardboard classicism, Leros does not have a lot going for it: except perhaps that not a lot of people do go for it, which means that Leros can truthfully be presented as peaceful. Although fairly fertile and populous (the asylums provide plenty of employment) it sees few tourists except, it is plausibly said, Greeks who make a holiday of visits to afflicted members of the family. They do not generate a very cheerful atmosphere, and Leros stands as a warning to all those who hold up undevelopment as the supreme criterion of desirability in a holiday destination.

It is a small island (about seven miles from top to toe, although the road is much longer) with a long coastline of deeply intruding bays separated by steep narrow ridges. The deepest intrusion is the almost enclosed west-coast bay of **Lakki**, the island's desolate modern port and for most visitors a first sight of Leros that will be quite enough to persuade them to sit tight on the ferry, or would be, if more ferries arrived in daylight. As things stand, Lakki tends to come as a nasty shock the next morning, like a hangover, which is what it is. It is perhaps the purest example of the Mussolinian style of town and as such not without interest, for a few minutes. A grand geometric plan of broad, shaded avenues is unfilled by the buildings which are themselves oversized and largely unoccupied and stand urgently demanding either to be kept up or pulled down. The result is an atmosphere of emptiness, which has a lot to do with the fact that Lakki appears to be used by the islanders neither as a place in which to live nor as an everyday harbour. A desultory scattering of tourists does little to fill the vacuum.

A wide road constitutes the water-front, which has no beach, no yachts, no fishing-boats and usually no strollers. A solitary palm tree outside the portholes of the far from palatial, although big, Leros Palace Hotel marks the town centre. The hotel itself is more a sightseeing curiosity than a place to inhabit, and there are more cheerful hotels set back slightly: the *Miramare* (a well-kept D) and the *Artemis* (C). Since most ferries arrive at Leros late at night, it is not always easy to avoid staying at Lakki. As well as being convenient for ferry travellers, it has most of the island's hotels and is the best, indeed probably the only, place at which to rent transport (cars, motor-bikes and bicycles), although this is by no means essential. The size of the island is about right for cycling, but the terrain is hilly. Lakki has not much cafe or taverna life, but the unpromising restaurant Pizza is surprisingly good. This and several other cafes show signs that Lakki has had a bit of a facelift recently; considering the town's run-down outward aspect, it is surprising to come across neat check tablecloths and polished pine furniture and panelling. The island's young bikers gather in an exotic bar towards the ferry quay, and the cafe nearest the ferries stays open late into the night for the benefit of travellers and a bleary-eyed collection of local insomniacs. Ferry tickets can be bought there, and the arrival of the agent with his briefcase full of tickets is the first sign of an impending arrival. Among the large public buildings are two hospitals. In case of need, avoid committal to the more obvious one, which sports a big red cross but does not dispense the sort of treatment tourists are likely to require, depressing though Lakki is. The new hospital is discreetly located at the end of the same road (westwards).

The island's main community is the conglomerate of Platanos/Agia Marina/Pandeli on the other side of the island, all of two miles away. Although not individually beautiful, the arrangement of the three is picturesque, with the central village of **Platanos**, the island's capital and main shopping and meeting place, straddling a ridge and spilling down to the sea on either side. Above Platanos, the hilltop dividing the two bays is crowned by a splendid **fortress**, which is still fortified, flag-flying and manned. This is the main sight on the island, impressive in itself and commanding a wonderful aerial view of the island. The castle can be reached by a long staircase from near Platanos (signposted) or by the road (accessible from Platanos or Pandeli) which skirts the southern side of the hill and runs along a windy ridge lined with old windmills. In its present form the castle dates mostly from the time of the Knights of St John (14th century), but the natural stronghold was certainly fortified in the Byzantine period and probably for many centuries before that. It is said to contain a chapel with frescoes and a miraculous icon, and to be often open to visitors, but we have not found it so. The icon arrived at Leros by boat during the period of Turkish occupation, and was carried by the islanders to the cathedral. Every night the icon made its way mysteriously into the castle's powder store, where it was found in the morning with a lighted candle. After a few nights of this potentially explosive miracle, the Turks chose to take no more risks, moved their powder elsewhere and gave the chapel to the Greeks. In the vicinity of the fortress, wield a camera with discretion, if at all.

Pandeli is the quieter of the two flanking bays, off the island's road. There is a taverna or two beside a smally scruffy sand and pebble beach, where fishing-boats are pulled up and nets mended on the shore. Pandeli has considerable tranquil charm, and its hotel, the *Pandeli* (C), beside the road down from Platanos, would be one of the best bases for a stay on the island. There are also rooms to rent.

On the northern side of the ridge, **Agia Marina** is the traditional island port and is still used by most of the excursion-boats (day-trips to Patmos, Kalymnos and Lipsi, and round-the-island boat-trips) and hydrofoils. Agia Marina has a more intimate atmosphere than Lakki, with tavernas by the port and some attractive balconied old houses, but it too is neglected and of limited appeal as a holiday base. The road continues northwards along the shore of Agia Marina bay, passing the British war cemetery from 1943, when the British forces were unable to hold on to the islands they had taken (Leros, Kos and Kalymnos) after the Italian surrender. The road runs alongside a

Getting around

The island has a bus or buses, but their comings and goings are largely uncharted. At the very least, there are services between Lakki, Xerokampos and Platanos/Agia Marina.

Car, motor-bike and bicycle hire is available at Lakki and, probably, Alinda.

long thin strip of beach, with a scattering of tavernas, pubs and mini-markets. There is a collection of holiday accommodation, including a couple of hotels, beyond the point where the main road heads inland and northwards to the airport. This peaceful holiday zone – it hardly qualifies as a village – is **Alinda**, by Leros's standards a blooming little resort, blessed with a beautiful view across the bay towards the hill village and fortress. Sheltered pebble beaches to the north of the bay can be reached on foot from Alinda.

The broad northern head of the island is mainly occupied by the army and the airstrip – again, airport would give a falsely grand impression of the facilities. There are no significant remains of an ancient sanctuary associated with the goddess Artemis who, in a curious act of pity for the grieving sisters of the slain Meleager, transformed them into guinea-fowls and gave them a home on Leros. There is a taverna at the gates of the army base but nothing on the shores of the main northern inlet, Partheni bay, which has no beach. All in all, exploring northern Leros has little to commend it.

Although most maps do not make it clear, there is an alternative route between Lakki and Alinda, passing the western bay of **Gournas**, which does have a beach, albeit more earthy than sandy. Most of the buildings around the wide bay are unconnected with tourism, but some hotel-building is under way and there is a taverna at the southern end of the bay. The road over the hill from Lakki to Gournas is now surfaced.

South from Lakki, the road follows a dreary stretch of Lakki bay and passes an institution and dismantled naval base at Lepida before crossing a hill and descending to the southern bay and village of **Xerokampos**, a well-kept and prosperous-looking little community in fertile surroundings, with palm trees and pomegranates in the gardens. Xerokampos is said to have the island's campsite and certainly has a caique ferry link with the west coast of Kalymnos (Myrties). Apart from the fun of travelling by caique rather than on one of the big ferries, this has the added attraction of enabling one to sail at a civilised hour, as the scheduled ferries often do not. There is not much of a village to Xerokampos, but the main street has a restaurant, a shop and rooms to rent. Unusually, it is set back a bit from the bay, where there is a small beach and a taverna in among the fishing-boats. The mountains of northern Kalymnos close the view southwards out of the long narrow inlet, which appears to be completely landlocked.

NISYROS (NISSIROS)

Volcanic Nisyros has been called the Polo Mint island. Like the sweets it has a fresh green and white wrapping with lush citrus and almond groves, huddles of white cube houses, and, of course, a hole in the middle – the crater of the bubbling Polyvotis volcano.

Myth has it that the Titans hurled a chunk of Kos at the giant Polyvotis and you can hear him groaning, still crushed beneath the weight of his burden.

Nisyros is prosperous and none of its people have had to emigrate to seek their fortunes. Their wealth is under their feet – pumice stone, quarried on the little neighbouring island of Giali and exported worldwide. From the ferry you can see workmen chipping away at it.

Although Nisyros has daily trips from Kos, the island doesn't rely on tourism for survival, and its tavernas and restaurants are geared to the locals. The islanders welcome visitors, however, and Nisyros stays lively, even in winter.

Mandraki, the main port and capital, is postcard pretty. From the long seaside promenade rises a maze of cool whitewashed alleys, too narrow for traffic, filled with pots of flowers and herbs. The houses are painted white or in bright contrasting colours; in some places their wooden balconies almost meet above you. There is a good variety of harbourside tavernas, with cheaper eating places in town. Small lively pensions near the harbour include the *Three Brothers Taverna* and the *Hotel Romantzo*, with a large vine-clad terrace.

Two Crusader castles stand guard. High above Mandraki the castle walls contain the lovely monastery of **Panagia Spiliana**, Our Lady of the Cave, hewn into the split rock above the sea. The church has a collection of Byzantine icons, framed in gold and silver. The other fortress, the **Kastro**, about half a mile inland, stands on the site of the ancient acropolis and has massive black walls of volcanic rock with glassy crystals.

Getting around

Nisyros has one taxi, mainly used for the local school run. There is also one bus which takes day-trippers up to the volcano. You can hire motorbikes, but you're probably safer on foot.

As well as daily excursions from Kardamena on Kos, the *Nisyros Express* links the island to Kos four times a week in the summer. The inter-island ferries also call in, so you can hop to Rhodes and other Dodecanese islands and to the Cyclades.

A mile or so to the east is a little spa, **Loutra**. Here you'll get a whiff of sulphur from the volcanic springs, whose healing mineral waters, piped to the nearby hotel, are supposed to work wonders on rheumatism and arthritis.

The island's beaches are mainly of black volcanic sand, shingle or pebbles. They are often crowd-free even in high summer. Just outside Mandraki there's a sandy bay at Miramare; but the best beach is at the fishing hamlet of **Pali** (or Skala), a couple of miles to the east of Mandraki, where rooms are available. On the way to Pali, on a steep hill, there's a new hotel, the *White Beach* (c), above a small beach.

The island is green and lush, even in summer, and is perfect walking country. Vineyards, olive groves, fig and almond trees flourish in the rich volcanic earth, and in spring Nisyros is ablaze with wild flowers. The volcano is the main tourist attraction. In the caldera, the deep cauldron-like crater at the summit, there's a moonscape of ashen grey and sulphur yellow – you need a peg on your nose for the bad-egg smell – and little blowholes puffing out jets of steam surrounded by crystals of pure sulphur. Up the zigzag road from Mandraki, two villages – **Emborio** and **Nikea** – cling perilously to the rim of the crater. The views are spectacular. Few people live in Emborio now, but Nikea is dazzling with blue and white painted houses and red geraniums. Pools of boiling water burst out from the volcano near the village – giant's tears. You can walk to it from Emborio, plunging down a steep path. The stench and the heat hit you as you approach (the temperature at the caldera is over 120°F).

After a visit, it's worth washing away the sulphur with the sweet local non-alcoholic drink, *soumada*, made from the island's almonds.

PATMOS

The northernmost of the Dodecanese Islands is where Saint
John, known locally as Theologos, was exiled in AD95 by the
Emperor Domitian. When 'in the spirit on the Lord's Day' he
heard a voice like a trumpet saying it was alpha and omega and
telling him to write what he saw in a book and not to seal it,
'for the time is at hand', John dictated his visions to his disciple
Procorus. The book is the Revelation (or Apocalypse, the Greek
word for revelation), the richest and most influential catalogue
of prophetic imagery ever recorded.

Renaissance paintings show a barren little rock scarcely large
enough to accommodate the holy man, a token indication of the
hardships of exile. Patmos is indeed a small island, although not
that small, and its barrenness is remarked upon in the accounts
of nearly all the island's many visitors down the centuries.
Although far from fertile, it no longer seems unusually bare,
especially if compared with the Cyclades, which it resembles
much more closely than it does the other islands of the eastern
Aegean. It has no Turkish buildings, and the style and position
of its old white hill village, clustered around the walls of a
perfectly preserved fortified monastery, make Patmos more
typically Cycladic than most of the Cyclades. The island has
terraces, trees, fields of passably healthy-looking cows in the
northern half of the island, and an unusual number of very
greedy ducks on the beaches. Exile on Patmos today would not
be too much of a hardship.

The island had been uninhabited for hundreds of years when,
in 1088, the Byzantine emperor of the day agreed to the
foundation of a monastery dedicated to St John under
Christodoulos, a hermit, scholar, soldier, long-distance pilgrim
and experienced founder of monasteries, who became the
island's 'absolute ruler in all eternity'. Christodoulos and his
successors did not rely on the imperial grant for their security
of tenure, but built a mighty fortress of a monastery in a
dominant position high above the sea.

For a variety of reasons – the poverty of the island, the
strength of the fortress and even, occasionally, respect for the
sanctity of the place – the monastery of St John on Patmos has
come through nine war-torn and piratical centuries physically
intact and with the continuity of its monastic community
unbroken. In the 18th century a seminary was founded. 'This
school is to the enslaved Greeks who bear the Turkish yoke a
substitute for ancient Athens,' wrote one of the early pupils.
The scholarship's foundation was the monastery's famous

library, now depleted but still immensely rich, especially in ancient manuscripts. The Patmos monastery is one of the great religious centres of Christendom.

It is also one of the country's great sightseeing attractions, without the restrictions on visiting that apply on Mount Athos. Grey monastery and white village crown the island magnificently and make a perfect half-day's visit, a lovely walk up from the port to the monastery via the cave of the Revelation. Along with Rhodes, Delos, Santorini and Crete, Patmos is a stop on the classic Greek cruise itinerary and the goal of day-trip excursion-boats and hydrofoils from islands as far away as Rhodes.

The great liners queue up every morning to enter the narrow bay of Skala and disgorge their cargo of tourists – a different generation, a different income bracket and often a different nationality from most Greek island travellers, who watch the cruiseloads pass through with unmitigated distaste, grumbling about the inflationary impact of these well-heeled culture vultures, scorning both the sheep-like nature of those who leap on to the bus for the monastery tour and the philistinism of those who prefer to spend their two hours ashore in the port. The locals take a different view and look after their short-stay visitors well. A fleet of little taxi-launches is always ready to scramble for the big ships that cannot dock, and a convoy of buses assembles on the quay ready to whisk the non-walkers up the hill without delay. It is all very, and uncharacteristically, well organised.

A tourist conveyor belt, then? Money changers in the temple? This is a common verdict, no doubt reflecting the travellers' anti-cruise prejudice. Certainly, in high season the sheer weight of numbers passing through Skala port and monastery is disconcerting. But the volume of tourism has done surprisingly little to compromise the peaceful beauty of the island. Few visitors stay overnight and few venture further from the port than Chora and the monastery. The island has no big hotels and sees very little beach holiday package tourism, although it has at least two suitable bays. Skala and the old village of Chora have souvenir sellers and tourist restaurants, of course, but both places remain essentially quiet and prices are not outrageously high. The monastery continues to flourish as a religious community, with an elaborate Easter ceremonial including, on Maundy Thursday, a famous re-enactment of the Washing of the Feet on one of the squares of Chora. Whenever you visit, long-haired monks in flowing black robes will be out and about swishing through the alleys and holding court in the cafes of Chora and Skala. Patmos is a wonderful island for photographers.

Although the monastery dominates the island, a visit need not be thought of as a deadly serious religious retreat. Skala is a cheerful little village resort with some totally contemporary nightlife. Grikou and Kampos are peaceful coastal places with simple accommodation in a rural setting near uncrowded beaches, unaffected by mass tourism of a style the island does not want and is lucky enough not to need. Patmos is a profoundly relaxing island, well worth more than the few hours it takes to tick off the monastery.

The island consists of three unspectacular hills of volcanic origin and only modest elevation, made scenically interesting by the intricate coastline and the splendid setting of the monastery, visible from most places on the island. The two main hills are linked by an isthmus no more than a few hundred yards wide, the site of the present port of **Skala**, tucked into a corner of a narrow east-coast inlet at the foot of the hill crowned by the monastery. Like many island ports, Skala dates back no further than the 19th century, earlier settlement having been ruled out by the vulnerability of the site to raids. The water-front has its share of typically unlovely Italian pre-war buildings, but the general impression is attractive, with low arcades on stumpy pillars making a lively, shady cloister of the central square, which opens on to the wide quay.

The village extends northwards along the shore, with a trio of comfortable and fairly expensive B-class hotels (the *Skala* is the best of them) in prime position, followed by a reasonable strip of roadside sand, not bad for a port beach and with a lovely view of the harbour and hill village behind, but littered. The *Rodos* (D) is a good cheap hotel in a quieter position on one of the alleys leading back from the quay.

Light sleepers may find that the day begins early at Skala, with the loud rattle of anchor chains and complicated multi-lingual instructions booming over the water from about 6.30 in the morning. Fortunately, Skala faces the morning sun, so it is no great hardship to sit on the quay waiting for a cafe to open and watching the grossly oversized liners carefully manoeuvring in the narrow bay.

In the evening Skala resembles many another island port, with a mixture of local and tourist bars and restaurants. The Garden cafe, under an arch near the ferry quay, is a splendid place for *meze*, fish or octopus from the grill, and a boisterous crowd of locals who are often in the spirit, to borrow Saint John's phrase. The Meltemi behind the beach is the most popular place for loud rock music.

Skala apart, the shore of the bay is an unattractive mixture of lava stones, litter and boatyard debris, but it is possible to wander around and sit in someone's private orange grove enjoying the evening sun and the view of Skala and Chora. Another tempting evening stroll is through the village to the bay on the western side of the isthmus. This too is disappointing, with a lot of building work on and around the stony beach. On the main village beach, early evening is feeding time for the ducks, who are joined by an assortment of confused, or perhaps canny, Patmiot cats and gulls when the lady duckherd appears with her tray of leftovers from the taverna. Unless you want a noisy and adhesive gaggle of friends for as long as you stay on the island, it is worth leaving the feeding to her. There is a campsite on Meloi bay (with beach and taverna), a short walk over the hill from the northern end of Skala bay.

The walk up to Chora takes less than half an hour from Skala and is recommended in preference to the bus: the path is shady, gives lovely views and involves not much walking along the road. The journey risks being seriously protracted if you succumb to all the offers of drinks, probably accompanied by some sales patter once you cross the threshold, from the pathside housewives. In the depressed period between the age of sail and the age of tourism, Patmos depended to a large extent on its women, who were specialist knitters of stockings famed throughout the Levant for their durability. Travellers wrote of women's singing, which carried from the workshops of Skala to the monastery ramparts.

About half-way up the hill a path leads to the steeply pitched, flower-filled **Apocalypsis monastery**, which has grown up around the cave of the Revelation, a rock-walled chapel at the bottom of the monastery, with tin haloes marking niches in the rock where the saint laid his head and placed his hand to get up, and an altar-cloth on a rock ledge used as a writing-desk. The buildings above the monastery are the famous Patmian seminary.

Chora is no ordinary Greek island village of basic white cubes. The houses are tall, handsome and beautifully maintained, with pillars and pediments and signs of the cross above many doorways. Many date from the 17th century, when the island was at the height of its prosperity, and illustrate the wealth accumulated by Patmian shipowners who, like many resourceful inhabitants of infertile islands, turned misfortune to profit through trade. As well as recording that Patmos had 20 times as many women as men, the early-18th-century traveller de Tournefort declared that the houses of the island (which meant Chora) were the finest and most solid in the Aegean. The maze of vaulted white alleys is unnaturally peaceful, with few shops (except the souvenir sellers flanking the route to the monastery), no cars and more donkeys than motor-bikes. Skala has now taken over as the main focus of everyday island life, and Chora is a bit of a showpiece and, one suspects, an exclusive place in which to have a second home. Sooner or later, wanderings will bring you to the square (Agia Levias), filled with the tables of two rival tavernas. Apart from the monastery, there are said to be over 50 churches in Chora. Many of them are old but few are open. Agios Vassilios, on the edge of the village to the east of the square, has good wall-paintings.

Finding the **monastery of St John** presents no problems, for it literally crowns the island with its many-faceted grim grey-brown crenellated walls, swelling towers and powerful buttresses: a fairy-tale castle entered through a 17th-century gateway complete with keyhole openings for dousings of boiling oil or molten lead to greet unwelcome visitors in a manner worthy of the Apocalypse. From the beautiful arcaded main courtyard one visits the church, which contains the marble tomb and reliquary of Christodoulos (to the right of the vaulted porch), an exceedingly ornate 19th-century iconostasis and a mass of dark frescoes (the best are in the right-hand Chapel of the Virgin, and date from the late 12th century); the refectory, with long built-in stone tables and fragmentary frescoes (mostly 13th century); the kitchen and some storage chambers; and an exhibition room, which costs extra but is well worth a visit (icons, vestments, manuscripts and silverware). The library is closed to the public, as is the highest roof-terrace, a celebrated aerial viewpoint (someone fell off). A detailed guidebook to the monastery is on sale and is recommended. The monastery is strict about dress requirements (no shorts or bare shoulders) but may be able to provide drapery if you forget.

Roads down from Chora and along the coast from Skala lead to **Grikos**, the island's main beach resort, at the top end of a splendid bay whose beauty makes up for the beaches, which are nothing special (a mixture of earth and stones), and for the village, which is no more than a few hotels, villas and tavernas, all closed out of season. Grikos beach has shade, windsurfing and pedalos, and is a popular place for rough camping. It is about an hour's walk around the bay and across an isthmus, where the island is even thinner than at Skala, to the western bay of Stavros, which has salt-marshes and some sand.

The main village in the more cultivated northern half of the island is **Kampos**, an ordinary, untouristy hill village with a few shops and a taverna near the bus-stop, about half a mile from Kampos bay. There are tavernas, rooms to rent and watersports beside the very sheltered beach, which is mainly stony. These

---

Getting around

There are lots of buses from Skala to Chora, either via Revelation (as the timetable charmingly puts it) or, less often, via Grikos. There are also a few buses a day to Kampos. Caique services operate from Skala to Kampos bay. Motor-bikes can be hired in Skala.

Patmos is small and not particularly steep, making exploring on foot quite practical, especially for those based in Skala. It is an island for incoming rather than outgoing excursions; very few are organised apart from boat-trips from Skala to various beaches along the east coast, which really come into the category of local transport rather than excursions.

---

seem to operate a longer season than at Grikos, or at **Lampi**, an exposed north-coast bay with views of the mountains of western Samos and an entertaining 'Flower Taverna' among the cultivations at the back of the stony beach. Rooms are available in season. Also near Kampos, a very pretty track leads down through vines and vegetable fields to the west-coast bay of **Lefkes**, overlooked by a grand old villa and a few farmhouses but without any taverna. The beach has some sand and trees, but most of it is earthy caked weed, springy and rather comfortable. From here the island in view, on a clear day, is Ikaria. South of Kampos, and easily accessible by track from the main road, is **Agriolivadi**. It is indeed an agri-beach, with a flock of goats on the hill behind, and ducks patrolling the stony beach for people to pester. As usual on Patmos, the scenery of the bay is lovelier than the beach itself, but there is a quiet taverna among the tamarisks.

SYMI

Symi lies between two Turkish peninsulas, one only six miles away, and fifteen miles north of Rhodes, which makes it eminently accessible for invasions. Nowadays, despite a military presence, the only hordes descending on the little island are day-trippers, who are responsible for a marked change in the atmosphere of the port and town between the hours of 11a.m. and 3p.m. Outside these hours, life is peaceful; fishermen mend their nets on the quayside in front of the Custom House, caiques land sponges, women pick over the vegetables outside the greengrocer's, and in little Harani bay boat-builders carry on their craft like their forefathers, who built the *Argo* for Jason and sent three triremes to the siege of Troy.

The boat-builders of Symi were renowned, and contributed to the island's wealth over the centuries (the other main industry was sponge-fishing). Under the Turks Symi became a privileged state in return for sending a yearly *machtou* or tribute in money and sponges to the sultan. At the turn of the century the population numbered 30,000, more even than in Rhodes town. But the Italian annexation of the Dodecanese during the Second World War took its toll; sponge-fishing stopped, sea trading suffered and thousands fled to make new lives elsewhere in Greece or abroad, following the pattern of many Greek islands. The fine mansions of the rich sponge-merchants and traders were bombed or deserted and fell into ruin. Despite a gradual return of Symiots, the population now numbers fewer than 3000; and it is tourism which is giving a much-needed boost to the economy.

Boat-building was responsible not only for the fine neo-classical mansions which form such an attractive aspect to camera-happy tourists leaning perilously over the rails of their excursion-boats, but also for the look of the interior of the island. Once well wooded, Symi is now one of the more rocky and barren of the Dodecanese Islands; there are a few farms and scattered shepherds' houses among the olive and almond groves, and the island is smothered with wild herbs – oregano, sage, thyme and camomile. Beaches are mainly pebble or shingle, in bays fringed by tamarisk trees.

Although long discovered by discerning British travellers as a holiday island, Symi has retained its character and a great deal of charm. Though stylish and cosmopolitan, it has managed to remain simple and unspoiled, having been saved from mass development by its greatest problem – a shortage of water. High-rise building is banned, and there is only one new hotel.

Symi town divides into two parts: the harbour, **Gialos**, and the ancient capital, **Chorio**, straddling a ridge immediately above. As the morning excursion-boats come into Gialos, an armada of little caiques leaves – people staying on Symi flee to the peace of beaches around the island, most accessible only by boat or by long and rough walks. With the arrival of the day-trippers, hooters sound and pandemonium reigns; tavernas tout for business and stallholders ply local herbs, sponges, lace and souvenirs. Groups of sun-seekers are herded off to the town beach, Nos (a small sand and shingle bay), by their multi-lingual couriers. After the afternoon departure, everyone closes up and has a siesta; once the taverna owners know you're staying, the ouzo is likely to be stronger.

Gialos is a favourite port of call with yachtsmen, and at night the harbourside tavernas and bars hum. Nightlife is jolly rather than raucous: one bar features jazz, a taverna has *bouzouki* nights, and there are two small discos. At Les Katerinettes taverna, the Treaty of the Dodecanese was signed in 1945 when Symi was restored to Greece following the Italian occupation.

Gialos and Chorio are linked by a tiered staircase of over 500 steps – the Kali Strata, bordered by fine houses (some still in ruins) in sugared almond shades, with terracotta pantile roofs and stucco pediments. Domed churches in rose pink, vanilla and peppermint, cypress trees, and stones and steps painted blue and white complete the vivid picture. Cars are banned from this part of town, and the only traffic up the steps are mule trains carrying building materials and other heavy goods. It's a gruelling slog in high summer when the sun beats off the surrounding rocky hills, and temperatures soar to over 100°F. Women sit on their doorsteps doing crochet, men play backgammon over coffee. Half-way up there are shops, tavernas and bars (including an English-run cocktail bar with a happy hour). There's also a well-preserved pharmacy with interesting bottles and jars, a small folk museum, and a four-storey restored Symiot house with murals. A further series of steps leads deeper into the old town, a labyrinth of narrow paths and alleys, where a torch is essential at night. At the top of the town are the remains of a castle of the knights containing a church, surrounded by windmills and small chapels.

Chorio looks out beyond the ridge towards **Pedi**, a sandy bay on the other side of the village, the main beach of the island. There are charming fishermen's cottages and some tourist development – a few beach bars and a new hotel, the *Pedi Beach* (B), right at the water's edge and good for families. On the road down from Chorio there are three tavernas.

There are several comfortable and reasonably priced pensions in Gialos; rather more luxurious is the *Hotel Aliki* (A), an elegant old Symiot mansion at the far end of the harbour and a short walk from Nos beach, which has been restored to a very high standard; it also has a roof-garden. Local women greet the boats with offers of rooms and apartments to let.

Accommodation offered by British tour operators varies from fishermen's houses at the quayside to restored Symian houses at various points up the Kali Strata – some gloriously atmospheric, with Turkish-style beds raised off the floor, high rooms with wooden floors and painted ceilings, cool mosaic courtyards and wrought-iron balconies. For those not on a package, Symian Holidays, at the beginning of the Kali Strata, and Symian Tours have a wide range of accommodation for independent travellers, from converted mansions to a windmill.

Getting around

Boats are the main means of transport. There are round-the-island tours which stop at Panormitis and a fishing cove on the way; an afternoon boat to Panormitis for those who wish to stay overnight; caiques from Pedi to a neighbouring cove where beach barbecues are held; trips to the neighbouring islets of Sesklia (which belongs to the Panormitis monastery) and Nimos; and water-taxis from Marathounda to Gialos. Inter-island ferries are useful for visiting other Dodecanese Islands, and it's easy to get to Rhodes. Excursions are offered to Kos, or you can organise one yourself via Rhodes using a hydrofoil. If there's enough interest, trips are offered to the islands of Tilos and Chalki.

Cars are still a rarity on the island, although plenty of locals have motor-bikes (which can be hired). There are two roads: one links Gialos to Chorio and Pedi; the other, in places only a roughly hewn track, twists along the spine of the island to Panormitis. A few taxis go up to Chorio, for those who can't face the Kali Strata; and there's an hourly bus during the day from Gialos to Chorio and Pedi. There's an excursion Pullman coach to Panormitis, a hair-raising trip in parts, and truck-trips along some of the inland tracks (one has recently been made to Marathounda) make for bumpy but amusing sightseeing.

A resident Englishman, Hugo, takes keen hikers on early-morning guided walks across the island, meeting up with a boat for the return journey.

The town beach, Nos, gets very crowded when the day-boats arrive. It's worth walking a mile or so west along the coastal path to **Nimborio**, a pretty bay with a taverna and fishing-boats at anchor. There are flat rocks and shingly coves all along the way. The other main beaches are in the east of the island: at Nanou, pretty and pebbly, with a chapel and plenty of trees; Marathounda, pebbly and fringed by fishermen's houses, with an old Symiot farmhouse which is being converted into a small holiday complex; Agia Marina, reached by a goat track from Pedi; and Agios Georgios, with spectacular cliffs. The neighbouring island of Sesklia has a pretty beach at Skomisa Bay, popular for barbecues and for naturists.

In the south of the island, the sheltered bay of **Panormitis** is a popular halt for day-trippers from Rhodes. The huge white enclave of the **monastery of the Archangel Michael** (patron saint of mariners), built in the 19th century on earlier foundations, takes up the whole bay. It's a place of pilgrimage for Greeks from far and wide, and contains a rich collection of offerings from sailors and overseas Symians. In the church is a fine iconostasis; there's a little museum which features bottles in which cash was floated from passing ships; the mosaic courtyard has pots of basil and bougainvillea (and is tranquil after the day-trippers have gone), and there are fine views across the bay from the pine woods above the monastery. The community has a taverna, a small coffee-shop, a bakery, and 200 rooms with 500 beds for visitors, either in cells or holiday homes in the grounds. You can stay, with the priest's permission, overnight or for a few days, and pay what you think fit. Accommodation is very basic – toilets but no washing facilities apart from the monastery pump, cells with camp beds. If you are a woman travelling alone, you'll be expected to stay within the cloisters, locked in at 9.30p.m. sharp.

The beautiful scenery goes some way towards making up for the fact that the locals here may find the constant stream of foreign visitors rather tiring, and seem less than welcoming.

TILOS

Remote and sleepy Tilos is quietly waking up to tourism. It offers little other than rugged beauty, lush valleys, deserted beaches and peace. Until now, Tilos has featured on the itinerary only of dedicated island-hoppers and intrepid travellers who sought few creature comforts.

Thanks to the volcanic eruptions of its neighbour, Nisyros, Tilos has pumice stone cliffs; it is also hilly, green and fertile, with fragrant vegetation, especially pretty in spring when the fruit trees are in blossom. To island-hoppers it can provide a colourful contrast with barren Chalki and Symi. Tilos boasts the remains of seven castles, outposts of the Knights of St John, a scattering of tiny whitewashed churches – some with frescoes – dotted about the fields and an attractive 15th-century monastery.

The port of **Livadia** has a big quayside restaurant, the hub of all life as the locals wait for ferries to dock or tourist-boats to arrive from Kos or Rhodes. There's a long sweep of tree-fringed multi-coloured pebble beach with four waterside tavernas, a leafy village square with white steps flanked by swan-headed pillars, two shops and a kiosk; but there's no bakery, and bread and other produce is shipped in from Rhodes. Gardens burst with roses and bougainvillea; and the low, stone, cottage-style houses, some with only one room, may be roofed with dry weeds and *patella* (a kind of green waterproof clay). Tourist accommodation consists of rooms, self-catering studios and two

---

Getting around

There is little transport on Tilos: a taxi service from Livadia to Megalo Chorio, and a bus which is usually packed with day-trippers when the boats come in. Bicycles may be available for hire in Megalo Chorio; otherwise a lift in a truck is the only way of getting around (and is usually offered willingly). Boats go around the island, and inter-island ferries call in; excursion-boats go to Rhodes, Kos, Nisyros and Chalki, but you should be prepared for overnight stays.

---

hotels – the *Livadia* (E) on the square and the smart new *Irini* (C) with a swimming-pool. Municipal beach bungalows can be rented (the mayor keeps the keys).

There's one metalled road into the interior of the island, winding through orchards past the deserted village of Micro Chorio, where you can see local pottery preserved within the ruins. Nearby, in the grotto of Harcadio near Misaria, are the fossilised bones of a species of mastodon, mini-mammoths. The road leads up to **Megalo Chorio** (7km), the island capital, dominated by a ruined knights' castle. There's an interesting Church of the Archangel Michael, built on the site of a classical temple, with a cool courtyard and pebble floor; it now houses silver icons from the ancient castle church. In the village are apartments and rooms to let and a small museum.

Tilos has lovely deserted beaches of pebbles or red sand; some of the best lie north-east of Megalo Chorio, reached by little tracks. That at **Agios Antonios** has a sweep of shingle with weird 'beach rocks' – the petrified remains of three sailors, 5th-century-BC skeletons – and a small hotel, the *Australia*. Further north-east, **Plaka** has a good beach, too, and is used by rough campers.

The main attraction on Tilos is the **Agios Panteleimon monastery**, perched high in the hills of the north-west, and surrounded by trees, vines and lush, cool gardens. It has an eastern look – circular chapels with red-tiled roofs, an intricate mosaic courtyard and rickety stairs leading to medieval cells. The church was built in 1470 and founded by the monk Jonas, a fresco of whom has recently been discovered. The fountain at the entrance, flanked by pots of basil, is memorable; so are the sunsets observed from the monastery's fortified battlements. The monastery, currently manned by an Albino monk who speaks good English, becomes a place of pilgrimage for expatriate Telians at the three-day festival from 25 July.

Between Livadia and Megalo Chorio, a track leads west to the pretty hamlet of **Eristos**, which has a jewel of a beach – a horseshoe of red sand – and rooms available in the *Pension Nausikka* and the *Tropicana Taverna*.

THE NORTH-EAST AEGEAN ISLANDS

Chios, Ikaria, Lesbos (Mytilini), Limnos, Samos, Thassos

Most of the islands described in this chapter are a long way from mainland Greece and a long way from each other (apart from Thassos and Samothrace in the far north, that is, and the very dissimilar neighbours Samos and Ikaria, and a few unvisited satellites – Psara off Chios and the two Fournoi off Ikaria). The large islands have their own history, landscape and island character, and do not form a coherent group, so there is no great advantage in the more conventional arrangement of separating the islands of the north (Thassos, Samothrace and Limnos) from those of the east. Quite apart from awkward travel connections between them (which are now by no means insuperable), the main islands are each large and interesting enough to merit a holiday on them.

An island for which it would be hard to make such a claim is the one whose name rings the loudest mythological bell, Ikaria, which recalls one of the most famous and universal of all Greek myths, the story of Icaros. Having made himself unpopular with Minos of Crete by constructing a pantomime-like cow costume that enabled Minos's wife Pasiphaë to realise her desire for union with a bull, the craftsman Daedalus made wings upon which he and his son Icaros escaped from prison. As every schoolchild knows, Icaros ignored his father's warnings and let the exhilaration of flight get the better of him, soaring ever higher until the sun's heat melted the wax where the wings' feathers were rooted, and sent the bold young aviator spinning to a watery grave in the Ikarian sea. Quite what the pair were doing so far north on their way from Crete to Sicily, where Daedalus reappeared, is not clear.

More intriguingly tied up with history are the numerous mythological associations of Limnos, a fertile although not very green island of volcanic origin, where archaeologists have uncovered a city (Poliochni) that flourished in the third millennium BC, thus long before the first foundation of Troy on the hills across the water in Turkey.

Limnos is the island of Hephaistos, god of fire and patron of smiths, who was cast down from Olympos by Zeus, landed on Limnos with a bump that broke at least one leg and subsequently went around on a metal crutch of his own making. Hephaistos taught the islanders the secrets of metal-working and was greatly honoured on the island where the capital (after the decline of Poliochni) was named after him. It was at Limnos that Prometheus stole fire and, in a different vein, the island won notoriety for a series of atrocities that gave rise to the expression 'Limnian deeds' – apparently commonplace in Greek. The original Limnian deed began with some offence caused by the ladies of Limnos to the goddess Aphrodite. She hit on the original punishment of clothing all the women in a foul odour, at which their husbands did not hesitate to make off for Thrace in search of more fragrant partners. The Limnian women murdered faithless husbands and Thracian paramours alike, all except King Thoas, whom Princess Hypsipyle pushed out to sea in a box. Soon afterwards, Jason and the Argonauts landed on Limnos, took a deep breath and did the necessary to repopulate the island.

Bad smells recurred, for Limnos was also the island where Philoctetes was abandoned by his fellow Greeks who could not endure the smell of his gangrenous snake-bitten leg. Philoctetes recovered on the island and rejoined the Trojan expedition. Throughout antiquity, Limnian earth was greatly valued for its therapeutic powers, which included healing snake bites. Squares of earth were wrapped up, stamped with an image of Artemis and exported.

According to Herodotus, Limnos was inhabited by non-Greek-speaking tribes. It also had an important shrine where the mysterious cult of the Cabiri was practised. The Cabiri belonged to the congregation of so-called Great Gods, whose main sanctuary was the lonely mountainous island of Samothrace (see page 253), to the north of Limnos. The island held a famous religious festival every summer, which reached the height of its fame in the Hellenistic age, following the meeting at Samothrace of Philip II of Macedon and Olympias, mother of Alexander the Great. The pre-Greek language was retained in the ritual and for the names of the Great Gods, adding to the occult nature of the initiation and purification ceremonies that participants underwent. The demonic Cabiri themselves were protectors of seafarers, and it may be no coincidence that Samothrace was a natural refuge for sailors in a notoriously stormy corner of the Mediterranean.

Despite the fame of the Louvre's Winged Victory, the beauty of its mountains and thick forests and the considerable interest of what remains on the site of the sanctuary of the Great Gods,

THE NORTH-EAST AEGEAN ISLANDS

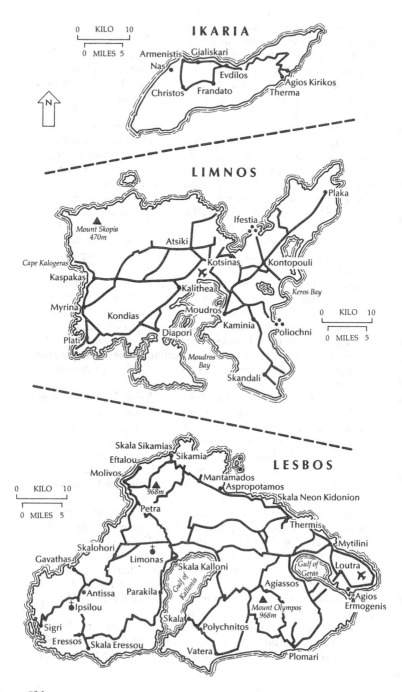

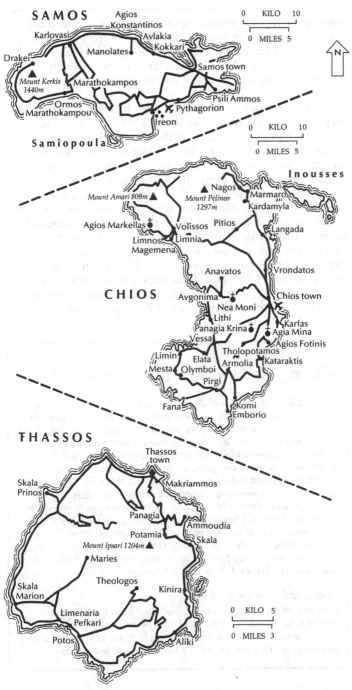

THE NORTH-EAST AEGEAN ISLANDS

SAMOS

Agios Konstantinos
Karlovasi
Avlakia
Drakei
Manolates
Kokkari
Samos town
Mount Kerkis 1440m
Marathokampos
Psili Ammos
Ormos Marathokampou
Pythagorion
Ireon
Samiopoula

0 KILO 10
0 MILES 5

N

0 KILO 10
0 MILES 5

CHIOS

Inousses
Mount Amari 809m
Nagos
Mount Pelineo 1297m
Marmaro
Kardamyla
Agios Markellas
Volissos
Pitios
Langada
Limnos
Limnia
Magemena
Anavatos
Vrondatos
Avgonima
Nea Moni
Chios town
Lithi
Panagia Krina
Karfas
Agia Mina
Vessa
Agios Fotinis
Limin
Tholopotamos
Kataraktis
Mesta
Elata
Armolia
Olymboi
Pirgi
Fana
Komi
Emborio

THASSOS

Thassos town
Skala Prinos
Makriammos
Panagia
Ammoudia
Potamia
Skala
Mount Ipsari 1204m
Maries
Skala Marion
Theologos
Kinira
Limenaria
Pefkari
Potos
Aliki

0 KILO 5
0 MILES 3

Samothrace remains something of a mystery island to which few are initiated. The reasons for this are entirely practical: it has very little accommodation, few beaches and no ferry links with other islands. The only frequent connection is with Alexandroupolis, a little-visited corner of north-eastern Greece.

The large and fertile islands of Chios, Lesbos and Samos lie very close to the coast of Asia Minor and feature large, like Rhodes and Kos to the south, in the ancient history of the Greek world, of which the coast of modern Turkey was an integral part. In political importance the leading island was Samos, largely thanks to its 6th-century-BC ruler Polykrates, whom Strabo described as the first to rule the Aegean since the time of Minos. Herodotus spent time on Samos during the rule of Polykrates and wrote that 'of all the Greeks the Samians have accomplished the three greatest projects'. These were a tunnel through the base of a mountain, bringing spring water to the city; a jetty built out to sea to protect the harbour; and the temple of Hera, which Herodotus reckoned to be the largest of all Greek temples. The splendid 12-gated ancient city stood on the hills above the modern resort of Pythagorion (which was its

Visiting the North-East Aegean Islands

Large fertile islands with a relatively modest amount of foreign tourism is an attractive formula for peak-season holidays. Limnos works particularly well in August, with good beaches around town, and a moderately lively atmosphere when many less attractive island resort towns are hectic. Chios is a sightseeing island without good beaches, so hardly the automatic midsummer candidate, although it too is no more than cheerfully animated in August. The same is true of Lesbos, which has a number of eight-weeks-a-year shanty beach resorts for locals. Here the drawback lies in the size of the island: exploring involves long hours at the wheel. Samos is a beautiful island whatever the season, but is not recommended to independent travellers in midsummer, when accommodation is very scarce indeed. On islands other than Thassos, few resorts are well equipped for watersports; exceptions are Molyvos and Eressos on Lesbos, Pythagorion and Kokkari on Samos.

Access and ferry connections
Reaching the main islands is not difficult despite the long distances involved, but Athens is not the ideal point of departure for a visit to Thassos or Samothrace. Nor does travelling between them present serious problems, provided you are not in a hurry and provided you do not want

harbour), where the tunnel can still be seen and, with some difficulty, explored.

After Polykrates was crucified by a Persian satrap who lured him to a banquet, the power of Samos declined, but not its great fertility nor the fame of its great temple of Hera, which occupied the legendary site of the goddess's birth and first union with Zeus. Antony and Cleopatra took statues from the temple, and the pillage was completed by the infamous Roman consul and collector, Verres. Enough remains on the site to give an idea of the enormous scale of the sanctuary, if not of the riches it once housed.

The islands were also great cultural centres. Pythagoras, founder of higher mathematics and first proponent of the idea that the earth revolves around the sun, was born on Samos in about 580BC but spent little time there, preferring to keep his distance from Polykrates. Chios is the island of Homer; and Lesbos, where the head and lyre of Orpheus were washed ashore at Antissa, was the birthplace of lyric, as opposed to epic, poetry. The name refers to a new prominence of music (which meant the lyre) in the composition and recitation of poetry, a development usually credited to Terpander of Antissa (7th

---

to miss out islands: sailing from Samos to Limnos, for example, would take many days unless you coincided with the one ferry that does sail all the way up and down the islands on its way from Rhodes to Kavala and back, the notoriously capricious *Kyklades*.

These are the islands where names can be particularly confusing: some islands have more than one ferry port, and timetables often indicate port rather than island names. Samos and Ikaria are the worst: boats on their way to and from Piraeus alternate between Ikaria's two ports (Agios Kirikos and Efdilos) and may or may not stop at Karlovassi as well as at Samos's capital, which is usually known as Vathy, not Samos. Lesbos is almost always referred to on timetables (and in conversation) as Mytilini, and Limnos very often as Myrina. There are no such problems with Chios.

Frequent excursion-boats and a few ferries sail to Turkey from Lesbos, where the main excursion target is Pergamon; from Chios (Izmir/Smyrna); and from Samos, which is well placed for day-trips to Ephesus. The rules governing visits to Turkey are important and changeable, and especially relevant to those using charter flights to and from Greece. Check the details carefully before you hop on an excursion-boat to Ephesus.

Charter flights operate from Britain to Lesbos and Samos; a few go to Limnos and Chios. Internal flights are available daily from Athens to Chios, Lesbos, Limnos and Samos. There are also daily flights from Athens to Kavala (for ferries to Thassos and Limnos) and to

century BC) who increased the strings of the lyre from three to seven. The expression of personal emotions took on new importance in poetry, especially in the work of the most celebrated of Lesbos poets, the 6th-century-BC contemporaries Alcaeus and Sappho. It is Sappho's love poetry, whose beauty does not survive translation, that has given the word Lesbian its modern connotation. Sappho's fame led to the establishment of a kind of finishing school in Mytilini, where well-bred young ladies came to be educated in the arts of poetry, music, dancing and good manners. The social climate on Lesbos was unusually liberal, and wealthy women like Sappho evidently led an emancipated life.

Lesbos remained an important cultural centre throughout the Roman period, and the island is very proud of its contribution to modern Greek art and literature. The names will mean little to most travellers, except perhaps that of Teriade (Stratis Eleftheriadis), a leading art patron and publisher in pre-war Paris. One of Teriade's discoveries was a folk artist from Lesbos, Theophilos, whose works became widely known through Teriade's magazines, where high-quality reproduction was pioneered. A museum on the island is devoted to Theophilos

---

Access and ferry connections continued

Alexandroupolis (for Samothrace); and from Salonika to Limnos and Lesbos, weekly to Samos.

There are several inter-island flights (all connections work in both directions); the approximate number of flights per week is given in brackets: Samos/Chios (one or two), Samos/Kos (one or two), Samos/Lesbos (one or two), Samos/Mykonos (two or four), Lesbos/Limnos (four), Lesbos/Mykonos (two or three), Lesbos/Rhodes (two), Lesbos/Chios (one), Chios/Mykonos (one or two).

Ferries operate daily from Piraeus to Ikaria/Samos and to Chios/Lesbos (occasionally continuing to Limnos and Kavala, or to Salonika). There is also a daily connection from Kavala to Limnos, often continuing to Lesbos, and there are numerous sailings every day from Keramoti and Kavala to Thassos (most Kavala boats use Prinos; all Keramoti boats go to Thassos town). There's a daily ferry to Samothrace from Alexandroupolis (weekly from Kavala); and occasional connections from Salonika to Lesbos/Chios.

Inter-island ferries operate daily between Samos/Ikaria, Chios/Lesbos; on most days between Lesbos/Limnos; twice a week between Chios/Samos, Chios/Psara, Samos/Ikaria/Paros; and infrequently between Lesbos/Limnos/Agios Efstratios/Evia (Kymi). There are ferries on most days in summer between Samos (Pythagorion)/Patmos.

and his works, which were often painted on a tablecloth in exchange for a free supper. Even when lionised by Teriade and persuaded to paint on canvas, Theophilos rarely took money for his work and remained true to the image of peasant artist, dying in poverty. Lesbos has other folk museums, craft centres, theatre groups and institutes of learning, and generally takes its culture and local traditions very seriously.

In post-classical times the islands suffered a catalogue of misfortunes, invasions and subjugations not dissimilar to those experienced all over the Aegean. Thassos was a profitable source of gold, silver, wood and marble, and still is for the latter two. In the Middle Ages Chios emerged not as a political force but as a uniquely prosperous island first under Byzantine and then Genoese control. Its well-managed economy, highly developed local culture and independent enlightened way of life under an aristocracy of mixed Byzantine and Genoese descent were little affected by Ottoman control in the 16th century and lasted until the War of Independence.

Chios had a flourishing silk industry and exported fruit, but its most prized product and the foundation of its economy was mastic, a natural chewing-gum tapped from lentisk bushes in the southern half of the island, greatly appreciated for purposes of oral hygiene. Lentisk bushes grow in many other places, but nowhere else does the sap solidify in the required way when it oozes out of the slashed trunks.

The main mastic villages in southern Chios were fortified in the Genoese period (14th and 15th centuries) and are still in a marvellous state of preservation. They would be top-flight sightseeing attractions even without the remarkable local tradition of decorating house exteriors with black and white geometric patterns as if on op-art canvases, known as *xysta* or by the Italian term *sgraffito*. The people of Pirgi, the largest of the mastic villages, still decorate their houses and new seaside villas in this way. Throughout southern Chios the lentisk bushes are still tapped and mastic produced, although the market for it is not what it was. The islanders make a very sticky liqueur, *masticha*, and a more palatable ouzo, *mastichato*. Curious travellers can also buy pellets of gum to chew, but it looks and tastes remarkably like the end of a biro.

In 1822 25,000 of the islanders were massacred in reprisal for having joined in the wave of rebellion against Turkish rule – the severity of the punishment said to have owed much to the fury in the harem at the interruption to its supply of chewing-gum. A famous painting by Delacroix (in the Louvre) and poetry by Victor Hugo publicised the atrocity and fanned public sympathy for the Greek cause.

Chios had prospered under the Ottoman Empire and its participation in the uprising had been at best half-hearted, largely incited by rebels from Samos. The same could not be said of the inhabitants of Chios's small neighbour Psara, an infertile island where refugees from an earlier age had built up a name for themselves as sailors, and a powerful fleet of 45 armed ships. Along with the similarly powerful navies of Spetses and Hydra, these formed the basis of the Greek revolutionary force. Rather than surrender when 14,000 Turks landed on their island in 1824, the Psariots blew themselves up. There is very little on the barren island today. It is a place to salute rather than visit.

In 1881 Chios was again victim, this time of severe earthquake, which destroyed the town and many of the most beautiful aristocratic mansions in the fertile citrus-growing hinterland, or Kambos. As a result, the modern town of Chios does not add greatly to the pleasure of a visit to the island. Home of many powerful shipping families (including Chandris), Chios is still a very rich island. Like Andros in the Cyclades, it sees relatively little foreign tourism but fills up with wealthy Greek-Americans in summer. Its lack of good beaches and charming resorts no doubt accounts for the small amount of organised tourism, although local reluctance to receive tourists may also have something to do with this. While most islands rely on charm and sand for their appeal, Chios has much more to offer and is one of the most rewarding of all the islands to visit, and quite unlike any other. As well as the mastic villages and crumbling aristocratic mansions of Kambos, Chios has a number of exceptionally beautiful Byzantine churches.

A glance at the map and the fact that these islands remained under Ottoman control until this century (1912) encourages the supposition that they must be more Turkish than Greek. Chios and Lesbos are separated from Turkey by a strait no more than a few miles wide, and at the eastern end of Samos the mainland is almost in spitting distance.

The men of Lesbos wear turban-like head-dresses; the skyline of Chios has its low domed mosque and slender minaret, and the old town has an old Muslim ghetto and graveyard; and the town of Mytilini has a ponderous 19th-century charm of its own which seems more oriental than Greek. But it cannot really be said that these islands are not Greek in atmosphere, not least because much of what we now consider to be typically Greek – music, food and so on – has its origins in Turkish influence.

The question of the extent to which Ottoman rule was intrusive, exacting and culturally oppressive is one of the most controversial aspects of national history. It is safe to say that it varied enormously from one area and one period to another, and in general compared favourably with the preceding period of Italian control, if only because Turkish rule meant freedom from Turkish raids. Many islands were left to run their own affairs without undue interference from their imperial overlords. During the 19th century, after the War of Independence, Turks and Greeks lived side by side on the islands, but in 1924 there was an enforced exchange of populations. The islands lost their Muslims and Turkey lost its Greeks.

At a local level, relations across the water are pretty relaxed, but not officially. Geography has decreed that the islands are at the sharp end of Greek nervousness about Turkish intentions, and, like all the islands close to the Turkish coast, Chios, Samos, Lesbos and Limnos are in a very obvious if not always very impressive semi-militarised state of semi-readiness for war. Signs prohibit photography and indicate the presence of mines. Promising-looking unsignposted rough roads down towards empty bays end abruptly at well-concealed look-out posts or gun batteries. Often, the soldiers seem to have bagged the best beaches. They do not allow tourists to share them and react extremely badly to cameras. Such is the general edginess that it is with hesitation that we hazard the information that the most heavily armed of all the islands is Limnos, although this impression may have something to do with the island's being so empty of anything other than soldiers.

Although its gently rolling landscape is peaceful in the extreme, the soldier's uniform is a familiar one to Limnos. The vast natural harbour of Moudros Bay and the island's position at the entrance to the Dardanelles have often earned it a place in the military history books, most famously in 1915, when it was the launching-pad for the Gallipoli campaign, many of whose victims lie commemorated in the island's well-kept war cemeteries. Many of the island's visitors are those who come to pay their respects to lost relatives.

Family connections of different kinds thus bring visitors to Chios and Limnos. Tourism on the other islands is equally diverse. The pine woods and sandy beaches of Thassos and its ideally convenient position for visitors arriving by car from the north have made Thassos the island of German campers par excellence. Even the most Europhile Briton may find it disconcerting not only to be addressed in German by all the natives on the assumption that all foreigners are German, but to have to speak German, unless he has good Greek, in order to make himself understood.

The large islands all have their own airports, but only Samos has become a large-scale package-holiday destination, with big hotels along the sandy south coast near Pythagorion. Here, too, nearly all the tourism is German and Scandinavian. Lesbos has two busy and a few peaceful international resorts. The capital is not one of them, and tourist development seems the exception rather than the rule on a very large and generally undisturbed island which has its own urban population and its own domestic tourism. Limnos and Chios have the attractions of infrastructure (international airport and a few very comfortable modern hotels each) and very little tourism. Ikaria has its own peculiarly ill-matched mixture of old-fashioned Greek spa tourism and naked beach-camping student tourism, on opposite sides of the mountainous island. Little Agios Efstratios has almost no one at all, stuck out in the middle of the open seas between Limnos and Skyros, which are themselves not on the main thoroughfare of Greek travel. There is not much to tempt visitors to Agios Efstratios, and the infrequency of ferry visits means that those who do disembark will not be able to leave in a hurry.

To a large extent the main islands are self-sufficient. Their working life is not always picturesque but it adds an unfamiliar and satisfying dimension of interest to a visit to an Aegean island, where so often colour comes down to little more than a few fishing nets and even the yoghurt is imported from Athens. All the large islands of the north-east Aegean have tastes and local specialities of their own, although once is often enough, as in the case of mastic. Thassos yields a delicious scented honey. Limnos has a golden fertility of corn, ploughed fields and fat cattle. Lesbos has 11 million olive trees and makes the best ouzo in Greece. Chios presents remarkable contrasts between its fertile citrus-growing plains and bare mountainsides. Samos is the most fruitful of them all, where Dionysos taught the islanders the arts of viticulture. They have not forgotten, although in the late Middle Ages the island became deserted almost to the point of being completely uninhabited. Samos brandy is excellent, and the clean white Samaina is one of the best Greek wines. The island's sweet muscatel is widely exported.

CHIOS

Chios is that rare thing: a beautiful, interesting, varied, easily accessible, all-mod-cons Greek island that features in few holiday brochures and on even fewer independent travellers' itineraries. Why? A common reply is that the Chiotes are wealthy enough to have no need for tourism and actively discourage tourist development. But there is no need to s⌣̲k refuge in conspiracy theories: the town, port and only serious candidate for a resort is modern, urban and without conventional Greek island charm; it has no beach to speak of, and the island as a whole has few. These shortcomings alone should suffice to ensure that mass-market sun and sand operators need not too much discouragement.

The ingredients of and background to Chios's historical interest – the development of the chewing-gum industry in the Middle Ages, when the island was under Genoese control from the mid-13th century until 1566 – have been outlined in the introduction to this chapter. Chewing-gum may not be the most obvious foundation stone for civilisation, but mastic, the product of the lentisk bushes (*Pistacia lentiscus*) of southern Chios, was a highly prized luxury commodity whose trade spilled over into a wealthy and highly civilised lifestyle for the whole island. This has survived, although shipowning has taken over from gum as the great provider. The great families of Chios are wealthy aristocratic patrons of arts and education in the mould of the philanthropists of the Industrial Revolution and 20th-century America.

Mastic was especially popular in the harems of Byzantium, it seems, not only because it freshened the breath and kept the dental regions in good order, but also because it provided something for the poor odalisques to do, which gives some idea of how tedious life must have been for them. The industry has declined today because mastic has been replaced by artificial substitutes in gum, toothpaste and other products of dental hygiene. But the farming and the production goes on in a modest way, and it will not now be allowed to expire. The bushes themselves are unremarkable and so familiar a part of the Greek island landscape that you may explore the mastic region of southern Chios for some while looking for something out of the ordinary before realising that those medium-sized dark green bushes are it. In spring they have reddish flowers and leaves.

A more beautiful landscape is the equally characteristic lush citrus-growing plain immediately south of Chios town, the so-called Kambos. With their rich dark green colour and seasonal scent, citrus groves are always attractive. On Chios they shelter behind the crumbling golden walls of aristocratic properties that reek of nostalgia for the island's golden age. The high mountains of the island's central spine and northern half are as starkly rocky and bare as the Kambos and southern Chios are lush. There is a no less abrupt contrast between barren mountains and pine forests in the north-west, and the transition from one to the other (at Agios Isidorus) is a surprising feature of the road from Chios to Volissos.

Chios town lies half-way down the island's east coast. Largely destroyed in 1881, it is an unpicturesque modern town of over 20,000 inhabitants, although the reddish-grey rocky peaks rising abruptly behind it lend some grandeur to the view from the approaching boat. Its heart is the long harbour-front, a place for ferries and freighters not fishing-boats and yachts. Workmanlike though it is, this is the best area for accommodation, with the prominent and very metropolitan-looking block of the *Hotel Chandris* (B) a landmark at the southern end of the harbour. It is expensive by Greek island standards, but its very good swimming-pool is quite an asset, considering the lack of decent town beach (there is a token man-made patch of beach just round the corner from the hotel). Breakfast, on the other hand, was awful when we visited. The Chandris's close neighbour the *Kyma* (B) has more old-fashioned charm and is less expensive. There is also a series of unusually comfortable rooming houses on the water-front itself, with balconies overlooking the very animated harbour scene. The *Ionia* and *Akropolis Inn* are recommended, as is Tassos's expensive restaurant near the Xenia hotel and beach.

The wide promenade is closed to traffic in the evening and positively swarms with strollers in summer: nowhere is the marvellous human spectacle of the early-evening *volta* more fun to watch. There are cafe terraces from which it can be comfortably enjoyed, to the accompaniment of ouzo and *meze*; pub-type bars, fast-food joints and car showrooms are here too. Untouristy though it is, Chios seems very Americanised, the result of expatriate families who return for the summer. Shops on the front sell Chios products – mastic to chew, *masticha* liqueur and ouzo, mastic jam and even Chios toothpaste made in the old-fashioned way.

At the northern end of the harbour rise the fine old walls of the medieval *kastro*, enclosing the old town, once the Turkish/ Jewish ghetto, which is entered by a very impressive and well-preserved old gateway. A vaulted chamber in the fabric of the wall was used as a dungeon; here, 70 leading Chiotes were held for over a month before their execution in 1822. Just inside the gates is the old Turkish graveyard. Its most elaborate tomb is that of the admiral who perished when the famous Kanaris of Psara used his fireship technique to destroy the Turkish flagship in 1822 in retaliation after the great massacre. There is cheap accommodation in this old part of town, but it is a fairly insalubrious quarter. There are good everyday restaurants at the northern end of the harbour.

The town's main grid of backstreets has no particular interest, apart from the shops. These include a number of good dairies and sticky pastry bars, which stay open late. Apart from the water-front the only focus is a big garden square at the back of the town (Vounaki square), the main bus terminal and afternoon idling spot. Nearby is the town's old mosque, no longer the home of the Chios archaeological museum, which now occupies a new building set back from the southern end of the harbour. There is another museum in the same building as the Korais library, one of the largest in Greece, with a collection of costumes and island crafts, a very crude reproduction of Delacroix' painting of the 1822 massacre, and portraits of some prominent Chiotes, including many members of the Argenti clan, whose villa in the Kambos has recently been restored and transformed into what is certainly the most exclusive hotel in Greece. The portraits do not all lend support to ancient travellers' reports of the exceptional beauty of the girls of Chios.

The most popular excursion from Chios is up into the hills directly above town to the **Nea Moni monastery**, famous for some of the finest medieval mosaics in Greece. The new monastery was founded in the 11th century by the Byzantine emperor Constantine the Dueller, whose elevation to the imperial throne had been prophesied by three hermits inhabiting an old monastery on the site, where a miracle-working icon (it resisted fire and even repelled an arrow shot at it) had been found in a myrtle bush.

Nea Moni appeals on several levels. It is in a lovely secluded wooded setting, looking down over the coast; there are a few picturesque old nuns and, in a chapel near the entrance, an ossuary where rows of bones are on display, including skulls split open in graphic illustration of the horrors of the 1822 massacre, when the monks and monastery's other defenders were killed and the buildings sacked. Then there is the church (or *katholikon*), severely damaged in the 1881 earthquake and remarkably well restored considering that the dome and vault collapsed. On a bright day, give your eyes plenty of chance to adjust to the light. The marvellous mosaics, the work of Byzantine artists soon after the construction of the church, are scenes from the Life of Christ and portraits of saints and hermits. The design of the church, with its dome supported by an octagonal drum, is unique to Chios and Cyprus and may have been modelled on a church in Constantinople, no longer standing.

If visiting Nea Moni independently on or in hired transport, it is well worth pursuing the excursion over the crest of the island to visit the magnificent ghost village of **Anavatos**, north of the also peaceful but still inhabited village of Avgonima. Rough grey ruined houses cover a steep hillside dominating a valley filled with olives. A few islanders sell herbs to the occasional visitors, who toil up the steep paths to the village's old hilltop fortress, where the main church is under restoration. The slopes of the hill fall away very steeply behind the acropolis, and there are horror stories of people being hurled off. Anavatos did not recover from the drastic decline in the island's population in 1822; although 25,000 is the conventional figure, some estimates of the overall loss are as high as 70,000 (out of 100,000), taking emigration, voluntary and enforced, into account.

Avgonima has a cafe, and a rough road leads steeply down to the west coast, which the road follows southwards to **Lithi**, making it possible to do a circuit of the south of the island, returning to Chios town via the mastic villages. There are several very peaceful pebble beaches between Avgonima and Lithi, and a small sandy one, very sheltered and gently shelving, but busy in midsummer, immediately below Lithi.

The coastal strip south of Chios town around the airport is the **Kambos** citrus grove and old-mansion zone, a maze of high-walled lanes without many signposts. The one old property to have been thoroughly restored is the Villa Argentikon, now a country-house-style hotel that may interest those who do not balk at £100 a night (for a double room with breakfast). Even the hotel is not signposted: presumably anyone going there takes a cab (it is about 100 yards from the Perivoli, a fashionable out-of-town restaurant which is signposted and well known). The international clientele, in blazers and golfing trews, sit among the fountainside statuary drinking Camparis served by white-suited waiters.

The coast road south from Chios town leads to the town's main Sunday afternoon beach resort, **Karfas**, not a conspicuously attractive location as resort or beach, although the sand is fine and there are tavernas and accommodation. There are a few other smaller beaches round the corner to the south of Karfas, where the coast is overlooked by the **Agia Mina monastery**, much visited in memory of the thousands killed there in 1822. As at Nea Moni, bones are on view. **Agia Fotini** is a stony beach with a taverna, rooms and windsurfing, all on a modest scale. Turkey is very close at this point, so mind the wind does not take you into hostile territorial waters. A separate road leads to the main coastal village in this part of the island, Kataraktis, which has balconied waterside houses, a couple of tree-shaded cafes, and fishing-boats. But there is no beach, and Kataraktis, while perfectly agreeable, does not exactly demand inclusion on every itinerary, nor win it on many.

The main road south (signposted to Pirgi) passes **Armolia**, a village known for its pottery, and which features as a stop on excursion-tours of southern Chios. There are some ceramics factories, but neither the village nor the factories' output has much charm. A more interesting diversion from the road south is the **Panagia Krina**, a delectable brick-red Byzantine church tucked away in the olive groves near a settlement called Sklavia, north-east of Tholopotamos. The church may well be closed (the frescoes were under restoration when we visited) but even so it is well worth finding. The farm tracks are narrow, but the church is signposted. Its plan is very similar to that of Nea Moni's church.

Pirgi is the biggest of the mastic villages and the main tourist centre in southern Chios, with accommodation and tourist shops as well as a healthy everyday life of its own. The 20th century has caught up with life, and much of the old street plan has been changed and the central keep, key element of the town's defences, has lost its dominance.

Instead, Pirgi takes the breath away with its astonishing *xysta* decoration on the houses – black and white bands of geometric motifs covering the outside walls. This technique is said to have its origins in Italy, although none of the painting now visible pre-dates the 19th century. To add colour to the composition the houseproud villagers hang tomatoes and other vegetables from their balconies. Nowhere is the *xysta* effect more dazzling than on the walls of the village's main church, which overlooks the delightful central square. On the north-east corner of the square a vaulted gateway leads to the tiny Byzantine church of Agii Apostoli, like Krina apparently modelled on Nea Moni, and with wonderful decorative patterns in its brick- and tile-work. Here the domes are intact and the scheme of frescoes complete, with the figure of Christ Pantokrator filling the vault. The paintings date from no earlier than the 17th century.

Pirgi has its beach resort at **Emborio**, due south of town. There is a small, well-kept stony beach just round the headland from the little harbour community, where new villas have been built in *xysta* style. A rough and unsignposted farm track leads north to a much better long sandy beach at **Komi**, a straggling villa community with a disco and a small hotel as well as a taverna or two. There is another beach at **Fana**, to the west, reached by a different road. Fana has no facilities and no palm trees, although Strabo reported that it had the latter. It also had a temple of Apollo, of which there is very little to be seen.

The other two mastic villages cannot offer the eye-catching op-art houses of Pirgi, but they have other compensations – fewer alterations to the original walled and gated plans of these fortress villages which were built to help the mastic-growers defend themselves against pirate attack in the 14th and 15th centuries. **Mesta** is the most celebrated of them, a wonderfully preserved maze of old vaulted streets, with some whitewash but mostly earth-coloured. Donkeys clatter and old women shuffle about picturesquely, and chess is played under the tall eucalyptus tree on the central square. Rooms can be rented and there are a few tourist shops, for Mesta is not a lost world – it merely looks like one. Not so many people visit the third village, **Olymboi**, and that is its charm. The old houses have been crudely modernised, but the street plan survives, as does the central keep, its chambers now occupied by two cafes and the local PASOK office. The menfolk idly turn cards while the old women sit in their open doorways spinning, and the younger ones return wearily from the fields at the head of a caravan of goats and donkeys all roped together.

Mesta's harbour, **Limin**, is a dreary little place without much shipping activity, but roads connect with Elata and the attractive farming village of Vessa, so retracing steps is not necessary.

Northern Chios is much less interesting than the centre and south, apart from some fine, impressively barren mountain scenery. North of Chios town, the capital almost merges with **Vrontados**, a sprawling coastal village with a strip of roadside beach and a slab of rock carved into a rough platform on the hillside, known as Homer's Stone but probably an ancient shrine. To the north of this is wild hill country, with very little vegetation until a rare oasis of greenery at **Langadas**, where a stream runs down to the sea. There are cafes under the trees and a few rooms to rent, but not much of a beach or any resort life. A tempting bay immediately to the north, visible from the road north, is occupied by the army.

The main northern village is **Kardamyla**, set about a mile inland from its small port and local resort of **Marmaro**. There are rooms to be rented at both, and a beachside hotel at Marmaro, but neither village has much to commend it. The road continues northwards to **Nagos**, a leafy spot with two peaceful beaches, one with a taverna. Nagos has quiet charm, but the fact that excursion-coaches come all this way from Chios for a day on the beach is a tribute to the island's poverty in the beach department.

From a few miles south of Kardamyla a road climbs steeply inland cutting across the mountains to join up with the main Chios–Volissos road at Agios Isidorus, no more than a church at a point remarkable for the sudden change of hill scenery from bare rock to dense pine woods. This is a splendid drive, and **Pitios** is a splendidly rough old subsistence farming village high

Getting around

Excursions are organised by water-front agencies and tour operators to the mastic villages (Mesta and Pirgi with a ceramics stop at Armolia), to Nea Moni, to Nagos (for swimming) and to Turkey (Izmir and Ephesus) for which a few days' notice is needed. Boat-trips to Inousses are also offered.

Car and motor-bike hire is available at Chios. Cars are booked well in advance in August. Garages are few (non-existent in the north) and distances are long on the island. Do not count on being able to get petrol other than at Chios town, Vrontados and Pirgi. The island guidebook *Chios*, published by the National Bank of Greece and available on the island in English, is recommended, especially for detail on churches and mosaics.

Buses travel more than once a day from Chios to Karfas; Vrontados; Kardamyla/Nagos and beyond; Kalamoti/Komi; Pirgi/Olymboi/Mesta; and Vessa/Lithi. There is a bus a few times a week to Volissos, and once a week to Anavatos.

up in the wilds, overlooked by a fortress tower and a ruined windmill. There is a shop-cum-cafe.

Continuing north-west, the Volissos road makes a splendid sweeping descent from the pine woods down towards the west coast, passing the abandoned buildings of Moni Moudon, in its day one of the most important foundations on the island. The broad coastal view includes a long stretch of sandy beach: this is **Magemena**, not signposted but easily reached by several rough tracks heading down towards the sea from not far south of Volissos. There are no tavernas on the beach, but the small harbour at **Limnia** has two, and rooms to rent, and is in walking distance of the northern end of the beach. **Volissos** is the main settlement of north-western Chios, an attractive white village at the foot of impressive medieval fortress walls. There are rooms to rent.

From Volissos an extremely long road winds its way round the mountainous north-western corner of the island high above the coast. Closer at hand, a road leads down to the sea at **Limnos**, not to be confused with neighbouring Limnia, and on to the **monastery of Agia Markellas**, which must be one of the most attractive retreats for keen swimmers with a vocation. The monastery buildings themselves are exceedingly ugly, but there is a long beach in front of them, and a midsummer cafe. Limnos also has a small beach and taverna and is a cheerful flower-filled roadside hamlet.

IKARIA

Few large Greek islands are less immediately appealing than ungainly Ikaria, a long mountain mass that projects far out across the Aegean from Samos towards Mykonos, bearing the full brunt of the *meltemi* in summer and southerly gales in winter. Its steep slopes drop gracelessly into the sea, and the island's long coastline has few shapely bays or good harbours. Ikaria has on several occasions been used as a place of exile, most recently under the Colonels, when it received 15,000 communists. Earlier this century Ikaria knew independence between July and October 1912 before joining Greece. The stamps and coins of the free State of Ikaria must have some rarity value.

'To write more about Ikaria would be like trying to write the Lord's Prayer on a penny,' wrote Lawrence Durrell after about 10 lines, which include the words 'unrewarding', 'rugged' and 'unkempt', all of which we would endorse. It is a thoroughly odd island, and in terms of tourism is something of a minority interest, almost entirely ignored by the mainstream of Mediterranean beach holiday-makers. Whether this will change when the island's airport, now at the planning stage, becomes operational remains to be seen. Certainly the island has a few good beaches. In its present state it hardly demands the stock advice in such circumstances, to rush out and catch the island before it is transformed.

The minority interests are the spas to the east and west of its main port, Agios Kirikos, which attract a number of ailing Greek visitors but almost no foreigners, as is the way with spas. The radioactive spring water is exceptionally powerful – one spring registers 792 degrees of radiation. Whatever this means it is deemed undesirable and the spring in question is not used. The life of the spa, especially Therma, the eastern resort, has its old-fashioned charm, but would soon become depressing unless one had need of the cure.

The contrast could hardly be more complete between the pale and arthritic figures swathed in towels from head to toe hobbling around Therma, and the bronzed young people, clad only in headphones, who colonise the sandy beaches near Armenistis on the northern side of the island. This is a fine species of the hippie colony in a much less decadent (in the sense of having sold out to mass tourism) state than on Ios, which it recalls. In smaller numbers a similar population camps near the little stony river-mouth cove of Nas to the west of

Armenistis, legendary home of the Naiads. Naked bodies draped round the rocks of the secluded cove re-create the legend very nicely.

The island's main port and administrative centre is **Agios Kirikos** in the south-east, a place for buses and boat-trips (to Fourni and Patmos), ferry tickets and convenient accommodation in a few small hotels and rooming buildings, nowhere outstanding. Well provided with gardens and trees, it is not an ugly village, but nor is it old, picturesque or in any way worth diverting for. To the east of the ferry quay is a small stony strip of pebbles where fishing-boats are beached, but few people swim. Water-taxis shuttle people to and fro between the port and the island's main summer resort of Therma, about five very agreeable minutes' ride along the cliff coast. There is also an overland route to Therma, which takes much longer.

Therma is prettier than Agios Kirikos, a narrow rock-enclosed cove with a row of tamarisk-shaded cafes (and a good fish restaurant, Zachos) looking out over a small but not overpatronised scruffy pebble beach, which abuts the caique quay and, from the smell of it, the sewage outlet. There are about half a dozen small hotels in the compact little village, which is likely to be totally overrun or deserted according to the season. The spa itself is a suitably gloomy-looking yellow building near the front, where all the bathrobed patrons queue up for admittance.

If the spa atmosphere seems a bit glum, there is rich entertainment in store when the fish-selling caique makes its daily appearance, especially if there is a bit of a swell running. In a marvellously Greek scene, the fisherman's wife on the heaving boat tries to weigh the fish in her scales, whose needle girates wildly with the movements of the boat. This manoeuvre complete and a price having been struck, the purchaser (who is ashore) and vendor have to manage the even more delicate business of reaching out over the water and swapping food for cash at precisely the same moment, for each party is convinced the other is an out-and-out swindler, ready to run or sail off with the fish or cash if given half the chance. After a few trial passes, when one party nervously withdraws, they somehow manage it.

The western spa, **Therma Lefkadas**, is of less interest, consisting of little more than a hotel (the most comfortable on the island) and the baths.

From Agios Kirikos the island's one main road climbs steeply, crosses the high scrub-covered mountainous spine of the island and descends through more attractive terraced country to the north coast, along which it runs westwards through Evdilos, the island's second port, and on to Armenistis, the young people's resort. **Evdilos** is a pleasant enough little port, with good beaches in walking distance to east and west. There are cafes round the harbour, and a comfortable small modern hotel (*Evdoxia*, B) beside the road above the village, not as bad a location as that sounds. Evdilos is not very tuned in to tourism and English is not widely spoken.

The coast road west of Evdilos passes a series of excellent sandy beaches, all clearly visible from the road. The two busy and camped-upon ones are on either side of a headland no more than a few hundred yards east of Armenistis, and are known as Gialiskari and Messakti. Young people build makeshift bamboo shelters (much more ideologically acceptable than tents) among the scrub at the back of the beach where a shower, lavatories and a new rock-blaring self-service cafe have been installed. One of the more surprising things about this colony is that it exists so close to the island's main road and beside the village, contrary to the usual Greek etiquette of naturism. Matters might change at no notice, and if you visit out of season the beaches will probably be empty, but the new services suggest the Ikarians are for the time being quite relaxed about their hippies. There is a good restaurant, with draught lager, on the rocks above the beach, so this is hardly the back of beyond.

The sand is brilliant and the water clear, but a number of signs (especially on the eastern beach, where fewer people camp) warn of dangerous currents. Access to the eastern beach is complicated by its forming a bank between the sea and a lagoon at the end of a river, a characteristic beach type on northern Ikaria, perhaps a result of the number of springs and year-round streams on the island, which is surprisingly well vegetated considering the mountainous terrain.

Armenistis is the service village for this beach colony, a tidy little collection of mostly new white houses (and a few restored old ones) looking out over fishing-boats and a small patch of beach towards the big beaches. The village has no hotels worthy of the name, but rooms to rent and a not unattractive mixture of old village Greeks and a slightly trendy style of bars and other tourist services, including an Ikarian arts display. Windsurf rental is advertised, and, considering the island's windy reputation, these north-facing beaches must be of considerable interest to expert practitioners, although the watersports vogue has not yet reached Ikaria in a big way.

A rough road continues south-west for a couple of miles to **Nas**, a beautiful coastal walk from Armenistis, rewarded by a delicious little place: a stream runs steeply down to the sea, with a very narrow rocky estuary where a pebble bank/beach

Getting around

Excursions are organised a few times a week in summer from Agios Kirikos to Patmos. These provide quite a useful (albeit expensive) ferry substitute for those wanting to change island groups, although the Samos/Patmos link is better. There are also daily boats from Agios Kirikos to Fourni, a cluster of islands (two of them inhabited) between Ikaria and Samos. The largest of the islands (Fourni itself) has a very cheerful port with rooms and good restaurants. Nearly all visitors are day-trippers from Ikaria.

Buses operate from Agios Kirikos to Armenistis via Evdilos, occasionally continuing to Nas. Motor-bike hire is available at Evdilos and Armenistis. Water-taxis ply between Agios Kirikos and Therma.

has a capacity for about 20 bathers. On the southern side of the river mouth a few vestiges of an ancient temple can be seen. It is quite a rough scramble down to the sea from the taverna beside the road. Another taverna (the Artemis) offers rooms and has a grassy campsite beside the stream. The rough road continues southwards from Nas, but monsters in the form of brutish dogs foaming at the mouth lurk here: proceed with caution. The wooded hills above Evdilos and Armenistis, indeed the whole western end of the island, are dotted with habitations and tiny villages. The main one and the most easily reached, by rough road from Armenistis, is **Christos Rachon**, which commands splendid views out over the sea. Rooms can be found if you ask around. To judge from the map (always a rash thing to do), it is possible to hike over the mountains from Evdilos to the south coast a long way west of Agios Kirikos and Therma Lefkadas. It may even be possible to make the same long journey by motor-bike, but the machines on offer for hire would not inspire confidence for such arduous and remote expeditions.

LESBOS (MYTILINI)

The island that has given us Sappho and Michael Dukakis is the third of the Greek islands in size, after Crete and Evia. Like the other great island out on its own in the Aegean, although unlike Evia, it has a proud character and cultural – one is tempted to say ethnic – identity of its own. In contrast to Crete, its moderately thriving varied economy does not depend to any great extent on tourism. Rather, it is an island of agriculture, with vast tracts of luxuriant olive growth around the shores of the two bottle-necked inland seas in the south, which give the island's outline on the map the spongy look of a minute submarine organism viewed through the microscope. The other local industry is the distilling of the national drink, the high-kicking aniseed-flavoured ouzo, which goes cloudy when mixed with water and clouds the brain rapidly, however you drink it.

For the tourist, Lesbos (pronounced Lesvos) presents a rounded appeal that will amount to more than the sum of its parts for those whose interest is in the everyday life of provincial Greece. It has an architectural style of its own, and rough villages of grey stone houses and pitched tile roofs, and many of the beautiful traditional overhanging upper storeys of polished wood survive, notably in Molivos, the island's architectural showpiece.

But for many visitors, the specific attractions of sightseeing, picturesque villages and beautiful beaches are likely to be too few and far between for a tour of the island to be very rewarding. Besides, touring the island by hired car (it is too big to be done sensibly by motor-bike) presents considerable problems, of which more later. This leaves the resorts themselves, which are very different and need to be evaluated individually, for Lesbos is too large to be taken in from one base.

One of the resorts, the old fortified town of Mithimna/ Molivos, is in itself a good reason to visit the island, and is one of the highlights on its modest sightseeing agenda. Eressos and Sigri in the far west are good beach resorts of their kinds: Sigri a very peaceful old village, and a fine place for an unwinding holiday; Eressos a small-scale and simple modern development, no more than a service area at the back of a vast and splendid sandy beach. In the south, the distillery town of Plomari reeks of aniseed and is not without its appeal, even to non-drinkers. But it does not work very well as a busy resort (which it is) mainly for beach reasons.

Lesbos is a peaceful island, even in midsummer, when many inhabitants of the capital and the inland villages disperse to bring life to numerous small shanty summer holiday colonies on the coast, which scarcely deserve the term resort. These are characteristic of the island, and add to the pleasure of exploring in July and August. Outside this short season they are abandoned. Another unusual, although not unique, feature of the island's coastline is rivers forming swampy lagoons behind the piled-up beaches of sand and stones. This means fertile cultivations and, often, a fascinating rich wildlife of birds, toads and terrapins. It can also make reaching the beaches unexpectedly complicated: on Greek islands river beds are normally dry in summer. Such coastal idylls can be found near Sigri, near Gavathas, near Kalloni and near Klio.

The capital, **Mytilini**, is a large, messy, noisy working port which has the considerable charm of appearing to look through tourists as if they were not there. Not many are, for long. It is not the only place on the island with industrial buildings – tall-chimneyed olive oil refineries are a special feature of the landscape. Mytilini is a finely situated town in the south-east, facing Turkey, with harbours on either side of a headland clothed in pines and very impressive fortifications which have been reinforced many times down the centuries from antiquity to the Turkish occupation. One cannot help feeling that they may not have seen their last action – nets camouflage eastward-pointing guns and there is plenty of warlike shipping in port. On a more leisured note, there is a small man-made town beach (with an entrance charge) below the woods on the southern side of the headland, only a short walk from the ferry quay.

The ferry harbour is the southern one, and its water-front is the busy focus of town life, not the most picturesque harbour frontage in Greece but well worth an evening. A narrow bazaar-like shopping street (Ermou) runs parallel to the water-front, one block back, and has a fascinating collection of shops (antiques, a taxidermist) at its northern end. Looming in elephantine fashion over the harbour is the domed, pedimented and pilastered orange church of Agios Therapon, built in the late 19th century. Other peeling buildings in similar inflated style include the old hotel Megali Britania, which may still be open for business, although most of it is now occupied by a bank. There is also a splendid palatial hall of a cafe on the water-front, echoing with the clink of glasses, the chink of billiard balls and the clamour of heated political argument. For accommodation, the best bet is probably the *Lesvion* (B), which has a smartly refurbished bar on the first floor and a good breakfast cafe next door. Small-hours ferry arrivals are a nasty feature of visits to Lesbos. The Lesvion remains open and attended all night. Between the town and airport, the *Xenia* (B) is comfortable, quiet and has a salt-water pool: not bad as a base for a few days, but not much use to passers through. The big *Blue Sea* (B) by the ferry quay has only the merit of convenience.

Mytilini has handsome gardens at the southern end of the harbour, a good archaeological museum close to the ferry quay and beach, a folklore museum and a good collection of icons in the Byzantine Museum near Agios Therapon, and an ancient theatre in a beautiful hillside position looking down over the town. Two no less interesting museums are at **Akrotiri**, not far south of town on the way to the airport, devoted to the Parisian pre-war patron Teriade and one of his protégés, the native, and naïve, wandering artist Theophilos, the Rousseau of Lesbos. Much of Theophilos's art was on cafe fronts and walls of houses and has succumbed to the weather and whitewash. Such is the glory of the artist 'to paint for himself not his posterior', as it is written in the museum. Perhaps fortunately, in view of this, there is not much more explanation in English.

The road out of town southwards passes a number of fairly grand 19th-century suburban villas. Although interestingly un-Greek in aspect – some of them would not look out of place on the coast of Normandy – they are no great architectural masterpieces.

The rest of the southern peninsula is not at all attractive, with the road following a very dreary stretch of shore near the makeshift airport. It would not be worth bothering with but for the lovely scenery on the southern tip of the peninsula and the secluded charms of **Agios Ermogenis**, two idyllic little beaches on either side of a chapel on a rocky outcrop, with a very good shaded taverna tucked away on the thickly wooded hillside above the sea. Needless to say, the inhabitants of Mytilini know all about this spot, and on a summer weekend it is ridiculously crowded. Agios Ermogenis stands at the entrance to the smaller of the island's two inland seas, the **Gulf of Geras**. There is a ferry service across the mouth of the gulf between Skala Loutron and Perama, a desolate and dilapidated olive-industry port with grey windowless factory buildings and chimneys. (It is a pretty safe bet in Greece that anywhere called Perama is exceedingly unattractive.)

With its perfectly calm water and surrounding mantle of deep-pile olive trees, the Gulf of Geras has a certain beauty. As a resort area it suffers from lack of beaches: the olive trees come right down to the sea in most places. However, proximity to Mytilini has led to the construction of several biggish new hotels along the road round the bay. Off the road, **Pyrgi** (the Pyrgi on the Mytilini side of the gulf, not the one near Perama) is a nice place at which to pause, with a quiet waterside taverna. Quitting the western shore between Dipi and Napi, the road charts a slow, tortuous course over the hills towards the main southern resort, Plomari, with luxuriant vegetation on the way down to the south coast via a cool river valley filled with flowers, butterflies, birdsong and the ripple of a fast-flowing stream. A rough road leads down to the alluring **Tarti**, a very pretty bay with a coarse sand beach, and a popular place for camping rough (very rough, considering the state in which we found the sanitation) in the olive groves. There are several tavernas. Over a mile before Plomari the road runs through Agios Isidoros, whose good long stretch of coarse sand is the main Plomari beach. Abandoned factories and tall chimneys give a semi-industrial look to the approach to Plomari. Tourist accommodation and assorted nightlife venues line the road.

This layout is the trouble with **Plomari**, combined with the fact that there is little alternative to the road, which is busy, for those walking from Plomari to the beach, their rooms or the disco, and vice versa. There is a small stony beach nearer to the resort centre, but it is very meagre. Boat-trips (to Vatera and Agios Ermogenis and beaches between) are the best solution.

This considerable inconvenience apart, Plomari is an attractive sheltered port, with most of the required ingredients of charm and liveliness. A middling-sized modern hotel (*Oceanis*, C) and tavernas are gathered around its peaceful palm-fringed harbour; and the dilapidated poky old heart of the village, where huge plane trees shade bars and cars parked in the dry river bed, is exceptionally picturesque. There are rooms to rent (mostly block-booked) and a few cocktail bars in this area, but its atmosphere is not unduly touristy. Houses have timbered overhanging galleries and the smell of ouzo hangs in the air. Several distilleries invite visitors. *Barbayianni* is the strongest local ouzo, which probably means the best for the purposes of most tourists.

Continuing by road from Plomari, either inland to Agiassos or, in very roundabout manner, along the coast to Vatera, is arduous and very slow. It is over an hour's bumpy driving to **Vatera**, an interminable coarse sand beach with a few tavernas. The best way to approach **Agiassos** is by the main road across the southern lump of island between the two gulfs. High on the pine-covered slopes of Lesbos's Profitis Ilias/Olympos, Agiassos is the biggest and most beautiful of the island's inland villages and a popular excursion target, with attractive old timbered houses, cobbled streets, leafy tavernas and tourist shops whose contents (pottery and olive-wood items), while not of outstandingly high quality, are one up from the usual beach-resort souvenirs. Rooms can be rented. There is a handsome 19th-century pilgrimage church in the middle of the village, with a marbled courtyard and an imposing neo-baroque church. The miraculous icon of the Virgin is supposedly by St Luke and was brought from Jerusalem in 803.

The main road continues west to **Polichnitos**, an uninteresting village with its own dreary villa community (Skala Polychnitou) on the weedy eastern shore of the larger inland sea, the Gulf of

Kalloni. This part of the island can be omitted at no great sacrifice.

Much the same could be said of the large village of **Kalloni** in the middle of flat farming country at the north of the gulf, and of its functional beach community, Skala Kallonis, only this is the main road to the far west, and on a hot day a swim may be necessary. Luckily, Skala Kallonis has one of the better beaches on the two gulfs, a long strip of unkempt coarse sand with some shade from tamarisks. There are tavernas, simple accommodation in modern rooming houses and small hotels, and no shortage of wildlife interest in the surrounding marshes, salt-pans and river mouth. The calm shallow water is no doubt splendid for small children, but none of all this should distract from the fact that Skala Kallonis would be a drab place for a prolonged stay.

On its way west from Kalloni the main road passes the vast 16th-century **Limonas** monastery, a somewhat austere and institutional red-brick place, which had the island's secret Christian school during the Turkish occupation and still serves as a boarding-school and summer camp for children of poor families. According to the ancient custom of the monastery, they say, ladies are not allowed into the church. Gents can inspect the coffered wooden ceiling and biblical murals of no special distinction. There is also a small museum of monastic miscellany.

As the road climbs and progresses west across the island, olives give way to pines, pines to planes and oak woods, and they in turn to open and boulderous country, in sharp contrast to the fertile south-east. From Skalochori a very rough track leads down to ancient **Antissa** on the north-west coast, passing some beautiful rural beaches on either side of a small headland (Limani), with a taverna on one side and a splendid view along the coast to Molivos from the fishing cove on the other side. There is similar topography at ancient Antissa itself, with longer beaches and even fewer people. Of the ancient site, on a headland by a river mouth, there is little to see. It was here that the head and lyre of Orpheus were washed ashore, since which moment the nightingales of Lesbos have sung extra sweetly. The road does not continue round to **Gavathas**, a larger and unremarkable coastal community reached from near the large village of Antissa, on the main road. Gavathas has a long weedy beach and a couple of tavernas. Tucked away in the woods beside the same river that runs down to old Antissa, high up near the main road, lies the verdant **Perivolis** monastery, its courtyard full of flowers. The church has 16th-century frescoes in the porch. The monastery shuts for a long lunch break, but

would make a lovely place for a leafy picnic outside the walls.
Listen out for nightingales.

The road south to Eressos descends through a mountain gorge
strongly reminiscent of western Crete (which is a
recommendation) in its wild grandeur and the way it opens out
into a fertile cultivated coastal strip between the village of
Eressos, birthplace of Sappho, and its beach resort, Skala
Eressou. The beach is vast, sandy and splendid, and the simple
resort at the back of it is a good example of its kind: simple
small-scale modern accommodation (nearly all rooms) on a
small grid of concrete streets at the back of the beach, tavernas
and tamarisks with their feet in the sand, and a moderately
cheerful package-holiday atmosphere, relaxed but not lifeless.
The tour operator Sunmed runs a watersports operation on the
beach and states plausibly in its brochure that winds are usually
ideal for windsurfing beginners – in other words, very light.
The ingredients of Skala Eressou are not so very different from
those of Skala Kallonis, admittedly, but the setting and the
beach are much finer.

The mountain country between Eressos and Sigri is the site of
one of Lesbos's more curious curiosities, the so-called **Petrified
Forest**, more accurately termed the petrified one or two tree-
stumps. The trees in question are not easily reached and seem
to disappoint almost everyone, since there is now very little left
to be seen of the intriguing phenomenon, for which souvenir-
hunters down the centuries are partly responsible. It seems that
the mountain on which now stands the Ipsilou monastery (see
below) erupted and covered the trees of a huge forest in ash.
Earthquakes led to the submerging of much of the forest, and
hydrothermic energy turned the wood to stone, soaking it with
silicon dioxide. Estimates of the age of the forest vary from
500,000 to 20 million years, which makes the eruption of
Santorini seem like the day before yesterday. A rough track
(too rough for cars) leads south from the main road not far west
of the Moni Ipsilou turning, and tour operators organise
excursions to the forest (boat-trip and hike) from Sigri and
Skala Eressou. The original forest must have been a mighty
one, for the remaining stumps are up to 8m round and almost
as high.

Mount Ordymnos (511m) wears **Ipsilou** monastery perched
slightly askew on its peak, a splendid sight from the road and an
even finer viewpoint over the western end of the island. The
mountain also has a cluster of buildings occupied, unlikely
though this may sound, by the navy, and they do nothing for
the beauty of the place. But the monastery is well worth
visiting, with an attractive courtyard full of plants, a couple of

wells and various bits of petrified tree. There is also a small museum of oddments – manuscripts, vestments, a handsome crown, and a more handsome old bearded monk who is not an exhibit but is there to sell postcards. He is not the most vigorous salesman, being much given to sleep.

Sigri is the pot of gold at the end of the long journey west across the island, a full 94km from Mytilini. The approach is climactic, a long descent from the mountain ridge into a broad coastal landscape with the long islet of Megalonissi sheltering the port and silhouetted against the setting sun. Sigri itself does not disappoint: a quiet fishing harbour, a fine 18th-century Turkish fortress of dark volcanic stone, a thin sheltered crescent of sandy beach, a cheerful central collection of tavernas (Kavalouros is recommended), and much more village life than at any of the Lesbos Skalas, for Sigri is its own place, not some other village's harbour community. The only minor let-down is the village centre itself: neither a picturesque huddle of old houses, nor cobbled streets and handsome balconied mansions in the style of Molivos. Sigri is just concrete streets and very ordinary small modern houses. The big name in Sigri tourism is the tour operator Timsway, which has quite a hold on the village rooms accommodation and on the one hotel, formerly the Nisiopi, now nameless. However, if there is space the proprietor, a charming and cultured individual, will happily rent you a room at no great expense. Like many tour operators, Timsway produces an information booklet for its visitors, which is likely to be on view in the hotel and includes extensive and detailed directions for those wishing to explore the nearby coast in search of bigger, better and emptier beaches than Sigri's, of which there are several to north and south. One, a very beautiful river-mouth beach (Faneromini) reached by farm tracks to the north of the village, is a perfect example of the terrapin-filled reedy lagoon type. People bathe naked on the sandy beaches to the south of the village, says Timsway.

If travelling between western and northern Lesbos, in other words between Sigri/Eressos and Molivos, the main road makes two sides of a triangle via Kalloni. There is a road along the third side between Skalochori and Petra, about three-quarters of an hour's drive (for 16km), of which about half is extremely rough. The main-road route is about 35km, so the short cut is not much shorter in time, and may be much longer if, as is not unlikely, you get a puncture. However, this is not a consideration to deter amateurs of Greek rock and roll roads, of which this is a fine example. It also passes a long grey sand beach with tavernas at Anaxos.

A few miles south of Molivos, a wide bay with another long

grey sand beach is overlooked by a prominent 18th-century church on top of an isolated rock, from which the village of **Petra** no doubt takes its name. A few beautiful old houses and a more interesting church (Agios Nikolaos, with good 16th-century frescoes) are gathered around the foot of the rock, but there is not much else old about Petra, which has recently become a sizeable resort sprawl along the back of the beach, with tavernas, discos, car-hire firms and all the usual tourist amenities. The lack of a good beach at Molivos brings a number of day visitors.

Molivos (or Mithimna, its classical name) is the main resort on the island and an exceptionally beautiful one, a meticulously preserved and restored old village of timbered or pastel-painted mansions on the steep slopes leading up to a very imposing flag-flying fortress, originally Byzantine but subsequently often reinforced. There are fine views out over the island and Turkish coasts from the ramparts, and a stage inside is used for evening drama in summer. Drama is not the only cultural event at Molivos, home of the ancient poet Arion; there are also poetry and folklore symposia and a summer school for art students.

The streets are narrow, cobbled and car-free, and would be traffic-free but for the few local bravos who insist on taking their motor-bikes up and down. Some of the streets are completely vaulted by vines and flowering creepers, and occupied by an attractive variety of souvenir shops, craft shops and galleries. All Molivos lacks is a square. At the foot of the steep village is a small and very pretty fishing harbour surrounded by tavernas, and to the south of the harbour stretches a long but not at all inviting narrow stony beach, with old industrial buildings and new watersports operators along it. Some accommodation is available in rooms in the old village, but hotels are mostly quite a walk from the centre, near the beach, as are the discos. The *Arion* and *Delfinia* (B) are the biggest and smartest, but a long walk from the village centre. The *Seahorse* (B) is a smaller hotel by the harbour, a much more attractive location.

Apart from the local beach and that at Petra, bathers at Molivos have the chance to go to the sands and pebbles of **Eftalou**, about an hour's walk or a short rough drive along the coast to the east, with a few hotels. The largest and best located of these is the unappealingly named *Molivos* 2 (B), with a swimming-pool, a good modern hotel for those who do not mind the isolation, for there is no village. Molivos 1 is near the town beach and main watersports unit. There are several more small coves to the east of the end of the road, with some nudism.

Getting around

Daily excursions are arranged from Mytilini to Turkey (Ayvalic and Pergamon), and also from Molivos and Plomari. The trip includes shopping (carpets, leather) and very worthwhile archaeological sightseeing. The excursion needs to be booked several days ahead. There are coach-excursions from Mytilini (including Kalloni, Limonos, Petra, Molivos; Sigri, Eressos; Agiassos, Plomari). Similar coach-trips to the main sites are available from Molivos. Local boat-trips go from Molivos, Eressos, Plomari.

Car and motor-bike hire is available in Mytilini, Molivos and Plomari (which also has bicycle hire). Tour operators at Sigri and Eressos can also make arrangements for hire of transport. Big-engined motor-bikes (125cc) are available, at Molivos and Plomari anyway.

Buses from Mytilini go to all corners: Mytilini–Kalloni–Molivos about twice a day; other services to Plomari, Sigri, Agiassos, Polychnitos and Eressos. Like many big towns, Mytilini has two bus terminals, one for local and the other for long-distance buses. They are at the northern (local buses) and southern (long-distance buses) ends of the main ferry harbour water-front.

In the natural course of events, independent travellers will arrive at Mytilini and set about hiring a car. There is no shortage of hire firms competing for your business, widely spread around town but mostly near the harbour and near the Olympic Airways office, a long walk away to the south. The problem is not the shortage of cars in midsummer,

---

No road runs east along the coast from Eftalou, but a fine rough road high on the northern slopes of the island's highest, or perhaps joint-highest peak, Lepetimnos (968m), leads to Sikamia and, much more interestingly, to its fishing harbour hamlet, **Skala Sikamias**, a place of irresistible charm. The road runs simply down to the harbour, where it expires beneath the disproportionately tall planes and limes. The harbour is closed by a rock-set chapel on one side and a single taverna jutting out on the other, with tables on the quay. 'Hampouker pitza and tost' are proudly advertised, but fortunately fresh fish is usually also on the menu. The taverna's looks have been spoilt a bit since a second storey with a few tourist rooms has been added to the once tile-roofed building. Tiny cats prowl around playing in the nets, to the annoyance of the fishermen, and, when the catch is brought in, hop smartly aboard the boats. It does not take many people to overcrowd Skala Sikamias, and boat-trips come here by day, but it is enchantment itself in the evening and early morning, with as many people as it takes to fill the two small pensions and the harbour taverna's rooms. The

although this may well be a problem, nor the time and effort involved in doing the rounds and comparing prices, although this is undeniably tedious. The real problem is insurance. For some reason the car hirers of Mytilini see red at the merest mention of the idea of renting a car with comprehensive or even third-party insurance. One understands that the island is big, there are many very rough roads and cars are very expensive: Lesbos hire cars must take an almighty beating. But the refusal to offer comprehensive cover and small print in the conditions of hire to the effect that 'bad driving' invalidates third-party cover indicate the need for great caution.

The problem (which stems from the lack of international car hire agencies on the island, in which it is not alone) is not insurmountable. Some hire firms do offer insurance and, very reasonably, make a big marketing pitch out of it. When we did the rounds, one of the few hirers offering full insurance was Mr Drakoulas, next door to the Blue Sea Hotel near the ferry quay. If you are unable to find a satisfactory deal in Mytilini, catch the bus to one of the international resorts (Plomari or Molivos) and try there. Pressure from tour operators tends to mean that insurance is more widely available. Hiring a car through a tour operator in advance should mean that you are insured, although it would be wise to check up on this.

Much the best map of the island, in fact the best map of any Greek island known to us, is in the free Greek National Tourist Organisation handout leaflet No. 23, published November 1984. It distinguishes pretty accurately between degrees of awfulness of road surfaces and even has contour lines.

Pension Gorgona is comfortable, friendly and inexpensive. Swimming is possible, but there is no real beach. One Mirivilis wrote a novel about the chapel on the rocks, Our Lady the Mermaid (this is the name of both the chapel and the novel), one of the masterpieces of modern Greek fiction, so they say.

A rougher kind of coastal idyll is what is signposted as **Plaz Tsonia**, a shanty summer community on a wide bay below Klio, a few miles south of Sikamia. A rough road leads down from the hill village to a fertile coastal strip of cultivations and a long coarse sand beach with a bench, changing-huts, a shower that works and, among the corrugated tinpot houses and tents, a couple of tavernas and a little shop. There is another beach at Limani, on the southern side of the same wide bay.

The rest of the east coast between Sikamia and Mytilini is much less appealing than this, although the black sheep are good looking, as is the very rustic old grey hill village of **Mantamados**. The village is locally famous for the Taxiarchis church, with its miracle-working icon, made out of blood and clay by the Archangel Michael, the setting for a big pilgrimage

three weeks after Easter. A bull is slaughtered after the priest
has blessed it, and 'does not usually resist', says the local guide.
Handkerchiefs are dipped in the blood and used to draw crosses
on children's foreheads. One way and another, Mantamados
sounds a good place to avoid on the third Sunday after Easter.
(A similar bull-slaughtering festival takes place over three days
leading up to the last Sunday in May at Mytilini.)

South of Mantamados, the road joins the coast at
Aspropotamos, which has a long stony beach and habitations but
no obvious taverna. The road follows the shore for much of the
way to Mytilini, not a very interesting drive and with no
outstandingly attractive resorts or beaches, although the sea is
accessible and bathing possible in many places and there is a
thin scattering of accommodation and tavernas. One of the
prettiest places for a pause is **Skala Neon Kidonion**. The nearest
thing to a resort is Paralia Thermis, but it has no great charm,
in fact none at all. There are impressive ruins of a Roman
aqueduct at **Moria**.

LIMNOS

It is not often that we find ourselves in wholehearted agreement
with the promotional tourist literature, in Greece or anywhere
else, so let us celebrate by quoting Thomas Sfounis, author of
the panegyric on the back of the island map: 'Welcome to the
island of Hephaistos. It does not offer you an impressive view
with sudden changes. However, the softness of the hills in
beautiful shades of colours, gliding slowly into the sea, without
a big contrast, will surely give you the impression of calmness
and peace. The inhabitants of the island are simple and
hospitable.' Spot on.

If anything, this undersells the island, since there is a real
contrast between the landscape of the west coast around the
capital, Myrina, where jagged rocky peaks form miniature
ranges no less mountainous for being only modestly elevated,
and the rest of the island, which does indeed glide slowly into
the sea. The island is unusually fertile, unusual in that its
fertility does not consist of woods, rivers and vineyards, but
fields of golden corn and ploughing cattle. There are few trees,
but fertile vegetable- and fruit-farming country in the
south-east.

This rich earth may bring to mind some famous lines of
Rupert Brooke's, and fields scarlet with poppies in spring may
underline the same train of thought. Brooke himself is buried

on another not very distant Greek island (Skyros), but many of his fellows (mostly Anzacs) who died at Gallipoli in the same year, 1915, are commemorated in the war cemeteries of Limnos, near Moudros, where the hills glide almost imperceptibly into the inert waters of a vast inland sea. From this great natural harbour the doomed expedition was launched, and to it the survivors straggled back, bearing the dead. As if in tribute, the plains around Moudros Bay still support a large number of military installations. Outside the immediate neighbourhood of Myrina, most of the island is dominated by the army and air force.

In so far as Limnos is known at all, it has the reputation of being a flat and boring island. Tranquil it undoubtedly is, and boring it may be for those in search of the bright lights. But it is not flat and does not seem dull. It has its archaeology – a good museum and sites of great antiquity which will not take the breath away but have a subtle enchantment, not so much monuments as integral parts of the island landscape.

At the site of the ancient city of Hefestia, for example, you will arrive quite alone, probably after much trial and error exploring unsignposted cart tracks, to find neither fences nor ticket offices. A few rough farm buildings by the baked muddy shore are the home of numerous dogs and chickens and the woman who acts as custodian of the hill and whom you will find on her bed but resigned to being roused by your arrival and the animal clamour it provokes. She takes a swig from the water bottle, applies her sensible big straw hat and plods silently off up the hill along thistly and rarely trodden paths through the excavations, at first leading then falling behind and finally stopping. She offers no explanations, just points this way and that. Having seen you safely to the top of the hillock, she leaves you to it and carries her considerable bulk back down again to her day-bed. On your way out she will offer you a swig from her bottle, and this is the cue for the purse to open.

Enjoying places like Hefestia depends a lot on your mood, for there is not a great deal to see. The charm of **Myrina**, the island's port and capital, is more tangible. Myrina is one of the most satisfactory of Greek island towns. Its setting at the foot of a very impressive and beautifully floodlit fortified acropolis is splendid. The commercial life of the small town and the island's emporium is interesting and animated but not too noisy or at all industrial. Myrina is enviably blessed with sandy beaches that can even take the discomfort out of arriving by ferry at four in the morning, and it is uniquely varied among Greek resorts in the accommodation it has to offer – from one of the smartest Luxury-class bungalow hotels in Greece to a couple of fine examples of the peeling quayside fleapit. Apart from these, the general standard of accommodation is unusually high, as is its cost.

The harbour, on the southern side of the *kastro*-crowned rocky headland, is also everything you could wish for in a Greek port, except that the rocky acropolis hides the sunset. Next to the old port hotel (the peeling Limnos) are a pair of cafe terraces where old men take their ouzo and snacks looking out over the water. Fishing-boats are crammed in to the sharp end of the harbour, where a couple of excellent fish restaurants are stationed by the water's edge; the Glaros is a good place for lobster. The beach to the south of the harbour is sandy but less good than those to the north of the fort. Floodlit, the battlements of the *kastro* make a splendid sight, a crown of fire hovering in the night sky. By day, Mount Athos may be visible from the walls, 35 miles away to the west. Some of the masonry dates back to antiquity, but most is medieval and later.

From the harbourside cafes the town's single narrow shopping street winds its way north behind the acropolis and through the town a block back from the northern water-front, which has a good sandy beach and bars with loud music, the main nightspots apart from a couple of out-of-town discos. The succession of poky little shops along the main street is full of old-fashioned interest, with tailors and cobblers stitching busily away into the evening, at least four barbers, shops dispensing local honey from big tubs, and a slightly eccentric bookshop. There are various bars, restaurants and car/motor-bike hire shops along the street, but few tourist shops and no broad central square, which function the harbour fulfils. Two good hotels near the road junction half-way along the street, cheaper than the smart new hotels and more comfortable than the quayside ones, are the *Sevdali* and *Astron* (both c). For smarter accommodation, the new *Kastro* (B), well placed on the main town beach, is recommended but expensive. Near the Hotel Kastro is the town's interesting archaeological museum, its top floor devoted to the excavations at Poliochni on the east coast of the island, with very good background explanations in English (as there are at the site). The main street ends with an alarmingly bow-walled billiard-hall cafe.

At its northern end the central beach is interrupted by a smaller headland occupied by the army; north of this is a more suburban part of town, and yet more good sandy beach, with tavernas. In the well-kept residential area near this beach is the comfortable and very well-run *Aphrodite* (c), a peaceful place no more than 10 minutes' walk from the heart of Myrina. Its owner is a useful chap to get to know: clued up, helpful and speaking good English. Some of the accommodation consists of apartments.

In the sheltered northern corner of the bay of Myrina, spread across the stony slopes of Cape Petassos, lies the *Akti Myrina* (Luxury-category), one of the best and most expensive hotels in the Greek islands, a surprising place to find on so untouristy an island. Of its kind it is undeniably good: little rough stone bungalows of no great luxury but secluded among well-watered and colourful gardens. There are good sports facilities (tennis and a good swimming-pool), an excellent, if very small, safe and sheltered sandy beach, and a big buffet bar for lunch by the sea. The hotel has its own watersports facilities (including dinghy sailing), its own excursion-yacht (trips to Mount Athos, Samothrace and Thassos) and caiques to rent; it also organises donkey rambles and even offers a baby-listening service.

Many visitors no doubt find the Akti Myrina a good self-contained place for a holiday and feel no need to venture outside except on an organised outing. For the few that do, it is no more than an amble of about 20 minutes along the beach to town. For independent travellers used to the Greek cost of living its prices (£150 and more per night for a bungalow) may seem ridiculous, but they do not put off package holiday-makers, and the atmosphere is not that of an exclusive hideaway for the jet set. With over a hundred bungalows in not a very large area, it can seem quite crowed at times (lunchtime at the buffet, for example).

The watersports are not available to non-residents, which is a pity because there is no other windsurfing in Myrina (or anywhere else on Limnos – at least at the time of inspection). Akti Myrina's protectionism was plausibly blamed for this state of affairs: the nearby beach taverna would not find it difficult to undercut the high prices charged by the hotel, and alert hotel patrons would only have to paddle round the low wall separating the hotel's from the town's sections of beach.

There are even better beaches to the north and south of Myrina, of which the least visited is a long strip of sand and pebbles at **Agios Ioannis** to the north, in tranquil farming surroundings (the local farmer uses a wonderfully antique plough). A small taverna shelters beneath a sandstone outcrop interrupting the beach, and the water shelves gently with sand underfoot: excellent family bathing. Between Akti Myrina and Agios Ioannis the long beach of **Avlonas** has no facilities at all, but another luxury hotel is threatened. If this would be bad news for the Akti, it would be disaster for the flourishing colony of terrapins in the river that runs down to the beach.

The more popular and spectacular beaches are the sweeping

wide bays below **Thanos** and **Plati**, two small villages in the
south-west corner of the island where the road makes its way
around the hills below volcanic rocky peaks of a kind very
characteristic of western Limnos, a grand mountain landscape in
miniature. Both bays have huge expanses of rather hard sand, a
few tavernas and no shade. Plati beach is the nearer to Myrina,
a quite manageable walk from town past an army camp, and has
showers and rooms as well as Jimmy's and Gregory's very
cheerful rival tavernas. There is also a desolate and
unconvincing hotel colony, with accommodation in bamboo huts
behind the big restaurant, the Fantasia, a not wholly
inappropriate name: in high season the pool was unfilled and
the whole place dusty and unpatronised, a shabby caricature of
Akti Myrina, where a night would cost more than two weeks at
the Fantasia. Thanos bay is much emptier and has two separate
beaches, signposted in Greek from the southern edge of Thanos
village.

The road continues unsurfaced around the south coast
through the most beautiful of the island's landscapes, passing an
empty beach (Agios Paulos bay) before reaching the handsome
but somewhat lifeless old village of **Kondias**. A track leads down
through fertile farmland to a tiny fishing hamlet at **Diapori** near
the isthmus between the bays of Kondias and Moudros. There is
a cafe and a muddy, agricultural beach. The track continues
southwards through the fields towards the round hill of Fakos,
with fine views over both bays, but access to the shore is not
obvious. The main track leads back towards the airport along
Moudros bay, passing several thoroughly unappealing villages
and bathing places.

From near the airport a surfaced road leads over the hills to
the northern bay of Bournia via Varos, reaching the coast at
Kotsinas, once an important settlement but now little more than
a few houses by the weedy shore, with a loud rock-blasting
Pizza Pub mainly patronised by soldiers from the big camp at
Romanou. On the hill behind, looking out over the bay,
Repanidi has big stone storage jars in the ground, said to be as
much as 400 years old and, in a few cases, still used for storing
wine. They also store rubbish. The once-celebrated therapeutic
red Limnian earth, rich in silica, was dug up from these slopes
above Kotsinas: one barrowload a year, on 6 August, was all
that was permitted.

From the main village of the island's north-eastern arm,
Kontopoulis, a poorly signposted track leads north to the coastal
site of **Hefestia**, already evoked. The site is on a promontory on
the eastern side of Bournia bay, overlooking a lagoon and mud-
flats. From the foot of the hill, the woman in the house nearest

Getting around

Boat-trips round the island are advertised in Myrina, but operate by
special arrangement, not as a matter of course. The Hotel Akti Myrina
runs its own excursions for guests.

  Car and motor-bike hire is available in Myrina. Cars are hard to come
by at short notice in midsummer and, unless there has been a very recent
re-equipment of the fleet, the motor-bikes are mostly antique.

  Buses go from Myrina to most villages. The bus services are timed to
bring villagers to town rather than the reverse, and are of limited value
for visits to the archaeological sites or more distant beaches. The main
road from Myrina to Moudros is good, but most other roads are rough.
Loose gravel and sand present considerable hazards.

the mud-flat will point you in the right direction. For the
inexpert visitor, about the only easily identified part of the
ancient city is the theatre. Hefestia was inhabited as early as the
Minoan period and was the main city on the island until it
succumbed to Athenian power in 490BC. Long before, according
to Herodotus, the Limnians had massacred a large number of
Athenian women and half-breed children on the island and had
been punished with infertility of women and livestock.
Consulting the Delphic Oracle for a remedy, the islanders had
been obliged to promise to yield their island to Athens if the
Athenians could sail to Limnos in a day. This became possible
when Athens controlled land in northern Greece and a summer
meltemi filled the sails. Hefestia gave in when Miltiades arrived
to claim his prize, but the rival city of Myrina put up some
unsuccessful resistance.

  There is another archaeological site, **Kavirio**, on the northern
side of Hefestia's bay. The name suggests a cult similar to that
celebrated at Samothrace's more important sanctuary (see page
253), here with more emphasis on fertility than protection at
sea. The archaeologists learnt much about the mysterious cult
from Kavirio, but there is not much to see *in situ*. A cave near
the sanctuary is traditionally associated with Philoctetes, the
Greek archer who was abandoned on Limnos because of the
smell of his gangrenous leg, but recovered to play an important
part in the siege of Troy.

  Continuing to the northernmost village of Plaka is not
rewarding, but there are huge empty beaches on the east coast
to the north and south of Cape Keros. Keros bay, a long drive-
in beach of caked sand, is a popular place for windsurfing
campers in Dormobiles and is easily reached from Kontopouli.
Unusually, though the beach is signposted (and not in Greek)
there is no taverna: buy provisions in the village.

The island's second town is **Moudros**, on the eastern shore of its wide, shallow gulf. It is a thoroughly unattractive town of interest only for its First World War associations. The main war cemetery, very well kept, is beside the road that leads out of town eastwards towards Roussopouli and the south-east.

The rough road south (16km, with some very treacherous sandy sections) runs through peaceful farming country, and the southern village of **Skandali** does not lack rough charm. Skandali has a cafe but little else to offer the visitor, and the nearby beaches are not good. The main attraction of this part of the island is the site of **Poliochni**, on the coast near Kaminia, looking out over a long beach of caked, almost petrified, weed (not bad for bathing). The excavations have good explanatory notices in English. As they make clear, Poliochni dates from the fourth millennium BC, a town of oval huts built at least seven times, which developed into a fortified city, one of the most important and sophisticated defensive and urban settlements of its day. The culture was apparently shared by inhabitants on the Anatolian coast across the water before the establishment of Troy. Whether as a result of enemy attack or earthquake, Poliochni came to a sudden end in about 2000 BC, and skeletons were found in the ruins.

SAMOS

Well watered, green and fruitful, prominent in the history books and spared the worst excesses of mass tourism, Samos is the enviable island that has everything – rough old hill villages, a perfectly charming pleasure-port resort, big beach hotels, imposing ancient monuments, a busy big town, miles of sand, towering grey peaks and excellent wine, dry or sweet. Think of a style of Greek holiday that suits you, from beach lounging to mountain hiking, and Samos will provide it.

The main reason for disappointment lies in the extent to which Samos has cashed in its chips. It remains a lovely holiday island, but some of the rough edges of Greek life have been rubbed smooth, especially at Pythagorion, which now seems almost too pretty and well organised, more a leisure centre than a village. Not only that, but the visitor attracted to Samos by its glorious ancient history and the acclaim Herodotus gave its great monuments will find that the great sightseeing zone has to a large extent fallen prey to the bulldozer. The foundations of the largest of all Greek temples can be inspected – a single wobbly column still stands – and there are interesting ruins at

Pythagorion, the ancient city's port, but between the two, where once a sacred highway ran, flanked by 2000 statues, now lie the airport and a big new crop of stark holiday-camp hotel complexes. It is hard to conjure up a vision of the grand scene this vast bay must have presented 2500 years ago when, in the words of Professor John Barron, 'Samos led Greece in science and technology, in the visual arts, in poetry and music'.

The obvious parallel is with Rhodes, where nothing remains of the fabulously wealthy Hellenistic city. On Rhodes there is plenty else for sightseers to enjoy, but the bulldozers and hotel-builders have been much more active on Samos, and most people find that enjoying the island takes some gritting of teeth. Holiday-makers simply have to make what they can of Pythagorion and the ancient city and then move off to enjoy the hills and mountains and peaceful undeveloped coastline, of which there is plenty. A bit like Crete, Samos is a long island with a wild, mountainous and beautiful west end, and nearly all its visitors and natives are concentrated in the east. Crowd-shunners and hikers will set their sights on the wild west.

Established resorts are surprisingly few and accommodation is largely taken up by package operators. Nearly all the accommodation is at (or near) Pythagorion, at the smaller beach resort of Kokkari, and in the capital, Samos/Vathy, an unlikely package-holiday resort but a busy one. Independent travellers should expect to find the island's beds 100 per cent occupied in midsummer, and the main resorts full for a much longer season. Enthusiastic sleeping-baggers may not be deterred, but should know that Samos is not the ideal place for their kind of holiday. This is not an island in the mould of the smaller Cyclades, with pint-sized ports, and beaches a few yards from the ferry quay.

The big ferries use the island's two north-coast ports, Karlovasi and the capital, **Samos town** – indeed a town, and a large one, spreading itself around the hills at the head of a long, narrow bay in the east. The names of Samos and Vathy are often used indiscriminately to refer to the whole agglomeration, but they are in fact different places, Vathy the old town on the hillside and Samos the port, which is younger. As a whole, town and bay make a splendid sight from the sea.

The main water-front and town centre are on the eastern side of the bay. The water-front is a wide and suitably urban main prom by the ferry quay, with self-important-looking official buildings, canopied cafe terraces, palm trees on Pythagoras Square, tourist offices galore and a number of convenient modern hotels, of which the best are the *Xenia* and *Samos* (both B). The *Parthenon* (E) is equally well placed and cheap.

Immediately behind the water-front is a steeply pitched area of wide staircase streets, with a large number of pensions, some of them attractive and comfortable. This is probably the first district that independent travellers will look at for accommodation – unless they prefer to entrust themselves to the water-front agencies, not a bad tactic on Samos – but even here many of the establishments are block-booked; Samos room lessors are not in the habit of greeting ferries to pick up business. North of the harbour the town straggles along towards the end of the promontory closing the north-eastern side of the bay, with a lot of package-holiday accommodation and a meagre town beach, Gaggou (entrance charge). Some of the hotels are adequate, but this is not an appealing part of town.

On the slopes above the head of the bay, the old town of **Vathy** is well worth exploring, older and more picturesque the higher you go, with narrow vaulted alleys and timbered houses at the very top. At the foot of the road up to Vathy is a lively collection of shaded tavernas, with a good evening atmosphere, and not without some bright new package hotels.

A popular short excursion from town is to the unremarkable 18th/19th-century Zoodochos Pigi monastery near Mourtia on the east coast, a scruffy little seaside village with a taverna but poor bathing. The best thing about the excursion is the coastal scenery. For bathers, there are more attractive coves on the south-eastern tip of the island, where Greek and Turkish hills confront each other across a strait little more than a mile wide, the Mikale. Unsurprisingly, the Greek side of the strait has a big military presence. **Posidonion** is a very sheltered cove with tavernas but only averagely inviting bathing. A mile or so to the west, but not directly accessible by car from Posidonion, lies **Psili Ammos**, a much more popular cove with a good sandy beach, several tavernas and some watersports. A notice ominously warns pedalo pedallers not to stray more than 100 yards from the shore. The little beach is very crowded by day, but is a delightful place for a quiet early-evening beach stop (the beach empties when the excursion-boats return to Pythagorion at about 4.30).

Pythagorion, often still referred to by its traditional name of Tigani, is the island's main resort and sightseeing attraction, the ancient capital of the island at the time of Polykrates (late 6th century BC), to whose order were constructed a five-mile circuit of town walls, which were never breached; a 400-yard mole, on the foundation of which the modern harbour wall rests; an aqueduct including a half-mile tunnel and escape route through the mountain; and, five miles away on the far side of the bay, a great temple of Hera, which was never completed.

The heart of the modern resort is a beautiful cobbled harbour-front with whitewashed trees shading the cafe tables. The port is always busy with fishing-boats, excursion-caiques and expensive yachts, but onshore traffic is kept at bay and the atmosphere is leisured and comfortable. Pythagorion in summer lacks only the breath of everyday life: even at early evening drinks time the water-front *volta* mainly consists of tourists. The *Pythagoras* (c) is an ideal hotel, comfortable and modern and at the eastern end of the harbour-front, only a short walk from the small town beach. There are many other comfortable little hotels and pensions along the rather dull main street leading down to the harbour, and dotted around town. Most of them are block-booked, and it is probably worth checking with the water-front agencies in case they know of any rooms.

Pythagorion benefits from not having any big modern hotels to spoil the looks of the harbour area: these places have grown up to the west of the town, more or less well placed for access to the interminable coarse sand beach that extends westwards. The smartest and best of these out-of-town beach hotel complexes is the *Doryssa Bay* (A), not too far to walk to and from town. Watersports facilities on the beach are plentiful.

On the eastern outskirts of Pythagorion, beside the Samos town road, two new hotels, the *Glicoriza* and *Princessa* (both c but fairly expensive), have good views and their own small secluded strips of pebble beach. A track leads down to a taverna and rooms at Karbovolos, also stony and peaceful and only a short walk from the resort centre.

From the same road out of Pythagorion a turning signposted left leads to the aqueduct tunnel, known as the Eupalinus tunnel after its engineer, and the scanty outline of the city's theatre. A few times a week for a few hours, the imposing monumental gateway is opened to give access to a very narrow staircase and initially equally narrow tunnel, which subsequently broadens out to about eight feet by eight, the funnel at the entrance perhaps designed to complicate matters for intruders. There is talk of illuminating the tunnel, but ask locally whether you need to take a torch. One of the most impressive aspects of the engineering was the precision, to within a foot or two, with which the diggers from each end of the tunnel met. Clay ducts in the tunnel brought water from a spring near Mytilini on the northern side of the mountain. From near the tunnel entrance there are paths across the scratchy hillside to the sporadically impressive remains of Polykrates' city walls.

Minor sights to be seen in Pythagorion are a small archaeological museum and the ruined fortress on the western side of the harbour, built at the time of the War of

Independence when the rebels of Samos fought bitterly, but without success, for their freedom.

Much greater interest lies at the far (western) side of the bay: the **temple of Hera** and surrounding excavations, a very ancient and important sanctuary on the legendary site of Hera's birth near a grassy river mouth. This was a place of worship in the second millennium BC and a flourishing Mycenaean settlement, and appears to have had a wooden temple in the 13th century BC. Of the great temple undertaken by Polykrates, which at 110m by 55m and 23m high was larger even than the great temple of Olympian Zeus at Agrigento in Sicily, a single column remains precariously erect, a famous spindly trademark of the island. The remains show fairly clearly the scale and layout of the temple, with impressive pillar heads and column drums lying around. But it is not always easy to distinguish between Polykrates' temple and a slightly earlier one, the work of a certain Roikos (8th century BC), knocked down during a Persian siege; the two temples overlap. The site also has the ruins of a 5th-century early Christian basilica.

The nearby resort community of **Irion**, which takes its name from the great sanctuary, is a scruffy little place, stretched out along a stony shore, with a few tavernas and basic resort facilities including simple block hotels.

Heading west from Samos town, the first sizeable village is **Kokkari**, a very pretty old fishing village, no more than a few cramped rows of old houses, overhung with creepers and flowers, between the coast road and the sea. A little rocky promontory divides the huddled old part of the village, with houses by the water's edge and fishing-boats pulled up on the stony shore, and the more modern and windswept resort sector, where a stony beach stretches away for a few hundred yards to the west. Here, too, rooming buildings and hotels give direct access to the beach and, less attractively, road. On this north-facing coast there is no shortage of wind and waves, and there is something unusually serious about the windsurfing school on the beach – smart boards, rigs and harnesses and all-in prices for a week's instruction. Most of Kokkari's accommodation is in rooms, but there are also a few hotels, nearly all set beside the main road, which, being busy, is Kokkari's big drawback. The central core of tavernas and bars around the harbour, however, is one of the most pleasing places on the island. Kokkari is full of young people and has a more intimate, laid-back atmosphere than Pythagorion.

The coast and steeply rising wooded hillsides to the west of Kokkari is perhaps the loveliest of all Samos landscapes, with vineyards down to the sea and thick woodlands on the slopes above, where rivers run down from the summits of central Samos's elongated massif, Ambelos (1150m). Roads lead steeply up to a few leafy hill villages (Vourliotes, Manolates and Stavrinides are the most attractive, and have tavernas and rooms), and this is excellent hiking country, with paths up to the peaks from all these villages. Near Vourliotes, reached by signposted rough road, lies the island's oldest extant monastery, Vrondiani, founded in 1566.

After Kokkari, the next bend in the island's very dorsal-looking north coast is **Avlakia**, a sheltered and delightfully peaceful clutch of tavernas looking out over the water and eastwards towards the bay of Vathy and the distant lights of Samos town by night. Adam's fish restaurant is recommended, as is the simple hotel *Avlakia* (D). There is a thin strip of beach near the restaurant, but for real bathing it is best to head for the long stony beach to the west of the headland, not too far to walk.

Platanakia takes its name from the splendid growth of plane trees shading a number of rural tavernas, rather surprisingly set on and near the rural junction of coast and Manolates roads. These places (especially the Aidone restaurant, not far up the road towards Manolates) are well known for traditional taverna nightlife (live music and dancing) and do a roaring excursion trade. This is also an excellent place for a cool picnic, for the Manolates road follows a shadowy river gorge, known for its nightingales, which strike up for a pre-dawn chorus once the *bouzouki* has gone quiet.

Agios Konstantinos is something of a resort, but not an attractive one, with a dreary concrete water-front and indifferent bathing. There is a campsite and at least one welcoming hotel, the *Atlantis* (E), above the main road.

Karlovasi is the island's second port and town, once a busy centre of the tanning industry, now a singularly desolate place of run-down grand old villas and derelict industrial buildings strung out for a considerable distance along the shore, with poor bathing and a bare concrete water-front. The only animated part of the seaside zone of town is the western end around the harbour, with some cheerful tavernas and a pair of nicely complementary hotels – the simple old *Aktion* (D) and smart new *Samaina* (B). Karlovasi is made up of several areas, including two older hill villages looking down over the sea, and a modern town centre, with banks and post offices and the like, near the vast and ugly modern church. The hilltop chapels have good views, but Karlovasi as a whole gets a low score, redeemed only by the beaches not far to the west, its convenience as a ferry port for western Samos and as a hiking base.

From the port, the road continues west for a mile or so beneath increasingly steep wooded mountains, to good stony beaches at **Potami** – good by the standards of northern Samos, anyway. Potami is a popular rough-camping area and, given the discomfort of the stony beach, the presence of discos booming out over the waves well into the small hours may be more consoling than annoying.

Beyond Potami the road dwindles into a hiking trail along the magnificent gorge-slashed coastline, where the sandy bays of **Seitani** (Mikro and Megalo) nicely punctuate the beautiful 3½-hour walk to Drakei, the terminal point of the long road from Marathokampos around the western end of the island. These remote bays are said to have colonies of the shy and increasingly rare monk seal. Identifying the right track is not always obvious: Marc Dubin's *Greece on Foot* gives detailed guidance to this and other hikes in western Samos. The easiest ascent of **Mount Kerkis** (1437m), whose great bulk dominates western Samos, is from Kosmadei (600m), accessible by road (signposted from the Kastania road out of Karlovasi) or on foot from Potami. From Kosmadei it is about four hours to the top, 'moderately challenging . . . fairly clear trail', according to Marc Dubin. The local guidebook says: 'difficult and dangerous . . . local guide certainly required . . . narrow trails, gorges and dangerous crevices . . . up to two days' efforts to reach the top,' probably referring to the more precipitous ascent from the south (Votsalakia). A route also runs from Kallithea in the far west.

A good road climbs south across the island from Karlovasi to the Agios Theodori junction, for Marathokampos or the overland route to Samos and Pythagorion running to the south of the central mountainous ridge of Ambelos/Profitis Ilias. A few miles south of the junction (heading for Samos) a turning south leads down to Komeikos, with a ceramics workshop, and **Ormos Komeikon**, also known as Valos beach, a very peaceful place with shaded stony beach, taverna and rooms. There is a rough-road connection with Ormos Marathokampos via another beach at Velanidia. Continuing towards Samos, a turning from **Pirgos** leads to Pandrosos, base camp for the southern ascent of Profitis Ilias.

Driving across central Samos is never less than beautiful, if rarely spectacular or specifically interesting: fine green hill country, with interspersed woodland and mixed cultivation around the various quiet country villages. There is extensive fire damage around **Marathokampos**, one of the largest of the inland villages and the most beautifully set, commanding its vast bay. This is undoubtedly the best location on the island for those in search of good beaches and simple accommodation,

Getting around

Excursions to Turkey (Ephesus) are organised from Pythagorion, Samos and Kokkari (advance notice must be given); to Patmos from the same resorts plus Ormos Marathokampos; and to Fourni from Karlovasi and Ormos Marathokampos. Local boat-trips go from Pythagorion to Psili Ammos (east) and the south-coast islet of Samiopoula, which is also served by caiques from Ormos Marathokampos. Walking tours are organised from Kokkari.

Cars, jeeps, beach buggies and motor-bikes can be hired from Samos town, Pythagorion, Karlovasi and Kokkari. Car hire is also advertised by agencies at Ormos Marathokampos and Votsalakia, via one of the big towns.

Buses are based in Samos town and run frequently along the north coast to Karlovasi, sometimes terminating at Kokkari (or Tsamadou, a beach to the west of it.) There are also frequent services to Pythagorion; several daily to Ormos Marathokampos/Votsalakia, to Irion, to Psili Ammos (east); and twice a week to Drakei. All the main inland villages also have bus services.

either in the little port of **Ormos Marathokampos** or somewhere along the miles of beach extending to the west, where clusters of rooms and tavernas make mini-resort communities in one or two places.

Ormos is a very relaxing little local port, the one coastal resort with a more local than international flavour to its tourism. On a busy summer evening villagers come down from the hill in large numbers to eat and dance on the water-front, drowning the rock music issuing from the one smart modern pub. The *Kerkis Bay* (B) is a straightforward modern hotel on the front. Ormos has its own stony beach, but the best bathing is some distance to the west, the huge expanse of sand and pebble beach generally known as **Votsalakia**, which improves the further west you go. Votsalakia itself (about 5km from Ormos) is the main mini-resort: a couple of tavernas, some rooms to rent and one very well-kept small hotel, the *Votsalakia* (D), reasonably priced, peaceful and recommended. Vines and flowers veiling the architecture account for much of the hotel's charm and pull in assorted stingers on the wing: watch out and stock up with repellent.

Asphalt gives way to rough track soon after Votsalakia, and leads past a couple more splendid sandy beaches, Psili Ammos (the finest of all) and **Limnionas**, both with tavernas. Limnionas has rooms to rent and a surprising colony of smart-looking villas announced as the Samos Yacht Club. From this point the track climbs and charts a spectacularly beautiful course around the western tip of Samos, high above the sea and far below the towering grey cliffs of Kerkis, which are pitted with caves, at least one of which has a chapel with medieval frescoes inside.

Considering the remoteness of this part of the island it is surprising to find that the two villages of **Kallithea** and **Drakei** (the end of the road) are by no means run down and primitive but quite well-to-do little farming communities. Between the two villages an extremely rough track leads very steeply down to **Agios Isidoros**, a rocky cove with a small but energetic community of boat-builders. A few people camp on the nearby small stony beaches. Kallithea has rooms and Drakei has a couple of cafes at the entrance to the village. As usual in Greece, the enchantment is likely to be rudely punctured by cowboy films and rock music. From Drakei it is a couple of hours' hike down to the sands of Megalo Seitani, and from there about an hour and a half on to Potami and civilisation in the dreary form of Karlovasi.

THASSOS

Only three miles from the Thracian coast near the beautiful old town of Kavala, Thassos is out of the way for the purposes of most island travellers but, for anyone arriving in Greece by car from the north, it is very much in the foreground, the closest and most accessible of all Greek islands and a very convenient place for a holiday provided your itinerary does not include any other islands. This spells German as well as large numbers of Greek holiday-makers.

A beautiful if slightly monotonous round island of pine-covered, well-watered mountains, its sandy coastline fills up with campers and beach holiday-makers. A good road makes a simple 100km circuit of the island, never departing far from the shore, except where it cuts a corner in the north-east, giving a rare taste of the mountain scenery of the interior. There are a few moderately interesting old inland villages, but no roads cross the island and in practice most people stick to the coast. It is a peaceful and relaxing island which, not being fanned by the summer *meltemi*, often verges on the torpid. Fanned or not, forest fires have ravaged the island in the recent past, and a large area of south-eastern Thassos – much of the coast between Limenaria and Skala Potamia – is no longer green and welcoming but charred. Thassos still likes to promote itself as the nation's emerald isle. In looks and in holiday atmosphere it resembles Skiathos and neighbours more closely than it does the other islands described in this chapter. As in the evergreen Sporades, bugs are plentiful.

Not all the vegetation is pines. There is small-scale farming along much of the gentler west coast, and a typical image of its homespun charm includes a little white and orange tile-roofed house, with chickens and goats scratching around under the nut trees, trays of newly made pots and plates drying in the sun, and a little backyard beach at the bottom of the garden. Very different images would be carried back from hikes up into the mountains that tower over the east coast.

Holiday accommodation is widely spread around the coast, but there are only two resorts of any size. One is the island capital, Thassos town, not wholly attractive but an interesting place, with remains of the ancient city and fortifications scattered around the edge of town and wooded hills behind: sightseeing at Thassos combines historical interest with a beautiful hill walk. At the opposite end of the island, Limenaria is a more straightforward, cheerful beach resort which serves the purpose. The best beaches are in the north-east (Chrissi Ammoudia), a very popular camping place, with a few hotels and rooms.

Thassos is rich in minerals – marble and various ores – and, fires and many centuries of ship-building notwithstanding, wood. Recently it has joined the ranks of the world's oil producers, with Greece's only rig not far offshore. The discovery of oil in these waters lies behind much of the recent argument between Greece and Turkey over rights in the north Aegean. In antiquity the island was an important source of gold or, more likely, a safe and defensible base for gold-prospecting (which involved filtering streams with a fleece) on the mainland. As if its own resources of marble were not enough, Paros greedily colonised the island for a spell in the 7th century BC following instructions from the Delphic Oracle: 'Found a far-seen city in the island of mists,' Telesikles was told. An important and profitable trade developed between Thassos and Attica and many distant Mediterranean shores, and Thassian coins have been found far afield, a sure indicator of a thriving and well-managed economy. Herodotus records that at the beginning of the 5th century BC the budgetary situation was healthy enough for public handouts of the surplus to the poor.

In later centuries the island's history is not exceptional: shifting allegiances during the Persian and Peloponnesian Wars, destruction of the island's powerful fleet, considerable renewed prosperity and new building in the 4th century BC (and later under Rome), integration in the Macedonian empire and

economic decline in the Middle Ages, when the island
population took to the hills in flight from destructive raids.
Unlike many remote islands, Thassos was colonised by the
Turks, although the story has a less familiar twist – in 1813 the
island was presented to the Egyptian Mehmet Ali Pasha, a
native and resident of Kavala. Egyptian rule, initially liberal and
affectionately remembered by the island's historians but
increasingly exploitative under subsequent governors, lasted
until 1902, when Turkey resumed control. The island joined
Greece in 1912 and was occupied by Bulgarians for three years
from 1941.

Thassos town (or Limin, confusingly) faces the Thracian shore
at its nearest point and is the port for the island's most frequent
ferry link, the Keramoti shuttle. Ferries to and from Kavala
usually use Skala Prinos, 15km to the west of town. The ferry
harbour's wide water-front – a road – and surrounding small
modern town are not delightful, although the narrow lanes full
of tourist shops set back from the harbour are colourful and
busy, with plenty of local produce on sale (honey, nuts, walnut
jam, local pottery and woven items) as well as the usual mass-
produced clothes and junk. Small modern hotels confront the
incoming ferry and are perfectly convenient if a shade expensive
by Greek standards. The *Timoleon* and *Poseidon* (both B) are
the most comfortable, the *Akti Pension* (B) simpler and cheaper.
The *Alkyon* (C) is a good small hotel at the quieter traffic-free
western end of the harbour, the main cafe terrace idling zone
and the base for boat-trips to nearby beaches.

Much more appealing is the old harbour immediately to the
east – fishing-boats, a beautiful old customs house beside the
port, tall trees shading the waterside, and some traditional boat-
building. Thassos has grown up on the site of the thriving
ancient city, and this was its harbour, built of local marble.
Extensive excavated remains of the city lie around the
backstreets and gardens of the town, and the ancient *agora* is set
back not far from the old port, with the town museum beside it.
The museum has good statues and pottery, and a brooding hawk
in its garden.

From the rocky headland to the east of the old harbour, the
line of the ancient city walls climbs the wooded hills behind
town. Much restored, the walls remain substantially intact,
especially on the western side, where there are two impressive
gateways, one of which, the gate of Silenus, stands close to the
main road leading west from Thassos. It is a lovely, fairly steep
walk, and a long one if you make the complete circuit – about
two miles – from the sea up to a height of 450 feet and down
again. But abbreviations are possible, and it is not far up to the

splendidly sited theatre, which is used for productions in summer. The finest views, naturally enough, are from the top where a ruined medieval *kastro* stands on the site of the acropolis and temple of Apollo, with another temple (of Athena) a short distance to the west. Having seen Thassos town, you will have finished sightseeing on the island, apart from the monastery in the south.

The town has only a small beach, nicely shaded, to the east of the old harbour. Three kilometres to the east, the secluded *Makriammos* bungalow hotel (A) has a good small sandy beach of its own and charges non-residents an entry fee. Watersports and tennis are accessible to all. Boats run trips here from town, as they do to Glyfada and Papalimani, small pine-backed beaches near the coast road to the west of town, with tavernas and campers. Papalimani has windsurfing.

Continuing anti-clockwise around the island – probably preferable if you plan a complete circuit, saving the more beautiful eastern coast until last – the road south runs through pleasantly fertile but rather featureless farming country, with neither interesting villages nor lively resorts, just a scattering of peaceful, off-road coastal campsites and a few hotels (around Skala Rachoni, for example), with watersports operators and even a tennis club not hard to find. **Skala Prinou** is little more than a ferry-port service area, with accommodation, cars and motor-bikes for hire, basic shopping and camping. Beaches around Skala Sotiros and Skala Kallirachis are not very inviting stony strips of beach with uncomfortable rock underfoot, but the landscape is pleasantly rural, with lots of farm animals at large. **Skala Maries** is the first village that invites a pause, with tavernas on a small fishing harbour and small beaches on either side of the village. A much better sandy beach (Tripiti) lies a few miles further on, just past the cape about half-way between Skala Maries and Limenaria.

Limenaria, the only coastal village of any size after Thassos town, and the island's main beach resort, grew up at the beginning of this century as the headquarters of the German ore mining and exporting industry. This may sound fairly unappealing, but it does mean that the village is, if not highly picturesque, less ugly than the standard Greek beach resort of small concrete box houses. Traffic is a nuisance along the lively main street, the long beach is thin, and the small harbour does not constitute much of a focus, although there are taverna terraces by the sea. Bar and disco life is quite animated.

Many of Limenaria's visitors plod along the coast to broader and better beaches to the east. **Pefkari** has pine trees and golden sands – two very pretty small coves – and one of the island's

Getting around

Motor-bikes and cars can be hired at Thassos town, Skala Prinos and Limenaria. Motor-bike hire is more expensive than usual. There are short-haul boat-trips from Thassos town to nearby beaches (Makriammos, Chrissi Amoudia, Glyfada, Papalimani).

Buses go from Thassos town around the island three times a day. More frequent services run to Skala Prinos/Limenaria and to Panagia/Skala Potamia. Buses go less often (but at least once a day) to Theologos, Rachoni and Kallirachi.

biggest campsites. There is no village, but rooms to rent and a couple of small hotels. Nearby **Potos** is another busy little beach resort, smaller than Limenaria, but otherwise not very different, with a similar long thin town beach. Its pre-tourism role was that of harbour for the largest and most attractive of the inland villages of Thassos, **Theologos**, a 10km drive up a river valley into the hills. Theologos is a well-watered and leafy village, with fine rough grey houses, mostly with roofs of old stone, not the usual modern substitute of clay tiles. The village has a small folklore museum and a few shops specialising in local produce.

Continuing on the coastal circuit, the road passes a few good beaches before rounding Cape Salonikos, the southernmost tip of the island; Psili Ammos, any old Greek hand will tell you, means a good sandy beach and this one is no exception. But it is small, popular with rough campers and likely to be crowded in season. There is a taverna. To the west of the cape lies a wilder landscape of cliffs and extensively burnt slopes. The **Archangelos monastery** is finely (and conveniently, for those on the road) situated high above a narrow bay with an olive-backed pebble beach, also popular with campers. Although not outstandingly interesting, the monastery is typically picturesque, flower filled and immaculately kept. A new church is under construction.

Alyki is the prettiest place on the island, promotional poster material: a small wooded promontory with a few old rough stone houses on the narrow isthmus, which has small beaches back to back and a few boats moored. The houses are tavernas, and there is nowhere on the island more pleasant for a lazy bathe, lunch, snooze and bathe again.

The south-eastern half of the coast makes a well-composed landscape, largely thanks to the nearby islet of Kinira. **Kinira** is also the name of a roadside community on the mother island, a straggling assortment of accommodation and a few tavernas. There is no village atmosphere and only a thin strip of stony beach. This is said to have been the gold-mining area.

After a fine forest drive through beehive country, the road heads inland from the southern end of the wide and beautiful Potamias bay. Streams run down from the island's highest peaks to water the cultivations behind a very long beach, which extends the full length of the bay, sandy at both ends, pebbles in the middle. There is road access to both northern and southern ends of the bay, but neither road nor drivable track along the back of the beach, which adds to the delights of camping rough among the olive groves, as not a few do. At the southern end, **Skala Potamias** is a peaceful collection of tavernas with a couple of hotels and a wide patch of sand. The northern end of the bay (**Chrissi Amoudia**) has much broader and better sands but also many more people and gets very crowded in midsummer. As well as hotels and rooms, all of which are straightforward, modern and beach-convenient, there is at least one campsite behind the beach, and a watersports school. High above the bay stands **Panagia**, an old grey village which is no less handsome than Theologos but a bit of a thoroughfare. It has tourist shops, tavernas and simple accommodation. From higher still, in the main marble-quarrying area of the island, the road makes a splendid sweeping descent through the woods to Thassos town, a succession of broad bends that must delight the big-bike brigade, which is well represented on Thassos.

Information

Travelling to Greece
Going independently
Air

Scheduled flights are available direct to Athens, Salonika and Corfu. To other destinations **charter** flights are the only direct flights available. The difference between charter and scheduled flights isn't always clear: many airlines sell blocks of seats on their scheduled services to tour operators, so you can buy a charter-type ('inclusive tour') fare on a scheduled flight. Not all charter fares are cheaper than the cheapest scheduled fares (APEX and SUPER APEX), which require advance booking and carry penalties for cancellation.

The following airports are served by charter flights. All have services from Gatwick; major cities or resorts (Athens, Corfu, Crete, Rhodes, Salonika) have services from many UK provincial airports: Athens, Aktion (Preveza), Araxos (Patras), Chios, Corfu, Crete (Heraklion and Chania), Kalamata, Karpathos, Kavala, Cephalonia, Limnos, Lesbos, Mykonos, Paros, Rhodes, Samos, Salonika, Santorini, Skiathos, Zante (Zakynthos).

Charter tickets for special flights are sold by tour operators holding an Air Travel Organiser's Licence (ATOL). Tickets are usually available only for stays of at least a week and less than a month. Many travel agents use computers which show what flights there are and whether there's room.

According to the rules, you can book a charter fare only as part of a package holiday, i.e. both travel and accommodation. But some operators offer a voucher system which is used by holiday-makers interested only in the cheap flight; it's not necessary to stay in the accommodation provided, and there may be only a small charge for it. However, it's vital to get and retain the accommodation voucher issued by the tour operator or agent (stating the name and address of the hotel, villa, room or campsite) which you may need to produce. For some time the Greek authorities have looked on the voucher system as a formality, but in 1988 it was announced that more stringent controls would apply. Students travelling on special student group charter flights are exempted from the accommodation voucher regulations.

Most charter flights operate only from May to mid-October. Exceptions are Crete and Rhodes, which are available in winter sun programmes; early specials for Greek Easter in March or April, usually from Gatwick; and winter flights offered by specialist operators, such as Grecian, to Athens, Salonika, Crete and Rhodes (which get booked up quickly by Greeks returning home for Christmas).

Charter flight regulations require you to remain within Greece for the duration of your stay, except for day excursions to Turkey and other countries (except for the island of Kos, from which not even day excursions to Turkey are permitted). If you stay overnight, you may forfeit your right to use the return portion of your charter ticket, and be made to pay a full scheduled fare.

It's well worth going independently to Athens if you plan to stay in

Arriving at Athens airport

Athens airport is on the coast to the south of the capital near Glyfada, about 25 minutes' drive from the city centre when traffic is light. The airport has two terminals, referred to as West (or Olympic) and East Airports, linked only by road all the way around the airport, a good 15 minutes by bus or taxi. The West terminal, on the coast road, is used by Olympic Airways international and domestic flights, East by all other airlines and all charter flights. This is one good reason for flying Olympic Airways to Athens if you have a domestic flight to catch afterwards. Olympic disclaims all responsibility for unmade connections unless there is at least 90 minutes between scheduled arrival and departure of flights. Although all domestic flights are booked on a straightforward scheduled basis, they are not fully transferable.

Various **buses** link the two terminals and run between the airport, city centre and Piraeus: 18 to East Airport from Amalias Street, at the top corner of Syntagma; 133 to West Airport from Syntagma. The latter is a straightforward Athenian bus that happens to go past the West terminal, stopping on the main road outside. As you come out of the terminal on to the main road, Athens is to the right and there is a bus stop almost immediately. Olympic Airways buses (dark blue) go from the West terminal itself to Syntagma. These are at least as frequent as the 133, but take a less direct route and stop at a terminal between Athens and Piraeus.

Yellow express buses link the two terminals and Piraeus docks. Going from one terminal to the other via Piraeus is a very long way round, so check before you set off. At the East terminal, tickets for the yellow buses must be bought at the kiosk outside. Do not leave luggage on the bus, even momentarily, or it will leave without you. The yellow bus stop is at the 'domestic flights' end of the West terminal.

There are usually long and ill-disciplined queues for **taxis** at the West Airport. Lots of people cheat by walking over to the main road outside the airport and hailing a taxi there.

To get from the airport to Piraeus, do not go through the city centre, unless you have to stay overnight, for which Piraeus is not recommended. The coast road is usually quick and the taxi ride does not cost more than a few pounds. Insist on travelling by the meter.

Travelling via central Athens is inevitable for other ferry ports except

simple hotels or pensions, since the choice of this type of accommodation is much wider than that offered by tour operators and there are plenty of cheap flights. For Luxury, A- or B-category hotels (see below), packages can be cheaper. For small islands, you can also save money by booking a charter flight and arranging accommodation (in simple hotels or rooms) independently; and cheap inter-island ferries and flights encourage independent island-hopping holidays. It's also well worth going

---

Lavrio, the port for the island of Kea. From the West terminal, cross the road and catch the orange bus along the coast (left).

Overnight stops

The airport is in the middle of a resort area with lots of hotels, but they are not recommended (except by taxi drivers who work on commission with some of them), even for the briefest of overnight stays. Nor is Piraeus outstandingly salubrious, although there is some accommodation near the Metro station and a number of cheap hotels in the backstreets at the southern end of the main harbour, near the customs buildings. On one of the main streets (Vassilios Kostantinou) in walking range of the ferry port, the *Noufara* (B) is seedy-looking but reasonably comfortable.

It is much more amusing to spend a night in Athens, preferably somewhere in walking distance of the Plaka if you are in time for an evening out (see Athens chapter for recommended accommodation). Athenian hotel prices are naturally high by Greek standards. Even so, it is worth trading up rather than down: air-conditioning is well worth the extra expense in summer. There are hotel booking offices at the airports, but it is preferable to book in advance from the UK and warn if you are likely to be arriving in the middle of the night.

To get to Piraeus from central Athens, either take the Metro (Omonia and Monastiraki are the most central stations) or green bus 40 from Syntagma.

Killing time

One big problem is the lack of left-luggage facilities at the airport. (An expensive solution is to hire a car for the day, though there are no reductions if you want the car for less than a full day.) If you can overcome this problem, you could:

- go to the beach in easy walking distance of the West terminal (turn left)
- take a trip into Athens to see the Acropolis and/or Archaeological Museum
- visit Cape Sounion, about an hour by bus from the West terminal, with a beautiful temple and a good beach. It's worth finding out from the tourist police at the airport how to get back from Sounion before setting off
- hop to the island of Aegina. Take a yellow bus to Piraeus, from where there are hydrofoils about every hour to and from the attractive island capital. There are also lots of excursion-boats to the island, leaving Piraeus in the morning.

independently to Crete, if you plan to tour or stay away from popular resorts. On Corfu and Rhodes, your chances of finding accommodation independently in high season are very limited.

There's an extensive network of **internal air services**, operated by Olympic Airways; most are to and from Athens, a few connect with Salonika, Heraklion on Crete, Rhodes and Santorini. Internal flights get very booked up in high season and vital legs of a journey should be pre-reserved as far ahead as possible (which is not to say that there is not often last-minute availability). Flights are cheap, and with more inter-island flights every year, travellers should be aware of them as a possible alternative to long ferry, train or bus journeys. Flying in the little 15-seaters used for some of the island flights is a great adventure. Many islands without airports have Olympic Airways agents who can find out about and sell tickets for the nearest airport. Olympic buses link the airport and local town.

Rail

There is little to recommend travelling to Greece by rail – unless you are eligible for a student pass or have plenty of time. There is no through service from Britain to Greece and you have to get to Germany (Munich or Dortmund) or Italy (Venice) before you can get a direct train. In summer carriages are very packed, so it's best to book a couchette in advance. There are three routes: the Hellas Express goes from Dortmund via Salzburg, Belgrade and Salonika to Athens; the Acropolis Express from Munich to Athens; and the Venezia Express from Venice via Trieste and Belgrade to Salonika. The journey takes about 3½ days. The leg through Yugoslavia can be tedious; it may be easier to travel through France and Italy, then catch a ferry from Brindisi to Patras.

The second-class fare is far higher than that for a charter flight, so it's worth going by rail only if you're under 26 and can get a cheap Interail Pass (from British Rail or travel agents), or a Transalpino or Eurotrain ticket – slightly more expensive but valid for two months. Details from Transalpino, 71–75 Buckingham Palace Road, London SW1; tel 01-834 9656; USIT-Eurotrain, London Student Travel, 52 Grosvenor Gardens, London SW1; tel: 01-730 8111.

Car

Going to Greece by car or camper can be an adventurous mini-tour of Europe if you have plenty of time and a co-driver. It's nearly 2000 miles from London to Athens, about 40 hours at the wheel, and although people boast of getting there in record time, it would be safer and wiser to allow five or six days to allow for pit-stops, rests and sightseeing *en route*.

The fastest and most direct motorway is via Brussels, Frankfurt, Munich, Austria, Yugoslavia, Salonika, Athens, 3255km in all. Or you can let the ferries take the strain and go down through Italy and by sea via Ancona, Bari or Brindisi to the islands of Corfu or Cephalonia, Igoumenitsa in Epirus or Patras in the Peloponnese (10–12 hours).

Although car fares on the ferries are modest, passenger fares can be steep and the cost of two people travelling to Greece and back overland could exceed bargain charter flights. But it is cheaper than a fly-drive holiday and enables you to take cumbersome sports gear and other essentials if you are going for a long stay.

Fares vary according to type of passage you want and seasons. Low season in Italy runs from 13 March–22 July or 16 August–29 October; high season is 23 July–15 August. The small print in the ferry line adverts is full of reductions, so check before you sail. There are special student and youth fares, in some cases for up to 26-year-olds, others up to 30. Children under two go free, children two to twelve pay half fare. Discounts are available for Automobile Club members. All prices are quoted one-way. Most firms offer discounts on return journeys. Full car ferry details are available from the Greek National Tourist Organisation.

The Automobile Association (AA) and Royal Automobile Club (RAC) can give information on recommended routes to members. If you live in the north it's worth travelling via the Hook of Holland or Ostend to save the drive to Calais or the other Channel ports. Otherwise the main jumping-off points are Dunkirk and Calais. If you opt for the European mini-tour then the quickest route is Calais, Liège or Ostend, Munich, then either via Villach and Ljubljana to Zagreb or via Klagenfurt and Maribor to Zagreb. From there the route goes via Belgrade to the frontier at Gevgelija with Evzoni, Greece, 342 miles from Athens; this is the most boring and dangerous route. Part of the slog from Zagreb to Belgrade has thundering heavy lorries and has been dubbed 'the death road'. The road from Evzoni to Salonika is a free motorway; from Salonika to Athens there's a toll road with three pay stages.

Alternative routes are via Paris, Basel, Innsbruck, Ljubljana and Belgrade to Athens; or via the Italian Adriatic ports – Brindisi, Bari or Ancona. The main ferry lines from Italy are: Minoan Lines, Karageorgis Lines, Marlines, Strinzis Lines, from Ancona; Hellenic Mediterranean, Adriatica, Fragline, Nausimar, from Brindisi; Ventouris Ferries from Bari.

Cars, caravans, campers and motor-bikes are allowed entry into Greece with a current customs card, the 'Carnet de Passage en Douanes', available from the AA, RAC or touring club of country of origin. Your vehicle must be entered on your passport. You will also need to prove third-party insurance so a Green Card International Motor Insurance Certificate is advisable. Under EC regulations you are covered by your British insurance, extended to a member state. But this extended cover gives only the minimum required by the host country, which may be less than third-party insurance, so it is best to play safe and go for fully comprehensive cover. You don't need an international driving licence if you hold a UK or Eire licence.

It's worth taking your vehicle registration documents and handbook, plus essential spares.

Package holidays

More than 100 British tour operators offer package holidays to Greece from a wide range of UK airports. Olympic (tel: 01-359 3500), Grecian (tel: 01-444 3333) and Sunmed (tel: 0293-519151) are three big companies who specialise in Greece, offering a particularly wide choice of resorts and types of accommodation. Thomson, Intasun and Cosmos have separate Greek programmes with a wide choice of budget accommodation.

For out-of-the-way places, many small specialist companies offer a wider choice of resorts and accommodation than the large companies. Some specialise in certain areas of mainland Greece, such as the Pelion Peninsula or the Peloponnese; others concentrate on island groups such as the Ionian, or a single large island; and a few offer remote destinations or lesser-known resorts on otherwise busy package-resort islands such as Rhodes or Corfu.

The type of accommodation offered ranges from smart hotels in the more developed resorts to simple hotels or pensions, rooms and self-catering accommodation in villas or studios; occasionally more unusual places are offered, such as converted mansions, windmills, old traditional houses, olive mills and fishermen's cottages.

Specialist operators include Aegina, Amathus, Corfu à la Carte, Falcon, Greek Islands Club, Houses of Pelion, Kosmar, Lancaster, Laskarina, Leisure Villas, Martyn, Jenny May, Simply Crete, Solair, Sporades Holidays, Sunvil, Timsway and Twelve Islands.

Operators who specialise in individual villas include Beach Villas, CV Travel, Greek Island Club, Meon and Starvillas.

Special-interest holidays available range from flotilla sailing to birdwatching, walking and cultural tours.

A comprehensive guide to tour operators in the UK and Eire is available from the **Greek National Tourist Organisation**, 195–7 Regent Street, London W1R 8DL; tel: 01-734 5997. They can give details of companies that offer self-catering accommodation, island-hopping tours, special-interest holidays, and facilities for disabled people. **Greco-File** (tel: Halifax (0422) 310204 or 37599) is an advisory service which can suggest an independent or tailor-made package holiday on the mainland or islands, including special-interest and out-of-season holidays.

Travel in Greece

Boats and hydrofoils

Ferries lie at the heart of travel in insular Greece, although nowadays many island holiday-makers fly in and fly out again without ever discovering the pleasure of sailing to an island by steamer, the island's link with Athens and the outside world, bringer of mail, news, food and long-awaited family and friends. Most small islands show their best profile to the approaching sailor, and the arrival of the Piraeus ferry is the great event of the day. Usually, the hubbub follows a long period of vague anticipation in the port, with all eyes trained on the horizon, for the ferries often get seriously behind schedule. At last it rounds the headland with a bellow, just in case anyone was asleep on deck or anywhere within a five-mile radius, and the water-front scrambles. As the captain skilfully backs his vessel towards the quay, passengers scan the port, identifying the hotels and the tourist bars, the ouzeries where the old men go for their evening tipple, and the tavernas by the fishing harbour. Down below, all is turmoil, with revving trucks, bleating goats and a stampede of passengers all determined to be first off the boat.

Being at sea in the Aegean is many a sailor's idea of heaven. A ferry is not quite the same as your own yacht or a luxurious cruise liner (although some of the ferries have done service as cruise ships), but is still a thoroughly agreeable place on a summer's day. On deck you pick your spot and settle down to sunbathe, read and doze to the pulse of the ship's engines. Nameless empty islands glide silently past, shearwaters dip and bank effortlessly in the troughs of the wake, and dolphins follow at a greater distance, occasionally leaping out of the water to delight their audience.

The Athenian port of Piraeus is the nerve-centre of the ferry network. Other mainland ports include Igoumenitsa and Patras for the Ionian Islands; Salonika, Volos, Agios Konstantinos and Kymi for the Sporades; Kavala and Alexandropouli for Thassos and the North-East Aegean; Rafina for the Cyclades; Porto Heli, Monemvasia and Gythion in the Peloponnese for Kithira and the Peloponnese Islands. Paros has taken over from Syros as the main port of the Cyclades, and you can hop to more than a dozen ports from there.

Island hopping is simplest within a group of islands (Cyclades, Dodecanese); the most popular, and easiest in terms of ferry connections, is the Cyclades, where it is possible to visit half a dozen small islands in a fortnight without undue rush. Ferry connections between the Ionian islands are not straightforward: the smaller islands link with Corfu but not with each other. The Sporades and the Peloponnese Islands have good ferry and hydrofoil connections between each other, and from the mainland; but there are no easy connections with other groups of islands. In the north-east Aegean, distances between islands are long; as the islands are large and interesting, island-hopping is less of a feature than in the Cyclades. The Dodecanese, however, lend themselves well to the island-hopping treatment, with good connections with each other, and links with the Cyclades and with Crete.

In the island sections of this guide we have tried to give information about ferry services specific enough for itinerary planning, without attempting detailed timetables which are out of date before publication and thus positively unhelpful. If you intend something more complicated than hopping within an island group (going from the Cyclades to the North-East Aegean, for instance) it's best to have at least thought about route possibilities before leaving Britain if you don't want to waste lots of holiday time waiting on quaysides.

Contrary to many rumours, Greek ferries are not hopelessly unreliable and captains do not alter their schedules at the slightest whim. However, comprehensive information about ferry schedules is very difficult to obtain and the timing of ferry sailings is never better than very approximate. Usually, boats are late, but you can never count on that: sometimes they arrive early and, if so, certainly don't hang around. Most ferries operate on short cycles – out from Piraeus and back every day – and are usually more or less on time. A few follow long meandering itineraries, calling at scores of islands; these are the boats that get seriously behind schedule. The grandest circumnavigator of them all is the *Kyklades*, which takes six days over its journey from Piraeus to Rhodes to Kavala to Rhodes to Piraeus, via such outposts as Kastellorizo, Astypalaia,

Tilos and Lipsi. Make enquiries about when the *Kyklades* is due in, and people simply shrug. For a couple of years the *Kyklades* was laid up in Piraeus, not sailing at all. On the islands, no one noticed: the *Kyklades* is late, so what's new?

Information on ferry services supplied by the Greek National Tourist Organisation in London, or anywhere else, has improved a lot but is still very incomplete and often out of date by the time it arrives. Occasionally, services mentioned on published timetables do not exist, but a much more common problem is the existence of lots of services not mentioned in any of the timetables, especially in summer when short-haul seasonal ferry operators fill gaps in the networks of big ferries. In general, you get hard information about ferry sailings only at the port itself. Whenever you arrive on an island, check that the information you're relying on for the next stage of the journey is correct. Checking means asking at least two different people; more, if they don't give the same answer. Facts about ferries are an elusive commodity.

Ferry services are not state-run, and ticket selling is not centralised, although prices are controlled. Most ports have several points of sale, with different agents selling tickets for different boats.

Agents are notoriously economical with information about boats whose tickets they do not sell: it won't do to walk into a travel agency and ask a simple question like 'When is the next boat to Mykonos?' On busy islands all the ferry agents tend to be clustered in the same area near the port and to advertise their boats' sailings in the window, translated and transliterated into English. On more remote islands information may be less easy to find and read. Always check the advertised information verbally.

Many agencies style themselves as information centres or tourist offices, which by our understanding of the terms they are not. If you want information and not a ticket, they are unlikely to have much time for you. Ask an agent on Paros how you can get from Samos to Chios, for example, and he will tell you (if in a polite and helpful mood) to go to Samos and ask. This makes it very difficult to plan ahead.

When asking for information or buying tickets, remember that local people are much more aware of boats than destinations and that many ferries have island names. This can lead to enormous confusion, especially when, like the *Limnos*, they never go to their eponymous island. In other words, if you go into a travel agency and say 'Limnos para kalo (please)' the agent is quite likely to assume that you want a ticket for the *Limnos*'s next sailing, not that you want to go to Limnos. Knowing the name of the ferry you have to catch also helps reduce the risk of boarding the wrong one, which is easily done. Usually, tickets are not checked until after the boat has sailed, by which time it is too late.

Locals are often not a very good source of information, especially when it comes to inter-island services. Their own knowledge is likely to be confined to the services to and from Piraeus or other mainland ports; since they rarely have reason to visit other islands, they have not the least interest in where else the ferries go *en route*. (The notion that on any island you will always be told quite seriously that the neighbouring islanders are a bunch of lazy untrustworthy crooks is a cliché that the

Greeks cheerfully perpetuate). Schedules change at the beginning and end of high season (early July and mid-September as a flexible rule) and locals may not cotton on to this immediately; advertising notices may also take some time to be changed.

Ferry timetables tend to detail only the outward itineraries of ferries (from Piraeus, typically) and not the return leg of a journey, which is often by a different route. An exception to this is the helpful (although far from complete) but very hard to obtain monthly *Key Travel Guide*, available from 6 Kriezotou Street, Athens 134 or BAS Overseas Publications, 45 Sheen Lane, London SW14. Another useful guide is the *Greek Travel Pages*, a monthly guide in English printed in Athens (from which timetables supplied in Britain by the Greek National Tourist Organisation are taken). This has the most up-to-date information and contains advertisements from all the main shipping lines. You can obtain it at *periptero* kiosks or direct from 4 Voukourestiou Street near Syntagma Square in Athens, or from Timsway Holidays, Nightingales Corner, Little Chalfont, Buckinghamshire HP7 9QS; tel Little Chalfont (024 04) 5541.

Bear in mind that timetables often refer to the ports of call without naming the island at all, for the good reason that some islands, like Samos and Ikaria, have more than one ferry port; and the Greek rather than anglicised names will be used (for instance, for Lesbos you'll need to look for the name Mytilini, for Corfu, Kerkyra, and so on). Note also that the terms a.m. and p.m. are as likely to stand for the opposite to what we would expect, a confusion arising when the Greek-letter equivalents are transliterated (but not translated) into English.

The Port Police (*Limnario*) are the sole disinterested source of information about ferry comings and goings, but they often don't (or won't) speak English and are rarely well informed about sailings more than 24 hours ahead.

Ticket prices are controlled and do not vary from one agent to the next. Tickets are not transferable from one boat to another, even for the same journey. This is one good reason not to buy tickets far in advance if two or more boats are due to call within a few hours of each other, bound for the same destination. Wait until the first one arrives and buy a ticket for that; it may well turn out to be the one scheduled to arrive later. It is not essential, not even always cheaper, to buy a ticket before boarding, but this is the usual form and usually more convenient than waiting until you board.

Long-distance ferries have at least two classes of accommodation and may have as many as four. You won't be sold the most expensive ticket if you don't specify which class you want to travel, but probably the cheapest. In general, the cheapest class is quite good enough, but for an overnight journey or any journey on a very crowded boat it may well be worth paying extra for A or B-class. Supplements to convert tickets can be paid on board. B-class is often a bad compromise, since a blind eye may be turned to an overspill of overcrowded C- and Deck/Tourist-class passengers into the B-deck areas and lounges. If you want to travel in some comfort, go for A-class, and enjoy the sight of the crew members gleefully allowing all the other tourists to settle before inspecting tickets and booting them out. When you get used to Greek prices, A-class seems outrageously expensive, but it still compares well with the cost for an hour and a half's trip to cross the English Channel. In general ferry travel costs about £1 an hour. An A-class ticket usually costs about double that. As an incentive to tourists, ferry tickets to some of the more remote islands are free in October and May. Contact the Greek National Tourist Organisation for details of this scheme.

Long-distance ferries all have cabins, often in several classes. At busy times, demand for berths far outstrips supply; this is the main exception to the rule that you should not buy ferry tickets far in advance of sailing. Booking cabin space can be very complicated, with agents unsure of their allocation. Overbooking is a common problem, and firm action once on board may be required. Certainly, you should not wait until bedtime to lay claim to your berth. Quality of berths, air-conditioning and shower/lavatory arrangements vary greatly from boat to boat, but are not always awful; it is often possible to sneak into the A-class facilities for civilised ablutions. The cheapest cabins are mostly foursomes and sex-segregated, but couples can usually share A-class cabins.

Sleeping on deck sounds a lot more attractive than it usually is, by night anyway: even in summer it tends to be cold in the small hours, and in midsummer the decks are very crowded. As the night progresses more and more people give up and go inside in search of a table to sprawl over. In the lounges the crackling videos and the smoking go on all night and prone bodies litter the aisles. All in all, a cabin space is a very worthwhile investment, as is a flight that saves having to make an overnight ferry journey.

Some ferries have restaurants with tables and waiter service: often these are quite good and, on a crowded ferry, the only place you're likely to be able to sit down. Evening meals are served early. If you board after 9p.m. you have little chance of a meal. Bar food is very limited and relatively expensive: *tiropitta* (cheese pie), under-filled toasted sandwiches ('toast'), pizza, crisps, packaged cakes, biscuits. For a long journey, take some provisions of your own.

It is not the case that all ferries are full in July and August. If you return to the mainland on Friday night or Saturday, you will probably find the boat empty. As you would expect, the busiest time for ferries away from the mainland is the weekend at the beginning of August, and the end of the month for ferries back to the mainland.

There is a fuzzy distinction between the different sorts of boats ferrying tourists and travellers across Greek waters. As well as the big car ferries, mostly operating from Piraeus, there are local car ferries, passenger boats and small boats that run day-trips. Most of these services are strictly local and few feature in any timetable. The most important distinction is between the excursion-boat, which will not (or should not, anyway) sell one-way tickets, and small ferries which do. The small local ferries go to and fro on short journeys, sail at a civilised time of day and on time, since they have no long itineraries on which to get behind schedule. The only drawback is that, like excursion-boats, they may well not sail at all if there is not enough demand or in windy conditions. Some of these services fill obvious gaps in the chain of big-ferry services – between Paros and Sifnos, for example, or Patmos and Samos. Excursion-boats can sometimes provide useful links that do not otherwise exist, but prices are inevitably high and, if you want a one-way ticket for the return leg of one of these trips, you must ask very nicely and be prepared to pay well over the odds. Outside the three-month period from July to September, travellers have to rely on the basic big-ferry services. The old myth of asking around for a lift with a fisherman is not a practical proposition any more than renting a donkey from a peasant.

Island-hopping may sound romantic, but old ferries belching diesel oil, lavatories blocked with paper, decks awash with vomit and the only available refreshments stale and overpriced doughnuts can put a different slant on things. Don't attempt it if you are a bad sailor – being seasick is no joke, and some small caiques give you a very rough passage. Don't try to pack too much travel in or you'll have a constant rolling feeling until you get your sea legs, and by then it may be time to come home. The golden rule is to give yourself plenty of time to catch your flight home – as the whole ferry system is prey to the whim of the gods, it is perfectly possible to miss your plane, and single-flight tickets are expensive. It's worth noting that ferry companies will not be held liable for delays.

High-speed **hydrofoils** supplement the ferry services on a number of routes – along the coast of the Peloponnese, in the Sporades and in the Dodecanese. It is often said that hydrofoils get fully booked and, although we have not experienced this, it seems likely, as they have a strictly limited capacity and are very popular for weekend-retreat islands. It makes sense to buy tickets in advance if you cannot afford to be delayed, but this is not always possible as island agents are not told of their seat allocation very far in advance. As usual, seek out information as soon as you arrive.

Hydrofoils are dreadfully stuffy, but the small area of outdoor seating at the back is not necessarily ideal. Not only are the benches hard; the ride can be very wet and windy, once the beast gets into its stride. People usually last 10 minutes or so before giving up and going inside.

Hydrofoils come and go very quickly and do not hang around at the quay. Do not assume that, as with a ferry, you can wait around in a cafe or on the beach, pack up your things and stroll along when the craft comes into view. Hydrofoils are usually more or less on time, if they sail at all: anything more than a force five wind is likely to confine them to port, which explains why they stick to the relatively sheltered island groups. Hydrofoils travel about twice as fast as ferries, and tickets are about twice as expensive. All the inter-island ferry hydrofoils are called Flying Dolphins.

Bus

Buses are an interesting way of getting round. There's a vast network nationwide, run by a private syndicate of companies known as KTEL. Buses are cheap, generally run on time and will take you anywhere that four wheels can venture.

Some drivers own their buses and give them special personal touches – family snapshots, dangling worry beads, icons of saints, and loud music. Local buses are usually packed to the gills but still pick up passengers between stops (long-distance buses are not supposed to stop *en route*). Main routes have air-conditioned buses which are usually faster than trains. On the islands and in rural areas the bus is not just a conveyance but a village lifeline purveying newspapers, packages and bread from towns to outlying areas. Buses do the school run, often linking with small ferries, and on market day they buzz as they become mobile Women's Institutes or meeting-places. You may have to share the vehicle with baskets of produce and wall-to-wall grannies in black, plus baby.

Local buses have conductors. On long-distance services you either get a ticket beforehand or pay as you enter. Athens and other cities have driver-only buses to the suburbs and you put the exact fare, 30 drachmas, in the ticket machine or honesty box.

In the big cities there are usually different bus stations for different destinations. The Greek National Tourist Organisation has details of bus services and timetables.

Information on details of provincial and international buses is also given in the *Greek Travel Pages*, available from Timsway Holidays, Nightingales Corner, Little Chalfont, Buckinghamshire; tel: Little Chalfont (024 04) 5541.

Train

The only advantage of letting the train take the strain is that it's even cheaper than the bus. The rail service (OSE) is limited, and much is on single track; trains are slow (about $7\frac{1}{2}$ hours from Athens to Salonika), and long-distance buses preferable.

Athens has its version of the Underground, a Metro line which runs from Piraeus to the suburb of Kifissia.

Car hire

There are several ways of hiring a car. Some tour operators and major airlines offer fly-drive deals which include a flight and a hire car for either one or two weeks. These deals are usually cheaper than if you were to do it yourself by organising your flight and then adding on the cost of the car hire. If you're going on a package holiday, it may be possible to hire a car through the tour operator, some of whom negotiate deals with car-hire companies (either a major international outfit or a local firm) in advance; the rates they quote in the package-holiday brochures may well be lower than the amount you would pay if you booked direct through the same car-hire company when you arrive in your resort, and cheaper even than a 'special deal' (see below).

If you don't go on a package, you will need to book direct with a car-hire company. If you want to be absolutely certain of getting a car at a certain place and time, you will do best to book in this country before you go. Some of the international car-hire companies offer special-price deals if you meet certain conditions – such as booking seven days in advance, and renting for a minimum period (three or seven days); these deals are generally cheaper than a straightforward rental done on the spot, and rates quoted are inclusive of insurance, local taxes and unlimited mileage (see below). But these inclusive rates mean that with some companies you don't have the option of declining insurance cover (see below).

If you are going on a touring holiday, it is generally better to hire a car from a company with several offices in the area – either an international company or a large local company. If your car breaks down, or you have an accident, it's best if there's an office nearby to come to your rescue. Large companies usually offer the facility of being able to pick up a car at one office and (usually for a charge) dropping it off at another.

Car rental in Greece is expensive; and quoted prices do not generally include extras such as insurance and local tax; your final bill could come to as much as 50 per cent more than you were first quoted. The main advantage of hiring a car from a small local firm is that of cost (an international company might charge as much as 35 per cent more on its 'standard rate') but the cost could work out the same or less if you get one of their 'special deals'. Don't assume, however, that if you hire from one of the big five rather than from a small local company you'll get better conditions of hire, or even a more roadworthy car.

When you hire a car, you will automatically get some form of minimum insurance cover. In fact, this may be very little cover indeed – either the type of cover or the amount you're insured for. Minimum insurance in Europe covers public liability – similar to the third party, fire and theft cover that we have in the UK.

If a car is involved in a collision, the car-hire company will take responsibility for damage to the hire car except for a specified amount (which varies) which you have to pay – called the 'excess' or 'deductible collision' charge. If you want to avoid paying this excess, which can be as much as several hundred pounds, you need to pay a daily or weekly Collision Damage Waiver (CDW) charge. Some small local companies don't offer this insurance.

The major companies and many large local firms offer personal accident insurance as an extra. It pays out if you or any of your party lose your sight, lose a limb or are killed while in the car. Some policies cover limited medical expenses: the amount you're insured for will usually be shown in a separate leaflet. The cost can add 15 per cent to the hire charge. However, a standard holiday insurance policy taken out at home will cover you for most things that personal accident insurance covers, and more besides (though some don't include death and disability). And the cover for medical expenses is almost always substantially higher than that offered by car-hire companies. Most credit cards used to pay for car hire give you automatic free accident insurance with higher cover (£25,000 to £50,000); you get even higher cover when you use a charge card (Amex, Diners) or a gold card.

The insurance cover offered by small car-hire companies varies a great deal. Beware of the term 'full insurance' – it usually means that you have cover for collision damage only, and even then you might still be liable for a small excess amount. What you may not be covered for are all the things that are normally included in personal accident insurance – which you may not be able to buy at all. And you may find yourself liable for extra costs – such as reimbursing the car-hire company for days of business lost as a result of the car being out of action after an accident (up to as much as 15 or 20 days).

Exclusion clauses crop up in the policies of both the large international companies and small local firms. You may find that your policy states that you will be held liable for all damage to the underside of the car caused by driving on non asphalt-coated roads, and for any damage to tyres, however caused.

Most car-hire companies state that the insurance may be invalidated under certain conditions – for instance, if you drink and drive, if you fail to lock the car and remove the keys when it is left unattended, and if you don't abide by *all* the conditions of hire. It is vital to read the small print of the contract before you hire a car: you will be bound by all the conditions even if you don't read them.

Car-hire contracts are complex legal documents, which can be unfairly loaded against you. Almost all will contain exclusion clauses which the company uses to deny liability for a wide range of things – from loss of or damage to your luggage, to loss or injury arising out of the use of the car, mechanical breakdown of the car, or damage caused when driving on non-asphalted roads. Your contract (and your insurance) may be invalidated if you break the law, or if you are guilty of 'misconduct' – such as driving under the influence of alcohol, even if the amount you have drunk is under the legal limit, or of 'fatigue' – or simply because you have failed to abide by all the conditions of hire. Some of these conditions are sensible: for instance, almost all companies say that you should not drive under the influence of hallucinatory drugs. But other conditions may not be as sensible; for instance, some contracts state that you are not allowed to use the car on non-asphalted roads. If you have an accident on such a road, your insurance would be invalid. Cars hired on islands are rarely allowed off the island.

When you sign a car-hire contract abroad, it is subject to foreign law. Your agreement is with a local company – or a subsidiary company, a licensee, or a franchise – even if that company has the same name as the UK one from which you thought you were hiring. No matter where you booked the car, or the fact that the contract looks much the same as it would have done in England, if there's a dispute between you and the car-hire company it will need to be settled in a Greek court. This will almost inevitably be a difficult and lengthy business.

On some islands it is possible to hire Suzuki SJ410 four-wheel drive jeeps. Tests carried out by *Which?* concluded that these were dangerously prone to rolling over. Other hazards of hire cars generally include poor-quality vehicles: dodgy brakes, malfunctioning lights and ropy tyres are commonplace. It's important to check that there's a spare tyre; Greek roads are perfect for causing punctures. Go slowly on rough roads, and be careful when you park on rough ground.

Motor-bike hire

The hired motor-bike plays almost as big a part in the Greek holiday scene as the taverna. Now all but the most remote islands have their backyard rent-a-moto operators with their motley fleet of Hondas, Vespas and Piaggis offering the irresistible promise of wind rushing through the hair, staying cool as you tan and the freedom to make your way to the most distant and undiscovered coves, all for £5 a day. Nobody bothers with a helmet and no questions are asked, provided you pay in advance, leave your passport at the desk and demonstrate the ability to pilot the bike for a few yards along the water-front without falling off.

The dangers are huge. Driving abroad demands great care and skills that have to be learned, as does riding motor-bikes, even Honda 50s. Often, the skills required are those of moto-cross. Good roads may suddenly deteriorate or present stretches of treacherous soft sand or loose gravel. Signposting in rural areas is often non-existent. Narrow winding roads may be little used, but the few users are mostly lorries and buses. Every year tourists are killed and thousands injured.

Most tour operators in their briefing booklets for clients take the safe line of strongly advising people against hiring motor-bikes. This lays them open to no criticism, except that it is totally unrealistic. Having done a large amount of research for this book on hired motor-bikes, we are bound to admit that a motor-bike is the ideal vehicle for exploring small islands in summer. Motor-bikes are very cheap, they take you places where even a four-wheel drive car won't, and they are great fun.

There are some simple rules which it is sensible to observe: never drink and drive, not even one beer. Never be in a hurry. Never take a good road surface for granted. Perhaps most important of all, do not choose Greece for your initiation into motor-cycling. If you, or your carefree and confident offspring, are likely to want or be tempted to rent a motor-bike on holiday, make sure the basic skills are mastered in advance.

Little single-seater automatic scooters with handlebar brakes (Piaggi, typically) are attractive to those who have no experience of riding and fine for short-range commuting between resort and beach, but are often incapable of conquering a moderate Greek hill. Simsons look like real motor-bikes but are weak on hills.

Vespas often have spare tyres, but their twist-grip gearing gives more problems on old bikes than the relatively simple Honda pedal gears. Honda 50s new and old, and their lookalikes (Yamaha, Suzuki), are comfortable, reliable and get up hills (eventually) even two-up; but the different gearing system on otherwise similar new and old Hondas is a hazard: changing into first instead of neutral can easily cause an accident. For some reason, large numbers of Greek Hondas seem to have been diverted from the British market, and have speedometers denominated in mph.

Bigger-engined motor-bikes are increasingly widely available on large islands. Thank goodness, the law is stricter than for small bikes and you will probably be required to show a licence as well as a brief demonstration of competence. The big bikes are also much more expensive, more difficult to ride and, because faster, more dangerous to all but experienced bikers.

Good firms give you the bike full of petrol and tell you to return it that way, but plenty of operators prefer to add to their profits by making sure all their machines go out empty, knowing that most will be returned half full. This is a fair indication of an operator with a generally unhelpful attitude, which is much more significant than the cost of a few drops of petrol. Before you set off, find out where petrol is available (garages nearly always stay open throughout the afternoon) and how to operate the machine's reserve tank, if it has one. Vespas need 'mix' (a mixture of oil and petrol), not petrol straight from the pump, and are relatively thirsty.

Plenty of Greeks bike around without sunglasses, but the number of insects on the wing makes this very hazardous. For the same reason, keep your mouth shut. A bag slung around your neck and resting on your lap increases the risk of a bee or similar becoming lodged somewhere intimate with very painful results. For some complicated aerodynamic reason, hats stay on better with the brim turned up.

You may reasonably be entirely confident in your ability to handle a small motor-bike of the kind widely available in Greece. The Greeks have ways of punishing such hubris: dogs, insects, gaping potholes, advancing buses, snakes on the road, or a topless sunbather can all result in a sudden instinctive braking or swerving manoeuvre, followed by a spill.

Some motor-bike accidents are extremely serious. The majority, however, consist of very unpleasant cuts and grazes which can ruin a holiday and which could be avoided by wearing more clothes. You might not think that a pair of jeans or a shirt could offer much protection in a fall, but they can. If you do suffer minor cuts, go to the nearest hospital or local doctor to be cleaned up and jabbed as soon as possible. Bathing in the Med is not a cleansing experience.

Insurance is rarely available for motor-bike hire, despite assurances to the contrary from travel agents. Even if third-party cover is included, the most important section relating to medical expenses and emergency repatriation will certainly not be. Generally you will be liable for any damage to the bike, including punctures, and will have to pay if the operator has to come out to rescue you. Obviously, there is rich potential for argument about responsibility for breakdown. If you are likely to hire a motor-bike or a moped, it is vital to take out a full holiday insurance policy (see Holiday insurance, page 674) which does not specifically exclude riding hired motor-bikes, as some policies do.

Taxis

Taxis are cheap. Licensed taxi drivers must abide by tariff regulations, and there is a fixed rate of charges and surcharges. Most meters have different rates for travel in and out of town – it may cost twice as much outside the city limits. There are surcharges for journeys from airports, bus and railway stations, and harbours, and travel late at night (after 1a.m.) or between 5a.m. and 6a.m. In some places, particularly on small islands, there are standard charges for standard journeys, and these may be advertised for tourists' convenience.

Off-meter travel can be negotiated: you and the taxi driver come to an agreement in advance on the rate to be charged for a particular journey. The general practice is to negotiate a rate for long journeys and go by the meter for city travel. But, unless you are experienced, the safest policy is to ask the taxi driver to use the meter, especially if, as is likely, you need the taxi and are in no position to haggle: it is thoroughly galling to watch the meter clock up a far smaller sum than you have already agreed to pay.

In Greece it is common practice to share a taxi cab with other passengers. At taxi ranks in Athens, there may be a self-styled attendant in charge, checking on people's destinations and doubling up passengers; in other places, other passengers may be added *en route*. The amount charged will depend, according to a mysterious and infinitely flexible formula, on how many others the taxi driver has managed to pick up on the way. For trips of a few kilometres, the consequences of being overcharged are not serious. If you strike too good a deal, the taxi driver will kerb-crawl for every roadside pedestrian, which gets extremely tiresome.

At certain times of the day it's almost impossible to find a taxi. They are scarce in the early afternoon when shops and offices close and people go home for late lunch and siesta; and in the early evening, when everyone is going back to work, shopping or out on the town. At these times there are giant queues at taxi ranks. You can try off-rank: hail the cab in the usual way and yell your destination at the driver. This might mean a scramble with other passengers, but if you show British politeness you'll be there for hours. Radio cabs are available in some cities, and a hotel can arrange a taxi in advance (there'll be an extra charge). On small islands, don't rely on being able to find the driver under the tree where he seems to spend most of every day asleep: book him in advance or he will have set off for the airport without you, five minutes before you came looking.

In big cities, particularly Athens, beware taxi touts. If you have no joy hailing a yellow cab, you might be approached by a private hire cab: these will not have a meter and you might be charged an outrageous price. Unlicensed cabs are prevalent in Piraeus, where they prey on unwary tourists getting off the ferries; it's wise to stick to taxis with meters to avoid being ripped off. Beware also helpful cabbies at Athens airport who offer accommodation: this may turn out to be in Glyfada rather than Athens, and will probably not be where you want to end up. According to our experience, a woman travelling alone should take the precaution of seeking a taxi herself rather than taking up an offer from a taxi driver. As a rule, do not imagine that every cabbie will try to rip you off; most Greek people are strictly honest and do not regard tourists as fair game.

Riding in taxis is not always relaxing. Athenian cabbies tend to drive aggressively and, if possible, very fast, while the proud owners of island taxis cruise sedately around, apparently oblivious to the possibility that there may be other road users. They drive on whichever side of the road has fewest potholes (blind corners are no exception), jabber away on the intercom to convey vital gossip, shopping lists and abuse from villagers who flag them down, and endlessly fiddle with their radio dials in the vain hope of being able to pick up some music. The dashboard and mirror will be smothered in family photographs, worry beads, icons and evil-eye charms. Smoking is prohibited in taxis, but the driver is more than likely to have a cigarette in his mouth. Some cabbies are great conversationalists and have an excellent command of English; others are taciturn or speak not a word of any foreign language. Do not assume that an Athens cabbie has any knowledge of the city: always carry a map so you can show him where to go, and, once he's driving, do the navigating yourself.

Accommodation

Hotels

Greek hotels are officially graded from E-category up to A and L (Luxury), and where possible we give in each area chapter the grade of the hotels we mention. Grades are not a reliable guide to standards, and depend on factors such as the size of the bedrooms, width of corridors, number of public rooms and bathrooms and the kind of building materials used. Minimum prices are set in each category except Luxury, and hotels are obliged to display rates on cards behind bedroom doors.

Prices may not include extras. Charges to watch out for include local taxes; a 10 per cent surcharge for stays of fewer than three nights (likely only in L-, A- or B-class in big resorts which specialise in package tours); heating or air-conditioning charges; 20 per cent high-season surcharge; municipal extras at festival times; and 6 per cent VAT. On the plus side, larger hotels may give up to 40 per cent discount out of season – it's worth asking for this.

In Athens and places such as Corfu, Crete and Rhodes, the range of accommodation includes stylish, comfortable hotels; elsewhere, simple standards prevail. Hotels in the C-, D- and E-categories are usually perfectly adequate family-run concerns, often with neat rooms even in the humblest pension. Although D- and E-class hotels are not required to have private bathrooms, many have very good ones. Some C-, D- and E-class hotels have their own restaurants, but in general they are places for bed and breakfast only. Inns (*pandokia*) offer similar budget accommodation, officially below E-class but often better. Pensions or boarding-houses, and tavernas or cafes with rooms are also classified, with controlled prices.

Resort 'beach hotels', generally used by tour operators, may be some distance from the nearest town or village, and are usually large, modern, low-rise buildings with extensive gardens, swimming-pool and lots of sports and entertainment facilities. Although many are well equipped and reasonably comfortable, there is little variety of architecture or character, and the most comfortable hotels are usually large and impersonal. Even in the top-grade hotels, bedrooms are usually simple and sparsely furnished; showers are more common than baths; and hot water and plumbing may be unreliable.

Children are welcomed anywhere and at any time. But only a few big hotels offer babysitting or daytime entertainment, and we have found several hotel play areas with old or even dangerous equipment. A serious safety problem in Greece is the fact that almost all hotels have three-sided lifts – that is, they lack a solid internal door, and have no barrier at all between the occupants of the lift-car and the 'moving wall' of the lift shaft. A recent investigation carried out by *Holiday Which?* pointed out that a gap of only half an inch or an inch between lift-car and shaft could be sufficient to trap a child's limb. It is vital to take great care over supervising children in hotel lifts.

Top-grade hotels offer full and half board, or B&B. In high season, some of the more expensive hotels insist you take half board. Some tavernas offer breakfast and may expect you to eat there at night. Breakfasts, except in the most expensive hotels, are usually very dull, and 'international-style' lunches and dinners are often little better. In a recent survey of package-holiday hotels in Greece, *Holiday Which?* encountered good food in only seven out of twenty hotels. Greek food seldom appears in hotel restaurants except in weekly gala dinners or barbecues. One hotel manager in Rhodes told us: 'People ask for Greek food – but when they try it, they say it's too heavy. Then they go back to their fish and chips.'

Part of the early modern tourist development of Greece was the building of government-run hotels, known as Xenias (from the Greek word for stranger, to whom Greeks were told by Zeus to be hospitable at all times), in some of the outstandingly attractive locations in the country. A generation later, most of these establishments look decidedly drab, with a typical pattern of neglectful and apathetic management and an optimistic official grading of comfort. Typical examples are at Koukounaries (Skiathos), Skyros, Chania (Crete), Paleokastritsa (Corfu), Spetses and Karpathos. However, many of the Xenias have now been semi-privatised and in some cases smartened up.

Rooms

Rooms to let (*dhomatia*) are widely available in Greece, and particularly prevalent on islands. They are graded from A to C categories. Old women, housewives and children meet incoming boats with offers of accommodation which can range from a room in the family house to purpose-built studios, parts of fine old villas, a room attached to a taverna, or Granny's spare bedroom. Following your would-be landlady up long staircases through the labyrinthine backstreets of town to who-knows-where is all part of the independent travelling lottery. If you don't like the accommodation when you finally see it, it may be too late to find anything else. Out of season, it is probably preferable to look around by yourself and select the most attractive location before knocking on doors (rooms to rent are usually advertised) but, at a busy time of year, this may be to sacrifice your only chance of finding a bed. You aren't obliged to take the first room you see, and haggling is acceptable. Obviously, in remote places where little English is spoken, it helps to have some basic Greek.

A few islands have a clearing-house system for accommodation in private rooms – typically, an office at the harbour – but not many. In many small resorts the best clearing-house is the local shopkeeper or taverna owner who will scratch his head and make a few phone calls, or simply bellow across the road to his sister, who may have a spare room or know someone who has. If someone offers to try to help, they are unlikely to give up until you have been seen right.

Travel agencies, typically sited near the port, may style themselves as accommodation agencies or information bureaux and have contacts with some room owners, but should not be relied on to give a true picture of bed availability. On a few islands (Spetses, for example), nearly all the accommodation is handled by the travel agencies, and allocated *en bloc* to tour operators. This does not mean that there are never rooms vacant, but it does mean that there is not much turnover during the week.

There can be no generalisation about the relative merits of rooms versus hotels or pensions. In all categories there is good, bad and squalid;

overpriced and outstandingly good value. Room owners may or may not live on the premises, be friendly, and decorate the rooms with more than the standard chair, bed and white walls bare but for the stains of squashed mosquitoes. Breakfast is almost never available in private rooming establishments, but some have fridges and, occasionally, cooking facilities. Prices vary enormously according to the facilities offered, the size of the room and the season. In low season it is well worth negotiating, especially if you plan to stay more than a day or two. Rooms in D- and E-class hotels may well be as cheap as accommodation in private rooms and, conversely, facilities in village rooms may well be just as good as in C- or even B-class hotels. Rooms in big hotels mainly used by package tourists tend to be very expensive if taken by the night, and half board is often compulsory. On some islands, it can happen that the police do not allow rooms to be rented in low-season months in order to protect the local hotel business. These are usually a better bet anyhow in winter, as village rooms generally have no heating.

It's not usually possible to book a room in advance unless you have personal contacts. 'Rooms to Let' signs are displayed in English and German, or in Greek – ENOIKIAZONTAI ΔΩMATIA. Prices vary throughout the season and go up in August, the Greek holiday time, when rooms are very scarce. Around 15 August, the Festival of the Assumption of the Virgin Mary, Greeks worldwide flock to their home islands, and you'll generally be lucky to find a mattress. Greeks are naturally hospitable, and staying in a room in a private house can be a bonus. While the room may be simple and facilities shared, extras might include home-baked bread, perhaps an egg from the hen, fresh figs from the tree, or the chance to join in local celebrations as a guest rather than a tourist.

Self-catering

There's quite a range of self-catering properties to choose from – simple apartments in resorts, modest villas, and a few quite luxurious places, including well-restored older buildings such as converted windmills or fishermen's cottages. Apartments are often in quite small buildings and don't have communal facilities such as a swimming-pool, bar or reception desk. Cooking facilities are often quite limited, and cheaper places might have shared facilities with a communal fridge and kitchen; but tavernas are so cheap that there is little incentive to cook for yourself. It's probably worth taking an electric travel kettle, as it's unlikely that you'll be supplied with a kettle in simple places – Greeks tend to boil water in saucepans.

Filling a modest villa with a party of four to eight people may be cheaper than taking a budget apartment for two. Relatively few villas are on large-scale complexes, or have pools; most are plain, modern concrete buildings. The more expensive ones can be quite isolated, making car hire essential. Villas are generally available through tour operators, who can organise car hire and maid service. Operators who specialise in self-catering holidays include Beach Villas, CV Travel, Greek Island Club, Meon and Starvillas.

Monasteries

Rooms, rather than cells, are available in Greek monasteries and convents, although overuse in the hippie 1970s has made some loath to open their doors as much as they did in the past. Act and dress respectfully and you should be welcome. Accommodation is generally very basic – just a camp-bed and a communal wc. There is no set charge, although you are expected to pay a donation. Those in charge usually speak English and can advise. Women travelling alone may get a frosty reception; but some big monasteries or places of pilgrimage – such as Panormitis on the island of Symi – have holiday homes in the grounds, and allow women to stay in the cloisters (the doors tend to be locked early, though). Mount Athos is banned to women, and accommodation needs to be booked in advance (see Visiting Macedonia and Thrace, page 234, for details of the admittance procedure).

Traditional settlements

In a bid to preserve the national heritage, the National Tourist Organisation of Greece has embarked on a programme of restoring ethnic village houses in certain parts of the country. The idea of the Traditional Settlements project is to conserve beautiful old rural buildings for Greeks themselves to enjoy, but tourists are also welcome to stay.

Some houses are available to rent; others are lived in and offer accommodation. At present there are settlements (*paradosiakos Ikismos*) at: Papingo and Zagorochoria, Epirus (for reservations the local telephone number is 0653-41088); Areopolis and Vathia, Mani, Peloponnese (tel: 0733-51233 and 0733-54225); Makrinitsa, Mount Pelion (tel: 0421-99250); Vizitsa, Mount Pelion (tel: 0423-86373); Mesta, Chios (tel: 0271-76619); Fiskardo, Cephalonia (tel: 0674-51398); Psaras, near Lesbos (tel: 0251-27908); and Ia, Santorini (tel: 0286-71234). You can book direct, or through the Greek National Tourist Organisation.

In the North-East Aegean, you can stay in rooms at Petra, Lesbos, or on Chios, under the first Women's Agricultural Tourist Co-operative Scheme in Greece. The women have their own taverna and offer traditional village hospitality. Details are available from the Greek National Tourist Organisation or tel: Blackpool (0253) 41238.

Camping

There are hundreds of Greek National Tourist Organisation and Greek Touring Club licensed campsites throughout the mainland and islands, often in attractive situations. Facilities range from basic pitches with few services in ramshackle compounds to sites with bungalows, huts, fishing and sports facilities; most, however, are relatively simple. A full list of sites with details of size and amenities is available from the NTOG. The monthly English-language guide *Greek Travel Pages*, available from *periptero* kiosks (or from Timsway Holidays, Nightingales Corner, Little Chalfont, Buckinghamshire HP7 9QS; tel: Little Chalfont (024 04) 5541) also lists campsites.

Charges vary from high to low season and according to the services available; in general, costs are relatively low.

American-style camper-vans can be hired in Athens from Camper Caravans, 4 Nikis Street; tel: 3230-552.

Camping outside official campsites is illegal. In 1977, after hippies and backpackers littered and fouled the beaches on Ios and Crete, 'freelance' or 'rough' camping was outlawed. But for many travellers camping in Greece still means pitching tent or simply unrolling a sleeping bag on a quiet beach or tucked away in an olive grove. The law may be enforced, particularly if it is thought that campers are causing a nuisance (or if there's any danger of a forest fire, easily sparked off by the negligent). In practice, many places (especially small islands) get so crowded in high season that there is simply no alternative to sleeping rough, and in practice rough campers are widely tolerated at this time of year. Out of season, however, you are quite likely to be moved on, if the local hotels and rooms are unfilled. The sight of tents pitched precisely beneath the No Camping signs is a very common one in Greece, and reflects the unsurprising fact that the authorities put their signs in those places most favoured by campers. The official attitude may well vary from one beach to another; and references in our descriptions to the presence of campers should not be taken to indicate that camping in these places is officially permitted.

From May to September it is warm enough to sleep under the stars without a tent. But a lightweight waterproof sleeping-bag is a must as nights can be damp and cool. Beware of camping near standing water – the mosquitoes it attracts can be torture. Also beware of ants and the odd snake.

Motoring

Greek road death statistics are much the worst in Europe, for three main reasons: cars that are not roadworthy, roads that are not carworthy, and dangerous drivers. On many islands, quite a few of the last category are tourists.

Although there has been a vast improvement in the road network during the last 10 years, roads vary considerably and the condition of secondary roads can range from reasonable to diabolical. Roads may be unsurfaced, narrow and tortuous, severely potholed or little more than a goat track. Local maps, particularly on small or remote islands, may be absurdly optimistic as to what constitutes a navigable road. Not surprisingly, punctures are common.

Driving regulations Seat belts must be worn. Children under 10 may not travel in the front of a car. Crash helmets must be worn by motor-bike riders and passengers (in practice, this regulation is largely ignored). All cars must carry a warning triangle, first-aid kit and a fire extinguisher. It is forbidden to carry petrol in cans in vehicles. Traffic coming from the right has priority at crossroads outside cities, and on roundabouts. Drinking and driving is illegal, and an offence carries up to six months in prison plus a fine; 50mg of alcohol in the blood is over the limit (it's 80mg in the UK).

Petrol Greece has two grades of petrol (*venzini*): Apli, 91–92 octane, and Super, 96–98 octane. Unleaded petrol (*amolivthi venzini*) is available from some petrol stations. Few stations will accept credit cards.

Motorways There are two motorways, both toll roads: linking Athens to Patras, and Athens to Salonika.

Speed limits Unless there are signs to the contrary, the speed limit for built-up areas is 50kph (31mph); outside built-up areas it's 80kph (49mph), and on motorways 100kph (62mph).

Parking Parking in cities can be very difficult, particularly at night. In Athens, you cannot park in the Green Zone except at a parking meter. Infringements may result in confiscation of the car's number plates, and a subsequent heavy fine. Garages may charge high rates.

Parking within 5m from an intersection, within 15m of a bus-stop or level-crossing, or within 3m of a fire hydrant is forbidden, as is parking on a road with a continuous white line unless it is a dual carriageway.

Accidents and breakdowns

The Automobile and Touring Club of Greece (ELPA) provides a free 24-hour assistance and light repair service. Dial 104 if you are within 60km of Athens, Salonika, Patras, Lamia or Larissa; or telephone the Tourist Police on 171, who can give information about other towns with ELPA facilities. ELPA also give tourist motoring information on 174. Their head office is at 2 Messogion Street, Athens (tel: 779–1615); and they have branches throughout the country and on Crete and Corfu.

In case of an accident involving injury to people or property, the police must be informed (dial 100 in most big cities, or consult local telephone directory; the Tourist Police can be contacted on 171).

For repairs, it's best to seek a garage listed as an authorised service agent for your make of car; your UK dealer should be able to provide you with a list. In its *Travellers' Guide to Europe*, the AA lists only around 10 recommended garages throughout the country: in Athens, Salonika, Kavala and on Lesbos. Some Greek garages charge high prices for repairing tourists' cars; others may display more enthusiasm than skill.

Useful words and phrases

Petrol	*venzini*	Brakes	*frena*	Exhaust	*exatmissi*
Tyres	*lastiha*	Battery	*bataria*	Lights	*fota*
Water	*nero*				

Fill it up	*Yemiste to*
I would like . . . litres of petrol	*The ithela . . . litra venzini*
Give me . . . drachmes worth	*Valte mou venzini . . . drahmon*
Can you check the . . .?	*Borite na kittaxete to . . .?*
My car won't start	*To aftokinito den xekinai*
I have had a puncture	*Emina apo lastiho*

Navigating and maps

Local maps are unreliable and, to make matters much worse, signposting is almost always inconsistent and often non-existent. Sometimes the maps fail to reflect recent road building (although most of the maps on sale are announced as a New Edition), but often the maps quite simply contain large elements of fantasy and wild inaccuracy. Most are too vague to be used for hiking.

Some individual island maps are on sale in Britain, but there is no great advantage in buying them here, as they are likely to be cheaper and are always widely available locally. An exception is the series of maps produced by Clyde Surveys of Maidenhead (tel: 0628 21371) whose output covers the Peloponnese, Peloponnese Islands and a few of the Cyclades; Crete; Corfu and the Ionian Islands; Samos, Rhodes and some of the Dodecanese. The Clyde Surveys maps are attractive, precise and far more informative than mere roadmaps, but by no means infallible; for many of the smaller islands local maps may be more useful, however amateurish they look by comparison. Freytag & Berndt maps (published in Greece by Efstathiadis) do much the same job and cover more of the islands, except the Ionians. On a recent visit to Crete we found lots of discrepancies between the Clyde Surveys map, the similar-scaled and more recent Freytag & Berndt map and a free handout map provided by Budget Rent-A-Car. None was consistently better than the others and often the handout came closest to the truth. Among local maps of individual islands, our experience has been to avoid the Welcome series: the maps cannot be recommended and the guidebooks that go with them are not good value for money.

When driving around, good signposts can go a long way to make up for a bad map. But in Greece good signs are the exception, not the rule, once you leave the main roads. In many rural islands and mainland areas, villages are not even identified when you reach them, let alone signposted along the way. In other places, a sign announces the next village as soon as you leave the one before, even if it is 10 miles down the road. Often villages have two different names, and maps may use a third.

Island maps in general tend to fudge the distinction between tracks strictly for donkeys and hikers, and rough roads practicable by car or motor-bike; and between a couple of houses and what we understand by a village. Some map problems may arise in translation: until recently the local map on Mykonos used one colour for roads 'of motorway standard', another for 'provincial highways'. After a lot of trial and error, we deduced that by 'motorway standard' they meant seriously rough and bumpy, but just about drivable. The provincial highways were admirable.

New road building continues apace in Greece, and in our travels we have found countless roads where all maps showed none. Unfortunately it is not safe to assume that new roads in good condition (tarmac or unsurfaced) lead somewhere worth visiting: more often than not they lead only to quarries, telecommunications stations (never pursue a road signposted to OTE) and military camps.

Road signs

International road symbols are used throughout the country, but some
signs are written in Greek. The following is a list of the most commonly
found:

ΑΔΙΕΞ ΟΔΟΣ	No through road
ΑΛΤ	Stop
ΑΝΩΜΑΑΙΑ ΟΔΟΣΤΡΩΜΑΤΟΣ	Bad road surface
ΑΠΑΓΟΡΕΥΕΤΑΙ Η ΑΝΑΜΟΝΗ	No waiting
ΑΠΑΓΟΡΕΥΕΤΑΙ Η ΕΙΣΟΔΟΣ	No entry
ΑΠΑΓΟΡΕΥΕΤΑΙ Η ΣΤΑΘΜΕΥΣΙΣ	No parking
ΑΠΑΓΟΡΕΥΕΤΑΙ ΤΟ ΠΡΟΣΠΕΡΑΣΜΑ	No overtaking
ΔΙΑΒΑΣΙΣ ΠΕΖΩΝ	Pedestrian crossing
ΕΛΑΤΤΩΣΑΤΕ ΤΑΧΥΤΗΤΑΝ	Reduce speed
ΕΠΙΚΙΝΔΥΝΟΣ ΚΑΤΩΦΕΡΕΙΑ	Dangerous incline
ΕΡΓΑ ΕΠΙ ΤΗΣ ΟΔΟΥ	Roadworks in progress
ΚΙΝΔΥΝΟΣ	Caution
ΚΥΚΛΟΦΟΡΙΑ ΕΠΙ ΜΙΑΣ ΛΩΡΙΔΟΣ	Merge
ΜΟΝΟΔΡΟΜΟΣ	One-way traffic
ΟΛΙΣΘΗΡΟΝ ΟΔΟΣΤΡΩΜΑ	Slippery road surface
ΠΑΡΑΚΑΜΠΤΗΡΙΟΣ	Diversion (detour)
ΠΟΡΕΙΑ ΥΠΟΧΡΕΩΤΙΚΗ ΔΕΞΙΑ	Keep right
ΠΡΟΣΟΧΗ ΠΕΖΟΙ	Caution pedestrians
ΠΡΟΣΟΧΗ ΠΟΔΗΛΑΤΑΙ	Caution cyclists
ΣΤΑΣΙΣ ΛΕΩΦΟΡΕΙΟΥ	Bus stop
ΤΕΛΟΣ ΑΠΗΓΟΡΕΥΜΕΝΗΣ ΖΩΝΗΣ	End of no-overtaking zone

It helps to have some knowledge of Greek letters, as signposts will
appear in Greek script, with a Latin version some 50m further on. The
spelling on signposts of main towns and cities will generally correspond to
those that appear on maps produced by the Greek National Tourist
Organisation.

Medical matters

In a survey of over 2000 travellers who returned from a holiday
abroad, 48 per cent of those who had been to Greece had been ill – four
out of five with vomiting and diarrhoea (see below). More seriously,
perhaps, in a similar survey of *Holiday Which?* members,
dissatisfaction with conditions in Greek hospitals was more acute than
in any other European country. The Department of Health warns that
'People seeking treatment under the Greek Social Insurance Scheme
[the Greek NHS] often have long waits for attention both in local offices
and surgeries/hospitals. Hospital wards are likely to be crowded and
may not give all the services usually found in other community

countries' – i.e. nursing may be poor, and you generally have to provide your own food and laundry services.

Greece, like other countries of the European Community, has a reciprocal health agreement with the UK, which means that you are entitled (subject to certain procedures) to treatment under the Greek National Health scheme, i.e. free treatment from a doctor registered with the Social Insurance Foundation (IKA), and a charge of 20 per cent for prescriptions. To obtain this entitlement, you need to contact the DSS in advance, and obtain a form E111 (by completing form CM1 at the back of leaflet SA30). When in Greece, you will need to find a local office (*upokotastinata*) or branch (*parioutimalta*) of the IKÀ, to show them your E111; they will direct you to a doctor or dentist registered with the scheme.

In practice, if you are in a remote part of Greece or on a small island there will be no IKA office. You will have to pay for private treatment, and then apply to the nearest IKA office before leaving Greece, submitting all receipted bills and any other documents; your refund will not be more than 50 per cent.

Even for an area covered by the Greek National Health scheme, the DSS states that 'private medical treatment is strongly recommended'.

Our advice to holiday-makers to Greece is to take out adequate private holiday insurance to cover every eventuality. You may prefer, or in fact need, specialist treatment back at home, and may need to be flown back quickly, either on a scheduled flight (where you may have to occupy several seats) or by air ambulance, so make sure that repatriation is covered, and that it applies to accompanying members of the family. Make sure that there are no exclusion clauses relating to the hire of a motor-bike or scooter if there is any chance of your using one, or to activities such as water-skiing; you may need to get a full policy statement – the summaries given in package-holiday brochures don't always make it clear what is or isn't excluded.

The following are some of the medical problems generally encountered by holiday-makers:

Stomach upsets

Though 'traveller's tummy' can be caused by an infection caused by contaminated food or water in places where standards of hygiene or sanitation are low (and cholera, typhoid and infectious hepatitis are not unknown in Mediterranean areas), in Mediterranean countries it may simply be as a result of oil used in cooking, and of increased consumption of wine. Current medical opinion is that you should avoid taking drugs to cure diarrhoea and vomiting. But if you're not prepared to take things easy for a couple of days while your system copes with the problem, try kaolin mixture or tablets (available without a prescription). Diarrhoea and vomiting cause dehydration: it's very important to replace lost water by drinking a lot of (non-alcoholic) fluids. You lose body salts too: to help this you can buy ready-mixed oral rehydration salts in sachets from a chemist here; or you can make your own mixture from one *level* teaspoon of salt and eight teaspoons of sugar added to one litre of drinking water. If diarrhoea or vomiting persists, or is accompanied by severe pain, bleeding or fever, get medical attention.

Diarrhoea and vomiting must be taken much more seriously in children because they can become dehydrated very quickly. Do not administer your own drugs as some will not be at all suitable. Dehydration is more serious than with adults; but increased salt intake may be inadvisable. If symptoms last for more than a day, seek medical advice. In the meantime, try to give the child as much fluid as possible – small amounts several times an hour are probably best. With babies or toddlers it's best to seek proper advice as soon as any trouble starts.

Brucellosis, an infection spread by unpasteurised milk, is fairly common around the Mediterranean.

The following precautions are advised:

- food should be well cooked and not poorly re-heated, or kept tepid, or left out where flies can get at it. Be wary of buffets or similar meals where food is left without refrigeration
- avoid raw or lightly cooked shellfish
- all uncooked fruit (and cucumbers and tomatoes) should be peeled
- drinking water (also ice-cubes and the water you use for cleaning your teeth) may not be safe, except perhaps to locals. If in doubt, boil it, use sterilisation tablets, or buy bottled water
- don't eat salads unless you're sure the ingredients have been washed in water which is safe to drink
- never drink unboiled milk unless you're sure it's pasteurised or sterilised
- ice-cream may be risky; to be on the safe side, buy only wrapped proprietary brands, however tempting the unwrapped local varieties seem.

Heat and sun problems

In hot conditions you sweat more to maintain your body temperature, but if you don't replace the fluid and salts lost you could suffer from heat exhaustion. Symptoms include giddiness, tiredness, headaches and vomiting; without treatment heatstroke could develop, which can be extremely serious. While everyone can suffer, certain people are more susceptible than others – the elderly and the very young, and those who are overweight or suffer from heart problems. It is especially important for children to be protected from heat and sun – dehydration and salt deprivation can occur very quickly.

For heat exhaustion, stay out of the heat and drink plenty of lightly salted liquid. If there's no improvement in a day, get medical attention.

It's easy to get sunburnt. The effects of sun don't appear immediately and you can be burnt even when there's a haze or it's slightly cloudy (ultra-violet rays can pass through cloud). Remember, too, that water reflects the rays, promoting even faster burning. If you do get burnt, take cool baths or showers, and apply calamine lotion; then cover up or keep out of the sun. Bear in mind that years of excessive sunbathing can lead to premature ageing of the skin or skin cancer.

The following precautions are advised:

- drink more than at home – one extra pint of (non-alcoholic) fluid a day for every 10°F
- take more salt than usual for the first week or so
- wear loose-fitting cotton, which allows the evaporation of perspiration, rather than man-made fibres
- in the sun wear white clothes – they can reduce by half the amount of heat your body absorbs – and a hat; if you're fair-skinned, wear a T-shirt when swimming or boating
- sunbathe for only short periods (as little as five to ten minutes when it's very sunny) at first and gradually build up. Remember that it's not only when you're on the beach that you're at risk. And avoid exposure to midday sun – take a siesta, like the locals
- use a sun-tan cream, particularly if fair-skinned, and for children. The higher the protection factor, the greater the protection: recently marketed creams have high factors of 12 to 20. If swimming or sailing, use a water-resistant cream
- young children should wear a hat, and a T-shirt when swimming.

Bites and stings

Jellyfish are a particular hazard for Mediterranean holiday-makers, particularly the dangerous Portuguese man-of-war, whose sting can be extremely painful and may cause severe shock. It is best to seek medical treatment if stung. Another hazard is inflammation or even poisoning from spiny creatures – including sea urchins.

There is a chance of getting rabies in several European countries – you don't even need to be bitten (even a lick or scratch from a rabid animal can infect you). Treatment needs to be immediate, and consists of a course of injections.

Holiday insurance

Whether you go on a package holiday or travel independently, the holiday insurance you're most likely to come across is an inclusive package policy. This covers several different sorts of risk in a ready-made policy; you can buy it when you book your holiday and are then covered until you get home.

Also available is the selective policy, which allows you to choose which risks you want to insure against. Some risks that form part of a holiday policy can be covered by other types of insurance, including a home contents policy, permanent health insurance or life insurance. Risks to do with motoring in your own car abroad are usually covered by a Green Card – an extension obtained on your UK car insurance – and by special breakdown insurance. And risks to do with driving a hired car will be covered in the hire-car insurance policy (but see Car hire, page 658, for advice on such insurance).

If you buy a package holiday, it's obviously tempting to go for the policy offered in the tour operator's brochure. Many operators do more than encourage holiday-makers to take out their policy, perhaps appearing to make it compulsory. Whatever the tour operator does, you should not be lulled into assuming that his policy is right for you. If you find it isn't, you have two options: to take out a separate insurance policy which does suit you (in addition to the one in the brochure) or to choose a holiday from another operator. One difficulty is that the brochure won't necessarily give you very much information on what it is you're buying. While most give at least basic details of the cover being offered, a few don't mention any exclusions at all. To make matters worse, you normally aren't sent fuller details of your insurance until your booking is confirmed – when the policy is already in effect. Most operators will send you full insurance details before you make your booking, if you ask. But some make it quite difficult to get details.

The main risks you need to insure against, and which form the main sections of an inclusive holiday insurance policy, are: cancellation or curtailment of your holiday; medical expenses; loss of or damage to baggage, money and valuables; personal liability; and accidents causing death or disability. Below we examine briefly what insurance policies cover, and give details of the sort of exclusion clauses you may find under each section. It's very important to scrutinise the small print very carefully when choosing an insurance policy.

Medical expenses

You should choose a policy that covers all reasonable medical, hospital and treatment expenses (including emergency dental treatment) incurred as a direct result of your injury, illness or death, and, if need be, your return to the UK by air-ambulance, or the repatriation of your remains. The limit of cover should be no less than £250,000.

Most policies boast of having 24-hour emergency services which can be contacted if you or a member of your party falls ill. The service can then provide help – perhaps by talking to the hospital to make it clear that the insurers will pay the medical costs – and may arrange for the sick person to be brought back to the UK for treatment, using special air-ambulances if necessary and providing trained staff to accompany the ill person.

Certain policies do not cover: repatriation; accidents caused while taking part in what the insurance company reckons to be a dangerous or hazardous activity (including skin-diving, yachting, waterskiing, parascending); accidents caused while riding a moped or motor-bike; some elderly people; pregnancy; costs incurred as a result of a pre-existing illness (which could refer to something quite trivial for which you have received minor treatment at home but which later develops into something serious).

Cancellation or curtailment

You should look for a policy which will refund your deposit and other charges paid in advance for your holiday if it is cancelled, or which will compensate you for part of the cost of the holiday and expenses incurred in getting home (such as the cost of a scheduled flight) if your holiday is cut short because of unforeseen circumstances. These should include: illness or death of yourself or of a close relative or business associate; being called to jury service or as a witness; redundancy qualifying for payment under current legislation; your home being uninhabitable after fire, flood or storm shortly before departure; your home or office being burgled, and the police requesting you to stay. All the above points should apply to your travelling companion, too.

The total amount of cover should be the cost of the holiday.

Some policies may not cover claims made as a result of: injury while taking part in certain 'hazardous activities', either before or during your holiday (including football, motor-cycling, yachting, waterskiing and so on); illness or death of less-than-very-close relatives; pregnancy; illness if it arises from a 'pre-existing' condition; or any of the points above.

Personal belongings and money

Policies cover loss or theft of or damage to all or part of your belongings or money. The total limit of insurance is generally up to £1000, with a maximum of £200 payable for any single article (or pair or set of articles). The overall maximum payable for loss of money (which includes travel tickets, passport and cash) is generally £200, with a maximum for cash of £150.

Some policies do not cover: breakage of fragile items or equipment such as cassette players; expenses you incur as a result of loss or theft – for instance if you have to travel to a consulate to replace your passport. You will probably not be able to claim unless you report a loss to the local police within 24 hours. And you are expected to take reasonable care of your property – for instance, leaving something unguarded while swimming, or in a car (even when locked), could lead to a claim being disallowed.

If the cover is too low for you, it's worth considering insuring some of your belongings under a different policy. Most 'home contents' insurance policies allow you to include valuables, cameras, and so on, in a special 'all-risks' part of the policy; you may need to take out a special extension to cover a holiday abroad.

Personal liability

Policies cover you for legal liability if you accidentally injure someone or damage their property. The sum insured is usually £500,000.

The policy will generally not cover claims caused by driving a motor-bike, or claims made in courts outside the UK.

Other cover

All the above sections form major parts of most holiday insurance policies. But many policies have sections which may or may not be useful extras. These include insurance for delayed luggage, delayed departure and alternative travel arrangements if you miss your plane.

A note to independent island-hoppers: missing your plane home through ferry complications is not something you'll be able to insure against.

Recommended books

Guidebooks

Blue Guides to *Greece* and *Crete*, A & C Black
Michelin, *Green Tourist Guide to Greece*
Companion Guides to *Mainland Greece* and *The Greek Islands*, Collins
Independent Travellers' Guide to *Mainland Greece* and *Greek Islands*,
    both by Victor Walker, Collins
Insight Guides to *Greece* and *Greek Islands*, APA Publications
Rough Guide, Routledge & Kegan Paul
Greece on Foot, Marc Dubin, Cordee, Leicester
Portrait of Southern Greece, Brian Dicks, Robert Hale

History and background

The *Odyssey* and the *Iliad*, Homer (around 8th century BC), Penguin
History of the Peloponnesian War, Thucydides (5th century BC), Penguin
The Guide to Greece (2 vols), Pausanias (2nd century AD), Penguin
The Pelican History of Greece, 1966, A. R. Burn, Penguin
The Greeks, 1951, H. D. F. Kitto, Penguin
Modern Greece: A Short History, 1968, C. M. Woodhouse, Faber & Faber
The Ancient Greeks, 1963, M. I. Finley, Penguin
The World of Odysseus, M. I. Finley, Faber & Faber (1954), Chatto &
    Windus (1977)
The Greek Myths, 1955, Vols I and II, Robert Graves, Penguin
The Bull of Minos, 1953, Leonard Cottrell, CUP
The Colossus of Maroussi, 1941, Henry Miller, Heinemann
The Mycenaeans, 1964, Lord William Taylor, Thames & Hudson
The Mycenaean World, 1976, John Chadwick, CUP
In Search of the Trojan War, 1985, Michael Wood, BBC Publications
Mistra, 1980, Steven Runciman, Thames & Hudson
Writing in Gold – Byzantine Society and its Icons, 1985, Robin Cormack,
    George Philip
The Glory that was Greece, 1911, J. C. Stobart, Sidgwick & Jackson
Land of Lost Gods, 1987, Richard Stoneman, Hutchinson
Crete: Its Past, Present and People, 1977, Adam Hopkins, Faber & Faber
The Villa Ariadne, 1973, Dilys Powell, Hodder & Stoughton
Travels in Crete, 1837, R. Pashley, Cambridge
The Cretan Runner, 1955, G. Psychoundakis (trans. Patrick Leigh
    Fermor), John Murray
Mani – Travels in the Southern Peloponnese, 1958, and *Roumeli – Travels
    in Northern Greece*, 1966, Patrick Leigh Fermor, Penguin
Prospero's Cell (Corfu), 1945, *Reflections on a Marine Venus* (Rhodes),
    1953, and *The Greek Islands*, 1978, Lawrence Durrell, Faber & Faber
Classical Landscape with Figures, 1947, Osbert Lancaster, John Murray
The Flight of Ikaros: Travels in Greece during a Civil War, 1984, Kevin
    Andrews, Penguin
Hill of Kronos, 1980, Peter Levi, Arena
Hellas, a Portrait of Greece, 1987, Nicholas Gage, Collins Harvill

INFORMATION

Novels

Zorba the Greek, 1959, *Christ Recrucified*, 1954, and *Freedom and Death*, 1956, Nikos Kazantzakis, Faber Paperbacks

The King Must Die, 1958, *The Bull from the Sea*, 1962, and *The Last of the Wine*, 1956, Mary Renault, Longmans Green

General

Flowers of Greece and the Aegean, 1977, A. Huxley and W. Taylor, Chatto & Windus

Greek Food, 1983, Rena Salaman, Fontana

Weather

In Greece there is always a long, hot, dry, brilliant summer, allowing maximum enjoyment of the sea and the scenery. Mainland coasts and all the islands have a 'Mediterranean' climate – summer holiday weather alternating with mild wet winters; only inland in the north of the country does a 'Continental' climate apply, with extreme cold in winter and an all-year tendency to storms.

There are really only three seasons in Greece: the green, the hot and the rainy. Everything comes to life in a natural explosion from March to June. Some islands are lusher than others, but all blossom with wild flowers. Then the green foliage parches and dwindles through the summer drought when evaporation exceeds rainfall – three or four months in northern Greece, five or six in the southern Aegean. At a point in October the first clouds gather and the rainy season's squalls begin, but even from November to February Greece has plenty of sunny days; rain usually falls in heavy showers rather than continuous overcast drizzle. More of it falls on the Ionian seaboard – consequently Greece's greenest areas – as Mediterranean depressions travel across from west to east; the central mountains partly protect the eastern side of the country. In all the mountains snow lies above 1000m, as far south as the Peloponnese and on the highest tops in Crete; snow and frost are severe and prolonged in the north, where cold winds can sweep down over plains and coast.

By March spring is blossoming and intermittently balmy but the squalls haven't finished, the sea is cold and ferry-boats face turbulent water. Things improve in April, and become extremely pleasant by May. After that two main factors influence summer comfort: the crowds and the wind. Excess people are chiefly a problem in July and August, when hotels and ferries, beaches and sites are crammed with both foreign tourists and holidaying Greeks. But while it is still possible to find an empty beach on a thinly visited island, dodging the wind is more difficult.

Wind

Greece's prevailing summer wind is the *meltemi*, a brisk dry northerly, which as a light persistent breeze mitigates the high temperatures throughout the Aegean. The near-constant supply of a cooling breeze is rightly considered one of the main attractions of the islands, along with the sea itself. When we read of midsummer heatwaves in Greece, the quoted temperatures nearly always refer to the mainland and often Athens, which is stiflingly sheltered. Maximum temperatures on the islands are usually about 5°C lower. The breeze makes the Greek islands idyllic places for windsurfers and sailing holidays. It also accounts for the brilliant clarity of Aegean light, as the lack of it accounts for the filthy haze that shrouds Athens.

That is the theory, anyway. In practice, the situation is less idyllic when the sea breeze turns into a howling gale. This may sound like a rough-with-the-smooth kind of warning, but deserves to be taken seriously because at certain times of year in certain parts of the Aegean a wind of force six or more is, if not normal, by no means exceptional. For days on end it whips up the sea, sand on the beach, dust and litter in the streets, and overturns taverna tables. Wonderfully invigorating and refreshing up to about force four or five, at greater strength the wind is intrusive, exhausting and comes between holiday-makers and many of their staple activities: sunbathing, boat-trips, watersports, sitting outside tavernas, reading out of doors, scootering. It can ruin holidays. It also plays havoc with ferry timetables, causing long delays and occasionally confining all shipping to port for days on end, although this happens more often during bad winter weather than in summer. The Aegean is shallow, and the sea that gets up in windy weather is short and steep: often it is enough to keep yachts, excursion-boats and hydrofoils confined to port, but it rarely causes severe disruption to the big ferries. Of course, if you do not allow a comfortable margin, a delay of half a day can mean severe disruption: missing the plane home. The wind and consequent travel uncertainties keep many tour operators away from islands without their own airports, for which many island travellers may be grateful.

August is known as the windy month, but strong winds should also be expected in July and September. The *meltemi* blows down from the north across the Aegean, buffeting the Cyclades, north-east Crete, and the Dodecanese most strongly. Summer winds are less constant in the Ionian Sea, with the southern Ionian (Zante and the west coast of the Peloponnese) much windier than the north (Corfu and Paxos which, with Thassos, are the least windy of Greek islands). The Peloponnese Islands are generally fairly sheltered, apart from Kithira. The Kos–Rhodes Sea and West Karpathian Sea (between Rhodes and Crete) seem to be especially notorious for wind and rough sea, with few calm periods between June and September.

At the height of the season, when the islands are at their most crowded, visitors may be in a state of siege, unable to venture out of doors in comfort. Visit Mykonos, one of the windiest of all the islands, in August and you may well not be able to visit Delos or learn to windsurf. It may be a good thing that the strongest winds coincide with the period of strongest sun, but this is also the period when travellers are most likely to have to resort to sleeping on the beach. Sleeping-bagging when the *meltemi* is blowing hard is no fun at all. In general, the summer wind gains strength through the day before subsiding in the early evening. But this is not always the case: sometimes the wind scarcely lets up for days on end.

The more mountainous the island, the more likely it is to have sheltered

Temperature in cities

	Jan	Feb	Mar	Apr	May	Jun	Jul	Aug	Sep	Oct	Nov	Dec	Total annual rainfall (mm)
Athens	12.9	13.9	15.5	20.2	25.0	29.9	33.2	33.1	29.0	23.8	18.6	14.6	402
Salonika	9.4	11.7	14.4	19.7	24.8	29.4	32.4	32.1	27.7	21.7	15.9	11.4	470
Heraklion	15.8	16.2	17.2	20.3	23.4	27.1	29.3	29.3	27.0	24.3	20.8	17.7	453
London	6.3	6.9	10.1	13.3	16.7	20.3	21.8	21.4	18.5	14.2	10.1	7.3	593

Temperature and rainfall on islands

	Apr		May		Jun		Jul		Aug		Sep		Oct		Total annual rainfall (mm)
Corfu	19.1	10	23.3	6	28.2	3	31.4	1	31.5	2	27.8	6	23.4	11	1352
N. Crete	20.3	6	23.4	4	27.1	1	29.3	0	29.3	0	27.0	2	24.3	6	453
Limnos	18.0	6	22.8	5	27.3	2	30.2	1	30.3	1	26.2	2	21.5	6	525
Naxos	19.5	4	22.7	3	25.6	1	27.3	0	27.6	0	25.5	0	24.0	1	475
Zante	20.2	6	24.7	3	28.7	2	32.2	0	32.3	1	28.7	3	24.9	8	922
Isle of Wight	12.9	11	15.9	11	18.9	9	20.5	11	20.8	12	18.7	14	15.2	14	769

Average daily maximum temperature in °C

Rain (second column) = average number of days it rains (0.1min or more); 0.25mm for Isle of Wight

stretches of coast. But from a watersports point of view an island's lee coast is often more dangerous than its windward side, with a deceptive area of inshore calm water and a strong offshore wind lurking not far out to sea. Coastal hills sheltering the beach often cause very awkward turbulence and patches of swirling wind, especially in a narrow bay. Windsurf renters are quick to close up shop when conditions are difficult and are required to have a rescue speedboat at the ready, but cannot be relied on to give the right advice about conditions, or to keep a lookout. On some islands that have plenty of wind and plenty of tourists, windsurfing may not be organised at all because of the lack of safe bays. Tinos is one such.

In general there are few north-facing resorts in the Aegean: those that there are may be popular among expert windsurfers, and sandy stretches of north coast tend to be colonised by camper vans piled high with boards and rigs. On both Kos and Rhodes there are busy holiday resorts in very exposed locations where it is more usual to see beach umbrellas used as windbreaks than as sunshades and where taverna terraces tend to face away from the sea.

General information

Greek National Tourist Organisation: 195–197 Regent Street, London W1R 8DL, tel: 01-734 5997. In Athens: 2 Karayeori Servias, tel: 01-322-2545; also at 4 Stadhiou, at Omonia station and at the airport. There are tourist offices in other main towns throughout Greece. Tourist police: tel 171 (English spoken).

Time

Greece follows the Orthodox calendar for the fixing of Easter, the largest festival which falls up to a month after ours. All movable festivals from Lent to Whitsun are governed by this date.

Greece is on Eastern European Time, which is two hours ahead of Greenwich Mean Time; in summer, their clocks are similarly two hours ahead of our Summer Time.

Money

The maximum cash you may take into Greece is 100,000 drachmas (about £380) and the maximum you may bring out is 20,000 drachmas (about £75). Sterling traveller's cheques are best. Eurocheques, credit and charge cards are useful in main tourist areas. No cash cards work.

Banks are generally open Monday to Friday (except public holidays) from 8a.m. to 2p.m. Post Offices (which close at 2.30p.m.) usually change money (including traveller's cheques) at much the same rate as the bank, and faster.

The drachma spends most of its time depreciating against the pound and other European currencies, which makes changing money an attractive speculation for Greeks. As a result, you will rarely have any difficulty changing sterling cash or traveller's cheques in the most modest resorts, even if there is no bank. A Eurocheque made out in drachmas is much less likely to be of interest. Changing money in banks can take hours, what with all the different forms to be filled in and the endless queues of old ladies arguing about the day's rate for their fistfuls of Australian dollars, or just arguing. The better rate you will probably get needs to be weighed against the extra speed and convenience of using unofficial money changers (shopkeepers or travel agents, usually) or hotels.

Shopping

Shops are generally open in summer from 8a.m. to 1.30p.m. and 5.30p.m. to 8.30p.m., on Tuesday, Thursday and Friday. On Monday, Wednesday and Saturday they close at 2.30p.m. or 3p.m. In winter the siesta is shorter, and shops close earlier in the evening.

Green kiosks (*periptero*) can be found throughout the country. They are open for about 18 hours a day, and sell all sorts of items including newspapers, sweets, toilet articles, film and stamps.

Telephoning

There are telephone and telegram offices (OTE) in many villages. It is not much more expensive to phone from one of the ubiquitous *periptero*, many of which have telephones with meters. The cheap rate is from 8p.m. to 8a.m. You are much more likely to be outrageously overcharged phoning from a hotel. Dial 0044 for the UK.

Museums and archaeological sites

Opening times for major archaeological sites and museums (including Athens Acropolis, Aegina, Corinth, Delphi, Epidavros, Mycenae and Olympia) are 8a.m. to 5p.m., 8.30a.m. to 3p.m. on Saturday, Sunday and holidays; and 11a.m. to 5p.m. on Monday. Opening hours for lesser sites are 8.30a.m. to 3p.m., closed Monday. It's wise to double-check, as there are a few local variations, particularly for museums.

Sites and museums are closed on 1 January, 25 March (except Palamidi Fortress in Nafplion), the morning of Good Friday, and Easter Sunday and Christmas Day. Holidays, on which the major sites and museums operate shorter hours, are 6 January, Shrove Monday, Easter Saturday and Monday, 1 May, Whit Monday, 15 August and Boxing Day. Half-holidays, when sites and museums are open only in the morning, are 2 January, the first Saturday of Carnival, Easter Thursday and Easter Tuesday, Christmas Eve and New Year's Eve.

Unless you are a Greek national, an archaeologist or an art historian, a foreign journalist or studying classics – and can prove it – there is an entrance charge for all museums and sites. If you qualify for a free pass, apply well in advance to the Ministry of Science and Culture, Museums Section, Aritidou 14, Athens. Fees vary, and there are reductions for foreign students and pupils. Some sites have free entrance on Sundays. Fees are payable for the use of tripod cameras.

Some museums and sites don't admit visitors in shorts or immodest dress.

Public holidays, festivals and events

1 January (Agios Vasillis, Feast of St Basil); **6 January** (Theophania, Epiphany); **25 March** (Independence Day); **Good Friday** and **Easter Sunday** (Orthodox calendar, so about a month after our Easter); **1 May** (Labour Day and the beginning of Summer); **Whit Sunday** and **Monday** (Orthodox calendar), 50 days after Easter; **15 August** (Panagia, Feast of the Assumption of the Virgin Mary, the most important religious holiday in the Greek calendar after Easter and Christmas; pilgrimages are held to the Aegean islands of Tinos and Paros); **28 October** (Ochi day); **25 December** and **26 December** (Agios Stephanos, Feast of St Stephen).

Easter is the most important festival in Greece, and this is a wonderful time to visit: traditional and colourful services are held in chapels and churches throughout the country, and Holy Week ends with feasting and dancing. Greeks fast in Lent, doing without olive oil and meat, and eating special Lenten dishes such as pickled vegetables. On Maundy Thursday, women dye the red eggs which will be eaten on Easter Day (apart from the first egg dyed, which belongs to the Virgin Mary). Good Friday is a day of total fast, and the evening Epitaphios the most moving ceremony of the Orthodox calendar. Christ's funeral bier, the Epitaphion, which has been lying in state decked with flowers during Holy Week, is taken from church and borne through the streets, followed by a candlelit procession. Many cafes and restaurants shut shortly after. On Easter Saturday crowds throng to churches for the midnight liturgy, clutching decorated candles and the red hard-boiled eggs. On the stroke of midnight, the priest lights the first candle from the Holy Flame to represent the light of the world, and intones *Christos Anesti* (Christ is risen). Bells ring, fireworks explode, and everyone lights their candles and cracks their eggs. At home, the fast is broken with a special Easter soup, Magiritsa, which is made from lamb's liver and entrails, egg, lemon and rice. On Easter Sunday the paschal lamb is roasted on a spit, and houses are decked with lilac.

Many other festival days are celebrated, including Rose Monday (Kathara Deftera, or Clean Monday), the first day of Lent in the Orthodox calendar; 23 April (St George's Day, Greece's patron saint); and 6 December (Agios Nikolaos, St Nicholas, celebrated in fishing villages and seafaring communities). Many places have local festivals: on Corfu the remains of the patron saint, Spiridon, are paraded on Palm Sunday and 11 August; there are big festivals in the Dodecanese on 29 August (Agios Ioannis, Martyrdom of St John the Baptist), and in the Cyclades on 20 July (Profitis Ilias, Festival of the Prophet Elijah). The Carnival takes place in the three weekends before Lent, and comes to a noisy climax on the seventh weekend before Easter; that at Patras is the most famous, and includes a chariot-race. Pre-Lenten boules or masques with pagan roots takes place particularly in Macedonia, around Naoussa, and at Veria, Thebes and Xanthi. On the islands there are special celebrations on Skyros, Zante, Chios, Lesbos, Karpathos, Crete (Heraklion) and Evia (Agia Anna).

The Greeks celebrate their name days (*yiorti*) rather than birthdays, and there are hundreds of saints' days. Churches dedicated to a particular saint will hold fêtes or festivals. On St John's or St Helen's Day, a large part of the population will celebrate.

Wine festivals are held at Daphni during July and August, at Rethymnon during July, and at Alexandroupolis. Cultural festivals include the Athens Festival, held from June to mid-September at the Herodes Atticus Theatre; the Epidavros Festival, from 23 June to 9 September; summer festivals at Philippi and Thassos, and an October festival at Salonika.

There are *son et lumière* shows and folk dance displays in Athens, Corfu and Rhodes from about May to September or October.

Laws and regulations

As soon as you arrive, you will probably become aware of an active military presence, as well as the fact that Greek police carry guns. However, the average Greek policeman is easy-going, and the authorities tend to turn a blind eye to laws and regulations which seem difficult to enforce. If this is confusing, it's as well to know that the following are illegal: camping outside official campsites, nude bathing, and the export of antiquities and works of art without a permit. Photography is forbidden near military barracks or lookout posts, and at airports; there are usually signs showing a camera crossed out in such areas. Underwater photography is not permitted in most parts of Greece, and the use of binoculars for bird-watching should not be undertaken without care. Drug offences are considered a very serious matter, carrying heavy sentences. Do not drink and drive, let a child sit in the front seat, or carry a petrol can in the car. Finally, it is an offence to abuse the Greek flag, as a group of British rowdies discovered when they dropped their trousers at the national emblem and ended up in court.

Public conveniences and plumbing

Greek public conveniences leave much to be desired. If you're unlucky enough to need one, the chances are that it will be a squat-over type, and will be devoid of paper. As public facilities are few and far between, and generally not for those of a delicate constitution, it is quite acceptable to use the facilities in tavernas, bars and hotels. Often these, as well as WCs at airports, ports and on ferries, are scarcely less depressing. Always carry plenty of tissues or paper napkins, and even a small torch, as there may be no light available.

Narrow-gauge Greek plumbing pipes cannot cope with paper, and attempts to flush it down the system may have much more unpleasant consequences than the only mildly unsavoury business of disposing of waste paper in lavatory-side waste-paper bins. Even ferries that began service on the Dover–Calais line have bins. Presumably, this is not because the plumbing has been customised to meet Greek standards of inefficiency, but simply because lavatory bins are part of Greek culture and no Greek could sit comfortably without one.

On the islands, facilities range from holes in the ground or squat-over privies flushing into the sea to palatial bathrooms with coloured suites – tributes to British sanitaryware – which are sometimes not connected to the water mains. Where water is scarce, supplies are often cut off, so you have to rely on a bucket of water and bleach.

According to the marvellous natural logic of solar power, hot water tends to be abundant in the middle of the day and unavailable in the morning or evening. Basins are often without plugs, because of the frequency of interruption to the water supply and the risk of overflow when the supply returns. Tapwater is usually drinkable, but does not always taste good.

Dogs

Greek shepherds and gypsies do not keep dogs simply for company. Being attacked by dogs has a long and distinguished pedigree: Odysseus's solution was craftily to sit down and drop all weapons until rescued by a shepherd. Otherwise pick up a stone or a stout stick and wield it threateningly. Greek dogs tend not to be distracted by things thrown for them to chase. As a rule it is not a good idea to take to your heels.

The nature of the canine problem has not changed much since George Bowen wrote about it in the last century. 'On approaching hamlets or sheepfolds the stranger is certain to find a certain disagreeable coincidence with Homer in being assailed as fiercely as was Ulysses by a pack of dogs. The number and ferocity of these descendants of the famous Molossian breed resembling in appearance a cross between an English mastiff and a sheepdog is one of the peculiarities of the country which first attracts the attention of the traveller and among the most curious illustrations of classical antiquity. Masters don't call them off – it would cow their spirit and make them useless. And if you shoot or injure them you are sure to get involved in a dangerous collision with the natives.' The feud between Herakles and Hippocoön, which resulted in the extermination of the latter and his entire family, began when Herakles's cousin Oenos killed a vicious dog belonging to Hippocoön and was himself beaten to death by Hippocoön's sons.

If you are bitten, however superficially, go straight to a doctor or hospital for anti-rabies treatment.

Greek language and alphabet

Greeks travel far and wide, and even in the most remote places you'll find someone who speaks English – even if it's in broad Australian or an American drawl. You can never escape from the fact that Greece is a seafaring nation with vast numbers of the male population working in the merchant marine. Even on the smallest islands former seamen will regale you with tales of Liverpool, Portsmouth and Cardiff Docks.

English is widely spoken in the main tourist resorts. But the most modest attempts at basic Greek can pay dividends. A simple 'Good morning' or 'How are you?' can open doors, and instead of being treated like a gawping tourist you'll be *xenos* – stranger, foreigner and guest.

The Greek you'll hear spoken on holiday is demotic Greek, *dimotiki* – the language 'of the people'. But many of the signs over shops will be in the old formal Greek, *katharevousa*. For instance, the bakery, although called the *fournos*, will have ΑΡΤΩΠΟΛΕΙΟΝ – bread seller – over the door.

Ancient Greek was the spoken word over 2500 years ago when the great classics were written. Over the centuries it evolved into *katharevousa*, the language of the educated. Among the rural population a separate vernacular developed, which became a substantially different form of Greek – *dimotiki*. Despite political battles which surfaced particularly at the time of Greece's struggle for independence and continued for over 150 years, *katharevousa* (literally 'pure Greek') became the official language used in documents, books and even newspapers, while at the same time *dimotiki* became used more and more for formal writing (in 1900 there were riots when a demotic translation of the New Testament appeared). Under the Colonels' Junta (1967–74) *katharevousa* was the only language allowed in secondary schools. Everything from textbooks to sweet wrappers had to be written in the pure form. The Great Language Question was finally solved in 1976 when demotic was adopted as the official Greek language. But there are still plenty of places where *katharevousa* is used: on signs, in timetables and on official announcements. As *katharevousa* approximates more closely to classical Greek than *dimotiki*, those who learned Greek at school will be more easily able to decipher it. However, even if a word is spelled the same as in classical times, the pronunciation is likely to be quite different.

Greek alphabet: pronunciation guide

Capital letter	Small letter	Name	Approximate sound
A	α	alpha	*c*at
B	β	beta	*v*an
Γ	γ	gamma	su*g*ar (before 'a' and 'o') *y*es (before 'e' and 'i')
Δ	δ	delta	*th*is
E	ε	epsilon	*e*gg
Z	ζ	zeta	*z*oo
H	η	eta	f*ee*t
Θ	θ	theta	*th*ick
I	ι	iota	f*ee*t
K	κ	kappa	*k*ing
Λ	λ	lambda	*l*ong
M	μ	mu	*m*an
N	ν	nu	*n*ot
Ξ	ξ	xi	bo*x*
O	o	omicron	d*o*t
Π	π	pi	*p*ick
P	ϱ	rho	*r*ed (rolled)
Σ	σ, ς*	sigma	*s*it
T	τ	tau	*t*ap
Υ	υ	upsilon	f*ee*t
Φ	φ	phi	*f*at
X	χ	chi	lo*ch*
Ψ	ψ	psi	la*ps*e
Ω	ω	omega	d*o*t

*Used at ends of words only

GESTURES

Greeks can speak volumes without saying a word. Facial expressions and gestures suffice, so it's worth getting to know how to read them, especially if you want to avoid a grave misunderstanding.

'No' is a sharp jerk of the head upwards, usually accompanied by raised eyes and eyebrows and a click of the tongue, much the same as our expression of impatience. It may be accompanied by the word ochi in one fell swoop, or it may be such a slight nod that you hardly notice.

'Yes' is indicated by a slight forward nod, slightly to the side.

For 'What do you want?' or 'What did you say?', a common gesture in Greece, the head is shaken from side to side, a bit like our 'no', with a quizzical expression and often raised eyebrows.

Greeks also wave their hands about a great deal; a circular movement of the wrist is used for emphasis of something good. Beware the outstretched palm: to hold up your hand as we would for a stop gesture is the very worst Greek insult.

Combinations of letters		Approximate sound
AI	αι	egg
EI	ει	feet
OI	οι	feet
YI	υι	feet
AY	αυ	have (-af- before mute consonants)
EY	ευ	ever (-ef- before mute consonants)
OY	ου	moon
ΓΓ	γγ	go (-ng- in the middle of a word)
ΓΚ	γκ	go (-nk- in the middle of a word)
ΜΠ	μπ	bat (-mb- in the middle of a word)
ΝΤ	ντ	dog (-nd- in the middle of a word)
ΤΖ	τζ	ads

Signs and abbreviations

Shop signs

ΑΡΤΟΠΩΛΕΙΟΝ	BAKER	ΟΠΩΡΟΠΩΛΕΙΟΝ	GREENGROCER
ΒΙΒΛΙΟΠΩΛΕΙΟΝ	BOOKSHOP	ΠΑΝΤΟΠΩΛΕΙΟΝ	GROCER
ΙΧΘΥΟΠΩΛΕΙΟΝ	FISHMONGER	ΦΑΡΜΑΚΕΙΟΝ	CHEMIST
ΚΑΠΝΟΠΩΛΕΙΟΝ	TOBACCONIST	ΧΑΡΤΟΠΩΛΕΙΟΝ	STATIONER
ΚΡΕΟΠΩΛΕΙΟΝ	BUTCHER		

INFORMATION

Other signs

ΑΦΙΘΕΙΣ	ARRIVALS	ΕΛΕΥΘΕΡΟ	VACANT
ΑΝΑΧΩΡΗΣΕΙΣ	DEPARTURES	ΚΑΤΕΙΛΗΜΜΕΝΟ	ENGAGED
ΤΟΥΑΛΕΤΕΣ	TOILETS	ΖΕΣΤΟ	HOT
ΓΥΝΑΙΚΩΝ	LADIES	ΚΡΥΟ	COLD
ΑΝΔΡΩΝ	GENTS	ΠΛΗΡΟΦΟΡΙΕΣ	INFORMATION
ΑΝΟΙΧΤΟ	OPEN	ΠΛΗΡΟΦΟΡΙΕΣ	RECEPTION
ΚΛΕΙΣΤΟΝ	CLOSED	ΑΝΕΛΚΥΣΤΗΡ	LIFT
ΕΙΣΟΔΟΣ	ENTRANCE	ΤΑΜΕΙΟ	CASH DESK
ΕΘΟΔΟΣ	EXIT	ΑΣΤΥΝΟΜΙΑ	POLICE
ΕΘΟΔΟΣ	EMERGENCY	ΝΟΣΟΚΟΜΕΙΟ	HOSPITAL
ΚΙΝΔΥΝΟΥ	EXIT	ΑΥΤΟΚΙΝΗΤΟ	MOTORWAY
ΚΙΝΔΥΝΟΣ	DANGER	ΔΡΟΜΟΣ	
ΜΗ ΑΓΓΙΖΕΤΕ	DON'T TOUCH	(ΕΘΝΙΚΗ ΟΔΟΣ)	
ΣΥΡΑΤΕ	PULL	ΔΙΟΔΙΑ	TOLL
ΟΘΗΣΑΤΕ	PUSH	ΠΩΛΕΙΤΑΙ	FOR SALE
ΤΕΛΩΝΕΙΟ	CUSTOMS	ΕΝΟΙΚΙΑΖΟΝΤΑΙ	ROOMS TO LET
ΑΠΑΓΟΡΕΥΕΤΑΙ	NO SMOKING	ΔΩΜΑΤΙΑ	
ΤΟ ΚΑΠΝΙΣΜΑ		ΙΔΙΩΤΙΚΟ	PRIVATE
ΑΠΑΓΟΡΕΥΕΤΑΙ	NO SWIMMING	ΕΙΣΟΔΟΣ	FREE
ΤΟ ΚΟΛΥΜΠΙ		ΕΛΕΥΘΕΠΑ	ENTRANCE
ΑΠΑΓΟΡΕΥΟΝΤΑΙ	NO		
ΟΙ ΦΩΤΟΓΡΑΦΙΕΣ	PHOTOGRAPHS	ΕΚΠΤΩΣΕΙΣ	SALES

Abbreviations

Α.Π.	Municipal Police	Ι.Κ.Α.	National Health
Ε.Ε.Σ.	Greek Red Cross		Insurance
Ε.Λ.Π.Α.	Automobile and Touring	Ο.Σ.Ε.	Railway Company
	Club of Greece		of Greece
Ε.Λ.Τ.Α.	Greek Post Office	Ο.Τ.Ε.	Telecommunications
Ε.Ο.Τ.	Greek Tourist		Company of Greece
	Organisation	Τ.Α.	Tourist Police

Basic phrases

The accent marks the stressed syllable

English	Pronunciation	Greek
Yes	né	Ναι
No	óhi	Όχι
Please/you're welcome	parakaló	Παρακαλώ
Thank you	efharistó	Ευχαριστώ
Good morning	kaliméra	Καλημέρα
Good afternoon/evening	kalispéra	Καλησπέρα
Good night	kaliníhta	Καληνύχτα
Hello and goodbye	yássas (*plural*)	Γειά σας
	yássoo (*sing.*)	Γειά σου
Goodbye (formal)	adío	Αντίο

English	Pronunciation	Greek
Pleased to meet you	héro polí	Χαίρω πολύ
Excuse me	me sinkhoríte	Με συγχωρείτε
Sorry	signómi	Συγνώμη
Good health! Cheers!	isigía/yámas	Εις υγεία/Γειά μας
OK	endáxi	Εντάξ ει
Today	símera	Σήμερα
Yesterday	hthés	Χθές
Tomorrow	ávrio	Αυριο
I understand	katalavéno	Καταλαβαίνω
I don't understand	dhen katalavéno	Δεν καταλαβαίνω
It's urgent	íne epígon	Είναι επείγον
Help!	voíthia	Βοήθεια
Go away	fíyete	Φύγετε

Questions

In Greek a semi-colon is used in place of a question mark

English	Pronunciation	Greek
Where?	pu	Που;
Where is (are)?	pu íne	Που είναι;
Left/right?	aristerá/dexiá	Αριστερά/δεξιά;
When?	póte	Πότε;
What?	ti	Τι;
How?	poss	Πως;
How many?	póssa	Πόσα;
How much?	pósso	Πόσο;
How much does it cost?	pósso káni	Πόσο κάνει;
Who?	piós	Ποιός;
Why?	yiatí	Γιατί;
What's your name?	poss se léne	Πως σε λένε;
What's that?	ti íne aftó	Τι είναι αυτό;
Do you speak English?	milate anliká	Μιλάτε αγγλικά;
What do you have? (*on the menu*)	ti éhete	Τι έχετε;
Do you have rooms?	éhete domátia	Εχετε δωμάτια;
For one person	yia éna átomo	Για ένα άτομο
For two people	yia dío atoma	Για δυο άτομα
The bill, please	to logariasmó parakaló	Το λογαριασμό παρακαλώ
What time is it?	ti óra íne	Τι ώρα είναι;
What time does it open, close?	ti óra aníyi/klíni	Τι ώρα ανοίγει/κλεινει;
Where are the toilets?	pu íne i toualétes	Που είναι οι τουαλέτες;

INFORMATION

Days and months

English	Pronunciation	Greek
Sunday	kiriakí	Κυριακή
Monday	deftéra	Δευτέρα
Tuesday	trití	Τρίτη
Wednesday	tetárti	Τετάρτη
Thursday	pémpti	Πέμπτη
Friday	paraskeví	Παρασκευή
Saturday	sávato	Σάββατο
in the morning	to proí	τό πρωί
in the afternoon	to apóyevma	τό ἀπόγευμα
in the evening	to vrádi	τό βράδυ
at night	ti nihta	τή νύκτα
January	januários	Ιανουάριος
February	fevruários	Φεβρουάριος
March	mártios	Μάρτιος
April	aprílios	Απρίλιος
May	máyos	Μάϊος
June	yúnios	Ιούνιος
July	yúlios	Ιούλιος
August	ávgustos	Αυγουστος
September	septémvrios	Σεπτέμβριος
October	októvrios	Οκτώβριος
November	noémvrios	Νοέμβριος
December	dekémvrios	Δεκέμβριος

Useful words

English	Pronunciation	Greek
airport	aerodrómio	αεροδρόμιο
aeroplane	aeropláno	αεροπλάνο
antiquities	arheótites	αρχαιότητες
beach	paralía	παραλία
bank	trápeza	τράπεζα
bakery	foúrnos	φούρνος
bus	leoforío	λεωφορείο
bus stop	stássi leoforíou	στάση λεωφορείου
bar	bar	μπαρ
boat	várka/kaïki	βάρκα/κάϊκι
bike (motor)	mikhaní	μηχανή
bicycle	podílato	ποδήλατο
centre	kéndro	κέντρο
castle	kástro	κάστρο

English	Pronunciation	Greek
cave	spíleo	σπήλαιο
chemist	farmakíon	φαρμακείο
church	eklisía	εακκλησία
cathedral	mitrópoli	μητρόπολη
café	kafeníon	καφενείο
cake shop	zakharoplastíon	ζαχαροπλαστείο
doctor	yatrós	γιατρός
dentist	odhontoyatrós	οδοντογιατρός
fortress	froúrio	φρούριο
ferry	plío/vapóri	πλοίο/βαπόρι
gardens	kípi	κήποι
hospital	nosokomío	νοσοκομείο
hotel	xenodokhío	ξενοδοχείο
harbour	limáni	λιμάνι
lake	límni	λίμνη
market	agorá	αγορά
monastery	monastíri	μοναστήρι
mosque	dzamí	τζαμί
museum	moosío	μουσείο
moped	véspa	βέσπα
park	párko	πάρκο
petrol station	venzinádiko	βενζινάδικο
police	astinomía	αστυνομία
post office	tahidromío	ταχυδρομείο
postcard	kárta	κάρτα
passport	diavatírio	διαβατήριο
road	droḿos	δρόμος
stamp	grammatósima	γραμματόσημα
sea	thálassa	θάλασσα
spring	pigí	πηγή
square	platía	πλατεία
street	odós	οδός
station	stathmós	σταθμός
steps	skála	σκάλα
temple	naós	ναός
tomb	táfos	τάφος
toilet	toualéta	τουαλέτα
telephone	tiléfono	τηλέφωνο
train	tréno	τρένο
ticket	isitírio	εισιτήριο
village	horió	χωριό

Glossary 1: Art and architecture

abacus slab crowning the capital of a column (also counting-board, antique aid to reckoning)

acanthus plant whose stylised leaves form part of the Corinthian capital's decoration

acropolis 'upper city', the citadel of an Ancient Greek city on a hill, containing temples, palaces

abaton, adytum innermost sanctuary of some temples, whence oracles were delivered

agora place of open-air assembly, market place; equivalent of Roman forum

ambo pulpit

amphora two-handed vessel for liquids

apse semi-circular (or polygonal) recess, in Roman basilica forming east end of church

architrave lowest part of entablature resting on abacus, spanning between columns

archontiko houses of notables; 'archon' was originally a magistrate

atlantes sculpted male figures serving as columns or supports

basilica large oblong hall with colonnades and apse; first royal, then commercial and judicial uses; later a Christian church

bema a raised platform, reserved for clergy in early Christian churches

bouleuterion senate house, council chamber

Byzantine (architecture) style evolved in 5th-century Constantinople, still that of the Greek Church

capital member at top of column which with the abacus supports the entablature, or arches in Byzantine architecture. See also ORDERS

caryatids sculpted female figures serving as columns or supports

cella inner enclosure of temple, room of cult statue

centauromachia fight between Centaurs and Lapiths, often depicted in sculpture

chryselephantine of gold and ivory on wood

cistern (artificial) reservoir or tank for holding water

Corinthian third Order of Greek architecture: capital formed of acanthus leaves and calyx

Cyclopean (walls of) irregular blocks so large that Ancient Greeks attributed them to the Cyclops (giants)

Doric first and simplest Order of Greek architecture

dromos passage into Mycenaean *tholos* tomb; public way lined with statues

entablature horizontal architrave, cornice, frieze, etc. carried by columns

entasis outward curve in the shaft of a column, to counteract the optical illusion whereby a straight column appears to curve inwards

fresco method of painting in watercolour laid on wall or ceiling before plaster is dry

frieze decorative band of carving above architrave, continuous (Ionic Order) or made up of metopes and triglyphs (Doric Order)

gigantomachia fight between gods and giants, often depicted in sculpture

Greek cross cross with all four arms of equal length

gymnasium school, often for physical training: courtyard surrounded by colonnades and rooms

Heraion temple or sanctuary of Hera

herm bust (originally of Hermes) on square pillar

heroön shrine of a hero

hieron whole sacred enclosure surrounding temple

hypocaust under-floor system of distributing heat from a furnace

iconostasis screen bearing icons separating off the sanctuary of a Byzantine church

Ionic second Order of Greek architecture: capital has pair of spiral volutes

INFORMATION

kalderimi paved track, sometimes up a hill

kastro castle (Byzantine, Venetian)

katholikon (chief) church of a monastery

kiosk pavilion, palace (Turkish)

kore (statue of) Ancient Greek maiden, clothed

kouros (statue of) Ancient Greek youth, nude

krater two-handled vessel with wide mouth in which liquids (wine and water) were mixed

Linear A still undeciphered Minoan script used in Crete, 2000–1400 BC

Linear B Mycenaean Greek script, found on clay tablets from before 1150 BC

loutrophoros large two-handled vessel used to carry water for the (bridal) bath

megaron rectangular main hall of a Mycenaean palace

metope plain or sculpted square panel alternating with triglyphs in a Doric frieze

naos inner space (*cella*) of temple; main space of Byzantine cruciform church

narthex long arcaded porch forming entrance across west end of Byzantine church

necropolis city of the dead: cemetery

nymphaion sanctuary of nymphs: building for retreat among fountains and plants

odeion roofed theatre or hall for music

orchestra most of the circular floor between stage and front seats of theatre, where the chorus performed

Order (style of) column and its entablature; see DORIC, IONIC, CORINTHIAN. A Composite Order combined Ionic and Corinthian features

palaestra open space, forecourt of gymnasium, for athletics practice

Panagia all-holy: Mother of God

Pantokrator ruler of all: Christ

parados entrance at side of orchestra

Parthenon temple of Athena Parthenos (Maiden) on the highest part of Athens' Acropolis

pediment triangular piece of wall filling space between entablature and end of sloping roof

pendentive concave triangle of vaulting supporting circular dome over square space

peripteral (building, temple) surrounded by colonnade

peristyle surrounding colonnade

podium continuous base of colonnade, low enclosing platform in amphitheatre

portico entrance-space with roof-supporting columns

pronaos entrance portico of temple

propylaia important, monumental version of propylon, gateway

proscenium narrow stage of theatre, behind orchestra, where protagonists performed

quadriga four-horsed chariot, often on top of a monument

refectory dining-hall in monastery

rhyton drinking-vessel characterised by animal-head shape

scene, skene back wall of stage in Greek theatre; loosely, whole stage area

stadion measure of length (stade, 600 feet); running track of that length; track (stadium) with enclosure of spectators' seats

stele upright (grave) stone, carved and inscribed

stoa long portico, colonnade; non-religious building with one

tessera small cube of stone, glass or marble used in mosaics

thermai (public) baths

thesauros treasury

tholos circular building, rotunda

tholos tomb (Mycenaean) mausoleum, with beehive-domed conical roof

triglyph 'three channels', blocks with three vertical grooves alternating with metopes in Doric frieze

trireme galley with three banked rows of oars

tympanum the triangular surface of a pediment

volute scroll, or spiral, shape distinguishing Ionic Order and also appearing in Corinthian.

Glossary 2: Food

The accent marks the syllable which is stressed

OPEKTIKA	Orektika	Starters/Appetisers
Αυγά (μπρουγέ, ομελέτα)	Avgá ('brouillé,' omelétta)	eggs (scrambled, omelette)
Διάφορα ορεκτικά	Diáfora orektiká	hors d'oeuvre
Εληές	Eliés	olives
Κοτόπιττα	Kotópitta	chicken pie
Ντολμάδες	Dolmádes	stuffed vine or cabbage leaves
Ντομάτες (γεμιστές)	Domádes (yemistés)	tomatoes (stuffed)
Χούμους	Hoúmmous	chickpea and oil dip
Μελιτζάνασαλάτα	Melitzánasaláta	aubergine puree
Μεζέδες	Mezédes	small, assorted appetisers
Πιπεριές (γεμιστές)	Piperiés (yemistés)	sweet peppers (stuffed)
Σπανάκοπιττα	Spanákopitta	spinach pasty
Ταραμοσαλάτα	Taramosaláta	cod's roe dip
Τσατζίκι	Tsatsíki	cucumber, garlic and yoghurt dip
Τυρόπιττα	Tyrópitta	cheese pasty

ZYMAPIKA	Zymarika	Pasta and rice dishes
Μακαρόνια	Makarónia	macaroni
Παστιτζιο	Pastítsio	macaroni, cheese and mince pie
Πιλάφι	Piláfi	pilaff
Ρύζι	Rísi	rice
Σπαγέτι	Spagéti	spaghetti

ΣΟΥΠΕΣ	Soupés	Soups
Χορτασουπα	Hórtasoupa	vegetable soup
Κοτοσουπα	Kotósoupa	chicken soup
Μαγειρίτσα	Magirítsa	tripe soup with rice, egg and lemon
Σουπα αυγολέμονο	Soúpa avgolémono	chicken broth with lemon, egg and rice
Σούπα φακές	Soúpa fakés	lentil soup
Σούπα χυλοπίττες	Soúpa hilopíttes	noodle soup
Φασολάδα	Fasoláda	kidney bean soup with tomatoes
Ψαρόσουπα	Psarósoupa	fish soup

ΨΑΡΙΑ	Psaria/Thalassina	Fish/Seafood
Αστακός	Astakós	lobster
Αχινός	Achinós	sea urchin
Γαρίδες	Garídes	prawns
Γλωσσα	Glóssa	sole
Καλαμαράκια	Kalamarákia	squid
Χταπόδι	Htapódi	octopus
Λιθρίνια	Lithrínia	bass, sea bream
Μαρίδες	Marídes	whitebait
Μύδια	Mídia	mussels
Μπαρμπούνια	Barboúnia	red mullet
Μπακαλιάρος	Bakaliáros	salt cod
Συναγρίδα	Sinagrída	sea bream
Στρείδια	Strídia	oysters
τηγανιτό	tiganitó	fried
ψητό	psitó	grilled
βραστό	vrastó	boiled
ΕΝΤΡΑΔΕΣ	Entrades	Entrees
Αρνάκι	Arnáki	lamb
Αρνι	Arní	mutton
Βωδινό	Vodinó	beef
Γουρουνόπουλο	Gourounópoulo	sucking pig
Κατζίκι; κατζικάκι	Katsíki; katsikáki	goat; kid
Κεφτέδες	Keftédes	meatballs
Κοτόπουλο	Kotópoulo	chicken
Κουνέλι	Kounéli	rabbit
Κοκορέτσι	Kokorétsi	kidneys, tripe and liver on a spit
Λαρδί	Lardí	bacon
Λαγός	Lagós	hare
Λουκάνικα	Loukánika	sausages
Μπριζόλα	Brizóla	chop, cutlet
Μοσχάρι	Moskhári	veal
Μουσακά	Moussaká	casserole of mince and aubergine with a bechamel and cheese sauce
Νεφρά	Nefrá	kidneys
Παϊδάκια	Païdákia	chops, usually lamb or goat
Παπί	Papí	duck
Σηκοτάκι	Sykotáki	liver
Τζουτζουκάκια	Tsoutzoukákia	sausage shaped meat balls with cumin, in a tomato sauce
Σουβλάκια	Souvlákia	meat kebab on a skewer
Χοιρινό	Hirinó	pork

ΛΑΔΕΡΑ/ΧΟΡΤΑ	Ladera/Horta	Vegetables/Greens
Αγγουράκι	Angouráki	cucumber
Αγκινάρες	Ankináres	artichokes
Κολοκυθάκια	Kolokithákia	courgettes
Κουνουπίδι	Kounoupídi	cauliflower
Λάχανο	Láhano	cabbage
Μαρούλι	Maroúli	lettuce
Μελιτζάνες	Melitzánes	aubergine (egg plant)
Μπάμιες	Bámies	okra, ladies' fingers
Μπιζέλια	Biséllia	peas
Ντομάτες	Domádes	tomatoes
Πατάτες	Patátes	potatoes
Πιπεριές	Piperiés	sweet peppers
Ραδίκι	Radíki	chicory
Ραπανάκι	Rapanáki	radish
Ρεβύθια	Revýthia	chick peas
Ρύζι	Rísi	rice
Σκόρδο	Skórdo	garlic
Σκορδαλιά	Skordaliá	garlic and potato puree
Σπανάκι	Spanáki	spinach
Φακές	Fakés	lentils
Φασολάκια φρέσκα	Fasolákia fréska	green beans

ΣΑΛΑΤΕΣ	Salates	Salads
Ρούσσικη σαλάτα	Rússiki saláta	Russian salad
Χωριάτικη σαλάτα	Horiátiki saláta	Greek village salad made of olives, tomatoes, cucumber, onions, herbs and *feta* cheese
Χόρτα σαλάτα	Hórta saláta	salad of (boiled) wild greens, with lemon and oil

ΤΥΡΙΑ	Tyria	Cheese
Φέτα	Féta	soft, white goats' milk cheese
Γραβιέρα	Graviéra	Greek gruyere
Κασέρι	Kasséri	hard, yellow cheese
Κεφαλοτύρι	Kefalotíri	strong and salty yellow cheese
Μανούρι	Manoúri	sort of cottage cheese
Μυζήθρα	Mizíthra	soft, salted ewes' milk cheese

INFORMATION

ΓΛΥΚΑ	Glyka	Puddings
Γαλακτομπούρεκο	Galaktoboúreko	custard pie
Γιαούρτι	Yaoúrti	yoghurt
Καταΐφι	Kataΐfi	shredded pastry with honey and almonds
Λουκουμαδες	Loukoumádes	hot fritters dipped in honey
Λουκούμια	Loukoúmia	Greek delight
Μπακλαβά	Baklavá	filo pastry with almonds and cinnamon
Παγωτό	Pagotó	ice cream
Ρυζόγαλο	Rizógalo	rice pudding
Χαλβά	Halvá	sweet made of sesame flour, almonds, honey and sugar

ΦΡΟΥΤΑ	Frouta	Fruit
Καρπούζι	Karpoúzi	water-melon
Πεπόνι	Pepóni	melon
Μήλο	Mílo	apple
Πορτοκάλι	Portokáli	orange
Ροδάκινα	Rodákina	peaches
Ρόδι	Ródi	pomegranate
Σταφίδα	Stafída	raisin
Σουλτανιά	Sultaniá	sultanas
Σταφύλια	Stafília	grapes
Σύκα	Síka	figs

Miscellaneous

beer	bíra	Μπύρα
bread	psomí	Ψωμί
butter	voútiro	Βούτυρο
chips	patátes tiganités	Πατάτες τηγανιτές
chocolate	kakáo	Κακάο
coffee	kafé	Καφέ
without sugar	skéto	σκέτο
slightly sweet	métrio	μέτριο
sweet	glykó	γλυκό
instant	Nes	Νες
fruit juice	himó froútou	Χυμό φρούτου
honey	méli	Μέλι
ice-cream	pagotó	Παγωτό
lemon	lemóni	Λεμόνι
mineral water	metalikó neró	Μεταλλικό νερό
milk	gála	Γάλα
mustard	moustárda	Μουστάρδα
oil	ládi	Λάδι
pepper	pipéri	Πιπέρι
salt	aláti	Αλάτι
sugar	záhari	Ζάχαρι
tea	tsáï	Τσάι
with milk/lemon	mé gála/lemóni	μέ γάλα/λεμόνι
water	neró	Νερό
wine	krassí	Κρασί
yoghurt	yaoúrti	Γιαούρτι

Index

Abram, Naxos 439
ACCOMMODATION
664–668
Acharavi, Corfu 275
Achillion Palace,
Corfu 287
Acrocorinth,
Peloponnese 140
Actium, Central
Greece 212
Adamas, Milos 416
Aegiali, Amorgos 476
Aegina town,
Aegina 329
AEGINA 321–334
Afandou, Rhodes 548
Agia Anna,
Mykonos 425
Agia Anna, Naxos 433
Agia Eleoussa
monastery,
Rhodes 548
Agia Evfimia,
Cephalonia 295
Agia Fotini, Chios 608
Agia Galini, Crete 504
Agia Irini, Paros 445
Agia Kyriaki, Tinos 471
Agia Marina,
Aegina 330
Agia Marina, Attica 123
Agia Marina, Crete 513
Agia Marina, Leros 578
Agia Marina,
Rhodes 547
Agia Marina,
Spetses 350
Agia Marina monastery,
Ios 411
Agia Marina monastery,
Milos 419
Agia Mina monastery,
Chios 608
Agia monastery,
Naxos 439
Agia Paraskevi, Evia 364
Agia Paraskevi,
Spetses 351
Agia Pelagia, Crete 490
Agia Pelagia,
Kithira 340

Agia Sophia cave,
Kithira 341
Agia Triada, Crete 503
Agia Triada monastery,
Crete 521
Agia Triada monastery,
Tinos 471
Agia Trias,
Macedonia 237
Agiassos, Lesbos 619
Agiassos, Naxos 435
Agii Anargyri,
Spetses 350
Agii Apostoli, Evia 366
Agios Andreas
monastery,
Cephalonia 293
Agios Antonios,
Tilos 592
AGIOS EFSTRATIOS 600,
604
Agios Fokas, Skyros 379
Agios Fokas, Tinos 471
Agios Georgios,
Cephalonia 293
Agios Georgios, Evia 361
Agios Georgios, west
Corfu 288
Agios Giorgios, north-
east Corfu 277
Agios Gordis, Corfu 285
Agios Ioanis, Central
Greece 204
Agios Ioannis,
Limnos 629
Agios Ioannis
monastery,
Chalki 556
Agios Ioannis
monastery,
Patmos 586
Agios Ioannis Porto,
Tinos 471
Agios Ioannis Siderianos
monastery, Milos 418
Agios Kiriakis,
Cephalonia 296
Agios Kirikos,
Ikaria 613
Agios Konstantinos,
Samos 637

Agios Nektarios
monastery,
Aegina 332
Agios Nikitas,
Lefkas 309
Agios Nikitas,
Tinos 473
Agios Nikolaos,
Crete 507
Agios Nikolaos,
Zante 319
Agios Nikolaos
monastery, Central
Greece 208
Agios Nikolaos
monastery,
Spetses 350
Agios Nikon,
Peloponnese 155
Agios Panteleimon
monastery, Tilos 592
Agios Prokopios,
Naxos 433
Agios Soulas monastery,
Rhodes 545
Agios Stefanos,
Mykonos 424
Agios Stefanos, north-
east Corfu 277
Agios Stefanos, north-
west Corfu 275
Agios Stephanos
monastery, Central
Greece 208
Agios Theodotis,
Ios 407
Agiou Dionisiou
monastery,
Macedonia 243
Agnontas, Skopelos 383
Agriolivadi, Patmos 586
Agros, Ithaca 301
Akrotiri, Crete 513
Akrotiri,
Santorini 455–457
Aktion see Actium
Alikanas, Zante 320
Alikes, Zante 319
Aliki, Kimolos 479
Aliki, Paros 445
Alinda, Leros 579

Index

ALONNISOS 353–359, 368–371
Alyki, Thassos 644
Amari Valley, Crete 518
Amarinthos, Evia 364
Ambelakia, Central Greece 189
Ambellas, Paros 444
Amfissa, Central Greece 188
Amopi, Karpathos 564
AMORGOS 384–397, 475–477
ANAFI 384–397, 480
Analypsi, Astypalaia 554
Andirrion, Central Greece 211
Andritsaena, Peloponnese 174
ANDROS 384–403
Andros town, Andros 401
Angali, Folegandros 478
Angelokastro, Corfu 284
Angistri, island, Aegina 333
Ano Boulari, Peloponnese 157
ANO KOUFOUNISSI 384–397, 480
Ano Mera, Mykonos 425
Ano Syros, Syros 466
Anoghi, Ithaca 302
Anogia, Crete 500
Antikira, Central Greece 187
Antimachia, Kos 574
ANTIPAROS 384–397, 479
Antipaxos island, Paxos 313
Antissa, Lesbos 620
Aperi, Karpathos 564
Apiranthos, Naxos 436
Apocalypsis monastery, Patmos 585
Apollo Coast, Attica 117–118
Apollon, Naxos 436
Apollonia, Sifnos 462
Arachova, Central Greece 187
Arcadia, Peloponnese 166–168, 174–176, 177
Archangel Michael monastery, Symi 590
Archangelos, Rhodes 549

Archangelos monastery, Thassos 644
Areopolis, Peloponnese 156
Argassi, Zante 318
Arginontas bay, Kalymnos 561
Argive Heraion, Peloponnese 144
Argolic Gulf, Peloponnese 167, 177
Argolid, Peloponnese 133–148
Argos, Peloponnese 143
Argostoli, Cephalonia 291
Arillas, Central Greece 215
Arillas, Corfu 277
Arkadi monastery, Crete 518
Arkassa, Karpathos 564
Armenistis, Ikaria 614
Armolia, Chios 609
Arni, Andros 400
Arta, Central Greece 213
Arvanitohori, Kasos 566
Arvi, Crete 506
Asklepion, Kos 572
Asomatos, Crete 519
Asselinos, Skiathos 374
Assos, Cephalonia 296
Astrakeri, Corfu 275
ASTYPALAIA 525–536, 553–555
Ateni valley, Andros 400
ATHENS AIRPORT, arriving at 648
ATHENS 79–112
Athos, Mount, Macedonia 240–243
Atsitsa, Skyros 379
Attaviros, Mount, Rhodes 546
Avgonima, Chios 608
Avlakia, Samos 637
Avlemonas, Kithira 341
Avlonas, Limnos 629

Barbati Beach, Corfu 274
Barlaam monastery see Varlaam
Bassae, Peloponnese 172–174
Batsi, Andros 399
Benitses, Corfu 287
Beroea see Veria

Blue Grotto of Perasta, Kastellorizo 567
BOOKS, RECOMMENDED 677
Boukari, Corfu 288
Brauron, Attica 121
Brooke, Rupert, grave, Skyros 379

Cape Gerakas, Zante 318
Cape Kommeno, Corfu 273
Cape Lefkatas, Lefkas 308
Cape Matapan see Cape Tenaro
Cape Tenaro, Peloponnese 158
CAR HIRE 658–660
Castello Rosso, Evia 368
Cathedral of Ekatontapiliani, Paros 442
CEPHALONIA 257–269, 290–298
Chalcidice see Halkidiki
Chalki, Naxos 435
CHALKI 525–536, 555–557
Chalkis, Evia 363
Chania, Crete 519–521
Chios town, Chios 606
CHIOS 594–611
Chlemoutsi, Peloponnese 167
Chora, Astypalaia 554
Chora, Ios 405
Chora, Kythnos 413
Chora, Patmos 585
Chorefto, Central Greece 204
Chorio, Chalki 556
Chorio, Symi 588
Chrissi Akti, Paros 445
Chrissi Amoudia, Thassos 645
Chrissopigi monastery, Sifnos 463
Christos Rachon, Ikaria 615
Commonwealth War Cemetery, Crete 513
Corfu town, Corfu 278–282
CORFU 257–290
Corinth, Ancient, Peloponnese 138
Corinth, Peloponnese 133

Index

Corinthian Gulf, Peloponnese 166
CRETE 482–524
CYCLADES, THE 384–481

Dafni, Evia 364
Danilia Folklore Village, Corfu 273
Daphni, Attica 112
Dapia, Spetses 347
Dassia, Corfu 273
DELOS 384–397, 426–430
Delphi, oracle, Central Greece 194–201
Diafani, Karpathos 565
Diakofti, Kithira 341
Diakofti, Mykonos 426
Diapori, Limnos 630
Diktaian Cave, Crete 501
Dimitsana, Peloponnese 175
Dion, Central Greece 210
Dirfis mountains, Evia 365
DODECANESE ISLANDS 525–593
Dodona, Central Greece 222–224
DONOUSSA 384–397, 480
Driopis, Kythnos 414
Drios, Paros 445
Drogerati, Cephalonia 295

Edessa, Macedonia 248
Eftalou, Lesbos 623
Elefsis see Eleusis
Eleftherna, Crete 518
Eleusis, Attica 114–115
Eleutherai, Central Greece 184
Elos, Crete 515
Elounda, Crete 508
Emborio, Chalki 555
Emborio, Chios 609
Emborio, Kalymnos 561
Emborio, Kasos 566
Emborio, Nisyros 580
Enos, Mount, Cephalonia 295
Ephyra, necromanteion, Central Greece 218
Epidauros see Epidavros
Epidavros, Peloponnese 146–148

Epirus, Central Greece 178–184, 210–230
Episkopi, Hydra 337
Episkopi, Kythnos 412
Epta Piges, Rhodes 548
Eressos, Lesbos 621
Eretria, Ancient, Evia 364
Eretria, Evia 364
Eristos, Tilos 593
Ermioni, Peloponnese 134
Ermones, Corfu 285
Ermoupolis, Sifnos 465
EUBOEA see Evia
Euripus Channel, Evia 363
Evdilos, Ikaria 614
EVIA 353–368
Exoghi, Ithaca 301
Exombourgo, Mount, Tinos 472

Faliraki, Rhodes 548
Fellos, Andros 399
Feraklos, Rhodes 549
FERRIES AND HYDROFOILS 652–657
FESTIVALS AND EVENTS 683
Filakopi, Milos 416
Filerimos, Rhodes 543
Filotheo monastery, Macedonia 242
Filoti, Naxos 436
Finikas, Syros 467
Finikione, Peloponnese 149
Finikounda, Peloponnese 149
Fira, Santorini 449
Fiskardo, Cephalonia 296
Flavourio, Kythnos 414
FOLEGANDROS 384–397, 477
Fotodoti monastery, Naxos 436
Fourka, Macedonia 239
Fourni, Rhodes 546
Frangokastello, Crete 516
Ftelia, Mykonos 425

Gaios, Paxos 311
Galataki monastery, Evia 361
Galatas, Peloponnese 134

Galaxidi, Central Greece 210
Galissas, Syros 467
Gavathas, Lesbos 620
Gavrion, Andros 398
Georgiopoulis, Crete 512
Geraki, Peloponnese 159
Gerolimena, Peloponnese 157
Gialos, Ios 405
Gialos, Symi 588
Gialova, Peloponnese 150
Glifada, Corfu 285
Glossa, Skopelos 383
Glyfada, Attica 117
Gorge of Samaria, Crete 521–523
Gortyn, Crete 501
Gournas, Leros 579
Gournia, Crete 510
Gouverneto monastery, Crete 521
Gouvia, Corfu 273
Grammatikon, Attica 124
Grand Lavra monastery, Macedonia 242
Great Meteoron monastery, Central Greece 207
GREEK LANGUAGE AND ALPHABET 685–691
Gregolimano, Evia 361
Grikos, Patmos 586
Gythion, Peloponnese 159

Halkidiki, Macedonia 236–243
Hanema, Skiathos 374
Haniotis, Macedonia 238
Hefestia, Limnos 630
Heraklion, Crete 492
Hersonisos, Crete 491
Hiliadou, Evia 365
Hora Sfakion, Crete 516
HOTELS 664
Hozoviotissa monastery, Amorgos 476
Hydra town, Hydra 335
HYDRA 321–328, 334–338

Ia, Santorini 451
Ialysos, Rhodes 543
Idaian Cave, Crete 500
Ierapetra, Crete 506

Index

Igoumenitsa, Central
  Greece 213
IKARIA 594–604,
  612–615
Ilia, Evia 361
INFORMATION 647–691
INSURANCE,
  HOLIDAY 674–676
Ioanina, Central
  Greece 219–222
IONIAN ISLANDS
  257–320
Ios 384–397, 403–407
Ipsilou monastery,
  Lesbos 621
Ipsos, Corfu 273
Ipsounda see Stemnitsa
IRAKLIA,
  Cyclades 480–481
Iraklion see Heraklion
Irion, Samos 636
Issos Beach, Corfu 288
Itanos, Crete 507
Itea, Central Greece 210
ITHACA 257–269,
  299–302
Iviron monastery,
  Macedonia 242
Ixia, Rhodes 543

Kalafatis, Mykonos 426
Kalamaki peninsula,
  Skiathos 373
Kalamata,
  Peloponnese 149
Kalambaka, Central
  Greece 208
Kalami, Corfu 275
Kalami, Crete 512
Kalamitsa, Skyros 379
Kalamitsi, Lefkas 308
Kalamos, Evia 365
Kalavria, Poros 344
Kalavrita,
  Peloponnese 176
Kalavrita Railway,
  Peloponnese 176
Kalithea, Rhodes 547
Kalives, Crete 512
Kallithea,
  Macedonia 238
Kalloni, Lesbos 620
Kalloni, Tinos 473
Kalogeros, Crete 519
Kalogria,
  Peloponnese 167
KALYMNOS 525–536,
  557–562
Kalythies, Rhodes 548
Kamares, Sifnos 461

Kamari, Kos 576
Kamari, Santorini 452
Kambos, Chios 608
Kaminaki, Corfu 275
Kaminia, Hydra 337
Kamiros, Rhodes 545
Kamiros Skala,
  Rhodes 545
Kampi, Zante 318
Kampos, Patmos 586
Kanala, Kythnos 414
Kanapitsa, Skiathos 373
Kantouni,
  Kalymnos 560
Kapparia, Andros 403
Kapsali, Kithira 339
Karababa fort, Evia 364
Karathona,
  Peloponnese 135
Kardamena, Kos 574
Kardamili,
  Peloponnese 153
Kardamyla, Chios 610
Karfas, Chios 608
Karistos, Evia 366
Karitaena,
  Peloponnese 175
Karlovasi, Samos 637
Karpathos town,
  Karpathos 563
KARPATHOS 525–536,
  562–566
Kassandra,
  Macedonia 239–241
Kassiopi, Corfu 283
Kastania,
  Peloponnese 176
Kastel Tornese see
  Chlemoutsi
Kastelli, Crete 514
KASTELLORIZO 525–
  536, 567–568
Kastellos, Rhodes 546
Kastoria, Macedonia 249
Kastraki, Central
  Greece 209
Kastraki, Naxos 434
Kastriani monastery,
  Ios 409
Kastro, Peloponnese 167
Kastro, Sifnos 462
Katakalo,
  Peloponnese 167
Katakoilos, Andros 400
Katapola, Amorgos 476
Katara Pass, Central
  Greece 217
Katavia, Rhodes 550
Kathara monastery,
  Ithaca 302

Kato Boulari,
  Peloponnese 157
Kato Katelios,
  Cephalonia 293
KATO KOUFOUNISSI
  384–397, 480
Katohora, Kithira 343
Kavala, Macedonia 250
Kavirio, Limnos 631
Kavos, Corfu 289
KEA 384–397, 407–411
Kechrovouni monastery,
  Tinos 472
Kefali, Crete 515
KEFALLINIA see
  CEPHALONIA
Kefalos, Kos 576
Kefalos, Paros 444
Kefalos Bay, Kos 575
Kefalos cave,
  Kalymnos 562
Kehria, Skiathos 375
Kehria monastery,
  Skiathos 376
Kepesovo, Central
  Greece 226
Kerkis, Mount,
  Samos 638
KEROS 384–397, 480
Khrisoskalitissa
  monastery, Crete 515
Killini, Peloponnese 167
Kimi, Evia 365
KIMOLOS 384–397, 479
Kionia, Tinos 471
Kipi, Central Greece 226
Kita, Peloponnese 157
Kithairon, Mount,
  Central Greece 184
Kithira town,
  Kithira 339
KITHIRA 321–328,
  338–342
Klima, Milos 420
Klima, Skopelos 383
Kliston monastery,
  Attica 124
Knossos, Crete 494–499
Kokkari, Samos 636
Kolimbia, Rhodes 548
Kolimbithra, Tinos 473
Kolimvari, Crete 514
Kolonna, Kythnos 413
Komi, Chios 609
Kondias, Limnos 630
Kontokali, Corfu 273
Koraka, Crete 516
Korissia, Ios 409
Koroni,
  Peloponnese 149

Korthion, Andros 403
Kos town, Kos 570
Kos 525–536, 568–576
Kotronas,
    Peloponnese 158
Kotsinas, Limnos 630
Koufa Bay,
    Macedonia 240
Koukounaries,
    Skiathos 374
Kouloura, Corfu 275
Koumbara, Ios 405
Kounistres monastery,
    Skiathos 375
Kounopetra,
    Cephalonia 296
Koutsounari, Crete 506
Krassas, Skiathos 374
Kremasti, Rhodes 543
Kria Vrisi, Evia 362
Krini, Corfu 284
Krios, Paros 443
Kritinia, Rhodes 546
Kritsa, Crete 509
Kynthos, Mount,
    Delos 428
Kyra Panagia,
    Karpathos 564
Kythnos town,
    Kythnos 413
KYTHNOS 384–397,
    411–414

Lafki, Corfu 274
Laganas beach,
    Zante 317
Lagia, Peloponnese 158
Lahania, Rhodes 549
Lake Korission,
    Corfu 288
Lake Megali Prespa,
    Macedonia 249
Lake Melissani,
    Cephalonia 295
Lake Mikri Prespa,
    Macedonia 249
Lake Stymphalia,
    Peloponnese 176
Lake Vouliagmeni,
    Attica 118
Lake Vouliagmeni, nr
    Loutraki, Attica 116
Lakka, Paxos 311
Lakkas, Peloponnese 177
Lakones, Corfu 284
Lamia, Central
    Greece 188
Lampi, Patmos 586
Langada,
    Peloponnese 155

Langadas, Chios 610
Langadha Pass,
    Peloponnese 165
Langadia,
    Peloponnese 174
Lardos, Rhodes 549
Larissa, Central
    Greece 189
Lasithi Plateau,
    Crete 501
Lassi promontory,
    Cephalonia 292
Lato, Crete 510
Laurion, Attica 120
Lefkadia,
    Macedonia 248
Lefkas town, Lefkas 304
LEFKAS 257–269,
    303–310
Lefkes, Paros 446
Lefkes, Patmos 586
Lefkos, Karpathos 564
Leonidion,
    Peloponnese 177
Lepeda, Cephalonia 296
LEROS 525–536,
    576–580
LESBOS 594–604,
    615–626
Levadia, Central
    Greece 184
Liapades, Corfu 285
Limani Hersonisou,
    Crete 491
Limeni,
    Peloponnese 156
Limin see Thassos town
Limni, Evia 361
Limnionas, Samos 639
LIMNOS 594–604,
    626–632
Limonas monastery,
    Lesbos 620
Linaria, Skyros 379
Lindos, Rhodes 550–553
Lithi, Chios 608
Litohoro, Central
    Greece 209
Livada, Tinos 472
Livadi, Peloponnese 177
Livadi, Serifos 458
Livadia, Astypalaia 554
Livadia, Tilos 591
Lixouri peninsula,
    Cephalonia 295
Loaras, Paros 444
Loggos, Paxos 312
Longovardas monastery,
    Paros 443
Loutra, Kythnos 413

Loutra, Nisyros 580
Loutra Edipsos, Evia 362
Loutra Kaiafa,
    Peloponnese 167
Loutra Killinis,
    Peloponnese 167
Loutraki, Skopelos 383
Loutro, Crete 516
Loutsa, Attica 121

MACEDONIA 231–252
Macherado, Zante 318
Madouri island,
    Lefkas 306
Magazia, Skyros 378
Maina Castle,
    Peloponnese 157
Makri Yialos, Evia 362
Makrinitsa, Central
    Greece 204
Maleme, Crete 514
Malia, Ancient,
    Crete 499
Malia, Crete 491
Maltezanas,
    Astypalaia 554
Mandraki, Hydra 337
Mandraki,
    Kastellorizo 567
Mandraki, Milos 420
Mandraki, Nisyros 580
Manganari, Ios 407
Mani, Peloponnese 148–
    149, 153–159
Mantamados,
    Lesbos 625
Mantinea,
    Peloponnese 177
Mantoudi, Evia 361
Marathias, Corfu 288
Marathokampos,
    Samos 638
Marathon, Attica 123
Marathon Plain,
    Attica 122
Marathon Tomb,
    Attica 123
Markopoulo,
    Cephalonia 293
Marmari, Evia 366
Marmari, Kos 573
Marmari,
    Peloponnese 158
Masouri, Kalymnos 560
Mastichari, Kos 573
Matala, Crete 504
Mati, Attica 122
MEDICAL MATTERS 671
Mega Amos, Central
    Greece 215

Index

Mega Livadi,
  Serifos 459
Mega Spileo monastery,
  Peloponnese 176
Megalo Chorio,
  Tilos 592
Megalo Papingo, Central
  Greece 227
Megalopolis,
  Peloponnese 175
Meganisi island,
  Lefkas 306
MEGISTI see
  KASTELLORIZO
Melidoni Cave,
  Crete 500
Menetes, Karpathos 564
Menites, Andros 401
Merichas, Kythnos 412
Mesavrisi, Corfu 288
Mesolongi see
  Missolonghi
Messanagros,
  Rhodes 550
Messara, plain,
  Crete 491
Messaria, Andros 401
Messene, Ancient,
  Peloponnese 165
Messini,
  Peloponnese 165
Messonghi, Corfu 289
Mesta, Chios 610
Metamorfossi,
  Macedonia 237
Meteora, monasteries,
  Central
  Greece 206–208
Methana,
  Peloponnese 134
Methoni,
  Peloponnese 152
Metohi, Evia 365
Metsovo, Central
  Greece 228–230
Mezapos,
  Peloponnese 157
Mikene see Mycenae
Mikinae see Mycenae
Mikri Papingo, Central
  Greece 227
Mikri Vigla, Naxos 434
Milatos, Crete 491
Milies, Central
  Greece 203
Milopotamos, Central
  Greece 204
Milopotamos,
  Kithira 341
Milopotas, Ios 406

Milos town, Milos 419
MILOS 384–397,
  414–420
Mirtidion monastery,
  Kithira 342
Mirtiotissa, Corfu 285
Mirtos, Cephalonia 296
Mirtos, Crete 506
Missolonghi, Central
  Greece 211
Mistra,
  Peloponnese 162–165
Mithimna see Molivos
Mogonisi, Paxos 311
Molivos, Lesbos 623
Molos, Paros 444
Monasteries of Mount
  Athos,
  Macedonia 240–243
Monasteries of the
  Meteora, Central
  Greece 206–208
Monastery of Agia,
  Naxos 439
Monastery of Agia
  Eleoussa, Rhodes 548
Monastery of Agia
  Marina, Ios 411
Monastery of Agia
  Marina, Milos 419
Monastery of Agia
  Mina, Chios 608
Monastery of Agia
  Triada, Crete 521
Monastery of Agia
  Triada, Tinos 471
Monastery of Agios
  Andreas,
  Cephalonia 293
Monastery of Agios
  Dionisios,
  Macedonia 243
Monastery of Agios
  Ioannis, Chalki 556
Monastery of Agios
  Ioannis Siderianos,
  Milos 418
Monastery of Agios
  Nektarios,
  Aegina 332
Monastery of Agios
  Nikolaos, Central
  Greece 208
Monastery of Agios
  Nikolaos, Spetses 350
Monastery of Agios
  Panteleimon,
  Tilos 592
Monastery of Agios
  Soulas, Rhodes 545

Monastery of Agios
  Stephanos, Central
  Greece 208
Monastery of
  Archangelos,
  Thassos 644
Monastery of Arkadi,
  Crete 518
Monastery of
  Chrissopigi,
  Sifnos 463
Monastery of Filotheo,
  Macedonia 242
Monastery of Fotodoti,
  Naxos 436
Monastery of Galataki,
  Evia 361
Monastery of
  Gouverneto,
  Crete 521
Monastery of Grand
  Lavra, Macedonia 242
Monastery of
  Hozoviotissa,
  Amorgos 476
Monastery of Ipsilou,
  Lesbos 621
Monastery of Iviron,
  Macedonia 242
Monastery of Kastriani,
  Ios 409
Monastery of Kathara,
  Ithaca 302
Monastery of
  Kechrovouni,
  Tinos 472
Monastery of Kehria,
  Skiathos 376
Monastery of
  Khrisoskalitissa,
  Crete 515
Monastery of Kliston,
  Attica 125
Monastery of Kounistres,
  Skiathos 375
Monastery of Limonas,
  Lesbos 620
Monastery of
  Longovardas,
  Paros 443
Monastery of Mega
  Spileo,
  Peloponnese 176
Monastery of Mirtidion,
  Kithira 342
Monastery of Nea Moni,
  Chios 607
Monastery of Ossios
  Loukas, Central
  Greece 193

Monastery of Panachrantos, Andros 401
Monastery of Panagia Spiliana, Nisyros 580
Monastery of Pantaleimon, Macedonia 243
Monastery of Perivolis, Lesbos 620
Monastery of Preveli, Crete 519
Monastery of Prodromos, Skopelos 383
Monastery of Roussanou, Central Greece 208
Monastery of Simonopetra, Macedonia 243
Monastery of Skiadi, Rhodes 547
Monastery of St John, Patmos 586
Monastery of Stavronikita, Macedonia 242
Monastery of Taxiachis, Serifos 459
Monastery of the Apocalypse, Patmos 585
Monastery of the Archangel Michael, Symi 590
Monastery of the Great Meteoron, Central Greece 207
Monastery of the Virgin Mary of Kalopetra, Rhodes 545
Monastery of Toplou, Crete 510
Monastery of Tourliani, Mykonos 425
Monastery of Tsambika, Rhodes 549
Monastery of Valsamonero, Crete 504
Monastery of Varlaam, Central Greece 207
Monastery of Vatopedi, Macedonia 242
Monastery of Vrondisi, Crete 504
Monastery of Ypsilos, Naxos 439

Monastery of Zoodochos Pigi, Andros 400
Monastery of Zoodochos Pigi, Corfu 287
Monastery of Zoodochos Pigi, Poros 346
Monemvasia, Peloponnese 159
MONEY 681
Moni, island, Aegina 332
Monodendri, Central Greece 225
Monolithos, Rhodes 546
Monolithos, Santorini 452
Moraitika, Corfu 289
Moria, Lesbos 626
MOTOR-BIKE HIRE 660
MOTORING IN GREECE 668–671
Moudros, Limnos 632
Mount Athos, Macedonia 240–243
Mount Attaviros, Rhodes 546
Mount Enos, Cephalonia 295
Mount Exombourgo, Tinos 472
Mount Kerkis, Samos 638
Mount Kithairon, Central Greece 184
Mount Kynthos, Delos 428
Mount Neritos, Ithaca 301
Mount Ohi, Evia 368
Mount Olympos, Central Greece 209
Mount Pantokrator, Corfu 274
Mount Parnassos, Central Greece 188
Mount Parnes, Attica 124
Mount Parnitha see Parnes
Mount Parnon, Peloponnese 161
Mount Pelion, Central Greece 201–206
Mount Profitis Ilias, Rhodes 545
Mount Skopos, Zante 318
Mount Spingion, Central Greece 184
Mount Stavrotas, Lefkas 306

Moutsouna, Naxos 436
Murteri, Evia 365
MUSEUMS AND ARCHAEOLOGICAL SITES 682
Mycenae, Peloponnese 140–145
Mykonos town, Mykonos 421
MYKONOS 384–397, 420–426
Myrina, Limnos 627
Myrties, Kalymnos 560
Mytilini, Lesbos 617
MYTILINI see LESBOS

Nafpaktos, Central Greece 210
Nafplion, Peloponnese 134
Nagos, Chios 610
Naoussa, Paros 443
Nas, Ikaria 614
Nauplia see Nafplion
Navarino see Pylos
Naxos town, Naxos 431
NAXOS 384–397, 430–439
Nea Anhialos, Central Greece 188
Nea Artaki, Evia 364
Nea Fokia, Macedonia 238
Nea Kameni island, Santorini 455
Nea Makri, Attica 122
Nea Marmaras, Macedonia 240
Nea Moni monastery, Chios 607
Nea Stira, Evia 366
Necromanteion of Ephyra, Central Greece 218
Nemea, Peloponnese 140
Neopirgos, Evia 361
Neritos, Mount, Ithaca 301
Nestor's Palace, Peloponnese 151
Nidri, Lefkas 305
Nikea, Nisyros 580
Nikopolis, Central Greece 212
Nimborio, Symi 590
Nissaki, Corfu 274
NISSIROS see NISYROS
NISYROS 525–536, 580–581

Index

Nomitsi,
Peloponnese 154
NORTH-EAST AEGEAN
ISLANDS 594–645

Ohi, Mount, Evia 368
Oia see Ia
Old Alonnisos,
Alonnisos 370
Olymboi, Chios 610
Olympia,
Peloponnese 168–173
Olympias,
Macedonia 237
Olympos,
Karpathos 564
Olympos, Mount,
Central Greece 209
Oracle of Delphi, Central
Greece 194–201
Oracle of Trophonios,
Central
Greece 184–187
Ormos Komeikon,
Samos 638
Ormos Marathokampos,
Samos 639
Ornos, Mykonos 424
Oropos, Attica 124
Ossios Loukas
monastery, Central
Greece 193
Othos, Karpathos 564
Otzias, Ios 409
Ouranopolis,
Macedonia 240

PACKAGE HOLIDAYS
651–652
Palaikastro, Crete 507
Paleohora, Aegina 332
Paleohora, Crete 523
Paleohora, Kithira 342
Paleohora, Milos 417
Paleokastritsa,
Corfu 286
Pali, Nisyros 580
Paliki peninsula see
Lixouri
Paliopolis, Andros 400
Panachrantos
monastery,
Andros 401
Panagia, Evia 366
Panagia, Kasos 566
Panagia, Serifos 459
Panagia, Thassos 645
Panagia Drossiani
church, Naxos 435

Panagia Episkopi,
Santorini 454
Panagia Kera, Crete 509
Panagia Krina,
Chios 609
Panagia Spiliana
monastery,
Nisyros 580
Pandeli, Leros 578
Panormitis, Symi 590
Panormos, Skopelos 383
Panormos, Tinos 473
Pantaleimon monastery,
Macedonia 243
Pantokrator, Mount,
Corfu 274
Paradissi, Rhodes 544
Paralia, Evia 365
Paralia Tirou,
Peloponnese 167
Paramona, Corfu 285
Parasporos, Paros 445
Parga, Central
Greece 217
Parikia, Paros 441
Parnassos, Mount,
Central Greece 188
Parnes, Mount,
Attica 124
Parnitha, Mount see
Parnes
Parnon, Mount,
Peloponnese 161
PAROS 384–397,
440–446
Patitiri, Alonnisos 368
PATMOS 525–536,
582–587
Patras, Peloponnese 166
PAXOS 257–269, 310–313
Pefkari, Thassos 643
Pefki, Evia 361
Pefkohori,
Macedonia 238
Pefkos, Skyros 379
Pelekas Beach,
Corfu 286
Pelion, Mount, Central
Greece 201–206
Pella, Macedonia 246
PELOPONNESE
ISLANDS 321–352
PELOPONNESE 127–177
Pera Kastro,
Kalymnos 560
Perachora, Heraion,
Attica 116
Perama, Corfu 287
Perama Caves, Central
Greece 222

Perigalos,
Astypalaia 554
Perissa, Santorini 454
Perithia, Corfu 274
Perivolis monastery,
Lesbos 620
Perkika, Aegina 331
Perkika, Central
Greece 215
Peroulades, Corfu 277
Petalia, Corfu 274
Petaloudes, Paros 446
Petaloudes, Rhodes 544
Petra, Lesbos 623
Petralona Cave,
Macedonia 237
Petrified Forest,
Lesbos 621
Petrochori,
Peloponnese 151
Phaistos, Crete 502
Pharos, Sifnos 463
Philippi, Macedonia 251
Phira see Fira
Phry, Kasos 566
Phyli, Attica 125
Pigadia, Santorini 452
Pighadia, Karpathos 563
Pili, Ancient, Kos 574
Pili, Evia 362
Piraeus, Attica 116
Piraievs see Piraeus
Pirgi, Chios 609
Pirgi, Corfu 273
Pirgos Dirou,
Peloponnese 156
Piso Livadi, Paros 444
Plain of Marathon,
Attica 122
Plain of the Messara,
Crete 491
Plaka, Milos 419
Plaka, Peloponnese 177
Plaka, Tilos 592
Plakias, Crete 517
Plantanistos, Evia 367
Platanakia, Samos 637
Platanias, Crete 513
Platanos, Crete 515
Platanos, Leros 578
Plati, Limnos 630
Plati Ammos,
Kithira 341
Plati Gialos, Sifnos 463
Plomari, Lesbos 619
Poli, Kasos 566
Polichnitos, Lesbos 619
Poliochni, Limnos 632
Polis, Ithaca 301
Pollonia, Milos 416

Index

Pondamos, Chalki 555
Poros, Cephalonia 294
Poros town, Poros 344
POROS 321–328,
    343–346
Portaria, Central
    Greece 204
Porto Carras,
    Macedonia 240
Porto Heli,
    Peloponnese 133
Porto Katsiki,
    Lefkas 308
Porto Kayio,
    Peloponnese 158
Porto Rafti 120
Porto Vromi, Zante 319
Posidonia, Syros 467
Posidonion, Samos 634
Potami, Evia 367
Potami, Samos 638
Potamos, Corfu 273
Pothia, Kalymnos 559
Prespa Lakes,
    Macedonia 249
Preveli monastery,
    Crete 519
Preveza, Central
    Greece 211
Prodromou monastery,
    Skopelos 383
Profitis Ilias, Mount,
    Rhodes 545
Prokopi, Evia 361
Psarrou, Mykonos 424
Psihro, Crete 501
Psili Ammos, Samos 634
Psilli Ammos,
    Serifos 459
PUBLIC HOLIDAYS,
    FESTIVALS AND
    EVENTS 683
Pyles, Karpathos 564
Pylos, Peloponnese 150
Pyrgaki, Naxos 434
Pyrgos, Santorini 454
Pyrgos, Tinos 472, 473
Pythagorion, Samos 634

Rafina, Attica 122
Reni Koskinou,
    Rhodes 547
Repanidi, Limnos 630
Rethymnon, Crete 517
Rhamnous, Attica 123
Rhodes town,
    Rhodes 536–542
RHODES 525–553
ROAD SIGNS 671
Robies, Evia 361

Roda, Corfu 275
Roussanou monastery,
    Central Greece 208

SALAMINA 321–328
SALAMIS see SALAMINA
Salonika,
    Macedonia 243–246
Samaria gorge,
    Crete 521–523
Sami, Cephalonia 295
Samos town, Samos 633
SAMOS 594–604,
    632–640
SAMOTHRACE 253,
    594–604
SANTORINI 384–397,
    447–457
Sarandi, Central
    Greece 188
Sarti, Macedonia 239
Savgia, Central
    Greece 215
SCHINOUSSA 384–397,
    480
SELF-CATERING 666
SERIFOS 384–397,
    457–460
Sfakia, Crete 516
Sfinario, Crete 515
Shinias, Attica 123
Siana, Rhodes 546
Sidari, Corfu 283
SIFNOS 384–397,
    460–464
Sigri, Lesbos 622
SIKINOS 384–397, 478
Simonopetra monastery,
    Macedonia 243
Sisi, Crete 491
Sithonia,
    Macedonia 239
Sitia, Crete 509
Sivota, Central
    Greece 213–215
Sivota, Lefkas 306
Skala, Cephalonia 294
Skala, Patmos 584
Skala Maries,
    Thassos 643
Skala Prinou,
    Thassos 643
Skala Sikamias,
    Lesbos 624
Skiadi monastery,
    Rhodes 547
Skiathos town,
    Skiathos 372
SKIATHOS 355–359,
    371–376

Skiviris, Macedonia 239
Skopelos town,
    Skopelos 381
SKOPELOS 355–359,
    380–383
Skopos, Mount,
    Zante 318
Skorpios island,
    Lefkas 306
Skyros town,
    Skyros 378
SKYROS 355–359,
    377–380
Soroni, Rhodes 545
Souda, Crete 513
Souda Bay, Crete 512
Sounion, Attica 119
Souvala, Aegina 331
Sparta, Peloponnese 162
SPETSAI see SPETSES
Spetses town,
    Spetses 347
SPETSES 321–328,
    347–352
Spingion, Mount,
    Central Greece 184
SPORADES ISLANDS
    353–359, 368–383
St John monastery,
    Patmos 586
Stafilos, Skopelos 383
Stavronikita monastery,
    Macedonia 242
Stavros, Ithaca 301
Stavros, Macedonia 237
Stavrotas, Mount,
    Lefkas 306
Stemnitsa,
    Peloponnese 175
Steni, Evia 365
Steni Vala,
    Alonnisos 370
Stenies, Andros 402
Stoupa,
    Peloponnese 154
Sykia, Macedonia 239
Symi town, Symi 588
SYMI 525–536, 587–591
SYROS 384–397,
    464–468

Tarti, Lesbos 618
Taxiarchis monastery,
    Serifos 459
TAXIS 662
Telendos, Kalymnos 560
Tembi, Vale of, see
    Tempe
Tempe, Vale of, Central
    Greece 190

Index

Temple of Aphaia,
  Aegina 331
Temple of Hera,
  Samos 636
Temple of Poseidon,
  Sounion, Attica 119
Thanos, Limnos 630
THASSOS 594–604,
  640–665
Thassos town,
  Thassos 642
Thebes, Central
  Greece 191–193
Theologos, Thassos 644
Thera, Ancient,
  Santorini 452
THERA see SANTORINI
Therma, Ikaria 613
Therma Lefkadas,
  Ikaria 613
Thessaloniki see
  Salonika
Thessaly, Central
  Greece 178–210
THIRA see SANTORINI
Thirasia island,
  Santorini 455
Thivai see Thebes
Tholos, Rhodes 545
Thorikos, Attica 120
THRACE 231–236,
  252–253
Thronos, Crete 519
Tigani, Peloponnese 157
TILOS 525–536,
  591–593
Tingaki, Kos 573
Tinos town, Tinos 470
TINOS 384–397,
  468–474
Tiryns, Peloponnese 145
Tolon, Peloponnese 137
Toplou monastery,
  Crete 510
TOUR OPERATORS 651
Tourliani monastery,
  Mykonos 425
Tragea, Naxos 435
TRAVEL IN
  GREECE 652–663
TRAVELLING TO
  GREECE 647–652
Trianda, Rhodes 543
Trikkala, Central
  Greece 189
Tripiti, Milos 419
Triple Way, Central
  Greece 187
Tripolis,
  Peloponnese 177

Troezen,
  Peloponnese 134
Trophonios, Central
  Greece 184–187
Troulos, Skiathos 374
Tsambika monastery,
  Rhodes 549
Tsangarada, Central
  Greece 203
Tsilivi, Zante 320
Tzermiadon, Crete 501

Vai beach, Crete 506
Vale of Souda,
  Crete 513
Vale of Tempe, Central
  Greece 190
Valley of the Butterflies,
  Paros 445
Valley of the Butterflies,
  Rhodes 544
Valsamonero monastery,
  Crete 504
Vari, Syros 467
Varkiza, Attica 118
Varlaam monastery,
  Central Greece 207
Vasses see Bassae
Vassilika, Evia 362
Vassiliki,
  Lefkas 306–308
Vatera, Lesbos 619
Vathi, Ithaca 300
Vathi, Kalymnos 561
Vathi, Sifnos 463
Vathia, Peloponnese 157
Vathy, Astypalaia 555
Vathy, Samos 634
Vatopedi monastery,
  Macedonia 242
Vergina, Macedonia 248
Veria, Macedonia 247
Veroia see Veria
Vikos Gorge, Central
  Greece 225
Virgin Mary of
  Kalopetra monastery,
  Rhodes 545
Visitsa, Central
  Greece 203
Vitina, Peloponnese 174
Vitsa, Central
  Greece 225
Vitylo, Peloponnese 156
Vlichada, Santorini 455
Vlicho peninsula,
  Lefkas 306
Vlichos, Hydra 337
Vliha Bay, Rhodes 549
Vohali, Zante 316

Volax, Tinos 473
Volimes, Zante 319
Volos, Central
  Greece 201
Vori, Crete 503
Vothini, Kalymnos 562
Votsalakia, Samos 639
Votsi, Alonnisos 369
Voula, Attica 118
Vouliagmeni, Attica 118
Vourkari, Ios 409
Voutakos, Paros 445
Vouvourou,
  Macedonia 239
Vravrona see Brauron
Vromolimnos,
  Skiathos 374
Vrondisi monastery,
  Crete 504
Vrontado, Syros 466
Vrontados, Chios 610
Vroukounda,
  Karpathos 566

WEATHER 678–681

Xanthi, Thrace 253
Xerokampos, Leros 579
Xilokastro,
  Peloponnese 166

Yialia, Andros 402
Ypsilos monastery,
  Naxos 439

Zagora, Andros 403
Zagora, Central
  Greece 204
Zagoria, Central
  Greece 224–227
Zakros, Crete 510
ZAKYNTHOS see ZANTE
Zakynthos town,
  Zante 314
ZANTE 257–269,
  313–320
Zia, Kos 573
Zitsa, Central
  Greece 216
Zogeria, Spetses 351
Zoodochos Pigi
  monastery,
  Andros 400
Zoodochos Pigi
  monastery, Corfu 287
Zoodochos Pigi
  monastery, Poros 346
Zouberi, Attica 122